CURRICULUM:
FOUNDATIONS,
PRINCIPLES, AND ISSUES

CURRICULUM:
FOUNDATIONS, PRINCIPLES, AND ISSUES

ALLAN C. ORNSTEIN
Loyola University of Chicago

FRANCIS P. HUNKINS
University of Washington, Seattle

ALLYN and BACON
BOSTON LONDON TORONTO SYDNEY TOKYO SINGAPORE

Library of Congress Cataloging-in-Publication Data

ORNSTEIN, ALLAN C. (DATE)
    Curriculum—foundations, principles, and issues.

    Includes indexes.
    1. Curriculum planning—United States.   2. Curriculum
evaluation—United States.   I. Hunkins, Francis P.
II. Title.
LB2806.15.O76   1988   375'.001   87-12442
ISBN 0-13-195777-5

Editorial/production supervision
    and interior design: Robert DeGeorge
Cover design: Ben Santora
Manufacturing buyer: Carol Bystrom

Printed in the United States of America

10 9 8 7   95 94 93 92 91

ISBN 0-13-195777-5 01

CONTENTS

12 CURRICULUM ISSUES AND TRENDS *299*

13 FUTURE DIRECTIONS FOR CURRICULUM *322*

NAME INDEX *337*

SUBJECT INDEX *342*

FOREWORD

I

The American people have an abiding faith in education. They want their sons and daughters to be informed, skilled, wise, and good. They also have a deep-seated belief that the schools can achieve these values. Like the teachers, the people look to the curriculum, particularly to the content and modes of teaching, as the primary source of learnings that produce informed, skilled, wise, and good members of society. Despite this fundamental consensus, there is widespread disagreement about what knowledge is of most worth, how such knowledge should be organized, and how teachers should perform as they carry on the activities of the classroom.

The issues that whirl about these differences of opinion, the contrasting views not only about the substance and organization of school programs but also about the specifics of the ultimate aims of education itself are the points on which the analysis of

the present book hinges. The book deals with the foundations (Part I), the principles (Part II), and the issues (Part III) of curriculum. In the foundations section, the authors introduce the field of curriculum. They discuss the philosophical, psychological, and social foundations of curriculum that serve to define and impact the dynamics of the field. They also in this section consider the evolution of the field. This first section sets forth the intellectual sources from which curriculum theory stems.

Part II addresses the principles that underpin curricular action. This section deals with the technical aspects of curriculum. It analyzes approaches to the purposes of education and the objectives of instruction. It treats the problems of curriculum design and development, giving in each case classical and current views of these topics.

The question of how to induce curricular changes has long plagued those who would improve the products of schooling. This part explores that question in light of what has been learned from past experience and from contemporary thought about social and institutional change. The authors, sensitive to public demands for evidence of curricular improvement, have analyzed the concepts and practices of curricular evaluation, drawing upon current as well as past conceptions of testing and evaluation.

Part III of the textbook treats those issues impacting curriculum and theory activity within the field. The issues discussed are ones that all involved in the various levels of curriculum activities need to consider. The final chapter, which deals with future directions for curriculum, leaves the reader with the realization that all involved in curriculum and educational programs need to understand the future and to engage in procedures that allow them to create visions and manage strategies for attaining those visions.

It should be emphasized that this book is not a nuts and bolt treatment of curriculum development. It deals with basic questions. This focus makes the book different from many on the market. Its range of topics also makes it different from other texts that address curriculum foundations. Rather than presenting recipes for dealing with curriculum questions, it urges the reader to contemplate what is required for fundamental curriculum thought and action. The authors have set forth a framework for understanding and for constructive thinking about curriculum foundations, curriculum principles, and curriculum issues.

B. Othanel Smith
Professor Emeritus,
University of Illinois and
University of South Florida

II

Those concerned with education and its improvement are giving increased attention to the curriculum and related learning activities. Efforts to improve schooling by legislation and policies voted by school boards of education have been found to have limited effects on what teachers teach and children learn. The curriculum as it is understood by the teachers and the learning activities they provide have been shown to be the major factors in stimulating and guiding student learning. Hence, students of education are well advised to study curriculum development and instructional practices.

In this volume, Allan Ornstein and Francis Hunkins provide comprehensive information about curriculum development, past and present. They also provide a rich overview of the foundations and issues of curriculum. Their approach is both theoretical and practical, and they synthesize the important research in the field. Students of education, and especially those who are concerned with curriculum, should find the material a useful basis for orientation as they work in this field.

Ralph W. Tyler
Director Emeritus, Center
for Advanced Study in the
Behavioral Sciences

PREFACE

Curriculum: Foundations, Principles, and Issues is a book for researchers, theoreticians, and practitioners of curriculum. It is intended to be a basic text for those studying curriculum development, design, and/or planning, as well as a reference for teachers, supervisors, and administrators who participate in curriculum making.

The book is a comprehensive and documented overview of the foundations, principles, and issues of curriculum: *Foundations* are the areas of study outside of curriculum that impact on the field; *principles* refer to the technical aspects, including techniques and methods, for developing, designing, implementing, and evaluating curriculum; *issues* are the theories and trends that influence the field.

The book consists of a one-chapter introduction to the field plus three major parts: foundations, principles, and issues. Part I has four chapters: one each on the philo-sophical, historical, psychological, and social *Foundations of Curriculum*. The next part, *Principles of Curriculum*, comprises five chapters: aims, goals, and objectives; design; development; implementation; and evaluation. The final part, *Issues of Curriculum*, includes three chapters that discuss theory, present issues and trends, and future directions.

This book differs from other curriculum texts in several ways. Most texts tend to focus on either theory or practice; we try to blend both aspects of curriculum. Most curriculum writers emphasize either the foundations, principles, or issues of curriculum; the majority focus on principles and many others focus on foundations. We have attempted to balance all three areas of curriculum. Most texts take a particular philosophical or theoretical position; we, however, have tried to present various philosophies and theories. We provide readers with alternatives and choices for formulating their own views and values on curriculum foundations, principles, and issues.

We have also attempted to maintain a foot in the past while keeping our eyes and ears open to the future by combining traditional concepts of philosophy, history, and sociology with emerging and futuristic perspectives of the field. We have analyzed several competing theories, models, and paradigms, and we have recommended several practical guidelines. In short, we have supplied a mix of material to help researchers, theoreticians, and practitioners develop their own interpretations of past, present, and future curriculum domains.

We extend a note of thanks to two valued contributors to the field of curriculum who, though both in their eighties, are still active in the field: Ralph Tyler and B. Othanel Smith, both of whom wrote the Foreword. We are also grateful to our respective mentors of curriculum: Virgil Clift, Hilda Grobman, and O. L. Davis. Finally, our sincere appreciation goes to the reviewers of the manuscript form of this text.

Allan C. Ornstein
Francis P. Hunkins

CURRICULUM:
FOUNDATIONS,
PRINCIPLES, AND ISSUES

chapter 1

THE FIELD OF CURRICULUM

Curriculum as a field of study is elusive and fragmentary, and what it is supposed to entail is open to a good deal of debate and even misunderstanding. Curriculum is both a subject to be taught at colleges and universities and a field in which practitioners work. Students who enroll in curriculum courses, as a minor or major field of study in education, usually study these courses at the graduate level. People who teach or train others, who engage in program development, instruction, supervision, and/or evaluation in schools and colleges, businesses, hospitals and health agencies, as well as governmental agencies are practicing curriculum.

What we mean by curriculum, what it involves, and who is involved are best understood by analyzing curriculum in a broad context. We thus look at curriculum in this text in terms of *approach* (or what others call an orientation, perspective, or position), and *definition*. We consider, also, the relationship and differences between the foundations and domains of curriculum, the theory and practice of curriculum, and curriculum and instruction.

In much of our discussion, we point to various curriculum texts published since 1980. This should not only help introduce the field, but it should also help put this text in context with other curriculum texts.

CURRICULUM APPROACHES

An individual's approach to curriculum reflects that person's view of the world, including what the person perceives as reality, the values he or she deems important, and the amount of knowledge he or she possesses. A curriculum approach reflects a *holistic* position or a *metaorientation*, encompassing the foundations of curriculum (the person's philosophy, view of history, view of psychology and learning theory, and view of social issues), domains of curriculum (common and important knowledge within the field), and the theoretical and practical principles of curriculum. An approach expresses a viewpoint about the development and design of curriculum, the role of the learner, teacher, and curriculum specialist in planning curriculum, the goals and objectives of the curriculum, and the important issues that need to be examined.

A curriculum approach reflects our views of schools and society; to some extent it may even become an all-encompassing outlook if we feel strongly about these views. By understanding one's curriculum approach, and the prevailing curriculum approach of the school or school district in which one works, it is possible to conclude whether one's professional view conflicts with the formal organizational view.

Although schools, over time, tend to become committed to a particular curriculum approach, many educators are not strongly committed to one approach. Many of them do not have a single or pure approach; rather, in some situations they emphasize one approach, and in other cases they advocate several approaches. In still other cases, they fail to recognize that they even reflect a particular attitudinal or behavioral curriculum approach, or that they are in fact influenced by many approaches. They need to recognize that curriculum textbook writers sometimes adhere to more than one curriculum approach. Moreover, curriculum specialists, even curriculum students, need to examine their approaches.

Curriculum approaches can be viewed from a technical and nontechnical, or scientific and nonscientific, perspective. (Note that the terms *nontechnical* and *nonscientific* do not suggest a negative or disparaging approach; rather, these two terms denote a contrast.) Technical-scientific approaches coincide with traditional theories and models of education, and reflect established and formal methods of schooling. Nontechnical and nonscientific approaches have evolved as part of avant-garde and experimental philosophies and politics of education: they tend to challenge established and formalized practices of education.

The remainder of this section outlines five curriculum approaches. The first three may be classified as technical or scientific, the latter two as nontechnical and nonscientific.

Behavioral-Rational Approach.

Rooted in the University of Chicago school (from Bobbitt and Charters to Tyler and Taba),[1] this is the oldest and still the major approach to curriculum. As a means-ends approach it is logical and prescriptive. It relies on technical and scientific principles, and includes models, plans, and step-by-step strategies for formulating curriculum. Goals and objectives are specified, content and activities are sequenced to coincide with the objectives, and learning outcomes are evaluated in relation to the goals and objectives.

This curriculum approach, which has been applied to all subjects for more than two-thirds of this century, constitutes a frame of reference against which other approaches to curriculum are compared.[2] Other names that have been used to identify this approach—including logical-positivist, conceptual-empiricist, experientalist, rational-scientific, and technocratic[3]—suggest that the approach is also technical and scientific and that it deals with principles for theoreticians and practitioners.

Textbooks written from this approach in the 1980s tend to stress other approaches as well.[4] Few pure behaviorists today are writing curriculum textbooks, because new, competing philosophies and learning theories are cropping up and expanding. Nonetheless, authors who cluster into the behavioral approach rely on prescriptive blueprints for curriculum making and consider the curriculum to be a plan with sequential and structured activities, and with predetermined roles among curriculum players. They are concerned with the technical issues of development and design. Theoretical issues that have merit are those that are related to technical matters from which to develop or design the curriculum. Practical issues are those that are concerned with logic, order, and rationality. Finally, most people who plan and develop curriculum utilize the behavioral-rational approach; regardless of how they may classify themselves or how others may classify them.

Systems-Managerial Approach.

This approach perceives the school as a social system, whereby students, teachers, curriculum specialists, and others, interact according to certain norms and behaviors. Curricularists who rely on this approach plan the curriculum in an organized way, and in terms of programs, schedules, space, materials, equipment, personnel, and resources. This approach advocates, among other things, selecting, organizing, and supervising people involved in curriculum decisions. Consideration is given to committee and group processes, communication processes, leadership methods and strategies, human relations, and decision making.

An offshoot of the behavioral-rational approach, the systems-managerial approach includes rational principles, but not necessarily behavioral approaches. The managerial aspect of the approach tends to zero in on supervisory and administrative aspects of curriculum, especially the organizational and implementation process. Advocates of this approach are interested in change and innovation, and in how curriculum specialists and supervisors can facilitate these processes. The curriculum specialist is considered to be a practitioner, not a theoretician, and an educational leader—a change agent, resource person, and facilitator.

The approach is rooted in the early school organizational and administrative models of the 1920s and 1930s, and combined a host of innovative curriculum and instructional plans that centered around individualization, departmentalization, grading, and work-study-social activities.

The systems-managerial approach became the dominant curriculum model in the 1950s and 1960s for the Association for Supervision and Curriculum Development and various school principals' and school superintendents' associations. During that era, Midwest school administrators and professors dominated the field of curriculum in terms of setting the priorities and agenda, establishing the direction of change and innovation, and planning and organizing curriculum.

The pacesetters for this era were such school superintendents as Robert Anderson (Park Forest, Illinois), William Cornog (New Trier Township High School, Winnetka, Illinois), Robert Gilchrist (University City, Missouri), Arthur Lewis (Minneapolis), Sidney Marland (Winnetka, Illinois), Lloyd Michael (Evanston, Illinois), Gordon McAndrew (Gary, Indiana) and J. Lloyd Trump (Waukegan, Illinois).[5]

These superintendents were very active politically. They used the administrative associations, and their respective journals and yearbooks, as platforms to publicize their ideas. Many, like Anderson, Gilchrist, Lewis, and Trump, became professors at major universities; others became active as board directors and executive committee members of the professional organizations that had major impact on curriculum, supervision, and administration.

These school administrators were less concerned about content than about organization and implementation. And they were less concerned about subject matter, methods, and materials than about improving curriculum in light of policies, plans, and people on a system-wide basis. They envisioned curriculum changes and innovation as they administered the resources and restructured the schools.

It was not far to leap from organizing people and policies, a managerial view, to organizing curriculum into a system such as *engineering:* processes necessary to plan the curriculum by such engineers as superintendents, directors, coordinators, and principals; *stages:* development, design, implementation, and evaluation; and *structures:* subjects, courses, units, and lessons. The systems approach in curriculum, somewhat technical and complex, was influenced by systems theory, systems analysis, systems engineering, and cybernetics. These concepts and principles, originally developed by social scientists in the 1960s, were used widely by school managers as part of administrative and organizational theory.

Most of the early curricularists who developed various curriculum systems, with the exception of professors George Beauchamp and Mauritz Johnson,[6] were once high-ranking school administrators (i.e., associate superintendent of curriculum). Some notable such innovators were Chester Babcock (Seattle Public Schools), Leslee Bishop (Livonia, Michigan, Public Schools), John McNeil (San Diego Public Schools), Stuart Rankin (Detroit Public Schools), Harold Shafer (Wyckoff, New Jersey, Public Schools), and Glenys Unruh (University City, Missouri, Public Schools). McNeil and Unruh are still active today. In fact, along with Ronald Doll, who also came from this era more than twenty-five years ago, they have published recent curriculum textbooks that express this systems-managerial point of view.[7]

Intellectual-Academic Approach.

Sometimes referred to as the traditional, encyclopedic, synoptic, or knowledge-oriented approach,[8] the intellectual-academic approach attempts to analyze and synthesize major positions, trends, and concepts of curriculum. The approach tends to be historical or philosophical, and, to a lesser extent, social in nature. The discussion of curriculum making is usually scholarly and theoretical (not practical), and concerned with many broad aspects of schooling, including the study of education. This expansion of curriculum boundaries relative to the subject of schooling, and the treatment of curriculum as intellectual thought, are reflected in a good deal of background in-

formation and broad overview of events and people.

This approach is rooted in the philosophical and intellectual works of John Dewey, Henry Morrison, and Boyd Bode.[9] It became popular between the 1930s and 1950s, and is illustrated by the lengthy and intellectual curriculum works of Caswell and Campbell, L. Thomas Hopkins, John and Mary Norton, B. Othanel Smith, and Florence Stratemeyer.[10] The influx of new topics related to curriculum during this period expanded the boundaries of the field to include a good number of trends and issues, and the integration of various instructional, teaching, learning, guidance, evaluation, supervision, and administrative procedures. The field became all-encompassing because the books published accumulated a great deal of curriculum knowledge and subject matter.

After the 1950s, major interest in curriculum centered around the structure of disciplines and qualitative methods. Thus the intellectual approach lost some of its glamor among curricularists. The texts in the 1980s that still reflect this approach frequently overwhelm beginning curriculum students who usually lack sufficient background information and philosophical and theoretical insights on the subject.[11] These texts tend to be more appreciated by advanced students of the field and by professors of curriculum.

Humanistic-Aesthetic Approach.

Other curricularists reflecting on the field contend that the just-described curriculum approaches are rigid. They propose that, in their attempt to be scientific and rational, curricularists miss the artistic and personal aspects of curriculum and instruction, do not consider the need for self-reflectiveness and self-actualization among learners, and ignore the sociopsychological dynamics of classrooms and schools. This view is rooted in progressive philosophy and the activities curriculum movement of the 1920s and 1930s, which highlighted the children's needs and interests and which was spearheaded by Teachers College of Columbia University by such people as Frederick Bosner, Hollis Caswell, William Kilpatrick,[12] and, to a lesser extent, by Ellsworth Collings, L. Thomas Hopkins, and Harold Rugg.[13]

From this movement, a host of curriculum strategies emerged, mainly at the elementary school level, including lessons based on life experiences, group games, group projects, dramatizations, field trips, social enterprises, interest centers, and child and adolescent needs. These activities included problem solving and active student participation; they emphasized socialization and life adjustment for students, as well as stronger family and school-community ties.

The humanistic-aesthetic approach became popular again in the 1970s as relevancy, radical school reform, and alternative education became part of the reform movement in education. Current texts that reflect the humanistic-aesthetic approach are authored by Elliot Eisner and Glen Hass.[14]

Various sociopsychological and child-centered theories to curriculum are derived from this approach. The formal or specified curriculum is not the only curriculum to consider; the informal and hidden curriculum are also worthwhile. Also, this approach considers the whole child, not only the cognitive dimension. Humanistic theories of learning are given equal billing, and sometimes greater emphasis, than behavioral and cognitive theories. Music, art, literature, health education, and the humanities are just as important as science and math (and other academic subjects).

Curriculum specialists who believe in this approach tend to put faith in cooperative learning, independent learning, small-group learning, and social activities as opposed to competitive, teacher-dominated, large-group learning and only cognitive instruction. Each child, according to this approach, has considerable input in the curriculum, and shares responsibility with parents, teachers, and curriculum specialists in planning that curriculum.

Today, demands for educational excellence and tougher academic standards put increasing stress on higher forms of cognition (i.e., problem solving, critical thinking, intellectual discovery, and divergent thinking), and on subjects such as science and math (not art or music). The humanistic-aesthetic approach thus represents a minority position in curriculum.

Reconceptualists.

Some curriculum textbook writers consider that reconceptualists represent an approach to curriculum.[15] But reconceptionalists lack a model for developing and designing curriculum (or for dealing with technical matters); rather, they tend to focus on larger ideological and moral issues of education (not only curriculum) and economic and political institutions of society (not only schools). For this reason, and because they lack a model for planning curriculum, we feel they should be discussed more in a philosophical or political context—not as a curriculum approach.

Reconceptionalists view schools as an extension of society. They hold that the purpose of curriculum ought to be emancipatory but that instead it has become controlling and preserving of the existing order. Most of these curricularists are not textbook writers (broad based, objective, nonpolitical, nonpartisan); rather, they tend to be educational critics—advocates of a particular philosophical and political position.[16]

Rooted in the philosophy and social activism of such early reconstructionists as Counts, Rugg, and Benjamin,[17] these new curricularists wish to rethink, reconsider, and reconceptualize the curriculum. Not only do they challenge the traditional, scientific, and rational views of curriculum, but they also criticize those holding them for embodying their own subjective and imperfect sets of values. They assert that other ways of knowing are not quantifiable or objective as the dominant notion of "good research" in education. Their approach to curriculum is subjective, political, and ideological, and they do not rely on either the hard sciences or empirical methods for answers.

DEFINITION OF CURRICULUM

What is curriculum? What is its purpose? How does it affect students and teachers? The way we define curriculum by and large reflects our approach to it. But the relationship between approach and definition is neither perfect nor mutually exclusive; approaches and definitions overlap. We can specify five basic views or definitions of curriculum. The first two, the most popular, delineate two extremes: specific and prescriptive versus broad and general.

A curriculum can be defined as a *plan* for action, or a written document, which includes strategies for achieving desired goals or ends. This position, popularized by Tyler and Taba, exemplifies the overlap previously mentioned between definition and approach. Most behavioral and systems-managerial people today agree with this definition. For example, J. Galen Saylor defines curriculum "as a plan for providing sets of learning opportunities for persons to be educated."[18] Writes David Pratt, "Curriculum is an organized set of formal educational and/or training intentions."[19] Wiles and Bondi view "curriculum as a plan for learning [whereby] objectives determine what learning is important."[20]

Curriculum can, however, be defined broadly—as dealing with the *experiences* of the learner. This view considers almost anything in school, even outside of school (as long as it is planned) as part of the curriculum. It is rooted in Dewey's definition of experience and education, as well as in Caswell and Campbell's view, from the 1930s, that curriculum was "all the experiences children have under the guidance of teachers."[21]

Humanistic-aesthetic curricularists and elementary school curricularists subscribe to this definition, which, over the years, has been interpreted more broadly by textbook writers. State Shepherd and Ragan, "The curriculum consists of the ongoing experiences of children under the guidance of the school." It represents "a special environment . . . for helping children achieve self-realization through active participation within the school."[22] Eisner points out that the curriculum "is a program [the school] offers to its students." It consists of a "preplanned series of educational hurdles" and "an entire range of experiences a child has within the school."[23] Finally, Hass contends that "curriculum is all of the experiences that individuals have in a program of education . . . which is planned in terms of . . . theory and research or past and present professional practice."[24]

Three other definitions fall in between these two common, almost extreme definitions. Curriculum can be considered as a *system* for dealing with people and the processes, or organization of personnel and procedures, for implementing that system. Most systems-managerial curricularists adopt this definition.[25] Curriculum can also be viewed as a *field of study*, comprising its own foundations and domains of knowledge, as well as its own research, theory, and principles. Intellectual-academics, such as Orlosky and Smith, Schubert, and the Tanners, often subscribe to this view of curriculum.[26]

Finally, curriculum can be considered in terms of *subject matter* (mathematics, science, English, history, etc.) or content (the way we organize and assimilate information). We can also talk about subject matter or content in terms of different grade levels. Nonetheless, the emphasis from this viewpoint would be on facts, concepts, and generalization of a particular subject or group of subjects, as opposed to generic concepts and principles of curriculum making that cut across the field of curriculum. There is no particular curriculum approach that adheres to this definition, and any curriculum approach could adopt this definition. Of all the current texts, only Shepherd and Ragan examine subject matter in depth, and at the elementary school level.[27]

George Beauchamp asserts that only

definitions involving a plan, system, and field of study represent "key" or "legitimate" uses of the word curriculum.[28] But the other two definitions (experiences and subjects) are also consistent with good theory and practice. Surprisingly, there are no real curriculum advocates of subjects and grades. Because most school systems across the country develop curriculum in terms of different subjects and grades, it would seem that we need to view curriculum more in line with this definition than others. The fact that practitioners use this form of curriculum on a daily basis, whereas theoreticians rarely do (usually professing that they wish to examine generic concepts and principles that are applicable to most subjects and grades) suggests that the two groups are not really talking to each other. Although many university curriculum departments offer courses in elementary and secondary school curriculum, they rarely offer curriculum courses by subjects—mathematics curriculum, science curriculum, and so on. (Curricularists commonly contend that too few students would enroll in these courses to justify them.)

The Problem of Definition.

The varied definitions of curriculum create confusion and trivialize the field. Definitional debates take away time and energy from substantive problems and issues; from research, theoretical, and practical approaches. Because curricularists cannot agree on just what is curriculum, it follows that they lack common terms and have trouble communicating with each other.

Consider the two most common definitions. The more precise one's definition of curriculum, and the more a person relies on a preconceived plan or document, the greater the tendency to omit, ignore, or miss relevant factors related to teaching and learning because they are not part of the written plan. As Doll points out, "Every school has a planned, formal acknowledged curriculum," but it also has "an unplanned,

informal and hidden one" that must be considered.[29] The planned, formal curriculum focuses on goals, objectives, subject matter, and organization of instruction; the unplanned, informal curriculum deals with social-psychological interaction among students and teachers, especially their feelings, attitudes, and behaviors.

If we only consider the planned curriculum, or if we are too prescriptive in our approach, we ignore the unintended and dysfunctional (negative) consequences of our plans and actions (i.e., suppose the student begins to dislike history or English, even though the teacher's intention was to teach Tolstoy). The point is, we cannot be too rigid or close-ended, and try to fill in all the boxes. There are too many gray areas in education, and too many human variables that we cannot control or plan for in advance. The curriculum must consider the smells and sounds of the classroom, the intuitive judgments and hunches of the teacher, and the needs and interests of the students that evolve and cannot always be planned by the student, teacher, or curriculum specialist.

On the other hand, a broad umbrella-like definition of curriculum as school experiences results in other problems. It assumes that almost everything that goes on in school can be classified or discussed in terms of curriculum. It even suggests that curriculum is synonymous with education. It also connotes that almost every field or discipline in schools of education has implications for curriculum or is part of the curriculum field. If nearly everything in schools and in the study of education is related to curriculum, classifying what is not curriculum is meaningless. The content of curriculum becomes so diffuse that no one can have sufficient knowledge, or knowledge that is agreed to be of sufficient value, in the field. Given this macro view of curriculum, it is extremely difficult to become a specialist or expert in the field. When the content and scope of any field become all-encompassing, or so enlarged that they overlap with those of many other fields, then it becomes too difficult to delineate that field (say, curriculum) and separate it from other fields.

Background Issues for Defining the Field.

Content or subject matter issues are relevant too. Is it appropriate to talk about a social studies or mathematics curriculum or about curriculum in general? Are there general principles of curriculum that apply to all subjects, or specific principles that apply to specific subjects? Should subject matter be organized around separate disciplines or based on interdisciplinary and core approaches? To what extent is subject a matter of student choice, professional choice, or parent choice? Should it be determined by the community, state, or nation? How should subjects be organized: around graded or nongraded approaches, behavioral objectives, student activities, social or community values, future jobs? What portion of subject matter should be classified as "general," "specialized," or "elective"? What is the appropriate mix of common subjects versus optional subjects? And what is the appropriate stress on facts, concepts, and principles of subject matter? As Beauchamp writes, "The posture . . . one assumes with respect to the content of a curriculum inevitably will be of great influence upon . . . theory and planning."[30] Actually, it has a major influence on everything that follows, from developing, designing, implementing, and evaluating the curriculum, from planning the policies and programs to determining the processes and products of the curriculum.

Other issues are related to people. Who are the major participants? To what extent should students, teachers, parents, and community members be involved in curriculum planning? Why are school administrators assuming greater roles in curriculum matters, and curriculum specialists assuming fewer roles? What are the roles and responsibilities of researchers and practitioners in curriculum making? And, how do we improve their communication?

Fundamental Questions.

Asking the right questions is crucial for addressing basic concerns in curriculum, and for determining the basic concepts, principles, and research methods of the field. If we ask the wrong questions, the discussions that follow (even the answers) are of little value. The danger in listing a host of fundamental questions, however, is that they tend to become translated as a set of principles or steps to be blindly followed. Indeed, appropriate questions can be used as a base for raising issues and problems that curriculum specialists need to address, whether they deal in theory or practice—or both.

The first list of fundamental questions was formulated by a famous twelve-person committee on curriculum making, organized for the Twenty-Sixth Yearbook of the National Society for the Study of Education (NSSE). This group of curriculum specialists, perhaps the most prestigious ever convened to present a general statement on the principles of curriculum making, started the second volume of the Yearbook with eighteen "fundamental questions" to serve as a basis for "viewing . . . the issues and problems of curriculum" for that era.[31] The eighteen questions focused on five major themes: (1) the role of the school in American Society; (2) the place and function of subject matter; (3) the methods and materials for facilitating learning; (4) the role of the professional curriculum specialist; and (5) organizational and administrative questions of curriculum development.[32]

With the exception of Schubert, current textbook writers in curriculum do not deal with these fundamental questions.[33] But such questions can help you, the reader, establish the basic concepts and principles of the field, and can serve as the basis for your dealing with the problems and issues in curriculum. The fundamental questions in Table 1-1 serve as bench marks for the remaining chapters of this text. The questions we raise are neutral, and they set the tone

TABLE 1-1 Fundamental Curriculum Questions

1. How is curriculum defined?
2. What philosophies and theories are we communicating, intentionally or not, in our curriculum?
3. What social and political forces influence curriculum? Which ones are most pertinent? Which constrain or impose limitations?
4. How does learning take place? What learning activities are most suitable for meeting the needs of our learners? How can these activities best be organized?
5. What are the domains of curriculum knowledge? What types of curriculum knowledge are essential?
6. What are the essential parts of a curriculum?
7. Why do changes in curriculum take place? How does change affect the curriculum?
8. What are the roles and responsibilities of the curriculum specialist?
9. How is curriculum best organized?
10. What are the roles and responsibilities of the teacher and student in organizing curriculum?
11. What are our aims and goals? How do we translate them into objectives?
12. How do we define our educational needs? Whose needs? How do we prioritize these needs?
13. What subject matter or content is most worthwhile? What are the best forms of content? How do we organize them?
14. How do we measure or verify what we are trying to achieve? Who is accountable, for what, and to whom?
15. What is the appropriate relationship between curriculum and instruction? Curriculum and supervision? Curriculum and evaluation?

for discussing (1) the foundations of curriculum; (2) the domains (including the development and design) of curriculum; (3) theory and practice in curriculum; (4) teaching and learning; (5) change and innovation in curriculum; and (6) issues and trends of the field.

FOUNDATIONS OF CURRICULUM

Debates continue on what is curriculum, and on how to outline the basic foundations (or boundaries) and domains (knowledge) of the field. An optimistic view would be that almost all, if not all, the knowledge con-

cerning curriculum is available in the literature, but at present it is "widely scattered" and is either "unknown or unread" by a majority of those who teach or practice curriculum.[34] A pessimistic view is that the field lacks purpose and direction because it has extensively "adapted and borrowed subject matter from a number of [other] disciplines," including its major "principles, knowledge and skills."[35] This is basically the same criticism that Joseph Schwab made some twenty years ago, when he complained that the field was "morbid [because] it has adopted theories from outside the field of education . . . from which to deduce . . . aims and procedures for schools and classrooms."[36]

Some argue that until these problems are resolved, curriculum as a field of study will be characterized by considerable confusion, conflict, and lack of coherence, and that it will continue to lack a well-organized professional and political constituency. A more optimistic view, however, considers this openness or lack of closure as a source of richness and challenge. It illustrates that curriculum is dynamic and subject to change, like schools and society.

Major Foundations: Philosophy, History, Psychology, and Sociology.

The foundations of curriculum set the external boundaries of the knowledge of curriculum and define what constitutes valid sources of information from which come accepted theories, principles, and ideas relevant to the field of curriculum.

The commonly accepted foundations of curriculum include the following knowledge areas: philosophical, historical, psychological, and social (sometimes cultural, political, or economical foundations are included as part of or separate from the social foundations). Although curriculum writers generally agree on the foundation areas, few attempt to analyze or discuss these four areas in depth. Of all the recent texts in curriculum, Miller and Seller put the most emphasis on the foundation areas—50 percent of their text deals with historical, philosophical, social, cultural, and psychological foundations.[37] They assert that the foundation areas serve as the basis for theory in curriculum, a view that corresponds somewhat with the intellectual-academic approach to curriculum. Not since Robert Zais, another intellectual-academic, has such emphasis been put on the major foundation areas of curriculum.[38] Other curricularists do not put as much emphasis on the foundation areas, but still seriously discuss the foundations in their respective textbooks.[39]

Most texts emphasize one or two foundation areas. The texts of Hunkins and Saylor et al., for example, emphasize the social foundations. They examine various social, as well as related political and economic issues.[40] Although Shepherd and Ragan examine some historical and social foundations, they also examine psychological principles and ideas (without the label foundations) extensively throughout the text. Elliot Eisner also puts strong emphasis on psychological foundations, especially the psychology of teaching and learning.[41] Schubert and the Tanners present an extensive historical overview of curriculum, but weave some social and philosophical overtones throughout their respective historical treatments of the field.[42]

Of course, merely examining the foundation areas is insufficient. Curricularists need to show the relationship of the foundation areas and curriculum. They must analyze and synthesize what is known about each of the foundations, and present implications that are relevant to curriculum. In this connection, Herbert Kliebard claims that the field of curriculum is a synoptic one. The specialist in curriculum brings perspectives from other fields to bear on curriculum. This means the curriculum person examines and uses the concepts, methods, and research tools of the philosopher, historian, psychologist, sociologist, economist, and political scientist.[43]

Regardless of their approach, or their philosophical, historical, social, or psychological views, it is natural for curriculum people to rely on the foundation areas as a means of studying and practicing curriculum. This text examines four foundation areas (in four chapters) with the intention of presenting important sources of information from other fields that are pertinent to curriculum. It is important that the readers analyze and interpret the knowledge of foundations presented to establish and clarify the external boundaries of curriculum.

The Growing Influence of Psychology.

We need to point out, also, the growing influence upon curriculum and instruction of one particular foundation area. Recent trends since the Sputnik era of the 1950s show the increasing impact of psychology. This was illustrated by the behaviorist and cognitive models of compensatory education in the 1960s, the humanistic models of learning in the 1970s, and the cognitive theories dealing with educational productivity and critical thinking in the 1980s. It is further evidenced by the shift of subject matter to disciplinary inquiry and modes of thinking, and from emphasis on traditional materials and media to language and reading processes. Finally, the growing influence of psychology is considered to be a major support of instruction, learning, and teaching—in the professional literature and research dealing with individualized learning, cooperative learning, academic learning time, direct instruction, mastery learning, and more effective schooling, as well as by the empirical emphasis on teaching methods, teacher behavior, teacher competencies, and teacher effectiveness. What has happened is that such instructional and learning theorists as Berliner, Bloom, Brophy, Doyle, Gage, Good, Evertson, Walberg, and Wang, who have strong research, measurement, and/or statistical backgrounds, seem to have filled a void left by curricularists who in the past addressed these twin areas and envisioned instruction and learning as integral to the discussion of curriculum.

This trend is especially exemplified by the educational psychologists, who dominate and deliver most of the papers at the American Educational Research Association (AERA) in Division C, "Learning and Instruction," and by· their growing influence even in Division B, "Curriculum Studies".[44] Even in two popular curriculum journals, *Educational Leadership* and *Phi Delta Kappan*, most of the papers on instruction and learning (as well as teaching) are increasingly written by educational psychologists.[45]

Indeed, some curricularists seem to have lost some of their initiative and influence in instruction and learning, what they did well (between the 1920s and 1950s) when the field of curriculum was expanding and including many aspects of instruction and learning. At that time, many curriculum leaders (Harold Alberty, Nelson Bossing, Gertrude Noar, John and Mary Norton, Hilda Taba, Ralph Tyler, B. Othanel Smith, etc.) had strong psychology backgrounds, and greater interest in educational measurement and assessment.

Some curricularists feel uncomfortable about the inroads of psychology; moreover, many appear to be less familiar with this foundation area compared with others. In this connection, we note the scant discussion of psychological foundations in curriculum texts. (Only two current curriculum texts, Eisner's and Shepherd and Ragan's, reflect a strong psychological approach; Doll and Hunkins's contain some psychological discussion).[46] Prior to these texts, one would have to turn back to Taba to find a basic text in curriculum that emphasized psychology.[47]

DOMAINS OF CURRICULUM

Whereas the foundations of curriculum represent the external boundaries of the field, the domains of curriculum define the internal boundaries, or accepted knowledge, of the field that can be derived from examining published textbooks, articles, and research papers. Although curriculum specialists generally agree on the foundation areas, they often do not agree on what represents the domains or common knowledge of curriculum. The latter problem suggests that the field is neither a disciplined body nor a full profession based upon a defined body of knowledge. Many efforts have been made to structure a matrix or map of the knowledge in curriculum so as to help conceptualize or set the boundaries within the field. According to some observers, the problem is that the knowledge is diffused in several sources, many unrecognized as curriculum sources. In addition, many known sources are unread because there is so much literature to read.[48]

The lack of consensus of the domains of curriculum is illustrated by the experts themselves. For example, Beauchamp divided curriculum knowledge into planning, implementation, and evaluation.[49] Foshay and Beilin divided curriculum knowledge into theory, design, and change.[50] More recently, Fenwick English viewed curriculum in terms of ideological (or philosophical-scientific), technical (or design), and operational (or managerial) issues.[51] Finally, Edmund Short outlines the domains of curriculum into policy making, development, evaluation, change, decision making, activities or fields of study, and forms and language of inquiry (or theory).[52]

Despite this lack of consensus, it is important to establish a framework for conceptualizing the domains of curriculum—that is, the significant and indispensable curriculum knowledge necessary to conduct research and make theoretical and practical decisions about curriculum. The problem is, however, that few curriculum writers can agree on the domains of curriculum knowledge; in some cases no framework exists that connotes curriculum as a distinct enterprise with its own boundaries, internal structures, relations, and activities. We maintain that, of all the domains of curriculum knowledge, the *development* and *design* of the curriculum—what some observers refer to as the theoretical aspects and what others call the technical aspects of curriculum—are crucial for any text.

Curriculum Development.

Analyzing curriculum in terms of development is the traditional and most common approach to the field. The idea is to show how curriculum evolves or is planned, implemented, and evaluated, as well as what various people, processes, and procedures are involved in constructing the curriculum. Such development is usually examined in a logical step-by-step fashion, based on behavioral and managerial approaches to curriculum and rooted in scientific principles of education. In other words, the principles are generalizable. Many curriculum texts today use the terms *development* and *plan* in their titles—and thus reflect this thinking.

Saylor et al., for example, outline a concise four-step planning model, which includes goals and objectives, curriculum design (or specifications), curriculum implementation (or instruction), and curriculum evaluation. The planning model is influenced by several social forces and three social sources of curriculum—society, learners, and knowledge.[53] Another easy-to-understand approach is by Unruh and Unruh, who outline five developmental steps: goals and objectives, needs assessment, content, implementation, and evaluation.[54] Francis Hunkins has designed a similar seven-step model, in seven corresponding chapters: curriculum conceptualization and legitimization, curriculum diagnosis, content selection, experience selection, curriculum implementation, curriculum evaluation, and curriculum maintenance.[55]

There are more complicated curriculum development models, but they are geared for the more advanced student of curriculum. All of these development models, however, attempt to show the relationship of curriculum to various decisions, activities, and processes. They provide us with guideposts, and structure to clarify our thinking. The models tend to be graphically or pictorially illustrated, and in terms of input, transformations, and output; they are se-quential and rational, the curriculum is viewed as a total system, and all enterprises within the model are conceived as subsystems. The development models are also theoretical and scientific, and they are designed to increase understanding of facts, correlates, and relationships of curriculum. Finally, the models are conceived in technical terms—with the assumption that one must be knowledgeable of the field to fully appreciate and understand them.

Many curriculum textbook writers tend to formulate developmental models. However, some curricularists use the term *development* in their respective textbook titles without either formulating their own developmental models or even paying much attention to other models.[56] But the emphasis on development is not without pitfalls. By basing their developmental models around scientific and technical terms, writers tend to overlook the human aspects of teaching and learning. By formulating steps that are concrete, prescriptive, and measurable, they tend to ignore processes that are not readily observable or measurable, that are not precisely consistent, or that are not applicable to a good deal of control. What they sometimes ignore are the personal attitudes, emotions, and feelings linked to teaching and learning, and the values and beliefs involved in curriculum making.

By adopting developmental models, curricularists tend to constrain curriculum choices and to limit flexibility in the various curriculum sequences or steps—from aims and objectives to evaluation of learning tasks and outcomes. They sometimes forget that the path to curriculum development is strewn with many concessions to social and political realities, qualitative judgments that require familiarity with teaching effectiveness and allowable choices in teaching methods and learning activities, and alternatives that recognize that one kind of curriculum may be more suitable and successful with one school (or with one population of students and teachers) than another.

However, adopting one or more of these developmental models does not prevent one from being mindful of these pitfalls. Some of the models' advocates would argue that by being systematic, they are able to consider students in all of their complexity and to manage the dynamics and decisions of curriculum activity; moreover, they might argue that their models consider multiple variables and permit choices.

Curriculum Design.

Curriculum design refers to the way we conceptualize the curriculum and arrange its major components (subject matter or content, instructional methods and materials, learner experiences or activities) to provide direction and guidance as we develop the curriculum. Most curriculum writers do not have a single or "pure" design for curriculum; they tend to be influenced by many designs, as they are by many approaches, and they are likely to draw bits and pieces from different designs. Unless they are highly motivated or compelled by one curriculum approach, or a set of values or tools for analyzing the world around them, they tend to use eclectic designs and to intermix ideas from several sources.

Nonetheless, the way someone designs a curriculum is partially rooted in his or her approach to and definition of curriculum. For example, those who view curriculum in behaviorist terms with a prescribed plan and set of learning outcomes and those who consider curriculum to be a system of managing people and organizing procedures will produce different curriculum designs. Those who have strong psychological views of teaching and learning will also present different designs for curriculum from those who have strong social or political views of schools. Whereas curriculum development tends to be technical and scientific, curriculum design is more varied, because it is based on curricularists' values and beliefs about education, priorities of schooling, and views of how students learn. Just asking questions such as what are schools for, what shall we teach, how shall we teach, and what learning theories should we stress evokes

considerable controversy. The positions writers adopt to these questions, however, reflect their preferred designs in curriculum.

A number of current curriculum texts focus on a particular curriculum design or a choice of designs. For example, Saylor et al. distinguish five curriculum designs: (1) subject matter/disciplines, which involve subject matter and knowledge; (2) competencies/technology, which are sequential, analytical, and behaviorist; (3) human traits/processes, which focus on human behavior and group behavior; (4) social functions/activities, which pertain to social living and societal needs; and (5) individual needs and interests, which comprise student-oriented or child-centered activities.[57]

Wiles and Bondi present six different designs: (1) conservative-liberal arts designs, which emphasize knowledge and intellectual pursuits; (2) educational technology designs, which focus on goals and ends, objectivity, and efficiency; (3) humanistic designs, which propose student-centered curricula; (4) vocational designs, which are concerned with vocational and economic aspects of schooling; (5) social-reconstruction designs, which are aimed at social improvement of society; and (6) deschooling designs, which emphasize the deemphasis of formal schooling.[58]

In general, a curriculum design should provide a basic frame of reference for planning—or more precisely, for developing—curriculum. A curriculum design is influenced to some extent by the writer's curriculum approach, but more precisely by his or her views of teaching, learning, and instruction.

The people who go into teaching, and eventually become curriculum specialists in schools, are often traditional and content oriented. This is good, because schools usually adopt conservative and cognitive designs to curriculum, highly liberal and humanistic designs are likely to encounter difficulty in most formal school settings. Schools in our society, and almost everywhere else, are given the traditional task of socializing students in accordance with the norms of society (a conservative function) and pursuing intellectual tasks (a cognitive function).

Other Domains of Curriculum.

Those who study curriculum, and who contribute to the professional literature, must constantly deal with other domains of curriculum. Opinions about what curriculum knowledge is essential vary from one scholar to another and from one textbook writer to another. There appears to be more disagreement than agreement in the status and scope of remaining domains of curriculum. As Rosales-Dordelly and Short assert, "The status of the body of curriculum knowledge has been described by scholars in the field as amorphous, diffuse, incoherent, and fragmentary. . . . Few advances have been made in conceptualizing the field."[59] In introducing his text, McNeil puts it another way: "Everything that ought to be known about curriculum has not been put into the book."[60]

The minimum consensus for which we can strive is that a curriculum text include a discussion of development and design. Some might argue that it is important to include, also, discussions of current policies, trends, and issues in curriculum; methods of curriculum change and innovation; methods of curriculum research and inquiry; basic language and concepts of curriculum; and other critiquing ways in which the field is understood.[61] Whatever other curriculum knowledge we can agree upon in the future as essential would facilitate theoretical and practical decisions in curriculum.

THEORY AND PRACTICE

A field of study basically involves theoretical and practical knowledge. By theory we mean the most advanced and valid knowledge available that can be generalized and applied to many situations. Theory often establishes the framework of the field and helps persons (researchers and practitioners) within the field analyze and synthesize data, organize concepts and principles, suggest new ideas and relations, and even speculate about the future. According to Beauchamp, theory may be defined as the knowledge and statements that "give functional meaning to a series of events [and] take the form of definitions, operational constructs, assumptions, postulates, hypothesis, generalizations, laws or theorems." In the case of curriculum theory, the subject matter involves "decisions about . . . the use of a curriculum, the development of curriculum, curriculum design and curriculum evaluation."[62] This definition suggests a scientific and technical approach that emphasizes the domain of knowledge which corresponds with curriculum development and also with most textbooks today.

Good theory in curriculum, or in education for that matter, describes and explains the various relationships that exist in the field. It also implies that there are elements of predictability, or that there are rigorous laws that yield high probability and control. Good theory should also prescribe actions to be taken; however, we do not always use theory productively in our practice or in education in general.

The more variable, complex, or unpredictable one views the teaching-learning process, the more one is impelled toward a belief that it is impossible to determine or agree upon generalizations or to obtain high predictability of outcomes. Curriculum, like other aspects of education, involves the use of judgments, hunches, and insights that are not always conducive to laws, principles, or even generalizations. A curriculum often does not emerge as a tightly regulated, predictable, or concise set of enterprises, or as a result of a single or theoretical mix of principles or processes; rather, it evolves as one act and one choice that lead to others, as interests emerge, and, finally, as educators reflect and quietly self-analyze their thinking.

Nonetheless, all curriculum texts should try to incorporate theory throughout the discussion to be systematic in their approach and to establish worthwhile practices. In fact, according to Taba, "any enterprise as complex as curriculum requires some kind of theoretical or conceptual framework of thinking to guide it."[63] There are many theories and theoretical constructs to examine, depending on the author's knowledge and interpretation of curriculum. Ideally, the data should be what we might call "hard" data—scientifically verifiable, quantifiable, and/or based on research principles that can be generalized in similar situations. *Model, paradigm*, or *system* referents can be developed, too, to show various relationships that exist. Most theoretical discussions in curriculum, in fact, rely on one or more of these three referents.

Most curriculum textbook authors would argue that their approaches are grounded in good theory, and that they examine the various theoretical structures and relationships that exist in curriculum. Some authors, such as Unruh and Unruh and Zais, include (like we do) separate chapters on theory.[64] Others, like McNeil, combine theory and research in one chapter.[65]

Recent reconceptualist curricularists, however, rely on nonverifiable and nonquantifiable data, what we might call "soft" data. Instead of presenting logical, rational, or so-called objective models, paradigms, or systems to show various curriculum relationships, they emphasize personal biographies, literary criticism, philosophical inquiry, psychoanalysis, and aesthetic and artistic knowledge, as well as ideological (or social and political) analysis—which can sometimes be construed as provocative and subjective. Their tools of inquiry are value laden, not objective; their emphasis is on qualitative matters, not quantitative data. By most social science standards, their perspective would not be considered scientific in terms of basic or traditional standards. They tend to focus on contemporary issues and to carefully select "proofs" and arguments that support preconceived beliefs.

Reconceptualists would argue that traditional social science methods have dominated, under the guise of certainty, logic, and objectivity, but that their methods introduce new knowledge, new ways of knowing, and new tools of research.[66] They argue that traditional curriculum thinkers and theorizers are ideological, and that their methods and models are also based on preconceived assumptions and values.[67]

From Theory to Practice.

The test of good theory is whether it can guide practice. In reverse, good practice is based on theory. By practice, we mean the procedures, methods, and skills that apply to the working world, where a person is on the job or actively involved in his or her profession. These procedures and methods are teachable and can be applied in different situations. When applied they should result in the practitioner being considered "successful" or "effective."

Regardless of the theories discussed in any book, those who work with, shape, or formulate curriculum in one way or another have to deal with practice. Such people include administrators, supervisors, and teachers; curriculum developers and curriculum evaluators; textbook authors and test makers; and individuals assigned to curriculum committees, accrediting agencies, school boards, and local, regional, state, and federal educational agencies. The idea is to present theories that are workable for these practitioners, that make sense, and that can explain and be applied to the real world of classrooms and schools.

According to Elizabeth Vallance, "much ado [is] made about the split between theory and practice in the dialogues and concerns about professional curriculum workers." The crux of the matter is to provide "practical answers to very practical questions having to do with design, development, implementation, and evaluation of curricula." The distinctions between theory and practice are secondary to Vallance, because both aspects of curriculum focus on the "same curriculum problems."[68]

The problem is, however, that most

curricularists, including those who write textbooks, have difficulty in fusing theory with practice. This is true even though many books in curriculum today emphasize "theory" and "practice,"[69] or "principles" and "processes"[70] to reflect some form of theory and practice, in their titles. Perhaps the reason curricularists have difficulty making the connection between theory and practice is that their methods of inquiry lend themselves more to theoretical discussions and less to practical matters. Also, good theory is recognized by professors of the field (and the research community in general) as a worthwhile endeavor; good practice is often misconstrued by theoreticians as a "cookbook" or as "dos and don'ts" that are second rate or unimportant.

Most curriculum texts are more theoretical than practical, but so are education textbooks in general. Despite their claims, curricularists seem unable to make the leap from theory to practice, from the textbook and college course to the classroom and school (or other organizations). Good theory in curriculum (and in other fields of education) often gets lost as practitioners (say, teachers) try to apply what they learned in college to the job setting in a search for practical solutions to common, everyday problems.

The problem of translating theory into practice is further aggravated by practitioners who feel that practical considerations are more worthwhile than theory; most teachers and principals view theory as unpractical and "how to do" approaches as helpful. In short, many theoreticians ignore the practitioners, and many practitioners ignore the theoreticians. Moreover, many theoretical discussions of curriculum are divorced from practical application in the classroom, and many practical discussions of curriculum rarely consider theoretical relationships.

Practice involves selecting strategies and rules that apply to various situations, like good theory, but all situations are not the same. This becomes especially evident when practitioners try to apply the theory they learn in their textbooks. Adopting the right method for the appropriate situation is not an easy task, and involves a good deal of common sense and experience, which no one can learn from theoretical discussions. No matter how scientific we think our theories are, a certain amount of art is involved in the practice of curriculum—intuitive judgments and hunches that cannot be easily predicted or generalized from one situation to another, and this confounds theory.

Just what, then, does curriculum practice involve? The response is open to debate. But we might say that curriculum practice includes understanding the constraints and specifics operating within the school (or organization in which one is working) and comprehending the goals and priorities of the school and the needs of the students and staff. It also involves planning and working with procedures and processes that can be implemented in classrooms (or any formal group setting) and schools (or any formal organization). A successful practitioner in curriculum is capable of developing, implementing, and evaluating the curriculum—that is, he or she can select and organize (1) goals and objectives; (2) subject matter; (3) methods, materials, and media; and (4) learning experiences and activities that are suitable for learners.

Curriculum Certification.

The fact that curriculum lacks certification—specified statewide or professional requirements—adds to the problem of defining and conceptualizing the field, and agreeing on curriculum courses at the college and university level. This lack of certification should be considered seriously, because we need competent people who can make wise curriculum decisions. Curriculum making is a complicated procedure that cannot be left to just anyone or any group. We need people qualified to serve as generalists and specialists in curriculum, both as resource agents and decision makers. And we need people who can maintain a curriculum balance—in terms of goals, subject matter, and learning activities—given the numerous special-interest groups who wish to impose their brand of education on schools.

Not only do minimum requirements for curriculum personnel vary among school systems within the same state, not to mention among states, but the programs in curriculum vary considerably among colleges and universities as well. Because there are no state or professional regulations, each school of education usually decides its own requirements and the courses it will use to meet these requirements. The result is a proliferation of elective courses in curriculum programs, and a lack of specialized and general, agreed-upon courses. Even when curriculum course titles are similar, wide differences in content and level of instruction are common.

The irony is that there is great confusion about content and experiences in a field that should be very clear about its curriculum. Although there are many good curriculum programs at the university level, there is little guarantee that curricularists who graduate from a program know how to develop, implement, and evaluate a curriculum—or that they can translate theory into practice. Some curriculum students may not have taken courses in development, implementation, or evaluation (especially students in administration), whereas others may have taken several. And, no test or screening device helps school systems or school board officials make choices about curriculum personnel, and their expertise in curriculum. This also adds to the problem of defining who curriculum specialists or generalists, and what their respective job titles, roles, and responsibilities, are. Is a supervisor a curriculum generalist or specialist? What about a principal who is supposed to be a curriculum and instructional leader? Is a resource teacher, consultant, or director a curriculum person? And what about the classroom teacher?

Professionals are certified in such other fields as teaching, counseling, school psychology, supervision, administration, and so on. Job descriptions and related course requirements are defined. Students can major

in curriculum but they are at risk, because curriculum jobs are not well defined and there are no certification requirements or licenses that protect their jobs. Curriculum positions are definitely available in schools, universities, and local, regional, state, and federal education agencies, but without certification someone other than a curriculum person can obtain the same job.

Actually, many curriculum specialists who work in schools are certified in other fields, which means that their loyalties are not often in curriculum or that their educational preparation and professional reading habits may be closely aligned to other fields. Similarly, professors of curriculum, unlike professors of elementary education, reading, counseling, educational administration, and so on, are usually schooled in many disciplines, not only curriculum per se. Thus, the field is open to several interpretations by the experts themselves—what curriculum should encompass, what knowledge is of tangible substance, and what content and experiences are essential.

The lack of certification weakens the role of curricularists in the schools, and the influence of curricularists at the university level. It also encourages local and state policy makers and legislators to develop and design the school curriculum—to impose standards and approve programs in terms of goals, content, and subject matter. This is especially true in large states like California, Florida, Illinois, New York, and Texas, where standards and programs are often changed and influenced by pressure groups. Because the field lacks certification, the responsibilities of curriculum leaders are vague and diffuse, and a strong and organized constituency is lacking at the school and university levels.

Hence, it behooves the professional organizations that perceive themselves as curriculum based (i.e., Association for Supervision and Curriculum Development, Division B of AERA), and leading professors of curriculum, as well as practitioners, to put pressure first on a national level, then state level, to formulate certification policy in curriculum. This is a call for reform.

CURRICULUM AND INSTRUCTION

The relationship between curriculum and instruction is not clearly defined in either professional literature or in current curriculum texts. This vagueness is reflected by the fact that about 40 percent of the curriculum departments in schools of education across the country use only the word *curriculum* in their department names, another 30 percent refer to *curriculum and instruction,* another 25 percent use the terms *educational leadership* or *curriculum leadership,* which suggest a curriculum-supervisory-administrative program, and about 5 percent use the term *curriculum and supervision.*[71]

Professional organizations avoid this issue. They are, in addition, unwilling to bring persons together to work through well-planned efforts or policy statements in this area of concern. Practitioners such as teachers often lack time to deal with the relationship because they are more concerned with classroom problems. Principals do recognize the importance of both curriculum and instruction, and they do consider their role to be that of *curriculum leader* and *instructional leader,* but they rarely have time to act on their concerns because of pressing managerial, community, and fiscal responsibilities.

Historical Context.

Eighteenth and nineteenth century European educators, from Locke and Rousseau to Spencer and Herbart, were pioneers in pedagogical principles. Their concern was not curriculum as we know it, because the term itself was unknown until the twentieth century. Their concern, rather, was with content and teaching methods, which they attempted to explore as scientific principles. But what they had to say was related to curriculum, even though the field of study did not exist.

The actual relationship between curriculum and instruction was touched on slightly in the works of Bobbitt and Charters, and later in a book by Henry Harap.[72] Then, in 1930, it was examined in detail when the famous committee for the Twenty-Sixth Yearbook of the NSSE formulated a composite statement about curriculum making. Of the twelve steps developed, two were linked to instruction: "the place of school subjects in instruction" and "measuring the outcomes of instruction."[73]

Both Tyler and Taba were concerned with instruction in their classic texts. This was especially true of Tyler, who considered instruction to be a plan for teaching the curriculum and "the procedures for organizing learning experiences into units, courses, and programs."[74] One of Tyler's four major questions (or chapters) examined "how learning experiences [can] be organized for effective instruction." By entitling his book *Basic Principles of Curriculum and Instruction,* he took the position that both components were equally important and part of a continuous and cyclical process, involving constant replanning and reappraisal.

Taba saw curriculum in a broader context than teaching, and teaching in a broader context than instruction. Curriculum represented the substance and content of what was to be learned; teaching was identified with the general behavior and methods of the teacher for imparting the subject matter to the learner; and instruction was viewed as the specific activities introduced while teaching at various stages of the curriculum. By taking this approach, Taba identified instruction as something apart from curriculum—and something that did not have equal weight with curriculum.[75]

In the 1960s a good deal of activity occurred over theories of instruction and the relationship between curriculum and instruction. Curriculum and instruction were defined as separate entities by Jerome Bruner, who developed a theory of instruction that focused on four factors: (1) facilitating learning; (2) structuring knowledge; (3) sequencing learning experiences; and (4) pacing rewards and punishments in the process of learning and teaching.[76] In this context, curriculum and instruction were considered as separate disciplines of education, and both had equal weight.

James Macdonald argued for clarification of terms associated with curriculum, instruction, teaching, and learning. Curriculum was defined as the "plans for action," instruction was "putting plans into action" (similar to Tyler), teaching was "the behavior of the teacher" (similar to Taba), and learning was the "desired responses" of the learner (similar to both Tyler and Taba).[77] Singling out instruction as a unique concept among the four terms, and basically as the "implementation" stage of curriculum, Macdonald advocated further research on instruction.

Finally, Harry Broudy and his colleagues spoke of curriculum as a total system; instruction and teaching were subsystems, and therefore not as important. Instruction was further categorized into five content or subject areas, what they termed "study areas," and teaching was further categorized into two methods or strategies, what they termed "modes."[78] They further claimed that even though "modes of teaching are not, strictly speaking, a part of curriculum, for practical purposes it is not useful to ignore them entirely in curriculum theory."[79] This statement would not significantly differ from most current theories of curriculum; moreover, the unequal weighting of curriculum and instruction would coincide with the majority of curriculum texts today.

Current Context.

Although Tanner and Tanner devote limited space to the relationship between curriculum and instruction, they assert that to describe both as separate components is not only misleading, but also impossible, because the dichotomy breaks down when the curriculum is implemented at the classroom or school level.[80] To examine them as separate components is like applying the old "doctrine of dualism," which was once criticized by John Dewey.[81] This doctrine conceives curriculum as a "means" for

achieving the "ends" of education; the ends and means are artificially separated or viewed as discontinuous functions. The Tanners conclude that the need is to *synthesize* curriculum and instruction as one problem, not to analyze them as separate problems. It is a view that corresponds with Tyler.

At the other extreme, among current textbook writers, is Zais. He *separates* curriculum and instruction along the views of Broudy and Taba. He views curriculum as a broad concept and instruction as a specific phenomenon or subsystem (with less importance). Instruction is to be introduced at some point along a curriculum continuum. The point of introduction is flexible, to permit subjective judgment on the part of the teacher: It "is to be selected according to the teacher's personality and teacher's style, and the students' needs and interests."[82]

Most current curricularists take a middle position between the Tanners and Zais. Although they separate curriculum and instruction for purposes of discussion, they consider one without the other incomplete. The two components are *fused* or brought together at times, but they still retain their original characteristics or independencies—a view similar to Bruner and Macdonald.

Saylor et al., for example, claim that the "two terms . . . are interlocked almost inextricably as the names . . . Romeo and Juliet. Without a curriculum or plan, there can be no effective instruction; and without instruction the curriculum has little meaning." However, both curriculum and instruction are separately defined; the latter is viewed "as the implementation of the curriculum plan."[83]

Similarly, Wiles and Bondi assert that "curriculum . . . interfaces with classroom instruction." Curriculum is defined as "a plan for learning, involving the selection and organization of both content and learning experiences." Instruction is viewed as "teachers making daily decisions about content, grouping materials, pacing and sequencing of activities."[84]

And Oliva considers curriculum and instruction "as two entities . . . like Siamese twins who are joined together [and] one may not function without the other." He points out that the relationship is *cyclical,* meaning that they "are separate entities with a continuing circular relationship. Curriculum makes a continuous impact on instruction and, vice versa, instruction impacts on curriculum."[85]

In the majority of cases, in which the two components are fused or depicted in a cyclical relationship (Oliva's term), curriculum is viewed as a written plan or program that serves as a guide; once the curriculum is acted upon or put into operation, the plan moves to instruction, which involves implementation and methodology. Although curriculum as a plan is *inert,* instruction as an act is *alive* and evolving. The curriculum takes place in the entire school (even outside the school) and instruction takes place in the classroom (or a specific setting such as an auditorium, ballfield, etc.). In this context, curriculum deals with the *what*: What we interpret students and society to need; the basis for our decisions is largely philosophical and social in nature. Instruction deals with *how* people learn, that is with the psychological foundations, and with methods, materials, and media. However, both curriculum and instruction modify each other in a continuous and multidimensional way: Curriculum decisions affect instruction, and instructional decisions affect curriculum.

The three approaches to curriculum and instruction have their own perspectives: The first (synthesis) is an interdisciplinary perspective; the second (separation) reflects a discipline approach to subject matter or a field of study; the third (fusion) is a more fluid approach. They all have their shortcomings, too. Those who wish to synthesize both components fail to provide answers about how curriculum and instruction can be combined; they merely provide theoretical insights without dealing with practice; they raise more questions than they resolve. A total synthesis of both components, for

example, could blur the principles and processes of both curriculum and instruction.

Those who separate the components fail to recognize that it is too simple and rigid to claim that one is the subsystem of the other or that one takes place prior to the other. Separating one component from the other does harm to both, because both become incomplete. Curricularists who separate both components tend to overemphasize curriculum at the expense of instruction, and instructional theorists and educational psychologists tend to overemphasize instruction at the expense of curriculum. Indeed, this model has potential for causing conflict and separation among people who have a strong interest in only curriculum or instruction.

On a theoretical level, we can make a good case for the fusion viewpoint, because it represents a compromise between syntheses and separation and because it suggests that both components continuously adapt and improve. But on a practical level, especially in the classroom, curriculum and instructional experiences come and go at a very rapid, complex, and amorphous level. The two components interface in the classroom in different ways under different circumstances (with different teachers, students, and subjects), and we cannot always observe or measure the relationship or show that they modify each other.

Whether people wish to synthesize curriculum and instruction, treat them as separate components, or take the middle position and fuse them reflects their own philosophical and psychological views on education. Curriculum students do not have strong views on this subject, and even the experts treat the matter briefly in their respective texts. Instructional experts (and learning theorists) have a definite position; their ideas reflect the growing influence of educational psychologists in the field of curriculum. The psychological school (Berliner, Bloom, Brophy, etc.), not curricularists, now dominates the field of instruction and provides much purpose and direction in the relationship beween curriculum and instruction.[86] In the fuure, we hope that curricularists will take a tronger and more precise view on instrucion.

ONCLUSION

Ve have discussed curriculum in a variety f ways. We have tried to define it, to show he relationship between foundations and omains of curriculum, to illustrate how heory and practice interrelate with curricuım, and to describe how curriculum and ıstruction can be viewed as separate or as elated components. In effect, we have told he reader that he or she can focus on aproaches and definitions, foundations and omains, theory and practice, or curriculum

and instruction. We feel that no one can fully integrate the entire field of curriculum. Eventually each individual should choose an approach and definition, a school of philosophy and psychology, developmental and design models, theory and practice relationships, and curriculum-instruction systems he or she wishes to promote. In this chapter, we outlined some options; we continue to do so in the remaining text.

In presenting this broad overview of curriculum, we have also tried to show how current texts in curriculum examine these theoretical dimensions or issues, and how, in terms of philosophy and direction, they fit into the field of curriculum. This information is summarized in Table 1-2. However, we caution the reader that it is not easy to categorize authors and textbooks into pure

ABLE 1-2   Overview of Curriculum Texts Since 1980

uthor	Curriculum Approach	Curriculum Definition	Curriculum Foundations	Curriculum Domains
eane et al. (1986)	Behavioral	Plan	Social	Change
oll (1986)	Systems	Plan	Social, psychological	Change
sner (1985)	Humanistic	Plan, experiences	Psychological	Teaching-learning
ass (1983)	Humanistic	Plan, experiences	Philosophical, social, psychological	Teaching-learning
unkins (1980)	Behavioral[a]	Plan, system	Social, psychological	Development-design
cNeil (1985)	Systems	System, field	Historical, social, political	Change, issues
iller & Seller (1985)	Intellectual	Field	Historical, philosophical, social, psychological	Development
liva (1982)	Behavioral	Plan, experiences	Social	Development
rlosky & Smith (1980)	Intellectual	Plan, field	Social, psychological	Development, change
att (1980)	Behavioral[a]	Plan, system	Historical	Development
ıylor et al. (1981)	Behavioral[a]	Plan	Social	Development-design, issues
hubert (1986)	Intellectual	Field	Historical, social	Development, issues
ıepherd & Ragan (1985)	Intellectual[b]	Field, experiences, subjects	Psychological	Teaching-learning
anner & Tanner (1980)	Intellectual	Field	Historical, philosophical	Change, issues
ınruh & Unruh (1984)	Systems	Plan, system	Social	Development, issues
iles & Bondi (1984)	Systems	Plan, grades	Philosophical, social	Development-design, change

otes: a = sometimes designated as a systems-managerial approach to curriculum.

   b = sometimes designated as a humanistic approach to curriculum.

types. Not only may overlap exist in some cases, but also some people may represent more than one category—at least on different issues. Finally, we have attempted to set the stage for the discussions that follow on the foundations of curriculum, the domains of curriculum, and the issues of curriculum.

Notes

1. Franklin Bobbitt, *The Curriculum* (Boston: Houghton Mifflin, 1918); W. W. Charters, *Curriculum Construction* (New York: Macmillan, 1923); Ralph W. Tyler, *Basic Principles of Curriculum and Instruction* (Chicago: University of Chicago Press, 1949); and Hilda Taba, *Curriculum Development: Theory and Practice* (New York: Harcourt, Brace, 1962).

2. Paul R. Feinberg, "Four Curriculum Theorists: A Critique in Light of Martin Buber's Philosophy of Education," *Journal of Curriculum Theorizing* (Spring 1985), pp. 5–164.

3. Herbert M. Kliebard, "Persistent Issues in Curricular Theorizing," in W. Pinar, ed., *Curriculum Theorizing: The Reconceptualists* (Berkeley, Calif.: McCutchan, 1975), pp. 39–88; William Pinar, "Notes on the Curriculum Field," *Educational Researcher* (September 1978), pp. 5–12; and William H. Schubert, *Curriculum Books: The First Eighty Years* (Lanham, Md.: University Press of America, 1980).

4. James A. Beane, Conrad E. Toepfer, and Samuel J. Alessi, *Curriculum Planning and Development* (Boston: Allyn and Bacon, 1986); Francis P. Hunkins, *Curriculum Development: Program Improvement* (Columbus, Ohio: Merrill, 1980); Peter F. Oliva, *Developing the Curriculum* (Boston: Little, Brown, 1982); David Pratt, *Curriculum: Design and Development* (New York: Harcourt, Brace, 1980); and J. Galen Saylor, William M. Alexander, and Arthur J. Lewis, *Curriculum Planning for Better Teaching and Learning*, 4th ed. (New York: Holt, Rinehart, 1981). Many of these authors can also be classified as representative of the systems-managerial approach.

5. A sample of their writings can be found in Francis S. Chase and Harold A. Anderson, *The High School in a New Era* (Chicago: University of Chicago Press, 1958).

6. George A. Beauchamp, *Curriculum Theory*, 2nd ed. (Wilmette, Ill.: Kagg, 1964); Mauritz Johnson, "Definitions and Models in Curriculum," *Educational Theory* (April 1967), pp. 127–140.

7. Ronald C. Doll, *Curriculum Improvement: Decision Making and Process*, 6th ed. (Boston: Allyn and Bacon, 1986); John D. McNeil, *Curriculum: A Comprehensive Introduction*, 3rd ed. (Boston: Little, Brown, 1985); and Glenys G. Unruh and Adolph Unruh, *Curriculum Development: Problems, Processes, and Progress* (Berkeley, Calif.: McCutchan, 1984). Also see Hunkins, *Curriculum Development: Program Improvement;* Pratt, *Curriculum: Design and Development;* and Jon Wiles and Joseph C. Bondi, *Curriculum Development: A Guide to Practice,* 2nd ed. (Columbus, Ohio: Merrill, 1984).

8. McNeil, *Curriculum: A Comprehensive Introduction;* Pinar, "Notes on the Curriculum Field"; and Schubert, *Curriculum Books: The First Eighty Years.*

9. John Dewey, *Democracy and Education* (New York: Macmillan, 1916); Henry C. Morrison, *The Practice of Teaching in the Secondary School* (Chicago: University of Chicago Press, 1926); and Boyd H. Bode, *Modern Educational Theories* (New York: Macmillan, 1927).

10. Hollis L. Campbell and Doak S. Campbell, *Curriculum Development* (New York: American Books, 1935); L. Thomas Hopkins, *Integration: Its Meaning and Application* (New York: Appleton-Century, 1937); John K. Norton and Mary A. Norton, *Foundations of Curriculum Building* (Boston: Ginn, 1936); B. Othanel Smith, William O. Stanley, and J. Harlan Shores, *Fundamentals of Curriculum Development* (New York: World Books, 1950); and Florence B. Stratemeyer et al., *Developing a Curriculum for Modern Living* (New York: Teachers College Press, Columbia University, 1952).

11. John P. Miller and Wayne Seller, *Curriculum: Perspectives and Practice* (New York: Longman, 1985); Donald E. Orlosky and B. Othanel Smith, *Curriculum Development: Issues and Insights* (Chicago: Rand McNally, 1980); William H. Schubert, *Curriculum: Perspective, Paradigm, and Possibility* (New York: Macmillan, 1986); Gene D. Shepherd and William B. Ragan, *Modern Elementary Curriculum,* 6th ed. (New York: Holt, Rinehart, 1985); and Daniel Tanner and Laurel N. Tanner, *Curriculum Development: Theory into Practice,* 2nd ed. (New York: Macmillan, 1980). Orlosky and Smith might also be categorized into the behavioral-rational approach, because there is a good deal of stress on technical issues such as development and design in their text.

12. Frederick G. Bosner, *The Elementary School Curriculum* (New York: Macmillan, 1920); Hollis L. Caswell, *Program Making in Small Elementary Schools* (Nashville, Tenn.: George Peabody College for Teachers, 1932); and William H. Kilpatrick, *Foundations of Method* (New York: Macmillan, 1925).

13. Ellsworth Collings, *An Experiment with a Project Curriculum* (New York: Macmillan, 1923); L. Thomas Hopkins and James E. Mendenhall, *Achievement at the Lincoln School* (New York: Teachers College Press, Columbia University, 1934); and Harold Rugg and Ann Shumaker, *The Child-Centered School* (New York: World Book, 1928).

14. Elliot W. Eisner, *The Educational Imagination,* 2nd ed. (New York: Macmillan, 1985); Glen Hass, ed.

Curriculum Planning: A New Approach, 4th ed. (Boston: Allyn and Bacon, 1983).

15. McNeil, *Curriculum: A Comprehensive Introduction;* Miller and Seller, *Curriculum: Perspectives and Practice.* (The latter uses the term *social change orientation* to classify the reconceptualists.)

16. One recent reconstructionist publication by Henry Giroux and David Purpel, *The Hidden Curriculum and Moral Education* (Berkeley, Calif.: McCutchan, 1981), is the closest to a textbook reconstructionist writings become.

17. George S. Counts, *Dare the School Build a New Social Order?* (New York: John Day, 1932); Harold O. Rugg, ed., *Democracy and the Curriculum* (New York: Appleton-Century, 1939); Rugg et al., *American Life and the School Curriculum* (Boston: Ginn, 1936); and Harold Benjamin, *The Saber-Tooth Curriculum* (New York: McGraw-Hill, 1939).

18. Saylor, Alexander, and Lewis, *Curriculum Planning for Better Teaching and Learning,* p. 10.

19. Pratt, *Curriculum: Design and Development,* p. 4.

20. Wiles and Bondi, *Curriculum Development: A Guide to Practice,* p. 135.

21. John Dewey, *Experience and Education* (New York: Macmillan, 1938); Caswell and Campbell, *Curriculum Development,* p. 69.

22. Shepherd and Ragan, *Modern Elementary Curriculum,* pp. 3–4.

23. Eisner, *The Educational Imagination,* p. 41.

24. Hass, *Curriculum Planning: A New Approach,* p. 41

25. Doll, *Curriculum Improvement: Decision Making and Process;* McNeil, *Curriculum: A Comprehensive Introduction;* and Unruh and Unruh, *Curriculum Development: Problems, Process, and Progress.*

26. Orlosky and Smith, *Curriculum Development: Issues and Insights;* Schubert, *Curriculum: Perspective, Paradigm, and Possibility;* and Tanner and Tanner, *Curriculum Development: Theory into Practice.*

27. Shepherd and Ragan, *Modern Elementary Curriculum.*

28. George A. Beauchamp, *Curriculum Theory,* 3rd ed. (Wilmette, Ill.: Kagg, 1975).

29. Doll, *Curriculum Improvement: Decision Making and Process,* p. 7.

30. Beauchamp, *Curriculum Theory,* p. 81.

31. Harold Rugg, "Introduction," in G. M. Whipple, ed., *The Foundations of Curriculum-Making,* Twenty-Sixth Yearbook of the National Society for the Study of Education, Part II (Bloomington, Ill.: Public School Publishing Co., 1930), p. 8.

32. "List of Fundamental Questions on Curriculum-Making," in Whipple, ed., *The Foundations of Curriculum-Making,* pp. 9–10.

33. Schubert, *Curriculum: Perspective, Paradigm, and Possibility.*

34. Carmen L. Rosales-Dordelly and Edmund C. Short, *Curriculum Professors' Specialized Knowledge* (New York: Lanham, 1985), p. 23.

35. Oliva, *Developing the Curriculum,* p. 15.

36. Joseph J. Schwab, "The Practical: A Language of Curriculum," *School Review* (November 1969), p. 1.

37. Miller and Seller, *Curriculum: Perspectives and Practice.*

38. Robert S. Zais, *Curriculum: Principles and Foundations* (New York: Harper & Row, 1976).

39. Doll, *Curriculum Improvement: Decision Making and Process;* Hass, *Curriculum Planning: A New Approach;* and McNeil, *Curriculum: A Comprehensive Introduction.*

40. Hunkins, *Curriculum Development: Program Improvement;* Saylor et al., *Curriculum Planning for Better Teaching and Learning.*

41. Shepherd and Ragan, *Modern Elementary Curriculum;* Eisner, *The Educational Imagination.*

42. Schubert, *Curriculum: Perspective, Paradigm, and Possibility;* Tanner and Tanner, *Curriculum Development: Theory into Practice.*

43. Herbert Kliebard, "Curriculum Theory as Metaphor," *Theory into Practice* (Winter 1982), pp. 11–17. See also Kliebard, *The Struggle for the American Curriculum* (Boston: Routledge & Kegan Paul, 1986).

44. About 75 to 80 percent of all Division C papers in the 1985 and 1986 AERA annual meetings were delivered by educational psychologists, especially research, measurement, and evaluation professors. The percentage was about 25 to 30 percent in Division B for the same period; moreover, the vice presidents in charge of Division B for 1980 and 1981 were educational psychologists, not curricularists.

45. In letters written to one of the authors of this text, Ronald Brandt (editor of *Educational Leadership*) concurs with this viewpoint about both journals. Bob Cole (editor of *Phi Delta Kappan*) is less enthusiastic about this viewpoint; his argument is basically that people like Bloom and Gage can be considered curricularists.

46. Eisner, *The Educational Imagination;* Shepherd and Ragan, *Modern Elementary Curriculum;* Doll, *Curriculum Improvement: Decision Making and Process;* and Hunkins, *Curriculum Development: Program Improvement.*

47. Taba, *Curriculum Development: Theory and Practice.*

48. Rosales-Dordelly and Short, *Curriculum Professors' Specialized Knowledge;* Edmund C. Short, "Organizing What We Know about Curriculum." Unpublished paper written at Pennsylvania State University, 1984; and Decker Walker, "Curriculum Theory Is Many Things to Many People," *Theory into Practice* (Winter 1982), pp. 62–65.

49. Beauchamp, *Curriculum Theory.*

50. Arthur Foshay and Lois A. Beilin, "Curriculum," in *Encyclopedia of Educational Research,* 2nd ed. (New York: Macmillan, 1969), pp. 275–278.

51. Fenwick W. English, "Contemporary Curriculum Circumstances," in F. W. English, ed., *Fundamental Curriculum Decisions* (Alexandria, Va.: Association for Supervision and Curriculum Development, 1983), pp. 1–17.

52. Short, "Organizing What We Know about Curriculum."

53. Saylor et al., *Curriculum Planning for Better Teaching and Learning.*

54. Unruh and Unruh, *Curriculum Development: Problems, Processes, and Progress.*

55. Hunkins, *Curriculum Development: Program Improvement.*

56. Beane, Toepfer, and Alessi, *Curriculum Planning and Development*; Orlosky and Smith, *Curriculum Development: Issues and Insights;* and Tanner and Tanner, *Curriculum Development: Theory into Practice.*

57. Saylor et al., *Curriculum Planning for Better Teaching and Learning.*

58. Wiles and Bondi, *Curriculum Development: A Guide to Practice.*

59. Rosales-Dordelly and Short, *Curriculum Professors' Specialized Knowledge*, p. 22.

60. McNeil, *Curriculum: A Comprehensive Introduction*, p. viii.

61. John I. Goodlad et al., *Curriculum Inquiry: The Study of Curriculum Practice* (New York: McGraw-Hill, 1979); Glenys G. Unruh, *Responsible Curriculum Development: Theory and Action* (Berkeley, Calif.: McCutchan, 1975).

62. Beauchamp, *Curriculum Theory*, p. 58.

63. Taba, *Curriculum Development: Theory and Practice*, p. 413.

64. Unruh and Unruh, *Curriculum Development: Problems, Processes, and Progress;* Zais, *Curriculum: Principles and Foundations.*

65. McNeil, *Curriculum: A Comprehensive Introduction.*

66. Feinberg, "Four Curriculum Theorists"; James B. Macdonald, "Curriculum and Human Interests," in W. Pinar, ed., *Curriculum Theorizing* (Berkeley, Calif.: McCutchan, 1975), pp. 283–294.

67. English, "Contemporary Curriculum Circumstances," pp. 1–17; Roger A. Kaufman and Fenwick W. English, "Conducting the Beta Needs Assessment," in R. A. Kaufman and F. W. English, eds., *Needs Assessment: Concept and Application* (Englewood Cliffs, N.J.: Educational Technology Publications, 1979), pp. 221–240; and William Pinar, "Reply to My Critics," *Curriculum Inquiry* (Summer 1980), pp. 199–206.

68. Elizabeth Vallance, "Curriculum as a Field of Practice," in English, ed., *Fundamental Curriculum Decisions*, p. 155.

69. Miller and Seller, *Curriculum: Perspectives and Practice*; Tanner and Tanner, *Curriculum Development: Theory into Practice*; and Wiles and Bondi, *Curriculum Development: A Guide to Practice.*

70. Doll, *Curriculum Improvement: Decision Making and Process;* Unruh and Unruh, *Curriculum Development: Problems, Processes, and Progress.*

71. There are about eighty departments in curriculum at the graduate level in universities across the country. These percentages are based on reviewing forty at random.

72. Bobbitt, *The Curriculum*; Charters, *Curriculum Construction*; and Henry Harap, *The Techniques of Curriculum Making* (New York: Macmillan, 1928).

73. "The Foundations of Curriculum Making," A Composite Statement by the Members of the Society's Committee on Curriculum-Making, in G. M. Whipple, ed., *The Foundations of Curriculum-Making*, p. 11.

74. Tyler, *Basic Principles of Curriculum and Instruction*, p. 83.

75. Taba, *Curriculum Development: Theory and Practice.*

76. Jerome S. Bruner, *Toward a Theory of Instruction* (Cambridge, Mass.: Harvard University Press, 1966).

77. James B. Macdonald, "Educational Models for Instruction—Introduction," in J. B. Macdonald, ed., *Theories of Instruction* (Washington, D.C.: Association for Supervision and Curriculum Development, 1965), pp. 5–6.

78. Harry S. Broudy, B. Othanel Smith, and Joe R. Burnett, *Democracy and Excellence in American Secondary Education* (Chicago: Rand McNally, 1964), p. 78.

79. *Ibid.*, p. 79.

80. Tanner and Tanner, *Curriculum Development: Theory into Practice.*

81. John Dewey, *Democracy and Education* (New York: Macmillan, 1916).

82. Zais, *Curriculum: Principles and Foundations*, p. 12.

83. Saylor et al., *Curriculum Planning for Better Teaching and Learning.*

84. Wiles and Bondi, *Curriculum Development: A Guide to Practice*, p. 135.

85. Oliva, *Developing the Curriculum*, pp. 10, 13.

86. See Allan C. Ornstein, "Teacher Effectiveness Research," *Education and Urban Society* (February 1986), pp. 168–175.

chapter 2

PHILOSOPHICAL FOUNDATIONS
OF CURRICULUM

Philosophy is an important foundation of curriculum because the philosophy advocated or reflected by a particular school and its officials influences its goals or aims and content, as well as the organization of its curriculum. Studying philosophy helps us deal with our own personal systems of beliefs and values: The way we perceive the world around us, and how we define what is important to us. It helps us understand who we are, why we are, and, to some extent, where we are going.

Philosophy deals with the larger aspects of life, the problems and prospects of living, and the way we organize our thoughts and facts. It is an effort to see life and its problems in full perspective. It requires looking beyond the immediate to causes and relationships and to future developments. It involves questioning one's own point of view as well as the views of others; it involves searching for defined and defensible values, clarifying one's beliefs and attitudes, and formulating a framework for making decisions and acting on these decisions.

Philosophical issues have always and still do impact on schools and society. Contemporary society and the schools in it are changing fundamentally and rapidly, much more so than in the past. The special urgency that dictates continuous appraisal and reappraisal calls for a philosophy of education. As William Van Til puts it, "Our source of direction is found in our guiding philosophy. . . . Without philosophy, [we make] mindless vaults into the saddle like Stephen Leacock's character who 'flung himself from the room, flung himself upon his horse, and rode madly off in all directions.' "[1] In short, our philosophy of education influences, and to a large extent determines, our educational decisions, choices, and alternatives.

PHILOSOPHY AND CURRICULUM

Philosophy provides educators, especially curriculum workers, with a framework or base for organizing schools and classrooms.

25

It helps them answer what schools are for, what subjects are of value, how students learn, and what methods and materials to use. It provides them with a framework for broad issues and tasks, such as determining the goals of education, the content and its organization, the process of teaching and learning, and in general what experiences and activities they wish to stress in schools and classrooms. It also provides them with a basis for dealing with precise tasks and for making such decisions as what workbooks, textbooks, or other cognitive and non-cognitive activities to utilize and how to utilize them, what homework to assign and how much of it, how to test students and how to use the test results, and what courses or subject matter to emphasize.

The importance of philosophy in determining curriculum decisions is expressed well by L. Thomas Hopkins:

Philosophy has entered into every important decision that has ever been made about curriculum and teaching in the past and will continue to be the basis of every important decision in the future.

When a state office of education suggests a pupil-teacher time schedule, this is based upon philosophy, either hidden or consciously formulated. When a course of study is prepared in advance in a school system by a selected group of teachers, this represents philosophy because a course of action was selected from many choices involving different values. When high school teachers assign to pupils more homework for an evening than any one of them could possibly do satisfactorily in six hours, they are acting on philosophy although they are certainly not aware of its effects. When a teacher in an elementary school tells a child to put away his geography and study his arithmetic she is acting on philosophy for she has made a choice of values. If she had allowed the child to make the choice she would have been operating under a different set of beliefs. Many persons believe that children can best be educated to live in a democracy by rigid authoritarian control through the adolescent period. Others believe that democratic interaction should be practiced as soon as the child is capable of distinguishing among subjects, situations, activities, which is a number of years before he usually enters school. When teachers shift subject matter from one grade to another, they act on philosophy. When measurement experts interpret their test results to a group of teachers, they act upon philosophy, for the facts have meaning only within some basic assumptions. There is rarely a moment in a school day when a teacher is not confronted with occasions where philosophy is a vital part of action. An inventory of situations where philosophy was not used in curriculum and teaching would lead to a pile of chaff thrown out of educative experiences.[2]

Hopkins's statement reminds us how important philosophy is to all aspects of curriculum decisions, whether it operates overtly or covertly, whether we know that it is operating or not. Indeed almost all elements of curriculum are based on philosophy. As John Goodlad points out, philosophy is the beginning point in curriculum decision making and is the basis for all subsequent decisions regarding curriculum.[3] Philosophy becomes the criterion for determining the aims, means, and ends of curriculum. The aims are statements of value, based on philosophical beliefs; the means represent processes and methods, which reflect philosophical choices; and the ends connote the facts, concepts, and principles of the knowledge or behavior learned, or what we feel is important to learning, which is also philosophical in nature.

Smith, Stanley, and Shores also put great emphasis on the role of philosophy in developing curriculum; it is essential, they posit, when (1) formulating and justifying educational purposes; (2) selecting and organizing knowledge; (3) formulating basic procedures and activities; and (4) dealing with verbal traps (what we see versus what is real).[4] Curriculum theorists, they point out, often fail to recognize both how important philosophy is and how it influences other aspects of curriculum.

Philosophy and the Curriculum Worker.

The philosophy of the curriculum worker reflects his or her life experiences, common sense, social and economic background, education, and general beliefs about him- or herself and people. An individual's philosophy evolves and continues to evolve as long as he or she continues to grow and develop, and as long as he or she learns from experience. One's philosophy is a description, explanation, and evaluation of the world as seen from one's own perspective, or through what some social scientists call "social lenses."

Curriculum workers can turn to many sources, but no matter how many sources they may draw upon or how many authorities they may read or listen to, the decision is theirs to accept or reject so-called explanations and truths presented. The decision is shaped by past and contemporary events and experiences that have affected them and the social groups with which they identify; it is based on values (attitudes and beliefs) that they have developed, and their knowledge and interpretation of causes, events, and their consequences. Philosophy becomes principles for guiding action.

No one can be totally objective in a cultural or social setting, but curriculum workers can broaden their base of knowledge and experiences, try to understand other people's sense of values, and analyze problems from various perspectives. They can also try to modify their own critical analyses and points of view by learning from their experiences and others. Curriculum workers who are unwilling to modify their points of view, or compromise philosophical positions, when school officials or the majority of their colleagues lean toward another philosophy, are at risk of causing conflict and disrupting the school. Ronald Doll puts it this way: "Conflict among curriculum planners occurs when persons . . . hold positions along a continuum of [different] beliefs and . . . persuasions." The conflict may become so intense that "curriculum study grinds to a halt." Most of the time, the differences can be reconciled "temporarily in deference to the demands of a temporary, immediate task. However, teachers and administrators who are clearly divided in philosophy can seldom work together in close proximity for long periods of time."[5]

The more mature and understanding one is, and the less personally threatened and ego involved one is, the more capable one is of reexamining or modifying his or her philosophy, or at least of being willing to appreciate other points of view. It is important for curriculum workers to consider their attitudes and beliefs as tentative—as subject to reexamination whenever facts or trends challenge them.

Equally dangerous for curriculum workers is the opposite: Indecision or lack of any philosophy, which can be reflected in attempts to avoid commitment to sets of values. A measure of positive conviction is essential to prudent action, even though total objectivity is not humanly possible. Having a personal philosophy that is tentative or subject to modification does not lead to lack of conviction or disorganized behavior. Curriculum workers can arrive at their conclusions on the best evidence available, and they can change when better evidence surfaces.

Philosophy as a Curriculum Source.

The function of philosophy can be conceived as either (1) the base or starting point in curriculum development or (2) an interdependent function with other functions in curriculum development. John Dewey represents the first school of thought. He contended that "philosophy may . . . be defined as the general theory of education," and that "the business of philosophy is to provide" the framework for the "aims and methods" of schools. For Dewey, philosophy provides a generalized meaning to our lives and a way of thinking; it is "an explicit formulation of the . . . mental and moral habitudes in respect to the difficulties of contemporary social life."[6] Philosophy is not only a starting point for schools, it is also crucial for all curriculum activities. For Dewey, "education is the laboratory in which philosophic distinctions become concrete and are tested."[7]

In Ralph Tyler's framework of curriculum, philosophy is commonly one of five cri-

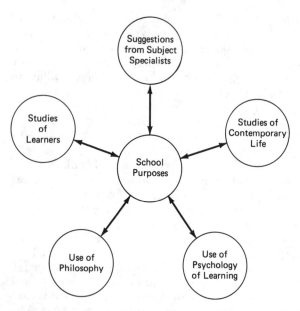

FIGURE 2-1 Tyler's View of Philosophy in Relation to School Purposes

teria for selecting educational purposes. The relationships between philosophy and the other criteria—studies of learners, studies of contemporary life, suggestions from subject specialists, and the psychology of learning—are shown in Figure 2-1. Although philosophy is not the starting point in Tyler's curriculum, but rather interacts on an equal basis with the other criteria, Tyler, highly influenced by Dewey, seems to place more importance on philosophy for developing educational purposes. He writes, "The educational and social philosophy to which the school is committed can serve as the first screen for developing the social program." He concludes that "philosophy attempts to define the nature of the good life and a good society," and that the "educational philosophies in a democratic society are likely to emphasize strongly democratic values in schools."[8]

For John Goodlad, there can be no serious discussion about philosophy until we embrace the question of what education is. When we agree on what education is, we can ask what schools are for. Then we can pursue philosophy, aims, and goals of curriculum. According to Goodlad, the school's first responsibility is to the social order, what

he calls the "nation-state," but in our society the sense of individual growth and potential is paramount, too.[9] This duality—society vs. the individual—has been a major philosophical issue in western society for centuries, and was very important in Dewey's works. As the latter claimed, we not only wish "to make [good] citizens and workers," but also we ultimately want "to make human beings who will live life to the fullest."

This duality—allegiance to the nation and fulfillment of the individual—is a noble aim that should guide all curriculum specialists—from the means to the ends. When many individuals grow and prosper, then that society flourishes since it is comprised of many individuals. The original question set forth by Goodlad can be answered now. Education is growth and the meaning that the growth has for the individual and society; it is a never ending process (so long as life exists), and the richer the meaning the better the quality of the educational process.

MAJOR PHILOSOPHIES

In any consideration of the influence of philosophical thought on curriculum, several classification schemes are possible; no superiority is thus claimed for the categories used in the following discussion. The cluster of ideas as organized here are those that often evolve during curriculum development.

Labeling a philosophical idea, method, or proponent may give rise to argument. Differences within philosophical groups are sometimes greater than differences between groups. Also, anyone who embraces an extreme point of view may very likely be critical of other views.

Four major philosophies have influenced education in the United States: Idealism, realism, pragmatism, and existentialism. Here, we present short overviews to define and identify each philosophy. The first two philosophies are traditional, and the latter two are contemporary.

Idealism.

Plato is often identified as giving classic formulation to idealist philosophy, one of the oldest that exists. The German philosopher Hegel created a comprehensive view of the historical world based on idealism. In the United States, transcendentalist philosophers Ralph Waldo Emerson and Henry Thoreau outlined an idealist conception of reality. In education, Fredrich Froebel, the founder of kindergarten, was a proponent of idealist pedagogy. William Harris, who popularized the kindergarten movement when he was Superintendent of Schools in St. Louis, Missouri, and who became U.S. Commissioner of Education at the turn of the twentieth century, used idealism as a source for this administrative philosophy. The leading contemporary proponent of idealism is J. Donald Butler.[10]

Idealism emphasizes moral and spiritual reality as the chief explanation of the world. Truth and values are seen as absolute, timeless, and universal. The world of mind and ideas is permanent, regular, and orderly; it represents a perfect order. Eternal ideas are unalterable and timeless. To know is to rethink the latent ideas that are already present in the mind. The teacher's task is to bring this latent knowledge to consciousness. As a primarily intellectual process, learning involves recalling and working with ideas; education is properly concerned with conceptual matters.[11]

The idealist educator prefers the order and pattern of a subject matter curriculum that relates ideas and concepts to each other. The most important subjects and highest form of knowledge recognize relationships and integrate concepts to each other. In this vein, the curriculum is hierarchical, and it constitutes the cultural heritage of humankind; it is based on learned disciplines, illustrated by the liberal arts curriculum.

At the top of this hierarchy are the most general or abstract subjects: Philosophy and theology; they cut across time, place, and circumstances, and they apply to a wide range of situations and experiences. Mathematics is important because it cultivates the power to deal with abstract thinking. History and literature also rank high because they are sources of moral and cultural models. Lower in the curricular ladder are the natural and physical sciences, which deal with particular cause and effect relationships. Language is also an important subject, because it is necessary for communication and facilitates conception of thought.

Realism.

Aristotle is often linked to the development of realism, another traditional school of thought. Thomas Aquinas's philosophy, which combined realism with Christian doctrine, developed an offshoot of realism, called thomism, on which much of Catholic education and religious studies today are rooted. Pestalozzian instructional principles, which began with concrete objects and ended with abstract concepts, were based on realism. Such modern educators as Harry Broudy and John Wild are leading realists.[12]

The realist views the world in terms of objects and matter. People can come to know the world through their senses and their reason. Everything is derived from nature and is subject to its laws. Human behavior is rational when it conforms to the laws of nature, and when it is governed by physical and social laws.

Like the idealist, the realist stresses a curriculum consisting of organized, separate subject matter, content, and knowledge that classifies objects. For example, the experiences of humankind comprise history. Animals can be studied as zoology. Like the idealist, the realist locates the most general and abstract subjects at the top of the curricular hierarchy, and gives particular and transitory subjects a lower order of priority. Logic and lessons that exercise the mind, and that cultivate rational thought, are stressed. Concepts and systems that can be organized into subjects—such as ethical, political, and economic thought—are also included in the curriculum. The three "Rs" (reading, writing, and arithmetic) are also necessary in a person's basic education.[13]

Whereas the idealist considers the classics to be the ideal subject matter, because the curriculum can be fixed and will not vary with time, the realist views subject matter experts as the source of authority. For the idealist, knowledge comes from studying the external ideas and universal truths found in the arts, but for the realist reality and truth emanate from both science and art.

Pragmatism.

In contrast to the traditional philosophies, pragmatism, also referred to as experimentalism, is based on change, process, and relativity. Whereas idealism and realism emphasize subject matter, disciplines, and content or ideas, pragmatism construes knowledge as a process in which reality is constantly changing. Learning occurs as the person engages in problem solving; problem solving is, moreover, transferable to a wide variety of subjects and situations. Knowing is considered a transaction between learner and environment. Basic to this interaction is the notion of change. Both the learner and environment are constantly

changing, as are the transactions or experiences. To disregard social change, and to consider only what is changeless, as the idealists do, or only our heritage, as the realists do, is unrealistic and unwise. Concepts of unchanging or universal truths, such as the traditional philosophies advocate, are senseless. The only guides that people have in their interaction with the social world or environment are established generalizations or tentative assertions that are subject to further research and verification.

To a pragmatist, nothing can be viewed intelligently except in relation to a pattern. The whole affects the parts, and the parts and the whole are all relative. The ideal teaching method is concerned not so much with teaching the learner what to think as with teaching him or her to critically think. Teaching is more exploratory than explanatory. The method is more important than the subject matter. What is needed is a method for dealing with change and scientific investigation in an intelligent manner.

Scientific developments at the turn of the twentieth century accelerated the pragmatic philosophy. Society's accepting scientific explanations for phenomena, and its recognizing the forces of change, challenged the long-standing traditional views of idealism and realism. In 1859 Charles Darwin's *Origin of the Species* shook the foundations of the classic view of human's notion of the universe. Charles Pierce, a mathematician, and William James, a psychologist, developed the principles of pragmatism, which (1) rejected the dogmas of preconceived truths and eternal values, and (2) promoted the method of testing and verifying ideas. The truth was no longer absolute or universal, but rather it had to be proven in relation to facts, experience, and/or behaviors.[14]

The great educational pragmatist was John Dewey, who viewed education as a process for improving (not accepting) the human condition. The school was seen as a specialized environment that coincided with the social environment. No demarcation exists between school and society. The curriculum, ideally, is based on the child's experiences and interests, and prepares him or her for life's affairs and for the future.[15] The subject matter is interdisciplinary, rather than located within a single or group of disciplines. The stress is on problem solving, not mastering organized subject matter, and using the scientific method, not a bunch of facts or a point of view.

The pragmatists consider teaching and learning to be a process of reconstructing experience according to the scientific method. Learning takes place in an active way as learners, either individually or in groups, solve problems. These problems, as well as the subject matter, will vary in response to the changing world. For the learner, it is most important to acquire the method or process of solving problems in an intelligent manner.

Existentialism.

Whereas pragmatism is mainly an American philosophy that evolved just prior to the turn of the twentieth century, existentialism is mainly a European philosophy that originated before the turn of the century but became popular after World War II. In American education, such people as Maxine Greene, George Kneller, and Van Cleve Morris are well-known existentialists who stress individualism and personal self-fulfillment.[16]

According to existentialist philosophy, people are thrust into a number of choice-making situations. Some choices are minor and others are significant, but the choice is the individual's, and the decisions lead to personal self-definition. A person creates his or her own definition and in doing so makes his or her own essence. We are what we choose to be. The essence we create is a product of our choices; this varies, of course, among individuals.

Existentialists prefer to free learners to choose what to study and also to determine what is true and by what criteria to determine these truths. The curriculum would avoid systematic knowledge or structured disciplines, and the students would be free

to select from many available learning situations. The learners would choose the knowledge they wish to possess. On both of these curricular points, some educators would criticize the philosophy as too unsystematic or laissez-faire to be included at the elementary school level.

Existentialists believe that the most important kind of knowledge is about the human condition and the choices that each person has to make, and that education is a process of developing consciousness about the freedom to choose and the meaning of and responsibility for one's choices.[17] Hence, the notion of group norms, authority, and established order—social, political, philosophical, religious, and so on—are rejected. The existentialists recognize few standards, customs or traditions, or eternal truths; in this respect, existentialism is at odds with the ideas of idealism and realism.

Some critics (mainly traditionalists or conservatives) claim that existentialism as a philosophy for the schools has limited application because education in our society, and in most other modern societies, involves institutionalized learning and socialization, which require group instruction, restrictions on individuals' behavior, and bureaucratic organization. Schooling is a process that limits students' freedom and that is based on adult authority and on the norms and beliefs of the mass or common culture. The individual existentialist, exerting his or her will and choice, will encounter difficulty in school—and in other large, formal organizations.

An existentialist curriculum would consist of experiences and subjects that lend themselves to philosophical dialogue and acts of choice making. Because the choice is personal and subjective, subjects that are emotional, aesthetic, and philosophical are appropriate. Literature, drama, film making, art, and so on, are important, because they portray the human condition and choice-making conditions. The curriculum would stress self-expressive activities, experimentation, and methods and media that illustrate emotions, feelings, and insights.

TABLE 2-1 Overview of Major Philosophies

Philosophy	Reality	Knowledge	Values	Teacher's Role	Emphasis on Learning	Emphasis on Curriculum
Idealism	Spiritual, moral, or mental; unchanging	Rethinking latent ideas	Absolute and eternal	To bring latent knowledge and ideas to consciousness; to be a moral and spiritual leader	Recalling knowledge and ideas; abstract thinking as the highest form	Knowledge based; subject based; classics or liberal arts; hierarchy of subjects: philosophy, theology, and mathematics are most important
Realism	Based on natural laws; objective and composed of matter	Consisting of sensation and abstraction	Absolute and eternal; based on nature's laws	To cultivate rational thought; to be a moral and spiritual leader; to be a source of authority	Exercising the mind; logical and abstract thinking are highest form	Knowledge based; subject based; arts and sciences; hierarchy of subjects: humanistic and scientific subjects
Pragmatism	Interaction of individual with environment; always changing	Based on experience; use of scientific method	Situational and relative; subject to change and verification	To cultivate critical thinking and scientific processes	Methods for dealing with changing environment and scientific explanations	No permanent knowledge or subjects; appropriate experiences that transmit culture and prepare individual for change; problem-solving topics
Existentialism	Subjective	Knowledge for personal choice	Freely chosen; based on individual's perception	To cultivate personal choice and individual self-definition	Knowledge and principles of the human condition; acts of choice making	Choices in subject matter, electives; emotional, aesthetic, and philosophical subjects

The classroom would be rich in materials that lend themselves to self-expression, and the school would be a place in which the teacher and students could pursue dialogue and discussion about their lives and choices.[18]

EDUCATIONAL PHILOSOPHIES

Although aspects of educational philosophy can be derived from the roots of idealism, realism, pragmatism, and existentialism, a common approach is to provide a pattern of educational philosophies. Four agreed-upon philosophies of education have emerged: Perennialism, essentialism, progressivism, and reconstructionism. Each of these four philosophies of education has roots in one or more of the four major philosophical traditions. For example, perennialism draws heavily on the principles of realism; essentialism is rooted in idealism and realism; and progressivism and recontructionism stem from pragmatism. Some reconstructionism has linkages to existentialist knowing and teaching.

Perennialism.

Perennialism, the oldest and most conservative educational philosophy, is rooted in realism. Much of colonial and post-colonial American education, up to the late nineteenth century, was dominated by perennialist thinking. At the elementary school level, the curriculum stressed the three Rs, as well as moral and religious training; at the secondary level, it emphasized such subjects as Latin, Greek, grammar, rhetoric, logic, and geometry.

As a philosophy of education, perennialism relies on the past, especially the past asserted by agreed-upon, universal knowledge and cherished values of society. It is a plea for the permanency of knowledge that has stood the test of time and for values that have moral, spiritual, and/or physical constancies of existence. It is a view of the unchanging nature of the universe, human

nature, truth, knowledge, virtue, beauty, and so on. As Robert Hutchins, a long-time advocate of perennialism, noted: "The function of man as man is the same in every society. . . . The aim of the educational system is the same in every age and in every society where such a system can exist; it is to improve man as man."[19] With this interpretation, education becomes constant, absolute, and universal.

For perennialists, the answers to all educational questions derive from the answer to one question: What is human nature? The perennialists contend that human nature is constant. Humans have the ability to reason and to understand the universal truths of nature. The goal of education is to develop the rational person and to uncover universal truths by carefully training the intellect. Character training is also important as a means of developing one's moral and spiritual being.

The curriculum of the perennialist is subject-centered; it draws heavily on defined disciplines or logically organized bodies of content—what proponents call "liberal" education—with emphasis on language, literature, and mathematics, on the arts and sciences. The teacher is viewed as an authority in the field whose knowledge and expertise are unquestionable. The teacher, accordingly, must be a master of the subject or discipline and must be able to guide discussion. Teaching is, in fact, the art of stimulating discussion and the inherent rational powers of the students. Teaching is primarily based on the Socratic method: oral exposition, lecture, and explication.

Students' interests are irrelevant for curriculum development because students are immature and lack the judgment to determine what are the best knowledge and values to learn. Whether the students dislike the subject matter is secondary.[20] There is only one common curriculum for all students, with little room for elective subjects, vocational, or technical subject matter.

Permanent Studies. The best way of obtaining enduring knowledge and truths today, according to perennialists, is through the permanent studies that comprise our intellectual heritage. This content is embodied in what is commonly called the liberal arts, or, according to Robert Hutchins the "Great Books" of the Western world that cover the foundations of Western thought and "every department of knowledge." The approach is to read and discuss the great works of great thinkers, which, in turn, should discipline the mind and cultivate the intellect. Among the great books are the works of Plato, Aristotle, St. Augustine, St. Thomas Aquinas, Erasmus, and Shakespeare.

The idea is to read these writers in their original languages, which is why students must learn Latin and Greek. In addition to the classics, and the study of language, Hutchins urges the study of the three Rs, as well as grammar, rhetoric, logic, advanced mathematics, and philosophy.[21] This is basically the curriculum of the past; it treats human nature as rational and knowledge as absolute and unchanging. For Hutchins, this type of education "develops intellectual power . . . it is not a specialized education or a pre-professional education; it is not a utilitarian education. It is an education calculated to develop the mind."[22] It is a universal, broad education that prepares the individual to think, to prepare for many possible jobs, and to deal with life and the real world. By studying the great ideas of the past, one can better cope with the future.

Paideia Proposal. A recent revival of perennialism appeared with the publication *Paideia Proposal* by Mortimer Adler. Adler developed three types of curriculum and instruction to improve the intellect: acquisition of *organized knowledge* to be taught by didactic instruction, development of basic *skills* by coaching and understanding of *ideas,* and *values* to be taught by the Socratic method.[23]

A broad liberal education is considered the best and only type of education for all students; in short, the same curriculum and quality of teaching and learning should be provided to all students. Among the subjects identified as indispensable for all students are language, literature, fine arts, mathematics, natural sciences, history, and geography. Although it emphasized fundamental subjects, the Paideia group did not consider subject matter as an end in itself but rather as the context for developing intellectual skills. Among the sought-after intellectual skills were the three Rs, speaking, listening, observing, measuring, estimating, and problem solving. Together, the fundamental subjects and intellectual skills lead to a still higher level of learning, reflection, and awareness. For Adler, like Hutchins, the purpose of education is to cultivate significant knowledge and thinking skills; the "best books"—great books, as they were called by Hutchins, are recommended by the Paideia program.

The education advocated by perennialists appeals to a small group of educators who tend to stress intellectual meritocracy. Such educators emphasize testing students, enforcing tougher academic standards and programs, and identifying gifted and talented students. Their education fosters a common curriculum, usually liberal arts, and offers little or no opportunity for students to choose electives related to their interests or goals. For the perennialists, genuine equality of education is maintained by providing quality education for all—of high intellectual fiber. To track some students into an academic curriculum and others into a vocational curriculum is to deny the latter genuine equality of educational opportunity. True equity can be satisfied only by access to quality education: A *common,* perennial curriculum.

Essentialism.

Another traditional and conservative philosophy is essentialism. This philosophy, rooted in both idealism and realism, surfaced in the 1930s as a reaction to progressivism and developed into a major position during the Cold War and the Sputnik era of the 1950s and early 1960s. The ideas of essentialism were formulated by William Bagley of Teachers College, Columbia University, and were later developed by Arthur Bestor of the University of Illinois and Admiral Hyman Rickover.[24]

According to essentialists, the school curriculum should be geared to the fundamentals or essentials: The three Rs at the elementary school level and five academic or essential subjects—that is, English, mathematics, science, history, and foreign language—at the secondary school level. Although subject-centered like perennialism, essentialism is not rooted in the past but is more concerned with the contemporary scene. Both perennialism and essentialism reject such subjects as art, music, physical education, homemaking, and vocational education as fads and frills, and thus appeal to those who favor limiting educational expenses (because these subjects are more expensive in terms of facilities, materials, and student-teacher ratios than academic subjects). Perennialists, however, totally reject these subjects as wasteful and senseless, whereas essentialists grudgingly award half credit for these so-called minor subjects, although they do limit the number and hours that students can take them. This latter requirement tends to parallel the present secondary school curriculum.

Perennialists tend to regard the student's mind as a sponge for absorbing knowledge; essentialists, too, are concerned with facts and knowledge, but they are also interested in conceptual thought and principles and theories of subject matter. Both groups feel that all students, regardless of abilities and interests, are to be offered the same common curriculum—intellectual in content—but with the quantity and rate adjusted to the capacity of the individual learner.[25] Just how far each student should go is related to his or her specific abilities. This, in fact, was the majority view before the turn of the twentieth century, when the perennialist era introduced many viable employment opportunities—farming, manual, and, later, industrial—that did not require formal educations.

Many essentialists, like the perennialists, embrace the past mental discipline approach that the educational process should emphasize the mastery of essential skills and facts that form the basis of the subject matter. Wrote Admiral Rickover, "For all children, the educational process must be one of collecting factual knowledge to the limit of their absorptive capacity."[26] A curriculum that takes into account student interests or social issues is wasteful, as are teaching methods that rely on psychological theories. As Bestor declared, "Concern with the personal problems of adolescents has grown so excessive as to push into the background what should be the schools' central concern, the intellectual development of its students."[27] The school is viewed as being sidetracked, when, at the expense of cognitive needs, it attends to the social and psychological problems of students. (Tanner and Tanner, *Curriculum Development*.) (Current task force reports on academic excellence, incidentally, agree with this assessment.) Tough discipline and training, and a good deal of homework and serious studies, permeate the curriculum. As Rickover asserted: "The student must be made to work hard" at his or her studies, and "nothing can really make it fun."[28]

The role of the essentialist teacher follows the perennialist philosophy. The teacher is considered a master of a particular subject and a model worthy of emulation. A teacher is to be respected as an authority because of the knowledge and high standards he or she holds. The teacher is very much in control of the classroom, and decides on the classroom curriculum with minimal student input (because the students do not really know what they want).

Essentialism today is reflected in the public demand to raise academic standards and to improve the students' work and minds. It is evidenced in such reports as *A Nation at Risk* (and other reports on excellence discussed in Chapter 5) and in the current proposals outlined in Ernest Boyer's *High School* and Theodore Sizer's *Hornace's Compromise* (also about high school). Although current essentialist philosophy is more moderate than it was during the Sputnik era—it provides, for example, for less able students—it still emphasizes academics (not play) and cognitive thinking (not the whole child). It is reflected in two current movements that emerged in response to the general relaxation of academic standards during the late 1960s and 1970s.

Back-to-Basics Curriculum. Automatic promotion of marginal students, the dizzy array of elective courses, and textbooks designed more to entertain than to educate are frequently cited as sources of the decline in students' basic skills. Today's concerns parallel, to some extent, those voiced immediately after the Sputnik era. The call is less for academic excellence and rigor, however, than for a return to basics. Annual Gallup polls have asked the public to suggest ways to improve education; since 1976 "devoting more attention to teaching the basics" and "improving curriculum standards" have ranked no lower than fifth in the list of responses; in the 1980s these suggestions surfaced as the number one, two, or three concern each year.[29]

By 1983, all of the states had implemented statewide testing programs for various grade levels; the tests were, in fact, mandated in twenty-seven states. In twelve states, mostly in the South, the test was required for high school graduation.[30] As an offshoot of this movement, as many as forty-four states in 1986 required beginning teachers to evidence minimum competencies in basic skills (spelling, grammar, mathematics), academic knowledge (English, social studies, science, mathematics, arts, etc.) and/or pedagogical practices.[31]

Although the back-to-basics movement means different things to different people, it usually connotes an essentialist curriculum with heavy emphasis on reading, writing, and mathematics. So-called solid subjects—English, history, science, and mathematics—are taught in all grades. English means traditional grammar, not linguistics or nonstandard English; it means Shakespeare and not Lolita. History means U.S. and European history, and perhaps Asian and African history, but not Afro-American history or ethnic studies. Science means biology, chemistry, and physics, not ecology. Math means old math, not new math. Furthermore, these subjects are required for everyone. Elective courses, minicourses, even the integrated social science and general science courses, are considered too "soft."

Proponents of the movement are concerned that too many illiterate students are passed from grade to grade and eventually graduate, that high school and college diplomas are meaningless as measures of academic performance, that minimum standards must be established, and that the basic skills and subjects are essential for employment and self-survival in modern society. Some of these advocates are college educators who would do away with open admissions, credit for life experiences or for remedial courses, and grade inflation. They would simply insist on reasonable high school and college standards, and they would use tests (a "dirty" word for some educators) to monitor educational standards over time and to pressure students, teachers, and parents to perform their responsibilities.[32]

Although the movement is spreading, and state legislators and the public seem convinced of the need for minimum standards, some unanswered questions remain: What standards should be considered minimum? What do we do with students who fail to meet these standards? Are we punishing the victims for the schools' inability to educate them? How will the courts and then the school districts deal with the fact that proportionately more minority than white students fail the competency tests in nearly every case? Is the issue minimum competency or equal educational opportunity? And, when all is said and done, are we not, educationally speaking, reinventing the academic wheel?

Excellence in Education. A spin-off to the back-to-basics movement is the demand, in the 1980s, for educational excellence and tougher academics. This trend is also in ine with the past Cold War-Sputnik era, when essentialists exerted a considerable influence on the school curriculum; today, it coincides with a broader theme of not only military defense but also technology and economic competition. The dimensions of the problem of academic quality are amply documented in several policy reports on academic excellence—the best known is *A Nation at Risk,* released in the mid-1980s—all calling for reform to improve the quality of education in the United States and emphasizing international "competition" and "survival"—themes reminiscent of the post-Sputnik era as well.[33]

Overall, the trend is for higher achievement (not just minimum competency) for all children (not just college-bound students) in the academic areas, which means that we need to stress cognitive achievement (not the whole child) and rigorous grading, testing, and discipline (not relaxed standards). The emphasis is on higher standards for passing courses and meeting graduation requirements.

For some this approach means more than emphasizing the basic ability to think, reason, and problem solve: It means promoting such serious subjects as calculus, physics, and advanced foreign languages at the high school level; it means upgrading our definition of basic skills to include advanced skills and knowledge, including computer skills as the fourth R—which are required for tomorrow's technological world. Stress is on increasing the time and improving the quality of instruction, upgrading our teachers and schools, and analyzing education in terms of *inputs* (improving the resources that go into the educational enterprise), *throughputs* (improving the allocation and use of resources), and *outputs* (raising expectations and standards for those who benefit from the resources). Unquestionably, the emphasis is on productivity. Moreover, the health and vitality of our country's economy and political position are linked to strengthening our educational institutions.[34]

Others allow wider latitude in defining excellence and permit various models or criteria of excellence. Some criticize the overemphasis on logical, mathematical, and scientific excellence in the schools, and the consequent underemphasis or ignoring of other conceptions of excellence—linguistic, musical, spatial, bodily kinesthetic, interpersonal, and intrapersonal areas.[35] Some are also concerned that equity and equality will be shoved under the rug, with too much stress on cognitive excellence—a return to a post-Sputnik-type emphasis on academically talented students but not high school dropouts.[36] Some fear that this emphasis on excellence will lead to disappointment; they say it is wrong to assume that increased testing and more course requirements will automatically raise the level of student performance. Students, teachers, and parents must also be motivated, and technical and financial support at the school and school district level must be evidenced.

In any event, the general theme of this movement is excellence, not adequacy, and many forms of it. The focus is on productivity, increased testing, more homework, better selection of textbooks, and more competent personnel. Both educators and the public agree that students must not only master basic or prerequisite skills, but they must also excel, think creatively, solve problems, and develop their fullest human potential. Finally, the public even seems willing to spend increased monies for real school reform and for upgraded curricula.

Progressivism.

Progressivism developed from pragmatic philosophy and as a protest against perennialist thinking in education. The progressive movement in education was also part of the larger social and political movement of reform that characterized much of American society at the turn of the twentieth century. It grew out of the political thought of such progressives as Robert La-Follette, Theodore Roosevelt, and Woodrow Wilson, as well as from the muckraker movement of the 1920s.[37] Progressivism is considered a contemporary reform movement in educational, social, and political affairs.

The educational roots of progressivism can be traced to the reform writings of Horace Mann and Henry Barnard of the nineteenth century, and later to the work of John Dewey in the early twentieth century.[38] In his most comprehensive work, *Democracy and Education*, Dewey claimed that democracy and education went hand in hand; democratic society and democratic education are participatory and emergent, not preparatory and absolute. Dewey viewed the school as a miniature democratic society, in which students could learn and practice the skills and tools necessary for democratic living.[39]

According to progressivist thought, the skills and tools of learning include problem-solving methods and scientific inquiry; in addition, learning experiences should include cooperative behaviors and self-discipline, both of which are important for democratic living. Through these skills and experiences the school can transmit the culture of society while it prepares the students for a changing world. Because reality is constantly changing, Dewey saw little need to focus upon a fixed body of knowledge, as did the perennialists and essentialists. Progressivism, instead, placed heavy emphasis on *how* to think, not *what* to think. Traditional education, with its "method of imposition from the side of the teacher and reception, [and] absorption from the side of the pupil," wrote Dewey, "may be compared to inscribing records upon a passive phonographic disc to result in giving back what has been inscribed when the proper button is pressed in recitation or examination."[40]

For Dewey and other progressivist thinkers, the curriculum was interdisciplinary in nature, and books and subject matter were part of the learning process rather than sources of ultimate knowledge. The role of the teacher was unique when operating under progressive thinking. The teacher served as a guide for students in their problem-solving and scientific projects. Dewey and William Kilpatrick both referred to this role as the "leader of group activities." The teacher and students planned activities to-

gether (although Dewey later affirmed tha the final authority rested with the teacher) but the teacher was to help students locate analyze, interpret, and evaluate data—to formulate their own conclusions.[41]

The progressive movement became splintered by several different wings, in cluding the child-centered, activity-centered, creative, and neo-Freudian groups Dewey criticized these groups for misinter preting and misusing his ideas. Just as he condemned the old philosophies that pur sued knowledge for its own sake, he at tacked those who thought knowledge had little or no value. Not only did he attack "traditional ideas as erecting silence as a vir tue," he also criticized those who sought to liberate the child from adult authority and social controls. He declared "progressive ex tremists" and "laissez-faire" philosophies to be destructive to the ideas of progressivism and he warned that "any movement tha thinks and acts in terms of an ism become so involved in reaction against other ism that it is unwittingly controlled by them."

Dewey was not alone in his criticism of pro gressive educators. As criticisms mounted Boyd Bode, another leading proponent o progressivism, warned his associates of th impending crisis in a book entitled *Progres sive Education at the Crossroads*.[43] He cau tioned that "progressive education stands a the parting of the ways." The movemen "nurtured the pathetic hope that it coul find out how to educate by relying on suc notions as interests, needs, growth and free dom." In its social and psychological ap proach to learning, in its "one-sided devo tion to the child, it betrayed the child," an deprived him or her of appropriate subjec matter. If progressivism continued its pre ent course without changing its focus, " would be circumvented and left behind." Bode's words proved prophetic. More an more, progressivists responded to the grow ing criticism and self-justifying theories an educational ideas that involved trivialitie and errors.

Although the progressive movement education encompassed many different the ories and practices, it was united in its oppo sition to certain traditional school practices: (1) the authoritarian teacher; (2) excessive reliance on textbook methods; (3) memorization of factual data and techniques by drill; (4) static aims and materials that reject the notion of a changing world; (5) use of fear or corporal punishment as a form of discipline; and (6) attempts to isolate education from individual experiences and social reality. However, the movement's inability to outline a uniform theory of the purpose of schooling, or even to establish a set of principles, contributed to its downfall.[45]

Progressive education was both a movement within the broad framework of American education and a theory that urged the liberation of the child from the traditional emphasis on rote learning, lesson recitations, and textbook authority. In opposition to the conventional subject matter of the traditional curriculum, progressives experimented with alternative modes of curricular organization—utilizing activities, experiences, problem solving, and the project method. Progressive education focused on the child as the learner rather than on the subject; emphasized activities and experiences rather than verbal and literary skills; and encouraged cooperative group-learning activities rather than competitive individualized lesson learning. The use of democratic school procedures was considered a prelude to community and social reform. Progressivism also cultivated a cultural relativism that critically appraised and often rejected traditional value commitments.

Although the major thrust of progressive education waned in the 1940s and 1950s, with the advent of essentialism, the philosophy did leave its imprint on education and the schools of today. Contemporary progressivism is expressed in several movements, including those for a relevant curriculum, humanistic education, and radical school reform.

Relevant Curriculum. As part of the student protest movement of the 1960s, students demanded relevant educations. The subject-centered curriculum of the essentialists was considered irrelevant to social re-

ality. (Allan C. Ornstein, "Curriculum Contrasts: A Historical Overview," *Phi Delta Kappan* (February 1982), pp. 404–408; Tanner and Tanner, *Curriculum Development*.) The shift was part of the progressive legacy. Learners must be motivated and interested in the learning task, and the classroom should build on real-life experiences.

The call for relevance came, in fact, from both students and educators. Proponents who advocate this approach see as needs: (1) the individualization of instruction through such teaching methods as independent study and special projects; (2) the revision of existing courses and development of new ones on such topics of student concern as environmental protection, drug addiction, urban problems, and so on; (3) the provision of educational alternatives, such as electives, minicourses, and open classrooms, that allow more freedom and choice; (4) the extension of the curriculum beyond the school's walls through such innovations as work-study programs, credit for life experiences, off-campus courses, and external degree programs; and (5) the relaxation of academic standards and admission standards to schools and colleges.[46]

Efforts to relate subject matter to student interests have been largely ad hoc, and many were fragmented and temporary, a source of concern to proponents and critics of relevance. In other cases, changes made in the name of relevance have in fact watered down the curriculum, and have led to lack of direction and focus.

Humanistic Curriculum. The humanistic curriculum also began as a reaction to what was viewed as an overemphasis on subject matter and cognitive learning in the 1960s and 1970s. In his best-selling book, *Crisis in the Classroom*, Charles Silberman advocated humanizing American schools.[47] He charged that schools are repressive, and that they teach students docility and conformity. He believed that schools must be reformed, even at the price of deemphasizing cognitive learning and student discipline. He suggested that elementary schools adopt the methods of the British infant schools. At the secondary level, he suggested independent study, peer tutoring, and community and work experiences.

The humanistic model of education stems from the human potential movement in psychology. Within education it is rooted in the work of Arthur Jersild, who linked good teaching with knowledge of self and students, and in the work of Arthur Combs and Donald Snygg, who explored the impact of self-concept and motivation on achievement.[48] Combs and Snygg considered self-concept the most important determinant of behavior.

A humanistic curriculum emphasizes affective rather than cognitive outcomes. Such a curriculum draws heavily on the works of Abraham Maslow and Carl Rogers.[49] Its goal is to produce "self-actualizing people," in Maslow's words, or "total human beings," in Rogers's. The works of both psychologists are laced with such terms as maintaining, striving, enhancing, and experiencing—as well as independence, self-determination, integration, and self-actualization.

Advocates of humanistic education contend that the present school curriculum has failed miserably by humanistic standards, that teachers and schools are determined to stress cognitive behaviors and to control students *not* for their own good but for the good of adults.[50] Humanists emphasize more than affective processes; they seek higher domains of consciousness. But they see the schools as unconcerned about higher planes of understanding, enhancement of the mind, or self-knowledge. Students must therefore turn to such out-of-school activities as drugs, yoga, transcendental meditation, group encounters, T-groups, psychotherapy, and sexual therapy.

But such activities lead many observers to put down the humanistic movement. Mario Fantini, an advocate of humanistic education, warns that too many Americans view the humanistic approach negatively. They are suspicious of what appears to be bizarre procedures and touch-feel-sexual experiences. "In certain professional circles, the movement is . . . referred to as the 'touch-

feeling crowd,' connoting an almost illegitimate status among the established disciplines."[51]

Humanists would attempt to form more meaningful relationships between students and teachers; they would foster student independence and self-direction, and they would promote greater acceptance of self and others. The teacher's role would be to help learners cope with their psychological needs and problems, to facilitate self-understanding among students, and to help them develop fully.

A drawback to humanist theory is its lack of attention to cognitive learning and intellectual development. When asked to judge the effectiveness of their curriculum, humanists generally rely on testimonials and subjective assessments by students and teachers. They may also present such materials as students' paintings and poems or talk about "marked improvement" in student behavior and attitudes. They present very little empirical evidence, however, to support their stance.

Radical School Reform. During the late 1960s and 1970s intense attacks were leveled on teachers and schools by radical critics of education, sometimes called "radical romanticists" or "neoprogressives." The criticisms were widely published in the mass media, especially in magazines that politically liberal and college-educated adults read (*Atlantic, Harpers, New Republic, The New York Times Magazine,* and *Saturday Review*). These radicals also published many popular books on their views; in fact, they were superverbalizers who enchanted their readers.[52]

Among the most prominent wave of radicals are John Holt, Paul Goodman, Edgar Friedenberg, A. S. Neill, and Ivan Illich. They expressed considerable disdain toward established methods of schooling, compulsory schooling, adult authority, and school rules. They referred to students as prisoners, to teachers as prison guards (who disliked their students), and to schools as prisons (which keep youths locked up, restricted from free expression and democratic procedures). In general, school is considered to be a highly discriminatory place that sorts and tracks students for various jobs that extend class differences in society.

In particular, Friedenberg argued that teachers "dislike and distrust" the students they teach, and that they "fear being involved with young people in any situation that is not under their complete control." Teachers have a "repressed hostility toward their students" and "resentment," a kind of ill temper, suppressed anger, and jealousy because of students' youthful energy and freedom.[53]

Holt's book, *How Children Fail*, is his most influential text.[54] There is nothing positive in it about teachers or the school processes; it deals instead with how teachers and schools turn off students. Holt describes the conventions of the classroom: Teachers' enforcing rigid rules and children's focusing on right answers, learning to be stupid, and learning not to learn. He goes into great detail about how children adopt strategies of fear and failure to please their teachers. The "successful" students become cunning strategists in a game of beating the system—figuring out how to outsmart the teacher, how to get the answer out of the teacher, or how to fake the answer.

Paul Goodman's thesis is that our society is sick and full of spurious and false values that have produced sick schools. He contends that schools have little to do with education; they provide jobs for millions of people and a market for textbook companies, building contractors, and graduates of schools of education. In the early grades, the schools provide "a baby-sitting service" for the parents and keep kids off the street. In the junior and senior years, "they are the arm of the police, providing cops and concentration camps paid for in the budget under the heading of 'Board of Education.'" From kindergarten to college, schools teach youth to adjust to a sick society and provide "a universal trap [in which] democracy begins to look like regimentation."[55] Goodman's solution is to do away with compulsory education, to which he refers as "miseducation" and to "drastically cut back formal schooling because the present extended tutelage is against nature and arrests growth."[56]

A. S. Neill, the fourth member of the earlier generation of romantic progressivists, recounts the way he operated his school, "Summerhill," in Suffolk, England. He wrote about the innate goodness of the child, and about the replacement of authority for freedom against which Dewey warned:

. . . we set out to make a school in which we should allow children to be themselves. In order to do this, we had to renounce all discipline, all direction, all suggestion, all moral training. . . . All it required was what we had—a complete belief in the child as a good, not an evil being. For almost forty years, this belief in the goodness of the child has never wavered; it rather has become a final faith.[57]

Neill claimed that the "child is innately wise and realistic. If left to himself without adult suggestions of any kind," he will develop on his own. Those "who are to become scholars will be scholars," and those "who are only fit to sweep the streets will sweep streets."[58] Neill is not concerned with formal teaching or instruction; he does not believe in examinations or in homework. Those who want to study will study, and those who prefer not to study will not—regardless of how teachers teach or what they say. If a child wants to go to class, great; if not, so what? Neill's criteria for success have nothing to do with school or economic outcomes; rather they relate to the ability to "work joyfully" and "live positively." Following these guidelines, most of the students who attend Summerhill allegedly turn out to be successful in life.

At Summerhill, a 6-year old has the same rights and same voting privileges as a teacher: One person, one vote. A child who breaks a window will come to Neill and tell the truth, we are told, because at Summerhill there is no fear—basically joy. In other schools, "discipline is used as a weapon of hate and obedience becomes a virtue." But at Summerhill, things are different; "classrooms are happy places."[59] What Summerhill provides is an alternative method of schooling that is highly child-centered and that places little emphasis on academic subjects or cognitive achievement. The school is, however, a private, middle- and upper-middle-class one with a small enrollment that rarely exceeds sixty students.

Ivan Illich, another radical critic, goes beyond his contemporaries in his plans for remaking schools. He argues for a new society that requires the prior deschooling of society.[60] In this sense Illich may also be a reconstructionist philosopher. Although the other radical critics are very angry and see little possibility of school reform, given the present educational process, Illich, who completely rejects school as a viable agency, is the center of controversy. His criticism of current schools is that they are coercive, discriminatory, and destructive toward their clients. If schools were eliminated, education could be open to all and could become a genuine instrument of human liberation: Learners would no longer have an obligatory curriculum imposed upon them; they would be liberated from institutional and capitalistic indoctrination. There would no longer be discrimination and a class society based on possession of a certificate.

In lieu of school, Illich recommends small learning networks characterized by the following: *Educational objects*—that is, shops, libraries, museums, art galleries, and so on—that are open to learners; *peer matching*—that is, identifying and bringing together students who wish to engage in a particular learning activity; *skill exchanges*—that is, exchanges between those who are competent in a particular skill, and who wish to teach it, and those who wish to learn it; and *educators-at-large*—that is, counselors who serve as advisors to students and parents and intellectual initiators and administrators who operate the networks.

Even though Illich is considered a neo-Marxist educator, he has stimulated large numbers of disciples to further the idea of deschooling, and a good deal of radical re-

form literature related to the political and economic concept of educational "revisionism."[61]

Reconstructionism.

Although the reconstructionist philosophy itself is based on early utopian ideas, the Great Depression of the 1930s stimulated a demand for social reconstructionism. The progressive educational movement was at its height in popularity then, but a small yet significant group of progressive educators still became disillusioned with American society and impatient for reform. This group argued that progressivism put too much emphasis on child-centered education that mainly served the individual child and the middle class, with its play theories and private schools. What was needed was more emphasis on society-centered education that took into consideration the needs of society (not the individual) and all classes (not only the middle class).

At the 1932 annual meeting of the Progressive Education Association, George Counts called for progressive educators to address the great social and economic issues of the day, to forge a new social reform platform, and to create a new vision of society and of the future. (Creanin, *The Transformation of the School*; Tanner and Tanner, *Curriculum Development*.) In his speech, "Dare the School Build a New Social Order?" (which was later published as a book), Counts suggested that the school lead society to realize democratic values, that it become the agent of change and institution for social reform. In a rhetorical and highly charged statement, Counts stunned his progressive colleagues with the following statement:

The weakness of Progressive Education thus lies in the fact that it has elaborated no theory of social welfare, unless it be that of anarchy or extreme individualism.... If Progressive Education is to be genuinely progressive, it must ... face squarely and courageously every social issue, come to grips with life in all its stark reality, establish an organic relation with the community, develop a realistic and comprehensive theory of welfare, fashion a compelling and challenging vision of human destiny, and become less frightened than it is today at the bogeys of *imposition* and *indoctrination*.[62]

The social issues of the 1930s, according to Counts, involved racial and class discrimination, poverty, and unemployment—and progressive education had ignored these issues. The social issues today are similar, although the list is larger: racial, ethnic, and sexual inequality; poverty, unemployment, and welfare; computers and technology; political oppression and war; the threat of nuclear disaster; environmental pollution; disease; hunger; and depletion of the earth's resources.

Theodore Brameld, who is often considered the originator of the term reconstructionism in 1950 (actually Dewey coined the term),[63] has asserted that reconstructionism is a crisis philosophy, appropriate for a society in crisis, which is the essence of our society and international society today.[64] According to Brameld, students and teachers must not only take positions; they must also become change agents to improve society. Neutrality in the classrooms or schools, that in which we often engage under the guise of objective and scientific inquiry, is not appropriate for the democratic process. Writes Brameld, "Teachers and students have a right to take sides, to stand up for the best reasoned and informed partialities they can reach as a result of free, meticulous examination and communication of all relevant evidence."[65] In particular, teachers must measure up to their social responsibilities. Brameld goes on:

In this vast, rumbling, clumsy infinitely powerful mass of hundreds of millions of human beings lies the great reservoir of strength for tomorrow's education. Here, indeed, is the fountainhead of all other utopian potentials presently emerging. The immediate task before the [teaching] profession is to draw upon this strength and thus to strengthen control of the schools by and for the goal-seeking interests of the overwhelming majority of mankind.[66]

As for the curriculum, it had to be transformed to coincide with a new social-economic-political education; it had, in other words, to incorporate realistic reform strategies. For reconstructionists, analysis, interpretation, and evaluation of problems are insufficient; commitment and action by students and teachers are needed. Society is always changing, and the curriculum has to change; students and teachers must be change agents. A curriculum based on social issues and social services is ideal.

The reconstructionists, including such recent proponents as Mario Fantini, Harold Shane, and Alvin Toffler, seek a curriculum that emphasizes cultural pluralism, internationalism, and futurism.[67] Students are taught to appreciate life in a world of many nations—a global village—with many alternatives for the future. A reconstructionist program of education: (1) critically examines the cultural heritage of a society as well as the entire civilization; (2) is not afraid to examine controversial issues; (3) is deliberately committed to bring about social and constructive change; (4) cultivates a future planning attitude that considers the realities of the world; and (5) enlists students and teachers in a definite program to enhance cultural renewal and interculturalism. In such a program, teachers are considered the prime agents of social change, cultural renewal, and internationalism. Teachers are organized not to strengthen their own professional security, but rather to encourage widespread experimentation in the schools and to challenge the outdated structures of society. They are considered to be the vanguard for a new social order—somewhat utopian in nature.

Reconceptualists. The reconceptualists have criticized the majority of curricularists as exemplifying a lock-step, means-ends approach, based on technocratic and bureaucratic school models that are not sensitive to the inner feelings and experiences of people. The majority of curricularists, in turn, have claimed that the reconceptualists are unable to quantify or verify the components of their curriculum and are unclear about their philosophical and methodological tools. Most people in the field, representing a conservative outlook, believe that the empirical-analytical and scientific approaches contribute the most to the field of curriculum; nonetheless, the reconceptualists's approach is enriching and introduces aesthetic, existentialist, and social science procedures previously not deemed appropriate.

Reconceptualists have expanded the field to include other dimensions of curriculum, including intuitive, personal, mystical, linguistic, political, and social systems of theorizing. They stress broad problems and issues—and they attempt to reflect, refine, rethink, reinterpret, and reconceptualize the field of curriculum. It is doubtful, however, that reconceptualists really reinterpret or reconceptualize anything. They are basically socially sensitive and politically concerned intellectuals who reflect and refine important issues that have philosophical, psychological, social, political, and economic implications. Unfortunately for the field of curriculum, they have been labeled reconceptualists.[68]

Reconceptualists accept many aspects of progressive philosophy, including learner-centered, relevant, humanistic, and radical school-reform models. However, they reiterate and detail a bit more of the dynamic, holistic, transcendental, linguistic, and artistic meaning of teaching and learning. They are more concerned with personal self-knowledge, inner self, personal reflection, psychologies of consciousness, and spiritual and moral introspection. They contend there is more to knowledge and knowing than empirical or even logical, verifiable data. Expanded ideas of inner consciousness, "third force" or humanistic psychology, and existentialist ideas serve as the foundations for their views.

Content and experiences that emphasize language and communication skills, personal biographies, art, poetry, dance, drama, literature, psychology, ethics, religion, and other aesthetic, humanistic, and spiritual subject matter comprise a good part of the reconstructionist curriculum—subjects not part of the normal curriculum

or certainly not the major foci. Maxine Greene advocates this curriculum, which she calls "personal expression," "intellectual consciousness," and "reflective self-consciousness."[69] Paulo Freire refers to this as a curriculum of "human phenomenon," "problematic situations," and "background awareness" that has the potential "to transform the world."[70] According to William Pinar, this subject matter deals with "personal becoming," "autonomy," the "soul" and "heart," "affiliative needs," "mature personality," "trust" and "love," "self-direction," "sensitivity," and "enjoyment"[71]—that is, psychological, philosophical, spiritual, and existentialist attitudes and behaviors.

Reconceputualists are also concerned with social, political, and economic ideas and ideology, and in this context reflect reconstructionist philosophy. Many of their ideas, rooted in the school of Dewey, Counts, and Rugg, deal with inequities and/or conflict concerned with socioeconomic relationships, sexual and racial roles and attitudes, the relationship between labor and capital, and the consequences of political power. Reconceptualists are also concerned with current technocratic and bureaucratic systems that dominate the individual, and that reduce the person to a powerless and manipulated cog. They envision schools as an oppressive instrument of society that controls and coerces, even oppresses, students through various customs and mores and teaching-learning practices.

Some reconceptualists have been labeled neo-Marxists. Michael Apple, for one, has tried to highlight the relationship between what he perceives to be political, economic, and cultural domination of the individual in relation to schools and society. Such domination "is vested in the constitutive principles, codes, and especially the common sense consciousness and practices underlying our lives, as well as by overt division and manipulation."[72] In other words, the everyday structures and institutions of our society, including schools, convey meaning and conditions that shape our lives and that take control over us; the dominant social, political, and economic system pervades in all critical aspects of the curriculum.

Elsewhere, Apple points out that just as there is "unequal distribution of economic capital in society, so, too is there a similar system of distribution surrounding cultural capital." In technological societies, schools become "distributors of this cultural capital."[73] They play a major role in distributing various forms of knowledge, which in turn leads to power and control over others.

Both Illich and Freire contend that the larger system is oppressive and in need of major overhaul. Illich, who is also considered to be a radical critic, outlines a curriculum that is less institutionalized, formal, and discriminatory for purposes of "emancipation." He relies on a "grass-roots" curriculum that seeks to engage students, teachers, and community members.[74] Freire develops a "pedagogy for the oppressed" for students and the poor, and describes how people can move through different stages to ultimately be able to take action and overcome oppression. To effect major change, at what Freire calls the "critical transforming stage," people must become active participants in changing their own status through social action that aims at changing the larger social order. Freire calls for a dialogue or match between students and adults who are sensitive to change. The curriculum is to focus on community, national, and world problems—and is to be based on a core or interdisciplinary approach.[75]

In general, the curriculum advocated by this wing of reconceptualists emphasizes the social sciences—history, political science, economics, sociology, and some psychology and philosophy—and not the hard sciences. The thrust is to develop individual self-realization and freedom through cognitive and intellectual activities, and then to liberate people from the restrictions, limitations, and controls of society. The idea is to move from knowledge to activity, from reflections to action. The curriculum attempts to create new conditions and environments that improve the human condition and the institutions of society. It is, according to James

Macdonald, "a form of 'utopianism,' a form of political and social philosophizing."[76] All the oppressed—youth, poor, minorities, women, and so on—are considered agents for change. The model, in essence, is an updated version of old reconstructionism, which viewed students and teachers as agents of change. In the new version, reconceptualism, the teacher is often construed as an agent of oppression, representative of the larger and coercive society.

Equality of Educational Opportunity.
No country has taken the idea of equality more seriously than ours. Politically, the idea is rooted in our Constitution—written more than 150 years prior to the emergence of reconstructionism as a philosophy. The origins of American public schools are also dominated by the concept of equal opportunity, and the notion of universal, free education. The rise of the "common school" was spearheaded by Horace Mann who asserted, "Education beyond all other devices of human origin is the greatest equalizer of the condition of men—the balance-wheel of the social machinery."[77]

Equality of opportunity in this context would not lead to equality of outcomes; this concept did not attempt a classless society. As David Tyack wrote, "For the most part, working men did not seek to pull down the rich; rather they sought equality of opportunity for their children, an equal chance at the main chance."[78] Equality of opportunity in the nineteenth and early twentieth centuries meant an equal start for all children, but the assumption was that some would go farther than others. Differences in backgrounds and abilities, as well as motivation and luck, would create differences in outcomes among individuals, but the school would assure that children born into any class would have the opportunity to achieve status as persons born into other classes. Implicit in this view was that the "schools represented the means of achieving the goal . . . of equal chances of success" relative to all children in all stratum.[79]

In retrospect, the schools did not fully

achieve this goal, according to some observers, because school achievement and economic outcomes are highly related to social class and family background.[80] Had the schools not existed, however, social mobility would have been further reduced. The failure of the common school to achieve social mobility raises the question of the role of school in achieving equality—and the question of just what the school can and cannot do to affect cognitive and economic outcomes.

The modern view of educational equality, which emerged in the 1950s through the 1970s, goes much further than the old view. In light of this, James Coleman has outlined five views of inequality of educational opportunity, the latter four of which parallel reconstructionist philosophy: (1) inequality defined by the same curriculum for all children, with the intent that school facilities be equal; (2) inequality defined in terms of the racial composition of the schools; (3) inequality defined in terms of such intangible characteristic as teacher morale and teacher expectations of students; (4) inequality based on school consequences or outcomes for students with equal backgrounds and abilities; and (5) inequality based on school consequences for students with unequal backgrounds and abilities.[81]

The first two definitions deal with race and social class; the next definition deals with concepts that are hard to define in terms of relevancy and starting and stopping points; the fourth definition deals with school expenditures and school finances. The fifth definition is an extreme interpretation: Equality is reached only when the outcomes of schooling are similar for all students—those in minority as well as dominant student groups.

When inequality is defined, in terms of equal outcomes (both cognitive and economic), we start comparing racial, ethnic, and religious groups. In a heterogeneous society like ours, this results in some hot issues—including how much to invest in human capital, how to determine the cost-effectiveness of social and educational programs, who should be taxed and how much, to what extent are we to handicap our brightest and most talented minds (the swift racers) to enable those who are slow to finish at the same time, and whether affirmative action policies lead to reverse discrimination.[82] Indeed we cannot treat these issues lightly, because they affect most of us in one way or another and lead to questions over which wars have been fought.

All these issues involve balancing acts, and what effect these balancing acts have on individuals, groups, and society. Many reconstructionists—not to mention perennialists and essentialists, who have their own ideas about excellence in education—have problems with these issues. Many of us are unable to agree on what is equitable and just, and how much we can stretch the embodiment of reform ideas or the fiber of society. Too much egalitarianism can lead to mediocrity, indifference, and economic decline within society. On the other hand, excellence carried too far can create wide social and economic gaps, hostilities among groups, and a stratified society. The idea is to search for the golden mean.

In his classic text on excellence and equality John Gardner describes the dilemma vividly:

We might as well admit that it is not easy for us as believers in democracy to dwell on the differences in capacity between men. Democratic philosophy has tended to ignore such differences where possible, and to belittle them where it could not ignore them. . . .

Extreme equalitarianism—or what I would prefer to say *equalitarianism wrongly conceived*—which ignores differences in native capacity and achievement, has not served democracy well. Carried far enough, it means . . . the end of that striving for excellence which has produced mankind's greatest achievements.

. . . no democracy can give itself over to extreme emphasis on individual performance and still remain a democracy—or to extreme equalitarianism and retain its vitality. A society such as ours has no choice but to seek the development of human potentialities at all levels. It takes more than educated elite to run a complex, tech-

TABLE 2-2 Overview of Educational Philosophies

Educational Philosophy	Philosophical Base	Aim of Education	Knowledge	Role of Education	Curriculum Focus	Related Curriculum Trends
Perennialism	Realism	To educate the rational person; to cultivate the intellect	Focus on past and permanent studies; mastery of facts and timeless knowledge	Teacher helps students think rationally; based on Socratic method, oral exposition; explicit teaching of traditional values	Classical subjects; literary analysis; constant curriculum	Great books; Paideia Proposal
Essentialism	Idealism, Realism	To promote the intellectual growth of the individual; to educate the competent person	Essential skills and academic subjects; mastery of concepts and principles of subject matter	Teacher is authority in his or her subject field; explicit teaching of traditional values	Essential skills (three Rs) and essential subjects (English, science, history, math, and foreign language)	Back to basics; excellence in education
Progressivism	Pragmatism	To promote democratic, social living	Knowledge leads to growth and development; a living-learning process; focus on active and relevant learning	Teacher is a guide for problem solving and scientific inquiry	Based on students' interests; involves the application of human problems and affairs; interdisciplinary subject matter; activities and projects	Relevant curriculum; humanistic education; radical school reform
Reconstructionism	Pragmatism	To improve and reconstruct society; education for change and social reform	Skills and subjects needed to identify and ameliorate problems of society; learning is active and concerned with contemporary and future society	Teacher serves as an agent of change and reform; acts as a project director and research leader; helps students become aware of problems confronting humankind	Emphasis on social sciences and social research methods; examination of social, economic, and political problems; focus on present and future trends as well as on national and international issues	Reconceptualism; equality of educational opportunity

nological society. Every modern industrialized society is learning that hard lesson.[83]

The issues that Gardner raised directly affected the social fabric of the country, and have echoed loudly in the past twenty-five years. They have given rise to educational equality and equal opportunity legislation that has permeated many aspects of school and society. The reconstructionists, among other educators, have raised many of the same issues, including school desegregation, compensatory education, multicultural education, handicapped education, more effective schooling, and affirmative action (who goes to college, who gets what jobs, and who manages society). These issues have no easy answers, and they will continue to plague us in the 1990s.

CONCLUSION

Philosophy gives meaning to our decisions and actions. In the absence of a philosophy, the educator is vulnerable to externally imposed prescriptions, to fads and frills, to authoritarian schemes, and to other "isms." Dewey was so convinced of the importance of philosophy that he viewed it as the all-encompassing aspect of the educational process—as necessary for "forming fundamental dispositions, intellectual and emotional, toward nature and fellow man."[84] If one accepts this conclusion, it becomes evident that many aspects of curriculum, if not most of the educational process in school, is developed around philosophy. Even if we believe that Dewey's point is an overstatement, we should still recognize the pervasiveness of philosophy in determining our views of reality, what values and knowledge are worthwhile, and decisions in education in general and curriculum making in particular.

Major philosophical viewpoints that have emerged within the curriculum field may be viewed along a continuum—traditional and conservative versus contemporary and liberal—idealism, realism, pragmatism, and existentialism. These general or world philosophies have influenced educational philosophies, sometimes called educational theories or views,[85] along the same continuum: Perennialism, essentialism, progressivism, and reconstructionism. Very few schools adopt a single philosophy; in practice, most schools combine various philosophies. Moreover, our position is that no single philosophy, old or new, should serve as the exclusive guide for making decisions about schools or about the curriculum. All philosophical groups (outlined in this chapter) want the same thing of education—that is, they wish to improve the educational process, to enhance the achievement of the learner, to produce better and more productive citizens, and to improve society. Because of their different views of reality, values, and knowledge, however, they find it difficult to agree on *how* to achieve these ends.

What we need to do, as curricularists, is to search for the middle road, a highly elusive and abstract concept, where there is no extreme emphasis on subject matter or student; cognitive development or sociopsychological development; excellence or equality. What we need is a prudent school philosophy, one that is politically and economically feasible, and that serves the needs of students and society. Implicit in this view of education is that too much emphasis on any one philosophy, sometimes at the expense of another, may do harm and cause conflict. How much we emphasize one philosophy, under the guise of reform or for whatever reason, is critical because no one society can give itself over to extreme "isms" or political views and still remain a democracy. The kind of society into which we evolve is in part reflected in our educational system, which is influenced by the philosophy that we eventually define and develop.

In the final analysis, curriculum workers must understand that they are continuously faced with curriculum decisions, and that philosophy is important in determining these decisions. Unfortunately, few school people test their notions of curriculum against the school's statement of philosophy.

It is not uncommon to find teachers and administrators developing elaborate lists of behavioral objectives with little or no consideration to the overall philosophy of the school.[86] (Ronald S. Brandt and Ralph W. Tyler . . . ; Tanner and Tanner, *Curriculum Development*.) Curriculum workers need to provide assistance in developing and designing school practices that coincide with the philosophy of the school and community. Teaching, learning, and curriculum are all interwoven in our school practices and should reflect a school philosophy. It is important, then, for school people, especially curricularists, to make decisions and take action in relation to the philosophy of their school and community.

Notes

1. William Van Til, "In a Climate of Change," in R. R. Leeper, ed., *Role of Supervisor and Curriculum Director in a Climate of Change* (Washington, D.C.: Association for Supervision and Curriculum Development, 1965), p. 18.
2. L. Thomas Hopkins, *Interaction: The Democratic Process* (Boston: D. C. Heath, 1941), pp. 198–200.
3. John I. Goodlad et al., *Curriculum Inquiry* (New York: McGraw-Hill, 1979).
4. B. Othanel Smith, William O. Stanley, and J. Harlan Shores, *Fundamentals of Curriculum Development*, rev. ed. (New York: World Book, 1957). See also B. Othanel Smith, "Curriculum Content," in F. W. English, ed., *Fundamental Curriculum Decisions* (Alexandria, Va.: Association for Supervision and Curriculum Development, 1983), pp. 30–39.
5. Ronald C. Doll, *Curriculum Improvement: Decision Making and Process*, 6th ed. (Boston: Allyn and Bacon, 1986), p. 30.
6. John Dewey, *Democracy and Education* (New York: Macmillan, 1916), pp. 186, 383–384.
7. Ibid., p. 384.
8. Ralph W. Tyler, *Basic Principles of Curriculum and Instruction* (Chicago: University of Chicago Press, 1949), pp. 33–34.
9. John I. Goodlad, *What Schools Are For* (Bloomington, Ind.: Phi Delta Kappan Educational Foundation, 1979). See also Goodlad, *A Place Called School* (New York: McGraw-Hill, 1984).
10. J. Donald Butler, *Idealism in Education* (New York: Harper & Row, 1966).
11. Morris L. Bigge, *Educational Philosophies for Teachers* (Columbus, Ohio: Merrill, 1982); Howard Ozman and Sam Craver, *Philosophical Foundations of Education*, 3rd ed. (Columbus, Ohio: Merrill, 1986).
12. Harry S. Broudy, *Building a Philosophy of Education* (Englewood Cliffs, N.J.: Prentice-Hall, 1961); John Wild, *Introduction to a Realist Philosophy* (New York: Harper & Row, 1948).
13. Broudy, *Building a Philosophy of Education*; William O. Martin, *Realism in Education* (New York: Harper & Row, 1969).
14. Ernest E. Bayles, *Pragmatism in Education* (New York: Harper & Row, 1966); John L. Childs, *Pragmatism and Education* (New York: Holt, Rinehart, 1956).
15. John Dewey, *Experience and Education* (New York: Macmillan, 1938).
16. Maxine Greene, *Existential Encounters for Teachers* (New York: Random House, 1967); George F. Kneller, *Existentialism in Education* (New York: Wiley, 1958); and Van Cleve Morris, *Existentialism and Education* (New York: Harper & Row, 1966).
17. Harold Soderquist, *The Person and Education* (Columbus, Ohio: Merrill, 1966); Donald Vandenberg, *Human Rights in Education* (New York: Philosophical Library, 1983). See also Israel Scheffler, *Of Human Potential: An Essay in the Philosophy of Education* (Boston: Routledge & Kegan Paul, 1986).
18. Maxine Greene, *Landscapes of Learning* (New York: Teachers College Press, Columbia University, 1978); Donald Vandenberg, "Human Dignity, Three Human Rights, and Pedagogy," *Educational Theory* (Winter 1986), pp. 33–44.
19. Robert M. Hutchins, *The Conflict in Education* (New York: Harper & Row, 1953), p. 68.
20. Bigge, *Educational Philosophies for Teachers*; Daniel Tanner and Laurel N. Tanner, *Curriculum Development: Theory into Practice* (New York: Macmillan, 1980).
21. Robert M. Hutchins, *The Higher Learning in America* (New Haven: Yale University Press, 1936).
22. Robert M. Hutchins, *A Conversation on Education* (Santa Barbara, Calif.: The Fund for the Republic, 1963), p. 1.
23. Mortimer J. Adler, *The Paideia Proposal: An Educational Manifesto* (New York: Macmillan, 1982); Adler, *Paideia Problems and Possibilities* (New York: Macmillan, 1983); and Adler, *The Paideia Program: An Educational Syllabus* (New York: Macmillan, 1984).
24. See William Bagley, "Just What is the Crux and the Conflict Between the Progressives and the Essentialists?" *Educational Administration and Supervision* (September 1940), pp. 508–511; Arthur Bestor, *Educational Wastelands* (Urbana, Ill.: University of Illinois Press, 1953); and Hyman Rickover, *Education and Freedom* (New York: E. P. Dutton, 1959).
25. See Daniel Tanner, "Curriculum History," in H. E. Mitzel, ed., *Encyclopedia of Educational Research*, 5th ed. (New York: Macmillan, 1982), pp. 412–420.
26. Hyman G. Rickover, "European vs. American Secondary Schools," *Phi Delta Kappan* (November 1958), p. 61.

27. Arthur Bestor, *The Restoration of Learning* (New York: Knopf, 1955), p. 120.

28. Rickover, "European vs. American Secondary Schools," p. 61.

29. Stanley M. Elam, "The Gallup Education Surveys," *Phi Delta Kappan* (September 1983), pp. 26–32. See also Gallup polls published in the September or October issues of *Phi Delta Kappan*, 1984 to 1986.

30. *Educational Governance in the States* (Washington, D.C.: U.S. Department of Education, 1983).

31. Daniel L. Duke, "What is the Nature of Educational Excellence and Should We Try to Measure It?" *Phi Delta Kappan* (June 1985), pp. 675–681; Allan C. Ornstein, "Teacher Accountability: Trends and Policies," *Education and Urban Society* (February 1986), pp. 221–229; and *Teacher Education Policy in the States* (Washington, D.C.: American Association of Colleges for Teacher Education, 1986).

32. Gregory R. Anrig, "Educational Standards, Testing, and Equity," *Phi Delta Kappan* (May 1985), pp. 623–625; Chester Finn, "The New Basics for Everyone," *Educational Leadership* (October 1983), pp. 28–29.

33. Allan C. Ornstein, "An Historical Look—How Do Educators Meet the Needs of Society?" *National Association of Secondary School Principals* (May 1985), pp. 36–47; Daniel Tanner, The American High School at the Crossroads," *Educational Leadership* (March 1984), pp. 4–13.

34. Duke, "What is the Nature of Educational Excellence?"; Albert Shanker, "The Real Crisis in Public Schools," *Educational Digest* (March 1983), pp. 10–11; and Herbert J. Walberg, "Can We Raise Standards," *Educational Leadership* (October 1983), pp. 4–6.

35. Howard Gardner, *Frames of Mind: A Theory of Multiple Intelligences* (New York: Basic Books, 1983).

36. Gary Natriello, Edward L. McDill, and Aaron M. Pallas, "School Reform and Potential Dropouts," *Educational Leadership* (May 1985), pp. 11–14; Charles V. Willie, "The Problem of Standardized Testing in a Free and Pluralistic Society," *Phi Delta Kappan* (May 1985), pp. 626–627.

37. Allan C. Ornstein and Daniel U. Levine, *An Introduction to the Foundations of Education*, 3rd ed. (Boston: Houghton Mifflin, 1985).

38. R. Freeman Butts, *Public Education in the United States* (New York: Holt, 1978); Lawrence A. Cremin, *The Transformation of the School* (New York: Knopf, 1961).

39. John Dewey, *Democracy and Education* (New York: Macmillan, 1916).

40. John Dewey, "Need for a Philosophy of Education," *New Era in Home and School* (November 1934), p. 212.

41. John Dewey, *How We Think*, rev. ed. (Lexington, Mass.: D.C. Heath, 1933); William Kilpatrick,

Foundations of Method (New York: Macmillan, 1925).

42. John Dewey, *The Child and the Curriculum* (Chicago: University of Chicago Press, 1902), pp. 30–31; Dewey, *Experience and Education* (New York: Macmillan, 1938), p. vii.

43. Boyd H. Bode, *Progressive Education at the Crossroads* (New York: Newson, 1938).

44. Ibid., p. 44.

45. Cremin, *The Transformation of the School.*

46. Herbert Kohl, *The Open Classroom* (New York: Random House, 1969); Jonathan Kozol, *Free Schools* (Boston: Houghton Mifflin, 1972). See also John P. Miller and Wayne Seller, *Curriculum: Perspectives and Practice* (New York: Longman, 1986).

47. Charles A. Silberman, *Crisis in the Classroom* (New York: Random House, 1971).

48. Arthur T. Jersild, *In Search of Self* (New York: Teachers College Press, 1952); Jersild, *When Teachers Face Themselves* (New York: Teachers College Press, 1955); and Arthur Combs and Donald Snygg, *Individual Behavior*, 2nd ed. (New York: Harper & Row, 1959). See also Arthur Combs, ed., *Perceiving, Behaving, Becoming* (Washington, D.C.: Association for Supervision and Curriculum Development, 1962); Combs, *A Personal Approach to Teaching* (Boston: Allyn and Bacon, 1982).

49. Abraham H. Maslow, *Toward a Psychology of Being* (New York: Van Nostrand Reinhold, 1962); Maslow, *Motivation and Personality*, 2nd ed. (New York: Harper & Row, 1970); Carl R. Rogers, *Client-Centered Therapy* (Boston: Houghton Mifflin, 1951); Rogers, *On Becoming a Person* (Boston: Houghton Mifflin, 1961); and Rogers, *Freedom to Learn for the 1980s*, 2nd ed. (Columbus, Ohio: Merrill, 1983).

50. Michael W. Apple, *Education and Power* (Boston: Routledge & Kegan Paul, 1982); Richard H. Willer, ed., *Humanistic Education: Visions and Realities* (Berkeley, Calif.: McCutchan, 1977).

51. Mario D. Fantini, "Humanizing the Humanistic Movement," *Phi Delta Kappan* (February 1974), p. 400.

52. For a discussion of these radical critics, see Philip W. Jackson, "Deschooling? No," *Today's Education* (November 1972), pp. 18–21; Allan C. Ornstein, "Critics and Criticism of Education," *Educational Forum* (November 1977), pp. 21–30. See also Diane Ravitch, *The Troubled Crusade: American Education 1945–1980* (New York: Basic Books, 1983).

53. Edgar Z. Friedenberg, *The Vanishing Adolescent* (Boston: Beacon Press, 1959), pp. 26, 91, 110. See also Edgar Z. Friedenberg, *Coming of Age in America* (New York: Random House, 1967).

54. John Holt, *How Children Fail* (New York: Pitman, 1964).

55. Paul Goodman, *Compulsory Mis-education* (New

York: Horizon Press, 1964), pp. 20–22.

56. Paul Goodman, *New Reformation* (New York: Random House, 1970), p. 86.

57. A. S. Neill, *Summerhill: A Radical Approach to Child Rearing* (New York: Hart, 1960), p. 4.

58. Ibid., pp. 4, 14.

59. Ibid., pp. 21, 157.

60. Ivan Illich, *Deschooling Society* (New York: Harper & Row, 1971).

61. See Samuel Bowles and Herbert Gintis, *Schooling in Capitalist America* (New York: Basic Books, 1976); Martin Carnoy, ed., *Schooling in a Corporate Society* (New York: McKay, 1975); and Alan Gartner, Colin Greer, and Frank Riessman, eds., *After Deschooling, What?* (New York: Harper & Row, 1973). See also Michael Dale, "Stalking a Conceptual Chameleon: Ideology in Marxist Studies of Education," *Educational Theory* (Summer 1986), pp. 241–258.

62. George S. Counts, *Dare the School Build a New Social Order?* (New York: Day, 1932), pp. 7–8. See also Robert R. Sherman, "Dare the School Build a New Social Order—Again?" *Educational Theory* (Winter 1986), pp. 87–92.

63. See John Dewey, *Reconstruction in Philosophy* (New York: Holt, 1920).

64. Theodore Brameld, *Ends and Means in Education* (New York: Harper & Row, 1950); Brameld, *Patterns of Educational Philosophy* (New York: World, 1950).

65. Theodore Brameld, "Reconstructionism as Radical Philosophy of Education," *Educational Forum* (November 1977), p. 70.

66. Brameld, *Patterns of Educational Philosophy*, p. 519.

67. Mario D. Fantini, *Regaining Excellence in Education* (Columbus, Ohio: Merrill, 1986); Harold Shane, *Educating for a New Millennium* (Bloomington, Ind.: Phi Delta Kappa, 1981); and Alvin Toffler, *Previews and Premises* (New York: Morrow, 1983).

68. Michael W. Apple, in a telephone conversation with one of the authors, August 8, 1985; Herbert M. Kliebard, in a personal conversation with one of the authors, April 17, 1986.

69. Maxine Greene, "Curriculum and Consciousness," in W. Pinar, ed., *Curriculum Theorizing* (Berkeley, Calif.: McCutchan, 1975), pp. 303–305; Greene, *Landscapes of Learning*, p. 163.

70. Paulo Freire, *Pedagogy of the Oppressed* (New York: Herder and Herder, 1970), pp. 75, 100, 108.

71. William Pinar, "Sanity, Madness, and the School," in Pinar, ed., *Curriculum Theorizing*, pp. 364–366; 369–373, 381.

72. Michael W. Apple, *Ideology and Curriculum* (Bos-

ton: Routledge & Kegan Paul, 1979), p. 4. See also Apple, *Teachers and Texts* (Boston: Routledge & Kegan Paul, 1986).

73. Michael Apple and Nancy R. King, "What Do Schools Teach?" in R. H. Weller, ed., *Humanistic Education* (Berkeley, Calif.: McCutchan, 1977), p. 30.

74. Illich, *Deschooling Society.*

75. Freire, *Pedagogy of the Oppressed;* Freire, *The Politics of Education, Culture, Power, and Liberation* (South Hedley, Mass.: Bergin and Garvey, 1985).

76. Macdonald, "Curriculum and Human Interests," p. 293.

77. Horace Mann, *The Republic and the School*, rev. ed. (New York: Teachers College Press, Columbia University, 1957), p. 39.

78. David B. Tyack, *Turning Points in American Educational History* (Waltham, Mass.: Blaisdell, 1967), p. 114.

79. Henry M. Levin, "Equal Educational Opportunity and the Distribution of Educational Expenditures," in A. Kopan and H. J. Walberg, eds., *Rethinking Educational Equality* (Berkeley, Calif.: McCutchan, 1974), p. 30.

80. See James S. Coleman et al., *Equality of Educational Opportunity* (Washington, D.C.: U.S. Government Printing Office, 1966); Christopher Jencks et al., *Inequality: A Reassessment of the Effect of Family and Schools in America* (New York: Basic Books, 1972).

81. James S. Coleman, "The Concept of Equality of Educational Opportunity," *Harvard Educational Review* (Winter 1968), pp. 7–22.

82. See Richard H. deLone, *Small Futures: Children, Inequality, and the Limits of Liberal Reform* (New York: Harcourt, 1979); Nathan Glazer, *Affirmative Discrimination: Ethnic Inequality and Public Policy* (New York: Basic Books, 1975); and Allan C. Ornstein and Steven I. Miller, *Policy Issues in Education* (Lexington, Mass.: D.C. Heath, 1976).

83. John W. Gardner, *Excellence: Can We Be Equal and Excellent Too?* (New York: Harper & Row, 1961), pp. 17–18, 83, 90.

84. Dewey, *Democracy and Education*, p. 383.

85. James A. Johnson et al., *Introduction to the Foundations of American Education*, 5th ed. (Boston: Allyn and Bacon, 1984); Ornstein and Levine, *Introduction to the Foundations of Education.*

86. Ronald S. Brandt and Ralph W. Tyler, "Goals and Objectives," in F. W. English, ed., *Fundamental Curriculum Decisions* (Alexandria, Va.: Association for Supervision and Curriculum Development, 1983), pp. 40–52.

chapter 3

HISTORICAL FOUNDATIONS
OF CURRICULUM

Because many scholars in the field of curriculum often lack historical perspective, they rely on the history of American education to analyze the heritage of our curriculum. By analyzing the first 200 years (or more) of curriculum, up to the turn of the twentieth century, we can view curriculum primarily in terms of evolving subject matter or content and the dominant philosophy of perennialism. Not until the rise of progressivism, followed by the early period of behaviorism and scientism in education (the use of empirical methods, analysis of human behavior, and generalizations), did attention in the curriculum field expand to include principles of curriculum development. This shift occurred in the early years of the twentieth century.

We begin our discussion with the colonial period and proceed through the eighteenth, nineteenth, and twentieth centuries. Most of our discussion focuses on the last 100 years. In the interest of brevity, we examine only

the broad sweep of curriculum, and how the curriculum evolved.

THE COLONIAL PERIOD:
1642–1776

The historical foundations of curriculum are largely rooted in the educational experiences of colonial Massachusetts. Massachusetts was settled mainly by Puritans who adhered to strict principles of theology. Unlike contemporary schools, the first schools in New England were closely related to the Puritan church. The major purpose of school, according to educational historians, was to teach children to read the Scriptures and notices of civil affairs.[1]

Reading, therefore, was the most important subject, followed by writing and spelling, for purposes of understanding the catechism and common law. Since colonial days, then, reading and related language skills have been basic to American education and basic to the elementary school curriculum.

Three Colonial Regions.

Colonial schools established in Massachusetts were derived from two sources: Legislation of 1642, which required parents and guardians of children to make certain that their charges could read and understand the principles of religion and the laws of the Commonwealth; and the "Old Deluder Satan" Act of 1647, which required every town of fifty or more families to appoint a reading and writing teacher. Towns of 100 or more families were to employ a teacher of Latin so that students could be prepared for entry to Harvard College.[2] The other New England colonies, except Rhode Island, followed the Massachusetts example.

These early laws reveal how important education was to the Puritan settlers. Some historians have regarded these laws as the roots of American school law and the public school movement. It is obvious that the Puritans did not want an illiterate class to grow in colonial America. They feared that such a class might comprise a group of dependent poor, an underclass, which would be reminiscent of that in England and other parts of Europe, and which they wanted to avoid. They also wanted to ensure that their children would grow up being committed to the religious doctrines.

In the middle colonies, unlike New England, no common language or religion existed. Writes George Beauchamp, "Competition among political and religious groups retarded willingness to expend the public funds for educational purposes."[3] No single system of schools could be established. What evolved instead were parochial and independent schools, related to different ethnic and religious groups, and the idea of community or local control of schools (as opposed to New England's concept of central or district-wide schools). The current notion of cultural pluralism thus took shape and form some 200 years ago. Just as the schools and the curriculum were uniform and centralized in the New England colonies, they were divergent and localized in the middle Atlantic colonies.

Until the end of the eighteenth century educational decisions in the Southern colonies were generally left to the family. Legislative action was taken, however, in behalf of poor children, orphans and illegitimate children—to ensure that their guardians provided private educational or vocational skills. Nevertheless, the plantation system of landholding, slavery, and gentry created a small privileged class of white children (children of plantation owners) who had the benefit of private tutors. For most poor whites who tilled the soil, formal education was nonexistent. Unable to read and write, many of them grew up to be subsistence farmers like their parents before them. Black slaves' children were forbidden to learn to read or write and were relegated as the underclass of the plantation system. In short, the economic and political system of the early South "tended to retard the development of a large-scale system of schools. This education [handicap] was felt long after the Civil War period."[4]

Despite the regional variations between the schools of New England, the middle Atlantic colonies, and the South, all three areas were influenced by English political ideas. And, despite differences in language, religion, and economic systems, religious commitment had a high priority throughout all schools and society; the family, too, played a major role in the socialization and education of all children. What was later to become the three Rs evolved from these schools as well.

"The curriculum of the colonial schools consisted of reading, writing, and [some] arithmetic along with the rudiments of religious faith and lessons designed to develop manners and morals."[5] It was a traditional curriculum, stressing basic-skill acquisition, timeless and absolute values, social and religious conformity, faith in authority, knowledge for the sake of knowledge, rote learning, and memorization. It was based on the notion of child depravity (children were born in sin, play was idleness, and child's talk gibberish), and thus the teacher needed to apply constant discipline. This approach to the curriculum dominated American education until the rise of progressivism.

Colonial Schools.

The colonial schools were important institutions for colonial society, as they are for today's. One difference is that a smaller percentage of the school-aged children attended elementary school on a regular basis compared to today, and a much smaller percentage of youth attended secondary school, much less graduated.

The Town School. In the New England colonies, the town school was a locally controlled and popular elementary school. Often it was a crude, one-room structure, dominated by the teacher's pulpit at the front of the room, and attended by both boys and girls of the community. Students sat on benches and studied their assignments until called on to recite by the schoolmaster. The children ranged in age from 5 or 6 to 13 and 14. Attendance was not always regular; it depended on weather conditions and on individual families' needs for their children to work on their farms.[6]

Parochial and Private Schools. In the middle colonies, parochial schools and private schools predominated; the elementary schools were established by missionary societies and various religious and ethnic groups to educate their own children. Like the New England town schools, these schools focused on reading and writing and religious sermons. In the South, upper-class children attended private schools oriented to reading, writing, arithmetic, and studying the primer and Bible; less fortunate children attended charity schools (if they were lucky) to be trained in the three Rs, to recite religious hymns (which was less demanding than reading the Bible), and to learn vocational skills.

Latin Grammar Schools. At the secondary level, the sons of the upper class attended Latin grammar schools, first estab-lished in Boston in 1635, to be prepared for entry into college. These schools catered to those who planned to enter the professions (medicine, law, teaching, and the ministry) or to spend their lives as business owners or merchants.[7]

A boy would enter a Latin grammar school at the age of 8 or 9 and remain for eight years. His curriculum consisted of studying the classics. "There were some courses in Greek, rhetoric . . . and logic, but Latin was apparently three-quarters of the curriculum in most of the grammar schools, or more . . ."[8] Little or no attention was given to the other arts and sciences. "The religious atmosphere was quite as evident . . . as it was in the elementary school" with the "master praying regularly with his pupils" and quizzing them "thoroughly on the sermons. . . ."[9] The regimen of study was exhausting and unexciting, and the school's role that of handmaiden of the church. As Samuel Morrison reminds us, the Latin grammar school was one of colonial America's closest links to European schools, and its curriculum resembled the classical humanist curriculum of the Renaissance (when schools were primarily intended for children of the upper classes and their role was to support the religious and social institution of that era).[10]

The Academy. The academy, established in 1751, was the second American institution to provide education at the secondary level. Based on the ideas of Benjamin Franklin, and intended to offer a practical curriculum for those not going to college, it had a diversified curriculum of English grammar, classics, composition, rhetoric, and public speaking.[11] Latin was no longer considered a crucial subject. Students could choose a foreign language based on their vocational needs—for example, a prospective clergyman could study Latin or Greek, and a future businessman could learn French, German, or Spanish. Mathematics was to be taught for its practical application to a job rather than as an abstract intellectual exercise. History was the chief ethical study, not religion. The academy also introduced many practical and manual skills into the formal curriculum; these formed the basis of vocational curriculum in the twentieth century: Carpentry, engraving, printing, painting, cabinet making, farming, bookkeeping, and so on.

College. Most students went to Harvard or Yale after they graduated from Latin grammar schools. College was based on the Puritan conception that those called to the ministry needed to be soundly educated in the classics and scriptures. The students had to demonstrate their competency in Latin and Greek and the classics.

Latin grammar schools prepared students for Harvard or Yale college—much like high school academic programs prepare students for college today. The current relationship between the course offerings of secondary school and college admission requirements was, in fact, set in motion more than 200 years ago. Writes Ellwood Cubberley, "The student would be admitted into college 'upon Examination' whereby he could show competency 'to Read, Construe, Parce Tully, Vergil and the Greek Testament; and to write Latin in Prose and to understand the Rules of Prosodia and Common Arithmetic' as well as to bring 'testimony of his blameless and inoffensive life.' "[12]

The Harvard/Yale curriculum consisted of courses in Latin, grammar, logic, rhetoric, arithmetic, astronomy, ethics, metaphysics, and natural sciences. The curriculum for the ministry or other professions also included Greek, Hebrew, and ancient history.

Old Textbooks, Old Readers.

Because the hornbook, primer, Psalter, Testament, and Bible were considered textbooks, they were widely read (depending on the reading ability of the students). By and large, most elementary textbooks, until the time of the American Revolution, were of English origin or were direct imitations of English texts.[13] Children learned the alphabet, Lord's Prayer, some syllables, words, and sentences by memorizing the *hornbook*—a paddle-shaped board to which was attached a single sheet of parchment covered by a transparent sheath made by flattening cattle horns.

When the *New England Primer* was published in the last decade of the seventeenth century, it replaced the English primer. It was not only the first American basal reader, it was also the most widely used textbook in the colonies for over 100 years; more than 3 million copies were sold. The *New England Primer* was permeated with religious and moral doctrines. The somber caste of the Puritan religion and morals was evident as students memorized sermons and learned their ABCs:

> A—In Adam's Fall
> We sinned all
> B—Thy Life to mend
> This book attend
> C—The Cat doth play
> And after slay . . .
> Z—Zacheus he
> Did climb the tree
> His Lord to see.[14]

In 1740 Thomas Dilworth published a *New Guide to the English Tongue,* which contained a mixture of grammar, spelling, and religious material. It was followed a few years later by the *School Master's Assistant,* a widely used mathematics text.

The narrowness of the elementary school curriculum, and the limited use of textbooks, were illustrated by Noah Webster, an ardent cultural nationalist, years later in a letter to Henry Barnard, then Commissioner of Education of Connecticut:

... before the Revolution ... the books used were chiefly or wholly Dilworth's Spelling Books, the Psalter, Testament, and Bible. No geography was studied before the publication of Dr. Morse's small books on that subject, about the year 1786 or 1787. No history was read, as far as my knowledge extends, for there was no abridged history of the United States. Except the books above mentioned, no book for reading was used before the publication of the Third Part of my Institute, in 1785. . . . The Introduction of my Spelling

Book, first published in 1783, produced a great change in the department of spelling.... No English grammar was generally taught in common schools when I was young, except that in Dilworth, and that to no good purpose.[15]

THE NATIONAL PERIOD: 1776–1850

A new mission for education, which began to emerge during the Revolutionary period, continued through the early national period. Many leaders began to link free public schooling with the ideas of popular government and political freedom. Wrote President Madison, "A popular government without popular information, or the means of acquiring it, is but a prologue to a farce or a tragedy or perhaps both." Jefferson expressed a similar belief when he asserted: "If a nation expects to be ignorant and free in a state of civilization, it expects what never was and never will be."

The emphasis on life, liberty, and equality was highlighted in the great documents of the era: The Declaration of Independence, the Bill of Rights, and the Northwest Ordinances. In 1785 these ordinances divided the Northwest Territory into townships and reserved the sixteenth section of "every township for the maintenance of public schools." In 1787, they reaffirmed that "schools and the means of education shall forever be encouraged" by the states. The federal government thus recognized its commitment to education and exhibited its willingness to advance its cause, while assuring the autonomy of state and local schools, guaranteed by the U.S. Constitution. As a result of these Ordinances, thirty-nine states received over 154 million acres of land for schools from the federal government.[16]

By the turn of the nineteenth century, secular forces had developed sufficiently to challenge and ultimately cause the decline of religious influence over elementary and secondary schools. Among these secular forces were the development of democracy, the development of a strong federal government, the idea of religious freedom, and new discoveries in natural sciences.

Even though some leaders of the country mistrusted the mass of the people and continued to favor the classical curriculum, the popular movement in government mobilized against the money class and the old curriculum based on English traditions. Accompanying this growing political liberalism was an emerging cultural nationalism—a demand for an American language, an American culture, and an American educational system free of English ideas from the past. As a new nation, America sought its own political system and culture—and this thinking spilled over into the schools.

Rush: Science, Progress, and Free Education.

Dr. Benjamin Rush (1745–1813) represented this new era. In 1791, he wrote that the emphasis on the classics led to the prejudice the masses felt for institutions of learning. As long as Latin and Greek dominated the curriculum, universal education beyond the rudiments was wishful thinking. In a new country, in which the chief task was to explore and develop natural resources, as well as to promote democracy, education should be functional to these concerns. "Under these circumstances, to spend four or five years in learning two dead languages, is to turn our backs upon a gold mine, in order to amuse ourselves catching butterflies." If the time spent on Latin and Greek were devoted to science, continued this champion pragmatist, "the human condition would be much improved."[17] For Rush, science was the chief instrument of social progress.

Rush went on to outline a plan of education for Pennsylvania and the new Republic: Free elementary schools in every township consisting of 100 families or more, a free academy at the county level, and free colleges and universities at the state level for the future leaders of society. The public would pay for the expenses, but, in the end, Rush argued, the educational system would reduce our taxes because a productive and well-managed workforce and entrepreneur force would result. Rush's curriculum emphasized reading, writing, and arithmetic at the elementary school level; English, German, the arts, and especially the sciences at the secondary and college level; and good manners and moral principles from the beginning to the end of the educational sequence.

Jefferson: Education for Citizenship.

Faith in the agrarian society and distrust toward the proletariat of the cities were basic in Thomas Jefferson's (1743–1826) idea of democracy. A man of wide-ranging interests that embraced politics, agriculture, science, and education, Jefferson assumed the state had the responsibility to cultivate an educated and liberated citizenry to ensure a democratic society. In "A Bill for the More General Diffusion of Knowledge," introduced in the Virginia legislature in 1779, Jefferson advocated a plan that provided educational opportunities for both common people and landed gentry "at the expense of all."[18] To Jefferson, formal education was largely a state or civic concern, rather than a matter reserved to religious or upper-class groups. Schools should be financed through public taxes.

Jefferson's plan subdivided the counties of Virginia into wards, each of which would have a free elementary school to teach reading, writing, arithmetic, and history. His proposal also provided for the establishment of twenty grammar schools at the secondary level, for which gifted students who could not afford to pay tuition would be provided scholarships. There, the students would study Latin, Greek, English, geography, and higher mathematics. Upon completing grammar school, half the scholarship students would be assigned positions as elementary or ward school teachers. The ten scholarship students of highest achievement would attend William and Mary College. Jefferson's plan promoted the idea of school as a selective agency to identify bright

students for continuing education, as well as the traditional idea of equality of opportunity for economically less fortunate students.

Neither Jefferson's proposal for Virginia nor Rush's proposal for Pennsylvania were enacted. Nonetheless, the bills indicate the type of educational theorizing characteristic of the young nation. Coupled with Franklin's academy, and its practical curriculum based on business and commercial principles of education rather than classical and religious principles, these bills demonstrated the purpose of education to be to promote good citizenship, social progress, and utilitarianism. The classical curriculum and religious influence were, in effect, beginning to decline. Rush and Jefferson (and to a lesser extent Franklin) were all concerned with equality of educational opportunity—that is, they proposed universal education for the masses of children and youth, and methods for identifying students of superior ability, who were to receive free secondary and college educations at public expense.

Webster: Schoolmaster and Cultural Nationalism.

The United States differed from most new countries struggling for identity in that it lacked a shared cultural identity and national literature. In its struggle against the "older" cultures and "older" ideas, the new nation went to great lengths to differentiate itself from England.[19] Noah Webster (1758–1843) called passionately upon his fellow Americans to "unshackle [their] minds and act like independent beings. You have been children long enough, subject to the control and subservient to the interests of a haughty parent. . . . You have an empire to raise . . . and a national character to establish and extend by your wisdom and judgment."[20]

In 1789, when the Constitution went into effect as the law of the land, Webster argued that the United States should have its own system of "language as well as government."

The language of Great Britain, he reasoned, "should no longer be our standard; for the taste of her writers is already completed, and her language on the decline."[21] By the act of revolution, the American people had declared their political independence from England, and now they needed to declare their cultural independence as well.

Realizing that a sense of national identity was conveyed through a distinctive national language and literature, Webster set out to reshape the English language used in the United States. He believed that a uniquely American language would: (1) eliminate the remains of European usage; (2) create a uniform American speech that would be free of localism and provincialism; and (3) promote self-conscious American cultural nationalism.[22] The creation of an American language would become the linguistic mortar or national union; it would, however, have to be phonetically simple to render it more suitable to the common people.

Webster directly related the learning of language to organized education. As they learned the American language, children also would learn to think and act as Americans. The American language that Webster proposed would have to be taught deliberately and systematically to the young in the nation's schools. Because the curriculum of these Americanized schools would be shaped by the books that the students read, Webster spent much of his life writing spelling and reading books. His *Grammatical Institute of the English Language* was published in 1783. The first part of the *Institute* was later printed as *The American Spelling Book*, which was widely used throughout the United States in the first half of the nineteenth century.[23] Webster's *Spelling Book* went through many editions; it is estimated that 15 million copies had been sold by 1837. Webster's great work was *The American Dictionary*, which was completed in 1825 after twenty-five years of laborious research.[24] Often termed the "schoolmaster of the Republic," Noah Webster was an educational statesman of the early national period whose work helped to create a sense of American language, identity, and nationality.

McGuffey: The Reader and American Virtues.

William Holmes McGuffey (1800–1873), who taught most of his life in Ohio colleges, also entered the debate on American cultural nationalism. The author of America's most popular textbooks of the period, called the *Readers,* McGuffey acknowledged with respect and gratitude America's "obligations to Europe and the descendants of the English stock" in science, art, law, literature, and manners. America had made its own contributions to humankind, however; they "were not literary or cultural, but moral and political." The seeds of popular liberty "first germinated from our English ancestors, but it shot up to its fullest heights in our land."[25] America had furnished to Europe proof that "popular institutions, founded on equality and the principle of representation, are capable of maintaining governments," that it was practical to elevate the masses, what Europe called the laboring and lower class, "to the great right and great duty of self-government."[26] Thus, McGuffey balanced the cultural indebtedness of the country with its political and social promise, the full realization of liberalism and traditions of the American common folk.

It is estimated that over 120 million copies of McGuffey's five *Readers* were sold between 1836 and 1920.[27] What McGuffey did was to combine the virtues of the Protestant faith with those of rural America—patriotism, heroism, hard work, diligence, and virtuous living. The tone was moral, religious, capitalistic, and pro-American; the selections of American literature included orations by George Washington, Patrick Henry, Benjamin Franklin, and Daniel Webster. Through his *Readers*, McGuffey taught several generations of Americans. He also provided the first graded *Readers* for our schools and paved the way for a graded system, which had its beginnings in 1840. So popular were his *Readers*, and so vivid and timeless his patriotism and faith in American institutions—home, work, church, and nationhood—that many of his *Readers* (also his *Pictorial Primer*) have been reintroduced today in some rural, conservative, and/or fundamentalist schools.

NINETEENTH-CENTURY EUROPEAN EDUCATORS

Even though much criticism was leveled against European thought, American education was greatly influenced by it. At the college level, German educators influenced the fields of natural science, psychology, and sociology; many of our research-oriented universities were based on the German model. At the public school level, K-12, German (and Swiss) thought introduced romantic and progressive ideas—and a curriculum and instructional method that were psychologically oriented and considered the needs and interests of the students. The English also impacted on American education by providing models of schooling that ranged from efficient to romantic.

However strongly American patriots may have desired a distinctive cultural life, they could not, as men and women of common sense and learning, turn their backs on the wealth and wisdom of European ideas. Moreover, the rising current of educational thought in the Old World was not all steeped in old-fashioned and classical ideas, because progressive and scientific principles were beginning to evolve.

The theme of reform characterized much of the educational discussions of the time. The limitations of the "traditional curriculum and typical school of this era were recognized by educational leaders in Europe and America, and many of the features that were now firmly established in [curriculum] theory and practice can be traced to the ideas of the men and women who were ahead of their time."[28] The traditional curriculum, which emphasized Latin, Greek, and the classics, was deemphasized. New pedagogical practices were developed that ran contrary to the methods of rote learning, memorization, and corporal punishment.

Pestalozzi: General and Special Methods.

During the early American period of education, educational reformers were influenced by Johann Heinrich Pestalozzi (1746–1827), a Swiss educator. According to one educational historian, "Pestalozzi, probably more than any other educational reformer, laid the basis for the modern elementary school and helped to reform elementary-school practice."[29] Pestalozzi maintained that the educational process should be based on the natural development of the child and his or her sensory influences—similar thinking to that of current progressives and environmentalists. Pestalozzi's basic pedagogical innovation was his insistence that children learn through the senses rather than with words. He labeled rote learning as mindless, and he emphasized instead linking the curriculum to children's experiences in their home and family lives.

Education, according to Pestalozzi, was to develop by considering the "general" method and "special" method. The general method called for educators, who were loving persons, to provide emotional security, trust, and affection toward the children. The special method considered the auditory and visual senses of the children in the teaching process. To this end, Pestalozzi devised the "object" lesson, in which children studied common objects that they saw and experienced in their daily environments—plants, rocks, artifacts, and so on. The object lesson enhanced three types of learning—form, number, and sound. Children would first determine the form of the object, then draw it, then name it. From the lessons in form, number, and sound came more formal instruction in the three Rs.

Pestalozzi's ideas had great impact on early nineteenth-century American education. William McClure and Joseph Neef, and later Horace Mann and Henry

Barnard, when he was U.S. Commissioner of Education, all worked to introduce his ideas into American schools.[30] His basic concepts of education became part of progressive schooling, and later appeared in the move for curriculum relevancy and humanistic curriculum. When educators discovered the "disadvantaged" in the 1960s and later promoted the ideas of Project Head Start and compensatory education, Pestalozzi's theories had special imprint.

Froebel: The Kindergarten Movement.

Friedrich Froebel (1782–1852), a German educator, is known for his development of the kindergarten, what he called the "child's garden." Froebel proposed that the educational process should start when children are 3 or 4 years old, and that it should be based on organized play. This obviously suggested a far less formal, rigid, or authoritarian school environment. (Daniel Tanner and Laurel N. Tanner, *Curriculum Development: Theory into Practice*, 2nd ed. (New York: Macmillan, 1980).)

Froebel's kindergarten was a prepared environment in which learning was based on the children's self-activities, and self-development, and on the children's trust and affection along the lines of Pestalozzi. Songs, stories, colorful materials, and games—what classical curriculum advocates would criticize as wasteful—were part of the formal curriculum. The children could manipulate objects (spheres, cubes, and circles), shape and construct materials (clay, sand, cardboard), and engage in playful activities (build castles and mountains, run and exercise).[31] Together these activities were to comprise the learning environment and provide a secure and pleasant place where children could grow naturally.

The kindergarten concept was brought to America by German immigrants, and the first American kindergarten was established in Watertown, Wisconsin, in 1855 by Margaret Schurz. William Harris, Superintendent of Schools in St. Louis, Missouri, and later U.S. Commissioner of Education,

was instrumental in implementing the idea on a broader scale. The kindergarten is now an established part of American education, and many of Froebel's ideas of childhood experiences and methods of play are incorporated into current theories of early childhood education and progressive schooling.

Herbart: Moral and Intellectual Development.

A famous German philosopher, Johann Freidrich Herbart (1776–1841) maintained that the main purpose of education was to develop moral character. This purpose could not be developed from the three Rs or the traditional curriculum because of their mechanical nature. (Tanner and Tanner, *Curriculum Development*; Robert S. Zais, *Curriculum: Principles and Foundations* (New York: Harper & Row, 1976).) Herbart specified two major bodies of subject matter: knowledge interests and ethical interests. Knowledge interests involved empirical data, factual data, and theoretical ideas; ethical interests involved personal convictions, benevolence, and regard for the social welfare of others, justice, and equity. Herbart urged that history, literature, mathematics, and science find a place in the curriculum at all levels of education. He also introduced the idea of "correlation" of all subjects to unify the curriculum, an idea that influenced curriculum specialists who favored a core curriculum in the 1940s and 1950s.

Herbart was instrumental in formalizing methods of instruction. Instruction, to be based on the teacher's building on the children's previous learning and on their interests and needs, was a psychological process that included the following steps:

1. *Preparation:* The teacher considers previous learning experiences and stimulates the readiness of the learner.
2. *Presentation:* The new lesson is summarized.
3. *Association:* The new lesson is related to ideas or materials previously studied.
4. *Generalization:* Rules, principles, or generalizations of the new ideas are mastered by the learner.

5. *Application:* The new lesson is given meaning by testing and applying the new ideas to specific instances.[32]

Speaking of Herbart's contribution to the instruction of teaching, John Dewey said: "Few attempts have been made to formulate a method, resting on general principles, of conducting a recitation. One of these is of great importance, and has probably had more influence upon the learning of lessons than all others put together; namely, the analysis by Herbart of a recitation into five successive steps."[33]

Herbart's formal steps of instruction were not only adopted by classroom teachers, they were applied to teacher training as well. In theory, teachers were asked to prepare their lessons by thinking of five steps, and asking: What do my students know? What questions should I ask? What events should I relate? What conclusions should be reached? How can students apply what they have learned? To a large extent, these instructional principles influenced the teaching-learning principles Dewey expressed in *How We Think;* they still serve as guidelines for teachers who use the developmental lesson approach.

Spencer: Utilitarian and Scientific Education.

Herbert Spencer (1820–1903) was an English social scientist who based his ideas of education on Charles Darwin's theories of biological evolution and survival of the fittest. Spencer maintained that social development takes place according to the evolutionary process by which simple societies had evolved to more complex social systems, characterized by an increased variety of specialized professions and occupations.[34] Because of the laws of nature, only intelligent and productive populations would adapt to environmental changes. Less intelligent, weak, or lazy people would slowly disappear. The doctrine had immense implications for education based on excellence, the notion of social-economic progress, and the idea of intellectual development based on heredity.

Spencer also criticized religious doctrines and classical subject matter in education as nonscientific and unrelated to contemporary society. Rather, he advocated a curriculum fit for industrialized society—one that was scientific and practical (utilitarian). He believed that traditional schools were impractical and ornamental, a luxury for the upper class that failed to meet the needs of the people living in modern society.

For Spencer, the major purpose of education was to "prepare for complete living." Curriculum needed to be arranged according to this purpose. Spencer constructed a curriculum by prioritizing human Activities so as to advance human survival and progress. His curriculum included the following activities, in order of importance: Activities that (1) sustain life; (2) enhance life; (3) aid in rearing children; (4) maintain one's social and political relations; and (5) enhance leisure, tasks, and feelings.[35]

In his famous essay, "What Knowledge Is Most Worth?," Spencer answered his own question. He maintained that science was the most important knowledge for self-preservation and for securing the necessities of life—even though it received scant attention in the curriculum. Spencer also believed that students should not be *told* what to think but should rather be encouraged to *discover* as much as possible.[36]

Although many of Spencer's ideas about religion, evolution, and social progress created a furor—and they still do among religious and political observers today—the ideas fitted well with those of thinkers in the second half of the nineteenth century, which was characterized by industrial growth, colonial expansion, and manifest destiny among European countries and the United States. Spencer's notion of discovery learning also influenced twentieth-century curricularists, both Deweyite progressive educators and later academic disciplinary educators. His demand for a curriculum steeped in science and linked with political survival and economic competition had special meaning during the Cold War-Sputnik era and still does—in light of present-day competition with Japan, Korea, and Germany.

THE RISE OF UNIVERSAL EDUCATION: 1820–1920

During the early nineteenth century America expanded westward. Life on the new frontier deepened America's faith in the common or average person, who built the new nation. Equality and rugged individualism were important concepts, expressed in the Declaration of Independence and reaffirmed by Westerners, who believed that all people were important and that in order to survive each had a job to do—despite different backgrounds. The common person, whether educated or not, was elected to various political offices; faith abounded in the capacity of humans to improve their lives. This kind of faith in the common people and in American civilization underscored to the frontier people the necessity of school.[37]

In the cities of the East, especially among the immigrant populations, there was also faith in the common person, in social mobility, and in the American dream of life, liberty, and equality. The upper class may not have had the same faith; nonetheless, the traditional argument (since Franklin, Rush, and Jefferson)—that mass education was necessary for intelligent participation in political democracy and that it must extend beyond the common school to high schools and colleges—helped convert the American populace to supporting free schooling.

Monitorial Schools.

The monitorial school was a European invention, based on Joseph Lancaster's model of education. It spread quickly to the large American urban centers, where the immigrant population was increasing, and to the frontier, where there was need for a system of schools. Its major appeal, in the 1820s and the following decades, was that it was cheap: bright student monitors were used as instructors. Each was usually as-signed to assist instruction to a row of about ten pupils. The teacher first taught the lesson to the student monitors, who then took their "stations" and taught their fellow classmates what they had just learned. The instruction was highly structured, and it was based on rote learning and drilling the three Rs.

Advocates of the monitorial method were quick to point out that besides being low cost, it kept students busy who would otherwise have had little to do while the teacher was listening to other groups. With the monitorial system, the students were engaged in constant recitation, and groups of students moved at their own pace, rather than spending their time being idle or mischievous.[38] As the teachers were relieved of some of their drill and recitation chores, their new roles were more as inspectors and supervisors. The monitorial system was thus also considered "efficient" education.

The monitorial system deemphasized classical education for the three Rs, and religious theory for moral doctrines and citizenship; demonstrated the need for and possibility of systematic instruction; acquainted many people with formal education; and made educational opportunities more widely available. Most important, it promoted mass education and tax-supported elementary schools.[39] At the peak of its popularity, in the 1840s, it was organized in some high schools and suggested for the colleges.

But the monitorial system was considered too mechanical, and it was criticized for using students who knew little to teach those who knew even less. By the middle of the nineteenth century, its popularity waned. One hundred years later, however, the virtues of mechanical education resurfaced with the notion of programmed instruction. Instruction through self-pacing and drill could now be measured.

Common Schools.

The common school was established in 1826 in Massachusetts, when the state passed a law requiring every town to choose a school board to be responsible for all the schools in the local area. Eleven years later, the Massachusetts legislature created the first state board of education, and Massachusetts organized the public common schools under a single authority. Connecticut quickly followed the example of its neighbor.[40] These common schools were devoted to elementary education with emphasis on the three Rs. The movement was spearheaded by Horace Mann and rooted in the ideas of progressive thought.

As a member of the Massachusetts legislature, and later as the first Massachusetts Commissioner of Education, Horace Mann skillfully rallied public support for the common school by appealing to various segments of the population. To enlist the business community, Mann sought to demonstrate that "education has a market value" with a yield similar to "common bullion." The "aim of industry . . . and wealth of the country" would be augmented "in proportion to the diffusion of knowledge."[41] Workers would be more diligent and more productive. Mann also established a stewardship theory, aimed at the upper class, that the public good would be enhanced by public education. Schools for all children would create a stable society in which people would obey the laws and add to the nation's political and economic well-being. To the workers and farmers, Mann asserted that the common school would be a great equalizer, a means of social mobility for their children. To the Protestant community, he argued that the common school would assimilate ethnic and religious groups, promote a common culture, and help immigrant children learn English and the customs and laws of the land.[42] He was convinced that the common school was crucial for the American system of equality and opportunity, for a sense of community to be shared by all Americans, and for the promotion of a national identity.

Although the pattern for establishing common schools varied among the states, and the quality of education varied as well, the foundation of the American public school was being forged through this system. The schools were common in the sense that they housed youngsters of all socioeconomic and religious backgrounds, from age 6 to 14 or 15, and were jointly owned, cared for, and used by the local community. Because a variety of subjects was taught to children of all ages, teachers had to plan as many as thirty or forty different lessons a day.[43] Teachers also had to try to keep their schoolrooms warm in the winter—a responsibility shared by the older boys, who cut and fetched wood—and cool in the summer. Schoolhouses were often in need of considerable repair, and teachers were paid miserably low salaries.

In New England, the state legislatures encouraged the establishment of school districts and elected school boards, and state laws to govern the schools. But it was on the frontier where the common school flourished, where there was faith in the common person and a common destiny. The common one-room schoolhouse "eventually led to one of America's most lasting, sentimentalized pictures—the 'Little Red Schoolhouse' . . . in almost every community." It had problems and critics, but it symbolized the pioneers' spirit and desire to provide free education for their children. "It was a manifestation of the belief held by most of the frontier leaders that a school was necessary to raise the level of American civilization."[44]

This small school, meager in outlook and thwarted by inadequate funding and insufficient teachers, nevertheless fit with the conditions of the American frontier—of expansion and equality. It was a "blab school," according to Abe Lincoln, but it was the kind of school in which the common person's children—even those born in log cabins—could begin their "readin," "writin," and "cipherin,"[45] and could advance to limitless achievements. It was a school local citizens could use as a polling place, a center for Grange activities, a site for dances, and a location for community activities; it was a school controlled and supported by the local community.

The traditions built around the common school—the idea of neighborhood schools, local control of schools, and government support of schools—took a firm hold on the hearts and minds of Americans. America's confidence in the common school helped fashion the public schools later in the nineteenth century; it also influenced our present system of universal education.

The Elementary School Curriculum Evolves. There was no agreement on an appropriate or common curriculum for the elementary school. The trend, throughout the nineteenth century, was to add courses to the essential or basic subjects of reading, spelling, grammar, and arithmetic. Religious doctrine changed to "manners" and "moral" instruction by 1825; the subject matter of textbooks was heavily moralistic (one reason for the popularity of McGuffey), and teachers provided extensive training in character building. By 1875 lessons in morality were replaced by courses in "conduct," which remained part of the twentieth-century curriculum. The traditional emphasis on curriculum was slowly altered, as more and more subjects were added—including geography and history by 1850; science, art (or drawing) and physical education by 1875; and nature study (or biology and zoology), music, and home and manual training by 1900. Table 3-1 shows this evolution of the elementary school curriculum.

Secondary Schools.

The common school created the basis for a tax-supported and locally controlled elementary school education. The American high school was established upon this base. By 1900 the majority of children aged 6 to 13 were enrolled in public elementary school, but only 11.5 percent of those aged 14 to 17 were enrolled in public secondary

TABLE 3-1   Evolution of the Elementary School Curriculum, 1800–1900

1800	*1825*	*1850*	*1875*	*1900*
Reading	*Reading*	*Reading*	*Reading*	*Reading*
	Declamation	*Declamation*	Literary selections	*Literature*
Spelling	*Spelling*	*Spelling*	*Spelling*	Spelling
Writing	Writing	Writing	*Penmanship*	Writing
Catechism	Good behavior	Conduct	Conduct	Conduct
Bible	Manners and morals	Manners		
Arithmetic	Arithmetic	*Mental arithmetic*	*Primary arithmetic*	*Arithmetic*
		Ciphering	*Advanced arithmetic*	
	Bookkeeping	Bookkeeping		
	Grammar	*Grammar*	*Grammar*	Grammar
		Elementary language	Oral language	*Oral langauge*
	Geography	Geography	Home geography	Home geography
			Text geography	*Text geography*
		U.S. history	U.S. history	History studies
			Constitution	
		Object lessons	Object lessons	Nature study
			Elementary science	Elementary science
			Drawing	Drawing
				Music
			Physical exercises	Physical training
				Play
	Sewing		Sewing	Sewing
				Cooking
				Manual training

Source: From E. P. Cubberley, *The History of Education* (Boston: Houghton Mifflin, 1920), p. 756.

Note: Italics indicate the most important subjects.

TABLE 3-2 Percentage of Students Enrolled in Secondary School and College, 1900–1980

	14–17 Year Olds Enrolled in Secondary Schools	17 Year Olds Graduating High School	18–21 Year Olds Enrolled in College
1900	11.5	6.5	3.9
1910	15.4	8.8	5.0
1920	32.3	16.8	7.9
1930	51.4	29.0	11.9
1940	73.3	50.8	14.5
1950	76.8	59.0	26.9
1960	86.1	65.1	31.3
1970	93.4	76.5	45.2
1980	93.7	74.4	46.3

Source: From *Digest of Educational Statistics, 1982, 1985–86* (Washington, D.C.: U.S. Government Printing Office, 1982, 1986), Table 35, p. 44; Table 9, p. 11. See also Allan C. Ornstein, *Education and Social Inquiry* (Itasca, Ill.: Peacock, 1978), Table 5.10, p. 177.

schools (and only 6.5 percent of the 17-year olds graduated). As shown in Table 3-2, not until 1930 did the secondary school enrollment figure exceed 50 percent. By 1980, the percentage of elementary aged children attending school was 99 percent, and the percentage of secondary aged children was 94 percent (and 75 percent were graduating). The great enrollment revolution for elementary schools took place between 1850 and 1900; for high schools it evolved between 1900 and 1980.

The Academy.

In the early nineteenth century, the academy began to replace the Latin grammar school; by the middle of the century, it was dominant. It offered a wide range of curricula, and it was designed to provide a practical program (for terminal students) as well as a college preparatory course of study. By 1855 more than 6000 academies had an enrollment totalling 263,000 students[46] (more than two-thirds of the total secondary school enrollment of that period).

"One of the main purposes" of the academy, according to Ellwood Cubberley, "was the establishment of . . . subjects having value aside from mere preparation for college, particularly subjects of modern nature, useful in preparing youth for the changed conditions of society. . . . The study of real things rather than words about

things, and useful things rather than subjects merely preparatory to college became prominent features of the new course of study."[47]

By 1828 as many as fifty different subjects were offered by the academies of the state of New York. The top fifteen, in rank order, were: (1) Latin, (2) Greek, (3) English grammar, (4) geography, (5) arithmetic, (6) algebra, (7) composition and declamation, (8) natural philosophy, (9) rhetoric, (10) philosophy, (11) U.S. history, (12) French, (13) chemistry, (14) logic, and (15) astronomy. By 1837, the state Board of Regents reported seventy-two different subjects.[48]

Although no typical academy existed, with so many different course offerings, the academy inadvertently served the major function of preparing students for college. The traditional curriculum, or the classical side of the academy, continued in the new setting. Writes Elmer Brown, "The college preparatory course was the backbone of the whole system of instruction" in the better academies. Although practical courses were offered, "it was the admission requirements of the colleges, more than anything else, that determined their standards of scholarship."[49] And, writes Paul Monroe, "The core of academy education yet remained the old classical curriculum . . . just as the core of the student body in the more flourishing academies remained the group preparing for college."[50]

The era of the academies extended to the 1870s, when academies were replaced by public high schools. The academies, nevertheless, served as finishing schools for young ladies—with courses in classical and modern language, science, mathematics, art, music, and homemaking. Also, they offered the "normal" program for prospective common school teachers by combining courses in the classics with principles of pedagogy. A few private military and elite academic academies still exist today.

The High School.

Although a few high schools existed in the early half of the nineteenth century (the first one was founded in 1821 in Boston), the high school did not become a major American institution until after 1874, when the Michigan court ruled, in the Kalamazoo decision, that the people could establish and support high schools with tax funds if they consented. There was some initial resistance—the fear that the taxes for the high schools would only benefit a small portion of the youth population—but after the court decision, the high school spread rapidly and compulsory attendance laws were established on a state-by-state basis. The idea of high school attendance for all youth, based on the notion of equality of educational opportunity, was a major educational reform.

Students were permitted to attend private schools, but the states had the right to establish minimum standards for all. By 1890, the 2525 public high schools in the United States enrolled more than 200,000 students, compared to 1600 private secondary schools, which had fewer than 95,000 students. By 1900 the number of high schools had soared to 6000, while the number of academies had declined to 1200.[51] The public high school system, contiguous with common schools, had evolved. Although as late as 1900 the high schools were still attended by only a small percentage of the total youth population, the inclusion of terminal and college preparatory students, as well as rich and poor students under one roof, was evidence that the American people had rejected the European dual system of secondary education.

The high schools stressed the college preparatory program, but they also served to complete the formal educations of terminal students. They offered, in addition, a more diversified curriculum than the academies. At the turn of the century, high schools began to offer vocational and industrial courses as well as commercial and clerical training courses. Despite all their problems and criticisms, the public high schools evolved into democratic and comprehensive institutions for social and political reform. They produced a skilled workforce in an expanding industrial economy, and they assimilated and Americanized millions of immigrant children in our cities. They emphasized that our society, unlike most others, could afford to educate the masses of 14 to 18 year olds. When the high school became a dominant institution, a student could attend a publicly supported and supervised institution from age 5 to 18. The high school, moreover, was a bridge to college and the university.

The Secondary School Curriculum Evolves. The curriculum of the Latin grammar school was virtually the same at the beginning and end of the colonial period. Table 3-3 lists the most popular courses. As indicated, Latin, Greek, arithmetic, and the classics were stressed. The academy introduced greater variation—courses for practical studies, for example—in the curriculum. By 1800, the academy offered about twenty-five different subjects (the table lists the seventeen most popular courses). Between 1850 and 1875, the peak period of the academy, estimates are that some 150 courses were offered.[52] The twenty most popular ones in rank order were as follows: (1) algebra; (2) higher arithmetic; (3) English grammar; (4) Latin; (5) geometry; (6) U.S. history; (7) physiology; (8) natural philosophy; (9) physical geography; (10) German; (11) general history; (12) rhetoric; (13) bookkeeping; (14)

TABLE 3-3 Evolution of Secondary School Curriculum, 1800–1900

1800–1825	1825–1850	1850–1875	1875–1900
Latin Grammar School			
Latin	Latin		
Greek	Greek		
Arithmetic	Arithmetic		
Classical literature	Classical literature		
	Ancient history		
Academy and High School			
Latin	Latin	Latin	Latin
Greek	Greek	Greek	Greek†
Classical literature	Classical literature	English literature	English literature
Writing*	Writing*	Composition*	Composition*
Arithmetic*	Arithmetic*	Arithmetic*	Arithmetic*
		Higher arithmetic	
Geometry	Geometry	Geometry	Geometry
Trigonometry	Trigonometry	Trigonometry	Trigonometry
	Algebra	Algebra	Algebra
Bookkeeping*	Bookkeeping*	Bookkeeping*	Bookkeeping*†
English grammar	English grammar	English grammar	English
Rhetoric	Rhetoric	Rhetoric	Rhetoric*
Oratory	Oratory†		
	Debating	Debating†	
Surveying*	Surveying*		
Astronomy*	Astronomy*	Astronomy	Astronomy*
Navigation*	Navigation*†		
Geography	Geography	Physical geography	Physical geography†
	Natural philosophy	Natural philosophy†	
		Meteorology	Meteorology†
		Chemistry	Chemistry
		Physiology	Physiology†
			Health education
		Botany	Botany†
		Zoology	Zoology†
			Biology
			Physics
Foreign language* (French, Spanish, German)	Foreign language* (French, Spanish, German)	Foreign language (French, Spanish, German)	Foreign language (French, Spanish, German, Italian)
Philosophy	Philosophy	Mental philosophy	
		Moral philosophy†	
	History	General history	World history
	Greek history	Greek history†	Ancient history
	U.S. history	U.S. history	U.S. history
			Civil government
			Political economy
			Manual training*
			Home economics*
			Agriculture*
			Music
			Art
			Physical education

Source: Adapted from Calvin Davis, *Our Evolving High School Curriculum* (New York: World Book, 1927), p. 38; Committee of Ten, *Report of the Committee on Secondary Studies* (Washington, D.C.: National Education Association, 1893), p. 4; Newton Edwards and Herman G. Richey, *The School in the American Social Order*, 2nd ed. (Boston: Houghton Mifflin, 1963), p. 250; and Gerald R. Firth and Richard D. Kimpston, *The Curricular Continuum in Perspective* (Itasca, Ill.: Peacock, 1973), pp. 102–104.

*Considered as part of Practical studies.

†All but disappeared; limited enrollments.

French; (15) zoology; (16) chemistry; (17) English literature; (18) geology; (19) botany; and (20) astronomy.[53]

There was no real philosophy or aim to these courses, except that most were college preparatory in nature, even though the original aim of the academy was to offer a practical program. It was believed then that a broad program with several course offerings was the hallmark of a better academy. The curriculum just expanded.[54]

After 1875, the high school rapidly grew and the academy rapidly declined. The secondary courses listed in Table 3-3 between 1875 and 1900 were high school courses. The curriculum continued to expand. The great variety in course offerings would allegedly allow the students to find where their interests and capabilities might be.[55]

THE TRANSITIONAL PERIOD: 1893–1918

From the colonial period until the turn of the twentieth century, the traditional curriculum—which emphasized classical studies for college-bound students—dominated at the elementary and secondary levels. The rationale for this emphasis was that the classics were difficult, and were thus the best source for intellectualizing and for developing mental abilities (a view later supported by the mental discipline approach to learning). The more difficult the subject, and the more the students had to exercise their minds, the greater the subject's value. Such ideas of knowledge and subject matter, as well as mental rigor, were rooted in the philosophy of perennialism.

Along with the classics, more and more subjects were added to the curriculum. As a result the need was growing to bring some unity or a pattern for curriculum organization out of the chaotic and confused situation, especially at the secondary level, where subject matter was expanding the most. According to two educators, "subjects taught varied from school to school. There was no uniformity as to time allotments, and grade

placements of topics or subjects pursued" differed from school to school.[56]

A companion problem existed. Most children, even as late as the turn of the century, completed their formal education at the elementary school level, and those students who did go to secondary schools usually ended their formal education upon graduation. As late as 1890, only 14.5 percent of the students enrolled in high school were preparing for college, and less than 3 percent went on to college.[57] Hence, the needs of more than 85 percent of these students were still being overlooked for only the top 15 percent; the discrepancy was more lopsided if college entry was considered. Reformers began to question the need for two curriculum tracks at the elementary level—one for high school-bound and the other for nonhigh school-bound children—the dominance of college over the high school, and the emphasis on mental discipline and the classics.

Reaffirming the Traditional Curriculum: Three Committees.

With these unsettled questions as background, the National Education Association (NEA) organized three major committees between 1893 and 1895: The Committee of Fifteen on Elementary Education, the Committee of Ten on Secondary School Studies, and the Committee on College Entrance Requirements. These Committees were to determine the specifics of the curricula for these schools. Their reports "standardized" the curriculum for much of this century. In the words of Ellwood Cubberley, "The committees were dominated by subject-matter specialists, possessed of a profound faith in mental discipline." No concern for student "abilities, social needs, interest, or capabilities . . . found a place in their . . . deliberations."[58]

The Committee of Fifteen. The Committee of Fifteen was heavily influenced by Charles Eliot, president of Harvard University, who had initiated vigorous discussion on the need for school reform in the years preceding, and by William Harris, then the U.S. Commissioner of Education, a staunch perennialist, who believed in strict teacher authority and discipline. Both Eliot and Harris wanted the traditional curriculum to remain intact. Eliot's plan, which was adapted by the Committee, was to reduce the elementary grades from ten to eight. The Committee stressed the three Rs, as well as English grammar, literature, geography, and history. Hygiene, culture, vocal music, and drawing were given sixty minutes, or one lesson, per week. Manual training, sewing, and/or cooking, as well as algebra and Latin, were introduced in the seventh and eighth grades.

In general, the Committee resisted the idea of newer subjects, and the principles of pedagogy or teaching that had characterized the reform movement of the European pioneers since the early 1800s. The Committee also rejected the idea of kindergarten and the idea that the children's needs or interests should be considered when planning the curriculum.[59] Any idea of interdisciplinary subjects or curriculum synthesis was rejected. Isolation of each branch of knowledge, or what John Dewey, in *Democracy and Education*, and Ralph Tyler, in *Basic Principles of Curriculum and Instruction*, later referred to as "compartmentalization" of subject matter, was considered the norm; it still is today, in most schools.

The Committee of Ten. The Committee of Ten was the most influential of the three committees. Its recommendations best illustrate the tough-minded, mental discipline approach supported by Eliot, who was the chair. The Committee selected nine academic subjects around which to organize the high school curriculum. As indicated in Table 3-4, they were: (1) Latin; (2) Greek; (3) English; (4) other modern languages; (5) mathematics (algebra, geometry, trigonometry, and higher or advanced algebra); (6) physical sciences (physics, astronomy, and chemistry); (7) natural history or biological sciences (biology, botany, zoology, and physiology); (8) social sciences (history, civil government, and political economy); and (9) geography, geology, and meteorology.

The Committee recommended four different programs or tracks: (1) classical; (2) Latin scientific; (3) modern languages; and (4) English. The first two required four years of Latin; the first program emphasized English (mostly classical) literature and math, and the second program, math and science. The modern language program required four years of French or German (Spanish was considered not only too easy, but also not as important a culture or language as French or German). The English program permitted four years of either Latin, German, or French. Both of these programs also included literature, composition, and history.

The Committee of Ten took a position and claimed that the latter two programs, which did not require Latin or emphasize literature, science, or mathematics, were "in practice distinctly inferior to the other two."[60] In taking this position, the Committee indirectly tracked college-bound students into the first two or superior programs and noncollege-bound students into the latter two or inferior programs. To some extent, this bias reflected the Committee's composition—eight of the ten members represented college and private preparatory school interests.

The Committee's unwillingness to recognize the value of art, music, physical education, and vocational education was based on the theory that these subjects had little mental or disciplinary value. In analyzing the effects of the Committee's action, Daniel and Laurel Tanner wrote: "The choice of these subjects and the omission of others from consideration was enough to set the course for secondary education" for many years and to indirectly set the tone at the elementary level, too. As "might be expected," the Committee suggested that "the nine subjects be taught sooner" and that all subjects except Latin and Greek be taught at the elementary school level.[61]

Even though very few students at that time went to college, this college prepara-

TABLE 3-4 Secondary School Programs and Subjects Proposed by Committee of Ten, 1893

1st Year	2nd Year	3rd Year	4th Year
Latin 5 p.*	Latin 4 p.	Latin 4 p.	Latin 4 p.
English Literature 2 p. ⎫ 4 p. " Composition, 2 p. ⎭	Greek 5 p.	Greek 4 p.	Greek 4 p.
German [or French] 5 p.	English Literature 2 p. ⎫ 4 p. " Composition, 2 p. ⎭	English Literature, 2 p. ⎫ 4 p. " Composition, 1 p. Rhetoric, 1 p. ⎭	English Literature, 2 p. ⎫ 4 p. " Composition, 1 p. Grammar, 1 p. ⎭
Algebra 4 p.	German continued 4 p.	German 4 p.	German 4 p.
History of Italy, Spain, and France 3 p.	French, begun 4 p.	French 4 p.	French 4 p.
Applied Geography (European political-continental and oceanic flora and fauna) 4 p.	Algebra,* 2 p. ⎫ 4 p. Geometry 2 p. ⎭	Algebra,* 2 p. ⎫ 4 p. Geometry, 2 p. ⎭	Trigonometry, ⎫ 2 p. Higher Algebra, ⎭
	Botany or Zoology 4 p.	Physics 4 p.	Chemistry 4 p.
	English History to 1688 3 p.	History, English and U.S. 3 p.	History (intensive) and Civil Government 3 p.
		Astronomy, 3 p. 1st ½ yr. ⎫ 3 p. Meterology, 3 p. 2nd ½ yr. ⎭	Geology or Physiography, 4 p. 1st ½ yr. ⎫ 4 p. Anatomy, Physiology, and Hygiene, 4 p. 2nd ½ yr. ⎭
25 p.	33 p.	34 p.	33 p.

*p. = periods.

Source: From Committee of Ten, *Report of the Committee of Ten on Secondary School Studies* (Washington, D.C.: National Educational Association, 1893), p. 4.

tory program established a curriculum hierarchy, from elementary school to college, that promoted academics and ignored the majority of students, who were noncollege bound. Today, even though we offer vocational, industrial, and/or technical programs, the academic program is still considered superior to, and of more status than, the other programs.

The Committee on College Entrance Requirements. When this Committee met in 1895, it reaffirmed college dominance over the high school, in terms of admission requirements and classical subjects for mental training at the high school and college levels. Consisting mainly of college and university presidents, including Eliot, the Committee recommended to strengthen the college preparatory aspect of the high school curriculum, believing that it best served all students. It also made recommendations regarding the number of credits required in different subjects for college admission; it served as a model for the Carnegie Unit, a means for evaluating credits for college admission, imposed on the high schools in 1909 and still in existence today in most high schools.

Pressure for a Modern Curriculum.

Gradually, demands were made for various changes to be made in the schools to meet the needs of a changing society. The pace of immigration and industrial development led a growing number of educators to question the classical curriculum and the constant emphasis on mental discipline and incessant drill. This shift in curriculum was influenced by the scientific movement in psychology and education in the late nineteenth century, particularly faculty psychology (that is, enhancing the "faculties" of the child through activities and stimulation of the senses); the social theories of Darwin, Herbart, and Spencer; and the impact of Pestalozzi, Froebel, and others on pedagogy.

Increased pressure against the traditional curriculum was evident at the turn of the century—with the educational ideas of John Dewey and Francis Parker, the Gestalt psychology and child psychology movements (which focused on the whole child), the learning theories of behaviorism and transfer learning (which involved connections between stimuli and responses), and the progressive movement in schools and society.

The argument eventually appeared that the classics had no greater disciplinary or mental value than other subjects, and that mental discipline (which emphasized rote, drill, and memorization) was not conducive to the inductive method of science or compatible with contemporary educational theory. Wrote Edward Thorndike, the most influential learning psychologist of the era:

The expectation of any large difference in general improvement of the mind from one study rather than another seems doomed to disappointment. The chief reason why good thinkers seem superficially to have been made such by having taken certain school studies is that good thinkers have taken such studies. ... Now that good thinkers study Physics and Trigonometry, these seem to make good thinkers. If abler pupils should all study Physical Education and Dramatic Art, these subjects would seem to make good thinkers.[62]

Even Latin came under attack, by none other than old-time perennialists. In 1917, for example, Charles Eliot, a former advocate of Latin, was saying Latin should no longer be compulsory for high school or college students.[63] Abraham Flexner, a former teacher of the classics who had become a celebrity with his exposé of the American medical schools, claimed that Latin had "no purpose" in the curriculum, and that the classics were out of step with scientific developments.[64] Flexner, who had become a strong advocate of utilitarianism, argued that tradition was an inadequate criterion for justifying subject matter. In short, society was changing and people could alter the conditions around them; the stress on psychology and science and the concern for social and educational reform made evident the need for a new curriculum.

Flexner: A Modern Curriculum. In a famous paper, "A Modern School," published in 1916, Abraham Flexner (1866–1959) rejected the traditional curriculum of the secondary school and proposed a "modern" curriculum for contemporary society. Flexner's curriculum consisted of four basic areas: (1) science (the major emphasis of the curriculum); (2) industry (occupations and trades of the industrial world); (3) civics (history, economics, and government); and (4) aesthetics (literature, languages, art, and music).[65] Modern languages would replace Latin and Greek. Flexner concluded that unless a utilitarian argument could be made for a subject, it had little value in the curriculum—regardless of traditional value.

Flexner's concepts of utility and modern subject matter tend to resemble Spencer's views on science and subject matter. The difference is that Flexner's timing was on the mark, and Spencer was ahead of his time. Flexner was tuned to the changing social and political times during which many educators were willing to listen to his proposals. In 1917, for example, Flexner's "Modern School" was established at the Lincoln School of Teachers College, Columbia University. The school combined the four core areas of study, with emphasis on scientific inquiry; it represented Dewey's type of progressivism and science of education, and it also reflected the fact that Dewey was now teaching at Columbia University.

Dewey: Pragmatic and Scientific Principles of Education. The same year Flexner published his modern school report, John Dewey (1859–1952) published *Democracy and Education,* in which can be found all elements of his philosophy as well as their implications for the educational process.[66] The book represented Dewey's attempt to link democracy to education and to present democracy as a social process that can be enhanced through the school. For Dewey, schooling was a "social process" that could fit into either a totalitarian state or a democracy. Thus, the aims of education went hand in hand with the particular type of society involved; conversely, the society that evolved influenced the aims of education.

Dewey argued that subjects could not be placed in a value hierarchy and that attempts to do so were misguided. Any study or body of knowledge was capable of expanding the child's experience, and "experiencing"—that is, being stimulated to develop and internalize intellectual capabilities—was the process of educating the child. Traditional subjects such as Latin or Greek were no more valuable than music or art.

One subject that may be more important to Dewey is science. Science, for Dewey, was another name for knowledge, and it represented "the perfected outcome of learning—its consummation. . . . What is known, certain, settled" and what "we think with rather than that which we think about" is science or rationalized knowledge. Dewey considered scientific inquiry to be the best form of knowledge for a society, because it consisted of the "special . . . methods which the race has slowly worked out in order to conduct reflection under conditions whereby its procedures and results are tested."[67] He thus elevated the place of science in education.

What is relevant to educating an individual to function well as a free person in a free society remained constant for Dewey. His emphasis on the "method of inquiry," which is really synonymous with "intelligent behavior," is as valued today as it was seventy years ago. Indeed, the connection between an enlightened citizenry, social change, and scientific principles advanced in Dewey's book played a major role in the theories of education that were evolving during this period. (Tanner and Tanner, *Curriculum Development*)

Commission on the Reorganization of Secondary Education. In 1918 the NEA Commission on the Reorganization of Secondary Education published the famous *Cardinal Principles of Secondary Education,*[68] a highly progressive document. Influenced by Flexner's "A Modern School" and Dewey's *Democracy and Education,* the Commission stressed the whole child (not just the cognitive area of study), education for all youth (not just college-bound youth), diversified areas of study (not classical or traditional studies), common culture, ideas, and ideals for a democratic society (not religious, elitist, or mental discipline learning).

The Commission noted the following:

1. Seven major aims or "Cardinal Principles" should comprise education: health, command of the fundamentals, worthy home membership, vocation, citizenship, leisure, and ethical character. These aims could be best met in a comprehensive and unified curriculum—a new kind of curriculum with no counterpart in the history of American schools.

2. High school should be a comprehensive institution based on the various social and economic groups that populate the nation.

3. The high school curriculum should offer various programs to meet various student needs—agricultural, business and commercial, vocational, and college preparatory.

4. The current ideas of psychology of education, principles of pedagogy, measurement, and evaluation should be applied to the curriculum and instruction of the high school.

5. American education comprises a set of defined institutions that should function in conjunction with, rather than in isolation from, each other.

Indeed, the high school was assuming its modern curricular patterns—combining academic programs with several nonacademic programs. The choice of subject matter was being fine tuned to emphasize five basic or essential subjects such as English, math, science, social science, and modern language. Classical languages and classical literature took a back seat to modern languages and English literature. Far from isolation, the aims and subjects were to be interrelated—not separated or compartmentalized. The idea of mental discipline was replaced by utilitarian modes of thought and scientific inquiry. There was a growing recognition that curriculum, too, should not be compartmentalized but interdisciplinary, and that it should not be static, but change as so-

ciety changed. The needs and interests of the students were now considered. Most important, there was recognition of the responsibility of schools (including the high school) to serve all children and youth, not just college-bound youth. The era of progressive education was about to begin impacting on the schools—and traditional education (which had dominated American education for so long) was vanishing.

CURRICULUM AS A FIELD IS BORN: 1918–1949

The early twentieth century was a period of educational ferment. Scientific methods of research, the influence of psychology, the child study movement, the idea of efficiency in industry, and the muckracker-progressive movement in society all influenced education. Many of the resulting ideas were applied to curriculum: From them evolved the process and how-to-do aspects of curriculum. Curriculum was now viewed as a science, with principles and methodology, not just as content or subject matter. The ideas of planning and designing a curriculum—as opposed to describing curriculum in terms of subjects and the amount of time needed to study each subject—appeared in the literature.

Bobbitt and Charters: Behaviorism and Scientific Principles.

Franklin Bobbitt (1876–1956) and Werrett Charters (1875–1952) were influenced by the idea of efficiency, promoted by business and industry, and the scientific management theories of Frederick Taylor, who analyzed factory efficiency in terms of time and motion studies and concluded that each worker should be paid on the basis of his or her individual output (as measured by the number of units produced in a specified period of time).[69] Efficient operation of the schools, sometimes called "machine" theory by sociologists and economists, became a major goal in the 1920s. Often ensuring efficiency meant eliminating small classes, increasing the student-teacher ratio, cutting costs in teacher salaries, and so on, and then preparing charts and graphs to show the resultant lower costs. Raymond Callahan later branded this idea the "cult of efficiency."[70] The effects were to make curriculum making more scientific, and to reduce teaching and learning to precise behaviors with corresponding activities and learning experiences that could be measured. These ideas were cultivated by Taylor's faithful followers: Bobbitt and Charters.

Bobbitt's book, *The Curriculum*, published in 1918, is considered by some observers as the first book devoted solely to curriculum as a science and to curriculum in all its phases.[71] Bobbitt outlined the principles of curriculum planning by focusing on an activities approach, which he defined as "a series of things which children and youth must do and experience by way of developing abilities to do things well and make up the affairs of adult life."[72] To Bobbitt the purpose of curriculum was to outline what knowledge was important for each subject, and then to develop various activities to train the learner and enhance his or her performance.

Bobbitt understood the importance of analyzing the process of curriculum making. Adherence to the traditional curriculum, which emphasized subject matter, did not provide educators with methods for developing curricula. Bobbitt described the problems as he set out to organize a course of studies for the elementary grades:

We need principles of curriculum making. We did not know that we should first determine objectives from a study of social needs. We supposed education consisted only of teaching the familiar subjects. We had not come to see that it is essentially a process of unfolding the potential abilities of [students]. . . . We had not learned that studies are means, not ends.[73]

Bobbitt further developed his objectives and activities approach in the early 1920s in *How To Make a Curriculum*. Here he outlined more than 800 objectives and related activities to coincide with student needs. These activities ranged from the "ability to care for [one's] teeth, . . . eyes, . . . nose, and throat, . . . ability to keep the heart and blood vessels in normal working condition, . . . to keep home appliances in good working condition . . . to spelling and grammar."[74]

Bobbitt's methods were quite sophisticated for the period. Moreover, his guidelines for selecting objectives can be applied today: (1) *eliminate* objectives that are impractical or cannot be accomplished through normal living; (2) *emphasize* objectives that are important for success and adult living; (3) *avoid* objectives opposed by the community; (4) *involve* the community in selecting objectives; (5) *differentiate* between objectives that are for all students and those that are for only a portion of the student population; and (6) *sequence* the objectives in such a way as to establish how far students should go each year in attaining them—that is, establish criteria for achievement.

Taken out of context, however, Bobbitt's list of hundreds of objectives and activities, along with the machine or factory analogy that he advocated, were easy to criticize.[75] Nevertheless, Bobbitt's insistence that curriculum making was a specialty based on scientific methods and procedures was important for elevating curriculum to a field of study, or what he called a "new specialization." His offer was that educators try his method with the intention of improving it or suggesting a better one. He was one of the first to propose the idea of a curriculum specialist, with special training.

Charters advocated the same behaviorist, precise approach, which he termed a "scientific" approach. He viewed the curriculum as a series of objectives that students must attain by way of a series of learning experiences. In his book on *Curriculum Construction*, Charters, who was influenced by the machine theory of business, envisioned curriculum as the analysis of definite operations—a process he termed *job analysis*—such as those involved in running a machine.[76]

Charters's statement about the weakness of curriculum is still relevant today—namely, that even though curriculum writers often begin "with the statement of aim, none has been able to derive a curriculum logically from his statement of aim." In almost every case, a "mental leap [is made] from the aim to the subject matter, without providing adequate principles such as would bridge the gap . . . and lead us from aim to selection of materials."[77] Charters attempted to bridge the gap by proposing a curriculum derived from specific objectives and precise activities. He considered objectives to be observable and measurable, an outlook that is similar to today's notion that behavioral objectives can be sound and definable. He felt the state of knowledge at that time did not permit scientific measurement that would specifically identify the outcomes of the objectives, but he set out to develop a method for selecting objectives, based on social consensus, and for applying subject matter and student activities to analysis and verification. Although Charters did not use the term *evaluation* during this period, he was laying the groundwork for curriculum evaluation, which surfaced twenty years later.

As prime initiators of the behavioral and scientific movements in curriculum, Bobbitt and Charters had a profound impact on curriculum. They (1) developed principles for curriculum making, involving aims, objectives, needs, and learning experiences (which they called activities); (2) highlighted the use of behavioral objectives, which has a legacy in various contemporary educational ideas, such as the use of instructional objectives and curriculum evaluation; (3) introduced the ideas that objectives are derived from the study of needs (later called needs assessment) and that objectives and activities are subject to analysis and verification (later called evaluation); and (4) emphasized that curriculum making cuts across subject matter, and that a curriculum specialist need not necessarily be a specialist in any *subject,* rather a professional in *method or process.*

Finally, Bobbitt and Charters taught at the University of Chicago when Tyler was a graduate student in the department of education (in fact, Tyler was Charters's graduate assistant). Tyler was highly influenced by their behaviorist ideas, particularly that: (1) objectives derive from student needs and society; (2) learning experiences relate to objectives; (3) activities organized by the teacher should be integrated into the subject matter; and (4) instructional outcomes should be evaluated. Tyler's stress on evaluation as a component of curriculum is rooted in the research background of Charters, who helped his graduate student get appointed to his first teaching and evaluation position in 1929 as Head of Testing and Evaluation for the Ohio State Bureau of Educational Research (Charters had assumed the Directorship of the Bureau the previous year). Tyler's principles of curriculum and instruction, especially his four major components (objectives, learning experiences, methods of organization, and evaluation), are rooted in Bobbitt's and especially Charters's ideas.

The Twenty-Sixth Yearbook.

In 1927, the National Society for the Study of Education (NSSE), an honor society with headquarters at the University of Chicago, published its twenty-sixth yearbook in two parts, *Curriculum-Making: Past and Present* and *The Foundations of Curriculum Making.*[78]

The Committee that developed the two volumes consisted of twelve members, including Harold Rugg (the chairperson) and William Bagley, Franklin Bobbitt, Werrett Charters, George Counts, Charles Judd, and William Kilpatrick, among others. Leaders of curriculum development during that period were scientific-oriented and progressive (including Bobbitt and Charters), and many were affiliated with the University of Chicago, which emphasized this science of education.

The Yearbook comprised two parts. The first part began as a harsh criticism of traditional education and its emphasis on subject matter, rote learning, drill, and mental discipline. It then became a synthesis of progressive practices and programs—the best and most innovative since the turn of the century—in public and private schools across the country. Part II has become a landmark text. It described the state of the art in curriculum making up to that period of time, and it included a consensual statement by the group on the nature of curriculum making. It is still relevant today.

The Committee recognized the need for curriculum reform and the need for "those who are constructing our school curriculum" to determine "an overview . . . [and] orientation . . . to curriculum making."[79] With this idea in mind, the Yearbook outlined characteristics of the ideal curriculum—a curriculum that:

1. Focuses on the affairs of human life.
2. Deals with the facts and problems of the local, national, and international community.
3. Enables students to think critically about various forms of government.
4. Informs and develops an attitude of open-mindedness.
5. Considers student interests and needs as well as opportunities for debate, discussion, and exchange of ideas.
6. Deals with the issues of modern life and the cultural and historical aspects of society.
7. Considers problem-solving activities and practice in choosing alternatives.
8. Consists of carefully graded organization of problems and exercises.
9. Deals with humanitarian themes, and purposeful and constructive attitudes and insights.[80]

This description of the ideal curriculum is basically one that might be developed today. The problems and issues identified by the Committee are chiefly those that another curriculum committee could recognize as important for the 1990s.

In the same vein, Harold Rugg maintained that the people should formulate the aims and purposes of education through committees or legislative groups; the appropriate materials and methods of instruction "through which to achieve those aims and purposes [were] . . . technical . . . demanding special professional preparation." The role of trained curriculum specialists was to plan the curriculum in advance and to include four tasks (which were later to become the basis of Tyler's four principles): (1) "a statement of objectives, (2) a sequence of experiences [to achieve] the objectives, (3) subject matter found to be . . . the best means of engaging in the experiences, and (4) statements of immediate outcomes of achievements to be derived from the experiences." Rugg concluded that curriculum was adapting scientific methods and that there was need "for specialization and for professional . . . training."[81] Experienced teachers and specialists in curriculum making should work together to organize the content and materials within the various fields of subject matter—what the schools do today.

The Yearbook represented a tremendous advancement in clarifying problems curriculum workers were encountering and in proposing procedures for the future in curriculum making. It had major influence in many school districts (both large and small, as well as city, suburban, and rural), as illustrated by the plan that was later called "The Eight-Year Study," and by the ideas that Ralph Tyler and Hilda Taba expressed in their classic texts twenty and thirty years later.

Rugg and Caswell: The Development Period.

During the late 1920s, the 1930s, and the early 1940s a number of important books were published on curriculum principles and processes, and on techniques for helping the teacher in curriculum making. Harold Rugg (1886–1960), the chairperson of the NSSE Yearbook, shared the faith of Bobbitt and Charters in a "science of curriculum." By training Rugg was an engineer, but, like Dewey, he had a broad view of curriculum that focused on the whole child and the way the child would grapple with the changing society. In this respect, Rugg was a progressive thinker as well as a forerunner of reconstructionism.

In 1928, Rugg coauthored his classic text, *The Child-Centered School,* with Ann Shumaker. In an era which stressed student input in planning the curriculum, the authors stressed the need for curriculum specialists to construct the curriculum.[82] He, also, wrote about the necessity of teachers' having at hand an outline of the knowledge, concepts, and generalizations that were to come from classroom instruction. Put in different terms, Rugg proposed that the curriculum should be planned by the teacher in advance.[83] The important point here is that Rugg (who was also progressive) rejected the idea of a curriculum based on the spontaneous needs or interests of the child. Such a curriculum, he believed, would have no sequence or predetermined outcomes. Even a play school had to have objectives and related organized activities; otherwise, education was wasteful. Finally, he advocated cooperation among educational professionals from different areas, including teachers, administrators, test experts, and curriculum specialists from various fields.

Rugg's attention in the 1930s and the 1940s shifted almost entirely to the integration of history, geography, civics, and economics—commonly called social studies. Some of his ideas about labor history and collectivism, and his criticisms of American life, compounded by his activities with the teachers' union, resulted in a great deal of criticism from Establishment groups. Like Counts and Dewey, Rugg, too, had the distinction of having an FBI file.[84]

During the mid-1920s and 1930s, most school districts and state education departments were developing curriculum guides. However, the selection of methods and activities was left to the teachers. Hollis Caswell (1901–   ), was concerned that this practice was limited; he wanted to shift emphasis from formulating a course of study to improving instruction. He envisioned curriculum making as a means of helping teachers coordinate their instructional activities with subject matter and students' needs and interests. He considered courses of study as guides or sources that teachers could use to plan their daily work, but not as plans they should follow in detail. He sought to combine three major curriculum components: content, teacher's instruction, and student's learning.

Caswell attempted to assist teachers by providing a step-by-step procedure for curriculum making. He and his colleagues outlined seven points, in question form, that still have relevancy today:

1. What is a curriculum?
2. Why is there need for curriculum revision?
3. What is the function of subject matter?
4. How do we determine educational objectives?
5. How do we organize curriculum?
6. How do we select subject matter?
7. How do we measure the outcomes of instruction?[85]

Influenced by Bobbitt's definition of curriculum as "that series of things which children and youth must do and experience," Caswell and Campbell, in their classic text on *Curriculum Development,* maintained that the curriculum must consider "all elements in the experience of the learner."[86] They thought curriculum should synthesize the fields of philosophy, psychology, and sociology—what other curricularists would later refer to as the foundations of curriculum. To a large extent, Caswell envisioned curriculum as a field with few limitations on content; rather, he thought curriculum represented a procedure or process that incorporated scientific steps of development, organization, instruction, and evaluation.

Caswell and Campbell believed that the curriculum must address three basic elements: Children's interests, social functions, and organized knowledge. The curriculum was to provide the proper scope and sequence of subject matter at every grade level. The *scope* was to represent broad themes based on social functions (similar to educational aims), such as conservation of natural resources, worthy home member-ship, democratic living, and so on. The *sequence* was based on experiences according to the children's interests. *Subject matter* was suggested to match the social functions and the learner's interests; the knowledge that was taught was to be measured as outcomes of instruction.

Caswell and Campbell's book "became heavily prominent during the next two decades, almost becoming synonymous with curriculum study at large."[87] Their three elements of curriculum, as well as scope and sequence, heavily influenced Taba's book on *Curriculum Development: Theory and Practice.* Their three foundations and elements of curriculum also influenced the classic textbook written by B. Othanel Smith and his colleagues, *Fundamentals of Curriculum Development.* Both textbooks served as bridges between Caswell and Campbell and many present curriculum textbooks (which stress foundations and principles of curriculum).

Tyler: Basic Principles.

An account of curriculum as a field is not complete without discussion of Ralph Tyler, (1902–   ). Although Tyler published more than 700 articles and sixteen books (eleven of which are coauthored) on the subjects of curriculum, instruction, and evaluation, he is best known for his small book, *Basic Principles of Curriculum and Instruction.*[88] Originally written as a course syllabus for his students at the University of Chicago, the book was published in 1949; it has already gone through over thirty-five printings. It is, in fact, considered by some as a "mini-Bible" of curriculum.

In 128 pages, Tyler outlines the basic questions that he believes should be answered by anyone involved in planning or writing a currriculum for any subject or grade level:

1. What educational purposes should the school seek to attain?
2. What educational experiences can be provided that are likely to attain these purposes?

3. How can these educational experiences be effectively organized?
4. How can we determine whether these purposes are being attained?[89]

Tyler was highly influenced by the progressive social theories of Judd and Dewey, as well as the learning theories of Thorndike and Piaget. He drew from the behaviorists, too, including Bobbitt and Charters. His philosophy and principles of curriculum were influenced by older contemporaries, such as George Counts (while Tyler was at the University of Chicago) and Boyd Bode (while he was at Ohio State University).

Not much in Tyler's model is new; we might consider it an elaboration of Rugg's four major tasks in curriculum and a condensed version of the NSSE's Twenty-Sixth Yearbook. One critic claims that "it clearly paraphrased, restated, and elaborated the position taken by the NSSE committee."[90] Others claim that the four questions and related discussions closely resemble the companion curriculum report, *Exploring the Curriculum,* submitted with "The Eight-Year Study."[91] The model was not fully developed at that time, however; Tyler fully developed it later.

To some extent, also, Tyler's model can be considered an elaboration of an earlier work he did with Douglas Waples, when Tyler was at Ohio State University. In their publication, Tyler and Waples outlined the major elements in curriculum and instruction: (1) defining objectives, organizing content, and adopting materials; (2) selecting learning experiences and diagnosing learners; (3) managing students; and (4) outlining techniques of instruction and evaluation.[92] Although Tyler does not mention the Waples publication in his book, in a recent interview he did give some credit to Judd, Dewey, and Thorndike, and minimal credit to Charters and Bode.[93]

Tyler, also, was highly influenced by Hilda Taba, his colleague for over twenty years at Ohio State and the University of Chicago. Tyler had a very close personal and professional relationship with Taba, and together they served on numerous research projects involving curriculum and evaluation. Because Taba's classic book on *Curriculum Development* was published several years after Tyler's book, most people think that Tyler influenced Taba. Actually, they influenced each other, but Tyler was the first to lay out four linear steps, which Taba further developed into seven linear steps.

The Tyler model depicts a rational, logical, and systematic approach to curriculum making. Although it embraces no philosophical or political bias in the sense that any subject can be organized around the model, its ideas are rooted in progressivism (it emphasizes the needs of the learner), scientific procedures (its principles are applicable in varying situations), and behaviorism (its objectives are the most important consideration, in Tyler's own words).

As the NSSE Yearbook put little emphasis on the teachers' role in curriculum making, Tyler said very little about the students' or the principals' roles. Although Tyler claims the book deals with principles and processes, the work is a "cookbook" approach to curriculum making. Nevertheless, the book is highly influential, because of its rational, no-nonsense, and sequential approach. In just over 100 pages, Tyler laid out a basic procedure to follow with easy-to-understand examples—different from the complex and cumbersome writings of other texts. Tyler gives students a manageable description, a series of concise steps, through which to plan curriculum.

Although critics have judged Tyler's model to be inadequate, naive, overly lockstep, and technocratic, and have censured it for its oversimplifying view of curriculum making as the collection of small bits of behavior,[94] it still works for many. Because it is simple to grasp, it serves as a starting point for curriculum students (which was its original intention). Remember that Tyler did not attempt anything more than to provide a basic guideline for students; his contemporaries inflated the significance of the book.

When a treatise in social science becomes popular, as this one did, it becomes fair game for analysis and criticism by others in the field—as this one did as well.

Perhaps the most important reason Tyler is so influential is that he worked closely with a number of influential colleagues, besides Taba, such as Paul Diederich, Harold Dunkel, Maurice Hartung, Virgil Herrick, and Joseph Schwab, who accepted many of his ideas and who also influenced curriculum. In addition, many of Tyler's students at Ohio State University—such as Edgar Dale, Louis Heil, Louis Raths, and Harold Shane—and at the University of Chicago—such as Elliot Eisner, Ned Flanders, David Krathwohl, Louise Tyler, and Thomas Hastings—were influenced by Tyler and also became prominent in the field. Most important, a number of Tyler's other students—including Ben Bloom, Lee Cronbach, John Goodlad, Ken Rehage, Ole Sand, and Herbert Thelen—were also his colleagues for many years.[95] With the exception of Eisner, these colleagues continuously praised Tyler's work in the professional literature. Like Tyler, these men and women were (or are) known for their scientific assumptions, systematic procedures, and traditional views on education.

CURRENT FOCUS

The Tyler model, despite its criticism, summed up the best principles of curriculum making during the first half of the twentieth century. The model has been utilized and adapted by many curricularists, including some of Tyler's students, like Taba and Goodlad.[96] Although Tyler and his predecessors did a great deal toward outlining a science of curriculum, the major concepts and principles of the field remain ill-defined and open to dispute. According to Bruce Joyce, there are "no agreed upon concepts or modes which are known and used. . . . The curriculum field has no overarching 'metasystem,' known to most of its practitioners, which enables comparisons of and choices between all alternative approaches which are taken." In general, curriculum people still "do their own thing."[97]

On the other hand, Elliot Eisner points out that the "kind of science that has dominated educational research, . . . including curriculum development . . . uses knowledge provided by the social scientist as the primary bases for . . . management and control."[98] This has led to prescriptive models of curriculum and instruction, uniform methods of teaching and testing, and outcomes of learning that can be standardized and measured. This tendency toward scientific principles of curriculum making, and educational research in general, has resulted in nonexpressive and nonemotional forms of education, according to Eisner, and what he labels as "value-neutral," "technical," "cool," and "dispassionate objective."[99] The inference is that the Bobbitt-Tyler era, and its science of curriculum, has taken the joy, humor, and fun out of teaching and learning.

Although this analysis may be construed as an overstatement, especially by those who believe in behavioral or managerial approaches to curriculum, several curricularists today—like Mike Apple, Dwayne Huebner, Herb Kliebard, James Macdonald, Gail McCutcheon, and Vincent Rogers—have lost faith in the ability of scientific principles and technical models to solve curriculum problems. Like Eisner, they have turned to various personal, aesthetic, and linguistic concepts to formulate—or better yet, to reformulate—curriculum.[100]

Even though we cannot agree on the concepts and principles of curriculum, much less on a science of curriculum making, the field of curriculum is expanding, and certain trends are taking shape. During the 1980s, the notion of international competition has resurfaced, along with the cry for tougher standards and educational productivity. The academic curriculum is also being expanded and upgraded, and the idea of academic excellence is once more being debated in educational circles. The notion of a fourth R—computer literacy for students—is also being seriously considered (the authors would introduce a fifth R, as well—namely, Spanish because of our country's ethnic population trends), along with a renewed emphasis on science, mathematics, and foreign languages—similar to the Sputnik period.

The field of curriculum is also maturing. It is moving beyond schools and including programs in business, industry, military, government, and health fields. It is also incorporating many disciplines, such as philosophy, psychology, sociology, and politics. Finally, the field is developing an international character, and curriculum specialists are adapting the tools of research methodology, computers, instructional technology, and systems analysis. In short, curriculum as a field of study is becoming more interdisciplinary, scientific, and qualitative.

CONCLUSION

From the colonial period to around World War I, curriculum was a matter of evolving subject matter. Some reform ideas concerned pedagogical principles, mainly as a result of European influence and the emerging progressive reform movement of the mid and late nineteenth century. But these ideas were limited to theoretical discussions and a few isolated and innovative schools. The perennialist curriculum, which emphasized the classics and timeless and absolute values based around religious and then moral doctrines, remained dominant for the first 150 years of our nation's history.

The idea of principles and processes of curriculum began to take shape after the turn of the twentieth century, along with emphasis on scientific principles and progressive philosophy. Curriculum as a field of study, with its own methods and theories and ways of solving problems, has made real advances ever since the 1920s. Most of the advances have actually taken place since Tyler wrote his basic text on curriculum.

Many of these advances are discussed elsewhere in this text.

Notes

1. John S. Brubacher, *A History of the Problems of Education* (New York: McGraw-Hill, 1947); R. Freeman Butts and Lawrence A. Cremin, *A History of Education in American Culture* (New York: Holt, Rinehart, 1953).

2. Warren H. Button and Eugene Provenzo, *History of Education and Culture in America* (Englewood Cliffs, N.J.: Prentice-Hall, 1983); Butts and Cremin, *A History of Education in American Culture*.

3. George A. Beauchamp, *The Curriculum of the Elementary School* (Boston: Allyn and Bacon, 1964), p. 34.

4. Allan C. Ornstein and Daniel U. Levine, *An Introduction to the Foundations of Education*, 3rd ed. (Boston: Houghton Mifflin, 1985), p. 151. See also Gerald Gutek, *Education in the United States: An Historical Perspective* (Englewood Cliffs, N.J.: Prentice-Hall, 1986).

5. Beauchamp, *The Curriculum of the Elementary School*, p. 36.

6. Paul Monroe, *Founding of the American Public School System* (New York: Macmillan, 1940); Samuel E. Morrison, *The Intellectual Life of Colonial New England* (New York: New York University Press, 1956).

7. Robert Middlekauff, *Ancients and Axioms: Secondary Education in the Eighteenth-Century New England* (New Haven: Yale University Press, 1963).

8. Elmer E. Brown, *The Making of Our Middle School* (New York: Longman, 1926), p. 133.

9. Newton Edwards and Herman G. Richey, *The School in the American Social Order*, 2nd ed. (Boston: Houghton Mifflin, 1963), p. 102.

10. Morrison, *The Intellectual Life of Colonial New England*.

11. John H. Best, *Benjamin Franklin on Education* (New York: Teachers College Press, Columbia University, 1962).

12. Ellwood P. Cubberley, *Public Education in the United States*, rev. ed. (Boston: Houghton Mifflin, 1947), p. 30.

13. R. Freeman Butts, *The American Tradition in Religion and Education* (Boston: Beacon Press, 1950); Gerald R. Firth and Richard D. Kimpston, *The Curricular Continuum in Perspective* (Itasca, Ill.: Peacock, 1973).

14. Paul L. Ford, *The New England Primer: A History of its Origins and Development*, rev. ed. (New York: Dodd, Mead, 1897), pp. 329–330.

15. Henry Barnard, *Educational Developments in the United States* (Hartford, Conn: Connecticut Department of Education, 1867), p. 367.

16. Cubberley, *Public Education in the United States;* Merle Curti, *The Social Ideas of American Educators* (New York: Littlefield, Adams, 1959).

17. Benjamin Rush, *A Plan for the Establishment of Public Schools* (Philadelphia: Thomas Dobson, 1786), pp. 29–30.

18. Thomas Jefferson, "A Bill for the More General Diffusion of Knowledge," in P. L. Ford, ed., *The Writings of Thomas Jefferson* (New York: Putnam, 1893), p. 221.

19. Merle Curti, *The Growth of American Thought*, rev. ed. (New York: Harper & Row, 1951).

20. Hans Kohn, *American Nationalism: An Interpretative Essay* (New York: Macmillan, 1957), p. 47.

21. Noah Webster, *Dissertations on the English Language* (Boston: Isaiah Thomas, 1789), p. 27.

22. Harvey R. Warfel, *Noah Webster: Schoolmaster to America* (New York: Macmillan, 1936).

23. Henry Steele Commager, ed., *Noah Webster's American Spelling Book* (New York: Teachers College Press, Columbia University, 1962).

24. Robert K. Leavitt, *Noah's Ark, New England Yankees and the Endless Quest* (Springfield, Mass.: Merriam, 1947); Richard M. Rollins, "Words as Social Control: Noah Webster and the Creation of the American Dictionary," *American Quarterly* (Fall 1976), pp. 415–430.

25. William H. McGuffey, *New Fifth Eclectic Reader* (Cincinnati: Winthrop Smith, 1857), p. 271.

26. William H. McGuffey, *Newly Revised Eclectic Fourth Reader* (Cincinnati: Winthrop Smith, 1853), p. 313.

27. John H. Westerhoff, *McGuffey and His Readers: Piety, Morality, and Education in Nineteenth Century America* (Nashville: Abingdon, 1978).

28. William B. Ragan and Gene D. Shepherd, *Modern Elementary Curriculum*, 4th ed. (New York: Holt, Rinehart, 1971), p. 20.

29. Edgar W. Knight, *Education in the United States*, 3rd ed. (Boston: Ginn, 1951), p. 512.

30. See Henry Barnard, *Pestalozzi and Pestalozzianism* (New York: Brownell, 1862).

31. Friedrich Froebel, *The Education of Man*, trans. W. Hailman (New York: Appleton, 1889).

32. Johann F. Herbart, *Textbook of Psychology* (New York: Appleton, 1894).

33. John Dewey, *How We Think*, (Boston: D. C. Heath, 1910), p. 202.

34. Andreas Kazamias, *Herbert Spencer on Education* (New York: Teachers College Press, Columbia University, 1966).

35. Herbert Spencer, *Education: Intellectual, Moral and Physical* (New York: Appleton, 1860).

36. Tanner and Tanner, *Curriculum Development*.

37. See Everett Dick, *Vanguards of the Frontier* (New York: Appleton-Century, 1940); William W. Folwell, *The Autobiography and Letters of a Pioneer Culture* (Minneapolis: University of Minnesota Press, 1923).

38. Tanner and Tanner, *Curriculum Development:*

Development: Theory into Practice, 2nd ed. (New York: Macmillan, 1980).

39. Button and Provenzo, *History of Education and Culture in America;* Monroe, *Founding of the American Public School System.*

40. Frederick M. Binder, *The Age of the Common School: 1830–1865* (New York: Wiley, 1974).

41. V. T. Thayer and Martin Levit, *The Role of the School in American Society,* 2nd ed. (New York: Dodd, Mead, 1966), p. 6.

42. Lawrence A. Cremin, *The Republic and the School: Horace Mann on the Education of Free Man* (New York: Teachers College Press, Columbia University Press, 1957); Jonathan Messerlie, *Horace Mann: A Biography* (New York: Knopf, 1972).

43. Andrew Gulliford, *America's Country Schools* (Washington, D.C.: National Trust for Historic Preservation, 1985).

44. James H. Hughes, *Education in America,* 3rd ed. (New York: Harper & Row, 1970), p. 233.

45. Carl Sandburg, *Abraham Lincoln: The Prairie Years* (New York: Harcourt, Brace, 1926), p. 19.

46. Theodore R. Sizer, *The Age of Academies* (New York: Teachers College Press, Columbia University, 1964).

47. E. P. Cubberley, *The History of Education* (Boston: Houghton Mifflin, 1920), p. 697.

48. Edwards and Richey, *The School in the American Social Order;* Firth and Kimpston, *The Curricular Continuum in Perspective.*

49. Brown, *The Making of Our Middle Schools,* p. 230.

50. Monroe, *Founding of the American Public School System,* p. 404.

51. Edward A. Krug, *The Shaping of the American High School: 1880–1920* (New York: Harper & Row, 1964); Daniel Tanner, *Secondary Education: Perspectives and Prospects* (New York: Macmillan, 1972).

52. Cubberley, *Public Education in the United States;* Edwards and Richey, *The School in the American Social Order;* and Monroe, *Founding of the American Public School System.*

53. Davis, *Our Evolving High School Curriculum.*

54. Krug, *The Shaping of the American High School.*

55. Issac L. Kandel, *History of Secondary Education* (Boston: Houghton Mifflin, 1930).

56. Thayer and Levit, *The Role of the School in American Society,* p. 382.

57. *Report of the Year 1889–90* (Washington, D.C.: U.S. Bureau of Education, 1893), pp. 1388–1389. See also Table 3-2.

58. Cubberley, *Public Education in the United States,* p. 543.

59. Daniel Tanner, "Curriculum History," in H. E. Mitzel, ed., *Encyclopedia of Educational Research,* 5th ed. (New York: Macmillan, 1982), pp. 412–420; Tanner and Tanner, *Curriculum Development: Theory into Practice.*

60. *Report of the Committee of Ten on Secondary School Studies,* book ed. (New York: American Book, 1894), p. 48.

61. Tanner and Tanner, *Curriculum Development: Theory into Practice,* p. 233. See also Edward A. Krug, *Charles W. Eliot and Popular Education* (New York: Teachers College Press, Columbia University Press, 1961).

62. Edward L. Thorndike, "Mental Discipline in High School Studies," *Journal of Educational Psychology* (February 1924), p. 98.

63. Charles W. Eliot, "The Case against Compulsory Latin," *Atlantic* (March 1917), pp. 356–359.

64. Abraham Flexner, "Parents and School," *Atlantic* (July 1916), p. 30.

65. Abraham Flexner, "A Modern School," *Occasional Papers,* No. 3 (New York: General Education Board, 1916); Flexner, *A Modern College and A Modern School* (New York: Doubleday, 1923).

66. John Dewey, *Democracy and Education* (New York: Macmillan, 1916).

67. Ibid., p. 190.

68. Commission on the Reorganization of Secondary Education, *Cardinal Principles of Secondary Education,* Bulletin No. 35 (Washington, D.C.: U.S. Government Printing Office, 1918).

69. Frederick W. Taylor, *The Principles of Scientific Management* (New York: Harper & Row, 1911).

70. Raymond E. Callahan, *Education and the Cult of Efficiency* (Chicago: University of Chicago Press, 1962).

71. See John D. McNeil, *Curriculum: A Comprehensive Introduction,* 3rd ed. (Boston: Little, Brown, 1985); John P. Miller and Wayne Seller, *Curriculum: Perspectives and Practice* (New York: Longman, 1985).

72. Franklin Bobbitt, *The Curriculum* (Boston: Houghton Mifflin, 1918), p. 42.

73. Ibid., p. 283.

74. Franklin Bobbitt, *How To Make a Curriculum* (Boston: Houghton Mifflin, 1924), pp. 14, 28.

75. Michael W. Apple, *Ideology and Curriculum* (Boston: Routledge & Kegan Paul, 1979); Callahan, *Education and the Cult of Efficiency;* and Elliot W. Eisner, *The Educational Imagination,* 2nd ed. (New York: Macmillan, 1985).

76. W. W. Charters, *Curriculum Construction* (New York: Macmillan, 1923).

77. Ibid., pp. 6–7. See also W. W. Charters, "Idea Men and Engineers in Education," *Educational Forum* (Spring 1986), pp. 263–272. Originally published in *Educational Forum* (May 1948), pp. 399–406.

78. Guy M. Whipple, ed., *Curriculum-Making: Past and Present,* Twenty-Sixth Yearbook of the National Society for the Study of Education, Part I (Bloomington, Ill.: Public School Publishing Co., 1927); Whipple, ed., *The Foundations of Curriculum Making,* Twenty-Sixth Yearbook of the National Society for the Study of Education, Part II (Bloomington, Ill.: Public School Publishing Co., 1930).

79. Harold Rugg, "Forward," in Whipple, ed., *Curriculum-Making: Past and Present,* p. x.

80. Harold Rugg, "The School Curriculum and the Drama of American Life," in Whipple, ed., *Curriculum-Making: Past and Present*, pp. 3–16.

81. Harold Rugg, "Three Decades of Mental Discipline: Curriculm-Making via National Committees," in Whipple, ed., *Curriculum-Making: Past and Present*, pp. 52–53.

82. Harold Rugg and Ann Shumaker, *The Child-Centered School* (New York: World Book, 1928), p. 118.

83. Ralph W. Tyler, "Curriculum Development in the Twenties and Thirties," in R. M. McClure, ed., *The Curriculum: Retrospect and Prospect*, Seventieth Yearbook of the National Society for the Study of Education, Part I (Chicago: University of Chicago Press, 1971), pp. 26–44.

84. David Pratt, *Curriculum: Design and Development* (New York: Harcourt, Brace, 1980).

85. Sidney B. Hall, D. W. Peters, and Hollis L. Caswell, *Study Course for Virginia State Curriculum* (Richmond: Virginia State Board of Education, 1932), p. 363.

86. Hollis L. Caswell and Doak S. Campbell, *Curriculum Development* (New York: American Book, 1935), p. 69.

87. William H. Schubert, *Curriculum Books: The First Eighty Years* (Lanham, Md.: University Press, 1980), p. 77. See also Schubert, *Curriculum: Perspective, Paradigm, and Possibility* (New York: Macmillan, 1986).

88. Ralph W. Tyler, *Basic Principles of Curriculum and Instruction* (Chicago: University of Chicago Press, 1949).

89. Ibid., p. 1.

90. Pratt, *Curriculum: Design and Development*, p. 34.

91. Tanner and Tanner, *Curriculum Development: Theory into Practice*, p. 83. See also Chapter 7, p. 166.

92. Douglas Waples and Ralph W. Tyler, *Research Methods and Teachers' Problems: A Manual for Systematic Studies of Classroom Procedure* (New York: Macmillan, 1930).

93. For a detailed discussion of who influenced Tyler and who he influenced, see Marie K. Stone, *Principles of Curriculum, Instruction, and Evaluation: Past Influence and Present Effects*. Ph.D. dissertation, Loyola University of Chicago, January 1985.

94. Elliot W. Eisner, *The Educational Imagination*, 2nd ed. (New York: Macmillan, 1985); Henry Giroux and David Purpel, eds., *The Hidden and Moral Curriculum* (Berkeley, Calif.: McCutchan, 1983); Herbert M. Kliebard, "Curricular Objectives and Evaluation: A Reassessment," *High School Journal* (March 1968), pp. 241–247; and Kliebard, "Reappraisal: The Tyler Rationale," in A. A. Bellack and H. M. Kliebard, eds., *Curriculum and Evaluation* (Berkeley, Calif.: McCutchan, 1977), pp. 34–69.

95. Stone, *Ralph W. Tyler's Principles of Curriculum, Instruction, and Evaluation*. Also from conversations by one of the authors with John Beck, April 2, 1985; Ken Rehage, March 21, 1985.

96. Hilda Taba, *Curriculum Development: Theory and Practice* (New York: Harcourt, Brace, 1962); John I. Goodlad et al., *Curriculum Inquiry: The Study of Curriculum Practice* (New York: McGraw-Hill, 1979).

97. Bruce R. Joyce, "The Curriculum Worker of the Future," in R. M. McClure, ed., *The Curriculum: Retrospect and Prospect*, Seventieth Yearbook of the National Society for the Study of Education, Part I (Chicago: University of Chicago Press, 1971), pp. 312–313.

98. Eisner, *The Educational Imagination*, pp. 17–18.

99. Ibid., p. 20.

100. See McNeil, *Curriculum: A Comprehensive Introduction*, Alex Molnar, ed., *Current Thought on Curriculum* (Alexandria, Va.: Association for Supervision and Curriculum Development, 1985).

chapter 4

PSYCHOLOGICAL FOUNDATIONS
OF CURRICULUM

How do people learn? Psychology is concerned with this question. Curriculum specialists, however, ask, How does psychology contribute to curriculum? Psychology provides a basis for understanding the teaching and learning process. As long as teaching and learning are important considerations for curriculum specialists, then psychology will be important as well. Other questions that interest psychologists and curriculum specialists are: Why do learners respond as they do to the efforts of the teachers? How should the curriculum be organized to enhance learning?

Teaching and learning are interrelated, and psychology cements the relationship; it provides the theories and principles that influence teacher-student behavior within the context of the curriculum. For John Dewey, psychology was the basis for understanding how the individual learner interacts with objects and persons in the environment. The process goes on for life, and the quality of interaction determines the amount and type of learning. Ralph Tyler considered psychology to be a "screen" for helping determine what our objectives are and how our learning takes place.[1] More recently, Jerome Bruner linked psychology with modes of thinking that underlie the methods employed in various bodies of knowledge comprising specific disciplines. The goal of utilizing these methods is to formulate concepts, principles, and generalizations that form the structure of the disciplines.[2] In short, psychology is the unifying element of the learning process; it forms the basis for the methods, materials, and activities of learning, and it subsequently serves as the impetus for many curriculum decisions.

Historically, the major theories of learning have been classified into two groups: (1) behaviorist or association theories, the oldest one of which deals with various aspects of stimulus-response and reinforcers;

and (2) cognitive-field theories, which view the learner in relationship to the total environment. Some texts, including this one, separate cognitive-field theories into cognitive-developmental and phenomenological-humanistic theories. When cognitive theories are discussed separately, the learning process focuses on developmental stages, hierarchies of learning, and various forms of problem solving and creativity. The phenomenological aspects of learning deal with attitudes and feelings and entail more alternatives in learning.

BEHAVIORISM

The behaviorists, who represent traditional psychology, are rooted in philosophical speculation about the nature of learning—the ideas of Aristotle, Descartes, Locke, and Rousseau. They emphasize conditioning behavior and altering the environment to elicit selected responses from the learner. This theory has dominated twentieth-century psychology, especially during the first half of the century; it has recently returned as a major school to explain the learning process.

Connectionism.

One of the first Americans to conduct experimental testing of the stimulus-response (or classical conditioning) idea was Edward Thorndike. At Harvard, Thorndike began his work with animals, a course of experimentation other behaviorists adopted as well.[3] Thorndike defined learning as habit formation—as connecting more and more habits into a complex structure. He defined teaching, then, as arranging the classroom so as to enhance desirable connections as bonds.

Thorndike developed three major laws of learning: (1) the *Law of Readiness*—when a "conduction" unit is ready to conduct, to do so is satisfying and not to do so is annoying; (2) the *Law of Exercise*—a connection is strengthened in proportion to the number

of times it occurs, and in proportion to average intensity and duration; and (3) the *Law of Effect*—responses accompanied by satisfaction are important for strengthening the connection; conversely, responses accompanied by discomfort weaken the connection.[4]

The Law of Readiness suggests that when the nervous system is ready to conduct, it leads to a satisfying state of affairs; this has been misinterpreted by some educators as referring to educational readiness, such as readiness to read. The Law of Exercise provides justification for drill, repetition, and review, and is best illustrated today by behavioral modification and basic-skill instructional approaches. Although rewards and punishments were used in schools for centuries prior to Thorndike's formulation of the Law of Effect, his theory did make more explicit, and furnished justification for, what was already being done. B. F. Skinner's operant model of behavior, programmed instruction, and many current ideas based on providing satisfying experiences to the learner, as well as reinforcement in the form of feedback, are rooted in this law.

Thorndike maintained that: (1) behavior was influenced more likely by conditions of learning; (2) attitudes and abilities of learners could change (and improve) over time through proper stimuli; (3) instructional experiences could be designed and controlled; and (4) it was important to select appropriate stimuli or learning experiences that were integrated and consistent—and that reinforced each other. For Thorndike, no one subject was more likely than another to improve the mind; rather, learning was a matter of relating new learning to previous learning. Thus, the "psychology" of mental discipline was attacked, and this attack meant that there was no hierarchy of subject matter.

Although connectionism no longer enjoys the wide appeal it once had in the schools, practices related to it continue under different behaviorist labels. And even though Thorndike's model of learning has minimal direct influence today, many of his assumptions related to learning are evident nonetheless.

Thorndike's Influence: Tyler, Taba, and Bruner.

Coinciding with Thorndike's (1874–1949) theories, both Tyler and Taba maintained that learning had application and thus could be transferred to other situations.[5] This meant that rote learning and memorization of knowledge were unnecessary. The student could organize and classify information into existing mental schemata or patterns and use it in different situations. According to Thorndike, the best way to learn something was by the most direct method possible, which coincided with the behaviorist and logical approach outlined by Tyler and Taba. However, both Tyler and Taba disagreed with Thorndike's view of connections between specific stimuli and specific responses. Rather, they outlined a more generalized view of learning, one that corresponds with a cognitive approach. Whereas Bobbitt and Charters opted for the more precise behavioral approach to learning, along Thorndike's lines, which viewed objectives in context with highly specific habits to be acquired, Tyler and Taba were inclined to take Dewey's and Judd's approach: That learning was based on *generalizations* and the teaching of important *principles* (terms used by the latter four educators) to explain concrete phenomena.[6]

Note that both Tyler and Taba gave credit to Thorndike in their classic texts. Tyler's notation of Thorndike was in passing; however, but this corresponds to his general reluctance to give credit to other authorities for his own ideas. Nevertheless, he spent considerable space discussing connectionism and organizing learning principles along Thorndike's transfer theories. Taba devoted an entire chapter to "the transfer of learning," as well as the influence that Thorndike and others had on this learning theory. Like Thorndike, Taba argued that practice alone does not necessarily strengthen memory or the transfer of learning, which served to free the curriculum from the rigid roteness and drill of the past. "Since no program, no matter how thorough, can teach everything, the task of all education is to cause a maximum amount of transfer."[7] The idea was to develop content or methods that led to generalizations and that had wide transfer value; this led to Taba's advocating problem-solving and inquiry-discovery techniques.

The notions of "learning how to learn" and "inquiry discovery," although popularized by Bruner, are rooted in Thorndike. Thorndike, and later Bruner, assumed that learning that involves meaningful organization of experiences can be transferred more readily than learning acquired by rote.[8] The more abstract the principles and generalizations, the greater the possibility of transfer. (This also corresponds with Dewey's idea of reflective thinking, and the steps that he outlined for problem solving).

For Bruner, learning the structure of a discipline provided the basis for the specific transfer of learning. The abilities to learn and to recall and use some information later are directly related to the learner's having a structural pattern by which information can be transferred to new situations. Transfer of learning is much more frequent when learning is of a basic, general nature. One difference between Thorndike and Bruner should be noted, however. Whereas Thorndike found that no one subject was more important than another subject for meaningful learning, Bruner gave great emphasis to science and mathematics as the major disciplines for teaching structure. In this context, Thorndike was more progressive than Bruner—he gave equal weight and equal importance to various subjects—and he broke from traditional thinking about the hierarchy of subject matter.

Classical Conditioning.

The classical conditioning theory of learning emphasizes that learning consists of eliciting a response by means of previously neutral or inadequate stimuli; some neutral stimulus associated with an unconditioned stimulus at the time of response gradually acquires the ability to elicit the response. The classical conditioning experiment by Ivan Pavlov is widely known. In this experiment, a dog learned to salivate at the sound of a bell. The bell, a biologically neutral or inadequate stimulus, was being presented simultaneously with food, a biologically nonneutral or adequate stimulus. So closely were the two stimuli associated by the dog that the bell came to be substituted for the food, and the dog reacted to the bell as he originally had to the food.[9]

The implications for human learning were important. Some neutral stimulus (bell) associated with an unconditioned stimulus (food) at the time of the response gradually acquired the association to elicit the response (salivation). The theory has led to a wealth of laboratory investigations about learning and has become a focal point in social and political discussions—for example, Aldous Huxley's futuristic novel *Brave New World* and the movies *Manchurian Candidate* and *The Deer Hunter*.

On the American scene, James Watson used Pavlov's research as a foundation for building a new science of psychology based on *behaviorism.* The new science emphasized that learning was based on the science of behavior, what was observable or measurable, and not on cognitive processes. The laws of behavior were derived from animal and then human studies and were expected to have all the objectivity of the laws of science.[10]

For Watson and others, the key to learning was to condition the child in the early years of life, based on the method Pavlov had demonstrated for animals. Thus, Watson once boasted:

Give me a dozen healthy infants, well-informed, and my own specified world to bring them up and I'll guarantee to take anyone at random and train him to be any type of specialist I might select—a doctor, lawyer, artist . . . and yes, even into beggarman and thief, regardless of his talents, . . . abilities, vocations, and race.[11]

Operant Conditioning.

Perhaps more than any other recent behaviorist, B. Frederick Skinner has attempted to apply his theories to the classroom situation. Basing a major part of his theories on experiments with pigeons, Skinner distinguishes two kinds of responses: *elicited,* a response identified with a definite stimulus, and *emitted,* a response that is apparently unrelated to an identifiable stimulus. When a response is elicited, the behavior is termed *respondent.* When it is emitted, the behavior is *operant*—that is, no observable or measurable stimuli explain the appearance of the response.[12] In operant conditioning, the role of stimuli is less definite; often, the emitted behavior cannot be connected to a specific stimulus.

Reinforcers can be classified, also, as primary, secondary, or generalized. A *primary* reinforcer applies to any stimulus that helps satisfy a basic drive, such as for food, water, or sex. (This reinforcer is also paramount in classical conditioning.) A *secondary* reinforcer is important for people, such as getting approval from friends or teachers, receiving money, or winning school awards. Although secondary reinforcers do not satisfy primary drives, they can be converted into primary reinforcers. Because of the choice and range of secondary reinforcers, Skinner refers to them as *generalized* reinforcers. Classroom teachers have a variety of secondary reinforcers at their disposal, ranging from words of praise or smiles to words of admonishment or punishment.

Operant behavior will discontinue when it is not followed by reinforcement. Skinner classifies reinforcers as positive or negative. A *positive* reinforcer is simply the presentation of a reinforcing stimulus. A student receives positive reinforcement when a test paper is returned with a grade of A or a note that says "Keep up the good work." A *negative* reinforcement is the removal or withdrawal of a stimulus. When the teacher shouts to the class, "Keep quiet," and the students quiet down, the students' silence reinforces the teacher's shouting. Punishment, on the other hand, calls for the presentation of unpleasant or harmful stimuli or the withdrawal of a (positive) reinforcer, but it is not always a negative reinforcer.[13] Although Skinner believes in both positive and negative reinforcement, he rejects punishment because he feels it inhibits learning. He maintains that a considerable amount of teaching and learning is based on punitive procedures and faulty reinforcement—a practice that has led to disappointing results.[14]

Acquiring New Operants: Behavioral Modification. Skinner's approach of selective reinforcement, whereby only desired responses are reinforced, has wide appeal to educators because he has demonstrated its application to the instructional and learning process. An essential principle in the reinforcement interpretation of learning is the variability of human behavior, which makes change possible. Individuals can acquire *new operants*—that is, behavior can be shaped or modified and complex concepts can be taught to students. The individual's capability for the desired response is what makes the shaping of behavior or the learning possible. Behavior and learning can be shaped through a series of successive approximations or a sequence of responses that increasingly approximate the desired one. Thus, through a combination of reinforcing and sequencing desired responses, new behavior is shaped; this is what some people today refer to as *behavioral modification.*

Although behavioral modification approaches vary according to the student and the behavior being sought, they are widely used in conjunction with individualized-instructional techniques and classroom-management techniques—whereby student activities are specified, structured, paced, reinforced by rewards (and punishments if necessary), and frequently assessed in terms of the learning or behavior desired. With this approach, curriculum may be defined

by Popham and Baker's definition—that is, "all planned outcomes for which the school is responsible" and "the desired consequences of instruction."[15]

Programmed Learning. The approach of selective and sequential reinforcement to learning has led to Skinner's supplementary theories of programmed instruction and learning. Programmed learning provides a step-by-step approach to instruction with immediate, frequent, and regular reinforcement, which encourages the continued expenditure of stimulus-responses and small step learning that the teacher cannot efficiently provide. Skinner argues that a skill subject, such as elementary mathematics, might have as many as 25,000 contingencies of reinforcement, and that each combination might have to be reinforced several times before the child learns the curriculum. A single teacher cannot provide so many reinforcements for each child and also time them with the child's responses, much less deal with the multiple number of combinations. But this could be done effectively through programmed instruction and teaching machines.[16]

Studies of programmed instruction in the 1960s and 1970s failed to show significant advantages for the procedure. Also, teachers' resistance to being replaced by machines, and their belief that the method ignored conceptual thought and affective aspects of learning, led to criticism of the approach. The idea of programmed instruction has resurfaced, however, in context of the larger trend of computer-assisted instruction.

Behaviorism and Curriculum.

Behaviorism, as mentioned previously, exerts a major impact on education. Educators who are behaviorists and who are in charge of curricula use many principles of behavior to guide the creation of new programs. Although what can reinforce individual students differs, curriculum specialists can adopt procedures to increase the likelihood that each student will find learning relevant and enjoyable. When new topics or activities are introduced, connections should be built on positive experiences each student has had. Things about which each student is likely to have negative feelings should be identified and modified, if possible, to produce positive results.

The behaviorists believe that the curriculum should be organized so students experience success in mastering the subject matter. Of course, all curriculum persons, regardless of their psychological camps, have this view. The difference is that the behaviorists are highly prescriptive and diagnostic in their approach, and they rely on step-by-step and structured methods for learning. For students who have difficulty learning, curriculum and instruction can be broken down into small units with appropriate sequencing of tasks and reinforcement of desired behavior.

Behaviorist theories, it should be noted, have been criticized as describing learning too simply and mechanically—and as perhaps reflecting overreliance on classical animal experimentation. Human learning involves complex thinking processes beyond respondent conditioning (or recall and habit) and operant conditioning (or emitted and reinforced behavior).[17] A further concern is that there is little justification to define learning in terms of a "collection of small bits of behavior each of which has to be learned separately." Although behavior consists of organized sequences, it is not a collection of tiny bits of behavior. The stress on prescribed, lock-step procedures and tasks—and a "belief that a behavioral science should be definable in terms of observable events—[are] hardly justifiable today."[18]

The latter criticism may be an overstatement, because many behaviorists today recognize cognitive processes much more than classical or S-R theorists, and they are flexible enough to hold that learning can occur without the individual's having to act upon the environment or exhibit overt behavior.[19] To the extent that traditional behavioral theory can be faulted for having

to rely on identifying all behavior, many behaviorists today are willing to consider that cognitive processes partially explain aspects of learning.

Behaviorism is alive and well; it is linked to many current educational practices impacting on classrooms and schools. Writes Robert Glaser:

... much of the application of psychological theory currently going on in schools represents the earlier behavioristic approach. The concepts of behavioral objectives, and behavior modification, for example, now pervade all levels of education, including special education, elementary school instruction in basic literary skills, and personalized systems of instruction ... [20]

To the preceding list, we must add that behaviorist theory today is evidenced in the theories, principles, or trends related to (1) behavioral objectives in writing and assessing teaching, learning, and evaluation; (2) basic-skill training programs in language and reading, such as Bereiter-Englemann's Scientific Research Association (SRA), Direct Instructional Training (DISTAR), Survey, Question, Read, Recite and Review (SQ3R), Continuous Progress, and Self-Directed Study, mainly but not exclusively geared for learning-disabled students; (3) individualized education, such as Individually Prescribed Instruction (IPI), Individually Guided Education (IGE), Team Assisted Individualization (TAI), individual learning contracts, adaptive instruction, direct instruction, and mastery learning; (4) instructional design or system design models, such as instructional systems, management systems, instructional training models, or cybernetic models used by training psychologists, management trainers, and educational planners; (5) teacher-training programs, such as simulation teaching, microteaching, competency-based teacher education, and performance-based teacher education; (6) educational technology, including the previously mentioned programmed instruction as well as instructional television, computerized instruction, and instructional materials centers; and (7) planning and evaluation programs, including accountability plans, cost-effective audits, Management by Objectives (MBO), Planning-Programming-Budgeting-System (PPBS), Program, Evaluation, and Review Technique (PERT), Planning and Controlling Technique (PACT), and several input-transaction-output models of education evaluation.

The emphasis with these behavioral approaches and programs is on: (1) remediation, skill acquisition, basic or advanced learning (from learning to read to flying an airplane); (2) well-defined, short-term and long-term objectives; (3) matching instructional materials and media to the learners' abilities; (4) shaping behavior through prescribed tasks, step-by-step activities, close supervision of activities, and positive reinforcers; and (5) diagnosing, assessing, and reassessing the learners' needs, objectives, activities, tasks, and instruction.[21] In general, emphasis is on careful analyzing and sequencing of learning needs and behaviors. Task analysis, principles of sequencing, testing and diagnosing, drilling, and feedback are also characteristic. The learning conditions needed for successful outcomes are carefully planned. Most of these steps and/or sequences are shown in Figure 4-1.

Finally, four basic behavioral principles are followed with these approaches and programs: (1) time on task—time attending to tasks varies with the learners' abilities to master learning; (2) repetition—practice and drill are related to eliciting correct responses; (3) reinforcement—direct and mastery learning are strengthened when built on previous learning; and (4) shaping—behavior and learning can be more easily acquired through "successive approximations," or a sequence of responses that increasingly approximate the desired behavior or learning. These basic principles tend to coincide with the current principles and methods of individualized instruction, direct instruction, and mastery learning. These step-by-step procedures are behaviorist in nature, although some observers

might also claim they are cognitive, too.

Many of the traditional and contemporary ideas of behaviorism are popular not only in classrooms and schools but also in business and industry, government, and allied health professions. With these behaviorist models, it is common to reject value-laden, qualitative influences and to accept fixed quantitative components. Stripped of their scientific and technocratic concepts, however, the models are sometimes viewed to be narrow and mechanistic.[22] On the other hand, they are the types of designs and models that people who deal in prescribed tasks, numbers, and cost-effectiveness, and in precise boxes and bottom lines are inclined to favor. Many behaviorists today are aware of these rigid doctrines and thus integrate cognitive developmental theory with their approaches to human learning.

COGNITIVE DEVELOPMENT

Today most psychologists classify human growth and development as *cognitive, social, psychological,* and *physical*—and they note that learning in school is mainly cognitive in nature. Growth and development refer to changes in the structure and function of human characteristics. The changes occur in a steady progression; they are not uniform, but result from the interaction of inherited potential (heredity) and environment. Whether a person is a rapid or slow learner, has a pleasing or disturbing personality, is tall or short largely depend on the interaction of hereditary tendencies and environmental influences.

There is no agreed-upon way to determine exactly to what extent the characteristics (cognitive, social, psychological, and physical) of an individual are the result of inherited limitations or potential, or the harmful or favoring circumstances in the person's environment. In fact, there is considerable controversy about the extent or role of heredity versus environment in determining cognitive outcomes (i.e., IQ

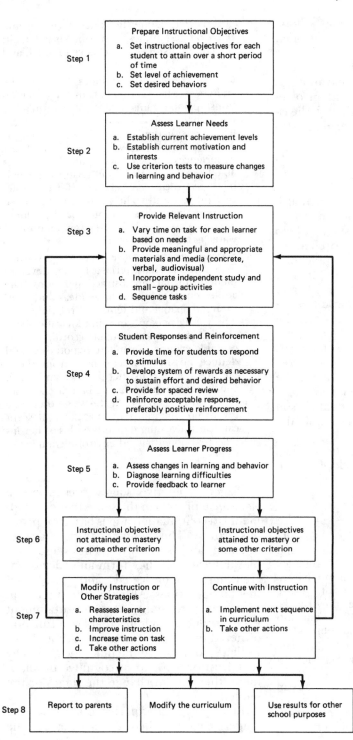

FIGURE 4-1 Elements of Behavioral Instruction*

*Implications for instructional design and instructional training models, individualized learning, direct instructional programs, mastery learning, etc.

scores and achievement scores) in school. Unfortunately, the evidence remains open to debate and to a variety of interpretations because of factors that cannot be adequately controlled and separated from one another. Most curriculum specialists avoid involvement in this controversy, even though the issue impacts on education and learning theories in general.

Cognitive Stages of Development.

Most cognitive theory is developmental— that is, it supposes that growth and development occur in progressive stages. Jean Piaget presents the most comprehensive view of this theory.[23] The Swiss psychologist's work camp came to the attention of American educators during the 1950s and 1960s—coinciding with the rising influence of cognitive developmental psychology, the environmentalist theories, and the compensatory education movement. (Remember, behaviorism was the first and foremost theory of behavior and learning during the first half of this century). Piaget is now probably the most quoted and influential person in the area of cognitive growth and child development.

Like many other investigators today, Piaget describes cognitive development in terms of stages from birth to maturity. The overall stages can be summarized as follows:[24]

1. *Sensorimotor Stage* (birth to age 2). The child progresses from reflex operations and undifferentiated surroundings to complex sensorimotor actions in relation to environmental patterns. The child comes to realize that objects have permanence; they can be found again. The child begins to establish simple relations between similar objects.

2. *Preoperational Stage* (ages 2 to 7). In this stage objects and events begin to take on symbolic meaning. For example, a chair is for sitting; clothing is what we wear. The child shows an increased ability to learn more complex concepts from experience as long as familiar examples are provided from which to extract

criteria that define the concept. (For example, oranges, apples, and bananas are fruit; the child must have the chance to touch and eat them.)

3. *Concrete Operations Stage* (ages 7 to 11). The child begins to organize data into logical relationships and gains facility in manipulating data in problem-solving situations. This learning situation occurs, however, only if concrete objects are available or if actual past experiences can be drawn upon. This child is able to make judgments in terms of reversibility and reciprocal relations (for example, that the left and right are relative to spatial relations) and conservation (that is, a long, narrow glass may hold the same amount of water as a short, wide one).

4. *Formal Operations Stage* (age 11 onwards). This stage is characterized by the development of formal and abstract operations. The adolescent is able to analyze ideas and comprehend spatial and temporal relationships. The young person can think logically about abstract data, evaluate data according to acceptable criteria, formulate hypotheses, and deduce possible consequences from them. He or she can construct theories and reach conclusions without having had direct experience in the subject. At this stage there are few or no limitations on what the adolescent can learn; learning depends on his or her intellectual potential and environmental experiences.

Piaget's cognitive stages presuppose a *maturation* process in the sense that development is a continuation and is based on previous growth. The mental operations are sequential and successive. The stages are hierarchical, and they form an order of increasingly sophisticated and integrated mental operations. Although the succession of stages is constant, stages of attainment vary within certain limits that are a function of heredity and environment. Although hereditary or environmental factors may speed up or slow down cognitive development, they do not change the stages or the sequence.

Environmental experience is the key to Piaget's cognitive theories, as it was also the crux of Dewey's learning principles. The educator's role involves "the shaping of actual experience by environing conditions" and knowing "what surroundings are conducive to having experiences that lead to growth."[25] Three basic cognitive processes form the basis of the environmental and experiential theories of both Piaget and Dewey. For Piaget, *assimilation* is the incorporation of new experiences into existing experiences; it represents a coordination of the child's experiences into his or her environment. But assimilation, alone, does not have the capacity to handle new situations and new problems in context with present cognitive structures. The child must organize and develop new cognitive structures in context with existing structures—that is, how he or she thinks. This is *accommodation,* whereby the child's existing cognitive structures are modified and adapted in response to his or her environment. *Equilibration* is the process of achieving balance between those things that were previously understood and those yet to be understood; it refers to the dual process of assimilation and accommodation of one's environment.[26]

This coincides with Dewey's "conceptions of situation and interaction [which] are inseparable from each other" and which form the basis of continuity.[27] For Dewey, a *situation* represents the experiences of the environment impacting on the child, similar to assimilation. *Interaction* is concerned with current or latitudinal transactions taking place between the child and his or her environment, including his or her capacities to establish meaning, similar to accommodation. *Continuity* refers to longitudinal learning or to situations and interactions that follow, similar to equilibration.

It is difficult to determine who influenced whom, because both Piaget and Dewey formulated most of their learning theories during the same period—in the 1920s and 1930s. Most authorities recognize Dewey's influence on Tyler, Taba, and Bruner, but Piaget had considerable influence on them, too.

Piaget's Influence: Tyler, Taba, and Bruner.

Piaget's (1896–1980) environmental theories (and Dewey's educational experiences) form the basis of Tyler's five principles of learning: (1) A student must have learning experiences that provide opportunity for practice and (2) satisfaction; (3) learning experiences must be appropriate for the student's present abilities; (4) many experiences can be used to attain the same educational objectives; and (5) the same learning experience will usually bring about several outcomes.[28]

Piaget's three cognitive processes (and Dewey's three educational experiences) also serve as a basis for Tyler's three methods of organizing learning experiences: (1) *continuity* suggests that the curriculum should possess vertical reiteration—that is, the skills and concepts should be "recurring" and there should be "continuing opportunity for these skills to be practiced"; (2) *sequence* suggests that the curriculum should include progressive development of understanding and that "each successive experience builds upon the preceding one [and] go more broadly and deeply into matters involved"; (3) *integration* "refers to the horizontal relationships of curriculum experiences" and means that the organization of experiences should be "unified . . . in relation to other elements" of the curriculum being taught and that subjects "should not be isolated . . . or taught as a single course" from the rest of the subjects.[29]

Taba not only spends considerable time reviewing Piaget's four stages of cognitive development, and the implications they have for intelligence and mental development, she also concludes that learning experiences must be "designed to match assessment of age levels at which certain processes of thought can occur." The idea is to transform complex concepts and subject matter into mental operations appropriate to the learner, and to develop a curriculum that provides for "increasing deeper and more formal levels" of thinking. "Building such a curriculum would naturally also involve a better understanding of the hierarchies [Piaget's stages] of concept formation and mental operations [and] a better understanding of the sequences in the development of thought."[30]

Similarly, Taba notes Piaget's cognitive processes—assimilation, accommodation, equilibration—in her discussion of generalizations and abstract thinking. She is concerned with organizing curricula and teaching new experiences so they are compatible with existing experiences (assimilation), moving from concrete experiences to concepts and principles (accommodation), and classifying and understanding new relationships (equilibration). The basis of what Taba calls "curriculum strategies for productive learning" are rooted in Piaget's synthesis of experiences into more complex forms and levels.

For Bruner, learning how things are related means learning the structure of knowledge. Such learning is based on Piaget's ideas of assimilation and accommodation.[31] The student who comes to grasp how bits of information within a subject area are related is able to continually and independently relate additional information to a field of study. Learning some "thing" should not be an end of learning, but, as Piaget and Dewey suggest, should be related to other aspects of subject matter and should be general enough to apply in other problems or situations. The structure of knowledge provides the basis for this kind of specific transfer of learning.

Piaget's equilibration forms the basis of Bruner's notion of a "spiral curriculum": Previous learning is the basis of subsequent learning, that learning should be continuous, and that subject matter is related to and built on a foundation (from grade to grade). Bruner is also influenced by Dewey, who uses the term *continuity* in learning to explain that what a person has already learned "becomes an instrument of understanding and dealing effectively with the situations that follow."[32] Bruner also uses the term continuity, in the same way as Piaget and Dewey, to describe the spiral curriculum: How subject matter and mental operations can be "continually deepened by using them in a progressively more complex form."[33]

Bruner considers that the act of learning consists of three related processes, similar to Piaget's cognitive processes:

1. *Acquisition* is the grasping of new information; it mainly corresponds to assimilation. Such information may be "new" to one's store of data; it may also replace previously acquired information, or it may merely refine or further qualify previous information.

2. *Transformation* is the individual's capacity to process new information so as to transcend or go beyond it. Means for processing such information are extrapolation, interpolation, or translation into another form. This process mainly overlaps with accommodation.

3. *Evaluation* is the determination of whether or not information has been processed in a way that renders it appropriate for dealing with a particular task or problem. It closely corresponds with equilibration.

What is educationally critical is that the teacher (in conjunction with learning psychologists and curriculum specialists) should determine the appropriate emphasis to be given to each of Piaget's stages of cognitive development and processes of thinking. Piaget's cognitive processes overlap with Tyler's methods, Taba's strategies, and Bruner's processes. The ability to match appropriate learning experiences with Piaget's four stages of development and three processes of thinking is especially important for elementary school teachers. It is during the elementary school period, to be sure, when children move from the second stage to the third and fourth stages.

Levels of Thinking.

Educators concerned with learning are also concerned with thinking. Thinking can be classified in various ways. One way is by levels that are both theoretical and developmental in nature. Levels of thinking are not necessarily hierarchical in nature, although we might expect them to be. Levels can also be neutral and not sequential. The first example here is hierarchical; the second is nonhierarchical.

Hierarchical Learning. Robert Gagné has presented a hierarchical arrangement of eight types of learning sets or capabilities that has become a classic model. The first five may be defined as behavioral operations and the last three may be considered cognitive operations. Problem solving is considered the highest form of thinking. The capabilities are based on prerequisite conditions, resulting in a cumulative process of learning. The seven types of learning and examples of each follow:[34]

1. *Signal Learning* (classical conditioning, a response to a given signal). Example: Fear response to a rat.
2. *Stimulus Response* (operant conditioning [S-R], a response to a given stimulus). Example: Student's response to the command, "Please sit."
3. *Motor Chains* (linking together two or more S-R verbal units to develop a more complex skill). Example: Learning a foreign language.
4. *Multiple Discriminations* (responding in different ways to different items of a particular set). Example: Discriminating between grass and trees.
5. *Concepts* (reacting to stimuli in an abstract way). Examples: animals, grammar, and so on.
6. *Rules* (chaining two or more concepts). Examples: Animals have offspring. An adjective modifies a noun.
7. *Problem Solving* (combining known rules or principles into new elements to solve a problem). Example: Finding the area of a triangle given the dimensions of two sides.

Structure of Intellect. The complexity of thinking permits alternative descriptions or what we call the structure of intellect or mental operations. A model of multiple cognitive factors by J. P. Guilford classifies mental abilities three-dimensionally.[35] It comprises:

1. *Operations:* mental operations dealing with the processing of certain content.
   a. Evaluation (making assessments or decisions)
   b. Convergent thinking (generating relationships and analogies)
   c. Divergent thinking (creative thinking and production)
   d. Memory (remembering of knowledge)
   e. Cognition (knowledge)
2. *Products:* mental operations related to the application of operations to content.
   a. Units (comprehending figural, symbolic, and semantic data)
   b. Classes (classifying units)
   c. Relations (perceiving connections between items)
   d. Systems (a coherent body of knowledge)
   e. Transformations (changes in preexisting data)
   f. Implications (association of previously unrelated items)
3. *Contents:* mental operations confined to information and comprehension.
   a. Figural (material perceived by the senses)
   b. Symbolic (letters and digits organized in a general system—that is, an alphabet or number system)
   c. Semantic (a form of ideas or verbal meanings)
   d. Behavioral content (social intelligence or understanding of oneself and others)

These three dimensions, represented graphically in Figure 4-2 by a $5 \times 6 \times 4$ geometric model of five operations, six products, and four contents, yield 120 cells or distinct mental abilities. By 1985, more than one hundred abilities had been recognized and separated by factor analysis. Guilford concluded that the vacant cells indicate uncovered mental abilities. It is possible, how-

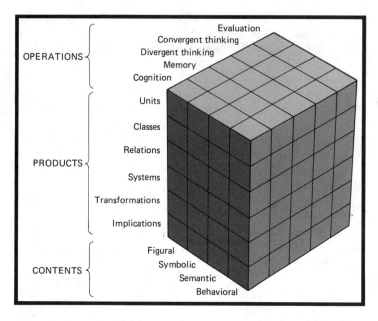

FIGURE 4-2 The Structure of Intellect
Source: From J. P. Guilford, *The Nature of Human Intelligence* (New York: McGraw-Hill, 1967), p. i.

ever, that our cognitive tests do not measure the other mental operations or that such abilities do not exist. The Guilford model is highly abstract and theoretical and involves administering and grading many extra tests. Rather than a single index of IQ (or of aptitude) we are required to report several scores. Thus, the theoretical issues surrounding intelligence and cognitive operations take on added complexity. The model of 120 specific abilities requires curriculum specialists, test specialists, and learning theorists to consider multiple thinking processes, as well as a three-dimensional model for learning with several categories under each dimension.

Problem Solving/Creative Thinking.

Since the Sputnik era, many curriculum theorists have renewed their examination of various aspects of problem solving and creative thinking. The common belief is that these methods of thinking constitute a highly sophisticated form of processing information. Some curricularists, especially those who talk about the structure of disciplines, feel they are complementary: Students must be given supportive conditions in which they can develop different forms of creativity, but at the same time they must be held responsible for confirming or disproving the value or correctness of their assumptions. Problem-solving procedures are their means of doing so, for they do not lead to creative discovery, but rather they establish the validity of the discoveries. In this context problem solving and creative thinking are considered methods of inquiry conducive of scholars and scientists.[36]

An opposing view is that problem solving (in the past referred to as reflective thinking and today called critical thinking) is based on inductive thinking, analytical procedures, and *convergent* processes. Creative thinking, which includes intuitiveness and discovery, is based on deductive thinking, originality, and *divergent* processes. Problem solving, in this second view, is conducive to rational and scientific thinking and is the *method* of arriving at a solution to a task or to a correct answer, whereas creativity is conducive to artistic and literary thinking and is a *quality* of thought. There is no right solution or answer when creativity is the goal.

Actually, problem solving and creativity may or may not go hand in hand. Some people perform well on problems without being creative, and others can be highly creative but do poorly in problem-solving tasks. But the fact that we can distinguish between both thinking processes does not necessarily suggest that they are mutually independent of each other; research does suggest that a creative individual is just as likely or unlikely to be a good problem solver, and, in reverse, that a good problem solver may or may not be creative.[37]

Perhaps the most important thing to note is that these complex cognitive tasks should be taught as generic skills and principles—relevant for all subject matter. The idea is to develop metacognitive strategies which students can transfer to many curriculum areas and content materials, as opposed to repeating the mistakes of an earlier period whereby experts claimed that each discipline had its own structure and thinking manner. The need is to develop reflective-thinking, critical-thinking, intuitive-thinking, and discovery-thinking strategies which fit a wide variety of course and content situations, not for mathematicians or historians to claim their own metacognitive strategies.

Reflective Thinking. Problem solving played a major role in Dewey's overall concept of education. Dewey not only believed that problem-solving activities in school developed intelligence and social growth, but also that the skills developed in problem solving could be transferred to resolving everyday problems of society. Dewey's concept of problem solving is rooted in his idea of the scientific method and has become a classic model:

1. Becoming aware of a difficulty (or a felt difficulty).
2. Identifying the problem.
3. Assembling and classifying data and formulating hypotheses.
4. Accepting or rejecting the tentative hypotheses.
5. Formulating conclusions and evaluating them.[38]

Dewey's problem-solving method encourages systemic interpretation of everyday experiences through the reasoning process. This method coincides with his strong belief in a science of education (see Chapter 3). Because Dewey considers that the chief function of the school is to improve the reasoning process, he recommends adapting this problem-solving method to other subjects at all levels. Problems selected for study should be derived from student interests, for a student who is not motivated will not really perceive a problem.

Others, however, criticize the problem-solving method as producing the misconception that scientists have a be-all and end-all formula for finding answers to practical problems. James Conant, for example, defines the problem-solving approach as a series of six steps that can be used both by experimental scientists in the laboratory and by laypersons confronted with everyday situations that need to be solved:

1. Recognizing a problem and formulating objectives.
2. Collecting relevant information.
3. Formulating an hypothesis.
4. Deducing from the hypothesis.
5. Using tests by actual trial.
6. Depending on the outcome, accepting, modifying, or discarding the hypothesis.[39]

Conant believes that problem solving is not enhanced by science. The scientific method is not readily applied to everyday problems, he claims; rather, science has simply borrowed the method of testing hypotheses from the practical person. Whereas Dewey's model, developed for all disciplines, involved social problem solving, Conant's model was used by the advocates of science and math (not social thinking) during the Sputnik era. The predominant notion then was that each discipline had its own method of problem solving.

Both models, and their derivatives, are considered by some researchers to be incomplete. First, the analysis occurs after the person has solved the problem. Second, the models ignore intuition, insight, and ideas that are nonlogical and perhaps even personal—in short, procedures that cannot be easily observed or tested but that are sometimes used successfully in problem solving. Present theories of cognitive processes suggest that logical and observable steps are not always used in problem solving, nor are the steps always related. Finally, different problem-solving techniques are used for different subjects or disciplines and different grade levels. Presumably, they have common features, but they also involve specific variance.

Critical Thinking. Critical thinking and thinking skills are the terms used today to connote problem solving. This old idea under a new label is endorsed by the outpouring of articles in the professional literature, by a host of conferences and reports on the subject, and by the majority of states' taking steps to bolster critical thinking for all students.

Although several teaching procedures, teacher-training programs, and taxonomies of critical thinking have surfaced in recent years, the latest opinion is that critical thinking is a form of intelligence that can be taught (it is not a fixed entity). The leading proponents of this school are Matthew Lipman and Robert Sternberg. Lipman seeks to foster thirty critical skills, generally designed for elementary school grades. Students are encouraged to develop, for example: (1) concepts; (2) generalizations; (3) cause-effect relationships; (4) allogistic inferences; (5) consistencies and contradictions; (6) analogies; (7) part-whole and whole-part connections; (8) problem formulations; (9) reversibility of logical statements; and (10) applications of principles to real-life situations.[40]

In a series of texts, called *Philosophy for Children,* Lipman outlines a strategy for teaching critical thinking. Children spend a considerable portion of their time thinking about thinking, and about ways in which effective thinking is distinguished from ineffective thinking. After reading the stories in the text, children engage in classroom discussions and exercises that encourage them to adapt the thinking process depicted in the stories.[41] The assumption behind Lipman's program is that children are by nature interested in such philosophical issues as truth, fairness, and personal identity. Children can and should learn to think for themselves, to explore alternatives to their own viewpoints, to consider evidence, and to make distinctions and draw conclusions.[42]

Sternberg seeks to foster many of the same intellectual skills, listed in Table 4-1, albeit in a very different way. He points out three mental processes that enhance critical thinking: (1) *meta components*—high order mental processes used to plan what we are going to do, monitor what we are doing, and evaluate what we are doing; (2) *performance components*—the actual steps or strategies we take; and (3) *knowledge-acquisition components*—processes used to relate old material to new material and to apply and use new material.[43] Sternberg does not outline a "how" approach like Lipman; rather, he outlines general guidelines for developing and/or selecting a program.

Note that some educators, including most phenomenologists and humanistic theorists, contend that teaching a person to think is like teaching someone to swing a golf club or tennis racket; it involves a holistic approach, not a piecemeal effort, as implied by Lipman and Sternberg. "Trying to break thinking skills into discrete units may be helpful for diagnostic proposals," according to two critics, "but it does not seem to be the right way to move in the teaching of such skills." Critical thinking is too complex of a mental operation to divide into small processes; the approach depends on "a student's total intellectual functioning, not on a set of narrowly defined skills."[44]

Perhaps the major criticism has been raised by the method's own proponent. Sternberg cautions that the kinds of critical thinking skills we stress in school, and the

TABLE 4-1   Principal Thinking Skills Underlying Intelligent Behavior

1. Recognizing and defining the nature of a problem
2. Deciding upon the processes needed to solve the problem
3. Sequencing the processes into an optimal strategy
4. Deciding upon how to represent problem information
5. Allocating mental and physical resources to the problem
6. Monitoring and evaluating one's solution processing
7. Responding adequately to external feedback
8. Encoding stimulus elements effectively
9. Inferring relations between stimulus elements
10. Mapping relations between relations
11. Applying old relations to new situations
12. Comparing stimulus elements
13. Responding effectively to novel kinds of tasks and situations
14. Effectively automatizing information processing
15. Adapting effectively to the environment in which one resides
16. Selecting environments as needed to achieve a better fit of one's abilities and interests to the environment
17. Shaping environments so as to increase one's effective utilization of one's abilities and interests

Source: From Robert J. Sternberg, "How Can We Teach Intelligence?" *Educational Leadership* (September 1984), p. 40. Reprinted with permission of the Association for Supervision and Curriculum Development and Robert J. Sternberg. Copyright (c) 1984 by the Association for Supervision and Curriculum Development. All rights reserved.

way we teach them, "inadequately prepares students for the kinds of problems they will face in everyday life."[45] We believe that because our critical skill programs stress "right" answers and "objectively scorable" test items, they are removed from real-world relevance. Most problems in real life have social, economic, and psychological implications. They involve interpersonal relations and judgments about people, personal stress and crisis, and dilemmas involving choice, responsibility, and survival. How we deal with illness, aging, or death (someone else's or even our own eventual demise), or with simple things like starting new jobs or meeting new people, has little to do with the way we think in class or on critical thinking tests. But they are important matters. By stressing cognitive skills in classrooms and schools, we ignore the realities and milieu of life. Except for college, being an A student or good problem solver in school guarantees us very little in real life.

Creative Thinking.   Standardized tests do not always accurately measure creativity; in fact, we have difficulty agreeing on what

creativity is and who is creative. There are many types of creativity—artistic, musical, scientific, manual, and so on—yet we tend to talk about creativity as an all-encompassing term. Creative students are often puzzling to teachers. They are difficult to characterize; their novel answers frequently seem threatening to teachers, and their behavior often deviates from what is considered "normal." Sometimes, teachers discourage creativity and punish creative students. Curriculum specialists also tend to ignore them in their curriculum plans (subject matter or course descriptions, subject guides, and subject materials and activities), because they represent only a small proportion (about 2 to 5 percent, depending on the definition) of the student population. Also, curriculum specialists have little money earmarked to support special programs and personnel for these students. Frequently, educators lump creative children in with highly intelligent or gifted children, even though high intelligence and high creativity are not necessarily related; and there are many types of creative children.

In a cross-cultural study, E. P. Torrance

used sixty-two statements to investigate elementary and secondary teachers' ratings of the "ideal" creative personality. From ninety-five to 375 teachers in each of the following countries were sampled: United States, Germany, India, Greece, and the Philippines.

Table 4-2 indicates some of the cultural values that encourage and discourage creativity. For example, the United States and Germany (technologically developed countries) both encourage independent thinking, industriousness, and curiosity; these traits do not appear important in the less developed countries. Greece and the Philippines reward remembering, which connotes convergent thinking, but many American researchers consider this type of thinking anticreative. Teachers in all the countries, especially the less developed ones, stress that being well-liked, considerate of others, and obedient are important ideals.

There is little agreement on a definition of creativity except that all believe it represents a quality of mind: It comprises both a cognitive and humanistic component in learning; although no one agrees upon an exact mix, it is probably more cognitive than humanistic. According to Carl Rogers, the essence of creativity is its novelty, and, hence, we have no standard by which to judge it. In fact, the more original the product, the more likely it is to be judged by contemporaries as foolish or evil.[46] The individual creates primarily because creating is self-satisfying and because the behavior or product is self-actualizing. (This is the humanistic side of creativity, even though the process and intellect involved in creating are cognitive in nature). Eric Fromm defines the creative attitude as (1) the willingness to be puzzled—to orient oneself to something new without frustration; (2) the ability to concentrate; (3) the ability to experience oneself as a true originator of one's acts; and (4) the willingness to accept conflict and tension caused by the climate of opinion or lack of tolerance for creative ideas.[47]

For teachers the definition of creativity

TABLE 4-2 Selected Characteristics of an "Ideal" Creative Personality as Rated by Teachers of Different Cultures

United States	Germany	India	Greece	Philippines
Independent thinking	Sincerity	Curiosity	Energetic	Industriousness
Curiosity	Sense of humor	Obedience	Strives for distant goals	Obedience
Sense of humor	Industriousness	Does work on time	Thoroughness	Courtesy
Consideration of others	Independent thinking	Courtesy	Sincerity	Health
Industriousness	Willingness to attempt difficult tasks	Health	Nonconforming	Consideration of others
Receptivity to others' ideas	Independent judgment	Self-confidence	Remembers well	Does work on time
Determination	Curiosity	Self-starting	Health	Self-confidence
Self-starting	Self-confidence	Industriousness	Altruism	Remembering well
Sincerity	Health	Affectionateness	Self-confidence	Willingness to accept judgments of authorities
Thoroughness	Adventurousness	Determination	Courtesy	Affectionateness

Source: From E. Paul Torrance, *Rewarding Creative Behavior: Experiments in Classroom Creativity*, 1965, p. 228. Reprinted by permission of Prentice-Hall, Englewood Cliffs, New Jersey.

comes down to how new ideas have their origin. We are dealing with both logical and observable processes and unconscious and unrecognizable processes. The latter processes give teachers trouble in the classroom, and sometimes lead to misunderstanding between teachers and creative students. For some students the methods of Edison and Einstein seem appropriate—theoretical, deductive, and developmental. For others, creativity may correspond more closely to the insights and originality of Kafka, Picasso, Bob Dylan, or Michael Jackson. Because few curriculum specialists think like the Edison or Kafka groups, there is a void, a real lack of attention to these students in our curriculum literature.

Intuitive Thinking.

Intuitive thinking is not new. But this thinking process was either discouraged, because traditional pedagogical practices relied instead on facts and rote, or ignored, because it was difficult to define and measure. Bruner popularized the idea in his book about the *Process of Education*. The good thinker not only has knowledge, but also an intuitive grasp of the subject. Intuitive thinking is part of a process of discovery that is similar to the scholar-specialist's engaging in hunches, playing with ideas, and understanding relationships so that he or she can make discoveries or add to the storehouse of new knowledge.

The following explanation by Bruner is a good description of how some people work with intuitive thinking:

Intuitive thinking characteristically does not advance in careful, well-defined steps. Indeed, it tends to involve maneuvers based seemingly on implicit perception of the total problem. The thinker arrives at an answer, which may be right or wrong, with little, if any, awareness of the process by which he reached it. He rarely can provide an adequate account of how he obtained his answer, and he may be unaware of just what aspects of the problem situation he was responding to. Usually intuitive thinking rests on familiarity with the domain of knowledge involved and with its structure, which makes it possible for the thinker to leap about skipping steps and employing short cuts in a manner that requires later rechecking of conclusions by more analytical means.[48]

This has very little to do with a convergent or step-by-step approach. It speaks of the revelation of discovery—the "sheer knowing the stuff"—but coupled with the ability to put knowledge to use and to find new ways in which to fit things together. According to this interpretation, problem solving and free discovery come together; knowledge is dynamic, built around the process of discovery, without precise steps or rules to follow.

Discovery Learning.

Since the Sputnik era, the inquiry-discovery method has been examined in conjunction with the discipline-centered curriculum—as a unifying element related to the knowledge and methodology of a domain of study. Taba, Bruner, Phenix, and Inlow were products of this era[49] (the latter's influence on curriculum planning and instructional methods is underrated and almost ignored by present curricularists). Taba was influenced by Bruner, Phenix was to a lesser extent influenced by both of them, and Inlow was influenced by all three. (Their respective books, including the content and citations, illustrate these relationships.) All four educators were more concerned about *how* we think than with *what* we think or what knowledge we possess.

Although Bruner went to great lengths to fuse the inquiry-discovery methods in the sciences and mathematics, Phenix, Taba, and Inlow claimed that the discovery method was separate from inquiry and that both methods of thinking cut across all subjects (not just science and math). Phenix, for example, proposed that discovery was a form of inquiry that dealt with new knowledge, hypothesis, and hunches. Most of his efforts were spent defining inquiry, which he claimed was the method of deriving, organizing, analyzing, and evaluating knowledge (like problem solving). Inquiry was considered to bind together all the separate aspects of knowledge into a coherent discipline; it was viewed as more important than discovery.

Taba and Inlow contrasted discovery learning with verbal and concrete learning. Most of traditional learning was described as a process of *transmitting* verbal and concrete information to the learner; it was authority-centered, subject-centered, highly organized, also flexible and open. Discovery, on the other hand, involved extensive exploration of the concrete at the elementary level. For older students, according to Inlow, it involved "problem identification, data organization and application, postulation, . . . evaluation and generalization."[50] For Taba, it meant "abstracting, deducing, comparing, contrasting, inferring, and contemplating."[51] All of these discovery processes are rational and logical, and thus infer a problem-solving or convergent component. Inlow and Taba, however, were quick to point out that discovery also included divergent thinking and intuitiveness; Taba also added creativity and limitless learning to help define discovery.

Bruner, who is well known for elaborating the idea of discovery, defined it as the learning that takes place when students are not presented with subject matter in its final form, when subject matter is not organized by the teacher but by the students themselves. Discovery is the formation of coding systems, whereby students discover relationships that exist among the data presented.

The most obvious characteristic of discovery as a teaching technique is perhaps that after the initial stages it requires less teacher input or guidance than do other strategies. Discovery is, in fact, less teacher-centered than other approaches to learning, and students assume more responsibility for their own learning.[52] Recall the influence of Thorndike's theory of transfer on Bruner. In order to be part of discovery, learning must be transferable. Increased transferability is evidenced by what Bruner calls "in-

tellectual potency"—an elusive term that infers a high degree of intelligence. Bruner also contends that discovery learning leads to greater skill acquisition in problem solving (in Bruner's terms, a learner acquires the heuristics of discovery) and motivation (a shift from extrinsic to intrinsic reward). Successful discovery experiences make the learner more capable of discovering new experiences and more willing to learn for the sake of learning.

Cognition and Curriculum.

Most curriculum specialists, and learning theorists and teachers, tend to be cognitive-oriented, because: (1) the cognitive approach constitutes a logical method for organizing and interpreting learning; (2) the approach is rooted in the tradition of subject matter; and (3) educators have been trained in cognitive approaches and better understand them. Even many contemporary behaviorists, as previously mentioned, incorporate cognitive processes in their theories of learning. Because learning in school involves cognitive processes, and because schools emphasize the cognitive domain of learning, it follows that most educators feel that learning is synonymous with cognitive-developmental theory.

The teacher who has a structured style of teaching would prefer the problem-solving method, based on reflective thinking and/or the scientific method. Most curricularists tend to be cognitive-oriented in their approach to learning, but we feel that this learning model is incomplete and that something gets lost in its translation to the classroom. For example, we feel that many schools are not pleasant places for learners and that the "quality of life" in classrooms can be improved.

We are reminded of John Goodlad's description of schools. After visiting more than 1000 elementary and secondary schools, Goodlad concluded that most students are not engaged in problem-solving tasks, but passive-rote tasks, and that they are rarely asked to "initiate anything . . . or create their own products."[53] In short, real and meaningful learning rarely takes place in schools. Although Goodlad is a cognitive curricularist, he finds that the teaching-learning process boils down to teachers' predominantly talking and students' mostly responding to the teachers. The workbook and textbook are the main sources of instruction; rarely are students permitted to talk to each other, and rarely do they become involved in problem-solving or creative activities. According to Goodlad, much of the so-called learning theories and educational reforms have been blunted at the classroom door.

We are also influenced by John Holt, a humanistic and radical critic of schools.[54] Holt points out that the schooling process encourages *producers* (students who seek to please adults and find right answers, but who, if they fail to obtain the right answers, plunge into despair) and discourages *thinkers* (students who are not concerned with pleasing adults, who can grapple with ideas, cope with uncertainty, and solve problems under consideration).

In a system run primarily on right answers, those who are thinkers find school an unpleasant place. Many students cannot bear to be wrong. They must be right; they wait for the magic words "right" or "wrong." According to Holt, those who produce the right answers are relieved. Those who are wrong no longer want to think about the problem; they give up. When teachers ask questions and they do not know the right answers, they stall, make up excuses, and, in some cases, become "paralyzed" with fear. Thinkers, on the other hand, are curious, challenged by problems rather than frustrated, and independent and inclined to risk—so that they do not need teacher approval. The trouble is, many teachers and schools do not know what to do with thinkers.

Curriculum specialists must understand that school should be a place where students are not afraid of asking questions, not afraid of being wrong, not afraid of not pleasing their teachers, and not afraid of taking cognitive risks and playing with ideas. With all our cognitive theory, we would expect students to want to learn and know how to learn, but we observe, both in the literature and in the real world of schools, that after a few years of school most students have to be cajoled to learn and have learned how not to learn. So-called "successful" students become cunning strategists in a game of beating the system and figuring out the teacher. To be sure, schools should be more humane places where students can fulfill their human potentials. With this in mind, we turn to humanistic learning.

PHENOMENOLOGY/HUMANISTIC PSYCHOLOGY

Traditional psychologists do not recognize phenomenology or humanistic psychology as a school of psychology, much less a wing or form of psychology. Their contention is that most psychologists are humanistic, because they are concerned with people and with bettering society. Moreover, they claim that the label *humanism* should not be used as a mask for generalizations based on little knowledge and "soft" research.[55] Nonetheless, a number of observers have viewed phenomenology, sometimes called humanistic psychology, as a "third force" learning theory—after behaviorism and cognitive development.[56] Phenomenology is sometimes considered a cognitive theory because it emphasizes the total organism or person. The distinct difference between the cognitive and affective aspects of learning, however, have led us to separate these domains.

The most obvious contrast with the mechanistic and deterministic view of behaviorism is the phenomenological version of learning, illustrated by the individual's awareness that he or she is an "I" who has feelings and attitudes, who experiences stimuli, and who acts upon the environment. We carry some sense of control and freedom to produce certain conditions in our environment. When we speak of this awareness, we are speaking of the self. The study of immediate experiences as one's reality is called "phenomenology" and is influenced by, and perhaps even based on, an existentialist philosophy. Most phenomenological ideas are derived from and for clinical settings; nevertheless, educators are becoming aware that they have implications for the classroom as well.

Phenomenologists point out that the way we look at ourselves is basic for understanding our behavior. What we do, even to what extent we learn, is determined by our concepts of ourselves.[57] If someone thinks he or she is Napoleon, he or she will act like Napoleon, or at least convey his or her concept of Napoleon. If someone thinks he or she is dull or stupid, his or her cognitive performance will be influenced by that self-concept.

Gestalt Theory.

Phenomenologist ideas are rooted in early field theories and field-ground ideas, which view the total organism in relationship to the environment, or what is called the "field," and the learner's perception of this environment and the personal meaning in a given situation. Learning must be explained in terms of the "wholeness" of the problem. Human beings do not respond to isolated stimuli, but to an organization or pattern of stimuli.

Field theories are derived from Gestalt psychology of the 1930s and 1940s. The German word *Gestalt* connotes shape, form, and configuration. In this context, various stimuli are perceived in relation to others within a field. What one perceives will determine the meaning he or she gives to the field; likewise, one's solutions to other problems will depend on his or her recognition of relationships between individual stimuli and the whole.[58] This is considered the "field-ground" relationship, and how the individual perceives this relationship determines behavior. Perception alone is not a crucial factor in learning; rather, the crucial factor is structuring and restructuring the field relationships to form evolving patterns.

On this basis, learning is complex and abstract. When confronted with a learning situation, the learner analyzes the problem, discriminates between essential and nonessential data, and perceives relationships. The environment is continuously changing, and thus the learner is continuously reorganizing his or her perceptions. In terms of teaching, learning is conceived as a selective process by the student. Curriculum specialists must understand that learners will perceive something in relation to the whole; what they perceive and how they perceive it is related to their previous experiences.

Maslow: Self-Actualizing Persons.

Abraham Maslow, a well-known phenomenologist, has set forth a classic theory of human needs. Based on a hierarchy, and in order of importance, the needs are:

1. *Pyschological Needs.* Those necessary to maintain life: needs for food, water, oxygen, and rest.
2. *Safety Needs.* Those necessary for routine and the avoidance of danger.
3. *Love and Belonging Needs.* Those related to affectionate relations with people in general and to a place in the group.
4. *Esteem Needs.* Those related to receiving recognition as a worthwhile person.
5. *Self-Actualization Needs.* Those related to becoming the best person one can be, to develop one's fullest potential.
6. *Knowing and Understanding Needs.* Those more evident in persons of high intelligence than those of limited intelligence, a wanting to learn and organize intellectual relationships.[59]

These needs have obvious implications for teaching and learning. A child whose basic needs—say, love or esteem—are not filled will not be interested in acquiring knowledge of the world. The child's goal to satisfy the need for love or esteem takes precedence over learning and directing his or her behavior. To some extent, Maslow's ideas that have classroom implications are based on Pestalozzi and Froebel, who believed in the importance of human emotions and a methodology based on love and trust.

Maslow coined the term *humanistic psychology*, which stresses three major principles: (1) centering attention on the experiencing person, and thus focusing on experience as the primary phenomenon in learning; (2) emphasizing such human qualities as choice, creativity, values, and self-realization, as opposed to thinking about people in mechanistic (or behaviorist) terms and learning in cognitive terms; and (3) showing ultimate concern for the dignity and worth of people and an interest in the psychological development and human potential of learners as individuals.[60]

The teacher's and curriculum maker's role in this scheme is to view the student as a whole person. The student is to be positive, purposeful, active, and involved in life experiences (not S-R or only cognitive experiences). Learning is to be a lifelong educational process. Learning is experimental, its essence being freedom and its outcome full human potential and reform of society.

The goal of education, for Maslow, is to produce a healthy and happy learner who can accomplish, grow, and actualize his or her human self. Self-actualization, and its attendant sense of fulfillment, is what the learner should strive for and what teachers should stress in the classroom situation. Self-actualizing people are psychologically healthy and mature. Maslow characterized them as: (1) having an efficient perception of reality; (2) being at ease and comfortable with themselves and with others; (3) not overwhelmed with guilt, shame, or anxiety; (4) relatively spontaneous and natural; and (5) problem-centered rather than ego-centered.[61] Rather than dealing with the scientific approach of isolating variables for research examination, as the behaviorists and cognition people do, Maslow preferred to deal with the "whole person," which accordingly he referred to as a holistic approach. This holistic approach guides Maslow's followers—both curriculum workers and teachers.

Rogers: Nondirective and Therapeutic Learning.

Carl Rogers, perhaps the most noted phenomenologist, has established counseling procedures and methods for facilitating learning. His ideas are based on those of early field theorists and field-ground theories; reality is based on what the individual learner perceives: "Man lives by a perceptual 'map' which is not reality itself."[62]

This concept of reality should make the teacher aware that the level and kind of response to a particular experience will differ among children. Children's perceptions, which are highly individualistic, influence their learning and behavior in class—for example, whether they will see meaning or confusion in what is being taught.

Rogers views therapy as a method of learning to be utilized by the curriculum worker and teacher. He believes that positive human relationships enable people to grow; therefore, interpersonal relations among learners are just as important as cognitive scores.[63] The teacher's role in nondirective teaching is that of a facilitator, very much like the existentialist teacher, who has close professional relationships with students and guides their human growth and development. In this role, the teacher helps students explore new ideas about their lives, their school work, their relations with others, and their interaction with society. The counseling method assumes that students are willing to be responsible for their own behavior and learning, that they can make intelligent choices, and that they can share ideas with the teacher and communicate honestly as people who are confronted with decisions about themselves and about life in general.

The curriculum is concerned with process, not products; personal needs, not subject matter; psychological meaning, not cognitive scores; and changing environmental situations (in terms of space and time), not predetermined environments. Indeed, there must be freedom to learn, not restrictions or preplanned activities. The psychological and social conditions of the environment limit or enhance a person's field or life space. A psychological field or life space is a necessary consideration in the curriculum, and everything that is taking place in relation to a specific learner at a given time gives meaning to the field and eventually to learning.

Value Clarification.

Value clarification, sometimes called value building, is part of the teacher-learning process. Value clarificationists have a high regard for creativity, freedom, and self-realization. They prefer that learners explore their own preferences and make their own choices.

The values a person holds depend on many factors, including environment, education, and personality. People often suffer from value confusion—whose symptoms are apathy, uncertainty, inconsistency, overconforming, or overdissenting.[64] Value clarification is designed to help persons overcome value confusion and become more positive, purposeful, and productive, as well as to have better interpersonal relations.

In a popular text, Louis Raths and his colleagues outlined the process of valuing: (1) choosing freely . . . ; (2) choosing from alternatives . . . ; (3) choosing thoughtfully . . . ; (4) prizing and cherishing . . . ; (5) affirming . . . ; (6) acting upon choices . . . ; [and] (7) repeating . . . as a pattern of life."[65] They developed various dialogue strategies, writing strategies, discussion strategies, and activity strategies for teaching valuing on a how-to-do basis. Table 4-3 illustrates some dialogue strategies for the seven valuing processes. These are actually instructional

TABLE 4-3 Clarifying Questions Suggested by the Seven Valuing Processes

1. Choosing freely
   a. Where do you suppose you first got the idea?
   b. How long have you felt that way?
   c. What would people say if you weren't to do what you say you must do? . . .
2. Choosing from alternatives
   a. What else did you consider before you picked this? . . .
   b. Are there reasons behind your choice?
   c. What choices did you reject before you settled on your present idea or action? . . .
3. Choosing thoughtfully
   a. What would be the consequences of each alternative available? . . .
   b. What assumptions are involved in your choice? . . . .
   c. Now if you do this, what will happen to that? . . .
4. Prizing and cherishing
   a. Are you glad you feel that way? [Why?] . . .
   b. What purpose does it serve? . . .
   c. In what way would life be different without it?
5. Affirming
   a. Would you tell the class the way you feel some time?
   b. Would you be willing to sign a petition supporting that idea? . . .
   c. Should a person who believes the way you do speak out? . . .
6. Acting upon choices
   a. Have you examined the consequences of your act? . . .
   b. Where will this lead you? How far are you willing to go?
   c. How has it already affected your life?
7. Repeating
   a. What are your plans for doing more of it?
   b. Should you get other people interested and involved? . . .
   c. How long do you think you will continue?

Source: From Louis E. Raths, Merrill Harmin, and Sidney B. Simon, *Values and Teaching*, 2nd ed. (Columbus, Ohio: Merrill, 1978), pp. 64–65.

strategies to be recommended by the curriculum specialist and used by the teacher.

It is possible to identify other ways of teaching valuing. The first is *inculcation*, teaching accepted values with the support of common law. Next is *moral development*, highlighting moral and ethical principles and application. Third is *analysis of issues* and situations involving values. Fourth is *clarification,* the method Raths emphasizes. Finally, is *action learning,* trying and testing values in real-life situations.[66] In addition, the approaches used by Abraham Maslow and Carl Rogers may be described as *evocation,* calling forth from the learner personal values and the ability to make choices and become self-actualizing.

Although the stress is on attitudes and feelings, and on human processes, there is a cognitive component in value clarification, just as in the *Taxonomy of Educational Objectives* there are corresponding cognitive components within the affective domain of learning.[67] One must think, and engage in various cognitive forms of analysis, synthesis, evaluation, and even problem solving, to engage in value clarification. The strategies for value clarification also involve what Raths calls "choosing" and "prizing," or what we see as a stress on attitudes, feelings, aspirations, self-concept, interests—and these are not easy to quantify or measure.

Phenomenology and Curriculum.

Phenomenologists view the individual in relation to the field in which he or she operates. But what determines behavior and learning is mainly psychological. The personal experiences of the individual are accessible to others only through inferences; thus such data are questionable in terms of scientific evidence. But to the phenomenologist, the raw data of personal experiences are vital to understand learning. Perhaps the data cannot be measured accurately, and perhaps they are vague, but they are "out there." The definitions and the processes are also subjective and evaluative, rather than precise and substantive. Besides the concept of humanistic psychology, the scope and subject matter are used synonymously with many other concepts—including existentialist psychology, neoprogressivism, creativity, love, higher consciousness, valuing, transcendentalism, psychological health, ego identity, psychoanalysis[68]— almost anything that suggests maximum

"self-fulfillment," "self-actualization," and "self-realization."

Although this umbrella aspect of phenomenology makes it difficult to provide a clear, agreed-upon definition of the term, the same broadness makes the concept acceptable to educational reformers of various psychological orientations. The fact that phenomenology means different things to different people is one reason for its easy acceptance, but it is also a basis for criticism. Nonetheless, phenomenologists attempt to rescue learning theory from the narrow and rigid behaviorists and from overstress on cognitive processes.

The Concept of Freedom. Phenomenologists seek to understand what goes on inside us—our needs, wants, desires, feelings, values, and ways of perceiving and understanding. The idea of personal freedom is an important issue in phenomenology or humanistic psychology. We may not always use the freedom we have, or we may misuse it, but it is there. One of the early humanistic psychologists put it this way: "I think people have a great deal more freedom than they ever use, simply because they operate out of habits, prejudices, and stereotypes. . . . [T]hey have a lot more self-determinism than is reflected in the traditional . . . view of humans as reactive beings. . . . [W]e have more freedom than most of today's psychology admits."[69]

The idea of freedom is the essence of Roger's thesis for learning. The more children and youth are aware of their freedom, the more opportunity they have to discover themselves and develop fully as people.[70] Freedom permits the learners to probe, explore, and deepen their understanding of what they are studying. It permits them latitude to accomplish goals and find the fit between goals and achievements and past learning and new learning—and the direction these new meanings have for additional learning. Freedom broadens the learners' knowledge of alternative ways of perceiving themselves and the environment.[71]

Freedom was the watchword of the radical school, free school, and alternative school movements of the 1960s and 1970s.[72] These movements increase various possibilities for learning and schooling and for enhancing diverse school environments that match the diversity of the needs, feelings, attitudes, and abilities of learners. The free school, alternative school, and radical school movements basically overlap; they were fueled by child-centered education and humanistic psychology. Even though they protested against established teaching and school practices, and knew they were against traditional education, they were never able to develop a constructive, detailed plan for reform.

Unquestionably, curricularists must enhance students' opportunities and alternatives for learning without lessening the teachers' authority. They need to find the "golden mean": student freedom without license and teacher authority without control—a very elusive ideal. The idea is to design a curriculum that helps learners realize their fullest potential in a behavioral, cognitive, and humanistic sphere of learning.

In Search of a Curriculum. Because each individual has specific needs and interests related to his or her self-fulfillment and self-realization, there is no generally prescribed humanistic curriculum. Rather, the learners draw on those experiences, subject matter, and intellectual skills necessary to attain full potential. The humanities and arts, especially philosophy, psychology, and aesthetics, would be appropriate content because they further introspection, reflection, and creativity. A curriculum of affect, one that stresses attitudes and feelings, would also be acceptable. Math and science would be considered unnecessary. Appropriate labels might be "relevant curriculum," "humanistic curriculum," "value-laden curriculum," or "existentialist curriculum."

Should the student reject the teacher's interpretation of subject matter, it is the student's right to do so. It is more important that the student-teacher relationship be based on trust and honesty, so that the student knows when the teacher's ideas of a subject are wise and deserve respect. Student choice would be crucial—the power to decide what to do and how to do it, a sense of control over one's ideas and work. School routine and rules would be minimal; learners would be left alone to do what they want to do, as long as it does not harm anyone or present a potential danger. Frequent evaluation, criticism, and competition would not be considered conducive to learning. The essence of many recent instructional trends—such as academic time, direct instruction, and mastery learning (which stress prescribed behaviors and tasks, well-defined procedures and outcomes, constant drill and testing) would be rejected as narrow, rigid, and high pressured.

Most reconceptualists would accept the phenomenologist-humanistic interpretation of learning because both these curricularists and learning theorists value the uniqueness of human personality and classrooms characterized by freedom, an existential educational experience, and subjects in the humanities and arts—not the hard sciences. Reconceptualists tend to approve this learning theory because it rejects the rational means-ends approach, the same processes that the traditional or hard curricularists follow.[73] Instead of presenting empirical data to justify the means, phenomenologists and reconceptualists rely on psychological and philosophical positions for validating ends proposed.

A drawback to the phenomenologist-humanistic theories is their lack of attention to cognitive learning. When asked to judge the effectiveness of their curriculum, both phenomenologists and humanists (like reconceptualists) rely on testimonials and subjective assessments by students and teachers. They may also present such materials as students' paintings, poems, interviews, reports, biographies, and projects, or talk about improvement in student behavior and attitudes.[74] They present very little empirical evidence or student achievement scores, however, to support their stance. Moreover, phenomenologists are not in agreement about how to teach self-actualization, self-determination, human striving, and so on, or about how to determine what subject matter is worthwhile, how to mesh the paintings, poems, and personal biographies with learning outcomes, and how to test or confirm many of their ideas.

There is great need to examine and construct a relevant, humanistic curriculum, and to enhance the self-actualizing, self-determining learning processes. However, until the just-described issues are resolved we shall continue to flounder in the phenomenologist area of learning. Those who trust the behavioral or cognitive-developmental process in teaching and learning, or the traditional or scientific spirit in curriculum making, will continue to distrust the "third force" in psychology and the "soft" approach to curriculum. Humanistic learning may enhance the mental health of the learners, personal feelings between students and teachers, and human awareness among students, teachers, and curriculum specialists. Sadly, however, their processes rely mainly on personal experiences and subjective interpretations that leave them open to criticism by traditional educators, including the majority of psychologists and curriculum specialists (who are either behaviorist or cognitive-oriented).

CONCLUSION

Psychology has had significant impact on curriculum, especially in recent years. This chapter has focused on *learning*—one of the major components of curriculum. Other aspects of psychology and curriculum are discussed in other parts of the book. As indicated in our discussion, as well as in Table 4-4, which serves as an overview of the chapter, learning can be examined in terms of three major theories: behaviorism, cognitive development, and phenomenology.

Behaviorism is the oldest theory of learn-

ing, and its continued popularity is illustrated by such teaching-learning trends as micro teaching, instructional training models, individualized learning, direct instruction, mastery learning, and so on. We explored the difference between classical and operant conditioning; traditional behavior is related to elicited responses (a well-defined stimulus-response association) and operant behavior is related to emitted responses (no well-defined stimulus-response association).

Cognitive-developmental learning theory represents the second school of thought, which has developed rapidly in the last twenty or thirty years. This corresponds with the increasing influence of Piaget among American psychologists, and the growing acceptance of environment (as opposed to heredity) as an explanation of cognitive growth and development. Cognitive learning theory is conducive for explaining various levels of thinking among humans, including concept thinking, problem solving, and creativity. Most learning theorists today are cognition-oriented.

Phenomenology or humanistic psychology can be considered the third and most recent learning theory. Its emphasis is on attitudes and feelings, self-actualization, freedom to learn, and value clarification; it overlaps with existentialist philosophy.

Most textbook writers, including the authors of this text, are cognition-oriented (by virtue of textbook organization and discussion of subject matter). However, we propose that the behaviorist component is needed for planning and developing curriculum. We also feel that the humanistic component of teaching and learning must also be incorporated into the curriculum—then into practice where it counts. We feel that each theory of learning is incomplete by itself, but all three theories have something to contribute to explain various aspects of behavior and learning in classrooms and schools. Readers should come to their own conclusions about what aspects of each theory they can use for their own teaching and curriculum development.

TABLE 4-4 Overview of Learning Theories and Principles

Psychologist*	Major Theory or Principle	Definition or Explanation
1. Thorndike	Law of effect	When a connection between a situation and response is made, and it is accompanied by a satisfying state of affairs, that connection is strengthened; when accompanied by an annoying state of affairs, the connection is weakened.
2. Pavlov-Watson	Classical conditioning	Whenever a response is closely followed by the reduction of a drive, a tendency will result for the stimulus to evoke that reaction on subsequent occasions; association strength of the S-R bond depends on the conditioning of the response and stimulus.
3. Skinner	Operant conditioning	In contrast to classical conditioning, no specific or identifiable stimulus consistently elicits operant behavior. Based on Thorndike's law of effect, operant conditioning means that if an operant response is followed by a reinforcing stimulus, the strength of the response is increased.
4. Piaget	Cognitive stages of development	Four cognitive stages form a sequence of progressive mental operations; the stages are hierarchical and increasingly more complex.
	Assimilation, accommodation, and equilibration	The incorporation of new experiences, the method of modifying new experiences to derive meaning, and the process of blending new experiences into a systematic whole.
5. Gagné	Levels of learning	Eight types of learning are identified, from simple to complex, both behavioral and cognitive; they are based on orderly, prerequisite, and cumulative processes of learning.
6. Guilford	Structure of intellect	Three major dimensions of thought—contents, operations, and products—each subdivided into several factors combine and interact to form 120 possible factors.
	Convergent-divergent thinking	A qualitative method of thinking; the first corresponds with problem solving, reflective thinking, and the scientific method; the second corresponds with creative thinking, intuitive thinking, and the artistic method.
7. Dewey	Reflective thinking	Being in a situation, sensing a problem, clarifying it with information, working out suggested solutions, and testing the ideas by application.
8. Lipman-Sternberg	Critical thinking	Teaching students how to think, including forming concepts, generalizations, cause-effect relationships, inferences, consistencies and contradictions, assumptions, analogies, etc.
9. Bruner-Phenix	Structure of a subject	The knowledge, concepts, and principles of a subject; learning how things are related is learning the structure of a subject.
	Inquiry-discovery method	A method or quality of thinking that uses a body of organized knowledge; the first method tends to be convergent and the second tends to be divergent.

TABLE 4-4 *(Continued)*

Psychologist*	Major Theory or Principle	Definition or Explanation
10. Maslow	Human needs	Six human needs related to survival and psychological well-being; the needs are hierarchical and serve to direct behavior.
11. Rogers	Becoming a person	Becoming a person means being open to experience, developing trust, and accepting oneself.
	Freedom to learn	Becoming a full person requires freedom to learn; the learner is encouraged to be open, self-trusting, and self-accepting.
12. Raths	Value clarification	Analysis of personal preferences and moral issues to reveal or clarify one's values—that is, beliefs, attitudes, and opinions.

*The first three psychologists and their respective theories (or principles) are behaviorist; the next group, numbers 4 to 9, are cognitive. However, some behaviorist principles are associated with Gagné. The last three psychologists and their respective theories (or principles) are humanistic.

Notes

1. Ralph W. Tyler, *Basic Principles of Curriculum and Instruction* (Chicago: University of Chicago Press, 1949).
2. Jerome S. Bruner, *The Process of Education* (Cambridge, Mass.: Harvard University Press, 1959).
3. Edward L. Thorndike, *Animal Intelligence* (New York: Macmillan, 1911).
4. Edward L. Thorndike, *Psychology of Learning*, 3 vols. (New York: Teachers College Press, Columbia University, 1913); Thorndike, *The Fundamentals of Learning* (New York: Teachers College Press, Columbia University, 1932).
5. Tyler, *Basic Principles of Curriculum and Instruction;* Hilda Taba, *Curriculum Development: Theory and Practice* (New York: Harcourt, Brace, 1962).
6. John Dewey, *How We Think* (Boston: D. C. Heath, 1910); Dewey, *My Pedalogic Creed* (Washington, D.C.: National Education Association, 1929); and Charles H. Judd, *Education and Social Progress* (New York: Harcourt, Brace, 1934).
7. Taba, *Curriculum Development: Theory and Practice*, p. 121.
8. Bruner, *The Process of Education.*
9. Ivan P. Pavlov, *Conditioned Reflexes*, trans. G. V. Anrep (London: Oxford University Press, 1927). The experiment was conducted in 1903 and 1904.
10. John B. Watson, *Behaviorism* (New York: Norton, 1939).
11. John B. Watson, "What the Nursery Has to Say about Instincts," in C. A. Murchison, ed., *Psychologies of 1925* (Worcester, Mass.: Clark University Press, 1926), p. 10.
12. B. F. Skinner, *Science and Human Behavior* (New York: Macmillan, 1953).
13. Ibid.; B. F. Skinner, *Reflections on Behaviorism and Society* (Englewood Cliffs, N.J.: Prentice-Hall, 1978).
14. B. F. Skinner, "The Science of Learning and the Art of Teaching," *Harvard Educational Review* (Spring 1954), pp. 86–97.
15. W. James Popham and Eva I. Baker, *Systematic Instruction* (Englewood Cliffs, N.J.: Prentice-Hall, 1970), p. 48.
16. B. F. Skinner, *The Technology of Teaching* (New York: Appleton-Century-Crofts, 1968).
17. David Ausubel, *Educational Psychology: A Cognitive View* (New York: Holt, Rinehart, 1968); N. L. Gage and David Berliner, *Educational Psychology*, 3rd ed. (Boston: Houghton Mifflin, 1984); and Hershel D. Thornburg, *Introduction to Educational Psychology* (St. Paul: West Publishers, 1985).
18. Robert M. Travers, *Essentials of Learning*, 5th ed. (New York: Macmillan, 1982), p. 505.
19. See Albert Bandura, *Social Learning Theory* (New York: General Learning Press, 1971); Robert M. Gagné, *The Conditions of Learning*, 4th ed. (New York: Holt, Rinehart, 1985).
20. Robert Glaser, "Trends and Research Questions in Psychological Research on Learning and Schooling," *Educational Researcher* (November 1979), p. 12. See also Glaser, "Education and Thinking: The Role of Knowledge," *American Psychologists* (February 1984), pp. 93–104.
21. Sigmund Tobias, "New Directions for Educational Psychologists," *Educational Psychologist* (Spring 1985), pp. 96–101.
22. Bruce Joyce and Marsha Weil, *Models of Teaching*, 3rd ed. (Englewood Cliffs, N.J.: Prentice-Hall, 1986); Travers, *Essentials of Learning.*
23. Jean Piaget, *Judgment and Reasoning in the Child* (New York: Harcourt, Brace, 1948).

24. Jean Piaget, *The Psychology of Intelligence*, rev ed. (London: Broadway, 1950). See also Hans Furth and Harry Wachs, *Thinking Goes to School: Piaget's Theory in Practice* (New York: Oxford University Press, 1974).

25. John Dewey, *Experience and Education* (New York: Macmillan, 1938), p. 40.

26. Jean Piaget, *The Child's Conception of Physical Causality* (New York: Harcourt, 1932). See also Piaget, *The Equilibration of Cognitive Structures*, trans. T. Brown and K. J. Thampy (Chicago: University of Chicago Press, 1985).

27. Dewey, *Experience and Education*, p. 43.

28. Tyler, *Basic Principles of Curriculum and Instruction*.

29. Ibid., pp. 84–86.

30. Taba, *Curriculum Development: Theory and Practice*, pp. 118–119.

31. Bruner, *The Process of Education*.

32. Dewey, *Experience and Education*, p. 44.

33. Bruner, *The Process of Education*, p. 13.

34. Gagné, *The Conditions of Learning*.

35. J. P. Guilford, *The Nature of Human Intelligence* (New York: McGraw-Hill, 1967).

36. Bruner, *The Process of Education;* Philip H. Phenix, *Realms of Meaning* (New York: McGraw-Hill, 1964); and Joseph J. Schwab, "The Concept of the Structure of a Discipline," *Educational Record* (July 1962), pp. 197–205.

37. See Jacob W. Getzels and Philip D. Jackson, *Creativity and Intelligence: Explorations with Gifted Students* (New York: Wiley, 1962); Robert J. Sternberg, ed., *Handbook for Human Intelligence* (New York: Cambridge University Press, 1982); and Michael A. Wallach and Nathan Kogan, *Modes of Thinking in Young Children: A Study of the Creativity-Intelligence Distinction* (New York: Holt, Rinehart, 1965).

38. Dewey, *How We Think*.

39. James B. Conant, *Science and Common Sense* (New Haven: Yale University Press, 1951).

40. Matthew Lipman, "The Cultivation of Reasoning through Philosophy," *Educational Leadership* (September 1984), pp. 51–56.

41. Matthew Lipman et al., *Philosophy for Children*, 2nd ed. (Philadelphia: Temple University Press, 1980).

42. Lipman, "The Cultivation of Reasoning through Philosophy."

43. Robert J. Sternberg, "How Can We Teach Intelligence?" *Educational Leadership* (September 1984), pp. 38–48; Sternberg, "Intelligence, Wisdom, and Creativity," *Educational Psychologist* (Summer 1986), pp. 175–190.

44. William A. Sadler and Arthur Whimbey, "A Holistic Approach to Improving Thinking Skills," *Phi Delta Kappan* (November 1985), p. 200.

45. Robert J. Sternberg, "Teaching Critical Thinking: Possible Solutions," *Phi Delta Kappan* (December 1985), p. 277.

46. Carl Rogers, "Toward a Theory of Creativity," in M. Barkan and R. L. Mooney, eds., *Conference on Creativity: A Report to the Rockefeller Foundation* (Columbus: Ohio State University Press, 1953), pp. 73–82.

47. Eric Fromm, "The Creative Attitude," in H. H. Anderson, ed., *Creativity and its Cultivation* (New York: Harper & Row, 1959), pp. 44–54.

48. Bruner, *The Process of Education*, pp. 56–57.

49. Bruner, *The Process of Education;* Gail M. Inlow, *Maturity in High School Teaching* (Englewood Cliffs, N.J.: Prentice-Hall, 1964); Philip H. Phenix, *Realms of Meaning* (New York: McGraw-Hill, 1964); and Taba, *Curriculum Development: Theory and Practice*.

50. Inlow, *Maturity in High School*, p. 78.

51. Taba, *Curriculum Development: Theory and Practice*, p. 156.

52. See David P. Ausubel, "The Facilitation of Meaningful Verbal Learning in the Classroom," *Educational Psychologist* (June 1977), pp. 162–178.

53. John I. Goodlad, "A Study of Schooling: Some Findings and Hypotheses," *Phi Delta Kappan* (March 1983), p. 468.

54. John Holt, *How Children Fail* (New York: Pitman, 1964).

55. Gordon H. Bower and Ernest R. Hilgard, *Theories of Learning*, 5th ed. (Englewood Cliffs, N.J.: Prentice-Hall, 1981); Travers, *Essentials of Learning*.

56. See Henry Misiak and Virginia Sexton, *Phenomenological, Existential, and Humanistic Psychologies* (New York: Grune and Stratton, 1973); Richard Schmuck and Patricia Schmuck, *A Humanistic Psychology of Education* (Palo Alto, Calif.: National Press Books, 1974); and Michael Wertheimer, "Humanistic Psychology and the Humane but Tough-Minded Psychologist," *American Psychologist* (August 1978), pp. 739–745.

57. Arthur W. Combs and Donald Snygg, *Individual Behavior*, 2nd ed. (New York: Harper & Row, 1959); Combs, *A Personal Approach to Teaching* (Boston: Allyn and Bacon, 1982).

58. Kurt Koffka, *Principles of Gestalt Psychology* (New York: Harcourt, 1935); Wolfgang Kohler, *Gestalt Psychology*, 2nd ed. (New York: Liveright, 1947); and Max Wertheimer, *Productive Thinking* (New York: Harper & Row, 1945).

59. Abraham H. Maslow, *Toward a Psychology of Being*, 2nd ed. (New York: Van Nostrand Reinhold, 1968); Maslow, *Motivation and Personality*, 2nd ed. (New York: Harper & Row, 1970).

60. Ibid.

61. Abraham Maslow, *The Farther Reaches of Human Nature* (New York: Viking Press, 1971); Maslow, *Motivation and Personality*.

62. Carl Rogers, *Client-Centered Therapy* (Boston: Houghton Mifflin, 1951), p. 485.

63. Carl Rogers, *A Way of Being* (Boston: Houghton Mifflin, 1981); Rogers, *Freedom to Learn for the 1980s*, 2nd ed. (Columbus, Ohio: Merrill, 1983).

64. Louise M. Berman and Jessie A. Roderick, eds., *Feeling, Valuing, and the Art of Growing* (Washington, D.C.: Association for Supervision and Curriculum Development, 1977).

65. Louis E. Raths, Merrill Harmin, and Sidney B. Simon, *Values and Teaching*, 2nd ed. (Columbus, Ohio: Merrill, 1978), pp. 27–28.

66. Ronald C. Doll, *Curriculum Improvement: Decision Making and Process*, 6th ed. (Boston: Allyn and Bacon, 1986); Alexander Frazier, *Values, Curriculum, and the Elementary School* (Boston: Houghton Mifflin, 1980).

67. David R. Krathwohl, Benjamin S. Bloom, and Betram Maisa, *Taxonomy of Educational Objectives, Handbook II: Affective Domain* (New York: McKay, 1964).

68. Charlotte Buhler, "Basic Theoretical Concepts of Humanistic Psychology," *American Psychologist* (April 1971), pp. 378–386; Arthur W. Combs et al., *Perceptual Psychology: A Humanistic Approach to the Study of Persons* (New York: Harper & Row, 1976).

69. Gordon Allport, "A Conversation," *Psychology Today* (April 1971), p. 59.

70. Rogers, *Freedom to Learn.*

71. See Berman and Roderick, *Feeling, Valuing and the Art of Growing*; Evan Simpson, "A Values-Clarification Retrospective," *Educational Theory* (Summer 1986), pp. 271–288.

72. See Allen Graubard, *Free the Children: The New Schools Movement in America* (New York: Pantheon, 1973); Jonathan Kozol, *Free Schools* (Boston: Houghton Mifflin, 1972); and Everett Reimer, *School is Dead: Alternatives to Education* (New York: Doubleday, 1971).

73. Michael W. Apple, "The Hidden Curriculum and the Nature of Conflict," in W. Pinar, ed., *Curriculum Theorizing: The Reconceptualists* (Berkeley, Calif.: McCutchan, 1975), pp. 95–119; Herbert M. Kliebard, "Persistent Curriculum Issues in Historical Perspective," in Pinar, ed., *Curriculum Theorizing*, pp. 39–50; and James B. Macdonald, "A Transcendental Development Ideology of Education," in J. R. Gress and D. E. Purpel, eds., *Curriculum: An Introduction to the Field* (Berkeley, Calif.: McCutchan, 1978), pp. 95–123. See also John McNeil, *Curriculum: A Comprehensive Introduction*, 3rd ed. (Boston: Little, Brown, 1985); Pinar, ed., *Curriculum Theorizing.*

74. Paul R. Feinberg, "Four Curriculum Theorists: A Critique in the Light of Martin Buber's Philosophy of Education," *Journal of Curriculum Theorizing* (Spring 1985), pp. 5–164; Maxine Greene, "Philosophy, Reason, and Literacy," *Review of Educational Research* (Winter 1984), pp. 547–559.

chapter 5

SOCIAL FOUNDATIONS
OF CURRICULUM

Any discussion of curriculum should consider the social setting, especially the relationship between schools and society and its influence on curriculum decisions. Social astuteness is essential for curriculum planners and developers today. Curriculum decisions take place in a complex social setting, through demands that are imposed by society and that filter down to schools. Indeed, curriculum workers need to consider and use social foundations to plan and develop the curriculum.

In many curriculum texts, a consideration of social foundations often leads to discussion of schools and society, as well as discussion of individual socialization, the social implications of knowledge and change, and the aims of education. This chapter, too, deals with such social issues. The last two chapters of the book examine other social issues—for example, those with a reconstructionist flavor: Issues dealing with compensatory education, bilingual and mul-

ticultural education, sex education, education of the handicapped, global education, and futurism.

SOCIETY, EDUCATION, AND SCHOOLING

Education is neutral. It can be used for constructive or destructive ends, to promote one type of political institution or ism or another. The kind of education our young receive determines the quality of our society. The transmission of culture is the primary task of a society's educational system. The values, beliefs, and norms of a society are maintained and passed to the next generation not merely by teaching about them, but also by embodying them in the very operation of the educational system.

For Dewey, education is the means of perpetuating and improving society, by properly organizing the experiences of the learners. It is "a primary responsibility of educators . . . [to] be aware of the general principle of the shaping of actual experiences by environing conditions" and to understand "what surroundings are conducive to having experiences that lead to growth." For Dewey, experience must be channeled properly "for it influences the formation of attitudes of desire and purpose."[1] It is up to educators, particularly those in charge of subject matter, to judge which content and activities (or what Dewey calls "experiences") enhance individual personal and social growth and improve society and which do not (or what he calls "miseducative").

Most of us regard education as synonymous with schooling. Actually, even a society that has no formal schools still educates its young through the family or special ritual and training. "Schooling plays a major role in education in modern industrial [societies]"; it becomes more important as societies become "more complex and as the frontiers of knowledge expand. In simple, nontechnological societies, almost everyone becomes proficient over the whole range of knowledge necessary for survival." In technological societies "people acquire different proficiencies and abilities; no individual can range over the entire body of complex knowledge or expect to be proficient in all areas of learning."[2]

In traditional and nonliterate societies, education is processed through ceremonies, rituals, stories, observation and emulation of older children, parents and elders, and by strict enforcement of codes of conduct and behavior. In modern and technological societies, the educational process starts at home but "school takes on greater importance as the child becomes older." The school is a vital institution "for helping the young acquire systematic knowledge," inculcating them with the proper attitudes and values, and "bonding the gap between generations." In contemporary society, the mass media also play a major role in processing knowledge and in "redefining values and ideas."[3] But it is the function of schools to serve a modern society by educating its children and youth. The curriculum worker who helps determine the content, activities, and environment of education plays a major role in shaping and indirectly socializing students.

Society and Modal Personality.

When social scientists speak of modal personality, they do not mean that all members of a particular society are exactly alike. As Ruth Benedict wrote, "No culture yet observed has been able to eradicate the differences in temperament of the persons who composed it."[4] However, members of a society do have much in common; they are nursed or fed on schedule, toilet trained a certain way, educated in similar fashion, marry one or several spouses, live by labor or perform common economic tasks, believe in one God or many deities. These shared experiences temper individual differences so that individuals behave in similar ways. According to Benedict, the norms of society govern interpersonal relations and produce a modal personality—that is, the attitudes, feelings, and behavior patterns most members of a society share.

In a study of the American modal personality, anthropologist Margaret Mead stressed that this is the land of unlimited opportunity. Whether or not this is true, the belief that anyone can become president, which is reinforced by our notion of equality of opportunity, places a heavy burden on most Americans.[5] By implication, those who do not become president (or doctors, lawyers, engineers, or corporate executives) have shirked their "moral responsibility to succeed." Most other people in the world blame poverty, fate, or the government for failure to succeed; Americans (except some minority groups) tend to blame themselves.

Whereas European parents usually raise their children to carry on family traditions, first- and second-generation American parents want their children to leave home for better lives. Americans tend to evaluate their own self-worth according to how high they have climbed above their father's status and how they compare with their friends and neighbors. At no point do Americans feel they have truly "arrived"; the climb is endless, but within reach, and it is very much a part of our American value system—and the nature of our schools and the traditional curriculum.

Sex Roles and Sex Differences.

Not only does society demand conformity to its basic values and mores, it also assigns specific roles to each of its members, and it expects them to conform to certain established behavioral patterns. A good example of this type of socialization is sex roles—that is, the way boys and girls and men and women are "supposed" to act. Sex roles vary from culture to culture, but within a given culture they are rather well defined; moreover, they are enforced through an elaborate schedule of selective reinforcement. For example, preschool boys are ridiculed for playing with dolls, and girls are supposed to be "feminine."

Both male and female children initially identify with the mother, but boys must shift their original mother identifications to establish masculine role identities. As this period begins, girls often have the same-sex parental models all day, but boys see their fathers only briefly.[6] Besides, fathers participate in some feminine roles—that is, roles that until very recently have been defined in American society as feminine (washing dishes, cleaning)—so boys must distinguish masculine roles from the stereotypes spelled out for them by society through a system of reinforcements and rewards. As boys' identification with their mothers diminishes, it is gradually replaced by learned identification with a culturally defined masculine role. This is accomplished mainly through such negative admonishments as "Don't be a sissy," which do not even tell them what to do instead.

Girls simply learn female identification as it is presented to them, partly through imitation and partly through the mothers' reinforcing and rewarding selective behav-ior. Boys have the problem of making the proper sex-role identification in the partial absence of male models at home; this is even more difficult in female-headed households in which the father is completely absent (increasingly common today, among all social classes). Girls acquire a learning method that basically involves developing a personal relationship and identification with their mothers. By contrast, boys must define their goals, restructure some of their experiences, and abstract underlying principles. The result is greater learning problems for boys and greater dependency on the part of girls.

Schools are largely staffed by females, especially at the elementary level, which is a critical period in child development. Schools are dominated by female norms of politeness, cleanliness, and obedience. The curriculum, tests, and classroom activities are female-oriented as well—safe, nice, antiseptic. Schools frown on vulgar language and fighting; they suppress boys' maleness and often do not permit action-oriented, tough sports. The disadvantages that boys find at home in developing masculine identities are sometimes compounded by the schooling process.[7]

Patricia Sexton presents controversial data showing that schools are feminizing institutions that discriminate against males and subvert their identity.[8] Her data show that approximately three out of four problem students are boys, and that because teachers tend to fail problem students, approximately two out of three students who fail are boys. Boys largely outnumber girls in school dropout rates, delinquent behaviors, mental illness, and suicides. Male students who are high achievers tend to be fat and flabby, especially at the elementary and junior high school level; those who gravitate to masculine activities, such as conflict sports and mechanics, tend to do poorly in academic areas—and they are often at odds with their teachers, who are predominantly female (but they conflict with male teachers, too, who, by virtue of their role, tend to enforce feminized school norms).

Although Sexton's conclusions may be

somewhat overgeneralized and extend beyond her data, there is no question that girls receive higher grades throughout elementary school, although the gap is gradually reduced in high school. More boys are nonreaders; more boys fail; more boys are disciplinary cases; more boys drop out of school; and more men than women are prisoners or have mental breakdowns. Men die younger, too. No doubt sex roles and sex differences in school are at least in part related to role expectations that are incorporated into the self-concept very early in life.

The problem that Sexton analyzes is highlighted by the fact that, on the average, according to biochemical research, boys are more active than girls almost from the time they are born, and that this difference is related, in turn, to hormone differences.[9] Boys are at a particular disadvantage in elementary school because they tend to learn through active manipulation of their environment (which schools tend to discourage), whereas girls tend to learn through verbal communication (which schools tend to stress). Writes one researcher, after a review of several studies:

By the time they are five or six, [all] children in . . . classrooms [are] expected to behave like girls. The system requires children to remain attentive to one task and stay seated in one place for a considerable period of time. . . . They must . . . persevere at tasks that are largely linguistic or symbolic in nature. Boys [usually] cannot sit still; they are distractible; they test the properties of objects. Such behavior interferes with the concentration they need to read and write.[10]

Sex Differences in Achievement. By way of contrast, the problems that girls experience in the schooling process generally reflect their socialization for dependency rather than aggressiveness. Until recently, most girls were not encouraged to prepare for high-status occupations in law, medicine, or business, or even for training beyond high school. Instead they were expected to prepare for roles as wives and homemakers.[11] Except for a few occupa-

tions, such as teaching, social work, or nursing (which have been classified as semiprofessions), girls traditionally were not expected to enter fields that require college preparation. Further, the few professions into which women were channeled tended to have relatively low pay and low status.

This socialization process was reinforced by the curriculum, which stereotyped women into "feminine" roles and "feminine" jobs. Textbooks also treated women as if they were invisible.[12] Girls were not motivated to achieve much beyond high school or to acquire skills that might contribute to later success in the economy. Furthermore, differences in mathematics and science scores between boys and girls in school were reinforced by schooling and socialization practices, which made females anxious and fearful not only of these courses, but of success in traditionally male activities and occupations as well. Some scholars have supported these conclusions by arguing that sex differences in math and science achievement, which usually are first evident in grade seven or eight, are largely a function of differential courses rather than the inability of women to learn analytical or spatial skills. They argue that if female enrollment in mathematics and science could be increased, most of the sex differences in achievement would be eliminated.[13]

The explanation for differences in math scores may be more complicated, however. A recent study of 10,000 gifted and talented seventh and eighth graders showed that boys scored consistently higher in math problems, even though the boys and girls in the survey had had essentially the same mathematical experiences in school.[14] The implications of the data are numerous: (1) ability may influence the kinds of courses students select, not the other way around; (2) sexism and sex stereotyping may not easily overcome other environmental influences (such as similar formal education); and (3) girls may have less innate math reasoning abilities than boys (which is not easy to accept). However, other researchers would merely conclude that sex-role limitations and stereotyping hamper the development of girls' mathematical abilities.[15]

SOCIAL AND DEVELOPMENTAL THEORIES

A number of theories have been originated that focus on global aspects of human growth and development. Because they emphasize the study of behavior as a totality, starting with infancy, in a sense they combine Gestalt psychology with socialization. Developmental theories address the cumulative effects of change that occur as a consequence of learning or failing to learn appropriate tasks during the critical stages of life. Failure to learn an appropriate task at a given stage of development tends to have detrimental effects on the developmental sequence that follows.

Development proceeds through a rather fixed sequence of relatively continuous stages, and it is assumed that maturation as well as appropriate societal experiences are necessary to move the individual from stage to stage. Shifts from one stage to the next are based not only on age but also on variations in the amount and the quality of social experiences an individual accumulates over long spans of time.

Human Tasks/Needs.

Robert Havighurst has identified six periods in human development: (1) infancy and early childhood; (2) middle childhood; (3) adolescence; (4) early adulthood; (5) middle age; and (6) late maturity. Developmental tasks are defined as "the tasks the individual must learn" for purposes of "healthy and satisfactory growth in our society." They are what a person must learn if he or she is to be judged and to judge him- or herself to be a reasonably happy and successful person. "A developmental task is a task that occurs at a certain stage or period in the life of that individual. Successful achievement . . . leads to happiness and to success with later tasks, while failure leads to unhappiness, disap-

proval by the society, and difficulty with later tasks."[16]

An individual's schooling is concerned with the developmental tasks of the second part of the first period and the next two periods of life. The tasks are:

1. Early Childhood
   a. Forming concepts and learning language to describe the social and physical reality.
   b. Getting ready to read.
   c. Learning to distinguish right from wrong and beginning to develop a conscience.
2. Middle Childhood
   a. Learning physical skills necessary for ordinary games.
   b. Building wholesome attitudes toward oneself.
   c. Learning to get along with age-mates.
   d. Learning appropriate male and female roles.
   e. Developing fundamental skills in reading, writing, and mathematics.
   f. Developing concepts for everyday living.
   g. Developing morality and a set of values.
   h. Achieving personal independence.
   i. Developing (democratic) attitudes toward social groups and institutions.
3. Adolescence
   a. Achieving new and more mature relations with age-mates of both sexes.
   b. Achieving a masculine or feminine social role.
   c. Accepting one's physique and using the body effectively.
   d. Achieving emotional independence of parents and other adults.
   e. Preparing for marriage and family life.
   f. Preparing for an economic career.
   g. Acquiring a set of values and an ethical system to guide behavior.
   h. Achieving socially responsible behavior.[17]

Although the Havighurst model is the best known, other models have been proposed to deal with student or adolescent needs. Havighurst uses the term *human* instead of *adolescent* to connote a wider range of ages, and the term *tasks* instead of *needs* to suggest a solution, but the other models are just as comprehensive and balanced as Havighurst's. For example, Harry Giles et al. outlined four "basic needs"—personal, social, civic, and economic—each of which has three to four subdivisions.[18] Florence Stratemeyer and her colleagues categorized "ten areas of living" into three "life situations"[19]; B. Othanel Smith and his colleagues classified twenty-nine "adolescent needs" into six major social-personal classifications,[20] and Henry Harap outlined thirty "life activities" needed for successful human development.[21]

Different as these classification schemes are, they clearly show that many common topics of concern tend to be social in nature and to include environmental, moral, civic, psychological, physical, and productive (or economic) dimensions of learning. Actually, it may well be that, in principle, this degree of broad agreement is the best we can aim for in the interest of developing a student-needs approach. All the models consider the *whole child* as opposed to only cognitive learning, tend to stress *achievement* categories—that is, tasks or needs—recognize the concept of *readiness,* and focus on the *individual* even though they do refer to social circumstances in which the person finds him- or herself. Whereas the Havighurst model professes to be developmental, and consists of a hierarchy of human needs called tasks, with no one curriculum emphasis, the other models tend to be organized around equally important student or adolescent needs and developed in context with a core curriculum and a social-issues curriculum. This does not mean that these models cannot be used for *all* curricula. Interestingly, all of the models can be used as a framework for a needs-assessment plan, discussed in greater detail in Chapter 7.

Note that the *needs-assessment* plan is basically rooted in the *student-needs* or *adolescent-needs* approach of the 1940s and 1950s. The needs-assessment plan evolved during the mid-1970s, when the federal government insisted that such a plan was required for federal funding. This requirement has filtered down to state and local guidelines and curriculum workers have adopted the idea. Whereas the student-needs approach focuses on the learner, a needs assessment may not always focus on the learner, although it often does. A needs assessment can include the needs of the professional staff, school, parents, and the community. The intent is to clarify the aims and goals of a school district; the assessment itself is conducted because school officials believe there is room for improvement.

Moral Development.

Any society depends on the presence of people who share its culture, who take active roles, who are tied together by a set of codes and laws that are in part determined by tradition, and who have a sense of morality and conscience.[22] Morality, in a practical sense, involves a strong social component, for what is considered morally right or wrong reflects the nature of a society—its customs, mores, and laws. How a person develops morally is partially, if not predominantly, based on the way he or she interacts with society—more precisely, on the social environment as well as the roles and responsibilities he or she learns and/or deems important via contact with people who are considered important. Although conscience and moral standards may start evolving in the preschool years, they do not begin to develop at a rapid rate until children are about 4. From about 4 to 6 years, conscience in most children is confined less to specific behaviors; it begins to incorporate more generalized abstract standards, and it becomes determined less by external rewards or punishments and more by internal sanctions.[23]

Jean Piaget's theories of moral development were based on investigations that included Piaget's questioning Swiss children about moral dilemmas and events in stories. For example, Piaget might have asked, "Why shouldn't you cheat in a game?" Piaget's observations suggested that from ages 5 to 12 the child's concept of justice passes from a rigid and inflexible notion of right and wrong, learned from his or her parents, to a sense of equity in moral judgments. Eventually, the concept takes into account the specific situation or circumstances in which behavior has occurred.[24] As the child becomes older, he or she becomes more flexible and realizes that there are exceptions to the rule—that is, there are some circumstances under which lying may be justifiable.

On the basis of numerous studies of these types, Piaget concluded:

... there are three great periods in the development of the sense of justice in the child. One period, lasting up to age 7–8 during which justice is subordinated to adult authority; a period contained approximately between 8–11, and which is that of progressive equalitarianism; and finally during which purely equalitarian justice is tempered by consideration of equality.[25]

More recently, Lawrence Kohlberg studied the development of children's moral standards and concluded that the way we think about moral issues is not simply a reflection of our society but is also based on stages of growth or age. Kohlberg outlined six developmental types of moral judgments grouped into three moral levels or stages, corresponding to Piaget's cognitive stages of development:

1. *Preconventional Level.* Children at this level have not yet developed a sense of right or wrong. The level is comprised of two types of children: (1) children who do as they are told because they fear punishment; and (2) children who realize that certain actions bring rewards.

2. *Conventional Level.* At this level, children are concerned about what other people think of them. As a result, their behavior becomes largely other-directed. There are two types in this level: (3) children who seek their parents' approval by being "nice"; and (4) children who begin thinking in terms of rules.

3. *Postconventional Level.* Children's morality is based on what other people feel or on their precepts of authority. This level also in-

cludes two types: (5) children who are able to view morality in terms of contractual obligations and democratically accepted laws; and (6) children who view morality in terms of individual principles of conscience.

Kohlberg and Piaget support the cognitive developmental view of morality—that is, there is a considerable amount of reasoning in moral judgments and behavior—although they differ on specifics. Whereas Piaget stresses that there are very real differences in the way children think about morality at different ages, Kohlberg found considerable overlap at the various ages. Both also believe that social arrangements and society play a major role; however, Piaget gives maturation more emphasis. Kohlberg says:

As opposed to Piaget's view, the data suggest that the "natural" aspects of moral development are continuous and a reaction to the whole social world rather than a product of a certain stage, a certain concept ... or a certain type of social relations.[26]

Existentialist educators, such as Maxine Greene and Van Cleve Morris, view morality as something beyond cognitive processes, akin to such social-psychological processes as personal sensitivity, feelings and openness to others, and aesthetic awareness.[27] One is free, but one's *freedom* is essentially an inner matter involving awesome *responsibility* of *choice* operating within the medium of humankind and human *awareness*. Freedom, responsibility, choice, and awareness all involve moral judgments, and are related to social standards and personal beliefs.

Philip Phenix, a strict cognitive curricularist, also maintains that moral development combines social standards or norms with personal choices. Moral action presupposes an "obligation of what is to be done ... self determination ... and freedom." Although we can discern personal knowledge in our moral behavior, it is questionable whether we can identify a subject matter or teach it. "By far the most significant sources of such influence are the laws and customs of society.... Accepted social standards "may not always be right or good, but they do embody much well-tested moral wisdom."[28]

Phenix outlines five basic moral traditions that encompass the foundations of society and that, although he does not say so, could be taught as part of the learning process to guide moral behavior: (1) human rights, which suggest conditions of life that ought to prevail, such as trial by jury, free speech and religion, and so on; (2) sex and family relations, whereby sex and family codes are carefully considered; (3) social relationships within and among class, ethnic, racial, and religious groups; (4) economic matters dealing with property rights and the distribution of goods and services; and (5) political matters dealing with distributive justice and power. Again, these concerns are mainly sociological in nature and involve social standards—various customs, mores, and laws.

In the final analysis, "moral conduct can be taught and is continuously taught, not by experts who profess the subject of ethics [or knowledge of any subject], but by participation in everyday life of society according to recognized standards of society."[29] Such learning connotes "ethical education," in Phenix's terms, not through formal schooling, but engendered by law, custom, and ritual. We can teach ethical theory in school, he maintains, and we can teach an array of standards (such as the Ten Commandments or the Golden Rule) to evaluate behavior, but an individual's final course of action is a matter of personal choice and is influenced by his or her view of what is right, good, or ideal. Phenix's position is a social and existentialist view of life—not cognitive.

Curriculum specialists, who must view moral development in conjunction with cognitive development, would probably feel more comfortable with Dewey's position. Dewey points out that subject matter has social and moral worth, which should be integrated "under conditions where their social significance is realized, [and] they feed moral interests and develop moral in-

sight."[30] But the actual decisions and behaviors related to morality involve social growth and social experiences, according to Dewey, which schools can help shape. He uses such descriptors as "character," "conditions," and "environment" to describe morality and the organization of subject matter.[31]

CHANGE AND THE CURRICULUM

Educators, in general, and teachers and curriculum workers have a choice that has been offered to them throughout the ages. They may uncritically accept the tendencies of the times in which they find themselves, and develop school programs that *mirror* current social and political forces; or they may appraise the times and develop school programs that respond to the dynamics of change. The curriculum can either reflect society or reflect upon and indirectly help *shape* society. Teachers may either serve as cogs in a bureaucratic school machine, keeping subject matter safe and sterile, or they may help students think and act—by offering specialized knowledge, raising controversial issues, and incorporating problem-solving activities.

The first approach views the school and educator as mirrors of society; the second approach views schools and school people as instruments of change. The former approach is based on the traditional conception of education; the latter is a progressive and reconstructionist conception of education. Sadly, the first approach tends to coincide with the *reality* of schools; the second approach borders on the *ideal*.

If we are unable to deal with change in a constructive and appropriate manner, then we become victimized by it. If we are unable to shape the world around us, then the whims of nature dictate to us and social and political forces overwhelm us. According to William Van Til, "There is a danger to individuals and to society in an education which accepts uncritically and reflects unthinkingly.... The danger is that some forces which mutually reinforce each other may take us down roads contrary to the American [ideal]"—the ideal of the individual who is free, morally responsible, and important. "Some tendencies of the times, if uncritically accepted and implemented by education, could lead to the powerless man in the powerful society."[32]

Society as a Source of Change.

Contemporary society is changing so swiftly that we have difficulty coping with it and adjusting ourselves to the present and preparing for the future. We are forced to look to the schools for help in understanding and living with social change, but schools are conservative institutions that usually lag behind change.

The differential rates of change in different parts of society give rise to the phenomenon known as *cultural lag*. Usually changes in the scientific, commercial, and industrial aspects of culture come first, followed by lags in the institutions of society. People seem to accept material changes more readily than institutional changes, and they seem to resist changes in fundamental ideological ideas.

The amount of cultural lag within a society varies with the amount of social change. If there is little or no social change, obviously the lag, if it exists, is small. In Western society, especially in the United States, consistent and fundamental change is occurring in many aspects of society. As our society has entered a period of rapid change (which has accelerated since World War II), and as each new change has set off a whole chain of other events, this lag has become acute.

Rate and Direction of Change. There are two basic ways to conceive change—rate and direction. The rate of change has implications that are quite apart from, and sometimes more important than, the direction of change.

One way to illustrate the *rate of change* is to divide the last 100,000 years of human existence into lifetimes of approximately seventy-five years each (equivalent to an average lifespan in our society), or a total of 1333 lifetimes. Only during the last sixty lifetimes has it been possible to communicate effectively from one lifetime to another through writing. Only in the last six lifetimes did humankind see a printed word. Only in the last two has anyone anywhere used a motor, and only in the last one have we used electricity.

Based on our present rate of change, Alvin Toffler notes that we are entering a period of *future shock:* We will have too many goods and services from which to choose, and our ability to choose wisely from all these options will become increasingly limited because of human overload (i.e., try choosing the best long-distance phone company).[33]

Another way of appreciating the rate of change is to consider that to a person born in 1940, who was 45 years old in 1985, the following occurred:

1. Telecommunications became, for practical purposes, instantaneous.
2. The speed of information processing increased a millionfold.
3. The rate of population increase went up more than a millionfold.
4. Jet aircraft, radar, space missiles, and space satellites became commonplace.
5. Major organs, such as the human heart, kidneys, and liver, were transplanted.
6. Moon and Martian landings were successfully completed.[34]

To this list, add the following:

1. Genetic engineering, test-tube babies, and sex selection became realities.
2. With a portable remote system (weighing less than one pound) a TV viewer can instantly (at the speed of light) tune into one or more of 100 channels and connect live to any part of the world through a satellite communication system.
3. More than 75 percent of the items on supermarket shelves today did not exist in 1940. Plastic money has since replaced paper money as the major medium of exchange.
4. Computers are common in everyday life, including in schools; robots are commonplace

in commerce and industry, and they will soon be in homes as well.

5. Whereas three-fourths of Americans employed by industry in 1940 were manufacturing goods, today more than 60 percent are providing services; we have changed from an industrial society to a "postindustrial society" or what some people call the "third technological revolution" or "third wave."[35]

One way to illustrate the *direction of change* is to consider world population growth. Philip Hauser estimated that for 600,000 years, the world population expanded by .02 per thousand per year. On a two-dimensional graph such as Figure 5-1, this growth appears as a straight horizontal line. During the past 500 years, however, the growth line has shifted essentially from a horizontal position to a vertical one. At the present time, population growth has expanded from 2 percent per millennium to more than 2 percent per year—a thousandfold increase.[36]

This shift in direction constitutes a fundamental change that simply cannot be comprehended as a mere quantitative change. (The quantitive shift represents only one dimension of change in population growth.) Other equally important directional changes in society involve advances in science, communication, transportation—all of which affect the quality of life and which have global impact. Actually, in these areas of society, as with population growth, the rate of change at a period in time reaches geometric or exponential proportions, and

causes a dramatic shift or change in direction. For population growth, as well as for science, communication, and transportation, the critical time period has been the present century.

Educators, especially curriculum specialists, need to reduce educational lag and to avoid planning schools for the 1990s that are suited for the 1970s—a typical twenty-year lag period that often exists between schools and society. The fact of rapid change and the need to plan schools today for tomorrow bring to mind serious questions: What policies govern our society? At a global level, what should be our educational aims? How do we identify the "good" life and what role do the schools play? How do schools reduce the gap between the "haves" and "have nots"? How do the schools prepare students for the world of tomorrow, when teachers who are trusted to do the job mainly rely on a knowledge base that is quickly becoming, if it is not already, dated?

Schools as a Source of Change.

If we take a broad, long view of schools— that is, a *macro* view—we can observe noticeable changes in schools over time. Historically, according to Philip Jackson, "one has only to think of the wooden benches and planked floors of the early American classroom as compared with the plastic chairs and tile flooring in today's suburban schools to note changes."[37] We can strengthen the contrast by looking back to the one-room schoolhouse: Students of many ages were

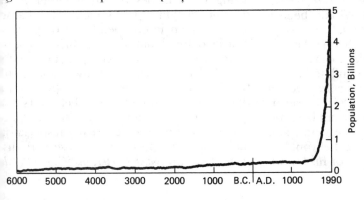

FIGURE 5-1 World Population Growth, 6000 B.C. to 1990 A.D.

crowded in one room; the teacher stood behind the pulpit (like the church minister) preaching the daily lessons; no blackboards or chalk were used; the desks and chairs were bolted down; the sun was the major source of light; and firewood was the main source of heat. Schools, today, are dramatically different.

If we look at the school during our lifetime—that is, a *micro* view—say, when we were attending elementary school, we note that the changes have been minimal. Unruh and Alexander have summarized the milieu of change since the 1950s: "Surface changes, small and isolated innovations and lack of comprehensive approaches to changes" have prevailed in the schools. The underlying assumption, or the reason for the lack of change, has been that "the school as an institution was headed in the right direction except that it needed to exert more effort toward its previous goals and make content and instruction more palatable to students. It was taken for granted that there was nothing wrong in the schools [and] . . . it was the student" and not the schools "that needed to be changed."[38]

Although the research in education may be impressive in quantity, very few noticeable changes have resulted in schooling since our days as students. We are basically using the same instructional methods in the classroom that we were using fifty years ago, according to one observer. On the other hand, the changes and improvements in science, technology, and medicine within the last five years have been impressive, and they have affected almost all of our lives in some way. "Had Rip Van Winkle been a teacher and slept for fifty years, he could return to the classroom and perform relatively well; the chalk, eraser, blackboard, textbook, and pen and paper are still, today, the main tools for most teachers, as they were a half a century ago—or longer." If, however, Mr. Van Winkle's occupation "had been related to one of the other three fields, and had he dozed off for five years, he would be unable to function effectively for his knowl-edge and skills would be dramaticall dated."[39]

We might expect educational aims an subject matter to change as society impose new social and political demands on th schools, and as new knowledge is created And they do! However, we should not ex pect the structure and organization c schools to change dramatically. This is wh Rip Van Winkle could function in th schools after sleeping for so long, or why teacher, after ten or twenty years of retire ment, could, if he or she wanted, go bac into the classroom and still be effective.

We must understand that schools ar highly bureaucratic and conservative (o traditional) institutions that operate wit standardized norms of behavior, writte rules and regulations, and well-define tasks dispersed among administrator teachers, and students. As parents and/o teachers who were once students, we can re turn to school and readily cope and functio almost immediately because the behavior and tasks, the rituals, rules, and regulation have not changed much since we were chi dren.

As teachers, curriculum specialists, ad ministrators, and students interact on daily basis in the operation of a school, a so cial order develops: A set of routines an rules surfaces and group norms and organi zational values become pervasive and shap individual personalities and behavior. Ho and Miskel describe this process: "Th school is a system of social interaction; it i an organized whole comprised of inter acting personalities bound together in a organic relationship." The school is "charac terized by an interdependence of parts, clearly defined population, differentiatio from its environment, a complex network o social relationships, and its own unique cul ture."[40] The outcome is a host of institu tional norms and patterns of behaviors tha govern the interaction between teachers an students and between curriculum specialis and other support staff. Observers us terms like *intrinsic character, institutional real ties,* or *cultural patterns* to describe these social characteristics and interactions.[41] When taken together they tend to result in a persuasive method of socializing and controlling the people who attend and/or work in schools, and they tend to inhibit change.

Knowledge as a Source of Change.

The accumulated body of organized knowledge about people and the world may be viewed as an extension of and interaction process with contemporary society. As society changes, so does our knowledge; in reverse, as our knowledge base increases, additional changes take place in society as well. The changes in Western society and growth in knowledge result from our striving to understand, control, and change the physical and social environment around us. (Changes take place in other societies, too, although today the growth in knowledge tends to be slower.) The schools should also be considered as a major data source for knowledge, especially for children and youth, in terms of: (1) screening knowledge against aims society sets for education; (2) identifying important kinds of knowledge; and (3) determining what can and should be taught.

Explosion of Knowledge. Since the 1950s, many educators have continued to call attention to the explosion of knowledge. Every fifteen years or so, our significant knowledge doubles, and this trend makes it important to continuously reappraise and revise existing curricula. "It can be affirmed unequivocally," says Bentley Glass, "that the amount of scientific knowledge available at the end of one's life will be almost one hundred times what it was when he was born." (This may be considered as an overstatement, because knowledge cannot continue to explode exponentially as it has in the past.) Moreover, 95 percent of all the scientists who ever lived are alive today.[42]

Similarly, Warren Ziegler maintains that: (1) more mathematics has been created since 1900 than during the entire period of history; (2) half of what a graduate engineer studies today will be obsolete in ten years; and (3) half of what a person learns is no longer valid by the time he or she reaches middle age.[43] We add to this list that nearly half of what we will need to know to function in scientific or technical jobs by the year 2000 is not even known today, by anyone.

The almost incredible explosion of knowledge threatens to overwhelm us unless we can find ways to deal with this new and growing wealth of information; new knowledge must be constantly introduced into the curriculum while less important material is pruned away. In assessing the ongoing rush of knowledge, Alvin Toffler asserts that knowledge taught should be related to the future. "Nothing should be included in the required curriculum unless it can be strongly justified in terms of the future. If this means scrapping a substantial part of the formal curriculum, so be it."[44] To deal with this knowledge explosion, as it shapes the future, curriculum specialists have two major problems that require continuous attention: (1) what knowledge to select and (2) how to organize it.

What Knowledge Is of Most Worth?
This question, which was raised by Spencer more than 100 years ago, has social implications; it is certainly more relevant today, because of the complexity of and changes in society, than it was during Spencer's time. In recent years, the question has, in fact, been repeated by many different curricularists.[45] Actually, the question dates back to ancient Greece, when Plato and Aristotle questioned the value of knowledge in relation to society and governmental affairs, and to ancient Rome, when Quintilian set forth the original seven liberal arts—grammar, rhetoric, logic, arithmetic, geometry, astronomy, and music—as the ideal curriculum for educated citizens of public life: Senators, lawyers, teachers, civil servants, and politicians. During the modern school period, these seven liberal arts have expanded to include many other subjects.

Table 5-1 shows a survey of enrollments in four basic subject areas for 1980. The percent of subjects for which high school seniors completed more than three years of coursework: English (including literature), 26 percent; history (or social studies), 10 percent; mathematics, 8.5 percent; and science, 6 percent. If these data appear alarming, the figures that show the seniors having completed one year or less are even worse: Mathematics, 24 percent; and science, 35 percent. Comparison data with other advanced, technological countries are disheartening. In any event, the percent for each subject area suggests what school officials, adult society, and students consider to be most worthwhile knowledge.

Considering that we live in a highly technocratic and scientific society, one in which knowledge has great impact on our standard of living, and in a world in which the push of a button can have enormous impact on our lives, the small enrollments in science and mathematics have serious implications for the future of our country. A similar concern was voiced nearly thirty years ago, when our standard of living was increasing more rapidly and when we were more influential as a superpower. Then, James Conant stressed that students needed to enroll in more courses in science, mathematics, and foreign language.[46] The seeds of the Sputnik era have resurfaced in the 1980s, under the theme of excellence in education, and there is the same feeling of urgency. Our failure to heed Conant's warning is viewed by some as one reason for our decline as the leading political and economic giant of the world, and for the general decline of our manufacturing capability and standard of living.

As a point of comparison, consider that Japanese students are required to take 23 percent of their total junior high school curricula in science and mathematics. In high school, they are required to take 1¼ science courses per year and 1½ math courses per year (including calculus and statistics). Because 94 percent of the Japanese attend high school, this requirement produces a

TABLE 5-1   Years of Coursework Completed by High School Seniors, 1980

	One year or less	More than three years
English	2.1%	26.0%
Mathematics	23.5	8.5
Science	35.0	6.1
History (Social Studies)	12.2	9.7

Source: From *The Condition of Education, 1983* (Washington, D.C.: U.S. Government Printing Office, 1984) Table 1.11, p. 34.

more scientifically literate public than ours.[47] In addition, Japanese students outperform American students in science and mathematics on the International Association for the Evaluation of Educational Achievement (IEA) study.

Knowledge Areas and Skills. Because our knowledge is changing so rapidly, we must continuously ask ourselves what is the most worthwhile knowledge, and we must continuously reappraise what we mean by worthwhile. A number of paradigms have been developed along these lines. Schwab, for example, takes an eclectic approach to organizing curriculum in context with change. He is willing to accept various curriculum modes, and he points out that there are limitations to almost any approach. We need to organize a curriculum that is conducive to change, and that enables scholars and practitioners to work together and test their ideas in the context of changing problems and issues of society.[48]

Weinstein and Fantini attempt to integrate a cognitive and humanistic view toward knowledge and learning. Referring to knowledge as "content vehicles," they contend that content should "include not only conventional subject areas (English, social studies, mathematics, science, and so on)," but also foundation disciplines such as "psychology, sociology, anthropology, philosophy," and so on, as well as "classroom situations, . . . out of school experiences, [and] the children themselves."[49] Weinstein and Fantini consider people more important than subject matter, but subject matter is still important for the self-actualization of people.

Elsewhere, Fantini argues that although educators talk about the relationship between cognition and affect, the curriculum limits the relationship. "Knowing something cognitively does not always result in behavior that follows on that knowing." This is because knowledge cannot always influence behavior, and "all kinds of knowledge are not equally influential." The missing link in the formula is that "knowledge [should be] related to the affective or emotional world of the learner. . . . Unless knowledge relates to feeling, it is unlikely to affect behavior appreciably."[50]

In a highly theoretical book, Joseph Tykociner suggests twelve basic areas of knowledge for dealing with change:[51] (1) *arts:* architecture, choreography, dramatics, graphic arts, industrial design, landscaping, literature, music, painting, sculpture, and so on; (2) *symbolics of information:* linguistics, mathematics, logic, and information theory; (3) *hylenergetics* (sciences dealing with matter and energy): physics, chemistry, astronomy, geology, and mineralogy; (4) *biological sciences:* botany, zoology, taxonomy, morphology, cytology, genetics, and physiology; (5) *psychology:* experimental, developmental, abnormal, animal, human, and industrial; (6) *sociology:* behavioral studies, human ecology, demography, social institutions, and ethnology; (7) *exeligmology* (sciences dealing with the past): the world at large, nations, states, ethnic groups, communities, family groups in historical, cultural, literary, scientific, and philosophical context; (8) *pronoetics* (sciences related to sustaining human life): agriculture, medicine, technology, and national defense; (9) *regulative area* (harmonizing human relations): jurisprudence, political science, economics, and public administration; (10) *disseminative area* (transmission of knowledge): education, vocational guidance, library science, journalism, and mass communications; (11) *zetetics* (how knowledge can be systematized and increased): problem solving, methodology, environmental conditions and incentives, research,

and development; and (12) *integrative areas* (the search for synthesis or a total picture): philosophical, aspirational, and general systems. This scheme is shown in Figure 5-2.

What Tykociner has achieved is to bind together the entire field of arts and sciences, with methods and processes for systematizing knowledge and for representing it in terms of growth, transformation, and integration. Knowledge is envisioned as a continuous process that shapes society—and links the past, present, and future. In more practical terms, Tykociner presents curriculum specialists with a total range of knowledge from which to select subject matter and organize curriculum. He provides us with various kinds of content and processes upon which the generalist or specialist can draw to develop an instructional program.

Knowledge and Future Learning. As we begin to cope with the many changes in our society, we need to organize certain knowledge skills and knowledge assumptions to deal with and evaluate the explosion of knowledge:

1. *Knowledge should comprise the basic tools.* This includes reading, writing, arithmetic, and oral communication, as well as computer literacy. The basic tools are means to an outcome, not an end in themselves. Students need to learn more than the basics, but without the basics they cannot move beyond simple knowledge or think critically in the subject fields.

2. *Knowledge should facilitate learning how to learn.* The school should help the learners acquire the skills, tools, and processes necessary to become more adept at learning and to use existing knowledge to learn new knowledge. Teachers must limit the temptation to teach a host of facts and right answers; they must encourage learners to assume responsibility for their own learning.

3. *Knowledge should be applicable to the real world.* Book knowledge that cannot be applied to everyday life is meaningless and easily forgotten. It does not help the learners participate productively in society. The schools must resist teaching theory that cannot be applied to practice. Good theory can be applied to practice.

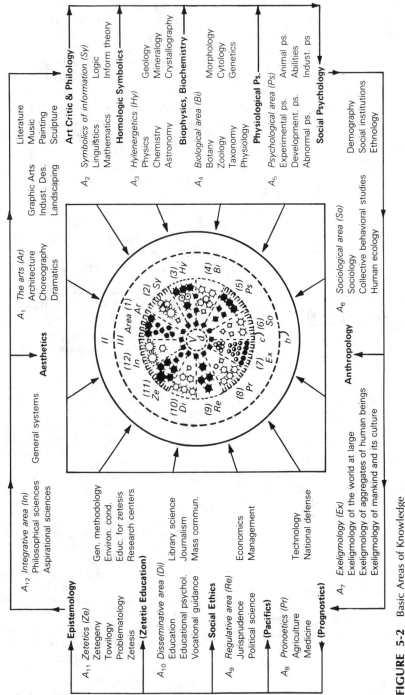

FIGURE 5-2 Basic Areas of Knowledge

Source: From Joseph T. Tykociner, *Outlines of Zetetics* (Philadelphia: Dorrance, 1966), pp. 35–51.

4. *Knowledge should improve the learners' self-concepts, awareness skills, and senses of personal integrity.* Stressing cognitive learning, or facts and figures, without considering the personal, emotional, and even spiritual state of the individual, is only considering half of learning. Knowledge should be used to develop the learners' feelings and personal integrity. It should enable them to get along with themselves and others, and to be relatively content with themselves and others. Unhappy or anxiety-laden individuals cannot make the best use of their cognitive skills.

5. *Knowledge should consist of many forms and methods.* There are many roads to learning and many avenues of inquiry. What works for one learner does not always work as well as for another, because there are many different styles of learning and patterns of thinking (in part related to sex, class, culture, and intelligence). Schools need to provide various options and alternatives for acquiring knowledge and learning. Schools must also recognize they are only one of many sources of learning and intellectual authority; they compete with the home, community, peer group, and mass media—which together have greater impact on the learners, on knowledge acquisition, and on thinking than the schools.

6. *Knowledge should prepare the individual for the world of technology.* The individual, in modern society, must learn to live with computers, robots, lasers, telecommunications, and space exploration. A truly educated, productive, and well-rounded individual will be able to function in an accelerating world of science and technology (i.e., individuals should be scientifically and technologically literate).

7. *Knowledge should prepare individuals for the world of bureaucracy.* Bureaucracy is a growing social phenomenon that also characterizes modern society. The school system is one of many formal institutions that is run by the complicated machinery of social organization; actually, it is the first of many bureaucratic organizations that the child will encounter in life. The individual in school, in church, in the military, in the hospital, on the job and in dealing with government must learn to cope with the enormous size of bureaucracy. He or she must be able to get along with others both on a horizontal basis (peers and colleagues) and on a vertical basis (subordinates and supervisors), in regard to rules and regulations, record keeping and "documentation," impersonal and abstract relations, experts, incompetents, seniority, and administrative hierarchy.

8. *Knowledge should permit the individual to retrieve old information.* No individual can accumulate all of the knowledge necessary to fully develop his or her human potential. The individual must understand how to retrieve old knowledge, and then to modify or transform it to gain new knowledge. Knowledge is a powerful tool and in an age of information processing, those able to retrieve and then apply information intelligently will be most productive and powerful and best able to compete in contemporary society.

9. *Knowledge acquisition should be a lifelong process.* It must be recognized that schools play a diminishing role as the learners grow and develop. Schools provide only a preliminary and temporary base of knowledge that is eventually superseded by other institutions and different forms of education. Other educational tools such as books, newspapers, television, videos, computers, etc. assume greater importance and more influence than textbooks or other school materials for continuing the educations of both youngsters and adults. As adolescents develop into adults, their experiences extend beyond schools. They acquire most new learning, in fact, outside of schools.

10. *Knowledge should be taught in context with values.* Knowledge is based on facts, which are objective, neutral, and quantifiable. The knowledge that is learned becomes processed through the social and philosophical lens of the individual; it therefore becomes value-laden. In a very real sense, what we learn, and what we do not learn, are based on a process of choosing—a filtering process—that is itself based on values. How we interpret knowledge, how we build and use it, partially reflect the act of valuing and the value structure we emphasize. The greatest danger in teaching knowledge is to ignore the values that shape the individual and society; this is teaching in a vacuum and without vision. Worthwhile knowledge cannot replace values, but must be incorporated into the values we cherish. The kind of society we are, and the kinds of people we become, reflect both the knowledge and values we

learn—more precisely, how we interpret knowledge amid our values.

Critical and Cautionary Choices.   All these knowledge skills provide learners with the basis for coping with change—and for understanding and analyzing the events and trends that impact on society. Those who possess these skills have an enormous advantage in dealing with themselves and others, and in the way they think and act in schools and society. Those who have such knowledge can deal with alternatives, possibilities, and probabilities—and can thus formulate and act upon convictions. Failure to achieve these knowledge skills leads to powerlessness in a powerful society.

On the other hand, we caution the reader on several fronts. Change for the sake of change is not good; change must be tempered with wisdom, compassion, and justice. Scholars throughout the ages have viewed their societies as being at the cutting edge of change and progress. We may be just as myopic, as we view our society; only the future will tell. New knowledge, indeed, is not necessarily better than old knowledge: Are we to throw away most of Aristotle, Copernicus, Galileo, Kepler, Darwin, and Newton—merely because they are not part of this century? If we stress only scientific and technological knowledge, we could languish physically, aesthetically, and spiritually. Also, we have no guarantee that a futuristic curriculum best prevents us from repeating the mistakes of the past; as a nation we seem to lack historical perspective, and we tend to rely on our youth and future.

What knowledge to select and how to organize it require continuing attention; we must learn to prune away old and irrelevant knowledge, and sequence, balance, and integrate new and relevant knowledge into subject matter. As we modify and update the curriculum, we must not, however, throw away time-tested, enduring subjects, such as literature, history, even music or art, because of pressure groups and special-interest groups. We must learn to screen our knowledge, with subsequent emphasis on certain subjects, against the values and educational aims that, as a society, we set for schools. These are difficult tasks. Curriculum workers need to help educators make choices in a climate of change.

ESTABLISHING SOCIAL/ EDUCATIONAL PRIORITIES

We look to the schools to help us cope with the elements of change. As a society, we react to change and social pressures by revising the aims or priorities of education. The schools, in turn, respond by changing their programs. The schools are also influenced by external or public groups who seek to further their interests and promote their causes, and who pressure the schools to teach particular subjects. Thus, rarely will there be complete agreement, much less agreement for any length of time, on the aims or priorities of education. Pressure, popular rhetoric, and slogans of the day, as well as concerns and demands of various public groups, must be balanced for the good of the general public and the nation at large.

Education for All Students.

Education prior to the turn of the twentieth century emphasized a perennialist outlook and stressed traditional subject matter, mental discipline, and academically able students. Influenced by the larger trends of society—namely, the muckracker movement and calls for social and economic reform—the period between World War I and World War II (some educators have extended the period from the *Kalamazoo* decision, in 1874, when the Supreme Court ruled that the states had the right to levy taxes for support of public schools,[52] to the Sputnik era) may be characterized by the rise and fall of progressive education. The educational aims of this progressive era, and the curriculum, reflected the growing child psychology movement and endorsed meeting the diverse needs of all students, providing a common ground for teaching, enhancing American ideas, and educating all citizens to function in a democratic society.

During this period, the *Cardinal Principles of Secondary Education* were formulated.[53] Only one of the seven principles or aims of secondary education was concerned with the fundamentals of cognitive learning. The aims cited in 1918 are still, in one form or another, the major aims and goals of contemporary education. The most important aspect of the document is that it emphasized that secondary schools should aim to educate all youth for "complete living," not just one segment of the student population, such as academically able students. Also, it did not emphasize subject matter or mental vigor. The Commission noted that more than two-thirds of entering high school students dropped out prior to graduation, and that an increasing number of immigrant children had to be educated, socialized, and provided with appropriate economic and civic skills.[54]

Twenty years later, the Educational Policies Commission of the NEA, which included the presidents of Harvard and Cornell Universities, the Commissioner of Education, and a number of progressive educators issued a report entitled *The Purpose of Education in American Democracy.*[55] Concerned with the problems of out-of-school youth and unemployment resulting from the Great Depression, these educators issued a comprehensive set of four goals: self-realization, human relations, economic efficiency, and civic responsibility. Each goal had several subcategories (see Chapter 6).

During the mid 1940s, the Educational Policies Commission continued to modify the aims of education. Influenced by World War II, it stressed aims related to democracy and world citizenship, as well as those related to the general needs of children and youth. According to another influential report, *Education for All American Youth,* youth must develop "Ten Imperative Needs":[56] (1) economic and vocational skills; (2) good health and physical fitness; (3) community

and citizenship duties; (4) family duties; (5) consumer skills; (6) scientific skills; (7) literature, art, and music skills; (8) leisure activities; (9) ethical values; and (10) rational abilities. These needs were mostly sociopsychological and physical in nature; only two were concerned with subject matter, and a third focused on cognitive learning in general.

Recapping from the 1918 Seven Cardinal Principles to the 1944 Ten Imperative Needs, the aims are representative of an era dominated by progressivism and by an offshoot science of child psychology. During this period, emphasis was placed on the "whole child" and "life adjustment." Subject matter was deemphasized, while social, psychological, vocational, moral, and civic responsibilities were stressed.

In general, the traditional concept of curriculum as a body of subjects came under attack by progressive educators; the major emphasis focused on the "child-centered," "experience-centered," and "activity-centered" curriculum. All three approaches were used by Pestalozzi and Froebel in the nineteenth century and by Dewey in his laboratory school at the University of Chicago from 1896 to 1904.[57] All three approaches emphasized adapting curriculum to student needs and interests, and ensuring that curriculum was relevant to the realities of the learner.

Focus on Academically Talented Students.

After World War II, during the era of the Cold War and the Soviet Sputnik flight, the aforementioned aims and curriculum focus became targets for criticism. Americans were appalled that our country was losing the space race to the Soviet Union, and that our skies were no longer impregnable.

Even though the influential Harvard Report, published at the end of World War II, looked optimistically to educating the whole person and providing a general education as means of developing the common understanding important to all citizens in a free society, powerful forces called for a return to academic essentials, and old-fashioned mental discipline. Historian Arthur Bestor stated that the main subjects in elementary school should be reading, writing, and arithmetic, with some emphasis on science and history. At the high school level, the curriculum should stress math, science, history, English, and a foreign language.[58] Admiral Hyman Rickover questioned why Johnny could not read while Ivan could and did. He demanded that, in the national interest, there be a return to the basics, a beefing up of our science and mathematics courses, and "a deemphasis on life-adjustment schools and progressive educational lists."[59]

Werner von Braun, a German-educated missile expert, testified before a U.S. Senate Committee in 1958 to urge ending "family life" and "human relations" subjects and adopting the European system of education, which emphasized "technical and scientific subjects" and academic excellence.[60] Lee DuBridge, then president of the California Institute of Technology, who testified before the committee on the same day, recommended that curriculum areas of science and mathematics be "singled out for federal support." DuBridge urged that schools recognize, encourage, and provide special programs for students who are "unusually gifted and ambitious," and, moreover, that a student's education persist "as far as his intellectual capacities and his ambitions should take him."[61] Unfortunately, the senators did not ask von Braun or DuBridge what schools or society should do with the intellectually less able students.

In 1952, as Chair of the Educational Policies Commission, James Conant had endorsed a progressive policy document that urged a student-centered, whole-child approach to schooling. By 1959 Conant's vision was still "to provide a good general education for *all* the pupils," but he now emphasized "educating those with a talent for handling advanced subjects." After visiting fifty-five high schools across the country that had "a good reputation," Conant concluded that "the academically talented student, as a rule, is not being sufficiently challenged, does not work hard enough, and his program of academic subjects is not of sufficient range."[62]

In the midst of intense criticism toward schools and school people, Conant came to the defense of the educational establishment and saw little need for radically changing schools. Conant's influential book, *The American High School Today,* was a blueprint for moderate reform: For upgrading the curriculum, especially mathematics, science, and foreign language; requiring more academic subjects; tightening standards and grades; pushing students to their maximum cognitive potentials; and grouping students according to their abilities. Although Conant gave some consideration to slow and average learners, his major emphasis for reform was related to serving the needs of the highly gifted (the intellectually highest 3 percent of the student population on a national basis) and the academically talented (the top 20 percent in terms of scholastic aptitude).[63] Indeed, many of Conant's ideas could be considered a return to the mental discipline approach under the modern version of essentialist philosophy.

Many policy statements issued during this period focused on academically bright students, the three Rs at the elementary school level, and traditional academic subjects at the high school level. For example, the White House Conference on Education in 1955 stressed quality and proposed that "educational programs [must] fully exercise and develop the abilities of especially bright students."[64] Five years later the President's Commission on National Goals gave top priority to science, mathematics, and foreign languages and called for "a testing program beginning in grade one if not before . . . and ability grouping from the earliest years of school. Every effort [was to be] made in and out of school to provide enrichment for the gifted student."[65] Indeed, these were rigorous and competitive times in schools, and testing and tracking of students were considered acceptable. Scholarships based on merit and ability, not on need or athletics, was the order of the day.

Focus on Subject Matter. Hard on the heels of Sputnik, and these national policy reports, came federal legislation supporting training, equipment, and programs in subject fields deemed vital to defense. The major legislation, called the National Defense Act (1958), singled out science, mathematics, modern languages, and guidance (often construed as a way of steering youth into the three academic fields and into college if they had the ability). The focus on certain subjects and academically talented youth was often couched in terms of a free people's surviving in a world in which Communism was spreading and in which the American sky was at risk.

Most important, large sums of money, for beefing up the curriculum, were readily available for the first time from both government and foundation sources. During the aftermath of Sputnik, William Van Til wrote, "The end result was that both national interest and available funds [in education] coincided. The scholars had a genuine opportunity to reconstruct the content of their separate subjects."[66] This was particularly true at the secondary level. To many leaders of this period, it was clear that the way to proceed to reconstruct subject matter was to call together the scientific community and university scholars, who most intimately knew the particular subject, along with some curriculum specialists, who might help with regards to methodology.

From this dialogue among scientists and scholars came a host of national curriculum projects that centered on science and math. These included the Biological Sciences Curriculum Study (BSCS), Chemical Education Material Study (CEMS), Physical Science Study Committee (PSSC), and the School Mathematics Study Group (SMSG). The new wave of curriculum reform emphasized the subject matter rather than students' needs or interests or societal problems. Most

of the leaders of this movement made sweeping claims for the superiority of the new curriculum, what they often called the "new science" and the "new math."

The subject matter was reconstructed around disciplines with special methods of inquiry (that is, around major concepts, principles, and generalizations), and, according to Tanner and Tanner, science and mathematics "came to occupy the highest rungs of the disciplinary hierarchy."[67] Proliferation of special projects in these subjects was followed by other projects in the social sciences and humanities intended to beef up the curriculum, especially the academic subjects of secondary schools, and to embrace the discipline approach for the science and math projects. But the search for structure in English, history, foreign language, and so on, proved unattainable. Even in science and mathematics, the idea of a disciplinary structure eventually declined.[68]

Focus on Disadvantaged Students.

The 1960s and early 1970s ushered in a period in which the social conscience of America burst forth—coinciding with our concern over poverty, racial discrimination, and equal educational opportunity. New aims and educational priorities surfaced to meet the climate of change. With the majority of students not going on to college, and with a large percentage of students dropping out of school or graduating as functional illiterates, serious problems could be anticipated if our aims and priorities continued to be narrowly directed at our most able students. The shift to the problems of disadvantaged students gradually accelerated until this population became the number-one concern in education. Exemplifying the change, James Conant, an early proponent of challenging the gifted students, gradually shifted his views.

In 1961, Conant wrote *Slums and Suburbs*. Only two years before, Conant had advocated academic rigor and upgraded academic subjects, as well as greater attention to the top 20 percent of high school students. Now he urged educators and policy makers to pay closer attention to the inner-city and disadvantaged children. He proposed that slum schools be upgraded and greater attention be paid to the less able students. Conant wrote:

I am concerned we are allowing social dynamite to accumulate in our large cities. . . . Leaving aside human tragedies, I submit that a continuation of this situation [youth out of school and out of work] is a menace to the social and political health of the large cities.

The improvement of slum conditions is only in part a question of improving education. But the role of the schools is of utmost importance. . . . Added responsibility, however, requires additional funds. Indeed the whole question of financing public education in the large cities is a major national concern.[69]

Conant's new position was a sign of the times—a shift in educational aims to focus on the disadvantaged. Historically a strong advocate of academic excellence, he was expressing a new viewpoint: One that would correct the educational discrepancies among students by placing greater emphasis on less able students, especially those in the inner city.

Given the student unrest and urban riots of the 1960s, it was easy to accept the arguments of an impacted crisis in schools and society. The government reports that were published in the 1960s strongly suggested an impending social upheaval. The needs of disadvantaged groups were stressed, both in schools and society, and these needs were reflected in such reports as the National Advisory Commission on Civil Disorders in 1967, the National Council on the Education of Disadvantaged Children in 1969, and the HEW Urban Task Force Report in 1970. A new political bias seemed to evolve; in education it overlooked the average and above-average student, and in social and economic arenas it overlooked what was later to be called "middle America."

The outcome was a host of compensatory programs funded by the federal govern-ment, although state and local money as well as foundation money was also available. The Elementary and Secondary Education Act (ESEA), passed in 1965, immediately provided $1 billion in Title I funds (sometimes called compensatory funding) to supplement and improve the education of poor and minority group children. Ten years later, Title I money totaled $2 billion per year, or about $200 extra per disadvantaged child. By 1980, Title I expenditures were more than $3 billion per year, and other federal compensatory expenditures totaled another $2 billion or more—a total of about $500 extra per disadvantaged child. During this fifteen year period, over $35 billion had been appropriated by the federal government.[70] Today, Chapter I funds have replaced most of the early ESEA money, and the amount of federal funding for the disadvantaged continues to increase: $3.7 billion in 1985, plus another $4 billion earmarked for vocational and postsecondary disadvantaged students.[71]

Expanded Priorities: New Disadvantaged Groups.

The focus on the disadvantaged extended into the 1970s; in fact, the definition of the disadvantaged was enlarged to include multicultural, bilingual, and handicapped students and to a lesser extent, women. Our multicultural and bilingual efforts were characterized by increased federal funding for Hispanic, Asian American, and Native American students; by the Bilingual Act in 1968, which expanded bilingual programs in American schools; and by the 1974 U.S. Supreme Court ruling in *Lau v. Nicholas,* which stated that schools must take steps to help students who "are certain to find their classroom experiences wholly incomprehensible" because they do not understand English. The courts, as well as policy makers and educators, took an active role in providing educational opportunities for limited-English speaking (LES) and non-English speaking (NES) students.[72] Despite controversies that have surfaced concerning specific approaches and programs and recruitment of personnel, bilingual and multicultural education grew in importance during the 1970s. Congressional appropriations for bilingual education increased from $6.1 million in 1970 to $156 million in 1980. In 1986, appropriations decreased to $143 million, illustrating that these funds have now leveled off.[73]

During the 1970s, much activity and concern also surfaced over special education, especially for the handicapped and for students with learning disabilities. New pressure groups, new courses, advanced degrees, new certification requirements, and new teachers and faculty at colleges and universities stimulated recognition of special education, as have new policies and programs. The Education for all Handicapped Children Act (PL 94-142) of 1975 is the cornerstone of these policies and programs.

Handicapped students are defined by this act as those who are mentally retarded, hard of hearing, deaf, orthopedically impaired, other health impaired, speech impaired, visually handicapped, emotionally disturbed, or learning disabled and, by reason thereof, require special education and related services. The legislation mandates a free and appropriate education for all handicapped children and youth. Handicapped students must be provided with special education and related services at public expense under public supervision and direction. Schools must not only adopt policies that serve all handicapped students, but they must conduct searches to locate such students as well.

Today, concern for the handicapped is very much alive, and the courts continue to take an active role in protecting the rights of and improving educational opportunities for the handicapped. Monies earmarked for the handicapped continue to increase in real dollars and in proportion to spending on nonhandicapped students; moreover, an increasing number of students are being identified as handicapped. Approximately 10 to 11 percent of the public school enrollments are considered handicapped, compared to 5 percent in 1975 (the year handicapped legislation went into effect).[74] This increase indicates that educators and policy makers recognize that many students who did not receive help in the past in fact need special help—not that contemporary students have more problems than students of earlier generations.

Concern for the gifted and talented students reached a low point during the 1960s and 1970s. The commitment to educating the gifted and talented was slight compared to efforts directed at the disadvantaged and at other special populations, such as bilingual, handicapped, or learning-disabled students. As two authorities stated, only "a very small percentage of the gifted and talented population [was] being serviced by existing programs, [about] 4 percent of the 1.5 to 2.5 million children."[75] A low funding priority and lack of trained personnel, coupled with few pressure groups for the gifted and talented, resulted in a scarcity of programs for these children—who, in terms of numbers, represent a real minority.

National priorities in the 1970s (like those in the 1960s) for the most part did not focus on the average, ordinary students who were nonrich, nonpoor, nonminority, nongifted, and nonnewsworthy. There was (and still is) very little in the educational literature on the cultural, social, and educational diversity of students in "middle" America—in Astoria, New York; Lombard, Illinois; or Whittier, California, for example. These students were rarely defined as a special group with special characteristics and needs, so remedial or special programs for them were minimal. In the late 1970s and early 1980s, some attention was unwittingly devoted to them as a result of other trends—such as the national testing program, minimum competency testing, basic-skills programs, and the theme of national excellence in schools—but special programs and services for average children remained minimal.

National Task Force Reports on Education.

In the mid-1980s, national attention turned to the need for educational excellence and higher academic standards for all students. The educational dimensions of this problem were amply documented in ten policy reports between 1983 and 1987, all calling for reforms to improve the quality of education in the United States. (The reports and their sponsoring agencies are described in Table 5-2.)

To support their alarming statements about the decline of American education and the need for academic reform, the policy reports detailed a host of gloomy trends and statistics about the decline of American education. Seven of the ten reports emphasized the need to strengthen the curriculum in the core subjects of English, math, science, foreign language, and social studies. The focus was thus on a *common curriculum.* Technology and computer courses were mentioned often, either as components of science or math or as separate subject areas (sometimes referred to as the fourth R). High-level cognitive and thinking skills were also stressed. All of the reports concerned all students: Providing various programs and personnel for disadvantaged and learning disabled students, as well as for average and above average students. The notion of *equity* was thus paramount. Nevertheless, the theme of *excellence* still seemed to stress academic, college-bound, and even gifted students; emphasis was still on core academic subjects and advanced science and mathematics.

All the reports emphasized tougher standards and tougher courses, and five out of the ten proposed that colleges raise their admission requirements. Most of the reports also talked about increasing homework, time for learning, and time in school, as well as instituting more rigorous grading, testing, homework, and discipline. They mentioned, too, upgrading teacher certification, increasing teacher salaries, increasing the number of and rewarding science and math teachers, and providing merit pay for outstanding teachers. Overall, they stressed excellence (not equity), academic achievement (not the whole child), and increased productivity (not relevancy or humanism).

Most of the reports expressed concern that the schools are pressed to play too many social roles; that the schools cannot meet all these expectations; and that the schools are in danger of losing sight of their key role—teaching the basic skills and the core academic subjects, new skills for computer use, and higher-level cognitive skills for the world of work, technology, and even military defense. Accordingly, many of the reports used such terms as "emergency," "urgency," "crucial to national survival," "global competition," "act of war," "educational disarmament" and the like—reminding us of the post-Sputnik era once again. Perhaps the number-one criticism of all these reports is who is to pay for all these reform measures given the decline of federal spending in education, the reported deficits at the federal level, and the weakening fiscal health among most states.

PLANNING FOR EDUCATIONAL CHANGE

As long as society is dynamic and composed of a conglomeration of cultural and social groups, the debate over the aims of education will stir up controversy and change. Perhaps this is good; perhaps this is what makes a society viable and able to resist decay.

In examining the aims or priorities of education from the turn of the century until today, we see considerable reiteration, but we also note considerable evolution—linked to sweeping social change. For example, the early twentieth-century adherents of mental discipline advocated rigorous intellectual training, as did the essentialist critics and conservative thinkers of the 1950s and mid-1980s. At the turn of the century public schools stressed an academic curriculum, and this priority reasserted itself during the

TABLE 5-2 Overview of Selected Recommendations of Ten Reports on Education, 1983–1987

Report and Sponsor	Curriculum Objectives	Content Emphasis	School Organization	Government-Business Role
Academic Preparation for College, The College Board	Improve student competencies in reading, writing, speaking, listening, reasoning, math, and study skills Raise college entrance standards	English, math, science, computers, foreign language	Stress study and independent learning . Incentives to students	Develop a national standard for academic achievement in secondary education
Action for Excellence, Education Commission of the States	Establish minimum competencies in reading, writing, speaking, listening, reasoning, and economics Strengthen programs for gifted students Raise college entrance standards	English, math, science, foreign language, history, computer literacy	Consider longer school day Emphasize order and discipline More homework More rigorous grading with periodic testing Independent learning	Foster partnerships between private sector and education Increase federal funds for education
Educating Americans for the 21st Century, National Science Foundation	Devote more time to math and science in elementary and secondary schools Provide more advanced courses in science and math Raise college entrance standards	Math, science, technology, computers	Consider longer school day, week, and/or year Twelve-year plan for math and science	Federal input in establishing national goals for education Increase NSF role in curriculum development and teacher training
High School, Carnegie Foundation for Achievement in Teaching	Mastery of language, including reading, writing, speaking, and listening Expand basic academic curriculum Student transition to work and further education Strengthen graduation requirements	Core of common learning, including English, history, civics, math, science, technology Computer literacy	Improve working conditions for teachers Utilize technology to enrich curriculum Flexible schedules and time allotments One track for students School-community learning activities Greater leadership role for principal	More "connections" between school and community, business, and universities Increase parent and community coalitions with and service to schools Utilize retired personnel from business and colleges Federal scholarships for science and math teachers

137

TABLE 5-2 (Continued)

Report and Sponsor	Curriculum Objectives	Content Emphasis	School Organization	Government-Business Role
Making the Grade, Twentieth Century Fund	Improve basic-skill programs Improve learning in English, math, and science Initiate general programs for students with learning problems and a voucher program for the disadvantaged	Basic skills English, math, and science Computer literacy	Reward teacher performance Special programs for poor, minority, handicapped, bilingual, and immigrant students	Increase federal aid for special programs for disadvantaged student populations Increase federal aid for programs to develop scientific literacy among all students and advanced math and science for academically able secondary students
A Study of High Schools, National Association of Secondary School Principals	Reduce traditional subject matter Emphasize higher-order thinking skills	Interdisciplinary curriculum Problem-solving activities and learning experiences	Eliminate age grouping Eliminate teacher specializations Incentives to students Out-of-school learning activities	Federal support for special students, including learning disabled and gifted
A Nation At Risk, National Commission on Excellence in Education	Improve textbooks and other instructional materials Provide more rigorous courses in vocational education, arts, and science Strengthen graduation requirements Raise college entrance requirements	Five new basics: English, math, science, social studies, and computer science	Consider seven-hour school day Tighten attendance and discipline More homework More rigorous grading and periodic testing Group students by performance rather than age	Federal cooperation with states and localities Meet needs of disadvantaged student populations as well as gifted and talented National standardized tests in context with national interest in education
The First Lesson: A Report on Elementary Education in America, The Secretary of Education	Improve basic skills for young children Improve complex learning tasks and abilities for higher-grade children Increase knowledge base essential for democratic society and national identity Improve textbook and workbook writing and selection Raise academic standards	Basic skills, especially reading through phonics Problem solving skills in mathematics and hands-on learning and discovery in science Unified sequence stressing history, geography, and civics Computer literacy and cultural literacy	Lengthen school day More homework More rigorous testing Parental choice in children's schools Reward teacher performance	Community-wide and parental responsibility in education Teacher and school accountability Improve training programs for elementary teachers; emphasis on arts and science rather than methods courses

Report	Focus/Aims	Curriculum/Skills	School Organization	Policy/Governance
The Early Years, Carnegie Foundation for the Advancement of Teaching	Focus on plight of "at risk" children, the nation's underclass Emphasis on basic skills Priority on childhood education	Language development, including reading, writing, and listening skills	Flexible school schedules reflecting changing family and work patterns Longer school day and school year Reward teacher performance; attract better teachers Parental choice for after school and summer programs; end of traditional summer vacation	Increased federal aid for education of "at risk" children Increased role of business and industry Greater involvement of teachers in decision-making, increased pay
Time for Results: The Governors' 1991 Report on Education, National Governors' Association	Focus on teenage pregnancy, school dropouts, adult illiteracy, and drug abuse Improve school leadership and management Better use of technology in the classroom Increase state role and responsibility in education Higher academic standards at all grade levels	Basic skills, math, science, and technology Research and development in education	Kindergarten for all children; early childhood programs for all "at risk" children Parental education programs Parental choice in selecting children's school Reliable and valid assessment of student performance Year-round schooling Reorganize and regulate schools and school districts that are "academically bankrupt"	National school board to certify teachers Increased pay and accountability for teachers and principals Improved teacher training and educational leadership programs Greater involvement in education of local leaders, teachers, parents, citizens, and business people Greater state role, regulation, and spending in education Annual progress reports until 1991 on what each state is doing to carry out educational reform

Source: From Allan C. Ornstein, "The National Reports on Education: Implications for Directions and Aims," *Kappa Delta Pi Record* (Winter 1985), p. 61; Allan C. Ornstein and Daniel U. Levine, *Introduction to the Foundations of Education,* 3rd ed. (Boston: Houghton Mifflin, 1985), pp. 466–467, 542–543. See also *Education Week,* September 10, 1986, pp. 1, 31–36.

era of the Cold War and the space race; it is reappearing, too, in 1980s as a result of concern over economic competition with foreign countries and foreign relations with the USSR. In the early 1900s progressive educators sought to broaden the aims of school to serve all children and youth, especially nonacademic and vocationally oriented students; beginning in the early 1960s and continuing into the 1970s, this priority reappeared with emphasis on poor and minority students, and later bilingual and handicapped students. Although concern for disadvantaged groups remains, the pendulum has now moved to the center. Our priorities are more diffuse, and we are concerned about various other students as well, including those in average and academic groups.

Appraising and Reflecting.

Educational aims should be as changeable as the changing social and political conditions and the groups of people that formulate them. Panels and commissions are often organized to formulate aims. They may operate at various government and educational levels—federal, state regional, and local—but those at the national level have the most influence and those at the local level have the least (in terms of overall impact). Such groups should include representatives of the following groups listed in Table 5-3.

Unquestionably, educational aims must be relevant or meaningful to the times. If the schools are not adaptable to changing conditions and social forces, how can they expect to produce people who are? This issue is pointedly illustrated in a satire on education entitled *The Saber-Tooth Curriculum*,[10] which describes a society whose major tasks for survival were catching fish to eat, clubbing horses, and frightening away saber-tooth tigers. The school in this society set up a curriculum to meet its needs—namely,

TABLE 5-3   Representative Groups for Setting Educational Priorities

1. *Students.* Most secondary students are mature and responsible enough to provide appropriate input in developing educational aims; moreover, they have the most at stake and thus deserve to be represented.

2. *Parents.* Because parents provide the students and taxes that support schools, custom and political astuteness on the part of school officials necessitates parental input.

3. *Educators.* Teachers, supervisors, and administrators must assume major responsibility in developing educational aims. To surrender this responsibility is to surrender their professional role—and is unjustifiable and naive.

4. *Research Community.* The role of the researcher or social scientist is important for providing objective data concerning trends and issues. These people should not serve as advocates, however, which they sometimes do.

5. *Community Members.* Whether they have children in school, whether their children have graduated, or whether they are childless, the citizens and taxpayers in the larger adult community have a civic responsibility to provide input in school matters. Their support is crucial, because they vote on school and fiscal matters—directly and indirectly and at various levels of government.

6. *Business Community.* Businesspeople are natural allies of school people, and the former groups should be aggressively enlisted in school affairs, because of their economic (and political) influence and stake they have in the outcomes of schooling in terms of human capital, technology, and industrial output.

7. *Government Officials.* Political officials are also natural allies of schools. They, too, should be enlisted because of their political (and economic) influence. Indeed, educational policy and politics go hand in hand as do school finance and governance.

8. *Pressure Groups.* People have the greatest impact by organizing into groups that promote special interests. The operation of such groups is clearly valid within the democratic process, but extreme views must be controlled and softened.

9. *Professional Organizations.* The input of the professional organizations is important in terms of obtaining support from the educational establishment. Although professional organizations may have agendas similar to those of pressure groups—that is, to see that educational aims benefit their memberships—the professional roles and responsibilities of the members warrant that what is good for schools should prevail.

10. *Governing Bodies.* Representatives from governing and legislative groups—at the federal, state, regional, and/or local levels—should be included because they have the power and authority to enact legislation (including the recommendations or policy statements, of commissions or panels designed to formulate educational aims.

Source: From Allan C. Ornstein, "How Are Educational Aims Determined?" *NASSP Bulletin* (May 1985), pp. 46–47.

teaching courses in these three areas of survival. Eventually conditions changed; the streams dried up, and the horses and tigers disappeared. Social change necessitated learning new tasks for survival, but the school curriculum continued to feature courses in catching fish, clubbing horses, and frightening saber-toothed tigers.

Today we live in a highly technical, automated, and bureaucratic society; we are faced with pressing social and economic problems—aging cities, the effects of centuries of racial and sexual discrimination, an aging population, unemployment and a displaced workforce, exhaustion of our natural resources, the pollution of the physical environment, and the threat of nuclear devastation. These forces and trends are highly interrelated; they mutually reinforce each other, and they are accelerating. In an era of space technology, telecommunications, computers, and robots, schools cannot continue to teach the skills that were appropriate for the Industrial Revolution. Whether we allow the times to engulf us, or whether we can cope with our new environment, will depend to a large extent on what kinds of skills are taught in our schools today, in addition to the development of appropriate aims of education.

CONCLUSION

Social forces have always had a major influence on schools and in turn on curriculum decisions. Some of these forces originate from society at large and others from the local community. In either case, educators are faced with a choice: To accept and mirror the tendencies of the times or to appraise and improve the times. One view represents a perennialist notion of education, the other a reconstructionist notion; however, we would like to view the choice in terms of a traditional versus futuristic way of looking at schools. The latter approach suggests that educators can analyze and evaluate the trends taking shape in society. In doing so, they can decide on appropriate

aims and curricula, and they can thus prepare students for the world of tomorrow by providing them with the knowledge and values they need to make wise decisions. Curriculum workers—indeed, all participants in curriculum decisions—play a major role in accomplishing these goals.

Notes

1. John Dewey, *Experience and Education* (New York: Macmillan, 1938), pp. 39–40.
2. Allan C. Ornstein and Daniel U. Levine, *Introduction to the Foundations of Education*, 3rd ed. (Boston: Houghton Mifflin, 1985), p. 325.
3. Ibid.
4. Ruth Benedict, *Patterns of Culture* (Boston: Houghton Mifflin, 1934), p. 253.
5. Margaret Mead, *And Keep Your Powder Dry* (New York: William Morrow, 1941).
6. Sarane S. Boocock, *An Introduction to the Sociology of Education*, 2nd ed. (Boston: Houghton Mifflin, 1980); Burton L. White, *The First Three Years of Life* (New York: Avon Books, 1984).
7. Robert J. Havighurst, "Sex Role Development," *Journal of Research and Development in Education* (Winter 1983), pp. 60–65; Catherine S. Chilman, "The Development of Adolescent Sexuality," *Journal of Research and Development in Education* (Winter 1983), pp. 16–26.
8. Patricia C. Sexton, *The Feminized Male* (New York: Random House, 1969).
9. Ray H. Bixler, "Nature versus Nurture: The Timeless Anachronism," *Merrill-Palmer Quarterly* (April 1980) pp. 153–159.
10. Diane McGuinness, "How Schools Discriminate against Boys," *Human Nature* (February 1979), pp. 87–88.
11. John E. Williams and Deborah L. Best, *Measuring Sex Stereotypes* (Beverly Hills, Calif.: Sage Publications, 1982).
12. Myra Sadker and David Sadker, "The Development and Field Trail of a Non-Sexist Teacher Education Curriculum," *High School Journal* (May 1981), pp. 331–336.
13. Daniel U. Levine and Allan C. Ornstein, "Sex Differences in Ability and Achievement," *Journal of Research and Development in Education* (Winter 1983), pp. 66–76; Harold W. Stevenson and Richard S. Newman, "Long Term Prediction of Achievement and Attitudes in Mathematics and Reading," *Child Development* (June 1986), pp. 646–659; and Sheila Tobias and Carol S. Weisslrod, "Anxiety and Mathematics: An Update," *Harvard Educational Review* (February 1980), pp. 63–70.
14. Camilla P. Benlow and Julian C. Stanley, "Differential Course-Taking Hypothesis Revisited," *American Educational Research Journal* (Winter 1983), pp. 469–473.

15. Karl L. Alexander and Aaron M. Pallas, "Reply to Benlow and Stanley," *American Educational Research Journal* (Winter 1983), pp. 475–477.

16. Robert J. Havighurst, *Human Development and Education* (New York: Longman, 1953), p. 2.

17. Robert J. Havighurst, *Developmental Tasks and Education*, 3rd ed. (New York: Longman, 1972), pp. 14–35, 43–82. All rights reserved.

18. H. H. Giles, S. P. McCutchen, and A. N. Zechiel, *Exploring the Curriculum* (New York: Harper & Row, 1942).

19. Florence B. Stratemeyer, Hamden L. Forkner, Margaret G. McKim, and A. Harry Passow, *Developing a Curriculum for Modern Living*, 2nd ed. (New York: Teachers College Press, Columbia University, 1957).

20. B. Othanel Smith, William O. Stanley, and J. Harlan Shores, *Fundamentals of Curriculum Development*, rev. ed. (New York: World Book, 1957).

21. Henry Harap, *The Changing Curriculum* (New York: Appleton-Century Crofts, 1937).

22. Benedict, *Patterns of Culture*; Kingsley Davis, *Human Society* (New York: Macmillan, 1948); and Edward Shorter, *The Making of the Modern Family* (New York: Basic Books, 1975).

23. Jerome Kagan, *The Nature of the Child* (New York: Basic Books, 1985).

24. Jean Piaget, *The Moral Judgment of the Child* (London: Routledge & Kegan Paul, 1932).

25. Ibid.

26. Lawrence Kohlberg, "Moral Development and Identification," in N. B. Henry and H. G. Richey, eds., *Child Psychology*, Sixty-Second Yearbook of the National Society for the Study of Education, Part I (Chicago: University of Chicago Press, 1963), pp. 322–323.

27. Maxine Greene, *Teachers as Strangers* (Belmont, Calif.: Wadsworth, 1973); Van Cleve Morris, *Existentialism in Education* (New York: Harper & Row, 1966). Also see Landon E. Beyer and George H. Wood, "Critical Theory and Moral Action in Education," *Educational Theory* (October 1986), pp. 1–14.

28. Philip H. Phenix, *Realms of Meaning* (New York: McGraw-Hill, 1964), pp. 220–221.

29. Ibid., p. 223.

30. John Dewey, *Democracy and Education* (New York: Macmillan, 1916), p. 414.

31. Ibid., pp. 411, 415–416.

32. William Van Til, "In a Climate of Change," in R. R. Leeper, ed., *Role of Supervisor and Curriculum Director in a Climate of Change* (Washington, D.C.: Association for Supervision and Curriculum Development, 1965), p. 16. See also Joe L. Frost, "Children in a Changing Society," *Childhood Education* (March/April 1986), pp. 242–249.

33. Alvin Toffler, *Future Shock* (New York: Random House, 1970).

34. *Curriculum Change toward the 21st Century*, an NEA Bicentennial Committee Report (Washington, D.C.: National Education Association, 1977), pp. 89–90.

35. See Daniel Bell, *The Coming of the Post-Industrial Society* (New York: Basic Books, 1976); Bell, *The Third Technological Revolution* (New York: Basic Books, 1984); and Alvin Toffler, *The Third Wave* (New York: Morrow, 1980).

36. Philip M. Hauser, "Urbanization: An Overview," in J. K. Hadden, L. H. Masotti, and C. J. Larson, eds., *Metropolis in Crisis* (Itasca, Ill.: Peacock, 1971), pp. 51–74.

37. Philip W. Jackson, *Life in Classrooms* (New York: Holt, Rinehart, 1968), p. 6.

38. Glenys G. Unruh and William M. Alexander, *Innovations in Secondary Education*, 2nd ed. (New York: Holt, Rinehart, 1974), p. 2.

39. Allan C. Ornstein, *Urban Education* (Columbus, Ohio: Merrill, 1972), p. 50.

40. Wayne K. Hoy and Cecil G. Miskel, *Educational Administration: Theory, Research, and Practice*, 2nd ed. (New York: Random House, 1982), p. 51.

41. Walter Doyle, "Academic Work," *Review of Educational Research* (Summer 1983), pp. 159–199; John I. Goodlad, "A Study of Schooling: Some Findings and Hypotheses," *Phi Delta Kappan* (March 1983), pp. 465–470; and Seymour B. Sarason, *The Culture of School and the Problem of Change*, 2nd ed. (Boston: Allyn and Bacon, 1982).

42. Bentley Glass, *The Timely and the Timeless* (New York: Basic Books, 1970), p. 39.

43. Warren L. Ziegler, *Social and Technological Developments*, rev. ed. (Syracuse, N.Y.: Syracuse University Press, 1981).

44. Toffler, *Future Shock*, p. 132.

45. Arno Bellack, "What Knowledge Is of Most Worth?" *High School Journal* (February 1965), pp. 318–332; Donald E. Orlosky and B. Othanel Smith, *Curriculum Development: Issues and Insights* (Chicago: Rand McNally, 1978); and Decker F. Walker and Jonas F. Soltis, *Curriculum and Aims* (New York: Teachers College Press, Columbia University, 1986).

46. James B. Conant, *The American High School* (New York: McGraw-Hill, 1959).

47. Masao Mikaye, "National Science Curriculum Case Studies," Unpublished paper, National Institute for Educational Research, Tokyo, 1981; Kay M. Troost, "What Accounts for Japan's Success in Science Education?" *Educational Leadership* (December–January 1984), pp. 26–29.

48. Joseph L. Schwab, *The Practical: A Language for Curriculum* (Washington, D.C.: National Education Association, 1970).

49. Gerald Weinstein and Mario D. Fantini, *Toward Humanistic Education: A Curriculum of Affect* (New York: Praeger, 1970), p. 50.

50. Mario D. Fantini, "Reducing the Behavior Gap," *NEA Journal* (January 1968), pp. 23–24.

51. Joseph L. Tykociner, *Outline of Zetetics* (Philadelphia: Dorrance, 1966). See also B. Othanel Smith

in a letter to Harold G. Shane, May 17, 1976; Orlosky and Smith, *Curriculum Development: Issues and Insights*, pp. 173–187.

52. Lawrence A. Cremin, *The Transformation of the School* (New York: Knopf, 1961).

53. Commission on the Reorganization of Secondary Education, *Cardinal Principles of Secondary Education*, Bulletin No. 35 (Washington, D.C.: U.S. Government Printing Office, 1918).

54. Allan C. Ornstein, "Aims of Education for Today and Tomorrow," *Educational Horizons* (Fall 1982), pp. 41–49.

55. Educational Policies Commission, *The Purpose of Education in American Democracy* (Washington, D.C.: National Education Association, 1938).

56. Educational Policies Commission, *Education for All American Youth* (Washington, D.C.: National Education Association, 1944).

57. Saylor and Alexander, *Planning Curriculum for Schools*; Gene D. Shephard and William B. Ragan, *Modern Elementary Curriculum*, 6th ed. (New York: Holt, Rinehart, 1985). See also Allan C. Ornstein, "Curriculum Contrasts: A Historical View," *Phi Delta Kappan* (February 1982), pp. 404–408.

58. Arthur Bestor, *The Restoration of Learning* (New York, Knopf, 1956).

59. Hyman G. Rickover, *Education and Freedom* (New York: Dutton, 1959), p. 190.

60. *Science and Education for National Defense*, Hearings before the Committee of Labor and Public Welfare, U.S. Senate, Eighty-Eighth Congress (Washington, D.C.: U.S. Government Printing Office, 1958), p. 65.

61. Ibid., pp. 39, 54.

62. Conant, *The American High School Today*, p. 15.

63. Ibid.

64. *Proceedings, White House Conference on Education* (Washington, D.C.: U.S. Government Printing Office, 1955), p. 12.

65. *Goals for Americans: The President's Commission on National Goals* (Englewood Cliffs, N.J.: Prentice-Hall, 1960), p. 85.

66. Van Til, "In a Climate of Change," p. 21.

67. Daniel Tanner and Laurel N. Tanner, *Curriculum Development: Theory into Practice* (New York: Macmillan, 1980), p. 546.

68. Ibid.; Alex Molnar, "Schools and their Curriculum: A Continuing Controversy," in A. Molnar, ed., *Current Thought on Curriculum* (Alexandria, Va.: Association for Supervision and Curriculum Development, 1985), pp. 1–30; J. Gaylen Saylor, *Who Planned the Curriculum?* (West Lafayette, Ind.: Kappa Delta Pi Press, 1982).

69. James B. Conant, *Slums and Suburbs* (New York: McGraw-Hill, 1961), p. 2.

70. Allan C. Ornstein and Daniel U. Levine, "Compensatory Education: Can It Be Successful? What Are the Issues?" *National Association of Secondary School Principals* (May 1981), pp. 1–15; A. Harry Passow, "Urban Education in the 1970s," in A. H. Passow, ed., *Urban Education in the 1970s* (New York: Teachers College Press, Columbia University, 1971), pp. 1–45.

71. *Digest of Educational Statistics, 1985–86* (Washington, D.C.: U.S. Government Printing Office, 1986), Table 163, advance copy.

72. Theresa Escobedo, *Early Childhood Bilingual Education* (New York: Teachers College Press, Columbia University, 1983); Allan C. Ornstein and Daniel U. Levine, "Multicultural Education: Trends and Issues," *Childhood Education* (March-April, 1982), pp. 241–246.

73. *Digest of Educational Statistics, 1982, 1985–86*, Table 155, p. 173; Table 163, advance copy.

74. *Digest of Educational Statistics, 1983–84* (Washington, D.C.: U.S. Government Printing Office, 1984), Table 30, p. 40; Table 68, p. 83; Daniel U. Levine and Allan C. Ornstein, "Some Trends in Educating Handicapped Students," *Journal of Curriculum Studies* (July 1981), pp. 261–265. See also *The School-Age Handicapped* (Washington, D.C.: U.S. Government Printing Office, 1985), Table 1, p. 61.

75. A. Harry Passow and Abraham J. Tannebaum, "Education of the Gifted and Talented," *National Association of Secondary School Principals* (March 1976), pp. 4–5; Donovan R. Walling, "Gifted Children: A Neglected Minority," *Curriculum Review* (September/October 1986), pp. 11–13.

76. Harold Benjamin, *The Saber-Tooth Curriculum* (New York: McGraw-Hill, 1939).

chapter 6

AIMS, GOALS, AND OBJECTIVES

Education is purposeful; it is concerned with outcomes that are usually expressed at several different levels. The most general level is reflected in statements of aims; the most specific is exhibited in statements of objectives. But, whatever the level of specificity, educators use these statements to guide their development, implementation, maintenance, and evaluation of educational programs.

Such statements, whether aims, goals, or objectives, are not created in a vacuum. Their formulation, which represents some point toward which educators are working, is influenced to a great extent by the philosophy they accept or follow. John Dewey argued that philosophy can be employed as a general theory of education: "If we are willing to conceive education as the process of forming fundamental dispositions, intellectual and emotional, toward nature and fellow men. . . ."[1] Although Dewey combines philosophy and theory as part of the educational process, we contend that philosophy also serves to illuminate the practice of education. This position is expressed by Boyd Bode: "If the younger generation is to [participate] in our social life the emphasis in curriculum construction and in teaching must be placed on social outlook, on reflective consideration of what constitutes a good life in the social order."[2]

If there were only one philosophy, only one way of viewing reality or interpreting societal needs, the tasks of curriculum specialists would indeed be easy, or so it would seem to some.[3] However, such is not the case. Indeed, because of the numerous philosophical positions, there are myriad ways to conceptualize and deliver curricula. The various philosophical positions curricularists hold influence all aspects of their curriculum decisions. Whether they look at the outcomes of schooling as "fixed terminal points" or as "points" in a never-ending series of points is influenced by their philosophies.

Dewey and others would argue that the ends to which people strive, when attained, only lead to other ends: "Ends when achieved become the means for proceeding to other ends." If we reach the end of learning to read effectively, this then becomes the means by which we can achieve the end of obtaining information about a particular topic. Dewey pointed out that ends and means are just two ways of regarding reality:

Ends are foreseen consequences which arise in the course of activity and which are employed to give added meaning and to direct its further course. They are in no sense ends of action. In being ends of deliberation they are redirecting pivots in action.[4]

Our purpose, however, is not to debate the various views of ends and means; it is to point out the role that philosophy plays in our interpreting and responding to reality and in our creating educational programs for students. We need to be well aware of the philosophical underpinnings of our curricular actions—perhaps even more so today than in past times, for today schools are existing in a society that is experiencing great waves of change that are impacting on the fundamental social fabric: Changes in family and personal relations, changes in levels of technology, changes in international relations.

In such times, educators need precise definitions of the endpoints of education, even if they view these endpoints as nothing more than the means of attaining other endpoints. When they are unsure of their purposes and ultimate objectives in education—and such imprecision currently exists in our society—educators tend to take on reactive postures. School officials—curriculum specialists in particular—react, they do not "pro-act." Many in society are dissatisfied with the schools because they have not pro-acted, have not anticipated developing needs, and have not articulated a clear philosophical posture to guide their educational decision making.

It seems especially important in these times that educators consider the worth of the "end" they suggest and also view it not as the final end but rather as leading to some other point of development or understanding, which in turn will lead to another. There is much information to consider, and there are many philosophical arguments to process. Curriculum workers would be well advised to conceptualize schooling as a philosophical enterprise. As J. Galen Saylor asserts, "Schooling is a philosophical venture, one that necessitates choosing . . . among innumerable possibilities. Those choices constitute the starting point in curriculum planning."[5]

AIMS OF EDUCATION

In times of great change, society looks to its schools to help its citizens adjust. Society often demands that the schools modify their programs so students will be able to function more effectively in the current times. To respond to such calls, educators rely on their philosophical foundations to guide their decisions regarding the purpose of school and the specifics and nature of their programs.

Few educators would dare respond to the myriad demands placed on the schools without some mention of educational aims. But often they are not precise in their use of educational language. The term *aims* is often used interchangeably with the terms, *goals, ends, functions, general objectives,* and *purposes.*[6] However, there are differences among the terms, and it is helpful to distinguish among them. David Pratt defines an aim as providing a basic orientation for the designer or user of a curriculum.[7] Komisar and McClellan define aims as general statements that provide both shape and direction to the more specific actions designed to achieve some future product or behavior.[8] Aims are starting points that allow educators to rally behind them. Aims are ideals functioning as inspirational visions of the Good.[9] Aims are slogans that excite people about a direction of education and get them to commit to various directions of schooling.

Aims serve the crucial function of guiding education, but they cannot be directly observed or evaluated. They are orientations, not specific quantifiable outcomes. They suggest endpoints, but they do not precisely define them. They are too general to guide particular instructional decisions; more specific objectives serve that function. Nonetheless, educators must first determine aims in order to match objectives with them.

Educators of every age are challenged to interpret the aims of society. Because of their global quality, only a few aims are necessary to guide education. For example, Ralph Tyler summarized the aims of American schooling as: (1) developing self-realization, (2) making individuals literate, encouraging social mobility, (3) providing skills and understanding necessary for productive employment, (4) furnishing tools requisite for making effective choices regarding material and nonmaterial things and services, and (5) furnishing the tools necessary for continued learning.[10] These all-encompassing aims reflect a progressive philosophy.

Ronald Doll notes that educational aims should address the intellectual or cognitive, the social-personal or affective, and the productive.[11] Aims dealing with the intellectual dimension focus on the acquisition and comprehension of knowledge, and problem-solving skills and various levels and methods of thinking. Aims in the social-personal dimension are concerned with person-to-society, person-to-person, and person-to-self interactions. These aims also subsume the emotional and psychological aspects of individuals and their adaptive aspects with regard to home, family, religion, and local community. Aims relating to the productive dimension of schooling center on those aspects of education that allow the individual to function in the home, on the job, and as a citizen and member of the larger society.

To these dimensions, we would add four others: (1) physical, dealing with the development and maintenance of strong and healthy bodies; (2) aesthetic, dealing with values and appreciation of the arts; (3) moral, dealing with values and behavior that reflect appropriate behavior; and (4) spiritual, dealing with the recognition and belief in the divine and the view of transcendence.

Sources of Aims.

During every period of contemporary history, society in general and educators in particular have formulated aims. These aims are usually developed by prestigious, nationwide commissions and task forces in the context of the overriding concerns and problems of a changing society. These commissions, which have been in existence for approximately 100 years, usually include descriptive studies of society to guide program creation.

Spencer's Report. We might denote the starting point for such reports as 1859, when Herbert Spencer published his essay "What Knowledge Is of Most Worth?" From his analysis of his contemporary society, Spencer concluded that for individuals to lead successful lives, they needed preparation in five realms of activities: (1) direct self-preservation; (2) indirect self-preservation (e.g., securing food, shelter, earning a living, etc.); (3) parenthood; (4) citizenship; and (5) leisure activities.[12]

Since Spencer's time, hundreds of descriptive studies of all aspects of society, many done by "blue ribbon" panels, have been utilized by educators to frame aims, as well as goals and objectives. Most of these reports have formulated aims to sustain our way of life—to allow students to be successful in life outside the school. Also, the aims are phrased to preserve our social and political institutions, to maintain the current society, and to improve it.

The Cardinal Principles. The National Education Association's Commission on the Reorganization of Secondary Education issued its report in 1918, when World War I ended. The report, called *The Cardinal Principles of Secondary Education,* spoke to the role of education in our democratic society in the following manner:

Education in a democracy, both within and without the school, should develop in each individual the knowledges, interest, ideas, habits, and powers whereby he will find his place and use that place to shape both himself and society toward even nobler ends.[13]

The Commission, perhaps being influenced by Spencer, employed the organizational principle of important life activities to organize categories of curriculum aims. Seven major areas were presented:

1. Health
2. Command of fundamental processes
3. Worthy home membership
4. Vocational education
5. Civic education
6. Worthy use of leisure
7. Ethical character[14]

Educational Policies Commission. After the Great Depression, the Educational Policies Commission of the NEA issued a report entitled *The Purpose of Education in American Democracy.* The commission noted:

In any realistic definition of education for the United States, therefore, must appear the whole philosophy and practice of democracy. Education cherishes and inculcates its moral values, disseminates knowledge necessary to its functioning, spreads information relevant to its institutions and economy, keeps alive the creative and sustaining spirit without which the latter is dead.[15]

A comprehensive set of four aims, each with several corresponding goals (which the Commission called objectives) was delineated: (1) self-realization; (2) human relationships; (3) economic efficiency; and (4) civic responsibility. The aim of *self-realization* was to encourage inquiry, mental capabilities, speech, reading, writing, numbers, sight and hearing, health knowledge, health habits, public health, recreation, intellectual interests, aesthetic interests, and character formation. The aim of *human relationships* included humanity, friendship, cooperation with others, courtesy, appreciation of the home, conservation of the home, homemaking, and democracy in the home. The aim of *economic efficiency* encompassed work, occupational appreciation, personal economics, consumer judgment, efficiency in buying, and consumer protection. The aim of *civic responsibility* related to social justice, social activity, social understanding, critical judgment, tolerance, conservation of resources, social application of science, world citizenship, law of observance, economic literacy, political citizenship, and devotion to democracy.[16]

Education for All American Youth. In 1944, the Educational Policies Commission, still concerned about the purposes of education, formulated several aims of education. Influenced by World War II, it stressed the overriding aims related to democracy and world citizenship, as well as those related to the general needs of children and youth. Its report, *Education for All American Youth,* listed ten aims, or what it called the "Ten Imperative Needs of Youth." All youth need to develop skills and attitudes that enhance the following:

1. Salable skills and those understandings and attitudes that make them intelligent and productive participants in economic life.
2. Good health and physical fitness.
3. Understanding of the rights and duties of citizens of a democratic society, and those necessary to serve as members of the community and citizens of the state, nation, and world.
4. Understanding of the significance of the family for the individual and society, and the conditions conducive to successful family life.

5. Knowledge of how to purchase and use goods and services intelligently, understanding both the value received by the consumer and the economic consequences of their acts.
6. Understanding of the methods of science, the influence of science on human life, and the main scientific facts concerning the nature of the world and humanity.
7. The development of capacities to appreciate beauty in literature, art, music, and nature.
8. The use of leisure time and the budgeting of it wisely, balancing activities that yield satisfaction to the individual with those that are socially useful.
9. Respect for other persons, insight into ethical values and principles, and the ability to live and work cooperatively with others.
10. Growth of their ability to think rationally, to express their thoughts clearly, and to read and listen with understanding.[17]

The Central Purpose of American Education.

Feeling the effects of Sputnik, the National Educational Association's Educational Policies Commission addressed the aims of education in 1961:

Many profound changes are occurring in the world today, but there is a fundamental force contributing to all of them. That force is the expanding role accorded in modern life to the rational powers of man. By using these powers to increase his knowledge, man is attempting to solve the riddles of life, space, and time which have long intrigued him.[18]

Educators were concerned that in a real sense we were losing excellence—especially in mathematics and science. Sputnik had caught us by surprise, and the schools were identified as the major cause of our coming up second. America had to meet the demands of the space race and the Cold War. The Educational Policies Commission's 1961 report essentially stressed intellectual excellence and thinking competencies. We needed to challenge our gifted and talented students.

The Nation at Risk. In 1983, the Commission on Excellence in Education was directed to examine the quality of American education and to report its findings. The commission concluded that our nation was at risk: Our educational system was delivering a mediocre performance and the schools had lost sight of the basic purposes of education. The commission argued that "learning is the indispensable investment required for success in the 'information age' we are entering."[19]

The Commission noted that educational reform should focus on the goal of creating a "system of education that affords all members the opportunity to stretch their minds to full capacity, from early childhood through adulthood." In the view of the commission, education was "the essential foundation . . . of one's life" and of society.[20]

The Commission made several recommendations that touched on the directions of education and how to address them. The first recommendation dealt with content. The commission stated:

We recommend that State and local high school graduation requirements be strengthened and that at a minimum, all students seeking a diploma be required to lay the foundations in the Five New Basics by taking the following curriculum during their 4 years of high school: a) 4 years of English; b) 3 years of mathematics; c) 3 years of science; d) 3 years of social studies, and e) one-half year of computer science. For the college-bound, 2 years of foreign language in high school are strongly recommended.[21]

The Commission focused on the need for higher standards and expectations by urging educators to "adopt more rigorous and measurable standards, and higher expectations, for academic performance and student conduct, and that 4-year colleges and universities raise their requirements for admission. . . ."[22] The Commission also made the recommendation that significantly more time be devoted to learning the New Basics. This would require more effective use of the existing school day, a longer school day, and a lengthened school year. Finally, the Commission also urged that citizens across the nation hold educators and lected officials responsible for providing he leadership necessary to achieve these re- orms, and that citizens provide the fiscal upport and stability required to bring bout the reforms it proposed.

This concern with excellence reflects the changing aims of education. Many recent eports have stressed the value of excellence n education; some reports have considered basic learnings for all students as well. Mortimer Adler, for example, argued that, o meet their obligation, schools must do hree things: (1) introduce the young to the world of learning; (2) teach the young all he skills of learning; and (3) give the young he incentives and the stimulation to con- inue learning after schooling is con- cluded.[23]

It is likely that educational aims will con- inue to be furnished by commissions and ignificant individuals. Educators still face he challenge of defining their purposes and addressing the demands placed on them. Groups of educators represent particular power factions: ethnic groups, women's groups, religious groups. The challenge for curriculum leaders is to process the data from these groups such that the aims of ed- ucation will be relevant to the present and he future and will furnish direction to hose who create educational programs.

GOALS OF EDUCATION

Goals are statements of endpoints or out- comes of education—in other words, state- ments of purpose. By analyzing a school's goals we can determine the scope of its en- ire educational program. Goals, in contrast o aims, are not open statements. They are pecific statements written so that those re- ponsible for program creation can use hem as guidelines to achieve particular purposes. Goals are derived from various aims and thus provide teachers and curricu- um decision makers with broad statements of what they should accomplish in terms of tudent learning as a result of a particular ubject or educational program.

Levels of Goals.

Goals can be written at several levels of generality. At one extreme, they can be writ- ten in such broad phrasing that they are similar to aims and reflect a philosophical base. At the other extreme, they can be writ- ten rather specifically to indicate a concern about a particular achievement.

The distinction between aims and goals of education is one of generality. Aims deal with the general process of education, such as "building worldmindedness" or "creating technological literacy." No particular pro- gram in the school will accomplish these aims; many aspects of the curriculum quite likely will address them. Aims become goals when they become more specific and refer to a particular school or school system and to a specific subject area of the curriculum. The aim of "building worldmindedness," for example, might become the social stud- ies goal that "students will become aware of the various nations of the world and the roles that they play in the world commu- nity."

Much discussion regards the proper phrasing of educational goals. Some indi- viduals prefer sentences, some phrases, some just a single word. The Association for Supervision and Curriculum Development identified ten major goals for youth that contain several words each: (1) learning self- conceptualization (self-esteem); (2) under- standing others; (3) developing basic skills; (4) encouraging interest in and capability for continuing learning; (5) becoming re- sponsible members of society; (6) devel- oping mental and physical health; (7) enhancing creativity; (8) being informed about participating in the economic world of production and consumption; (9) using accumulated knowledge to understand the world; and (10) coping with change.[24] Each of these goals contained several subgoals.

Some educators are more comfortable with goal statements that start with infinitive verbs. These persons would rewrite the pre- ceding list as follows: (1) to develop in stu- dents positive self-concepts; (2) to develop in students understanding of others; (3) to develop in students command of basic skills; (4) to stimulate students' interests and capabilities for continual learning, and so forth.

The Phi Delta Kappa honor society has distributed a list of goals that was created by the Program Development Center of Northern California. A partial list appears next:[25]

1. Learn how to be a good citizen.
2. Learn how to respect and get along with people who think, dress, and act differently.
3. Learn about and try to understand the changes that take place in the world.
4. Develop skills in reading, writing, speaking, and listening.
5. Understand and practice democratic ideas and ideals.
6. Learn how to examine and use information.
7. Develop skills to enter a specific field of work.
8. Develop a desire for learning now and in the future.
9. Practice and understand the ideas of health and safety.
10. Appreciate culture and beauty in the world.

Many model lists of goals seem to be variations of the above list.

Creating educational goals is really a continuing activity in which educators engage as they consider the philosophies of their schools and work to clarify their educational aims. The needs of society, of students, or of the particular community commonly give rise to initial statements of curriculum goals. When school districts have identified current students' learning and behaviors, they often match those with their views of what an educated person is. When persons analyze their philosophies and the aims of their schools, they come up with general statements of outcomes—results they expect to occur in consequence to educational activity. People then make a final match between students' learnings and behavior and the goals they have generated. The goals are sometimes rank-ordered in light of importance or feasibility, or both. Persons involved in goal development—

teachers, community members, and even students—are asked to decide if these are the goals they wish to address—if these are the endpoints to which the program should strive. If they answer "yes," then these goals are accepted by those who are creating and delivering the curriculum.

OBJECTIVES OF EDUCATION

Within the context of educational aims and goals, it is necessary to formulate objectives that will indicate in more specific terms the outcomes of the curriculum or project being considered. Throughout much of our history objectives have been stated vaguely; they are often confused with goals and aims. To keep aims, goals, and objectives clearly separated it is perhaps helpful to remind ourselves that in translating aims into goals and finally into objectives, we proceed from the very general—couched in a long-term framework—to the more specific—couched in a short-term time sequence. The sequence is illustrated as follows:

Philosophy → Aims → Goals → Objectives

For a particular program or project, then, curriculum developers may state a general objective like "improving students' skill in information processing when dealing with science material." Under this rather general objective, which some might call a goal, they must have a series of more specific objectives.

Types of Educational Objectives.

When proceeding from the most general statements to the more specific, as illustrated in the sequence above, some curriculum planners denote several levels or types of objectives. These begin with general objectives (which indicate general outcomes relating to specific areas of the curriculum, often courses or subjects and particular grade levels) and go to specific outcomes resulting from classroom instruction.

Hilda Taba asserted that educational objectives can be of two sorts; those that describe school-wide outcomes and those that are more specific and describe behaviors to be attained in a particular unit, a subject course, or a particular grade-level program.[26] Robert Zais classifies the school-wide objectives as curriculum goals and the more specific objectives as curriculum objectives.[27] Baker and Popham point out that such specific objectives can be called instructional objectives.[28] Bruce Tuckman and Robert Mager note that objectives are often called performance objectives and that they include a proficiency level.[29]

Whatever they are called, objectives are more specific than goals, and this specificity increases in the progression from general curriculum objectives (subject or grade level), to unit objectives (classroom level), to lesson objectives (also classroom level). Objectives are statements that enable curriculum decision makers—curriculum developers, teachers, and even students and members of the general public—to identify the particular intent of a particular action. Both Gronlund and Mager state that a meaningful objective is one that communicates effectively to the reader the instructional intent or behavior of the objective as well as specific learning outcomes.[30]

Behavioral Educational Objectives. In our previous discussion, we referred to educational objectives as general or specific statements of expected learner outcomes. Advocates of both types of objectives have, for the past decade or so, debated their value. But, the general public and, so it seems, the majority of educators have accepted the view that specific statements are the most effective for educational objectives. Mager and others who hold this view believe that objectives that are stated precisely will improve the quality of teaching and learning.

For an objective to be meaningful, and therefore useful in guiding educators (whether or not it has been achieved) it should be measurable. To the extent that educators are unable to measure achieve-

ment, the meaningfulness of the objective is diminished. Put simply, this means that a behavioral objective is a statement of outcomes in terms of observable behavior expected of students after instruction.

Mager contends that an educational objective must describe: (1) the *behavior* of the learner when demonstrating his or her achievement of the objective; (2) the *conditions* imposed upon the learner when demonstrating mastery of the objective; and (3) the minimum *proficiency* level that will be acceptable.[31] A behavioral objective in science following Mager's counsel might read as follows:

After studying the unit on energy, the student must complete a 100 item multiple-choice text on the subject. The student must answer correctly 75 items and respond to this exam within a one-hour period.

An example for mathematics might be as follows:

Given a worksheet dealing with the process of multiplication, the pupil will be able to multiply sets of three-place numbers at the rate of one problem per minute with 80 percent accuracy.

Most behaviorists are advocates of such objectives. They counsel all who formulate objectives to use verbs in the objectives to signify *observable behaviors*, such as "name," "describe," "solve," "write," "build," "recall," and so on. They urge educators to avoid such verbs as "appreciate," "understand," and "know," because such words are vague and really cannot be easily observed as outcomes of education.

Nonbehavioral Objectives. Perhaps the greatest advantage of behavioral objectives is the clarity of communication they foster. People reading such objectives know precisely what they mean and can determine the extent to which they have been attained. But advocates of nonbehavioral objectives, who are somewhat general in wording, and use such words as "appreciate," "know," and "understand," contend that stating objectives too specifically restricts learning opportunities to those situations that require measurement. Objectives that address higher-order learning (e.g., analytic thinking, appreciation of literature) are likely to be eliminated because they frequently do not lend themselves to precise measurement. Many opponents of behavioral objectives reject precise objectives as expressions of behaviorism. They insist that much learning can occur that does not result in overt, measurable pupil behavior. Learning in the affective domain is a more subtle form of learning—and teachers cannot detect the attainment of positive affective states by having pupils take 100-item tests and get eighty responses correct.

Behavioral objectives are also criticized for not taking into account what Michael Polanyi has called *tacit knowing:* Having knowledge that we are perhaps unable to verbalize or demonstrate specifically.[32] One example of tacit knowing is being able to recognize a familiar face in a crowd, yet not being able to describe in any detail the person's appearance.

Advocates of nonbehavioral objectives point out that educators must realize that there are many indicators of attainment of an educational outcome. With behavioral objectives, the educational outcome may be considered attained *if, and only if,* such a behavior is demonstrated. Knowledge of subtraction, for example, is attained if and only if a child completes eight out of ten subtraction examples in a twenty-minute period. Are we willing to state that 80 percent is the only indicator of achieving this goal? What of the student who gets seven out of ten? Are curriculum designers really willing to enunciate such a narrow interpretation?

Some advocates of behavioral objectives realize the dangers of such a system. They realize that if we followed the Magerian method for stating objectives we would have trivia—and an unmanageable number of objectives. These persons do not reject behavioral objectives, but they advise curriculum makers to create comprehensive lists

of *behavioral indices.* The behaviors indicated are only to be guides that indicate that a learning outcome has been attained. Other behaviors could also attest that a learner has been successful.

This still is not acceptable to those who completely reject the behaviorist posture. These people still prefer nonbehavioral objectives. Because objectives should indicate intended learning outcomes such words as "know," "understand," and "appreciate" are appropriate for objectives. The intent of the program is for the student to know something or to appreciate something—not to be able to do twenty pushups or run ten laps. Doing twenty pushups or ten laps, or correctly processing twenty subtraction examples, indicates performance, not an intended learning outcome. As Lorin Anderson asserts, "A well-written instruction objective specifies the desired learning outcome in conceptual terms." It focuses on learning outcomes. "Test items, on the other hand, specify the desired learning outcome in operational terms." They focus on skills and tasks, and are more specific.[33]

Those who favor nonbehavioral objectives are not unconcerned with being precise. All educational objectives should be stated with sufficient precision to make clear what pupils are supposed to learn. The verbs "to know," "comprehend," "be able to," "enjoy," and "encounter" are all clear—they just are not behavioral! Words like "be familiar with" or "become aware of," or "have a feeling for" are vague and are rejected.

Teachers who believe in nonbehavioral objectives sometimes prepare such objectives in broad general terms indicating what students are to do. Some examples follow:

As a result of this course, the learner will:

Be able to interpret the various map symbols found on the particular types of map projections.

Understand that a community is a place where people work and play together.

Understand the syntax of a sentence and the functions of nouns and verbs.

Be able to perform long division of numbers.
Demonstrate the ability to do back flips.
Discriminate between various geometric forms.
Enjoy folk music.

Components of Objectives.

All objectives, whether behavioral or nonbehavioral, have components. Some components are characteristic of both types of objectives—the target individuals or learners for whom the objectives are intended, for example. Both types have, or at least imply, an *environmental condition* in which the student is to perform. And both types have an *operation*—a behavior to be performed, stated in general terms. Where there is a difference is in what Baker and Schutz call the *behavior mode*.[34] Behavioral objectives usually indicate this component specifically. This component identifies the terminal behavior by name. Nonbehavioral objectives do not have the behavior mode—the specific listing in precise terms of just what is to be done and how it is to be performed. Another component that behavioral objectives have and nonbehavioral objectives do not is the *statement of the criterion* or level of acceptable performance.[35] This component indicates the degree of mastery or achievement required.

Means and Ends. Much of the argument between behaviorists and nonbehaviorists revolves about the nature of and need for these components. Just how precise must the language in educational objectives be? Maritz Johnson and David Pratt make an interesting and useful distinction between educational intent and the realization of the intent. They note that many educators fall prey to the belief that the objective is in reality the statement that indicates its measure of achievement.[36] They state that an educational objective is really a statement of intent, an expected endproduct, not an actual product.

Drawing on these arguments, consider the following objective: "The student will write three statements, three questions, three commands, and three exclamations within a fifteen-minute time period and will have at least ten of the sentences correct as to type and with regard to subjects, predicates, and punctuation."

A person charged with curriculum development should raise the question, "Why do I want the student to do this?" A likely response is that by engaging in this activity, the student will show a basic understanding of the four types of sentences and punctuation. But does this answer the question? *Why* should a student need to understand these types of sentences? Johnson and Pratt would argue that the real reason is that a student will be able to apply such knowledge of sentence types and write what accurately and effectively expresses his or her feelings or interpretations of a subject. The real objective is not writing three statements, three questions, three commands, and three exclamations; rather, it is writing effectively on subjects of the student's own choosing.

Guidelines for Formulating Educational Objectives.

Because objectives indicate endpoints or expected outcomes or points that lead to other significant outcomes or points in the educational process, careful thought must be given to the creation of educational objectives. Indeed, giving careful thought to objectives increases the probability that a particular program will be judged successful. Educators should consider the following points when creating objectives.

Matching. Objectives should relate to the goals and the aims from which they are derived. Many curriculum guides include objectives that, although perhaps having merit, are unrelated to the goals. An objective of students' "understanding" certain science contents, for example, is not in alignment with a goal that students be able to utilize particular information-processing approaches to uncover scientific understanding.

Worth. It is often debatable which educational objectives have worth and which do not. Many schools overemphasize detail, especially in the skills subjects such as reading and mathematics. As a result many objectives are written that have little worth. Even in such subjects as social studies we see evidence of trivial objectives. "The student knows that the Mississippi River empties into the Gulf of Mexico." Does such an objective have value? Is it essential to know such information? Worth also relates to whether attaining an objective will have value to the student at present and in the future. Indeed, certain subject knowledge needs to be eliminated, modified, or updated because our knowledge base is constantly changing.

Wording. Objectives are only effective if the persons who are to use them as curriculum guides are able to understand from them the same intended outcomes as their writers. Objectives, brief and trimmed of excessive wordiness, are easy to understand and agree upon. How appropriately an objective is worded also depends on its level and its scope. Some objectives are written as general subject or grade objectives, some are written as unit objectives, and some, as lesson-plan objectives. Because lesson-plan objectives should be worded to indicate rather specifically the intended outcomes, they may include performance criterion statements. This type of precision is not necessarily needed at the first two levels (subject or grade level and unit plan level).

Appropriateness. Not all objectives need to be attained by all students. Curricularists must ask, What are the needs of the students? What type of learning outcomes do they need to achieve? To determine appropriateness, educators must consider the students who are to receive the instruction and the content within which the curriculum is to be delivered. Some objectives might not be appropriate because they demand of students behavior that they are incapable of performing. Some are not appropriate because they do not cater to the students' interests. Some objectives might be more suitable for students in a particular subject than

for students interested in a general orientation. Some objectives might list outcomes that students have already attained.

Logical Grouping. Objectives should be grouped logically so as to make sense when units of instruction and evaluation are being determined. Frequently, statements of objectives lack organizational coherence. In many cases, objectives that address a general understanding of self—such as understanding the particular effects of lack of exercise on the body—are grouped with objectives that are more specific. Often such general objectives as students' understanding how to process information are listed alongside objectives of students knowing how to write complete sentences. The need is to group objectives according to some common thread or idea; what some observers call a "domain."[37]

Periodic Revision. No objectives should stand for all times; objectives require periodic revision. This is necessary because students change, society changes, the realm of knowledge changes, and instructional strategies change. Educators should occasionally analyze their objectives to determine if they are still of value to the program. At times, the objective may perhaps still be of value in regard to its implied content, but the activities, or the behavioral guideline incorporated, may no longer be appropriate.

TAXONOMIC LEVELS

When making curricular decisions, especially when generating objectives, educators ideally consider all domains of learning: The cognitive, the affective, and the psychomotor. Fortunately, several well-known classifications of learning exist for them to use. These classifications have organized various types of learning into taxonomies.

Perhaps the best-known taxonomic classifications of learning in education are those developed by Benjamin Bloom,[38] David Krathwohl,[39] and Anita Harrow.[40] Bloom and his colleagues developed the

Taxonomy of Educational Objectives: Cognitive Domain. Krathwohl and others created the *Taxonomy of Educational Objectives: Affective Domain*. Harrow was responsible for *A Taxonomy of the Psychomotor Domain*.

The Cognitive Domain.

Of all the classifications of realms of objectives, Bloom's *Taxonomy* is perhaps the most familiar, and certainly has the greatest influence on the formation of objectives. The *Taxonomy* categorizes cognitive learning into six major divisions; each upper division subsumes the previous lower ones: (1) knowledge; (2) comprehension; (3) application; (4) analysis; (5) synthesis; and (6) evaluation.

When forming objectives, effective curriculum makers keep in mind at which cognitive level the objectives are placed. Following is a brief listing, along with illustrative examples, of the types of objectives at each level of the cognitive taxonomy:

1. *Knowledge*. This level includes objectives that are related to knowledge of (1) specifics, such as specific facts and terminology; (2) ways and means of dealing with specifics, such as conventions, trends and sequences, classifications and categories, criteria and methodology; and (3) universals and abstractions, such as principles, generalizations, theories, and structures. Example: The student will name the highest mountain range in Asia.

2. *Comprehension*. This level involves objectives that deal with (1) translation; (2) interpretation; and (3) extrapolation of information. Example: When given various geometric concepts in verbal terms, the student will draw the correct geometric form.

3. *Application*. This level includes objectives that are related to using abstractions in particular situations. Example: The student will be able to predict the effect on a container of exhausting its air contents.

4. *Analysis*. This level includes objectives that relate to the breaking of a whole into parts and distinguishing (1) elements; (2) relationships; and (3) organizational principles. Example: When given a document to read, the student will be able to distinguish facts from hypotheses.

5. *Synthesis*. This level includes objectives that relate to putting parts together in a new form such as (1) a unique communication; (2) a plan for operation; (3) a set of abstract relations. Example: When confronted with a report on pollution, the student will be able to propose ways of testing various hypotheses.

6. *Evaluation*. This is the highest level in the cognitive taxonomy in terms of complexity. Objectives at this level would address making judgments in terms of (1) internal evidence or logical consistency; and (2) external evidence or consistency with facts developed elsewhere. Example: The student will appraise fallacies in an argument.

A key assumption many educators bring to this cognitive taxonomy is that we should proceed from the lower levels to the higher levels. Another is that the higher levels of learning should be stressed. Most of our objectives should be addressing thinking skills rather than the recall of knowledge. However, we sometimes think that we need to spend a great deal of time on knowledge since it has so many categories compared to the other levels in the taxonomy. We believe mistakenly that students first need vast amounts of facts before they can process information and problem solve. If we keep in mind that the upper categories subsume the knowledge category, then we will write objectives that stress the higher mental processes realizing that we are not really ignoring the dimension of knowledge.

The Affective Domain.

Krathwohl and others presented to the educational community a taxonomy of objectives, consisting of five major categories, in the affective domain. Following is a brief listing, along with examples, of objectives of the categories of the affective domain:

1. *Receiving*. Objectives at this level refer to the learner's sensitivity to the existence of stimuli. This includes (1) awareness; (2) willingness to receive; and (3) selected attention.

Example: From studying various cultures of the Eastern world, the student develops an awareness of aesthetic factors in dress, furnishing, and architecture.

2. *Responding.* Objectives at this level refer to the learner's active attention to stimuli such as (1) acquiescence; (2) willing responses; and (3) feelings of satisfaction. Example: The student displays an interest in the topic of conversation by actively participating in a research project.

3. *Valuing.* Objectives in this level refer to the learner's beliefs and attitudes of worth. They are addressed in the form of (1) acceptance; (2) preference; and (3) commitment. Example: The student will take a viewpoint on advantages or disadvantages of nuclear power.

4. *Organization.* Objectives at this level refer to internalization of values and beliefs involving (1) conceptualization of values; and (2) organization of a value system. Example: The student forms judgments about his or her responsibilities for conserving natural resources.

5. *Characterization.* This is the highest level of internalization in the taxonomy. Objectives at this level relate to behavior that reflects (1) a generalized set of values; and (2) a characterization or philosophy of life. Example: The student develops a regulation of his or her personal and civic life based on ethical principles.

Although many educators find these categories useful, other educators, and many parents, view the taxonomy with concern. They feel that the school is responsible for the cognitive dimensions of learning, but has little or no responsibility in the affective or values domains. Arthur Combs has been an effective spokesperson for affective education: "Education must be concerned with the values, beliefs, convictions, and doubts of students. These realities as perceived by an individual are just as important, if not more so, as the so-called . . . facts."[41]

The Psychomotor Domain.

The psychomotor domain has received much less emphasis than either the cognitive or affective domains. Also, fewer per-

sons have worked on delineating it. Anita J. Harrow has, however, developed a psychomotor taxonomy with several categories:

1. *Reflex Movements.* Objectives at this level include (1) segmental reflexes (involving one spinal segment); and (2) intersegmental reflexes (involving more than one spinal segment. Example: After engaging in this activity, the student will be able to contract a muscle.

2. *Fundamental Movements.* Objectives in this category address behaviors related to (1) walking; (2) running; (3) jumping; (4) pushing; (5) pulling; and (6) manipulating. Example: The student will be able to jump over a two-foot hurdle.

3. *Perceptual Abilities.* Objectives in this division address (1) kinesthetic; (2) visual; (3) auditory; (4) tactile; and (5) coordination abilities. Example: The student will categorize by shape a group of building blocks.

4. *Physical Abilities.* Objectives included at this level are related to (1) endurance; (2) strength; (3) flexibility; (4) agility; (5) reaction-response time; and (6) dexterity. Example: The student will do at least five pushups more at the end of the year.

5. *Skilled Movements.* Objectives at this level of the domain are concerned with (1) games; (2) sports; (3) dances; and (4) the arts. Example: The student can correctly perform a series of somersaults.

6. *Nondiscursive Communication.* Objectives at this final level of the taxonomy relate to expressive movement through (1) posture; (2) gestures; (3) facial expressions; and (4) creative movements. Example: The student will be able to create his or her own movement sequence and perform it to music.

The categories of the three taxonomies are arranged in a hierarchy in which the levels increase in complexity from simple to more advanced. In the cognitive domain, levels two through six connote various problem-solving skills and abilities. Each level depends on the acquisition of the previous level. For example, for a student to analyze an issue, he or she must be able to apply information, must comprehend information, and must have some level of knowledge. For a student to express a value preference, he or she must be able to respond to situations and must be willing to receive information—that is, he or she must be sensitive to a particular situation. For a child to be skilled at the level of perceptual abilities, he or she must have mastered fundamental movements and reflex movements.

The taxonomies, as has already been noted, are useful for developing educational objectives and for grouping sets of objectives. One difficulty educators may have is making decisions identifying objectives between adjacent categories. This is particularly true if the objectives are not clearly stated. But, if educators carefully reflect on their objectives, they should find the taxonomies valuable tools for creating objectives. Mindful of these taxonomies, they should be able to move their learners from the lower to the higher levels of learning in each domain. Ideally, effective education calls into play all three major domains of learning.

APPROACHES TO EDUCATIONAL OBJECTIVES

Objectives, stated more specifically than goals, are designed to communicate to involved parties—students, teachers, laypersons—the intents of particular actions. However, diverse views exist regarding approaches to curriculum objectives. Some attention was given to defining these approaches in Chapter 1.

Behavioral-Rational Approach.

In the last two decades much attention has been given to behavioral objectives. Although such objectives are rather new to educational dialogue, the theoretical basis for them is not; it has been borrowed from behaviorist learning theory (see Chapter 4) in psychology and from the concept of "operationalism" in science (by which people operationalize or give a tangible or observable condition to a particular learning or dis-

position of a human being). For example, you may wish to indicate that a person appreciated good art; however, no one has ever seen an "appreciation." What you need to do is to indicate those tangible or observable ways of behaving that comprise "appreciation." Armed with such a tangible definition of appreciate, you have a better indication of what you are looking for or intending with your objectives.

In this connection, B. F. Skinner views the curriculum as being formulated according to behavioristic objectives.[42] To Skinner, the teacher's role is primarily a mechanical one of arranging contingencies of reinforcement, in a sequenced and step-by-step procedure, under which the students are automatically conditioned toward specific terminal ways of behaving. Taking this approach to objectives, we view method as the scheduling of reinforcement contingencies established by the teacher or the curriculum developer.

This concern for high levels of behavioral specificity has some history in American business and education. It is tied closely to the notion of curriculum as a production system in which the student is a product to be acted upon. This view of the curriculum received attention during the early decades of this century, when educators were attempting to relate scientific management to education.[43]

Franklin Bobbitt (along with his contemporary W. W. Charters) developed activity analysis, a means of obtaining objectives efficiently. Activity analysis is a variation of job analysis, by which the basic components of a job are noted in order to determine how someone might be trained to do that job.[44] Bobbitt argued that life consisted of performing specific activities. If education was preparation for life, it must prepare students to be skilled in the performance of these activities. The educator's task was to analyze these activities and make their component parts definite and particular. Once the parts were identified, they could then be taught. Bobbitt reasoned that such activities would be the basis for the objectives of the curriculum. "The curriculum will then be that series of experiences which children and youth must have by way of attaining these objectives."[45]

Popham and Baker defined the curriculum as "all planned learning outcomes for which the school is responsible."[46] They viewed curriculum as the ends and instruction as the means. This separating of curriculum and instruction as ends and means continues to affect behavioral objectives. Popham argued: "Measurable instructional objectives are designed to counteract what is to me the most serious deficit in American education today, namely a preoccupation with the process without assessment of consequences." He lists three areas in which "measurable objectives have considerable potential—in curriculum (what goals are selected); in instruction (how to accomplish those goals); and in evaluation (determining whether objectives of the instructional sequence have been realized)."[47]

Gagné and Briggs made a similar point. They stated that greater precision in the definition of objectives meets two needs: The need for communication of the purposes of instruction and the need for evaluation of instruction.[48] They note that in achieving precision in stating objectives "one is said to be 'defining objectives in terms of human performance [or human behavior].' " When objectives are so stated, an individual is "informed as to what must be observed" in order to determine the achievement of the course's purpose.[49]

Intellectual-Academic Approach.

Behaviorism influences greatly the writing of objectives; nonetheless, the intellectual-academic approach is also an important approach to curricular activity. Although when this approach to forming objectives actually started is debatable, few would contest Dewey's influence on it. Dewey identified the fundamental factors to which the educator should attend as: (1) the learner; (2) society; and (3) organized subject matter. He cautioned educators not to consider these three factors as separate, for when this

happens this "interaction is transformed into an unreal, and hence insoluble, theoretical problem. Instead of seeing the educative process steadily and as a whole, we see conflicting terms. We get the case of child vs. the curriculum; of the individual nature vs. social culture."[50]

Despite Dewey's admonition, educators over the years have continued to separate these factors, and to thus switch allegiances in succeeding periods from discipline-centered studies to learner-centered curricula, from curricula with a social relevance thrust to curricula stressing basic skills. Each of these three sources has at various times become the primary source of doctrine for a particular approach to the curriculum. Dewey's view of these three sources of the curriculum were and continue to be considered by educational thinkers.

Thus, when Ralph Tyler provided a method for formulating objectives, he relied on three sources of the curriculum: (1) studies of the learner; (2) studies of contemporary life; and (3) suggestions from subject matter specialists. Many today give Tyler the credit for formulating these three sources. But, Dewey had discussed them as three sources forming an interacting dynamic. Actually, Tyler's model of curriculum development is an ends-means (or behavioral) approach. In this approach, the setting of purposes or objectives as ends affect the kinds of content and activity, and their organization, that most likely will assist education in reaching its goal. These objectives also affect the means of evaluation and what will be considered standards of acceptable performance.

The Systems-Managerial Approach.

The systems-managerial approach to curriculum is a way of thinking. In Figure 6-1, Roger Kaufman notes that a systems approach is an overall process by which needs are identified, problems selected, requirements for problem resolution determined, solutions chosen from alternatives, actual methods and means obtained and implemented, results evaluated, and revisions en-

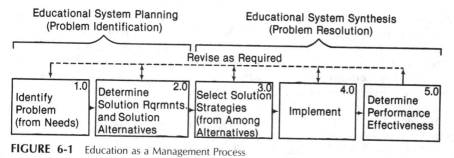

FIGURE 6-1 Education as a Management Process

Source: From Roger A. Kaufman, "A System Approach to Education: Derivation and Definition," *A V Communication Review* (Winter 1968). Reprinted by permission of the Association for Educational Communications & Technology.

acted. These various states can be divided into two major stages: problem identification and problem resolution.[51]

Sometimes the systems-managerial approach appears in educational instructions under the guise of management by objectives. Management by objectives (MBO) can be considered as a philosophical approach whereby all school personnel identify their common and uncommon goals as a basis for defining successful criteria for evaluating the degree of goal attainment. Some people call this approach behaviorist. MBO rests on the assumption that school operations can be conducted in a logical and effective pattern. One can identify directions, plot action, implement such action, and evaluate the success of such implementation.[52]

Although MBO is not a complex process, it still includes an acceptance of the systems-managerial posture. When the school functions as a system it consists of a number of components, each differentiated from the others in terms of particular functions to be performed; all of these components contribute in some way to the accomplishment of the organization's purpose. Further, the term *system* implies that the relationships among the various components are characterized by interdependence, regularity, order, and predictability.[53]

Humanistic-Aesthetic Approach.

Humanists believe that the function of the curriculum is to provide each learner with intrinsically rewarding experiences that will foster personal liberation. Humanists view the goals of education as personal growth, integrity, and autonomy. The goals and objectives of the humanist are to enable individuals to actualize their human potential. The resulting curriculum program should contain experiences through which individuals can expand their awareness of being human. Humanists deal with such questions as: What is real? What is human? What is good? In processing such questions educators can arrange educational objectives and experiences to allow students to attain personal dignity and self-worth. Weinstein and Fantini embrace the notion that education in a free society should have a broad human focus, which is best served by educational objectives resting on a personal and interpersonal base and dealing with students' concerns.[54]

The idea of self-actualization is central to the humanistic-aesthetic approach to education. Earl Kelley asserts that the self has to be achieved; it is not given. The self is, however, achieved through social contact, and therefore it has to be understood in terms of others.[55] Carl Rogers, a recognized spokesperson for this approach, indicates that the goals and objectives of such a curriculum should be geared to enabling the individual student to gain an openness to experience, to view living as a process, and to trust his or her own experiencing. The individual is thus able to view himself or herself as becoming a more fully functioning individual.[56]

Abraham Maslow, a major figure in the development of humanistic psychology, viewed self-realization as multidimensional, as relating to life achievement, as continually evolving. Thus, the curriculum was constantly changing as well. Every learner is, in part, "his own project" and makes the currriculum fit his own needs.[57] The objectives and goals that humanists favor address openness and tend to be stated in humanistic rather than behavioral or rational terms. The prime criterion is that such objectives must encourage self-actualization; they must relate to peak experiences. For Maslow such experiences are those that give rise to love, hate, anxiety, depression, and joy. Maslow noted that the peak experiences of awe, mystery, and wonder are both the end and the beginning of learning.

Philip Phenix has expanded some of Maslow's thinking. Phenix believes that the curriculum must do more than concentrate on academic knowledge. It must stress transcendence—the limitlessness of experience. Stressing transcendence, the student will experience every event within a context of wider relationships and possibilities. Phenix indicated that certain qualities are associated with transcendence—hope, creativity, awareness, doubt and faith, wonder, awe, and reverence.[58] Focusing on these dimensions permits optimal individual development.

Objectives in the humanistic-aesthetic camp direct the teachers to furnish learners with opportunities to become their own persons, and to gain control over their processes of learning, to realize the complexity of existence. Some teachers in this camp do not write explicit or precise objectives. They allow the objectives, if there are any, to "evolve" from the experiences that students have. If we were looking at a curriculum guide for a humanistic-aesthetic curriculum, for example, we might find such objectives as: (1) students will have experiences that will help them become self-directed and involved in the learning process; (2) students will gain in self-confidence; and (3) students will become more considerate of

others. Such objectives do not list specific behaviors that the students are to demonstrate, nor do they indicate any criteria of performance. But, these so-called "vague" statements are still objectives, for they do present educational outcomes.

Reconceptualist Approach.

The questions asked by advocates of the behavioral-rational, systems-managerial, and intellectual-academic approaches to the formation of objectives and the creation of curriculum are not considered by the reconceptualists to be the key questions. Reconceptualists think that curricularists are preoccupied with the practical and technical modes of understanding and action. William Pinar asserts that the key question is not what are the purposes of the school, but rather Why do I as an individual identify with particular people or certain situations? Why do I read these authors and not those? Why am I fascinated with this play and not that play?[59]

In a sense, reconceptualists are like humanists; reconceptualists, however, are much more critical of education and view the educational arena from an existential, aesthetic, and spiritual framework. For this reason, the objectives of the reconceptualists are open ended. Macdonald indicates that the objectives of the curriculum should be to foster the individual's development of interests.[60]

Most reconceptualists have not provided specific advice on creating objectives. Rather, they have critiqued the field of curriculum and reinterpreted its major issues. Because there is a tendency to stress philosophical and ideological issues, the reconceptualists have little time to worry about the smaller issues, or the mechanics, of writing objectives.[61]

Challenges.

Educators are certainly being challenged by these various approaches to objectives and to the resulting curricula. Although many of them will not have to decide among these approaches, they will need to know that such approaches to objectives do exist, and that each makes various assumptions regarding the schools, education, the curriculum, the students, and the teachers. Quite likely, those faced with making decisions about objectives will draw on different aspects of each of these approaches. Those using the behavioral-rational approach will write their curriculum objectives in behavioral terms; those confronted with ensuring that the school program is delivered according to plans, schedules, and programs will draw on the systems-managerial orientation to objectives and their delivery. For certain teaching and learning aspects of the curriculum, some will draw heavily on the humanistic-aesthetic approach, and a few may learn to be reconceptualists.

Considering goals and objectives as statements of endpoints in students' learning raises the issue of how to determine whether the competency implicit or explicit in an objective is stated appropriately. Although behavioral objectives have the "virtue" of clarity, they usually only indicate the observable levels of learning—some would argue only the trivial or lowest outcomes of the curriculum.[62]

Expanding on this point—that objectives tend to trivialize important issues—Joseph Schwab asserted that curriculum developers who overrely on endless strings of objectives tend to separate what should be held together. "They atomize, not only subject matter, but teachers' thoughts about it, the pattern of instruction used to convey it, the organization of textbooks, and the analysis and construction of tests."[63]

Behavioral objectives can easily denote logical and rational thought, but they cannot easily describe creative and intuitive learning or internalized value systems. Behavioral objectives seem to indicate that behavior is unidimensional rather than multidimensional. Advocates assume, for instance, that all students who list the major river systems in the United States have the identical understanding or are exhibiting the same competency at the same level. The objectives developed seem to be for all students, but for those students who are able to

specialize and excel, they would be limiting.

Many curriculum specialists are concerned that behavioral objectives do not seem to focus on higher-order tasks and skills. Other educators, however, are concerned that the focus on precise objectives is likely to cause educators to ignore the unintended consequences—either positive or negative—of the curriculum on the learners.[64]

Curriculum development also deals with the issue of competencies. Educators must question, What competencies? Competencies in what subject areas? An individual's approach to curriculum will influence how he or she processes such questions. The behavioral-rationalists will respond, "Those skills necessary for working in the world." Intellectual-academics may say, "Those subjects necessary for earning a living and meeting responsibilities as a citizen." Those involved in systems-managerial approaches might respond, "Those subjects that enable one to obtain a better understanding of the world and its many systems and subsystems." Humanistic-aesthetics might respond, "Those competencies that enable individuals to know who they are, and that contribute to the development of positive self-concepts." Reconceptualists, on the other hand, might say, "Those competencies needed to engage in self-inquiry and to seek out meaningful relationships in life."

All of the approaches to creating objectives have shortcomings. The behavioral-rational approach might be viewed as too structured and trivial. The systems-managerial approach could be viewed as technocratic, and an offshoot of behaviorism. The intellectual-academic approach could be viewed as middle of the road, where a position is avoided. The very strength of the humanistic-aesthetic camp is perhaps also its major weakness; the wording of such objectives is "vague" and open to interpretation and misinterpretation. A program following such objectives might well lack internal consistency—that is, the program under one teacher's direction might differ radically from the "same" program following the same general objective taught by another teacher.

The reconceptualists' approach can also be criticized as not furnishing enough specific guidance about how to form objectives. We might also fault such objectives as being directed more toward political and social realities than educational concerns.[65]

Both the humanistic-aesthetic and the reconceptualist approaches are difficult to assess: When have we attained the endpoint, the expected outcome? Even though educators can agree that endpoints are only points that lead eventually to other points in a continuum of existence, they still need some indication that they are at least on the correct track with regard to their purposes. It is not likely that advocates of these approaches will come to any agreement in the near future, because persons in these camps are not just arguing about the wording of objectives, but are debating the basic purpose of education itself—and they are coming up with different answers as a result of their inherent philosophical orientations.

CONCLUSION

We have presented in great detail information on aims, goals, and objectives. The chapter began with a discussion of the nature of aims. We presented aims that have been created by various groups and commissions. Aims essentially guide and direct our educational efforts. Aims are generated in response to general societal concerns at particular times.

Goals are statements that are more specific than aims; they indicate endpoints or outcomes of education. It was pointed out that often goals are generated by commissions, but that educators do and can take more active roles in creating goals. It was also mentioned that creating goals is a continuous activity.

The major portion of the chapter dealt with the objectives of education. We attempted to present a complete picture of objectives, giving much attention to both behavioral and nonbehavioral objectives. Discussion centered on the common components of the various types of objectives, which illustrates that objectives differ perhaps more in degree than in kind. But, careful attention must be given to the formulation of objectives. Guidelines were presented to assist this process.

The diversity of levels of objectives was presented in a discussion of the various taxonomies that are available for guiding the creation of objectives. Such taxonomies help educators write objectives. The various philosophical approaches assist as well. We presented these to show the "richness" of views that we really need to consider when formulating objectives.

Notes

1. John Dewey, *Democracy and Education* (New York: Macmillan, 1916), pp. 383–384.
2. Boyd H. Bode, "Education at the Crossroads," *Progressive Education* (November 1931), p. 548.
3. Decker Walker and Jonas F. Soltis, *Curriculum and Aims* (New York: Teachers College Press, Columbia University, 1986).
4. John Dewey, *John Dewey on Education: Selected Writings*, D. Archambault, ed. (New York: Random House, 1964), p. 74.
5. J. Galen Saylor, William M. Alexander, and Arthur J. Lewis, *Planning Curriculum for Schools*, 4th ed. (New York: Holt, Rinehart, 1981), pp. 144–145.
6. Allan C. Ornstein, "How Do Educators Meet the Needs of Society?" *National Association of Secondary School Principals* (May 1985), pp. 36–47.
7. David Pratt, *Curriculum: Design and Development* (New York: Harcourt, Brace, 1980).
8. B. P. Komisar and J. E. McClellan, "The Logic of Slogans," in B. O. Smith and R. H. Ennis, eds., *Language and Concepts in Education*, (Chicago: Rand McNally, 1961), pp. 195–214.
9. Walker and Soltis, *Curriculum and Aims*.
10. Ralph W. Tyler, "Purposes of Our Schools," *National Association of Secondary School Principals* (May 1968), pp. 1–12.
11. Ronald C. Doll, *Curriculum Improvement: Decision Making and Process*, 6th ed. (Boston: Allyn and Bacon, 1986).
12. Herbert Spencer, *Education: Intellectual, Moral and Physical* (New York: Alden, 1885).
13. Commission on the Reorganization of Secondary Education, *Cardinal Principles of Secondary Education*, Bulletin 35 (Washington, D.C.: United States Office of Education, 1918), p. 9.
14. Ibid., pp. 11–16.

15. Educational Policies Commission, *The Purpose of Education in American Democracy* (Washington, D.C.: National Educational Association, 1938), p. 89.

16. Ibid.

17. Educational Policies Commission, *Education for All American Youth* (Washington, D.C.: National Educational Association, 1944), pp. 225–226.

18. Educational Policies Commission, *The Central Purpose of American Education* (Washington, D.C.: National Educational Association, 1961), p. 89.

19. Commission on Excellence in Education, *A Nation at Risk* (Washington, D.C.: U.S. Government Printing Office, 1983), p. 1.

20. Ibid., pp. 13–14.

21. Ibid., p. 24.

22. Ibid., p. 27.

23. Mortimer J. Adler, *Paideia: Problems and Possibilities* (New York: Macmillan, 1983), p. 9.

24. ASCD Committee on Research and Theory, *Measuring and Attaining the Goals of Education* (Alexandria, Va.: Association for Supervision and Curriculum Development, 1980).

25. Program Development Center of Northern California, *Phase III of the Educational Planning Model* (Bloomington, Ind.: Phi Delta Kappa Educational Foundation, 1976).

26. Hilda Taba, *Curriculum Development: Theory and Practice* (New York: Harcourt, Brace, 1962).

27. Robert S. Zais, *Curriculum Principles and Foundations* (New York: Crowell, 1976).

28. Eva Baker and James W. Popham, *Expanding Dimensions of Instructional Objectives* (Englewood Cliffs, N.J.: Prentice-Hall, 1973).

29. Bruce W. Tuckman, *Evaluating Instructional Programs*, 2nd ed. (Boston: Allyn and Bacon, 1985); Robert F. Mager, *Preparing Instructional Objectives* (Palo Alto, Calif.: Fearon, 1962).

30. Mager, *Preparing Instructional Objectives*; Norman E. Gronlund, *Stating Behavioral Objectives for Classroom Instruction* (New York: Macmillan, 1970); and Gronlund, *Measurement and Evaluation of Teaching*, 5th ed. (New York: Macmillan, 1985).

31. Mager, *Preparing Instructional Objectives*.

32. Michael Polanyi, *The Tacit Dimension* (New York: Doubleday, 1966).

33. Lorin W. Anderson, "Mastery Learning: One Approach to the Integration of Instruction and Measurement." Paper presented at the annual meeting of the American Educational Research Association, Toronto, March 1978, p. 4.

34. Robert L. Baker and Richard E. Schutz, eds., *Instructional Product Development* (New York: Van Nostrand Reinhold, 1971).

35. Jon Wiles and Joseph C. Bondi, *Curriculum Development: A Guide to Practice*, 2nd ed. (Columbus, Ohio: Merrill, 1984).

36. Mauritz Johnson, "Definitions and Models in Curriculum Theory," *Educational Theory* (April 1967), pp. 127–139; Pratt, *Curriculum: Design and Development*.

37. Saylor, Alexander, and Lewis, *Curriculum Planning for Better Teaching and Learning*.

38. Benjamin S. Bloom, ed., *Taxonomy of Educational Objectives, Handbook I: Cognitive Domain* (New York: McKay, 1956).

39. David R. Krathwohl, ed., *Taxonomy of Educational Objectives, Handbook II: Affective Domain* (New York: McKay, 1964).

40. Anita J. Harrow, *A Taxonomy of the Psychomotor Domain* (New York: McKay, 1972).

41. Arthur W. Combs, ed., *Perceiving, Behaving, Becoming: A New Focus for Education* (Washington, D.C.: Association for Supervision and Curriculum Development, 1962), p. 200.

42. B. F. Skinner, *The Technology of Teaching* (New York: Appleton, 1968).

43. Raymond E. Callahan, *Education and the Cult of Efficiency* (Chicago: University of Chicago Press, 1962).

44. Franklin Bobbitt, *How to Make a Curriculum* (Boston: Houghton Mifflin, 1924).

45. Ibid., p. 132.

46. W. James Popham and Eva I. Baker, *Systematic Instruction* (Englewood Cliffs, N.J.: Prentice-Hall, 1970), p. 48.

47. W. James Popham, "Practical Ways of Improving Curriculum via Measurable Objectives," *National Association of Secondary School Principals* (May 1971), p. 48.

48. Robert M. Gagné and Leslie J. Briggs, *Principles of Instructional Design*, 2nd ed. (New York: Holt, Rinehart, 1979).

49. Ibid., p. 47.

50. John Dewey, *The Child and the Curriculum* (Chicago: University of Chicago Press, 1902), pp. 4,8.

51. Roger A. Kaufman, *Educational System Planning* (Englewood Cliffs, N.J.: Prentice-Hall, 1972).

52. James Lewis, *School Management by Objectives* (West Nyack, N.Y.: Parker, 1974); George B. Redfern, *Evaluating Teachers and Administrators: A Performance Objectives Approach* (Boulder, Colo.: Westview Press, 1980).

53. Max G. Abbott and Terry L. Eidell, "Administration Implementation of Curriculum Performance," *Educational Technology* (May 1970), pp. 62–64. See also Robert G. Owens, *Organizational Behavior in Education*, 2nd ed. (Englewood Cliffs, N.J.: Prentice-Hall, 1981).

54. Gerald Weinstein and Mario D. Fantini, *Toward Humanistic Education: A Curriculum of Affect* (New York: Praeger, 1970).

55. Earl C. Kelley, "The Fully Functioning Self," in Combs, ed., *Perceiving, Behaving, Becoming*, pp. 9–20.

56. Carl R. Rogers, "Toward Becoming a Fully Functioning Person," in Combs, ed., *Perceiving, Behaving, Becoming*, pp. 21–33.

57. Abraham H. Maslow, "Some Basic Propositions of a Growth and Self-Actualization Psychology," in Combs, ed., *Perceiving, Behaving, Becoming*, pp. 34–49.

58. Philip H. Phenix, "Transcendence and the Curriculum," in E. W. Eisner and E. Valance, eds., *Conflicting Conceptions of the Curriculum* (Berkeley, Calif.: McCutchan, 1974), pp. 117–135.

59. William Pinar, "Currere: Toward Reconceptualization," in Pinar, ed., *Curriculum Theorizing: The Reconceptualists* (Berkeley, Calif.: McCutchan, 1975), pp. 396–414.

60. James Macdonald, "Curriculum and Human Interests," in Pinar, ed., *Curriculum Theorizing*, pp. 283–294.

61. Michael Apple, "Making Knowledge Legitimate: Power, Profit, and the Textbook," in A. Molnar, ed., *Current Thought on Curriculum* (Alexandria, Va.: Association for Supervision and Curriculum Development, 1985), pp. 73–90.

62. Gail Delicio, "Teaching Alliteration Inductively: Taba's Deductive Thinking Model in Practice." Paper presented at the annual meeting of the American Educational Research Association, San Francisco, April 1986.

63. Joseph Schwab, "The Practical Four: Something for Curriculum Professors to Do," *Curriculum Inquiry* (Fall 1983), pp. 239–266.

64. John C. Ory, " A Study of the Relationship Between Affective and Cognitive Performance." Paper presented at the annual meeting of the American Educational Research Association, San Francisco, April 1986; Schwab, "The Practical Four."

65. Jerry L. Patterson, Stewart C. Purkey, and Jackson V. Parker, eds. *Productive School Systems for a Nonrational World* (Alexandria, Va.: Association for Supervision and Curriculum Development, 1986).

chapter 7

CURRICULUM DESIGN

The concept of curriculum design brings into focus the way in which curricula are created, especially the actual arrangement of the parts of the curriculum plan. In this chapter the term *curriculum design*—sometimes called *curriculum organization*—refers to the arrangement of the elements of a curriculum into a substantive entity. Which design someone actually selects is influenced by his or her curriculum approach and philosophical orientation.

The parts, sometimes called components or elements, that are arranged in a curriculum design are: (1) aims, goals, and objectives; (2) subject matter; (3) learning experiences; and (4) evaluation approaches. The nature of these components and the manner in which they are organized in the curriculum plan comprise what we mean by curriculum design. Although most curriculum plans have within their design these four essential elements, often they are not given equal weight. Frequently, content or

subject matter receives the primary emphasis. But, sometimes schools do create designs that stress primarily objectives and evaluation approaches. Some designs give primary emphasis to learning experiences or activities.

COMPONENTS OF DESIGN

When considering curriculum design, the curriculum decision maker confronts the question: What general structure of the curriculum can I develop so that autonomy of the parts does not confuse the design as a whole?[1] As already mentioned, curriculum design is concerned with the nature and arrangement of four basic curricular parts. These parts are rooted in the classic work of H. Giles, an offshoot of "The Eight-Year Study." He used the term "components" to show the relationship, and included learning experiences under "method and organization."[2] The relationship is shown in Figure 7-1.

The design's four components suggest to the curriculum maker four questions: What is to be done? What subject matter is to be included? What instructional strategies, resources, and activities will be employed? And what methods and instruments will be used to appraise the results of the curriculum? According to Giles, the four components interact with each other; decisions made about one component are dependent on decisions made about the others.

While Giles presented the paradigm, it is very similar to a model that Tyler developed several years later. Tyler's model, however, denotes a linear attention to the key elements of the curriculum, while Giles's paradigm shows ongoing interaction among the components. Tyler, who also worked on "The Eight-Year Study," claims to have influenced Giles in his conceptualization of the curricular framework.[3]

Curriculum design involves various philosophical or theoretical issues as well as practical issues. A person's philosophical stance will have an impact on his or her interpretation and selection of objectives; influence the content he or she selects and how he or she will organize it; affect his or her decisions about how to teach or deliver the curriculum content; and guide his or her judgments about how to evaluate the success of the curriculum developed.

Not all designs need to have the four components noted by Giles. But a curriculum design does need to provide a consistent framework of values and priorities for

dealing with the operational decisions nec essary for delivering the curriculum.

If a curriculum is designed adequately, i defines for the curriculum decision make the nature and scope of the components i the curriculum that are to receive particula attention.[4] Hilda Taba noted that most cu riculum designs contain Giles's four compo nents, but that many lack balance, becaus the elements are poorly defined or are nc considered in relation to a theoretical ra tionale.[5] Indeed, the various types of de signs that we discuss in this chapter are re ally the result of loading on a particula component or element of the curriculum

Sources for Curriculum Design.

Those charged with curriculum desig must clarify their philosophical and soci views of society and the individual learn er—or what is commonly called the sourc of curriculum. To determine the influenc of curriculum design, attention must t given to how such sources will influence e ucation. How the curriculum planner r sponds to the question: "What are t sources of ideas for education?" will impa his or her views of curriculum design. F this reason, it is essential for curriculum d signers to identify their philosophical ar social orientations. If they ignore philosop ical and social questions, their curriculu designs will have limited or confused ratio ales. Taba notes that "much of the distan between theory and practice may be caus by just such lack of rationale."[6]

Ronald Doll describes four sources ideas that undergird curriculum designs science, society, eternal verities, and Divi Will.[7] These sources are somewhat similar those sources of curriculum; identified Dewey and Bode and popularized by Tyler knowledge, society, and the learner.[8]

Science as a Source. Persons who vie science as a source for curriculum rely hea ily on the scientific method for determinir truth. They select and arrange in the curr ulum those elements of reality that can t observed and quantified. The subje centered designs discussed later usua

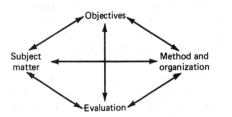

FIGURE 7-1 The Components of Design.
From H. H. Giles, S. P. McCutchen, and A. N. Zechiel, *Exploring the Curriculum* (New York: Harper, 1942), p. 2.

come from persons who view science as the prime source of ideas.

Society as a Source. Curriculum designers favoring society as a source for the curriculum believe that because the school is an agent of society, the school should draw its ideas for the curriculum from the analysis of the social situation.

Although Dewey certainly thought of education as enabling people to improve society, he was mindful that it was necessary for educators to consider society as a source. He wrote: "Whenever we have in mind the discussion of a new movement in education, it is especially necessary to take the broader, or social view." If we fail to consider the broad, social view, then the change will be "looked at as the arbitrary inventions of particular teachers, at the worst transitory fads, and at the best merely improvements in certain details." The modification going on in curriculum and instructional matters is as much a product of the changed social situation, and as "much an effort to meet the needs of the new society that is forming, as are changes in modes of industry and commerce."[9]

But Bode pointed out years later, "The purpose of education is not to fit the individual for a place in society, but to enable him to make his own place. . . ."[10] Some persons consider that the government should lead the way in deciding how to design the curriculum—so our curricula would be similar to European national curricula. In this view, the curriculum would only change in response to legislative or judicial mandates. Other persons believe that curricular design should be intended to perpetuate society. Reconstructionists take an opposite stance; the curriculum should emphasize ideas that would change and/or improve the social order.

Eternal and Divine Sources. Some people consider that designers should simply draw on the past for guidance as to what is appropriate content. This traditional view, which reflects a perennialist philosophy, proposes selecting those eternal truths advanced by great persons in the past. Such designs stress the content element.

Divine will as an undergirding factor for curriculum design, related to eternal truth, notes that the elements of the curriculum are revealed to humans through the Bible or through other religious documents. Although this was a popular view during the colonial period in New England, it is not followed by public schools today because of mandated separation of church and state. But, many private and parochial schools do consider this source of the curriculum design most important.

Knowledge as a Source. Some might interpret science as the source of the curriculum design as too limiting because it ignores content from other fields of study. If we consider knowledge itself as one of the prime sources of curriculum, we certainly will not leave out any particular content. Hunkins has gone so far as to suggest that knowledge is perhaps the only source of curriculum, and that society and what we know about learners really serve as filters in the selection of content.[11] Certainly knowledge cannot be ignored. Herbert Spencer placed knowledge within the framework of curriculum when he asked "What knowledge is of most worth?" It is the same question that Arno Bellack raised eighty years later when he examined knowledge in relationship to the various disciplines and structure of a curriculum.[12]

Those who place knowledge at the center, or as a key source, realize that it is organized in specialized ways. Disciplined knowledge has a particular structure and a particular method or methods by which its scholars extend its boundaries. Undisciplined knowledge does not have unique content, but has content that is "clustered" according to the focus of the investigation. Physics has a unique conceptual structure and a unique process. But home economics is undisciplined in that its content is not unique to itself but is drawn from various other disciplines and adapted to a special focus.

The Learner as a Source. Some believe that the curriculum should be derived from what we know about the learner: How he or she learns, and forms attitudes, generates interests, forms values. Progressive curricularists and educators who favor learner-centered and experience-centered curriculum designs (we discuss both designs later in this chapter) consider the learner as the primary source.

Those who put emphasis on the learner tend to ignore subject matter and knowledge, at least the latter are given secondary emphasis. Today, with the current stress on academic excellence, learner-centered curricularists are on the defensive and perceived as outdated. Elementary school teachers, however, still recognize the importance for dealing with the needs and interests of the child as the major source of curriculum design. At the secondary school level, learner-centered designs are waning—a reversal from the 1960s and 1970s, when "relevancy" and "humanism" were faddish.[13]

Conceptual Framework: Horizontal and Vertical Organization.

Curriculum design, the organization of the components or elements of curriculum, exists along two basic organizational dimensions—horizontal and vertical. *Horizontal* organization engages the curriculum worker with the concepts of scope and integration—that is, the side-by-side arrangement of curriculum elements. For instance, arranging content from the separate subjects of history, anthropology, and sociology into a course dealing with contemporary studies involves horizontal organization. Taking content from one subject, such as mathematics, and relating it to content in another, such as science, is another example of horizontal design.

Vertical organization, which centers on the concepts of sequence and continuity, is concerned with the longitudinal placement of curriculum elements. Placing "the family" in first grade social studies and "the community" in second grade social studies is an example of vertical organization.[14] Frequently, curricula are organized so that the same topics are introduced and treated in different grades, but at increasingly more detailed and difficult levels. This also is vertical organization. For instance, in mathematics the concept of set is introduced in first grade and reintroduced or mentioned at each succeeding year in the elementary curriculum. This corresponds with Bruner's idea of the "spiral curriculum."[15]

Even though design decisions are essential it appears that curricula in schools are not the result of careful design deliberations. In most school districts, overall curricular designs receive little attention. Most school curricula, regardless of school level, are not really closely related either vertically or horizontally. Curricular elements, in fact, often give the appearance of a patchwork quilt.[16] As one patch in the quilt has nothing to do with the next patch, except that it is sewed to it, so the element, for example, of curriculum objectives has no relation to the element of content. Curriculum often exists as disjointed clusters of content organized as particular items that frequently duplicate and/or conflict with other items. Robert Zais has noted that many courses in the schools' curricula are really the result of current "educational" fashion and not careful deliberations about design.[17]

DESIGN DIMENSION CONSIDERATIONS

As already noted, curriculum design is a statement noting the relationships that exist among the components or elements of a curriculum. Curricularists must, when considering design, view it on several dimensions—scope, integration, sequence, continuity, articulation, and balance.

Scope. When considering the design of a curriculum, educators need to address the breadth and depth of its content—that is, its scope. J. Galen Saylor defines scope in the following manner: "By scope is meant the breadth, variety, and types of educational experiences that are to be provided pupils as they progress through the school program. Scope represents the latitudinal axis for selecting curriculum experiences."[18] What content should be included in the curriculum? What activities should be included? What will be the extent and arrangement of such curricular elements?

Integration. The major challenge in dealing with scope is integrating the myriad learnings that students are to encounter at a particular level of the curriculum. Ideally, those designing curricula realize that learning is more effective when content from one field is related meaningfully to content from another field. Integration emphasizes *horizontal* relationships among various content topics and themes. It is an attempt to interrelate content with learning experiences and activities to ensure that students' needs are met. If ideas and concepts are used as basic threads for showing relationships, integration can be achieved in several ways, including but not limited to combining subjects and/or showing how content cuts across subject matter.

Sequence. When considering sequence, curricularists are challenged to deal effectively with the curricular elements so that the curriculum fosters cumulative and continuous learning, or what is referred to as the *vertical* relationship among curricular areas. Taba has noted that people dealing with sequence have addressed content but have given little or no attention to the sequences of processes—those skills requisite for dealing with the content.[19] She argued that this failure to pay serious attention to sequence in terms of the cumulative development of intellectual and affective processes has resulted in less-than-optimal curricula as well as problems articulating among the levels of schooling.

Persons addressing sequence have been aware of the longstanding controversy over whether the sequence of content and expe-

riences should be based on the logic of the subject matter or on the way in which individuals process knowledge. Those arguing for sequence based on psychological principles draw on an understanding of and research on human growth, development, and learning. Piaget's research has provided a framework for sequencing content and activities and relating expectations to what we know about how individuals function at various cognitive levels.[20] Kohlberg's research has provided a similar service regarding individuals' moral development and the ways in which individuals process types of moral issues and concepts.[21]

Certainly, in organizing content into a productive sequence, we cannot totally disregard how individuals develop and learn. But, neither can we neglect the substantive structure or logic of the content. Nor can we forget that learners have individual and group interests and needs, and that these concerns must also be addressed.

Curricularists faced with sequencing content have drawn on some fairly well-accepted learning principles. Smith, Stanley, and Shores introduced four such principles: simple to complex learning, prerequisite learning, whole to part learning, and chronological learning.[22]

1. Simple to complex learning indicates that content is optimally organized in a sequence going from simple subordinate components or elements to complex components depicting interrelationships among components. It draws on the idea that optimal learning will result when individuals are presented with easy, often concrete, content and then with more difficult, often abstract, content.

2. Prerequisite learning is similar to part to whole learning. It works on the assumption that bits of information or learning must be grasped before other bits of learning can be comprehended.

3. Whole to part learning receives support from educational psychologists.[23] They urged that the curriculum be arranged so that the content or the experience is presented first in an overview (abstract) fashion

to furnish students with a general idea of the information or situation.

4. Chronological learning is another favored organizer for sequencing content. Frequently, history, political science, and world events are organized in this manner. Curricularists refer to this type of organization as "world-related": The content is sequenced as it seems to or does occur in the world.

Posner and Strike also furnished the field of curriculum with four other organizers for determining sequence: concept-related, inquiry-related, learning-related, and utilization-related learning.[24] The *concept-related* method draws heavily from the structure of knowledge. It focuses on the interrelationships among and between concepts rather than on the real world. Mathematics and logic are in large measure organized in this manner. The *inquiry-related* sequence is derived from the nature of procedures employed by scholars in the field. The steps they would take in processing a sequence of concepts and principles in their investigations would become the sequence of topics in the curriculum. The *learner-related* sequence concerns how individuals learn or should experience content and activities. *Utilization-related* learning draws on how people who use some knowledge or engage in a particular activity in the world actually proceed through it. Although it may appear to be a novel way of considering sequence, it closely resembles the "activity analysis" proposed by Bobbitt and Charters many years ago.

Continuity. Continuity deals with the vertical manipulation or repetition of curriculum components. Tyler indicated that if, for example, reading skills is an important objective, then "it is necessary to see that there is recurring and continuing opportunity for these skills to be practiced and developed. This means that over time the same kinds of skills will be brought into continuing operation."[25]

Continuity accounts for the reappearance in the curriculum of certain major ideas or skills about which educators feel students should have increased depth and breadth of knowledge over the length of the curriculum.

Continuity is most evident in Bruner's notion of the "spiral curriculum." Bruner noted that the curriculum should be organized according to the interrelationships between or structure of the basic ideas of each major discipline. For students to grasp these basic ideas and structures, "they should be developed and redeveloped in a spiral fashion"—in increasing depth and breadth, as a pupil progresses through the grades. Wrote Bruner, "A curriculum as it develops should revisit these basic ideas repeatedly, building upon them until the student has grasped the full formal apparatus that goes with them."[26]

The concept of the spiral curriculum relates not only to the vertical integration of knowledge but also to the horizontal integration, or the adding of breadth. When educators seek to improve the linkages among topics within a given discipline or subject field, they are dealing with the vertical articulation of the curriculum. When they are organizing the curricular elements to stress the interrelationships between and among different elements, disciplines, subject fields, or experiences, they are concerned with the horizontal articulation of the curriculum.

Articulation and Balance. Articulation refers to the interrelatedness of various aspects of the curriculum. The relation can be either vertical or horizontal. Vertical articulation depicts the relationships of certain aspects in the curriculum sequence to lessons, topics, or courses appearing later in the program's sequence. For instance, a teacher might design introductory or ninth grade algebra so that concepts in the algebra class are related to key concepts in a geometry course. Horizontal articulation refers to the association between or among elements occurring simultaneously. Horizontal articulation takes place, for instance, when curriculum designers attempt to develop interrelationships between eighth grade social studies and eighth grade English courses.

Articulation is difficult to achieve, and few school systems have mapped out procedures by which the various interrelationships among varied and distinct parts can be made evident to the planners or to the teachers and learners. One reason for the difficulty is that it is sometimes a difficult task to determine just what are the interrelationships among subjects. Curricula arranged by subjects often pay no attention to connections with any other subject matter.

When designing a curriculum, educators are also concerned that appropriate weight be given to each aspect of the design so that distortions do not occur. A *balanced* curriculum is one in which students have opportunities to master knowledge and to internalize and utilize it in ways that are appropriate for their personal, social, and intellectual goals. Because the curriculum can be viewed from different frames of reference—subject matter, discipline, student interests, student experiences, values, persistent problems— the curriculum components that are to be balanced will take on different forms and dimensions. However, regardless of the design, the components must be balanced.

John Goodlad argues that the curriculum should be balanced in terms of subject matter and the learner. He comments:

Much recent and current controversy over the curriculum centers on the question of what kind and how much attention to give learners and subject matter, respectively. The prospect of stressing one to the exclusion of the other appears scarcely worthy of consideration. Nonetheless, the interested observer has little difficulty finding school practices emphasizing one component to the impoverishment of the other.[27]

Perhaps the curriculum will never be fully balanced, because schools are slow to adapt to the changing needs of the individual and society, and because they are influenced by whim and fads. Educators tend to put too much emphasis on one subject, or a group of subjects, at the expense of others. The criteria for emphasis are often based on pressure and subjectivity, not systematic planning and objectivity. The latest fad often dominates the direction of curriculum design.

REPRESENTATIVE CURRICULUM DESIGNS

Curriculum components can be organized in numerous ways. However, all curriculum designs are modifications and/or integrations of three basic design types: (1) subject-centered designs; (2) learner-centered designs; and (3) problem-centered designs. Each category comprises several examples. Subject-centered designs include subject designs, discipline designs, broad field designs, and correlation designs. Learner-centered designs are those identified as child-centered designs, experience designs, romantic/ radical designs, and humanistic designs. Problem-centered designs consider life situations, core designs, and social problem/ reconstructionist designs.

Subject-Centered Designs.

Subject-centered designs are by far the most popular and widely used curriculum designs. This is because knowledge and content are well accepted as integral parts of the curriculum. Schools have a strong history of academic rationalism; furthermore, the materials available for school use also reflect content organization.

The category of subject-centered designs has the most classifications of any of the designs. This richness may result from our greater understanding of knowledge, or from the very strong tradition knowledge or content has in our culture. Concepts central to a culture are more highly elaborated than peripheral ones. In our culture, content is central to schooling; we thus have many concepts to depict our diverse organizations.

Subject Design. The subject design is both the oldest school design and the best known—to both teachers and laypeople. It is so well known because teachers and laypersons are usually educated and/or trained in schools employing it. It is also popular because it corresponds to textbook treatment and how teachers are trained as subject specialists.[28] This design is based on a belief that what makes humans unique and distinctive is their intellect; the searching for and the attainment of knowledge are the natural fulfillment of that intellect.

An early spokesperson for the subject curriculum was Henry Morrison, who was the state superintendent of public instruction in New Hampshire before he joined the University of Chicago. Morrison argued that the subject matter curriculum contributed most to the literacy of the individual and that literacy skills should be the focus of the elementary curriculum. This orientation to subject matter reflected a mental discipline approach to learning and a perennialist orientation to subject matter. Morrison also felt that such a design could allow a student at the secondary school level to develop interest and competence in one subject area. However, he proposed that a variety of courses should be offered to address the needs of different students.[29]

William Harris, superintendent of the St. Louis schools in the 1870s, also receives credit for fostering this curriculum design. Under Harris's guidance, the St. Louis schools established a subject-oriented curriculum that took firm hold there well into this century. Indeed, some would argue that the subject design is still alive and well. One educator notes that most Americans would recognize this curriculum design, which he classifies as the conservative liberal arts design, as the type they experienced in school.[30] In the mid-1930s Robert Hutchins indicated what subjects would be part of such a curriculum design: (1) language and its uses (reading, writing, grammar, literature); (2) mathematics; (3) sciences; (4) history; (5) foreign languages.[31] Arthur Bestor urged that a curriculum containing similar content divisions be offered all students.[32] Several observers point out that the back-to-basics movement and the current focus on

educational excellence in the United States are reflections of the subject matter orientation.[33]

In the subject-matter design, the curriculum is organized according to how knowledge has been developed in the various subject areas. With the explosion of knowledge and the resulting specializations in the various fields of knowledge, subject divisions have not only become more numerous but also exceedingly complex. For instance, history has been divided into cultural history, economic history, and geographic history. English, at least at the college level, has become even more complex; attention is paid to literature, writing, oral expression, reading, linguistics, and grammar as major subject divisions.

To the purest educators, each separate subject represents a specialized and unique body of content. The basis for content organization is primarily the division of labor accepted by academic scholars, who have, over the years, agreed on ways in which to organize subjects: History, anthropology, literature, economics, mathematics, chemistry, and so on. Dewey, however, cautioned that dividing knowledge into separate subjects isolates and compartmentalizes knowledge.

This organization of curricular content also assumes that these subjects are systematized primarily on (1) a chronological basis; (2) prerequisite learning; (3) whole to part mastery; and (4) deductive learning. The teacher usually assumes the active role. Lecture, recitation, and large group discussion are major instructional techniques utilized with this design.[34] Usually discussion proceeds from simple to complex ideas. Logic is emphasized.

Advocates of this design defend the emphasis on verbal activities. They argue that knowledge and ideas are best communicated and stored in verbal form. Many educators today, in fact, agree that learning is primarily a verbal activity. Advocates also note that a prime advantage of the design is that it introduces students to the essential knowledge of society. Also, the design is easy to deliver because complementary text-books and support materials are commercially available. Tradition, too, is on its side. People are familiar with this format, having gone through schools using it.

Critics, however, say that the design prevents individualization of the program, and deemphasizes the notion of the learner.[35] Other critics contend that stress on subject matter fails to foster social, pscyhological, and physical development, and to some extent fosters a scholarly elite—a ruling class based on knowledge.

Another drawback of this design is that learning tends to be compartmentalized and to stress mnemonic skills. Subjects are thus not related to the reality of the students. Perhaps the major problem is, then, that this design stresses content and neglects students' needs, interests, and experiences. Another danger is that, in delivering such a curriculum, the teachers tend to foster in students a passivity for learning.

Dewey was concerned about isolating subject matter from the learner's reality. He was also concerned about compartmentalization of subject matter, and adherence to the organization of subject matter "that was almost completely contemptuous of [the learner's] experience."[36] Tyler went one step further, arguing that overemphasis on subject matter resulted in a curriculum that was "too technical, too specialized, or in other ways . . . inappropriate for a large number of . . . students."[37] Indeed, the need is for balance. The idea is to ask: What can your subject contribute to students who are not going to be specialists in a given field? How can the subject be best organized to meet the needs of the majority of students, the average layman, the citizen in general? Specialization and compartmentalization should be reflected only in elective courses and advanced courses as students major in a field of study. If education is life, all life has, from the outset, a scientific aspect, an aspect of art and culture, and an aspect of communication.[38]

Discipline Design. The discipline design that appeared in the post World War II era evolved from the separate-subject design. This new design grew rapidly in popularity during the 1950s and reached its zenith during the mid-1960s. Its popularity was tarnished somewhat during the student protests of the 1970s, but it is still present in much curriculum organization in the elementary and secondary schools and especially in colleges and universities.

Like the separate-subject design, the discipline design's basis is the inherent organization of content. However, whereas the subject design does not make clear the foundational basis upon which it is organized or established, the discipline design's orientation does specify its focus on the academic disciplines.

King and Brownell, proponents of this design, indicate that a discipline is specific knowledge that has the following essential characteristics: A community of persons, an expression of human imagination, a domain, a tradition, a mode of inquiry, a conceptual structure, a specialized language, a heritage of literature, a network of communications, a valuative and affective stance, and an instructive community.[39]

Disciplined knowledge is the key aspect of this curriculum design. Content for the school curriculum is determined in part by identifying or creating a discipline's structure and using this foundation as a guide for selecting the school content and organizing it for learning. This stress on disciplined knowledge can be likened to a "command" to only teach the disciplines—science, mathematics, English, history, and so on. The assumption used by advocates to support their advice is that the school is a microcosm of the world of intellect, and that the disciplines reflect that world.[40] This means that the manner in which the content is to be learned is suggested by the methods scholars employ to study the content of their fields. Students in history would approach the subject matter as would a historian, and students in biology would investigate biological topics following procedures advocated by biologists.

This point is important. Even though

proponents of the discipline design view as necessary experiencing the disciplines in the school, they stress understanding the conceptual structures and the processes of the disciplines. This is perhaps the essential difference between the disciplines design and the subject matter design. In the discipline design, students experience the disciplines so that they can comprehend and even conceptualize, whereas in the subject matter design the students are considered to have learned if they just acquire knowledge and information. Sometimes, it is difficult to determine whether in fact a classroom has a subject matter or a discipline design. The key distinguishing characteristic seems to be whether students are involved in actually using some of the methods of the discipline to process information.

In the discipline design, students are encouraged to see the basic logic or structure of each discipline—the key relationships, concepts, and principles—and to understand the discipline's modes of inquiry— what Joseph Schwab calls the "syntactical structure."[41] This approach allows students "to attack unfamiliar problems and to grasp the relationship of new phenomena not previously encountered [with] phenomena already experienced."[42]

Jerome Bruner perhaps can be credited with making the term *structure* a common educational term. His book, *The Process of Education*, became the "gospel" for those advocating the disciplines orientation. Bruner asserted that those charged with curriculum development must focus on the structure of subject matter and the transfer of learning. What Bruner meant by structure is that the student is able to transfer what he has learned to new problem situations. "He is in the position to recognize wherein 'new' [problems] to be solved are not new at all, but variants on a familiar theme already learned."[43]

To Bruner, learning occurs when the student recognizes the key ideas and fundamental principles of a discipline and notes the interrelationships of these ideas and also their applicability to many situations. The learner, by recognizing the fundamental and general ideas that constitute the structure of the discipline, will be able to continually broaden and make more sophisticated his or her knowledge. In effect, he or she will have learned how to learn. Bruner maintains, "The continuity of learning that is produced by the second type of transfer, transfer of principles, is dependent upon mastery of the structure of the subject matter." He continues, "The more fundamental or basic is the idea he has learned . . . the greater will be its breadth of applicability to new problems."[44]

A most attractive notion of the disciplines approach expounded by Bruner was that "any subject can be taught in some effectively honest form to any child at any stage of development."[45] Contrary to what many persons had held, Bruner argued that students are able to comprehend the fundamental principles of any subject at almost any age. And children can thus understand the structure and operations of a discipline at any age—such understanding does not need to await adolescence or adulthood.

Bruner has been criticized as having a romantic notion of students as scholars. Developmentalists have disagreed with his thesis that "intellectual activity anywhere is the same," and point out that the processes of the young child, for example, differ in kind and in degree from the thinking processes of adolescents and adults. There are also small differences between sexes in the early grades in terms of how children process cognitive information.[46]

Dewey also spoke against the tendency to make students into "little scholars." He noted that there are qualitative changes in the intellectual development of children. Moreover, he argued that when "working" with content, children have a style of learning that is directly productive rather than investigative; they want to use the information rather than advance their realms of knowledge. Children are concerned with discovering facts already known to scholars.

Their activity is regulated by practical interest, not research or hypothetical thinking.[47]

Another proponent of the disciplines, Philip Phenix, noted, in contrast, that by drawing on or arranging knowledge in discipline format, we actually simplified the knowledge. In drawing out key elements for the purposes of generalization, we abstract information in order to simplify and reduce its complexity. In recognizing patterns among a great diversity of information, we make it easier to say something about the information. For Phenix, the disciplines also enabled the student to continue his or her search for more understanding. This, for Phenix, was the characteristic of dynamism. "Disciplines do not merely simplify and coordinate; they also invite further analysis and synthesis. A discipline contains a lure to discovery."[48]

The discipline design did not escape criticism. It was challenged by many for the same reasons that the separate-subject design was questioned. Curricula designed according to the structure of a discipline focused on acquiring knowledge for its own sake and organizing information into isolated and self-serving domains. Knowledge in the disciplines was not related to the lives of the students. Its detachment from the students' experiences and interests weakened the motivational quality of the content. Many educators criticized the design for assuming that the students must adapt to the curriculum, rather than that the curriculum must adapt or be modified to meet students' requirements.[49] Additionally, the design was attacked for assuming that all students have a common or at least a similar type of learning style. The design tended to emphasize academically oriented students and to ignore nonacademic students. This later evolved as a major criticism, as educators turned to the needs of the disadvantaged in the mid-1960s and 1970s. Perhaps the greatest shortcoming of the design was that it caused the schools to ignore the vast amount of information that could not be classified as disciplined knowledge. Such

knowledge—dealing with aesthetics, humanism, personal-social living, and vocational education—is important and needs to be part of the school's curriculum.

Broad Fields Design. The broad fields design, another variation of the subject-centered design, appeared as an effort to correct the fragmentation and compartmentalization caused by the subject design. Essentially, this design permits the melding of two or more related subjects into a single broad or fused field of study—a curriculum design that deviated from the traditional subject pattern of the perennialists and essentialists.

In the 1930s and 1940s, broad fields were part of the movement for integrated studies. At that time, the design served as a response to society's demands for integration of knowledge and more comprehensive models of knowledge.[50] The justification for the design is the same today. One reason for its continued popularity is that it dissolves subject boundaries in ways that make the information meaningful to the pupils. Also, it allows the teacher to have more flexibility in choosing content. But, perhaps it is most popular because, by integrating separate subjects, it enables learners to see relationships among the various subjects of the curriculum. Knowledge thus comprises a meaningful whole.

Early in this century the design first appeared at the college level. Courses so organized allowed students to experience the methods of inquiry and to generalize knowledge across broad fields of information rather than single disciplines. Students were thus able to gain understanding of an entire field.

Even though the broad fields design has a long history, its use in secondary schools is relatively recent. At the secondary level, this design in fact shares the spotlight with the separate-subjects design. But, the broad fields design has become the standard pattern for most elementary school curricula. In these schools, biology, chemistry, and physics are integrated into general science. Literature, grammar, composition, and speaking are part of the language arts curriculum. History, geography, sociology, political science, anthropology, and economics are the foundations for the elementary social studies curriculum.

Harry Broudy et al. offered a unique broad fields design during the Sputnik era. They suggested that the entire curriculum be organized into the following categories: (1) symbolics of information—English, foreign language, and mathematics; (2) basic sciences—general science, biology, physics, and chemistry; (3) developmental studies—evolution of the cosmos, evolution of social institutions, and evolution of human culture; (4) exemplars—modes of aesthetic experience that would include art, music, drama, literature; and (5) molar problems that would address typical social problems.[51] This last category would have a yearly variety of courses depending on the social problems of the times.

This broad fields design still receives attention from curriculum specialists. The National Society for the Study of Education recently discussed this design for all students. Its curriculum included mathematics, natural sciences, language and literature, aesthetics and fine arts, and social studies.[52]

The broad fields approach usually combines separate subjects from within a domain of knowledge; sometimes, however, this curriculum design enables the blending of content from two or more branches of knowledge into an entirely new field of study. Futuristics is such a new field of study. It synthesizes knowledge from mathematics, sociology, statistics, political science, economics, education, and various other fields. Multicultural education is another new content area; it draws information from sociology, psychology, history, and anthropology.

Like any design, this one has its problems. One is the issue of breadth versus depth. Having students spend a year studying social studies teaches them a greater and more varied range of social science concepts than they would learn if they just took a year of history. But, is their knowledge of the various social sciences superficial? Certainly a year of history will furnish more historical knowledge than a year of social studies. But then the question arises, at least at the elementary level, is it necessary to have great depth? Is not the purpose of the curriculum to have students understand the entire field of social science knowledge? How this question is answered depends in part on the particular philosophical posture of the school.

Correlation Design. Correlation is a design employed by those who do not wish to go as far as creating a broad fields design, but who do realize that there are times when separate subjects require some linkage in order to reduce fragmentation of curricular content. Correlation is an attempt to eliminate the isolation and compartmentalization of subjects without radically overhauling the subject curriculum. For example, a science teacher might wish to collaborate with the social studies teacher by having students write papers dealing with the history of some particular scientific theory. Or these teachers might cooperate in getting students to uncover the history behind a particular environmental problem. Often, when courses are organized in a problems approach, such linkages are formalized. But, the divisions between the subjects are maintained—at no time does the science course become unrecognizable or the history course lose its identity.

Almost any part of the curriculum can be organized in this design. Courses in literature can be correlated with courses in art and music by connecting them through various themes, such as Romanticism. Science and mathematics are easily correlated because mathematics provides a powerful tool for dealing with science content. But, not all correlated designs link content from different subject fields. Courses from within the same field—such as history and geography or history and sociology—can be correlated as well. Because correlated subjects maintain their identity, however, a true curriculum synthesis does not take place.[53]

The notion of a correlated design was attractive to many. Alberty and Alberty were famous for their discussion of the correlated core, which was usually English and American history at the secondary level or social studies and language arts at the elementary level. They presented a variant of this design that employed an "overarching theme." This version of core retained the basic content of the subjects, but the content was selected and organized with reference to broad themes, problems, or units.[54]

This variation of core required that classes be scheduled in a block of time. So scheduled, teachers of the various content areas to be correlated could work together and have students working on assignments that drew from the correlated content areas. Thus, if teachers were having students investigate the history of industrialization in the United States, they would have students emphasize topics that dealt with science—perhaps the chemistry involved in making iron ore into steel, for example.

Today, few teachers are actually using the correlated design, possibly because it requires that they plan their lessons cooperatively. This is usually very difficult to accomplish because teachers have self-contained classes at the elementary level and do not have time for such collaboration. At the secondary level, teachers are organized into separate compartments that tend to encourage isolation. Teachers must also meet time schedules dictated by specified classes, and so may have little time to work with other teachers in team-teaching arrangements. Further, most class schedules do not allow a sufficient block of time for students to meaningfully study correlated subjects. Modular scheduling, which would allow for this, really never received wide acceptance.

Learner-Centered Designs.

All curricularists are concerned with creating curricula that are valuable to students. In response to those educational planners who consider that in creating curricula of value one must emphasize subject matter, educators early in this century asserted that students are the center or focus of the program. Supporters of this posture, largely progressives, advocated what have come to be called learner-centered designs.

Child-Centered Designs. At times, especially when the learner-centered design was first gaining a foothold in educational thinking, its advocates insisted that virtually all school learning activities should be centered around the felt needs and interests of the child. Many of these early advocates rejected the traditional notion of the child as a miniature adult and accepted the romantic metaphor of the child as a flower that would unfold naturally with the proper "educational gardening."[55]

Much of this thinking originates from Rousseau's version of education, espoused in his book *Emile*, published in 1762. Rousseau wrote, "God makes all things good; man meddles with them and they become evil."[56] But Rousseau was not for child anarchy. He called for "well-regulated liberty" that was to be assumed within the competence levels of the child. Teachers were thus to pique a child's curiosity by providing direction using means that were appropriate for the development for the age of the child. Rousseau noted that as a child approaches adolescence, "much skill and discretion are required to lead him towards theoretical studies." Teachers were to provide the pupil with opportunities to observe nature and learn on his own. "Put the problems before him and let him solve them himself. . . . Let him not be taught science, let him discover it."[57]

Proponents of this design also drew on the thinking of some other early pedagogical giants. Heinrich Pestalozzi and Friedrich Froebel argued that children would attain self-realization through social participation; they voiced the principle of learning by doing. Their social approach to education furnished a foundation for much of the work of Francis Parker.

The child-centered design, often attributed to John Dewey, was really conceived by Parker, who laid the foundations for this movement. Parker had studied pedagogy in Germany, and he knew well the work of Pestalozzi and Froebel. He tried out his ideas while he was superintendent of schools in Quincy, Massachusetts.[58]

Parker believed that the methods of instruction should be patterned by the child's natural approach to learning.[59] He suggested that because children learn to speak a language by using words, they should be taught reading by a "word method." Thus, teachers were encouraged to perfect ways of involving children in conversations in order to teach reading. To teach geography, Parker urged teachers to take children on field trips and have them make sketches of landscapes and simple maps. This would be more productive than reading a textbook. This approach, which became known as the Quincy system, attracted national attention.

Dewey deduced similar notions in his early thinking. In 1896, he had a chance to put some of his ideas, and Parker's, into action in his laboratory school at the University of Chicago.[60] The curriculum was organized around human impulses—the impulse to socialize; the impulse to construct; the impulse to inquire, to question, to experiment; and the impulse to express or to create artistically. Dewey, like Parker, viewed education as a social process that served a social function. Through education the individual had his or her capacities freed so as to achieve social aims. Dewey viewed the development of individuality in the child, the person, as something developing continuously, not something given all at once and ready made.

William Kilpatrick, a colleague of Dewey's when the latter changed his affiliation to Teachers College, Columbia University, attempted to merge the behaviorist psychology of the day, particularly Thorndike's S-R psychology and connectionism (see Chapter 4), with Dewey's progressive philosophy.[61]

Kilpatrick combined four steps in methodology, which were actually behaviorist steps—purposing, planning, executing, and judging—with highlighted projects (ranging from school classroom projects to community projects). The one major criterion for what came to be known as the "Project Method" was the presence of a dominating purpose.[62]

Although Kilpatrick's Project Method and the experience movement in general were applied in the elementary schools, and were often indistinguishable from each other, Kilpatrick argued that the difference was that his doctrine had "social purpose" whereas the experience-centered curriculum had only "child purpose." Nevertheless, when forced to choose who would plan the curriculum, the child or teacher, Kilpatrick chose the former, arguing that "if you want to educate the boy to think and plan for himself, then let him make his own plan."[63] In this respect, he differed from Dewey, who emphasized the guidance of the teacher.

The emphasis on the child displaced the emphasis on subject matter. In addition, when subject matter was presented, it was no longer separated into "narrow" divisions but was "integrated" around units of experience or social problems. The idea that a solution to a problem required using methods and materials from several subject fields was inherent in the child-centered, experience-centered curriculum. This new emphasis on the learner also led to "life needs,"[64] "life-adjustment education,"[65] "persistent life situations,"[66] "common learnings,"[67] and "core"[68] methods for organizing bodies of knowledge and subject matter. Curriculum specialists of the day gradually turned to problem-centered and broad fields courses—that is, they integrated subject matter from various fields as needed for the understanding and solution of social problems.

The child-centered design of curriculum really flourished in the 1920s and 1930s, primarily under the work of the progressives, but its foundations had been laid earlier. In 1904, Junius Merian established a school that stressed the child and his or her activities. The school, located at the University of Missouri, used observation, play, stories, and children's handwork as the basis for organizing curriculum experiences. Ellsworth Collings, in 1917, introduced the child-centered curriculum in the public schools of McDonald County, Missouri. He advocated using play projects, excursion projects, and story projects to organize for learning activities.[69] Even though these schools were quite successful within their own confines, and the movement did appear in much educational literature, it really only gained limited acceptance. Educators, in fact, have never seriously considered this design for secondary schools.

Experience-Centered Designs. Experience-centered curriculum designs closely resembled the child-centered designs in that they used the concerns of children as the basis for organizing the children's school world. However, they differed from child-centered designs in their view that the interests and needs of children cannot be anticipated and, therefore, a curriculum framework cannot be planned for all children. After the children arrived at school, programs could then be created that were geared to their unique interests. The needs and interests of the children would determine the actual curriculum. Growth and learning were considered to be completely dependent on the active participation of children in activities that were congruent with their needs. Subjects were only furnished to help children solve problems of their own choosing. This notion—that a curriculum could not be preplanned, that everything had to be done "on the spot" by each teacher reacting to each child—made this design almost impossible to implement. It also put people in a posture of ignoring the vast amount of information they had about children's growth and development—cognitively, affectively, emotionally, and socially.

Those favoring the child-centered or experience-centered curriculum placed heavy emphasis on the learners' interests. Pupils' interests have received much attention throughout this century. However, cautions about relying solely on children's interests have been made frequently. Harold Rugg and Ann Shumaker wrote in 1928, "We do not dare leave longer to chance—to spontaneous, overt symptoms of interest on the part of occasional pupils—the solution of this important and difficult problem of construction of a curriculum for maximum growth."[70]

In 1934 Dewey noted that "interests" had come to be equated with choices delineated by the child. Dewey said that some of the current thinking was transferring the responsibility of creating curricula from educators to children. Educators needed to be aware that children's interests tended to be transitory or accidental, rather than enduring and of major significance.[71] The teacher was responsible for identifying and cultivating children's interests, even forming new ones, that were prized by the community and compatible with the evolution of society. Many years later, Boyd Bode cautioned that it was major educational folly to build the curriculum on the quicksand of students' ephemeral interests.[72] It seems that many current advocates of this design have forgotten or chosen to ignore these cautions.

Many current advocates of the learner-centered design have, however, taken an adversarial position when considering their design in relation to the subject-center design camp. They assume an either-or posture—one either supports a design with content at the center or a design with the child at the center. Many have counseled against such an either-or stance. For example, Dewey pointed out that there were fallacies in both camps. The learner was not a "tabula rasa," a passive receiver of established subject matter content. Neither was the learner "the starting point, the center, and the end" of school activity.[73]

Dewey argued that educators had to attend to the subject matter of the curriculum. The various studies "embody the cumulative outcomes of the efforts, the strivings, and the successes of the human race generation after generation."[74] But, educators could not ignore the child in curriculum design because the child had to be viewed as fluent, embryonic, and vital: "Abandon the notion of subject-matter as something fixed and ready-made in itself, outside the child's experience; cease thinking of the child's experience as something hard and fast . . . and we realize that the child and the curriculum are simply two limits which define a single process. Just as two points define a straight line."[75]

Several current curriculum specialists have argued that we need to meld our curricular concerns as relating to *both* the subject matter or content of the curriculum and the child and his or her experiences. In their definition, Tanner and Tanner identify the curriculum as the reconstruction of knowledge and experience, systematically developed under the auspices of the school. Other curriculum reformers have translated the ideas of the experience movement into courses emphasizing touching, feeling, and Gestalt psychology. Still others have emphasized life experiences, with credit for working in community-based and career-based activities intended to prepare students for adult responsibility and work and courses that deal with social problems and personal experiences.[76]

Romantic (Radical) Designs. The view of the child has been carried to more recent times by reformers who advocate radical school modification. These individuals have adopted the tenets of romantic naturalism. Rarely do they note, however, that their ideas have a rather long history, dating back to at least the time of Rousseau. They do not credit Parker's and Dewey's contributions to educational thinking and to progressive education. Indeed, some have stated that Dewey was really in favor of maintaining the social status quo, even though Dewey had cautioned that "the conception of education as a social process and function has no

definite meaning until we define the kind of society we have in mind."[77]

The radical school reformers are eloquent proponents of learner-centered designs. Contemporary romantics present the case that there actually can be no curriculum development before the students arrive in the classroom and their needs and interests are accessed. Some romantics even state that it is fruitless to plan the content of the program in advance of the children's arrival. John Holt argues this point:

The notion of a curriculum, as an essential body of knowledge, would be absurd even if children remembered everything we "taught" them. . . . We don't and can't agree on what knowledge is essential. . . .

The idea of the curriculum would not be valid even if we could agree what ought to be in it. For knowledge changes. Much of what a child learns in school will be found, or thought, before many years, to be untrue. . . .[78]

Paul Goodman argued that when educators attempt to influence children's growing up according to a preconceived curriculum with articulated methods, they adversely affect individuals' capacities for learning and living. The teacher is not to furnish carefully structured situations determined useful by adult standards. Rather, the school is to provide "incident education, taking part in the ongoing activities of society" if learning is to be indeed meaningful. Goodman even claimed that it might be better if many children from the poor and middle class did not go to school at all.[79]

Goodman, like Rousseau, considered the larger society as corrupt and repressive. He argued that children have the innate ability to determine what experiences are best for their own learning. In a sense students do not need adults. Educators must realize that children are innately good and have the ability, when provided with freedom, to make choices meaningful to their education and development.

These radical reformers really seek to do away with the notion of a planned curriculum; they propose instead to center all experiences in the school on the children's present needs. The school would provide opportunities to learn and possible contents to be considered, but all would be arranged as a "smorgasbord."[80] The children would pick what they need and decide what they need. As Holt argued, "We cannot know, at any moment, what particular bit of knowledge or understanding a child needs most . . . and best fits his model of reality. Only he can do this." The child may not be expert at these decisions, "but he can do it a hundred times better than we can." For Holt, adults don't plan the learning experiences, rather they let the child "know . . . what is available and where he can look for it."[81]

A major weakness of the learner-centered design, especially the romatic designs according to its critics, is its educative inefficacy. A curriculum based on children's own needs and interests certainly cannot adequately prepare those children for life. Students have not had the experiences necessary to understand what is needed to function effectively in the current and future world. Also, such a decision may not even consider social goals.

A second weakness of the design is that it lacks a definitive horizontal structure. If subjects or disciplines are eliminated as the key organizers, what organizing principle can be used instead? Smith, Stanley, and Shores pointed out, "Merely to say that the curriculum will be based on children's interests does not provide a framework of categories for a curriculum pattern."[82]

A third criticism of this design is that it lacks continuity (sequence). Basing a design on students' interests, which shift unpredictably over time, makes establishing and maintaining continuity difficult. Attempts have been made to address this weakness by looking at the "natural" sequence order in which children develop their mental capacities.

The design also has some other weaknesses or limitations. Perhaps a most practical limitation is that commercial materials are neither available nor producible if the educational assumption is that individuals bring idiosyncratic needs and interests to the school. Also, the design assumes that teachers have an extraordinary range of skills and competencies. Teachers would have to be renaissance persons, psychologists, and masters of the unique dimensions of individuals in order to foster effective teacher-pupil interactions.

Humanistic Designs. This design gained prominence in the 1960s and 1970s, partly in response to the excessive emphasis on the disciplines during the 1950s and early 1960s. Other names for this orientation have been affective education, open education, and existential education. As with other learner-centered designs, the focus of humanistic designs has been on the learners—especially students' self-concepts. Much of the underpinning for this design has been "third force" psychology and the humanities. Abraham Maslow's concept of self-actualization furnished the theoretical support for designing the curriculum along these lines.[83]

Carl Rogers's work has been another major force. He assumes that people can enhance self-directed learning by drawing on their own resources to improve self-understanding, to learn self-concepts and basic attitudes, and to guide their own behavior. The educators' task is to set the educational environment such that these personal resources can be tapped. Such an environment encourages genuineness of behavior, empathy, and respect for self and others.[81]

Individuals given such an environment will naturally develop into what Rogers termed a fully functioning person. Individuals able to take self-initiated actions and responsibility for those actions are capable of intelligent choice and self-direction. Furthermore, having acquired knowledge relevant to the solutions of problems, these persons are critical learners. They also are able to approach problem situations with flexibility and intelligence and to work cooperatively with others. They are internally guided with regard to their socialization process; they do not wait for or work for the approval of others.[82]

Humanistic education took on a major form in the 1970s with the notion of "confluence." Essentially, confluence education is a melding of the affective domain (feelings, attitudes, values) with the cognitive domain (intellectual knowledge and abilities). This approach adds the affective component to the conventional subject matter curriculum that is already in place.[83] Those who support this design do not favor either content or experience or intellect or feeling; rather, they strive to blend the subjective or intuitive with the objective. They urge that the curriculum be so organized as to provide students with more alternatives from which they can choose what to feel. Students are challenged to take responsibility for and to appreciate their choices, and to feel comfortable knowing that they have the power to make choices.

Confluent education stresses participation; it emphasizes power sharing, negotiations, and joint responsibility. It is essentially nonauthoritarian. It also stresses the whole person and the integration of thinking, feeling, and acting. It centers on the relevance of subject matter in light of students' basic needs and lives. Throughout the curriculum, students are confronted with situations that make them realize that the development of self is a legitimate objective of learning.

Weinstein and Fantini have presented a type of confluent education in which students' basic concerns determine what concepts they will study.[84] The authors carefully distinguish between concerns and interests. Interests are activities that attract students. Concerns are students' basic physiological and sociological drives. The authors organized concerns into three major classifications: concern about self-image, concern about disconnectedness, and a concern about control over one's life.

They also consider the curriculum to exist as a three-tiered structure. One tier is comprised of reading, computation, and writing skills. The basic subject matter of the subject matter curriculum is found at this tier. The second tier consists of those activities designed to draw out the learners' latent talents and abilities. This tier is highly individualized, as is the first tier. It stresses the development of individual creativity and the exploration of interests. The third tier is concerned with group inquiry. It consists mainly of societal issues and problems that are related to the self in society. Here students get a chance to explore who they are as individuals and as members of a group. They analyze issues and identify common themes. They can develop their own personalities, increase their skills in interpersonal relations, and become more cognizant of their feelings and concerns. The nature of this tier perhaps explains why Weinstein and Fantini call their approach a curriculum of affect.

Advocates of the humanistic curriculum design realize that there is more to education than addressing the rational dimension of humans. Indeed, some would argue that because feelings and attitudes function as they do, the emotions of the youth must be the primary target of public education.[85] Children need to understand their feelings and attitudes; they need to recognize those feelings that are liberating and those that are debilitating. In a real sense, educators of this camp believe that education and its attendant curriculum design should be such that the individual is liberated to pursue his or her own goals.

Humanistic educators realize that the cognitive, affective, and psychomotor domains are interconnected and that the curriculum design should address these dimensions. Some educators in this camp—and in the subject-centered camp—would argue that in addition to these three domains, the two domains of socialization and spirituality should also be addressed.[86]

Humanistic curriculum designs stress the development of positive self-concept and interpersonal skills. A related design, the transpersonal or transcendence orientation—the consciousness aspect of the humanistic design—takes this orientation a bit further. Here the stress, though still on the individual, encourages intuition and transcendence. Through intuition a person is able to access his or her creative thinking and to generate a holistic perception of reality. An individual's inner and outer worlds tie his or her inner self to the environment. This orientation suggests a curriculum that highly regards the uniqueness of the human personality. According to Philip Phenix, "A curriculum of transcendence provides a context for engendering, gestating, expecting and celebrating the moments of singular awareness and of inner illumination when each person comes into the consciousness of his inimitable personal being."[87] The curriculum is not characterized so much by the objective content of studies as by the atmosphere created by those who comprise the learning community.

This curriculum is open to human spirituality, which, as used by such curricularists, refers to the links between a person's inner life and the infinite. Transcendence and spirituality are experienced through quality experiences. As Phenix notes, in such a curriculum reality is experienced as a "single interconnected whole, such that a complete description of any entity would require the comprehension of every other entity."[88]

Transcendent education is lured by the concept of wholeness or comprehensiveness of experience. To be sure, certain contents do need to be incorporated into the curriculum, but the stress is on giving the students the opportunity to take a journey, to contemplate on that journey, and to relate that journey to others—past, present, and future. It emphasizes the general dispositions of humans for hope, creativity, awareness, doubt and faith, wonder, awe and reverence.[89]

Humanistic curriculum designs have many of the same weaknesses as learner-centered designs. They require of the teacher great skill and competence in dealing with individuals. Moreover, available educational materials are often not appropriate.

One serious charge against this design is that humanists focus on their methods and techniques and do not adequately consider them in light of the consequences for learners. Another criticism leveled at the design concerns its apparently inconsistent emphasis on both the human as unique and on activities that all students experience. In contrast, some say that the design places far too much emphasis on the individual and ignores the needs of the overall society. A final criticism is really of third force psychology itself. Critics charge that it does not integrate what we know about behaviorism and psychiatry or about cognitive developmental theory. Rather, it seems to splinter our knowledge base about human learning and development.

Problem-Centered Designs.

The third major type of curriculum design, which is problem-centered, focuses on the problems of living—on the perceived realities of institutional and group life—both for the individual and for society in general. Problem-centered curriculum designs are organized to reinforce cultural traditions and also to address those community and societal needs that are currently unmet. They address individuals' problems as well.

Even though these designs place the individual in a social setting, they are unlike learner-centered designs in a major way. Problem-centered designs are planned before the arrival of students. However, problem-centered curricularists realize that because their concern is with genuine life problems, they will sometimes have to adjust to cater to the concerns and situations of learners.

How a curriculum is organized with this design depends in large part on the nature of the problem areas to be studied. Contents selected must be relevant to the problem under consideration. For this reason, the content often cuts across subject boundaries. It must also be based, to a major extent, on the needs, concerns, and abilities of the students. This dual emphasis on both content and the development of learners distinguishes problem-centered designs from the other major types of curriculum designs.

Because problem-centered designs draw on social problems and the needs, interests, and abilities of learners, several variations exist. Some focus on persistent life situations, others center on contemporary social problems, others address areas of living, and some are even concerned with the reconstruction of society. What seems to distinguish these various types is the relative degree of emphasis they place on social needs as opposed to individual needs.

Life-Situations Design. The persistent life-situations design is perhaps the best-known variation of the problem-centered designs. Interest in this curriculum approach can be traced to the nineteenth century and to Herbert Spencer's seminal essay "What Knowledge Is of Most Worth?" and later to Dewey's concept of growth and education and social participation in school and society.[90] A similar advocacy statement was made in 1918 by the Commission on the Reorganization of Secondary Education. During the 1930s and 1940s this viewpoint was expressed in an approach that addressed adolescent needs. The life-situations design as we know it today, proposed by Florence Stratemeyer and her associates in the early years after World War II, was based on a principle derived from studies on the transfer of learning. Stratemeyer and her colleagues concluded that students would find their school learning more meaningful, and would thus be able to directly apply it to life, if the problems they studied in school were in fact similar to those they faced out of school.[91]

Using such a design, based on recurring life situations, educators could assist students in broadening their insights and deepening their generalizations about problems relating to the "real" world. Stratemeyer created a master list of *persistent life situations* for educators to follow. The key aspects of this list are presented next:[92]

A. Situations calling for growth in individual capacities
  1. Health
  2. Intellectual power
  3. Responsibility
  4. Aesthetic expression and appreciation
B. Situations calling for growth in social participation
  1. Person-to-person relationships
  2. Group membership
  3. Intergroup relationships
C. Situations calling for growth in ability to deal with environmental factors and forces.
  1. Natural phenomena
  2. Technological phenomena
  3. Economic-social-political structures and forces

In addition to drawing on these persistent life situations, Stratemeyer believed that the needs of children and youth also supplied a basis for determining the curriculum. But Stratemeyer, like Kilpatrick, noted that not all children's interests were of equal value. Good curriculum planners had to distinguish between superficial interests and those useful in fostering the development of meaningful generalizations. It was considered preferable for the problems studied to be based on the children's immediate concerns rather than on adults' views of what was necessary. In this respect, the design proposed by Stratemeyer was child-centered.

One of the strengths of the life-situations design is its focus on the problem-solving procedures for learning. Process and content are effectively integrated into the curricular experience. Some critics point out that the students do not learn subject matter. However, proponents are quick to counter that the design draws heavily from content, and from traditional content at that. What makes the design unique is that the content is organized in ways that allow students to clearly view problem areas.

Another strong feature of this design is that it utilizes the past and current experiences of learners as a means of getting them to analyze the basic areas of living. In this respect, the design is very different from the activities/experience design, which uses the learners' felt needs and interests as the sole basis for content and experience selection. The life-situations design uses students' immediate concerns, as well as pressing immediate problems in the larger society, as a starting point.

The design has definite strengths. It presents subject matter in an integrated form by cutting across the separate subjects and centering on related categories of social life. Because it centers on social problems and personal concerns, it encourages students to learn and apply problem-solving procedures. The linking of subject matter to real situations increases the relevance of the curriculum.

But, like the previous designs, life-situation designs have deficiencies and challenges. Perhaps the greatest challenge is to determine what are the scope and sequence of the essential areas of living? Are the major activities of the current time also going to be the essential activities of future times?

Another criticism of this design has been that it does not adequately expose students to their cultural heritage. Moreover, it tends to indoctrinate youth into the existing conditions and thus perpetuates the social status quo. However, if students are educated to be critical of their social situations, then not the status quo but rather intelligent processing of the social scene is fostered rather than adherence to the status quo.

There are always some who point out that the life-situations design cannot be mounted by teachers for they lack adequate preparation for it. Others argue that textbooks and other teaching materials inhibit the implementation of this design. Furthermore, many citizens are uncomfortable with it because it departs too much from their school experiences. Finally, this organization departs from the curricular tradition maintained by colleges and universities.

Core Design. This particular curriculum design, sometimes called "social functions" core, is carefully planned. It centers on general education and is based on problems arising out of common human activities. There are several variations of core designs. Subject matter core designs, for example, would be classified as subject-centered designs. Areas-of-living core designs are rooted in the progressive education tradition. However, making areas of living the core of the curriculum leaves no doubt about the focus of the curriculum.

This type of core is problem-centered rather than learner-centered. It is carefully planned before the students arrive, but with the notion that adjustment can be made if necessary. This design is usually taught in a block-time format, whereby two or more normal periods for teaching the core component are scheduled together. One teacher assumes responsibility for this block of time and also manages a counseling function. Although content is part of this design, the common needs, problems, and concerns of learners comprise the central focus.

The focus on problems proceeds in different ways in each core class, but certain characteristics for problem solving are recommended by the advocates of core, as illustrated below. These recommendations make sense today, as they did when core was popularized by Faunce and Bossing.

1. The problem is selected by either the teacher or students.
2. A group consensus is made to determine important problems and interest of the class.
3. Problems are selected on the basis of developed criteria for selection.
4. The problem is clearly stated and defined.
5. Areas of study are decided, including dividing the class by individual and group interests.
6. Needed information is listed and discussed.
7. Resources for obtaining information are listed and discussed.
8. Information is obtained and organized.
9. Information is analyzed and interpreted.
10. Tentative conclusions are stated and tested.

11. A report is presented to the class on an individual or group basis.
12. Conclusions are evaluated.
13. New avenues of exploration toward further problem solving are examined.[93]

The advantages of the core design are that it unifies content, presents subject matter relevant to students, and encourages active processing of information. Further, because it presents subject matter in a relevant form, it fosters intrinsic motivation in students. Alberty and Alberty state that this design makes it possible for students to attack directly problems they consider crucial in the contemporary society. It encourages students to view the community as a laboratory for learning.[94] Because the design encourages cooperative learning, its advocates claim it fosters democratic practices in the classroom.

But, the design has weaknesses, too. Perhaps the major one, which may also be its strength, is that it departs too significantly from the traditional curriculum. People attack it as ignoring the fundamentals. It also requires materials that are hard to find. Conventional textbooks, in fact, do not support this core design. Nor is it commonly used because the general population has not accepted the idea that general education is worthwhile. Furthermore, it requires an exceptional teacher, well versed in subject matter, problem-solving skills, and general knowledge.

Social Problems and Reconstructionist Designs. Whereas some educators, such as Stratemeyer, have urged that children's interests should guide the selection of curriculum content and experiences, other educators still feel that the curriculum should address contemporary social problems and even social action projects aimed at reconstructing society. Many such educators consider themselves to be in the social orientation camp, or what some have called social reconstructionism. These individuals, interested in the relation of the curriculum to the social, political, and economic development

of society, believe that through the curriculum, educators will effect social change and ultimately create a more just society. Interestingly, even though many of the schools' current critics are of this opinion, aspects of reconstructionism actually first appeared in the 1920s and 1930s.

Perhaps this concern for reconstructionism, or social reconstruction, was a response to the Great Depression. To many reconstructionists, the problems lay with the schools, as did the solutions. Many educators during this period classified the reconstructionists as "leftists" or communists who were plotting the overthrow of the government by their urgings for actions in the classroom. Indeed, Theodore Brameld, starting out his teaching career at Long Island University, urged teachers to "influence their students, subtly if necessary, frankly if possible, toward acceptance of . . . the collectivist ideal."[95]

It is always difficult to place precisely in time the beginning of any movement or countermovement. But, perhaps George Counts of Teachers College can be given the credit for initiating reconstructionist designs. Counts gave a speech that was entitled "Dare Progressive Education Be Progressive?" In his speech, Counts accused the members of the Progressive Education Association of having narrow views of education and of mirroring the values and goals of the middle class. If the progressives really wished to be progressive, he charged, they would have to free themselves of middle-class bias, face the social realities of the time, and "fashion a compelling and challenging vision of human destiny."[96] Counts elaborated on his theme in his book *Dare the Schools Build a New Social Order?*[97] He noted that the schools had to involve students in a curriculum that would enable the creation of a "new" and "more equitable" society.

Harold Rugg also believed that the school should engage children in a critical analysis of society in order to improve it. Rugg's criticisms were directed to those who favored child-centered schools. He stated that their laissez faire approach to program building only produced chaos, and their programs were disjointed and unarticulated. "Rarely are they designed in the light of a review of a careful record of the program of earlier years and of the most probably effective year-programs to follow it in the school career of the child."[98] In the 1940s Rugg observed that the Progressive Education Association still overemphasized the child. All seven purposes of the Association referred to the child, and not one took into consideration "man's crucial social conditions and problems."[99]

Brameld continued to be a spokesperson for the reconstructionists' view. In the early 1950s, he outlined the major features of this approach to curriculum. He noted that reconstructionists were committed to creating a new culture. Brameld was convinced that we were in the midst of a revolutionary period—the times demanded that educators harness the school for social reconstruction. The continuing problems at the national and global level—war, poverty among affluence, crime, racial conflict, unemployment, political oppression, and disregard for the environment—all called for a major shift in society. If Western society was to survive, it would be because the common people in the industrial system—and the public service system—would gain control. Once in control, these persons would release and equitably use society's resources to solve the problems of democracy. Brameld placed the working people, in a new sense of collective strength, in control of all principle institutions and resources. This was necessary if the world was to become genuinely democratic. He challenged teachers to join forces with these organized working people.[100]

Brameld also believed that the school should help the individual to develop as a social being and also as a skilled planner of the social reality. The individual must come to learn that he or she must satisfy his or her personal needs through social consensus. The group would be paramount. The schools not only had this obligation to educate children in the value of the collective;

they also needed to point out the urgency for the change.

The fact that reconstructionists stress the notion of change and the needs to plan for tomorrow bring in mind a series of pressing questions raised by two current reconstructionists, Virgil Clift and Harold Shane, as they explore new directions for American educators and new decisions for curriculum specialists.

1. What policies shall govern our future use of technology?
2. At a global level, what shall be our goals, and how can we reach them?
3. What shall we identify as the "good life"?
4. How shall we deploy our limited resources in meeting the needs of various groups of people?
5. How shall we equalize opportunity, and how shall we reduce the gap between the "haves" and "have-nots"?
6. How can we maximize the value of mass media, especially television?
7. What shall be made of psychological, chemical, and electronic approaches to behavior modification?
8. What steps can we take to ensure the integrity of our political, economic, and military systems?
9. What, if anything, are we willing to relinquish, and in what order?
10. And, what honorable compromises and solutions shall we make as we contemplate the above questions?[101]

These questions deal with social issues that are generic—meaning they were relevant yesterday, they are relevant today, and they will be relevant tomorrow, and they are relevant for most school subjects and grade levels. The way we deal with these issues or problems will make the difference about the society we are and will become.

The social reconstructionist curriculum has the primary purpose of engaging the learner in analyzing the many severe problems confronting humankind. However, the exact content and objectives are to be decided by those who actually create such a curriculum. The curriculum is to engage students in a critical analysis of the local, national, and international community. Also, attention is to be given to the political practices of the business and government groups and their impact on the economic realities of the workers. Such a curriculum must propose industrial and political changes that will ultimately modify the social fabric of the nation and perhaps the world.

CONCLUSION

Curriculum design is more than just making sure that the parts of a curriculum are neatly organized in a document. Design is a complex phenomenon requiring of educators careful attention so that the curriculum conceived will have merit and will succeed in getting students to learn those concepts, attitudes, and skills considered worthwhile and essential.

The issue of design is likely to continue to draw the attention of curriculum specialists and generalists. Designing a curriculum is really dealing with a vision, which most educators have. The concepts related to design help them put "flesh" on their visions and to increase their probability of becoming reality.

Various design options exist from which curricularists can select—subject-centered, learner-centered, and problem-centered. Each of these, as has been noted in this chapter, has a history and philosophy associated with it. Each has ardent advocates. Each, when implemented, gives the school a particular character. However, many schools meld these designs, often so much that it is almost impossible to determine just what the curriculum design is.

Advocates of each design face the same design decisions as advocates of all the others. Regardless of the particular design, educators must be concerned with the scope and sequence of the curriculum elements. They must also pay attention to articulation, continuity, and balance. Overall, their understanding of curriculum design is requi-

site knowledge for the building of a curriculum, the topic of the next chapter.

Notes

1. Arno A. Bellack, "What Knowledge Is of Most Worth?" *The High School Journal* (February 1965), pp. 318–332.
2. H. H. Giles, S. P. McCutchen, and A. N. Zechiel, *Exploring the Curriculum* (New York: Harper, 1942), p. 2.
3. Ralph W. Tyler, Conversation with one of the authors, April 16, 1986.
4. George A. Beauchamp, "Curriculum Design," in F. W. English, ed., *Fundamental Curriculum Decisions* (Alexandria, Va.: Association for Supervision and Curriculum Development, 1983), pp. 90–98.
5. Hilda Taba, *Curriculum Development: Theory and Practice* (New York: Harcourt, Brace, 1962).
6. Ibid., p. 423.
7. Ronald C. Doll, *Curriculum Improvement, Decision Making and Process*, 6th ed. (Boston: Allyn and Bacon, 1986).
8. Ralph W. Tyler, *Basic Principles of Curriculum and Instruction* (Chicago: University of Chicago Press, 1949).
9. John Dewey, *The School and Society* (Chicago: University of Chicago Press, 1900), p. 94.
10. Boyd H. Bode, *Modern Educational Theories* (New York: Macmillan, 1927), p. 237.
11. Francis P. Hunkins, *Curriculum Development: Program Improvement* (Columbus, Ohio: Merrill, 1980).
12. Herbert Spencer, *Education: Intellectual, Moral, and Physical* (New York: Alden, 1885); Bellack, "What Knowledge Is of Most Worth?"
13. Laurence Iannaccone and Richard Jamgochian, "High Performing Curriculum and Instructional Leadership in the Climate of Excellence," *National Association of Secondary School Principals* (May 1985), pp. 28–35; Allan C. Ornstein, "Curriculum Contrasts: A Historical View," *Phi Delta Kappan* (February 1982), pp. 404–408.
14. Hunkins, *Curriculum Development: Program Improvement*.
15. Jerome S. Bruner, *The Process of Education* (Cambridge, Mass.: Harvard University Press, 1959).
16. Francis P. Hunkins, "Splintering the Curriculum," *Educational Forum* (Winter 1982), pp 193–201.
17. Robert S. Zais, *Curriculum: Principles and Foundations* (New York: Crowell, 1976).
18. J. Galen Saylor, William M. Alexander, and Arthur J. Lewis, *Planning for Better Teaching and Learning*, 4th ed. (New York: Holt, Rinehart 1981), p. 7.
19. Taba, *Curriculum Development: Theory and Practice*
20. John Piaget, *The Psychology of Intelligence* (Paterson, N.J.: Littlefield, Adams, 1960).

21. Lawrence A. Kohlberg, "The Cognitive-Developmental Approach to Moral Education," *Phi Delta Kappan* (October 1975), pp. 670–677; Clark Power and Lawrence A. Kohlberg, "Moral Development: Transforming the Hidden Curriculum," *Curriculum Review* (September-October 1986), pp. 14–17.

22. B. Othanel Smith, William O. Stanley, and Harlan J. Shores, *Fundamentals of Curriculum Development*, rev. ed. (New York: Harcourt, Brace, 1957).

23. David P. Ausubel, *The Psychology of Meaningful Verbal Learning* (New York: Grune & Stratton, 1963). N. L. Gage and David C. Berliner, *Educational Psychology*, 3rd ed. (Boston: Houghton Mifflin, 1984).

24. G. J. Posner and K. A. Strike, "A Categorization Scheme for Principles of Sequencing Content," *Review of Educational Research* (Fall 1976), pp. 401–406.

25. Tyler, *Basic Principles of Curriculum and Instruction*, p. 86.

26. Bruner, *The Process of Education*, p. 52.

27. John I. Goodlad, *Planning and Organizing for Teaching* (Washington, D.C.: National Education Association, 1963), p. 29.

28. Allan C. Ornstein, "How Do Educators Meet the Needs of Society?," *National Association of Secondary School Principals* (May 1985), pp. 36–47.

29. Henry C. Morrison, *The Curriculum of the Common School* (Chicago: University of Chicago Press, 1940). See also Howard Ozman and Samuel M. Craver, *Philosophical Foundations of Education*, 3rd ed. (Columbus, Ohio: Merrill, 1986).

30. Christopher J. Lucas, *Challenge and Choice in Contemporary Education* (New York: Macmillan, 1976).

31. Robert M. Hutchins, *The Higher Learning in America* (New Haven: Yale University Press, 1936).

32. Arthur Bestor, *The Restoration of Learning* (New York: Alfred A. Knopf, 1956).

33. Ornstein, "Curriculum Contrasts: A Historical Overview"; Ronald Podeschi and David Hackbarth, "The Cries for Excellence: Echoes from the Past." *Educational Forum* (Summer 1986), pp. 419–432.

34. Smith, Stanley, and Shores, *Fundamentals of Curriculum Development*.

35. John I. Goodlad, *A Place Called School* (New York: McGraw-Hill, 1984); Zais, *Curriculum: Principles and Foundations*.

36. John Dewey, *Experience and Education* (New York: Macmillan, 1938), p. 82.

37. Tyler, *Basic Principles of Curriculum and Instruction*, p. 26.

38. Dewey, "My Pedagogic Creed," p. 434.

39. Arthur R. King and John A. Brownell, *The Curriculum and the Disciplines of Knowledge* (New York: Wiley, 1966).

40. Ibid.; Taba, *Curriculum Development: Theory and Practice*.

41. Joseph J. Schwab, "Structures and Dynamics of Knowledge,"in M. Levitt, ed., *Curriculum* (Urbana, IL.: University of Illinois Press, 1971), pp. 181–214.

42. John I. Goodlad, "Directions of Curriculum Change," *NEA Journal* (December 1966), pp. 23–31.

43. Bruner, *The Process of Education*, p. 8.

44. Ibid., p. 6.

45. Ibid., p. 33.

46. Patricia Arlin, "Piagetian Tasks as Predictors of Reading and Math Readiness in Grades K-1," *Journal of Educational Psychology* (October 1981), pp. 712–721; Anita M. Meehan, "A Meta-analysis of Sex Differences in Formal Operational Thought," *Child Development* (June 1984), pp. 1110–1124.

47. Dewey, *The School and Society*.

48. Philip Phenix, "The Uses of the Disciplines as Curriculum Content," in D. Purpel and M. Belanger, eds., *Curriculum and the Cultural Revolution* (Berkeley, Calif.: McCutchan, 1972), p. 87.

49. Elliot W. Eisner, *The Educational Imagination*, 2nd ed. (New York: Macmillan, 1985); Vincent Rogers, "Qualitative and Aesthetic Views of Curriculum and Curriculum Making," in A. Molnar, ed., *Current Thought on Curriculum* (Alexandria, Va.: Association for Supervision and Curriculum Development, 1985), pp. 103–118. Daniel Tanner and Laurel N. Tanner, *Curriculum Development: Theory Into Practice*, 2nd ed. (New York: Macmillan, 1980).

50. Edward A. Krug, *Curriculum Planning*, 2nd ed. (New York: Harper & Row, 1957).

51. Harry S. Broudy, B. O. Smith, and Joe R. Burnett, *Democracy and Excellence in American Secondary Education* (Chicago: Rand McNally, 1964).

52. Gary Fenstermacher and John I. Goodlad, eds., *Individual Difference and the Common Curriculum*, Eighty-Second Yearbook of the National Society for the Study of Education, Part I (Chicago: University of Chicago Press, 1983).

53. Tanner and Tanner make similar points in their discussion of this design, as do others in the curriculum field. See Tanner and Tanner, *Curriculum Development: Theory Into Practice*, 2nd ed. (New York: Macmillan, 1980).

54. Harold B. Alberty and Elsie J. Alberty, *Reorganizing the High School Curriculum*, 3rd ed. (New York: Macmillan, 1962).

55. Tanner and Tanner, *Curriculum Development: Theory Into Practice*, 2nd ed.

56. Jean Jacques Rousseau, *Emile* (London: Dent, 1911), p. 5. Originally published in 1762.

57. Ibid., pp. 130–131.

58. Francis W. Parker, *Talks on Pedagogics* (New York: E. L. Kellogg, 1894).

59. Tanner and Tanner, *Curriculum Development: Theory Into Practice*, 2nd ed.

60. John Dewey, *Democracy and Education* (New York: Macmillan, 1916).

61. William H. Kilpatrick, "The Project Method,"

Teachers College Record (September 1918), pp. 319–335; Kilpatrick, *Foundations of Method* (New York: Macmillan, 1925).

62. Kilpatrick, "The Project Method."
63. Kilpatrick, *Foundations of Method*, p. 212.
64. Frederick G. Bonser, *Life Needs and Education* (New York: Teachers College Press, Columbia University, 1932).
65. Charles Prosser, *Life Adjustment Education for Every Youth* (Washington, D.C.: U.S. Government Printing Office, 1951).
66. Florence B. Stratemeyer et al., *Developing a Curriculum for Modern Living* (New York: Teachers College Press, Columbia University, 1947).
67. Wilford M. Aikin, *The Story of the Eight-Year Study* (New York: Harper, 1942).
68. Roland C. Faunce and Nelson L. Bossing, *Developing the Core Curriculum*, 2nd ed. (Englewood Cliffs, N.J.: Prentice-Hall, 1958).
69. Lawrence A. Cremin, *Public Education* (New York: Basic Books, 1976).
70. Harold Rugg and Ann Shumaker, *The Child-Centered School* (New York: World Book, 1928), p. 118.
71. John Dewey, *The Child and the Curriculum* (Chicago: University of Chicago Press, 1902), pp. 8–9.
72. Boyd H. Bode, *Progressive Education at the Crossroads* (New York: Newson, 1938). Tanner and Tanner in their book, *Curriculum Development: Theory Into Practice*, have made similar comments about Dewey's views of students' interests.
73. Dewey, *The Child and the Curriculum*, pp. 8–9.
74. Ibid., p. 12.
75. Ibid.
76. Daniel Tanner and Laurel N. Tanner, *Curriculum Development: Theory Into Practice*, 2nd ed. (New York: Macmillan, 1980); Gloria A. Castillo, *Left-Handed Teaching*, 2nd ed. (New York: Holt, Rinehart, 1978); Mario D. Fantini, *Regaining Excellence in Education* (Columbus, Ohio: Merrill, 1986).
77. Dewey, *The Child and the Curriculum*, p. 12.
78. John Holt, *How Children Fail* (New York, Pitman, 1964), pp. 175–177.
79. Paul Goodman, *Compulsory Mis-education* (New York: Horizon, 1964).
80. For a helpful additional discussion, see Tanner and Tanner, *Curriculum Development: Theory Into Practice*, 2nd ed.
81. Holt, *How Children Fail*, p. 178.
82. Smith, Stanley, and Shores, *Fundamentals of Curriculum Development*.
83. Abraham H. Maslow, *Toward a Psychology of Being* (New York: D. Van Nostrand, 1962).
84. Carl Rogers, "Toward Becoming a Fully Functioning Person," in A. Combs, ed., *Perceiving,*

Behaving, Becoming (Washington, D.C.: Association for Supervision and Curriculum Development Yearbook, 1962), pp. 21–33.

85. Ibid.
86. Castillo, *Left-Handed Teaching*.
87. Gerald Weinstein and Mario D. Fantini, *Toward Humanistic Education: A Curriculum of Affect* (New York: Praeger, 1970).
88. Gail McCutcheon, "Curriculum Theory/Curriculum Practice: A Gap or the Grand Canyon," in A. Molnar, ed., *Current Thought on Curriculum* (Alexandria, Va.: Association for Supervision and Curriculum Development, 1985), pp. 45–52; Vincent Rogers, "Qualitative and Aesthetic Views of Curriculum and Curriculum Making," in A. Molnar, ed., *Current Thought on Curriculum*, pp. 103–118.
89. Paul R. Feinberg, "Four Curriculum Theorists: A Critique in the Light of Martin Buber's Philosophy of Education." *Journal of Curriculum Theorizing* (Spring 1985), pp. 1–164.
90. Philip H. Phenix, "Transcendence and the Curriculum," in Eisner and Vallance, eds., *Conflicting Conceptions of Curriculum*, pp. 118–119.
91. Ibid., p. 123.
92. Ibid.
93. Spencer, *Education: Intellectual, Moral, and Physical*; Dewey, *Democracy and Education*.
94. Stratemeyer et al., *Developing a Curriculum for Modern Living*.
95. Ibid.
96. Faunce and Bossing, *Developing the Core Curriculum*.
97. Alberty and Alberty, *Reorganizing the High School Curriculum*.
98. Theodore Brameld, "Karl Marx and the American Teacher," *Social Frontier* (November 1935), p. 55.
99. George S. Counts, "Dare Progressive Education Be Progressive?" *Progressive Education* (April 1932), p. 259.
100. George S. Counts, *Dare the Schools Build a New Social Order?* (Yonkers, N.Y.: World Book, 1932).
101. Harold Rugg, *Culture and Education in America* (New York: Harcourt, 1931), pp. 302–303.
102. Harold Rugg, *Foundations for American Education* (New York: Harcourt, 1947), p. 745.
103. Theodore Brameld, *Toward a Reconstructed Philosophy of Education* (New York: Holt, Rinehart, 1956).
104. Virgil A. Clift and Harold G. Shane, "The Future, Social Decisions, and Educational Change in Secondary Schools," in W. Van Til, ed., *Issues in Secondary Education*, Seventy-fifth Yearbook of the National Society for the Study of Education, Part II (Chicago: University of Chicago Press, 1976), pp. 295–315.

chapter 8

CURRICULUM DEVELOPMENT

Successful education requires careful planning. Educators have come to recognize that without planning, disorder and friction are likely to characterize curriculum activity. Educators originate curriculum development strategies. They should formulate a master plan prior to creating or implementing a program for students. How they conceptualize the plan will be influenced by their awareness of and sensitivity to issues—both present and anticipated. Certainly, few people can construct a curriculum without giving some thought to goals; to content; to learning experiences, methods, and materials; and to evaluation.

The need to plan effective curricula is obvious; the difficulty, however, is that there are various ways to define curriculum development. Also, several curriculum designs dictate what factors should receive attention: subject matter, students, or society. Also, it is difficult to be precise or to plan what is not defined with any universality.

Not everyone agrees what curriculum is or what is involved in curriculum development. We present here a broad definition to allow the different views and interpretations to coexist with ours—which posits that curriculum development draws on the principles (usually technical or scientific) and consists of those processes (humanistic, humane, and artistic) that allow schools and school people to realize certain educational goals.

Ideally, all those who are to be affected by a curriculum should be involved in the process of development. But, like with most aspects of education, there is some debate about what formula to follow in order to achieve particular educational goals. Although there are numerous models from which to choose, most models can be classified as either technical-scientific or nontechnical-nonscientific. These two general organizers were presented in Chapter 1, which identified specific curriculum ap-

191

proaches. Technical-scientific approaches were (1) behavioral-rational; (2) systems-managerial; and (3) intellectual-academic. The two nontechnical-nonscientific approaches were (1) humanistic-aesthetic, and (2) reconceptualist.

Although these specific approaches are appropriate, in this chapter we refer to the more global categories. As we pointed out in Chapter 1, classifying an approach as nontechnical or nonscientific does not mean presenting it in a negative manner. Rather, it means contrasting the two basic postures. Persons who believe in some subject matter curriculum design usually advocate the technical-scientific approach to curriculum development. Those individuals who favor a learner-centered design frequently advocate the nontechnical-nonscientific approach. Problem-centered designs can fall within either approach.

TECHNICAL-SCIENTIFIC APPROACH

The technical-scientific approach to education and to curriculum is a way of thinking. To those who believe in the approach, it is not a vehicle for dehumanizing education, but rather a way of planning curricula to optimize students' learning and to allow them to increase their output, including their humanness. According to this point of view, "Curriculum development . . . is basically a plan for structuring the environment to coordinate in an orderly manner the elements of time, space, materials, equipment and personnel."[1]

A technical-scientific view can enable us to comprehend curriculum from a macro or broad view and to understand it as a complex unity of parts organized to serve a common function—the education of individuals. It also allows us to have a plan in mind.

The technical-scientific approach requires that educators use an intellectual and rational approach to accomplish their tasks and that they believe that it is possible to outline systematically those procedures that will facilitate the creation of curricula. The

various models employ a means-end paradigm that suggests that the more rigorous the means, the more likely the desired ends will be attained. Followers of this approach indicate that such a systematically designed program can be evaluated. However, others question just how precise the evaluation can be.

The various technical-scientific models exhibit what James Macdonald would call a "technological" rationality as opposed to an "aesthetic rationality." Macdonald notes that there is a press for this rationality in the way schools are organized.[2] Persons who have this orientation tend to believe that there is a large body of educational knowledge and that efforts should be made to ensure that students are presented with opportunities to gain such knowledge. Macdonald wrote that those with a technological consciousness prize optimum growth, maximum efficiency, and effectiveness of the system in delivering education.

Larry Cuban indicates that because the bureaucratic organization of our schools is rooted in rationality, this technological-scientific approach to curriculum development will probably continue to grow. Cuban states that goals, objectives, problem solving, planning, and evaluation are simply outward signs exhibited by a bureaucracy trying to embrace rationality.[3]

History of Technical-Scientific Approach.

Students of the history of curriculum development have located the origin and substance of the technical-scientific model in the schools' attempt, at the turn of the century, to adapt the principles of bureaucracy to methods that could be considered scientific. Early educators reasoned that using empirical methods (surveys and analysis of human conduct) would answer the curriculum question: What shall be taught? The push for a science of curriculum making paralleled the rise of science—biology, physics, and chemistry—during the nineteenth and twentieth centuries, and also the notion of "machine theory"—time and motion studies—evolving in the world of business and industry. Scientific principles were also being applied to agriculture, manufacturing, and government, as well as to other phases of practical life. In education, especially in curriculum, these models evolved with the work of Bobbitt and Charters. Standards for the various educational products needed to be established. "The ability to add at a speed of 65 combinations per minute, with an accuracy of 94 percent, is as definite a specification as can be set up for any aspect of the work of the steel plant," Bobbitt argued.[4]

Bobbitt viewed the process of curriculum development as perhaps even more important than the details of the curriculum itself. Bobbitt compared the curriculum maker to an engineer. This "educational engineer" was to use his or her "educational surveying instruments" to locate particular objectives in the various subject fields. From such surveying, the educator could map out appropriate content and experiences to prepare the student for the future. The curriculum worker was to define the major fields of adult experience and to then analyze and consequently divide them into smaller and smaller units until they became part of specific curricular activities.

For Bobbitt, the source of the content for the curriculum was "reality" uncovered by scientific analysis. For his contemporary, Charters, the source was really in the realm of philosophy. The philosopher set the aim whereas the analyst only created the technique for translating the aim into the reality of the curriculum.[5]

Philosophy supplied the ideals that were to serve as objectives and standards for actions. For Charters, the curriculum consisted of both ideas and activities. Unlike Bobbitt, Charters discussed the issue of knowledge. He argued that subject matter had to be useful and motivational.[6]

These two men firmly established the scientific movement in curriculum making. They pointed out that curriculum development is a process that will, if followed, result in a meaningful program for pupils. They initiated a concern for the relation of goals, objectives, and activities, pointing out that the selection of goals is a normative process whereas the selection of objectives and activities is empirical and scientific. They indicated that curricular activity can be planned and systematically studied and evaluated.

Through the efforts of men like Bobbitt and Charters, concern grew for curriculum as a field of study. The area achieved independent status upon the establishment of the Society for Curriculum Study in 1932. In 1938, Teachers College at Columbia University established a department of curriculum and teaching. For the next twenty years, Teachers College dominated the field of curriculum, even surpassing the earlier influence of the University of Chicago.

The Tyler Model: Four Basic Principles.

Without doubt, Tyler's is one of the best known technical-scientific models. In 1949, Tyler published *Basic Principles of Curriculum and Instruction,* in which he outlined a rationale for examining the problems of curriculum and instruction.[7] He mentioned that those involved in curriculum inquiry must try to define the: (1) purposes of the school; (2) educational experiences related to the purposes; (3) organization of these experiences; and (4) evaluation of the purposes.

By "purposes," Tyler was referring to objectives. He indicated that curriculum planners should identify these general objectives by gathering data from three sources—the subject matter, the learners, and the society. After identifying numerous general objectives, the curriculum planners were to refine them by filtering them through two screens—the philosophy of the school and the psychology of learning. What resulted from such screening were specific instructional objectives. Note, however, that even though Tyler used the term *instructional objectives,* he was not advocating the narrow behavioral objectives that have been advocated in recent years.

Tyler then discussed how to select educational experiences that would allow the attainment of objectives. Learning experiences had to take into account both the previous experience and the perceptions that the learner brings to a situation. Also, the experiences were to be selected in light of what educators know about learning and human development.

Tyler next talked about the organization and sequencing of these experiences. He purported that the ordering of the experiences had to be somewhat systematic so as to produce a maximum cumulative effect. He thought that organizing elements, such as ideas, concepts, values, and skills, should be woven as threads into the curriculum fabric. These key elements could serve as organizers and means and methods of instruction, and they could relate different learning experiences among different subjects. The ideas, concepts, values, and skills could also link content within particular subject courses—for example, English and mathematics. Indeed, much of the discussion today on the conceptual structures of courses or curricular content is drawn from Tyler.

Tyler's last principle deals with evaluating the effectiveness of planning and actions. Tyler considered evaluation to be important in curriculum development. He realized that it was necessary if educators were to find out whether the learning experiences actually produced the intended results. Also, it was necessary to determine whether the program was effective or ineffective. It could guide where the program should be maintained or modified. An evaluation should relate to all of the objectives.

Although Tyler did not display his model of curriculum development graphically, several other people have. The authors' diagram of this procedure follows in Figure 8-1.

The Taba Model: Grass-Roots Rationale.

Hilda Taba believed that those who teach curriculum should participate in developing it. She advocated what has been called the grass-roots approach,[8] a model whose steps or stages are similar to Tyler's. Although

Tyler did not advocate that his model only be employed by persons in the central office, educators during the early days of curriculum making thought that the authorities really had the knowledge requisite for creating curricula. This was the "top-down" or what some have called the administrative or line-staff model. Ideas from curriculum experts were frequently given to teachers to develop, and then administrators supervised the teachers to ensure that the ideas were implemented.

Taba felt that the administrative model was really in the wrong order. The curriculum should be designed by the users of the program. Teachers should begin the process by creating specific teaching-learning units for their students. She advocated that teachers take an inductive approach to curriculum development—starting with specifics and building to a general design—as opposed to the more traditional deductive approach—starting with the general design and working toward the specifics.

Taba noted seven major steps to her grass-roots model in which teachers would have major input:

1. *Diagnosis of Needs.* The teacher (curriculum designer) starts the process by identifying the needs of the students for whom the curriculum is to be planned.

2. *Formulation of Objectives.* After the teacher has identified needs that require attention, he or she specifies objectives to be accomplished.

3. *Selection of Content.* The objectives selected or created suggest the subject matter or content of the curriculum unit. Taba pointed out that not only should objectives and content match, but the validity and significance of the content chosen needed to be determined as well.

4. *Organization of Content.* A teacher cannot just select content, but must organize it in some type of sequence, taking into consideration the maturity of the learners, their academic achievement, and their interests.

5. *Selection of Learning Experiences.* Content must be presented to pupils or pupils must engage in an interaction with the content. At

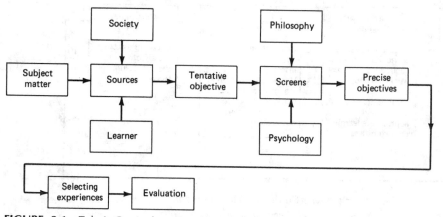

FIGURE 8-1 Tyler's Curriculum Development Model

this point, Taba discussed the instructional methodologies that will involve the students with the content.

6. *Organization of Learning Activities.* Just as content must be sequenced and organized, so must the learning activities. Often the sequence of the learning activities is determined by the content that is sequenced. But the teacher needs to keep in mind the particular students whom he or she will be teaching.

7. *Evaluation and Means of Evaluation.* The curriculum planner must determine just what objectives have been accomplished. Evaluation procedures need to be considered by the students and teachers.

Taba's model has much merit. Nonetheless, according to some educators, putting such an effort into a grass-roots framework weakens it. Robert Zais maintains that the primary weakness is that it applies the concept of participatory democracy to a highly technical, complex, and specialized process. This does not mean that teachers cannot be involved—indeed, they must if curricula are to be actually used in the classroom. It does mean, however, that a "one person-one vote" rationale will not guarantee effective curricula.[9] Also, the grass-roots design assumes that teachers have the expertise, and perhaps more importantly, the time to engage in such extensive curricular activity. However, we do need to recognize that the grass-roots approach has made it abundantly clear that a broad base of involvement is essential for curriculum decision making.

Curriculum making requires compromise among administrators from the central office, supervisors from the local school, and teachers, students, and community members. Traditionally, the central office staff is charged with directing those actions that enable the various participators to engage in curriculum development. In a nontraditional approach members of the community and teaching profession are given primary responsibility for developing the curriculum.

Saylor and Alexander Model: Planning Process.

Saylor and Alexander have presented a systematic approach to curriculum development that is illustrated in Figure 8-2.

1. *Goals, Objectives, and Domains.* Curriculum developers start their work, according to this model, by specifying the major goals and objectives they wish to address. Each major goal depicts a curriculum domain. There are four major domains that should receive attention: personal development, human relations, continued learning skills, and specialization. However, the reader is cautioned that the school should not be limited by just these domains.[10]

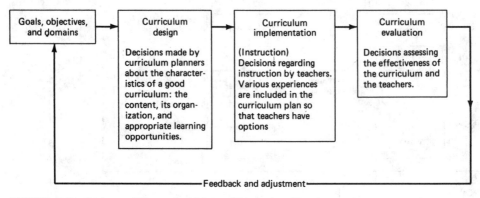

FIGURE 8-2 Saylor and Alexander's View of Curriculum Development.
From J. Galen Saylor and William M. Alexander, *Planning Curriculum for Schools*
(New York: Holt, Rinehart, 1974).

The goals, objectives, and domains selected evolve from careful consideration of external variables, among which are the views and demands of the community, the legal requirements of the state, research findings, and the philosophical views of the curriculum specialists.

2. *Curriculum Design.* Once this first major step has been accomplished, the curriculum planners are ready to engage in curriculum designing. Here curriculum decision makers decide on the content, its organization, and appropriate learning opportunities for the content selected. The manner of delivering these learning opportunities and tying them into the particular domain are also considered at this juncture. The philosophical views are taken into consideration. Will the curriculum be designed to emphasize the academic disciplines, the learner, or the needs and patterns of society?

3. *Curriculum Implementation.* When the curriculum design or designs have been decided upon and created, the teachers create instructional plans, or, in other words, implement the curriculum. Teachers select the methods and materials to use to help the students learn the content.

4. *Curriculum Evaluation.* This is the final stage in the model. At this stage, curriculum planners and teachers choose from myriad evaluation techniques those that will furnish an accurate picture of the value and success of the curriculum and its delivery. It is urged that evaluation be approached comprehensively. Evaluation should focus on the curriculum

plan, the quality of the instruction, and the learning behaviors of the students. Through such comprehensive evaluation curriculum developers determine whether to keep the program, modify it, or discard it.[11]

Goodlad Model: Learning Opportunity, Organizing Center.

Figure 8-3 depicts Goodlad's and Richter's approach to curriculum development. In this model, all educational aims are drawn from the analysis of the values of the existing culture. These educational aims are then translated into educational objectives stated behaviorally. These objectives then suggest learning opportunities (LO) that are to exist as "a situation created within the context of an educational program or institution for the purpose of achieving certain educational ends."[12] Particular courses or even certain readings are examples of learning opportunities.

Curriculum planners then deduce from the educational objectives and the suggested learning opportunities more specifically stated educational objectives. From these objectives, the curriculum planners design and/or select organizing centers (O.C.). Goodlad defined an organizing center as "a specific learning opportunity set up for identifiable students or for a student."[13]

The model is technical-scientific because

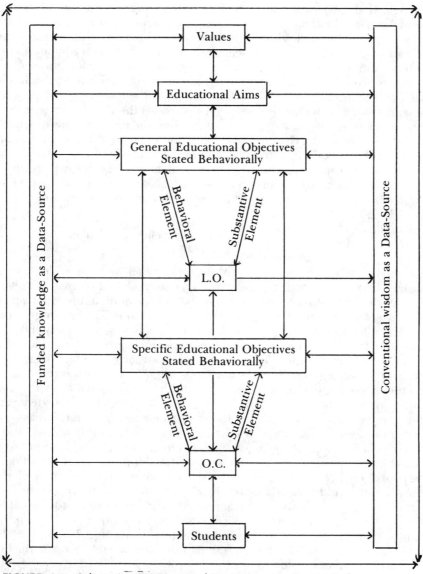

FIGURE 8-3 Substantive Decisions and Derivations in a Conceptual System for Curriculum.

Source: from John L. Goodlad and Maurice N. Richter, *The Development of a Conceptual System for Dealing with Problems of Curriculum and Instruction* (Los Angeles: Institute for Development of Educational Activities, University of California, 1966), p. 65.

its various parts are connected and because feedback and adjustment of the entire model result from analyzing the students' performances and relating them to the values of the general society.

Hunkins's Developmental Model.

Hunkins's model, also a technical-scientific model, has seven major stages—curriculum conceptualization and legitimization;

diagnosis; content selection; experience selection; implementation; evaluation; and maintenance.[14] A schema of the model follows, as illustrated in Figure 8-4.

This model differs from some of the previous ones in two major ways. First, it incorporates a feedback and adjustment loop—the dashed line—and second, it includes a conceptualization and legitimization stage and a maintenance stage. The feedback and adjustment loop allows those working with the model to continually adjust their decision making about curricular actions. For instance, when designers are at the stage of content selection and see that, for example, no appropriate content exists for certain pupils, they can return to the curriculum diagnosis stage, at which objectives were created, and modify the objectives. Or they can go back to the beginning stage and rethink the curriculum in light of the new information. The feedback and adjustment loop is central to a technical-scientific approach; it allows the process of curriculum decision making to be "circular" rather than linear.

The conceptualization and legitimization stage is unique to the model because, in addition to determining needs to be addressed and identifying the student audience, it allows philosophical questions to be raised and answered, and it relates those questions to the tentative selection of a curriculum design. Frequently, people engage in curriculum development without considering what their philosophical orientations are—that is, whether they are essentialists, or progressivists, or existentialists, or whatever.

The curriculum maintenance stage is also unique. Usually, curriculum evaluation is the last stage. Once data suggest that a curriculum has been successful, curricularists "rest." They rarely consider anything else. But curriculum programs that are not consciously maintained usually disappear or become part of a patchwork of courses. Curriculum maintenance outlines various means of managing the curriculum system and the support systems necessary for the continuation of the program.

The other stages draw from the legacy of the technical-scientific orientation. Curriculum diagnosis is the creation and selection of objectives. Content selection means the selection and organization of content. Experience selection is the selection and organization of various instructional approaches in relation to the content selected. Curriculum implementation is the initial pilot testing of the curriculum, the modifications of curricular units, and the final diffusion of the curriculum to the total school population. Curriculum evaluation is engaging in those activities necessary for formative process and summative product evaluation.

Miller and Seller: Curriculum Orientations.

Miller and Seller introduce the notion that the various models of curriculum development exhibit orientations toward the purpose of the curriculum. The first orientation is the transmission position. They indicate that the curriculum can emphasize that education should transmit facts, skills, and values to students. The stress is on mastery of competencies and carrying on the culture. The second orientation they delineate is the transaction position. In this view, the individual is perceived as rational and as capable of intelligent action. Education is viewed as a dialogic process between student and the curriculum. Actually, most of the technical-scientific models represent the transmission and transaction positions. The third position, transformation, centers on personal and social change. It would be the position most likely taken by those in the humanistic camp.[15]

These three orientations serve as another means by which we can consider curriculum development models. While Miller and Seller seem to advocate the transformation orientation, their model is very much like technical-scientific models. Their model has five stages: (1) orientation; (2) aims, developmental goals, instructional strategies; (3) teaching models; (4) implementation plan; and (5) evaluation. They present it in a circular format so that evaluation data feed-

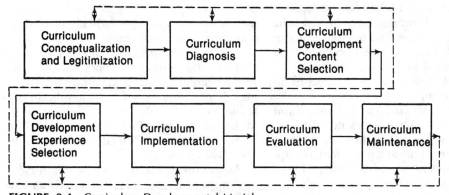

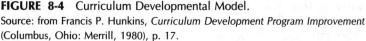

FIGURE 8-4 Curriculum Developmental Model.
Source: from Francis P. Hunkins, *Curriculum Development Program Improvement*
(Columbus, Ohio: Merrill, 1980), p. 17.

back to the orientation stage and the cycle can repeat.

The stages are rather self-evident. The orientation stage deals with considering one's philosophy, one's view of psychology and learning theory, and one's view of society. This tends to coincide with our notion of curriculum approach. From this orientation, one then determines what aims, goals, and specific objectives will be addressed. After this, learning experiences and teaching strategies are selected. It is interesting that these two authors leave out the content dimension of the curriculum. One goes from objectives to experiences and teaching methods. Teaching methods include teacher behavior and teacher effectiveness. The implementation stage refers to incorporating the curriculum into the teacher's repertoire of behavior. Evaluation is testing to determine if the curriculum is being taught effectively.

Other examples of technical-scientific models exist, but all of them are incomplete by themselves. It is not possible for every model to show every detail and every nuance of a process as complicated as curriculum development. However, the models do show—in graphic form—those aspects of curriculum development essential for consideration.

We should realize that even though these model types tend to be used by advocates of subject-centered designs, who are perhaps more in the traditional philosophical and technological camps, the models really can be employed to develop a curriculum for any and all of the curriculum design orientations. Curricularists can be systematic in creating subject-centered, child-centered, or problem-centered curricula. Although good planning cannot guarantee programs of quality, quality programs rarely result from unplanned actions.

NONTECHNICAL-NONSCIENTIFIC APPROACH

The danger in noting that one set of approaches is systematic or rational is the implication that the other camp is nonsystematic or nonrational. Advocates of methods of curriculum development not in the technical-scientific camp, however, are not suggesting disorder. Rather, they are taking issue with some of the key assumptions underlying the technical-scientific approach and questioning some of the consequences that result from utilizing this approach to curriculum development.

The technical-scientific approach to curriculum suggests that the process of curriculum development has a high degree of objectivity, universality, and logic. It works on an assumption that reality can be known, understood, and represented in symbolic form. It states that the aims of education can be made known, can be stated precisely, and can be addressed in a linear fashion.

In contrast, those in the nontechnical-nonscientific camp stress the subjective, the personal, the aesthetic, the heuristic, and the transactional. They stress not the outputs of production but rather the learner, especially through activity-oriented approaches to teaching and learning. Those favoring this approach note that not all ends of education can be known nor, indeed, do they need to be known in all cases. This approach considers that the curriculum evolves rather than being planned precisely.

In this approach, those persons who are to be most affected by the curriculum are involved in its planning. Individual learners know themselves better than anyone else, and therefore are capable of identifying and selecting those learning experiences that will facilitate their cognitive growth and social development. This approach to curriculum development focuses on individuals' self-perceptions and personal preferences, their own assessments of self-needs, and their attempts at self-integration. These are the data points for the curriculum decision-making process.

This differs to some degree from the technical-scientific persons, who rely more heavily on the view of experts and the demands of subject matter and society for determining students' needs. Indeed, some have criticized Taba for being too subject-oriented and Tyler for being too accepting of the values of society in determining the direction of the curriculum.[16] The "top-down" tradition of the technical-scientific advocates is challenged by the nontechnical-nonscientific persons. The teacher and the learner have some roles—some autonomy for "running" the curriculum. Advocates of the nontechnical-nonscientific view stress that curricula deal with humans, both at the teaching and learning levels.

Those favoring this view place high priority on educational objectives that are person- and process-oriented and that allow individuals to grow as individuals and as members of a social order.

The technical-scientific view toward curriculum development relies heavily on rationalism (thinking) and empiricism (sensing). The nontechnical-nonscientific orientation relies heavily on intuitionism (feeling), and on what Macdonald has called an "aesthetic rationality" in contrast to a "technological rationality."[17]

Advocates of the nontechnical-nonscientific approach to designing curricula are likely to support child-centered and to a lesser extent problem-centered designs. But as some examples of nontechnical-nonscientific designs will hopefully show, these are still purposeful approaches that can be employed systematically. In fact, even though the difference between a technical-scientific and a nontechnical-nonscientific plan is real, the major issue is really determining what element of curriculum receives the greatest attention in the curriculum planning, designing process. Technical-scientific approaches usually focus on subject matter, keeping in mind the student and the society on a secondary basis. Nontechnical-nonscientific approaches, in contrast, focus primarily on the learner and his or her needs and interests, and with secondary attention to subject matter and society.

Nontechnical-nonscientific approach advocates challenge assumptions about whether all aims and goals of education can be known. They do not accept the position of the logical positivists—that if something exists it can be perceived and measured. If it cannot be measured, then it does not exist or, if it does, it still is of no concern to the school. There are various ways of knowing and processing reality. This applies to formulating conclusions about the world, and it also applies to relating questions to the curriculum and to the procedures for creating curricula. Perhaps the difference between the technical-scientific and the nontechnical-nonscientific people can be summed up in the recognition that they are looking at curricular realities from different frameworks or paradigms.

Open-Classroom Model.

Much discussion favoring a nontechnical-nonscientific approach to curriculum appeared during the early 1970s in what has come to be known as the open-classroom or open-school movement. This reform effort was patterned after reforms being made in English primary schools. Advocates heralded it as the answer to the imbalance placed upon the schools by their emphasis on disciplines during the 1960s. The open classroom was touted as the means of humanizing our elementary schools.

The open classroom was based on an activity curriculum in which the activities were often treated as ends in themselves. The curriculum was not necessarily put into place for any particular social rationale. The activity curriculum, also known as the activity movement and activity program, has had a long history in this century. In the 1930s, it had become an integral part of educational dialogue. To some degree, those who favored the activity curriculum were averse to making any plan in advance that might stifle the development and learning of children. These persons stated that the formal preparation of plans before the arrival of children would most likely stultify the children's learning. This aversion to planning the curriculum prior to students' arriving was encouraged by William Kilpatrick, the chair of philosophy at Teachers College. Kilpatrick believed that planning a curriculum in advance was simply inappropriate educational behavior.

The activity curriculum was a reaction to the then current practice of conducting much school learning with only the teacher actively engaged and the learner remaining passive and silent unless given permission to move. In contrast, persons urging the activity curriculum thought of educational activity as gross, overt movement. Children learned by doing and by actively moving around the room.

As was true of the early disciples of the activity movement, current advocates of this approach do not want either a rigid, systematically developed curriculum or tightly organized curriculum content. Herbert Kohl, one of the most popular current spokespersons, considers the open classroom to be an arena in which pupils can " . . . make choices and pursue what interests them." The teacher finds that "the things that work best for him are the unplanned ones, the ones that arise spontaneously because of a student's suggestion or sudden perception."[18] For Kohl, the classroom is in constant flux. The direction of learning and the focus of the curriculum take their direction depending on what happens to be gaining the attention of both pupils and teachers at a particular moment.

John Holt is another supporter of the open classroom. He considers the open classroom to be an environment in which pupils' activities derive from their interests. The teacher is not to control the curriculum, but is rather to arrange the environment so that pupils' activities evolve from their interests. The teacher facilitates the curriculum "evolving" from the children in natural situations. Holt argues that curriculum planning is a type of intervention by adults on the learners. "The more we intervene in children's lives, however intelligently, kindly, or imaginatively, the less time we leave them to find and develop their own ways to meet their true needs. The more we try to teach them, the less they can teach us."[19]

The open classroom could be characterized by "child freedom" and progressive ideals. But the freedom issue is approached not as something to be attained in order to fully develop the child. Rather, it is approached as freedom from certain things—from teacher domination, from a tightly structured curriculum, from the imposition of goals by others.

This model places great faith in children. Left to their own devices they are to somehow select the proper curriculum and the proper educational experiences, and they are to come from the encounters as persons better than those from previous generations. They would be self-actualized individuals with well-adjusted personalities, primarily because of their ability to communicate effectively with others without self-consciousness. Paul Goodman argued that "we must drastically cut back formal schooling because the present extended tutelage is against nature and arrests growth."[20] He noted that "the effort to channel the process of growing up according to a preconceived curriculum and method discourages and wastes many of the best human powers to learn and cope."[21] Goodman also argues that we do not have to plan a curriculum—we only need to allow a curriculum to evolve from the interaction of pupils within the classroom context.

Although some persons believe in such nonplanning of the curriculum, most of them also advance some consistent ways of creating a program. They present, for example, stages of actions that need to be considered systematically.

Weinstein and Fantini Model: A Curriculum of Affect.

Weinstein and Fantini presented a model by which teachers can generate new content and techniques and assess the relevance of existing curriculum, content, and techniques. They note that it is a way of linking sociopsychological factors with cognition so that the learners can cope with their concerns. For this reason, these authors consider their model one for a "curriculum of affect."[22] In viewing the model (Figure 8-5), one might at first consider it part of the technical-scientific model. But it is in a way a shifting away from the deductive organization of the curriculum and more toward an inductive orientation. The individual learner is central to the development process.

The first step is determining just who are the learners as a group. The authors are careful to point out that they are concerned with the group because most students are taught in groups. Therefore, knowledge of their common interests and characteristics is considered a prerequisite to differentiated

diagnosis and individualized teaching. In the next step, student concerns are identified that actually determine the curriculum. This focus on student concerns is what places this model into the nontechnical-nonscientific camp. The concerns of the learner will influence the content and its organization, as well as the teaching procedures employed. Because concerns are deeper and more persistent than interests, they give the curriculum some consistency over time. These authors focus on enhancing self-image and gaining control over one's life. The content of the curriculum is to be employed—is, in fact, to be instrumental—in getting students to gain control of their lives. This—not specific content learned—is the deserved outcome.

Weinstein and Fantini next discuss outcomes in their model, an indication of their technical propensity. But, even though they are interested in learner behavior, they are more concerned with broad educational aims and the concept of liberation than those curriculum developers who emphasize specific subject matter.

Once educators have determined outcomes, they select organizing ideas—those generalizations, ideas, principles, and concepts around which specific curriculum content can be developed. Here these authors are very much in line with many mainstream curricularists. But the difference is that the organizing ideas are selected on the basis of learner concerns rather than on the "demands" of academic subjects. Also, these ideas must help the learners gain the skill to cope with their concerns.

After organizing ideas, educators confront the key task of selecting the content vehicle. In Weinstein and Fantini's model, the content can come from the traditional sources or from out-of-school experiences or from the children themselves. Content is organized into three divisions in addition to the traditional cognitive material. The first is content gained from experiences one has as a growing person. Here content addresses student identity, power, belonging, and connection. The second type of con-

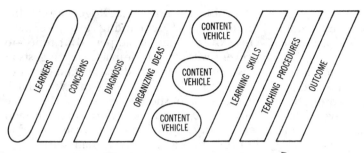

FIGURE 8-5 From Gerald Weinstein and Marco D. Fantini, *Toward Humanstic Education.* (New York: Praeger, 1970). Reprinted with permisson.

tent—affective—also relates to the learner's feelings about his or her experiences in relation to his or her major underlying interests. Examples would be feelings about friends, sports, and social activities. The third type of content is that which the student has learned from the social context in which he or she lives—his or her "experimental content." These contents leave no doubt that this model is within the nontechnical-nonscientific family.

The types of content selected influence the types of skills selected as well. What skills will the learner require in order to deal with the content and with him- or herself as a person with power? The basic skills content of reading, writing, and arithmetic can be included. But students must also acquire the skill of learning how to learn. Another set of concepts is related to the self: Self-skills and "other awareness" skills are employed to enable the pupil to recognize and describe him- or herself and others multidimensionally, particularly in terms of feeling.

Teaching procedures is the last major stage considered. What means can the teacher employ to get the pupils to learn the appropriate contents and to gain the necessary skills for power over their own lives? The procedures necessary are those that will address the learning styles of individuals and that will also have the greatest impact on their affective dimensions. The learners, from interacting with the teachers, with themselves, and with their peers, should develop emotionally and strengthen their feelings of self-worth. A critical concern in using this model is fostering self-control of one's educational experience. The individual must come from this curricular experi-

ence as a person feeling in control of his or her own destiny and believing that his or her ideas, values, and decisions are indeed important.

Rogers's Model: Interpersonal Relations.

Although Carl Rogers is not a curriculum specialist, he has developed a model for changing human behavior that can be used for curriculum development. His emphasis is not on content or learning activities, rather on human experiences; it does not focus on products, rather on processes for solving personal and group problems.[23]

Since curriculum is planned and implemented by educators who must be flexible and open to change, his model is relevant to us in that it fosters personal growth, group rapport, and system-wide innovation and change. Rogers's model is used for exploring group experiences, whereby people examine themselves and others, through T-groups, encounter groups, and sensitivity training groups—rooted in the ideas of the National Training Laboratories and the human relations theories of management in the 1950s and 1960s.[24] With the aid of a trained facilitator, each participant in the group is encouraged to put aside his or her own defenses, to communicate honestly, and to explore his or her own feelings and the feelings of others. Rogers contends that the group experience permits "individuals . . . to know themselves and each other more fully than is possible in the usual social or working relationships; the climate of openness, risk-taking, and honesty generates trust," which permits each participant to "test out and adopt more innovative and constructive behaviors."[25] In short, the model promotes curriculum change by changing the participants involved in curriculum development.

According to Rogers, a week-long intensive group experience should produce noticeable changes among school administrators. They become (1) less protective of their own beliefs and are more willing to listen to others, (2) less threatened by innovative ideas, (3) less bureaucratic and more democratic and people oriented, (4) more willing to communicate with superiors and subordinates, (5) more open with staff members, and (6) more willing to accept feedback, both positive and negative, and learn from it. A week-long intensive group experience for teachers should produce the following outcomes: they become (1) more willing to listen to students, (2) more willing to accept novel ideas from students rather than insist on conformity, (3) more willing to explore relationships with students, (4) more willing to change the course content or learning activities to meet the interests of students, (5) more willing to work with students and help them resolve their problems, as opposed to disciplining them, and (6) more democratic and less authoritarian in teaching and running the classroom.[26]

Rogers's model can be used for improving the attitudes, behaviors, and personal relations of students, parents, community members, and school board members, too. It can be used not only among peers (people of the same status), but also to effect relations between members of different status roles—such as a curriculum committee consisting of school board members, community members, parents, administrators, teachers, and students. In this manner, members of the curriculum committee can learn to better understand themselves and others, to become more flexible and willing to work for constructive change. It is this kind of change in human attitudes and behavior that should produce results in a curriculum team effort and for curriculum development.

It should be noted that Rogers asserts the importance of scheduling group experiences over a reasonable period of time—to prevent withering of impact. He suggests at least ten sessions for educators and community people during an academic year. Each group session should consist of the same participants, and no more than fifteen members. Although there is obvious need to improve human relations in all work situations, including schools, it needs to be stated that the model does not direct change, rather it facilitates change; it does not provide specific outcomes or answers, rather it permits people to explore processes and experiences. The improvement in human relations, in theory, will indirectly lead to more effective changes, outcomes, and answers. Rogers never answers the crucial questions: What content? What learning activities? What values? What are the roles of administrators, teachers, etc. in making curriculum decisions? The participants must work out these questions, and the answers will differ among different curriculum groups. But by getting an honest and open picture of how one feels and how others feel, and in communicating in a supportive manner, these kinds of questions can be answered in a way that leads to improving curriculum development—actually in improving most aspects of the educational process.

COMPONENTS TO CONSIDER IN DEVELOPING A CURRICULUM

Curricularists deal with the question, "*What* shall be included for purposes of learning?" After that they deal with *how* to present or arrange the *what* that is selected for learning so that students can learn or experience it. In other words, first they deal with knowledge and content specifically, and then they deal with teaching and learning experiences. Regardless of their philosophical orientation, they should not ignore these two elements.

Curriculum Content.

All curricula have content, regardless of their design or developmental model. How individuals view the content is impacted by their view of knowledge and reality—their philosophical postures. Those who believe in the traditional philosophies "discover" knowledge by using their senses. Also, to them knowledge is "objective"; it can be measured and therefore tested.

Those who view the world from a progressive posture "invent" knowledge according to their relationships with others and the environment. The meaning and truth of a child's experience depend on their relationship to the situations in which he or she is acting.

Those who are part of the romantic position view knowledge and likewise content from an existential or phenomenological epistemology. To these individuals, knowledge and reality refer to the immediate inner experience of the self. Knowledge and truth in this view are self-awareness or self-insight. This form of truth is extended beyond the self as a person attempts to understand other human beings.

Conceptions of Content. Groups charged with curriculum planning have options in content selection that are influenced by their philosophical outlooks. Actually, they have the problem of overchoice. There is too much content to include, and they must somehow make sense of what is available and select that which will enable students to learn the most—whatever curriculum design or developmental model they implement. This task can perhaps be made a bit easier if curricularists think of just how they define curriculum content. Parker and Rubin have noted that when educators speak of content, they refer "to the compendium of information which comprises the learning materials for a particular course of a given grade." This information may consist of "facts, laws, theories, and generalizations," as in the case of mathematics or science courses, or it may consist of "a description of events" trends, or categories, as in the case of a history course.[27]

Some educators argue that it is more important to learn process than content. Such a statement dichotomizes content and process, when in reality they should receive equal emphasis in the school's curriculum. In truth, process is a type of specialized content, related to methodology and procedures. Parker and Rubin indicate that process suggests "random or ordered operations which can be associated with knowledge and with human activities." Varied processes can help "create" knowledge, as well as "communicate" and "utilize" knowledge.[28]

Emphasis on process does not reduce the value of students' gaining knowledge, but rather affirms that students need to be active in their learning. Furthermore, such underscoring of process indicates that students must progress beyond the simple acquisition of knowledge; they must use the knowledge, if they are to gain appreciation and understanding of it.

Content is more than just information to be learned for school purposes. Dewey argued long ago that if content is to be more than information for school purposes it must bear some relationship to "some questions with which the learner is concerned," and it must "fit into his more direct acquaintance so as to increase its efficacy and deepen its meaning."[29] When selecting content the curriculum planner must take into account the potential of the content to address all the cognitive, social, and psychological dimensions of the individual student.

Some curricularists might conclude that content is really another term for knowledge. Content (subject matter) is a compendium of facts, concepts, generalizations, principles, and theories similar to disciplined knowledge. Additionally, school content does incorporate methods of processing information. But, knowledge, whether disciplined, like chemistry, or non-disciplined, like environmental education, is concerned with the

KNOWLEDGE⎯⎯⎯⎯⎯⎯⎯⎯→ Content ⎯⎯⎯⎯⎯⎯⎯⎯→Knowledge
(formal organization of   (selected from knowledge   (understanding of school
information)   source for educational   content at levels sufficient
                            purposes)   for use)

advancement of understanding and the exploration of unknown areas. In contrast, content and processes arranged in school subjects do not provide students with opportunities for advancing the realm of knowledge, but rather opportunities for discovering knowledge that is new to them but known by scholars and practitioners outside of the school. School content, then, is distinguished from knowledge by its purpose.

All curriculum content—that is, facts, concepts, generalizations, and so on— should enable students to gain understanding and to apply that understanding to daily living—present and anticipated. Content selected should contribute to the students' knowledge or levels of understanding. Considering content in terms of its meaning as knowledge allows or enables the curriculum planner to be more effective in the content-selection process. The diagram above might make these distinctions clearer.

Organization of Content. The capitalized version of knowledge in the previous diagram is all information that has been organized by scholars for the advancement of understanding. Such knowledge is organized according to various knowledge theories. Paul Hirst has advanced a "forms of knowledge" theory that organizes knowledge into distinct domains with unique types of concepts in specialized relationships. For instance, he observes that mathematics has unique categorical concepts of number, integer, and matrix. Physics has unique concepts of matter and energy. These concepts are organized into specialized networks whose relationships influence the particular types of meanings that can be derived from them. These specialized organizations of knowledge can be distinguished by the different types of tests, or processes, utilized to determine the truth or validity of the propositions.[30]

How knowledge is organized in "reality" depends on the philosophical views of the scholar. Curriculum planners who favor subject-centered designs would accept most, if not all, of what Hirst discusses. However, those who accept learner-centered curriculum designs might consider that the school curriculum organizes personal knowledge rather than what some would call objective knowledge. Persons like Hirst and subject-centered advocates in many cases view knowledge as things and relationships that are real and awaiting discovery in the outer world. To the learner-centered design champion, however, knowledge relates to the individual's process of personalizing the outer world as his or her inner potential interacts with outer reality.[31]

Perhaps the best posture for curriculum designers is to recognize the many variations among interpretations of knowledge and its organization. They would be wise to remember what Bruner was quick to point out—that the knowledge they identify and create cannot be conceived of in terms of absolute truth: "Knowledge is a model we construct to give meaning and structure to regularities in experience." The way we organize knowledge is an invention for "referring experiences economical and connected. We invent concepts such as force in physics, . . . motive in psychology, style in literature as a means to the end of comprehension.[32]

Faced with organizing content for the curriculum, program planners usually use two organizers—logical and psychological. In following the *logical* organization, they organize content according to certain rules, to make it manageable. Certain concepts are central to the content, and others are prerequisite to other concepts. In economics, for example, the concepts of supply and demand are major conceptual organizers. Without these concepts, the concepts of capital and labor or the marketplace cannot be grouped. Arranging economics content in this manner makes sense—but it really does not denote the way an individual might actually learn economics.

To detail this process, curricularists consider a *psychological* organization: How do people learn or process information? Most educators assume that content should be organized by going from the students' immediate environment to a more distant environment. Content, in other words, should be organized so that the concrete is experienced first, then the more abstract. This psychological factor is a key principle of sequencing content.

Criteria for Selecting Content.

Regardless of their curriculum design preferences or their philosophical orientations, curriculum planners have to apply criteria in choosing curriculum content. Although the criteria are common to most curricular orientations, persons in the various philosophical camps might place greater emphasis on particular criteria.

SELF-SUFFICIENCY. Israel Scheffler argues that the prime guiding principle for content selection is helping the learners to attain maximum self-sufficiency in the most economical manner. He elaborates three types of economy—economy of teaching effort and educational resources; economy of students' efforts; and economy of subject matter's extent of generalizability.[33]

This criterion—helping learners to attain maximum self-sufficiency—is also supported by many humanists, radicals, and reconceptualists as a means by which learners can actualize their potential and crystallize their identities.

SIGNIFICANCE. Content to be learned is significant only to the degree to which it contributes to the basic ideas, concepts, principles, generalizations, and so on, of the overall aims of the curriculum, and to the development of particular learning abilities, skills, processes, and attitude formation.

Taba noted that we should not just select content based on the cognitive aspects of learners, but also on their affective dimensions.[34] Even though most curriculum planners note that significance is central, they often disagree as to what is significant. Those who favor subject matter designs think of significance in terms of what knowledge needs to be transmitted to students. Those who favor learner-centered designs think of significance in terms of how it contributes to the meaningful experiences of the pupils. Those who advocate problem-centered designs would consider significance in terms of particular social, political, and economic issues.

VALIDITY. Validity is the authenticity of the content selected. In this time of information explosion, knowledge selected for school content can quickly become obsolete, and even incorrect. As new knowledge is discovered, content assumed valid may become misleading at best and false at worst. Validity must be verified at the initial selection of curriculum content, but it also needs to be checked at regular intervals through the duration of the curricular program to determine if content originally valid continues to be so.

Validity would seem to be a rather straightforward criterion. Something is either accurate or inaccurate; something either happened or it did not. Nevertheless, the ideological stance that any individual brings to a situation vastly influences what he or she perceives as valid. This is why some can state that certain information in school content is valid or truthful, while others can consider the same information invalid. Revisionists, radical school critics, and reconstructionists would state that much of the curriculum offered to students is invalid.[35]

Another way of looking at validity is in relation to selected goals and objectives. Is the content sound in relation to such goals and objectives? People can come to different conclusions about the validity of the content in light of the various philosophies they support and the curriculum designs they prefer. The content they choose will be valid to the extent that it coincides with the goals and objectives of the curriculum.[36]

INTEREST. Another criterion is interest. To those who favor the learner-centered design, this is a key criterion. These persons note that knowledge exists in the learner when it is meaningful to his or her life. When it fails to be meaningful, it dehumanizes education.[37]

The interest criterion has been with us since the times of the child-centered school in the 1920s. Radical advocates of this movement urged that the child should be the source of the curriculum—that, in other words, the children's interest should determine the curriculum.

Dewey's concern was that interest had come to be interpreted narrowly as choices expressed by children. He noted that waiting for children to express their interests, what they wanted and needed, "transferred the responsibility of the teacher to those taught."[38] Children's interests are transitory and sometimes accidental. The teacher has the responsibility of identifying and cultivating those interests that are prized by the community and that will, if addressed, allow the individual to function in ways that will facilitate successful participation in society.

Those currently advocating a learner-centered curriculum point out that the content of the curriculum must be selected with students' interests in mind. But, the school experience should create and broaden interests as well as address them. A key question is: "Are students' current interests of long-lasting educational value for both the students and society?" Dealing with this question is difficult because it assumes educators possess some degree of perception regarding future society and students' places in that future. The criterion of students' interests should be weighted and adjusted to allow for students' maturity, their prior experiences, the educational and social value of their interests, and the way they are expected to interact within society.

UTILITY. Utility concerns the usefulness of the content. Again, how a person defines usefulness is influenced by his or her philosophical view and favored curriculum design. Usefulness to those favoring the subject-centered design is often judged in terms of how the content learned will enable students to use that knowledge in job situations and other adult activities. Usefulness to those in the learner-centered camp is related to how the content enables the individual to gain an accurate perception of his or her self-identity and to attain meaning in his or her life. Is the content useful for the learner developing his or her human potential? Proponents of the problem-centered mode would think of content as having utility if it has direct application to ongoing life and to social and political issues.

LEARNABILITY. Could anyone select content without considering this obvious criterion? Some critics of the schools say yes. Certain contents are selected that are out of the range of experiences of particular students and are thus difficult, if not impossible, to learn. Further, selected contents are sometimes arranged and presented in ways that make their learning difficult for some students. Critics often say that content selected reflects a middle-class bias and that it is organized to favor those who have convergent (and right-answer) learning styles. The learnability criterion relates to the optimal placement and appropriate organization and sequencing of content. Further, it addresses the issue of appropriateness for the intended student audience.

FEASIBILITY. Feasibility, the last criterion, forces curriculum planners to consider content in light of the time allowed, the resources available, the expertise of current staff, the nature of the political climate, the existing legislation, and the amount of public monies available. Although educators may think that they have an entire world of content from which to choose, they do have limitations on their actions. Even the number of days in the school calendar, for example, limits what can be taught. So do the size of the classroom and the personnel of the school. Content selection has to be considered within the context of the existing reality—which usually boils down to economics and politics.

In this connection, David Pratt analyzes economic and political feasibility in terms of "constraints." The curriculum, he argues, is "largely governed by [such] constraints, [and] unfeasibility is commonly due to the magnitude of the constraints." It may be necessary to "ask whether any of the constraints can be changed."[39] Here we allude to economic compromises, shifting funds, altering public opinion, compromising or negotiating with pressure groups, and/or becoming involved in school-community politics.

Curriculum Experiences.

Curriculum content is the "meat" of the curriculum plan, but we can consider the experiences planned for the students as the "heart." Experiences are the key factors that shape the learners' orientations to the content and, ultimately, their understanding of it. Taba noted that "perhaps the first important consideration in achieving a wider range of objectives is the fact that the learning experiences, and not the content as such, are the means for achieving all objectives besides those of knowledge and understanding."[40]

Curriculum experience involves the instructional component of the curriculum. Instruction refers primarily to the human interaction between teacher and student in ways that are designed to achieve the goals of the school. It is specialized behavior planned in light of particular objectives. It consists of teaching methods and activities that take place in the classroom for the purpose of attaining the schools' goals. There are a multitude of both teaching methods and educational activities. Examples of teaching methods are inquiry strategies, lecture, discussion, and demonstration. Examples of educational activities are viewing films, conducting experiments, viewing videos, interacting with computer programs, taking field trips, and listening to speakers.[41] Both are integral parts of the curriculum and must be carefully considered in light of the content selected.

At a theoretical level, instruction includes all the actions of teachers necessary to influence the students' behavior and, ultimately, their learning. The particular actions of a teacher may vary according to the teaching method and/or educational activities, but they all have the purpose of influencing students' behavior and learning.[42]

EXPERIENCES VERSUS ACTIVITIES. When discussing curriculum we do not make a fine distinction between teaching methods and educational activities. Rather, we group all the actions of both teachers and students under the title learning experiences. But this was not always the case. At the turn of this century, the terms *learning activities* and *learning experiences* were absent in the educational literature. One read instead about *recitations, exercises,* and *projects.* But with the evolution of the field of psychology, and also the work of progressivism led by Kilpatrick and Ellsworth Collings (a doctoral student of Kilpatrick's), the activities of the learners received more attention in the educational equation.[43]

Educators began to realize that the term *learning activities* did not describe adequately the dynamics of the teaching-learning situation. Many children could be engaged in the same learning activities, but the experiences each pupil derived might be quite different. By 1935, the term *learning activities* was being replaced with the term *learning experiences*. Most writers of curriculum today talk of learning experiences, especially since Tyler used the term in his classic text.[44]

The shift in terms is more than a mere change of words. It also indicates a difference in intent and result—a focus on processes or products. This dichotomy is still debated in the curriculum field. Sometimes the discussion seems to be an argument between those who value the journey of education (the means, the learning process) and those who prize the destination (knowledge, understanding, ends). Maxine Green favors learning experiences, not activities, for their potential of having personal significance for learners.[45] Others with this view want students to encounter the curriculum content through experiences that will enable them to do something with it and to create meaning from it.

WHOLENESS AND CONTINUITY. Students' curriculum experiences should be such that they see life's wholeness and continuity in activity.[46] Students should see "that every concrete entity is experienced within a context of wider relationships and possibilities. Conscious life is always open to a never-ending web of entailments and unfoldings. No content of experience is just what it appears to be here and now without any further prospects or associations.[47]

MEANS AND ENDS. Persons who favor learner-centered designs and problem-centered designs tend to view learning experiences as means—as valuable in themselves. These persons consider learning experiences to be expressions of individuality. In their analysis of the curriculum, they tend to focus on the learning process and to charge the curriculum designer with offering the best of conditions: encounters that allow individuals to be liberated to fully achieve their human potential.

But many in the curriculum field, though they do not necessarily ignore completely the process aspect of the educational experience, place major emphasis on the ends of education. These individuals favor subject-centered curriculum designs. Curriculum-development activities and implementation strategies are performed with the intention of achieving the aims and goals of the school. Instruction is the means for attaining the content that has been selected and the overall goals of the program. Ends-oriented curricularists view learning opportunities not as valuable in themselves but as instrumental in attaining specified consequences. These persons are product-oriented. They look at the outcomes resulting from the interface of students, teachers, and the curriculum. They are interested in results; not just inherent attributes of experiences.

Means-oriented curricularists, in contrast, seem to be looking at effects that are more personal and individual and that perhaps address human needs. They are looking at the effects of the experiences to determine whether or not students gain a sense of personal fulfillment and power over their own lives and a commitment to responsible action. Those favoring the ends orientation are interested in effects that seem to be academic: Did the students "learn" the content of the curriculum?

Relationship of Content and Experiences.

No curriculum—regardless of its design—can ignore content and experiences. Although subject-centered designs stress content, they also consider its delivery. Learner-centered designs focus on the centrality of the students and their experiences, but they, too, consider the experiences in relation to what is learned.

What educators need to remember is that, in reality, content and experiences do not exist apart. If students are thinking, they are usually thinking about something—some content. If they are engaged in some experience, such as reading a book, they are combining both an experience and content. Content and learning experiences always comprise curriculum unity. Students cannot just engage in learning, or in studying, without experiencing some activity and some content. Likewise, students cannot deal with content without being engaged in some experience or some activity.

Curriculum planners sometimes separate content from experience. However, they realize that in the actual delivery of educational programs both elements coexist. Taba noted, "One can speak of effective learning only if both content and process are fruitful and significant."[48]

Criteria for Selecting Experiences.
Some criteria are useful for considering po-

tential content and experiences. Validity, especially congruence of objectives and goals, is an appropriate example. Other criteria are expressed by the question: "Will the experience do what we wish it to do in light of the overall aims and goals of the program and specific objectives of the curriculum?" Following are specific extensions of this question. Are the experiences:

1. Valid in light of the ways in which knowledge and skills will be applied in out-of-school situations?
2. Feasible in terms of time, staff expertise, facilities available within and outside of the school, community expectations?
3. Optimal in terms of students' learning the content?
4. Capable of allowing students to develop their thinking skills and rational powers?
5. Capable of stimulating in students greater understanding of their own existence as individuals and as members of groups?
6. Capable of fostering in students an openness to new experiences and a tolerance for diversity?
7. Such that they will facilitate learning and motivate students to continue learning?
8. Capable of allowing students to address their needs?
9. Such that students can broaden their interests?
10. Such that they will foster the total development of students in cognitive, affective, psychomotor, social, and spiritual domains?

Educational Environments.

As we cannot separate content from experiences in the actual delivery of a curriculum, neither can we divorce the experiencing of content from the space within which experience occurs. Until recently educators have not given much attention to the environment of the school other than to make sure that the children had adequate light, places to sit, desks upon which to write, and places to hang their clothes. As John Holt points out, "We would have to worry a lot less in our schools about 'motivating' children, about finding ways to

make good things happen, if we would just provide more spaces in which good things *could* happen." Space, Holt notes, creates activity; it allows students "to generate places and moods."[49]

Educational space is crucial to meaningful educational experiences. Children who experience a creative environment are much more likely to be stimulated, to realize their potential, and to be excited about learning.[50]

Presently, there is increasing concern about educational space, namely how to define it, classify it, and organize it. The environments educators design should facilitate students' attending to the experiences and content that they have selected and organized. The environments should stimulate purposeful student activity. They should allow for a depth and range of content and experiences that facilitate learning.

Persons who favor subject-centered designs might give only scant consideration to the educational environment. They might feel that it matters little where learning is to occur. But, even these persons would have to admit that if, for example, a teacher were presenting science information, the laboratory environment would, at times, be more appropriate than the lecture hall. Persons who favor learner-centered designs, on the other hand, might be more inclined to take seriously the planning of meaningful environments. Spaces need to allow individuals to grow; they are part of the quality of experience for students. Ideally, persons creating programs, regardless of their design preference, will take into consideration the nature of the space in which the curriculum is to be realized by both teachers and students.

Criteria for Environment. Educational environments should address social needs, security needs, and belongingness needs, as well as the development of inner awareness, appreciation, and empathy for others. In addition, they should enable students to master intended learnings. The environments should stimulate purposeful student activity, and they should allow for a depth and range of activities that facilitate learning.

Brian Castaldi has suggested that, when contemplating and designing educational environments, planners keep in mind four criteria—adequacy, suitability, efficiency, and economy.[51] *Adequacy* refers to the space planned: Is it of sufficient size to accommodate the students for whom the space is intended? Adequacy also refers to environmental controls: Is the light sufficient so that students can read with ease? Are the visual displays big enough so that students can see them? Are the materials serviceable for the learning styles of the students? Are the acoustics appropriate so that students can hear?

Closely related to adequacy is *suitability*. Is the shape of the environment suitable for the type of activity planned? If some information is going to be demonstrated, is the environment such that all students can see with ease? If students are to engage in discovery, does the environment help or hinder such activity?

When dealing with the criterion of adequacy, we also consider the relationships between the various spaces within a school. How do spaces designed for individual investigation relate to spaces planned for storage and retrieval of educational materials? How do spaces created for small-group investigation relate to spaces designed for small-group viewing of educational media? Will students be able to move around the room without disrupting other students?

Ensuring *efficiency* involves attending to those characteristics of educational space that are likely to improve its instructional effectiveness or operational characteristics: Does the environment as planned allow the educational activity to be carried out with a minimum of effort? Will the environment as planned facilitate the greatest amount of learning with the least amount of effort by students and teachers? If students are to listen to audio tapes at their desks, can they be placed where they will not be disturbed by unnecessary noise or by students engaged in other activities?

Castaldi's final criterion, *economy*, relates to actual savings, in terms of capital outlay, that can be achieved by the initial architectural design or by a modification of an existing environment for a particular aspect of the curriculum. Economy deals with the cost of teaching some part of the curriculum in the environment provided. It also relates to economy of students' and teachers' efforts. Time is a resource, and curricula are designed to make maximum use of time to achieve basic program goals and objectives. Sometimes, for example, students spend a major part of their day just waiting for the teacher to get to them. Sometimes, teachers spend too much time going from one part of the school to another to engage in a different school activity. It could be that planners can design educational environments so that students and teachers are very near to the appropriate spaces for their different activities.[52]

PARTICIPANTS IN DEVELOPING THE CURRICULUM

Developing or designing a curriculum involves a large number of persons, both school-based and community-based. It also involves different levels of planning: The classroom level, the school level, the national level, and even the international level. Sometimes the designers work in harmony, and sometimes they are at odds with each other. In fact, the competition among them for certain types of curricula is what makes curriculum development largely a political activity in which there is competition for authority and control, for scarce resources, and for primacy of certain values.

Political-Arena Participants.

This competition for control involves struggles among educators and policymakers and the public. Most educators are workng to have their particular views of purpose of education and the curriculum become dominant. All curriculum developers are concerned with attaining the greatest benefits from the curriculum. The politics of education is concerned with who benefits and how those benefits are determined. Curriculum is concerned with providing programs to benefit learners. Curriculum participants—both leaders and followers—have to determine what types of curricula will benefit what students, how to select those curricula, how to determine who will receive the benefits of particular curricula, and how to deliver those benefits.[53]

School-Arena Participants.

Macdonald advocated that all parties affected by the curriculum should be involved in deciding its nature and purpose. He presented a model that showed several groups, all directing their thinking, feelings, and knowledge to curriculum activity. The model, shown in Figure 8-6, depicts the players in continuous interactions.

Teachers. The teacher occupies a central position in curriculum decision making. Michael Kirst points out that the teacher decides what aspects of the curriculum, newly developed or ongoing, to implement or stress in a particular class. The teacher also determines whether to spend time, and how much of it, on developing thinking skills or basic skills.[54]

At the classroom level, teachers set the stage and determine the direction and quality of the curriculum. They define what curriculum objectives within the overall framework of the curriculum to teach. The content and experiences they select will reflect their views of the curriculum design. Teachers also decide who will get what kind of curriculum content and what types of experiences.

In addition to being curriculum participants at the classroom level, teachers are also involved with curriculum committees. Some of these committees are organized by grade level—for example, an elementary curriculum committee; others are organized by subject area. Some might be organized according to the type of student under consideration—for example, a committee for the gifted or a committee for the learning disabled. The committee format is the standard way of involving teachers in curriculum activity outside of the classroom level.[55]

Actually teachers are involved, or should be involved, with every phase of curriculum development. Although not all teachers wish to be involved in all stages of curriculum development, all teachers, by the nature of their role, are involved in the implementation of the curriculum: Teaching is implementing the curriculum. Teachers need to be part of the total curriculum-development activity—from the formation of aims and goals to the evaluation and maintenance of the curriculum. They need to help develop curriculum packages, conceptualize resource designs, design educational environments, assist in piloting curriculum units, and communicate with the general public on new curricular projects.

Students. If we accept that all who are impacted by the curriculum need to be involved in its planning, we cannot ignore the students. Students seldom have formal influence on what they will learn or even on the manner of their experiencing the content. This is, however, changing in some schools. Students, especially at the secondary level, are sometimes involved in curriculum committees. Some schools are also involving secondary students in conducting surveys and needs assessments. As Ronald Doll notes, students are the "consumers" of education and they deserve to supply input to educators regarding curricular matters.[56]

Principals. Principals are often considered to be the curriculum leaders in the school setting. Although this is the ideal notion, principals are frequently little more than go-betweens from the central office to the parents and the school staff developing

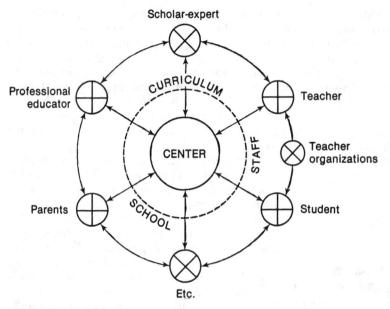

Scholar-expert

Professional educator

Teacher

CURRICULUM

CENTER

STAFF

Teacher organizations

Parents

SCHOOL

Student

Etc.

FIGURE 8-6 Continuous Interaction Model for Curriculum Activity. Source: from James B. Macdonald, "Responsible Curriculum Development," in E. W. Eisner, ed., *Confronting Curriculum Reform* (Boston: Little, Brown, 1971), p. 71.

and implementing the curriculum. Often principals just do not have the time to engage in "real" curriculum development. Principals who are actively engaged in curriculum development and implementation delegate to others portions of their usual managerial responsibilities of running their schools. In most cases, however, the managerial functions of the school—not curriculum issues—take up most of the principals' time.

The principal must be supportive of curricular activity within the school and must actively work to help the staff and others create the program. John Goodlad and others have noted that the school is the arena for curriculum development and that the role of the principal is essential for curriculum change and curriculum reform.[57] The principal should be a key participant because he or she is in daily contact with teachers and thus knows their needs and their reactions, both positive and negative, to the existing or developing curriculum. This educational leader can serve to interpret local as well as national trends. In addition to setting the stage, this person also serves a crucial role as supervisor by ensur-

ing that the instructional component of the program is viable.[58]

Some argue that the principal should initiate curriculum change; others think the principal should facilitate implementation of curriculum decisions already made. As a facilitator, the principal furnishes time for curricular activity; arranges for in-service training; sits on a curriculum advisory committee as a resource agent; and orders necessary support materials. In small schools we would expect principals to serve more actively as curriculum initiators, developers, and implementers.

Curriculum Specialists. Curriculum specialists play a major role in curriculum-development and implementation activities. They are known by many titles: coordinators, supervisors, directors, or chairpersons. An individual's title usually gives some idea of his or her responsibilities. Persons called curriculum directors or coordinators are usually educators who are known as curriculum generalists.[59] They have a broad knowledge of the nature of curriculum and are experts in creating and implementing curricula. They usually do not have a content major. Other generalists in a school district are known as directors of elementary or secondary education. Usually, these persons have expertise in administration as well as curriculum, but their focus is either elementary or secondary.

Persons with specific content specialties are often titled as supervisors, chairs, or heads of a particular subject area, for example supervisor (chair, head) of science. These persons have some background in curriculum, but they have a content major and are often more concerned with supervising instruction.[60]

Curriculum specialists are responsible for ensuring that programs are conceptualized, designed, created, and implemented. This requires a high level of understanding of curriculum and skill in managing people. Curriculum specialists need knowledge of curriculum design and development, in translating curriculum theory into practice, and in supervising and evaluating instruction. Unruh and Unruh have noted that curriculum specialists must be versatile, sensitive, patient, and skilled in human relations. Additionally, they need competence in decision making and leadership. The authors identified ten tasks of the curriculum specialist: (1) defining goals and objectives; (2) developing needs and problems; (3) creating conceptual models of curriculum development; (4) developing plans, strategies, and procedures that encourage people to work together; (5) fostering interrelationships and comprehensiveness in curriculum development; (6) involving people in curriculum development; (7) communicating within and outside of the schools; (8) increasing professionalism regarding curriculum; (9) planning implementation; and (10) evaluating the curriculum.[61]

The Assistant (Associate) Superintendent. In many school systems, the person with the primary responsibility for curriculum activity is the assistant or associate superintendent. This person, a line administrator, reports directly to the superinten-

dent, who is in the forefront. In many school districts curriculum directors or coordinators report to the assistant or associate superintendent. Ideally, this assistant or associate superintendent: (1) chairs or serves as advisor to the general curriculum advisory committee; (2) is responsible for informing the superintendent of the major trends occurring in the field of curriculum and how these trends are being translated in the school system; (3) works with elementary and secondary directors or coordinators regarding curricular activity; (4) is in charge of the budget for curricular activity; (5) provides input in the statement of philosophy, aims, and goals; (6) guides evaluation relevant to aims and goals; and (7) manages long-term and short-term activities designed to strengthen programs.[62] This educator also helps formulate policies concerning curriculum innovation.

The Superintendent. The chief administrator of the school system is the superintendent, who is charged with keeping the system running. The superintendent responds to matters before the school board, initiates curriculum activity, starts programs for the in-service training of teachers, informs all district personnel of changes occurring in other schools, and processes demands coming from outside the system for change or maintenance of educational offerings.

Good superintendents also inspire change and enable curricula to be responsive to changing demands. They are directly responsible to the school board for the total educational action in the district. They must establish the means for curricular action, interpret all aspects of the school's program to the board, and set up communication networks to inform the public of and involve the public in the curriculum process.

Boards of Education. Boards of education are the legal agents for the schools. Comprised of laypersons usually elected as representatives of the general public, these boards are spokespersons for the community, who are responsible for the overall management of the schools. They are also responsible for being informed about the realm of curriculum and for relating the existing curriculum to the goals of the school system. They are involved as new curricula are being proposed so they can be aware of the rationale for changes recommended. The school boards, in fact, have the final say about whether a new program piloted is finally implemented district-wide. They enact district policies that facilitate the development and implementation of new curricula. They vote the funds that enable curricula to go from an idea to reality.

School boards, along with the central administrative staffs, do seem to be losing control of the "running" of the school districts. In some cases, control has been taken away by the actions of legislatures defining just what basic education is. In other cases, special-interest groups have gone to court to alter board policies if such policies are found unacceptable.[63] In many school districts the school board, rather than being the leader in determining curriculum and policy, plays a secondary role. Federal, state, and local professionals carry the charge for creating new curricula.

Lay Citizens. Few people would contest that the schools belong to the public. But although laypeople have been assuming increasing roles in curriculum activity, the role of the lay community in curriculum matters is still minimal. Most of the public, though perhaps concerned in general terms with the schools, are really not interested in becoming actively engaged in curriculum development.[64] Most possess little knowledge about course content, course designs, or models of curriculum development.

Research indicates that citizen participation in curriculum policy making tends to be superficial and reactive. Citizens do participate, however, when goals are being determined and often when the changes have been completed.[65] This may be because considering and implementing new programs involves needs analysis, and so receives me-

dia coverage. In general, however, even though lay groups may not be actively involved in curriculum development, a major conflict between the citizens and the school board is usually won by the citizens.

Most authorities maintain that the lay public should be involved in curriculum activity. However, there is still some discussion as to the extent and manner of their participation. Ideally, citizens should be involved in real problems and should be members of formal committees or groups established by the school district. They can, for example, be members of school-sponsored "overall" or "phase" committees. Overall committees attend to the total school program whereas phase committees focus on a particular aspect of education. Citizens for effective schools would comprise an overall committee; citizens for bilingual education would be a phase committee.[66]

Participants Outside the School District.

Many participants outside the school district impact the nature and scope of the curriculum and influence who will receive the curriculum. These participants exist at various levels. Figure 8-7 shows decision making in curriculum planning according to levels. It starts with level one, the individual teacher, and proceeds upward and outward. The in-district participation ends at the school district level, but beyond that are the state, the national, and international levels (the latter is not shown in the figure). In particular, various social and political forces (left side of the figure) and legal structures and agencies (right side) impact on the different curriculum levels.

The Federal Government. For much of this century, the federal government was content to allow the states and the local districts to deal with curricular matters. But beginning in the 1960s the federal government became a powerful factor in determining the kinds of educational materials for and their uses in the schools. This corresponded with the Sputnik and Great

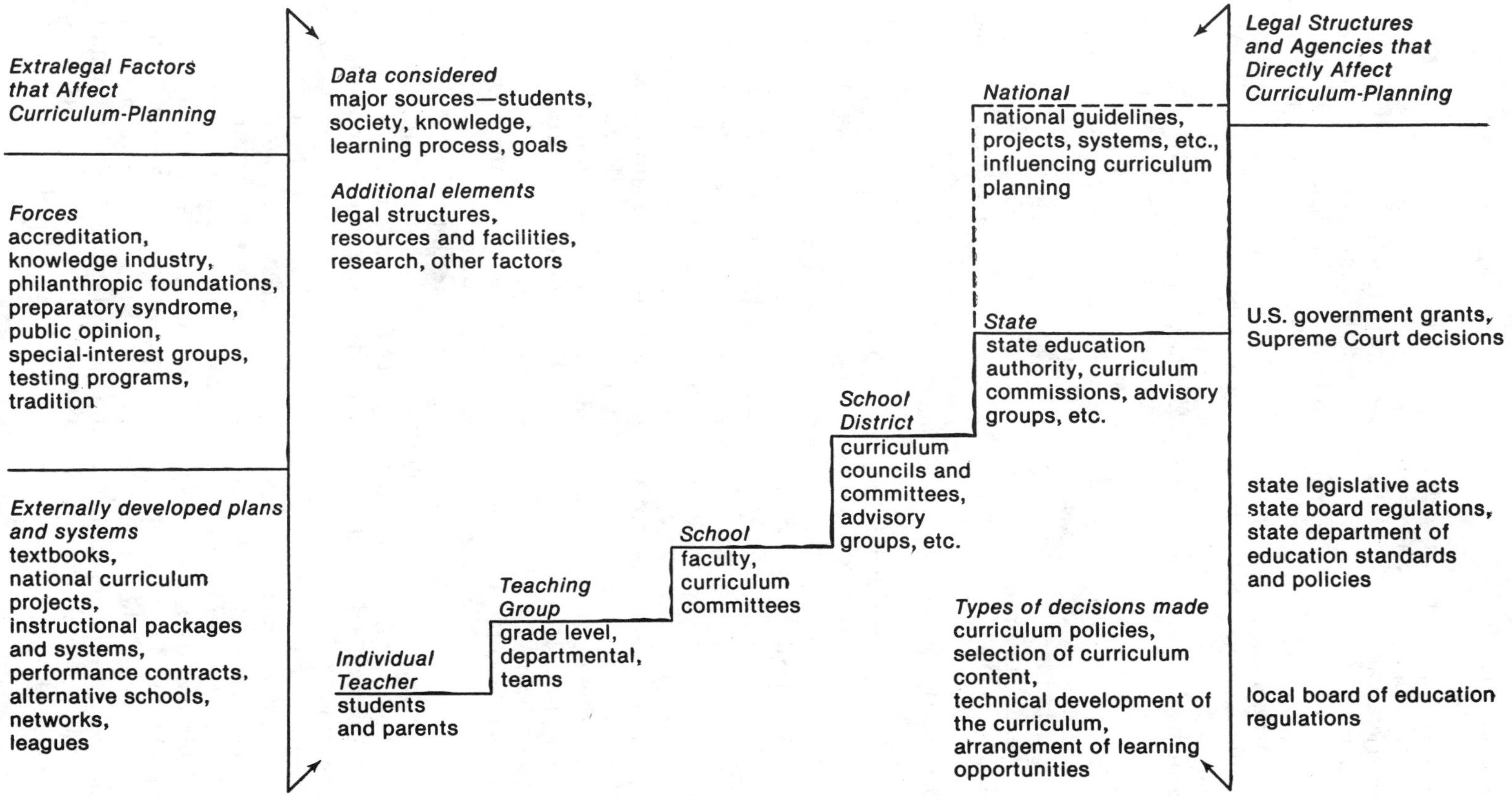

Extralegal Factors that Affect Curriculum-Planning

Forces
accreditation, knowledge industry, philanthropic foundations, preparatory syndrome, public opinion, special-interest groups, testing programs, tradition

Externally developed plans and systems
textbooks, national curriculum projects, instructional packages and systems, performance contracts, alternative schools, networks, leagues

Data considered
major sources—students, society, knowledge, learning process, goals

Additional elements
legal structures, resources and facilities, research, other factors

Individual Teacher
students and parents

Teaching Group
grade level, departmental, teams

School
faculty, curriculum committees

School District
curriculum councils and committees, advisory groups, etc.

Types of decisions made
curriculum policies, selection of curriculum content, technical development of the curriculum, arrangement of learning opportunities

National
national guidelines, projects, systems, etc., influencing curriculum planning

State
state education authority, curriculum commissions, advisory groups, etc.

Legal Structures and Agencies that Directly Affect Curriculum-Planning

U.S. government grants, Supreme Court decisions

state legislative acts, state board regulations, state department of education standards and policies

local board of education regulations

FIGURE 8-7 Decision-Making Levels in Curriculum Planning.
Source: from J. Galen Saylor and William H. Alexander, *Planning Curriculum for Schools*, 3rd ed. (New York: Holt, Rinehart & Winston, 1974), 52. Reprinted by permission of Holt, Rinehart & Winston.

Society eras. Federal dollars established and maintained regional laboratories and innovations, first for science and math and then later for most subject areas.

Today controversy exists over the role and extent of involvement by the federal government in curriculum matters. It has been suggested, for example, that the federal government might well assume five specific roles. The federal government:

1. Could identify critical educational issues, many of which are related to curriculum, such as the demand for back to the basics or a common curriculum for all students.
2. Could synthesize the vast amount of knowledge regarding education, specifically curriculum.
3. Could promote research regarding curriculum materials.
4. Could support the application and dissemination of knowledge, especially about curriculum.
5. Could encourage the preparation of persons interested in the field of education, including curriculum.[67]

State Agencies. During the last decade and continuing into this one, states increased their role in educational policy making. Much of this growth has been at the expense of the local school district. In many states, the state board of education has made formal recommendations and issued guidelines as to what the curriculum should contain and how it should be organized. The growing involvement of the states is based in part on the position that the management of education is truly a state function, a posture that is augmented by the decrease in federal funds.[68]

States impact the curriculum in many ways. State legislatures frequently publish guidelines on what shall be taught. They also mandate such courses as driver education and drug education to deal with perceived social problems. Pressure groups operating on a state basis, who frequently vie to have their interests represented in the curriculum, affect curriculum decisions as well. Often these associations or groups lobby in the legislatures for the curriculum to treat particular content and/or address certain students.

With the publication of the numerous reports on the reform of education in the 1980s, state agencies throughout the nation have initiated minimum competency movements aimed at academic reform. Much legislation regarding the testing of competency skills has been passed. By 1983 as many as forty-two states sought to increase the rigor of such curriculum areas as mathematics, science, English, and foreign language, and forty-four states had increased high school graduation requirements.[69]

Regional Organizations. States often participate voluntarily in curriculum matters. Two regional organizations have become formalized to ensure such participation: Regional educational laboratories and research and development (R and D) centers. Regional educational laboratories influence school curricula by providing guidance in the production of materials and by furnishing consultants who serve on planning teams. R and D centers investigate specific curricular problems, among other problems, whose results can be of value to curriculum planners. R and D centers also aid curriculum specialists by documenting the effectiveness of particular programs or approaches.

Another type of regional organization is the intermediate school district. The term "intermediate district" or "educational service agency" (ESA) refers to an office or agency in a middle position between the state department of education and local school districts. Thirty-nine states have some form of intermediate school district. The average intermediate district comprises twenty to thirty school districts in about fifty square miles.[70]

In recent years, intermediate districts have provided school districts with resource personnel in such general areas of education as curriculum, instruction, and evaluation; in specialized areas, such as education of the handicapped, gifted and talented, and bilingual students; and in more specific areas, such as prekindergarten education, vocational education, data processing, and computer education.

Other Participants.

1. *Educational Publishers.* In large part, publishers have given the country an unofficial national curriculum. In most schools, the textbooks used frequently determine the curriculum. The power of the textbook is particularly evident when we realize that nearly 75 percent of the students' total classroom time is spent engaged with instructional materials. An even greater percentage of time—90 percent—is spent with instructional materials when students are doing homework. What students "know" usually reflects their textbooks' content.[71]

2. *Testing Organizations.* Along with educational publishers, testing organizations, such as the Educational Testing Service or Psychological Corporation, have also contributed to the making of a "national" curriculum. By standardizing the content tested, these organizations have impacted what content the curriculum will cover and how much emphasis will be given to particular topics.

3. *Professional Organizations.* Organizations such as the Association for Supervision and Curriculum Development, the National Council of Teachers of English, the National Council for the Social Studies, and the American Educational Research Association have indirectly influenced the curriculum. Their members bring messages and goals set forth at state and national conferences "back home," to be tried out in the local schools. Increasingly, such professional organizations are actually formalizing networks of schools to communicate curricular concerns and also to mount studies whose published reports set guidelines and standards for the creation of curricula.

Other professional organizations, such as the National Education Association and the American Federation of Teachers, have tried to involve teachers more directly in curriculum decision making. State affiliates of these organizations have worked with local districts to set up curricular goals. In some school districts, teacher organizations have made curriculum a negotiable matter.[72]

Many other people and groups outside of the schools also influence the curriculum in one way or another. Colleges and universities directly and indirectly influence curriculum development. Many educational consultants to the schools come from the colleges, for example. Pressure groups often organize to impact the curriculum too. Sometimes, individual educators and lay critics assume the role of educational reformers, and they attempt, mostly through their writings, to give direction to curriculum development.

Various foundations have also impacted curriculum formation, largely by supplying funds. The Ford, Rockefeller, Carnegie, and Kettering Foundations have made the most active efforts to modify the curriculum through pilot and experimental programs.

CONCLUSION

Curriculum planners faced with creating curricula really have an overchoice of curriculum development models from which to choose. Which models they select are influenced by their philosophical orientations and approaches to curriculum. Several subject-centered development models emphasize a technical-scientific approach to curriculum development—the major approach to curriculum creation today.

Likewise several models of a nontechnical-nonscientific approach to curriculum exist; these consider curriculum from a more "evolutionary" viewpoint. Persons who accept learner-centered designs tend to favor these models.

Diversity of approach characterizes curriculum creation. Most in the field of curriculum admit, however, that certain curriculum elements are universal; they require attention or at least awareness from all curricularists. Contents, experiences, and environments, for instance, are constants regardless of design or development—that is, whether a particular curriculum is being systematically planned or evolving naturalistically. A curriculum without content is no curriculum. A curriculum without experiences cannot be delivered or encountered by students. And a curriculum without a planned environment cannot be implemented.

The various models available, and the numerous elements of curriculum, present challenges to a vast array of participants, who exist at many levels—from the local to the national. People will no doubt continue to argue about who should have the major part in curriculum decision making.

Notes

1. Kathryn Feyereisn, A. John Fiorino, and Alene Nowak, *Supervision and Curriculum Renewal: A System Approach* (New York: Appleton-Century-Crofts, 1970), p. 204.
2. James B. Macdonald, "The Quality of Everyday Life in School," in J. B. Macdonald and E. Zaret, eds., *Schools in Search of Meaning* (Washington, D.C.: Association for Supervision and Curriculum Development, 1975), pp. 76–94.
3. Larry Cuban, "Determinants of Curriculum Change and Stability, 1870–1970," in J. Schaffarzick and G. Sykes, eds., *Value Conflicts and Curriculum Issues* (Berkeley, Calif.: McCutchan, 1979), pp. 139–196.
4. Franklin Bobbitt, *The Supervision of City Schools: Some General Principles of Management Applied to the Problems of City School Systems*, Twelfth Yearbook of the National Society for the Study of Education, Part I (Bloomington, Ill.: 1913), p. 11.
5. W. W. Charters, "Functional Analysis as the Basis for Curriculum Construction," *Journal of Educational Research* (October 1924), pp. 214–221. See Tanner and Tanner, *Curriculum Development: Theory Into Practice*, 2nd ed. (New York: Macmillan, 1980) for a discussion on Bobbitt and Charters.
6. W. W. Charters, *Curriculum Construction* (New York: Macmillan, 1923).
7. Ralph Tyler, *Basic Principles of Curriculum and Instruction* (Chicago: University of Chicago Press, 1949).
8. Hilda Taba, *Curriculum Development: Theory and Practice* (New York: Harcourt Brace, 1962).
9. Robert S. Zais, *Curriculum: Principles and Foundations* (New York: Crowell, 1976).
10. J. Galen Saylor and William M. Alexander, *Planning Curriculum for Schools* (New York: Holt, Rinehart, 1974). See also J. Galen Saylor, William M. Alexander, and Arthur J. Lewis, *Curriculum Planning for Better Teaching and Learning*, 4th ed. (New York: Holt, Rinehart, 1981).
11. Ibid.
12. John I. Goodlad and Maurice N. Richter, *The Development of a Conceptual System for Dealing with Problems of Curriculum and Instruction* (Los Angeles: Institute for Development of Educational Activities, University of California, 1966), p. 65.
13. Ibid.
14. Francis P. Hunkins, *Curriculum Development: Program Improvement* (Columbus, Ohio: Merrill, 1980); Hunkins, "A Systematic Model for Curriculum Development," *National Association of Secondary School Principals Bulletin* (May 1985), pp. 23–27.
15. John P. Miller and Wayne Seller, *Curriculum: Perspectives and Practice* (New York: Longman, 1985).
16. Herbert M. Kliebard, "The Tyler Rationale," in J. R. Gress and D. E. Purpel, eds., *Curriculum: An Introduction to the Field* (Berkeley, Calif.: McCutchan, 1978), pp. 256–267.
17. James Macdonald, "Curriculum Theory," in W. Pinar, ed., *Curriculum Theorizing: The Reconceptualists* (Berkeley, Calif.: McCutchan, 1975), pp. 5–13.
18. Herbert R. Kohl, *The Open Classroom* (New York: Random House, 1969), pp. 20, 40; see Tanner and Tanner, *Curriculum Development: Theory Into Practice*, 2nd ed. (New York: Macmillan, 1980) for a helpful discussion of the open-classroom model.
19. John Holt, *Freedom and Beyond* (New York: Dutton, 1972), p. 91.
20. Paul Goodman, *New Reformation* (New York: Random House, 1970), p. 86.
21. Ibid.
22. Gerald Weinstein and Mario D. Fantini, *Toward Humanistic Education: A Curriculum of Affect* (New York: Praeger, 1970).
23. Carl Rogers, *On Becoming* (New York: Delacorte, 1979); Rogers, *Freedom to Learn for the 1980s*, 2nd ed. (Columbus, Ohio: Merrill, 1983).
24. See Chris Argyris, *Integrating the Individual and the Organization* (New York: Wiley, 1964); Daniel Katz and Robert L. Kahn, *The Social Psychology of Organization* (New York: Wiley, 1966); and Rensis Likert, *New Patterns of Management* (New York: McGraw-Hill, 1961).
25. Carl Rogers, "A Plan for Self-Directed Change in an Educational System," *Educational Leadership* (May 1967), p. 718.
26. Ibid.
27. J. C. Parker and Louis J. Rubin, *Process as Content: Curriculum Design and the Application of Knowledge* (Chicago: Rand McNally, 1966), p. 1.
28. Ibid., p. 2.
29. John Dewey, *Democracy and Education* (New York: Macmillan, 1916), p. 186.
30. Paul Hirst, *Knowledge and the Curriculum* (London: Routledge & Kegan Paul, 1974).
31. James Macdonald, "A Transcendental Developmental Ideology." Gress and Purpel, eds., *Curriculum: An Introduction to the Field*, pp. 95–123.
32. Jerome S. Bruner, *On Knowing: Essays for the Left Hand* (Cambridge, Mass.: Harvard University Press, 1963), p. 120.
33. Israel Scheffler, "Justifying Curriculum Divisions," in J. Martin, ed., *Readings in the Philosophy of Education: A Study of Curriculum* (Boston: Allyn and Bacon, 1970), pp. 27–31.

34. Taba, *Curriculum Development: Theory and Practice*.
35. Bernice J. Wolfson, "Psychological Theory and Curricular Thinking," in A. Molnar, ed., *Current Thought on Curriculum* (Alexandria, Va: Association for Supervision and Curriculum Development, 1985), pp. 53–72.
36. A. Nicholls and S. H. Nicholls, *Developing a Curriculum: A Practical Guide* (London: Allen and Unwin, 1972).
37. Zvi Lamm, "The Status of Knowledge in the Radical Concept of Education," in Gress and Purpel, eds., *Curriculum: An Introduction to the Field*, pp. 124–142.
38. John Dewey, "Comments and Criticisms by Some Educational Leaders in Our Universities," in G. M. Whipple, ed., *The Activity Movement*, Thirty-Third Yearbook of the National Society for the Study of Education, Part II (Bloomington, Ill.: Public School Publishing Co., 1934), p. 85.
39. David Pratt, *Curriculum: Design and Development* (New York: Macmillan, 1980), p. 116.
40. Taba, *Curriculum Development: Theory and Practice*, p. 278.
41. John Wiles and Joseph Bondi, *Curriculum Development: A Guide to Practice* (Columbus, Ohio: Merrill, 1985).
42. Nancy J. Lee and Gary L. Obermeyer, "Mastering School Reform," *Educational Leadership* (September 1986), pp. 64–66; John E. Penick, Robert E. Yager, and Ronald Bonnstetter, "Teachers Make Exemplary Programs," *Educational Leadership* (October 1986), pp. 14–21.
43. See Allan C. Ornstein, "Curriculum Contrasts: A Historical View," *Phi Delta Kappan* (February 1982), pp. 404–408.
44. Tyler, *Basic Principles of Curriculum and Instruction*.
45. Maxine Green, "Public Education and the Public Space," *Educational Researcher* (June–July 1982), pp. 4–9.
46. James B. Macdonald and Ester Zaret, eds., *Schools in Search of Meaning* (Washington D.C.: Association for Supervision and Curriculum Development, 1975).
47. Philip H. Phenix, "Transcendence and the Curriculum," in E. W. Eisner and E. Vallance, eds., *Conflicting Conceptions of Curriculum* (Berkeley, Calif.: McCutchan, 1974), pp. 117–135.
48. Taba, *Curriculum Development: Theory and Practice*, p. 290.
49. John Holt, "Children Are Sensitive to Space," in T. G. David and B. D. Wright, eds., *Learning Environments* (Chicago: University of Chicago Press, 1975), p. 83.
50. P. Curtis and R. A. Smith, "A Child's Exploration of Space," in David and Wright, eds., *Learning Environments*, pp. 145–154.
51. Brian Castaldi, *Educational Facilities: Planning, Remodeling and Management* (Boston: Allyn and Bacon, 1977).
52. Ibid.
53. Ann Lieberman, *Rethinking School Improvement: Research, Craft, and Concept* (New York: Teachers College Press, Columbia University, 1986).
54. Michael W. Kirst, "Policy Implications of Individual Differences and the Common Curriculum," in G. D. Fenstermacher and J. I. Goodlad, eds., *Individual Differences and the Common Curriculum*, Eighty-second Yearbook of National Society for the Study of Education, Part I (Chicago: University of Chicago Press, 1983), pp. 282–299.
55. Richard D. Kimpston and Douglas H. Anderson, "The Locus of Curriculum Decision Making and Teachers' Perceptions of Their Own Attitudes and Behaviors Toward Curriculum Planning," *Journal of Curriculum and Supervision* (Winter 1986), pp. 100–110.
56. Ronald Doll, *Curriculum Improvement: Decision Making and Process*, 6th ed., (Boston: Allyn and Bacon, 1986).
57. John Goodlad, *A Place Called School* (New York: McGraw-Hill, 1984). Also see Thelbert L. Drake and William H. Roe, *The Principalship*, 3rd ed. (New York: Macmillan, 1986).
58. Allan C. Ornstein, "Curriculum, Instruction, and Supervision: Their Relationship and the Role of the Principal." *National Association of Secondary School Principals* (April 1986), pp. 74–81.
59. James A. Beane, Conrad E. Toepfer, and Samuel J. Alessi, *Curriculum Planning and Development* (Boston: Allyn and Bacon, 1986).
60. Ben Harris, *Supervisory Behavior in Education*, 3rd ed. (Englewood Cliffs, N. J.: Prentice-Hall, 1985); Wayne K. Hoy and Patrick B. Forsyth, *Effective Supervision: Theory into Practice* (New York: Random House, 1986).
61. Glenys G. Unruh and Adolph Unruh, *Responsive Curriculum Development*, 2nd ed. (Berkeley, Calif: McCutchan, 1984).
62. Roald F. Campbell et al., *The Organization and Control of American Schools*, 5th ed. (Columbus, Ohio: Merrill, 1985); William B. Castetter; *The Personnel Function in Educational Administration*, 4th ed. (New York: Macmillan, 1986).
63. Michael A. Robell and Arthur R. Block, *Educational Policy Making and the Courts* (Chicago: University of Chicago Press, 1982).
64. Joyce L. Epstein, "Parent Reactions to Teacher Practices of Parent Involvement," *Elementary School Journal* (January 1986), pp. 277–294.
65. Bruce R. Joyce, Richard H. Hersh, and Michael McKibbin, *The Structure of School Improvement* (New York: Longman, 1983); Jon Schaffarzick, "Teacher and Lay Participation in Local Curriculum Change Considerations." Paper presented at the annual meeting of the American Educational Research Association, San Francisco, 1976.
66. M. R. Sumption and Y. Engstrom, *School Community Relations* (New York: McGraw-Hill, 1966).
67. Keith Goldhammer, "The Proper Federal Role in Education Today," *Educational Leadership* (February 1979), pp. 350–353.

68. Michael Fullan, *The Meaning of Educational Change* (New York: Teachers College Press, Columbia University, 1982).

69. *Meeting the Challenge: Recent Efforts to Improve Education Across the Nation* (Washington D.C.: U.S. Department of Education, 1983).

70. Allan C. Ornstein and Daniel L. Levine, *Introduction to the Foundations of Education*, 3rd ed. (Boston: Houghton Mifflin, 1985).

71. Sherry Keith, *Politics of Textbook Selection* (Palo Alto: Stanford University Press, 1981).

72. See Kathleen D. Morin, "The Classroom Teacher and Curriculum Developer," in K. K. Zumwalt, ed., *Improving Teaching* (Alexandria, Va.: Association for Supervision and Curriculum Development, 1986), pp. 149–168.

chapter 9

CURRICULUM IMPLEMENTATION

It makes little difference how appropriate or valued a school curriculum is if it does not get "delivered" to students. A curriculum, however well designed, must be implemented throughout a school district if it is to make any impact or if students are to attain its goals and objectives. Much that is planned and developed often does not get implemented. Many new programs do nothing more than gather dust on shelves. They get blunted at classroom doors.[1]

Part of the problem is that implementing a curriculum has not been considered a crucial stage. Also, many charged with curriculum activity have neither had a good macro view of the process nor realized that innovations need to be monitored. Implementation should not be viewed as a clear-cut yes or no—to use or not use a new program. The process is developmental and occurs at different levels. Successful implementation of a curriculum, regardless of its design, rests upon delineating at the outset of the

development process the stages necessary for implementation.[2]

THE NATURE OF IMPLEMENTATION

Leslie Bishop stated that implementation requires restructuring and replacement. It requires reorganizing and adjusting personal habits, ways of behaving, program emphases, learning spaces, and existing curricula and schedules. It means getting educators to shift from the current program to the new program, a modification that can be met with great resistance. The ease with which a curriculum leader can trigger such behavior changes in staff depends in part on the quality of the initial planning and the precision with which the steps of curriculum development have been carried out up to this point.[3]

Although experienced leaders of curriculum activities have realized that implementation is an essential aspect of curriculum

223

development, only in the last ten or fifteen years has implementation become a major educational concern. Such interest has evolved partly because even though millions of dollars have been spent developing curriculum projects, especially for reading, math, and science, many of these projects have not succeeded.

When evaluating implementation, we need to consider the various assumptions educators bring to the process. Many assume that implementation is simply another step in the curriculum planning process and that they can expect to proceed from the planning and design stages to the actual implementation stage with relative ease. After reviewing several innovative projects, Fullan and Pomfret presented some sobering comments:

If there is one finding that stands out in our review, it is that effective implementation of . . . innovations requires time, personal interaction and contacts, inservice training, and other forms of people-based support. Research has shown time and again that there is no substitute for the primacy of personal contact among implementers, and between implementers and planners/consultants, if the difficult process of unlearning old roles and learning new ones is to occur. Equally clear is the absence of such opportunities on a regular basis during the planning and implementation of most innovations.[4]

In order for implementation of a program or process to occur, changes must be made in the behaviors of all affected parties. Fullan and Pomfret point out that teachers must be clear about the purpose, the nature, and the benefits of the innovation.

A high degree of district-wide and school-wide implementation involves educating individuals about the worth of a new program or program component, such as a new content area or a new type of student material. Several years ago social scientists furnished a definition of total implementation that is still useful: (1) the acceptance, (2) over time, (3) of some specific item—an idea or practice, (4) by individuals, groups, or other adopting units linked, (5) to specific

channels of communication, (6) to a social structure, and (7) to a given system of values, or culture.[5]

Keith Leithwood also considers implementation to be a process—involving the reduction of the differences between existing practices and practices suggested by innovators or change agents. Implementation attempts to influence behavioral change in a direction or directions deemed necessary. It occurs in stages; it takes time to win people over to an innovation.[6]

The present authors view implementation as a separate component in the curriculum action cycle. It is the logical step once a program has been developed and piloted. It involves extensive actions by many parties— not just, for example, an offer to staff one workshop. Note, however, that implementation also involves attempts to change individuals' knowledge, actions, and attitudes. This takes time. It also suggests that implementation is an interaction process between those who have created the program and those who are to deliver it.

Relationship of Implementation to Planning.

Successful implementation of curricula results from careful planning. Planning processes address needs, changes necessary, and resources requisite for carrying out intended actions. It involves establishing and determining how to administer policy that will govern the planned actions. Planning takes place prior to program creation and/or delivery. Edgar Morphet et al. have indicated that if the processes of planning and implementation are to be effective and meaningful, the relationship between the two must be carefully considered. Effective planning must relate to a desired and identifiable change that is to be implemented.[7] Essentially, the planner—whether a politician, a businessperson, or an educator—is the agent of change. He or she must be concerned with instituting change in an orderly fashion.[8]

Implementation, then, requires planning, and planning focuses on three factors: People, programs, organizations or processes, and institutions. Although these three factors are inseparable, some individuals consider that dealing primarily with only one factor will facilitate implementation. Some persons feel, for example, that to really facilitate implementation of a major change, educators must deal primarily with people. If the people change, so does the program and/or the organization. Others consider that the primary focus should be the program. People will adapt if they are furnished with different ways to meet the objectives of the schools' programs.[9] Still others think that attention should center on the organization within which the people work. If departments are reorganized, if spaces are remodeled, then people will adjust in the directions necessary for successful implementation.[10]

Curriculum leaders really need to consider working with all three factors: People, programs, and organizations. Certainly, a leader may wish to stress one factor more than another, but no skillful leader will ignore any one factor altogether. Many school districts have failed to implement their programs because they ignored the people factor and spent time and money modifying only the program or organization. One reason that many of the curriculum projects of the 1960s failed to take "root" was that the curriculum innovators, essentially scholars from universities, centered most of their energies on changing the program but paid scant attention to the needs of teachers, and minimal attention to the organization of American schools.[11]

Incrementalism.

People want to change; yet they are also afraid of change, especially if it comes quickly or if they feel they have little control or influence over it. People become accustomed to the status quo and prefer to make modifications in new behavior in small and gradual steps.[12]

The world of the teacher does not allow for much receptivity to change. Both Fullan and Goodlad have described the teacher's daily routine as presenting little opportunity for interaction with colleagues.[13] This isolation results partly from the school's organization into self-contained classrooms and partly from the teaching schedules. Seymour Sarason has also commented on the isolation of teachers in the school organization and on how that isolation negatively impacts change. Sarason has stated that the reality of the school has made teachers feel that professionally, they are on their own. It is their responsibility, and theirs alone, to solve their problems.[14] This posture causes teachers to view change introduced into the program as an individual activity. Viewing their struggles as solitary, teachers often develop a psychological loneliness that results in hostility to administrators and outside change agents who seem insensitive to the teachers' plight. Dan Lortie has noted that, in fact, many factors affect the teachers' receptivity to change:

Teachers have a built-in resistance to change because they believe that their work environment has never permitted them to show what they can really do. Many proposals for change strike them as frivolous and wasteful—not addressing the real issues which deal with student disruptions or discipline, student reading problems, administrative support, etc.[15]

In an investigation of maturation during adulthood, one investigator noted that several principles can guide changing adults' behaviors. These principles include fostering multiple perspectives, allowing time for integration of ideas, and creating a supportive environment in which learning becomes more autonomous.[16] Drawing on these principles, the curriculum implementor facilitates the active involvement of teachers to allow for experiential learning, fosters the creation of an environment that encourages openness and trust, and gives feedback so that participants realize that their contributions are appreciated and their talents considered worthwhile.

Teachers need time to "try" the new program to be implemented. They need time to reflect on new goals and objectives, to consider new contents and learning experiences, and to try out new tasks. They need time to map out their tactics for meeting the challenges of the new program, and they need time to talk to their colleagues. They can handle new programs if the changes demanded in their attitudes, behaviors, and knowledge are to be attained in manageable increments.[17]

Implementation does not occur all at once with all teachers. Ideally, an implementation process allows sufficient time for certain groups of teachers to try out the new curriculum in "pieces." Loucks and Lieberman have found that teachers go through levels of use with a new curriculum.[18] First, they orient themselves to the materials and engage in actions that will prepare them to deliver the curriculum. Their beginning use of the new curriculum is mechanical. They follow the guide with little deviation. Planning is largely day-by-day. Their delivery of the curriculum becomes rather routine, and they take little initiative to make any changes in the curriculum. As they become more comfortable with the curriculum, they may begin to modify it, either to adjust it to their own educational philosophies or to better meet students' needs.

Successful implementors appreciate that it takes time for teachers to "buy into" a new curriculum, and it takes time for them to become skilled in delivering the new program. Curriculum leaders should anticipate teachers' questions and concerns. And they should plan potential strategies for addressing them.

Communication.

It is almost an axiom that whenever a new program is being designed, communication channels must be kept open so that the new program comes not as a surprise. Frequent discussion about a new program among teachers, principals, and curriculum workers is a key to successful implementation.[19]

But communication is a complex phenomenon. It has been defined as the transmission of facts, ideas, values, feelings, and attitudes from one individual or group to another. Put simply, communication deals with message processing between the sender and the receiver of a message. The receiver can either accept or reject the message. Communication is not a one-way street; however, the process can be reversed to make a two-way channel. One administrator charted communication as in the chart at the bottom of this page.[20]

Knowing that communication deals with messages and message sending and receiving is not sufficient to ensure that communication will be effective or that messages sent will be accurate or of high quality. The curriculum specialist must be sure that the communication network is comprehensive and that avenues for message sending exist in all levels of the system. An effective system is not rigid but allows different population members input opportunities and vehicles.

If curriculum leaders only want to communicate facts about a new program being implemented, they can communicate such facts by means of letters, memos, articles, books, bulletins, research reports, or speeches.[21] Sometimes they need to communicate to staff the underlying assumptions, values, and points of view imbedded in a new curriculum. If the new program is a major change from the existing program, then the curriculum leader may wish to use such communication vehicles as workshops, meetings, role-playing situations, and demonstrations.[22]

Despite the various sophisticated and

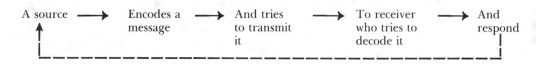

simple means available for communication, the key to communication is the individual. Communication involves messages among people, not hardware. Philip Phenix made this point in the late 1950s: "The real barriers to communication are not technical, but persons." Thus, the curriculum leader needs to create a climate conducive to effective communication among all members of the educational staff and community (both person-to-person and mass communication). He or she needs to inform all persons of the avenues that are established for communication. He or she also needs to inform all persons that their "views are welcome and that they all have a responsibility to participate" in sending and processing messages.[23] This is especially true at the implementation stage of curriculum activity.

Cooperation.

Cooperation between all persons who are to be involved with program implementation must occur if change is to be successful and to become institutionalized. Ample research supports the practice of engaging teachers in new ideas and programs that will find expression in their classrooms. In many ways, teachers are the experts, and so their commitment to the new curriculum is especially necessary. Such commitment depends heavily on how active they have been in conceptualizing and developing the new program.[24]

A review of research indicates that if teachers actively participate in curriculum development and implementation, the likelihood of successful implementation is increased.[25] This may be partly because emotion as well as rationality are inevitably elements of change. People require the involvement of their total beings—their feelings, sentiments, and values—if they are to accept, tolerate, or support change.[26]

Charles Silberman noted that many of the reforms of the 1950s actually "wrote" the teachers out of the educational process. Teacher-proof materials were designed by innovators,[27] which meant that basically all

teachers had to do was to "hand out" the materials. Also, teachers viewed the programs as invasions over which they had no control. This is, in fact, a key reason these programs did not reach the levels of implementation intended for them.

Educators have come to learn, sometimes the hard way, that for change to be effective, the teachers must be committed to it, and they must see that it has professional value to them. Teachers often judge change by how it will address the immediate needs they encounter in their daily work: "An important lesson of . . . reform is that even the best educational practice is unlikely to fulfill its promise in the hands of an inadequately trained or unmotivated teacher." We have learned the hard way that successful "reform or change is more a function of people and organizations than of technology" or even money.[28]

Indeed, educators need to consider teacher needs, level of commitment, and skills when determining when and how to involve teachers in implementation. It appears that even though teachers indicate that they want involvement, what most of them really want is input into the decisions. They want programs that reflect their philosophies and curriculum orientations to education.[29]

Other participants in curriculum development need to cooperate in the process as well. Those who favor learner-centered designs want to involve the students in the curriculum development and implementation processes. They wish to incorporate students' ideas about how to test and modify, if necessary, the new program. Those who advocate reform in the schools raise the issue of involving community members in the development and implementation of programs.[30] Various minority groups are requesting that they too be involved in the implementation and development stages in order to ensure that their views are represented and that their children are not discriminated against in the initial implementation of the new program.

Support.

Implementation costs, in terms of both time and materials. Curriculum designers need to provide the necessary support for their recommended programs or program modifications to facilitate their rapid implementation. They have to do this so as to build self-confidence among those affected. Educators often require in-service training and time to feel comfortable with new programs. In analyzing the results of the Rand Corporation's Change Agent Study, in fact, McLaughlin and Marsh indicated that in-service training was crucial. Research efforts have catalogued the characteristics of effective professional in-service programs. Such programs must be designed so that they can be integrated into and supported by the organizations within which they are designed to function. In-service programs that work have resulted from collaborative efforts and have addressed the needs of those who are to be impacted by the new curricula.[31] Effective in-service training has the necessary flexibility to respond to the changing needs of the staff. Not all details of in-service training can be planned prior to implementation; nor can all problems and concerns be anticipated.

Because in-service programs must reach their intended audiences, they should be accessibly scheduled for curriculum implementors. Open discussions on the new programs should, in fact, be scheduled throughout the implementation process. Such discussions allow implementors to voice their objections or concerns, and consequently reduce opposition. Effective in-service programs must also evaluate whether they are achieving their objectives and whether they are in harmony with the underlying philosophy and approach of the district.[32]

Without adequate financial support, efforts to get a program "going" district-wide will fail. When federal monies were flowing, many school districts were quite innovative, but they failed to add funding for their innovations into their regular school budgets. When the federal monies ran out, which

were essentially meant to be start-up monies, the districts discontinued their new programs, citing lack of necessary funds. If school districts, today, create new programs using federal or state grant money, called "soft money," they need to devise ways to support these programs once implemented with "hard money"—money that is part of the regularly allocated school budget.

Money is required for materials and equipment to institutionalize a new program. Money is also necessary to provide often-overlooked human support for the implementation effort. A trusting relationship must exist among all parties in the school, especially the administration and the teachers. The principal is a key guarantor of successful innovation and implementation.[33] Disagreement does exist, however, on how principals should furnish human support. Still, those considered to be successful principals are knowledgeable of and committed to the curriculum; they also view their role as providing encouragement for it on one end of the continuum, and to serving as the "curriculum leader," on the other end of the continuum.[34]

Implementation is a collaborative and emotional effort. Peer support is vital if implementation is to be successful. Dan Lortie points out that teachers spend the majority of their working time in individual classrooms with their students, therefore, they have minimal communication with their peers. By and large, they are left on their own with little input or assistance from colleagues or supervisors, unless a crisis develops.[35] Opportunities for teachers to work together, share ideas, jointly solve problems, and cooperatively create materials greatly enhance the probability of successful curriculum implementation.

IMPLEMENTATION AS A CHANGE PROCESS

The purpose of curriculum development, regardless of level, is to make a difference—to enable students to attain the chool's, the society's, and, perhaps most importantly, their own (students) aims and oals. Implementation, an essential part of urriculum development, brings into reality nticipated changes. Simply put, curriculum ctivity is change activity.

But, what is change? What happens when hange occurs? What is the source of hange? Can people predict the consequences of change? Can educators control hose changes that directly impact them? We assert that people can exert some conrol over the process of change, but to do so equires that they understand change. Understanding the concept of change, and the arious types of change, allows individuals o determine sources of change. It also helps hem realize that even though they cannot eally predict the consequences of change, hey can make "best-guess" forcasts about its esults.

Change can occur in several ways. The wo most obvious differences are slow hange (as when minor adjustments are nade in the course schedule, when some ooks are added to the library, or when the unit or lesson plan is updated by the eacher) and rapid change (say as the result f new knowledge or social trends impacting on schools—such as computers being introduced into classrooms).

According to the research, for curriculum change to be successfully implemented, either slowly or rapidly, five guidelines hould be followed to help avoid mistakes of he past.

1. *Innovations designed to improve student achievement must be technically sound.* This means that changes should reflect research about what works and what does not work, as opposed to whatever designs for improvement happen to be popular today or tomorrow.

2. *Successful innovation requires change in the structure of a traditional school.* By structural change, we mean major modification of the way students and teachers are assigned to classes and interact with each other.

3. *Innovations must be manageable and feasible for the average teacher.* We cannot innovate ideas concerning critical thinking or problem sol-

ving when students cannot read or write basic English or refuse to behave in class.

4. *Implementation of successful change efforts must be organic rather than bureaucratic.* Strict compliance, monitoring procedures, and rules are not conducive for change; this bureaucratic approach needs to be replaced by an organic or adaptive approach that permits some deviation from the original plan and recognizes grass-roots problems and conditions of the school.

5. *Avoid the "do something, do anything" Syndrome.* The need is for a definite curriculum plan, to focus one's efforts, time, and money on content and activities that are sound and rational, not a scam or simplistic idea.[36]

The data indicate that the guidelines "are systematically interrelated, and that with the possible exception of the guideline regarding structural change, they apply equally well to all levels of education." Curricularists will benefit by "considering their applicability in the particular context of their own schools and school districts."[37]

A Theory of Change.

Change results from new knowledge; however, the presence of new knowledge is not sufficient for changes. People must recognize a need for change. And they are more likely to recognize that need if they understand change and how it works. Lovell and Wiles present a model of change that incorporates the social and psychological concepts (see Figure 9-1).[38] Even though they relate their model to instructional supervision, it is still valuable to those considering curriculum change.

This model implies that teachers and students constitute teacher-pupil systems and that they are bound by the belief that they can achieve certain goals more effectively as a system than as individuals. The model shows that various processes of change can be employed; some of these processes are listed as leadership, communication, and problem solving. These specific strategies are available for use by the participants involved in the change. The system's processes for change are affected by external

PROCESSES OF CHANGE

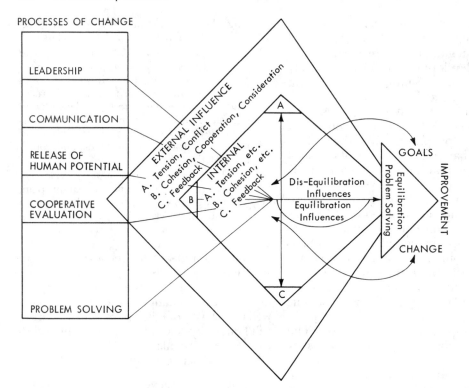

FIGURE 9-1   Model for Change.
Source: from John T. Lovell, "A Perspective for Viewing Instructional Supervisory
Behavior," in W. H. Lucio, ed. *Supervision: Perspectives and Propositions,*
(Washington, D.C. Association for Supervision and Curriculum Development,
1967), p. 15; John T. Lovell and Kimball Wiles, *Supervision for Better Schools*
(Englewood Cliffs, N.J.: Prentice-Hall, 1983), p. 117.

systems and forces. "Feedback" from the external environment, for instance, furnishes information on the effect the system is having on external systems, new expectations, allocation of resources, and rewards for system members. It also relays information about outside threats to the working of the system. Such data inputs from external factors can cause tension within the system and generate a state of disequilibration among members within the system. This condition then sets in motion an attempt by the system to achieve a new state of equilibration.

Lovell and Wiles point out that change is achieved through the continuous process of disequilibration and reequilibration through problem-solving activities. Curriculum leaders should work to facilitate this change process through leadership, communication, the release of human potential and cooperative problem solving and evaluation. The consequence of successfully employing these approaches is creating new external and internal forces that will further stimulate change and improvement in the system—in this case, the curriculum system.

Change Typologies.

Persons charged with curriculum activity specifically implementation, need to understand the nature of change. Warren Bennis has identified several useful types of change:

1. *Planned change* is change in which those involved in the change process have equal power and function in a prescribed fashion. People identify and follow precise procedures for dealing with the activity at hand. Planned change is the ideal.
2. *Coercion* is characterized by one group determining the goals and intentionally excluding others from participating. The group in control has the major power and works to maintain the unequal power balance.
3. *Interaction change* is characterized by mutual goal setting and a fairly equal power distribution among groups. But those involved often lack a deliberateness of effort; they are uncertain how to follow through with the plans of development and implementation. Few procedures are carefully developed; people are more or less left on their own.[39]

The opposite of planned change is *natural* or *random change*. This type of change occurs with no apparent thought and no goal setting on the part of the participants. Often natural change is what occurs in schools. Curricula are adjusted or modified and implemented not as a result of careful analysis, but as a response to unanticipated events. For example, demands by legislatures or pressure groups that certain programs be implemented, often receive inconsistent reactions.

Robert Chin has discussed three types of change strategies that can be considered as change typologies as well:

1. *Empirical-rational* strategies stress the importance of knowing the need for change and having the competence to implement it. Often schools lack this approach to change because they neither know they need a change nor have the skill to implement it.
2. *Normative-reeducative* strategies are based on the rationality and intelligence of humans. Humans will change if they are approached rationally and made to see that they need to modify their values, attitudes, understandings, and skills.
3. *Power strategies* require that individuals comply with the wishes of those who are in positions superior to theirs. Although outright strategies of coercion are rarely used in schools, it is not uncommon for those in power to "coerce" people into compliance by offering material and symbolic rewards in exchange for accepting new programs.[40]

Change According to Complexity.

We can also consider change according to its complexity. Those involved in investigating the change process have identified five kinds of change using complexity as the organizer:

1. *Substitution.* This depicts alteration in which one element may be substituted for another. A teacher can, for example, substitute one textbook for another. By far, this is the easiest and most common type of change.
2. *Alteration.* This type of change exists when someone introduces into existing materials and programs new content, items, materials, or procedures that appear to be only minor and thus are likely to be adopted readily.
3. *Perturbations.* These changes could at first disrupt a program, but can then be adjusted purposefully by the curriculum leader to the ongoing program within a short timespan. An example of a perturbation is the principal's adjusting class schedules, which would affect the time allowed for teaching a particular subject.
4. *Restructuring.* These changes lead to modification of the system itself—that is, of the school or school district. New concepts of teaching roles, such as differentiated staffing or team teaching, would be a restructuring type of change.
5. *Value-Orientation Changes.* These are shifts in the participants' fundamental philosophies or curriculum orientations. Major power brokers of the school or participants in the curriculum must accept and strive for this level of change for it to occur. However if teachers do not adjust their value domains, any changes enacted are most likely going to be short-lived.[41]

Although change that occurs in the schools cannot be fit into precise categories, curricularists need to realize that types do exist and that planned change is the ideal. But change is not synonymous with improvement. Education is a normative activity. A person's advocating and then managing change means, in effect, making a statement about what he or she thinks is valuable. This is why people can use the same change procedures and generate different curricula. They have different values and different perceptions of what education should be.

Resistance to Change.

A curriculum leader who accepts that people are the key to successful curriculum activity and implementation is cognizant of the barriers that people place between themselves and change efforts. Perhaps the biggest barrier is inertia—among the staff, the administration, or the community. Many people think it is just easier to keep things as they are. If we think of ourselves as systems, we realize that we like to maintain steady states. We have traditions to which we adhere and institutions that we cherish—and we do not wish to change them. Many people are happy with the current school setup as a bureaucracy.

Wanting to keep things as they are is often mixed with believing that things do not need to be changed or that the change being suggested is unwise and will thus be unproductive in meeting the objectives of the school. Educators themselves argue this point. Some say that the schools are fine and just need to be maintained, whereas others posit that the schools are not responsive to the times and require major modification. The status quo tends to be maintained if those suggesting change have not presented precise goals of the new program being suggested—that is, they have not planned adequately what the new program will look like or indicated ways in which the new program will be superior to the existing one.[42]

Often, teachers have not been able or willing to keep up with scholarly developments. They have not stayed abreast of the knowledge explosion which would allow them to feel committed to curriculum change and the implementation of new pro-

grams. Teachers frequently view change as just signaling more work—something else to add on to an already overloaded schedule for which little or no time is allotted. Usually no extra money or reward is earmarked for the extra work either. Many educators, in fact, are overwhelmed by changes proposed and their implications. Often they view new curricular programs as requiring them to learn new teaching skills, develop new competencies in curriculum development and the management of learning resources, or acquire new skills in interpersonal relations. In some instances, even teacher education programs fail to develop those competencies necessary for teachers to become active participants in innovation.

Another reason curriculum leaders have difficulty getting teachers to accept innovation is, according to Edgar Friendenberg, that people who go into teaching tend to be conformist in nature—not innovative. These people have succeeded in the school system as it has existed. They have learned to play it safe and to keep a low profile in a bureaucratic system run by administrators who do not like to create "waves."[43] They have found success and fulfillment as students and now as teachers in this system, and for this reason many see no reason to change it. To many beginning teachers, the bureaucracy in place is a welcome and familiar support system—and they are often slow to change it.

Can educators cope with the demands for more change, or for assuming new roles? Uncertainty fosters insecurity. Often educators who feel comfortable with the present are reluctant to change for a future they cannot comprehend or see clearly. People often prefer to stay with certain known deficiencies than venture forth to uncertain futures, even if the changes most likely would be improvements. Bringing new students or parents or content into the curriculum realm, or organizing the program in new ways, makes many teachers uneasy.

Another factor that causes people to resist change is the rapidity of change. Many people feel that if something is implemented this year, it will most likely be abandoned when another innovation appears, and will thus make all their efforts useless. There have, in fact, been enough "bandwagons" in education to make educators "innovation shy."

Sometimes people resist innovation and its implementation because they lack knowledge. They either do not know about the innovation at all or they have little information about it. Curriculum leaders must furnish all affected parties—teachers, pupils, parents, community members—with information about the nature of the program and its rationale. Ideally, all affected parties should be informed either directly or indirectly by school representatives of the reasons for the new program.

People often resist change, too, if no financial or time support are given the effort. A project for which no monies are budgeted is rarely destined to be implemented. Often, school districts budget monies for materials but fail to allocate funds for the creation of the curriculum plan, its delivery within the classroom, or necessary in-service training.[44] Finally, we raise the question whether a person who earns $20,000 to $35,000 is supposed to be a change agent. Teachers are not paid enough to innovate; that is not the role of a teacher—rather of a leader. Teachers are required to help implement change, but the school leader (principal) or school district leader (superintendent) should be the one to initiate change and provide the ingredients and processes for constructive change. On the other hand, teachers are virtually an untapped source of energy and insight, capable of profoundly changing the schools if they act as a group and direct their energies to local and state policy matters.

Several years ago, Everett Rogers listed some key obstacles to getting people involved in change. They are still current:

1. There is little reward to being an innovator in education.
2. Education is not set up with change agents who provide assistance or answer questions.

3. Educational innovations have cloudy advantages over the existing ideas or programs they are to replace.
4. Innovative matters in schools are frequently not individual responsibilities, and few processes and formal structures for change exist in schools.
5. Diffusion methods are not clearly defined in schools; there are few avenues of communication and follow-up for new programs.[45]

It may seem that curriculum specialists face insurmountable problems. But resistance to change is good, because it requires change agents to think carefully about the innovations and to consider the human dynamics involved in implementing programs. Having to "fight" for change protects the organization from becoming proponents of just random change and educational fads.

Improving Receptivity to Change.

Curriculum activity involves people thinking and acting. Leaders of curriculum development, and especially implementation, realize that the human equation is of paramount importance and that, therefore, they must understand how people react to change. Often, people say they are willing to change, but act as though they are unwilling to adjust. A successful change agent knows how people react to change and how to encourage them to be receptive to change.

Curriculum implementation requires face-to-face interaction—person-to-person contact. Those persons charged with implementation must understand the interpersonal dimension of leadership. Curriculum implementation is also a group process involving individuals working together. Not only does the group enable certain actions to occur, it also serves to change its individual members.

Of course, if a group is to change individuals, it must be attractive to its members. The ideas and values the group expresses must be acceptable to them. This is why curriculum leaders need to make sure that the members of the group are clear about the platform upon which they are to build the curriculum. This is why members must understand the rationale for the various curriculum designs and the consequences of accepting a particular design. As groups talk about the need to change and the strategies for implementation, they create a pressure for change within the educational system.[46] Creating a well-formed group with a clear sense of mission and confidence that it can bring about change is one way to make individuals receptive to the notion of change.

Curriculum leaders can also increase educators' willingness to change by "linking" the needs and expectations of the individuals with those of the organization. Each person has certain needs and expectations that he or she expects to fulfill within the school organization. Rarely, however, are institutional expectations absolutely compatible with individual needs. Getzels and Guba have created a model (Figure 9-2) that depicts the major relationships between the individual's personality and needs and the institution's role expectations.

Every individual who comes into a system plays a multitude of roles; each professional brings to his or her role his or her personality as well. Each person has certain needs he or she expects to fulfill within the system—in this discussion, the school—or the school district. Rarely is there absolute congruence between institutional roles and expectations and individual personality and needs. Misalignment can cause conflict. Curriculum leaders need to recognize that they cannot always avoid this conflict; they must manage it. The way they manage it is reflected in the social behavior of the individual.

Following the guidelines outlined next

can help individuals increase their receptivity to curriculum innovations:

1. *Curriculum activity must be cooperative.* If any program is to be implemented and institutionalized, it should be perceived by all parties as their program. This sense of ownership is achieved by involving people directly and indirectly with the major aspects of curriculum development and implementation. When people participate in planning and implementing a program they gain understanding of it and commitment to its goals and underlying philosophical basis.

2. *Some people like to change; some people do not like to change.* Resistance to any new idea is often natural. Curriculum leaders should anticipate it, and should prepare procedures for dealing with it. They must also identify well in advance of the action questions that will arise about the innovation being implemented: How will people feel about the change? What worries will people have? What are some likely points of conflict? What can be done to lessen the anxiety levels of individuals who will be affected by the change?

3. *Innovations are subject to change.* Nothing should be viewed as permanent. A new curriculum is presented as a response to a particular time and context. As time passes and contexts change, other modifications, sometimes even new programs, will be required. Change is a constant, and people need to realize that all programs will be constantly reviewed to determine if they should be continued.

4. *Proper timing is a key to increasing peoples' receptivity to an innovation.* If the school community is demanding that a new program be created to respond to a perceived national need, then a new program addressing that need is likely to meet with success and acceptance. However, if people are satisfied with the current program, and there is little demand for change from either the staff or

FIGURE 9-2 The Dimensions of Social Behavior.

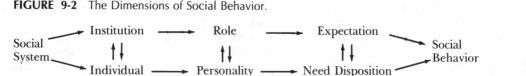

Source: From Jacob W. Getzels and Egon G. Guba, "Social Behavior and the Administrative Process," *School Review* (December 1957), p. 429.

community, then a major curriculum change should not be attempted. Also, if staff have just completed a major revision or created a major program, it is most likely not a good idea to involve the same people in another major curriculum development effort.[47]

CURRICULUM IMPLEMENTATION MODELS

We live in a time of overchoice—overchoice not only of products, but also of orientations to action, as well as of models for guiding our actions. Considering the total process of curriculum activity can help educators select a particular approach to implementation. Their views are often influenced by their overall curriculum approaches and philosophical preferences.

Ben Harris has pointed out that strategies for improving educational offerings are not easy to identify.[48] But, scholars and practitioners continue to dialogue about the need for effective means of improving the curriculum and its delivery. Harris observes that from the present dialogue we can ferret out common suggestions for possible strategies of change: (1) clarifying lines of authority; (2) involving affected parties in goal setting, staff selection, and evaluation; (3) specifying roles and responsibilities of teachers; (4) training personnel in change strategies and conflict-resolution techniques; and (5) furnishing impacted parties with necessary support.

Implementing change in any organization, and schools are no exception, requires a multitask approach. Those involved in implementing new programs should be encouraged by the fact that much of the work of the last two decades has furnished tactics on how to effect change in schools. Change agents can employ several strategy types to solve a variety of specific problems and to enhance change. We examine a number of change models next.

Overcoming Resistance to Change Model.

The Overcoming Resistance to Change (ORC) Model rests on the assumption, ac-

cording to Neal Gross, that the success or failure of planned organizational change efforts is basically a function of the ability of leaders to overcome staff resistance to change that is present just prior to, or at the time of, the introduction of the innovation.[49]

One observer describes this approach to change as follows: In social organizations, "patterns of behavior become established and are great stabilizers because individuals . . . fear that any change will be to their disadvantage in some way." Most people in organizations are concerned about change because "they will be paid less or have to work harder for the same amount." Even managers resist change "because they are afraid their positions will be weakened somehow or that they will be further from the centers of power."[50]

If we desire change we must address people's fears, misgivings, misapprehensions, or other factors. We must point out to persons that their values, assumptions, and beliefs are included in the new program proposed. In addressing persons within the system we should remember that "the main principle . . . is that the subordinates should be persuaded and motivated rather than ordered—so that they actually want to behave in a new way."[51]

One strategy to overcome resistance to change is power equalization between management and organizational members—school administrators and teachers in this case. The leaders of an innovation accept that subordinates will initially be negatively predisposed toward the innovation and will hence resist it. This resistance can be avoided if staff members are involved in the deliberations that initially create the program and in the deliberations to develop it. Educational curriculum leaders, mindful of this fact, share their power with subordinates by allowing them to participate in decisions about program change. When leaders take this tack, staff members tend to view the innovation as self-imposed, and thus express ownership of it and commitment to it. According to one educator, power equalization has thus become a key concept in several of the prevalent people theories, a first step in the theoretical causal chain leading toward organizational change. It has been constructed as an initial subgoal, a necessary predecessor to creative change in structure.[52]

Curriculum leaders using the ORC Model realize that they must address—that is, identify and deal with the concerns of the staff. In their research on the implementation of innovations in schools and colleges, Hall and Loucks have noted that concerns can be grouped into four broad developmental stages:

Stage 1: Unrelated Concerns. At this level teachers do not perceive a relationship between themselves and the suggested change. For example, if a new science program is being created in a school, a teacher at this stage would be aware of the efforts, but would not consider that he or she would be affected by or concerned with the effort. The teacher would not resist the change, because he or she really does not perceive the change as impacting on his or her own personal or professional domain.

Stage 2: Personal Concerns. At this stage, the individual reacts to the innovation in relation to his or her personal situation. He or she is concerned with how the new program compares to the ongoing program—specifically, to what he or she is doing. In the science example, the teacher would perceive that he or she would have to be involved with the new program. He or she would face the question of how well he or she could teach the innovation. Sometimes, a teacher might question how much latitude he or she will have in delivering the curriculum to his or her class.

Stage 3: Task-Related Concerns. Concerns raised at this level relate to the actual use of the innovation in the classroom. Continuing the science example, the teacher would now be concerned with how to actually implement the new program in his or her classroom. How much time will be required for teaching this new program? Will adequate materials be provided? What are the best strategies for teaching the new program?

Stage 4: Impact-Related Concerns. When reacting at this stage, a teacher is more concerned with how the innovation will impact others—the to-tal organization. He or she is interested in how the new program might influence students, colleagues, and the community. He or she might want to determine the program's impact, too, on what he or she is teaching. Will the new science program, for example, enable students to live in the future world?[53]

When working with the ORC Model educators must deal directly with the concerns at stages 2, 3, and 4. If they ignore them, then people will either not buy into the innovation, or will deal with it in ways that are not intended in the program's conception. Often such concerns can be addressed by curriculum leaders' keeping all staff informed of the innovation and by their involving those persons who will be directly impacted in the early decisions regarding the innovation. Often, faculty can be called together to share concerns and to map strategies for dealing with those concerns. Sometimes information on concerns can be gathered from questionnaires that allow for open-ended questions. When concerns are shared, often persons with some insecurity regarding the program find that they really have nothing about which to worry. This does not mean that they do not have to make changes. Perhaps teachers will find that they do have to change their strategies and that they do have to teach different content. By sharing concerns, they may realize, however, that they are capable of making any changes necessary in order to deliver the new program in its intended fashion.

Leadership-Obstacle Course Model.

Another model for dealing with implementation is the Leadership-Obstacle Course (LOC) Model. This model grew out of work by Neal Gross to determine the success or failure of organizations.[54] In essence, the LOC Model extends the Overcoming Resistance to Change Model. It treats staff resistance to change as problematic and proposes that data should be gathered to determine the extent and nature of the resistance. The idea is for leaders to neutralize this obstacle. They can do this by making sure that five conditions or stages exist:

1. The organizational members must have a clear understanding of the proposed innovation.
2. Individuals within the organization must be given the skills and possess the capabilities requisite for carrying out the innovation.
3. The necessary materials and equipment for the innovation must be furnished.
4. The organization—the school in this case—must be modified so that it is compatible with the innovation being suggested.
5. The participants in the innovation must be motivated to spend the required time and effort to make the innovation a success.

Curriculum leaders are responsible for guaranteeing that these five conditions are present during the period of attempted implementation. Management alone possesses the authority to establish these conditions; it is the only agency with the power to change the existing organizational arrangements and to furnish the necessary rewards.

The LOC Model extends the ORC Model of change in several respects. The ORC Model conceptualizes educational change as a two-stage process: (1) initiation, and (2) incorporation or inclusion of the innovation as part of the ongoing processes of the organization. The LOC Model considers educational change as a three-stage sequence: (1) initiation, (2) attempted implementation, and (3) incorporation.

Implicit in this model is that management is not just responsible for overcoming resistance at the outset of the change effort; management must also establish and maintain conditions such that necessary tasks can be accomplished during attempted implementation, and also during maintenance of the established program.[55]

Let us assume that we are introducing a new social studies curriculum for an elementary school. Using the LOC Model, we would have, at the outset of the curriculum development effort, made sure that all members of the organization—that is, the

social studies teachers—had a clear understanding of the proposed innovation. They would know what specific needs were being addressed by its implementation. They would know who the intended audience was. If teachers do know the reasons and justifications for the new social studies program, it is more likely that they will accept and be willing to implement it.

In the second stage of this model, the new skills and capabilities teachers would need to implement the new program would be identified. Teachers would have a role in suggesting what these are. The social studies teachers, either all of them at the elementary level or their representatives would, through deliberation, indicate essential skills and capabilities. They would suggest ways in which those skills, if lacking, could be developed through in-service activities.

New programs require new materials, as indicated by the third stage. In this example, teachers would be involved in suggesting what materials would be necessary. Leaders would guarantee that funds would be such that these materials, and the necessary equipment for teaching the new social studies program, would be forthcoming.

As part of the fourth stage, space and schedules might be adjusted. Cooperative learning might be part of the new social studies program. If so, then classrooms would have to be modified to allow for such activity. If teachers will need to engage in team planning for many of the new units, then office space may need to be provided for such cooperative efforts.

In the last stage, those in charge of the new social studies program should make sure that rewards are built into the social studies effort so that teachers are committed to the program. Teachers must be motivated not only to plan the curriculum, but also to take the time and to make the effort to deliver the social studies program as developed.

Some individuals have noted that this implementation model could be strengthened by engaging people in an exploratory stage at the outset of the innovation effort. Participants could look at the current situation and brainstorm to determine what is needed to address the current situation. In the social studies example, people to be involved in creating the program, and to be impacted by it, would explore the current scene in social studies. What are the current social studies issues? What issues are likely to continue? What issues are likely to arise in the future?

Another way of strengthening this model is to remember that many of the obstacles to be processed will come from outside the system—in this example, from outside the school. External barriers, such as community attitudes, values, and views of what is necessary, might be considered. Many impediments to local change in schools are located in federal, state, or local government. For example, in a social studies program, we might discover that a major obstacle is a state regulation indicating what topics must be covered and how much time must be allowed. We might also discover that the local community disapproves of a particular topic. In order for an innovation to take hold, the community's attitude and perception regarding the topic must be considered and resolved. Another major obstacle to a new social studies program might be individual school board members.

To overcome resistance to change—or, put another way, to foster acceptance of an innovation—it is necessary to take into consideration all the reasons why people resist change. These points were indicated earlier. However, school personnel can hinder educational change efforts in ways other than outright refusal to accept them. Some schools have a high faculty turnover. If a school is trying to implement a new math or science program, for example, it will have serious difficulty if it continually loses a large percentage of its staff. Many school districts across the country have released large numbers of staff from their responsibilities because of enrollment and budgetary problems. Often many of the newer teachers, who advocated the innovative programs, were the ones released because they had the least amount of tenure in the system. In general, then, a school should consider the stability of its workforce when attempting to implement a new curriculum.

Note that implementation obstacles solved at one point in time using this model may arise again at another point. This model really needs to include a feedback and monitoring mechanism to determine if problems, once solved, are reappearing. Perhaps, for example, while working to develop an elementary social studies program, curriculum leaders solved the problem of securing adequate materials to teach the new program. Suppose, however, that more students come into the system during the implementation process; materials now are in short supply. Likewise, a budgetary crisis could occur, so monies promised for the purchase of materials cannot be disbursed.

Innovation involves political action. People are primarily political entities, and they can be pressured to adopt new programs or not to adopt new programs by others who possess power. The school is an arena in which vested interest groups do jockey for power to influence particular changes or to champion their views of curriculum.[56] Innovations are value-laden, and curriculum leaders must be mindful of this. Innovations will be accepted if people find their values, assumptions, and beliefs in the programs. If these preferences are absent, people will work to adjust the programs until the values and beliefs align with their own.[57]

Those in charge of curriculum innovation—in this example, the directors of social studies education—need to keep in mind that they must secure and maintain the support of the change effort by members of the central administration, the school board, and community residents and officials. It is not sufficient just to have the social studies teachers committed to the new program.

Linkage Model.

The linkage model developed by Ronald Havelock recognizes that there are innovators in research and development centers, universities, and school systems. Educators in the field, however, find some of their attempts at innovations inappropriate for solving school problems. What is needed is a match between school problems and innovations—the establishment of linkages.[58]

The starting point for educational change is in the problem-solving process of the user. If change is to occur, the user must uncover information relevant to his or her identified problems. Useful interaction is most likely to get to the user if a resource system is effectively linked to the user system. The resource system must have a clear picture of the user's problems if it is to retrieve or create appropriate knowledge or educational packages. The resource system must also transmit possible solutions to the user. As shown in Figure 9-3, a successful resource system must proceed through a cycle of diagnosis, search, retrieval, fabrication of solution, dissemination, and evaluation in order to test out its product. Going through such stages allows the resource system to then document that the system or curriculum being suggested as appropriate to the user is in fact appropriate.

In the linkage model, the basic process is knowledge transfer. In schools that use this model, the entire purpose of developing and piloting is to go through the stages of problem diagnosis, search, retrieval, and so on, so that knowledge can be transferred to the entire school staff in a manner that will enable them to see the relevance of the innovation and to feel comfortable with and skilled in implementing it.[59] This is also shown in Figure 9-3. How an individual employs the linkage model depends in part on the nature of the school district, the characteristics of the students, the nature of the innovation itself, the amount of time available, and the means available for communicating the innovation to the various impacted parties.

A school district faced with creating or implementing a new language arts curriculum, for example, might employ this model in the following manner. The school would first analyze its existing language arts curriculum to identify problems. Once it has determined a problem and the reasons for it, it would search for possible solutions. At this juncture, the school would send a message regarding its problem to the resource system. The resource system, which can either be within the school system or external to it, would also diagnose the problem and then search for a solution.

The resource system would then generate a solution to the language arts curriculum problem and send messages to the user—the school system. Meanwhile the school system has been analyzing various language arts curricula and has also retrieved from the search potential solutions. The school feeds its information to the resource system. Throughout the process, both the resource system and the user system are linked because they are addressing the same problem—creating a language arts curriculum appropriate for identified needs.

Once the solution has been identified, through the suggestions of either the school system or the resource system, it is disseminated to the school for implementation. The various stages can be recycled as necessary.

Organizational Development Model.

Schmuck and Miles hold the positions that many approaches to educational improvement from the 1960s and 1970s did not succeed because the leaders assumed that adoption was a rational process.[60] Taking such a view forced leaders to overrely on the technical aspects of innovation and diffusion. They assumed that systematic properties of local school districts were constants. They did not perceive that the organizations needed self-renewal or that various parts of the districts experienced change as a result of interaction with the environment. Schmuck and Miles suggested Organizational Development (OD) as a better approach.

To understand this model for change,

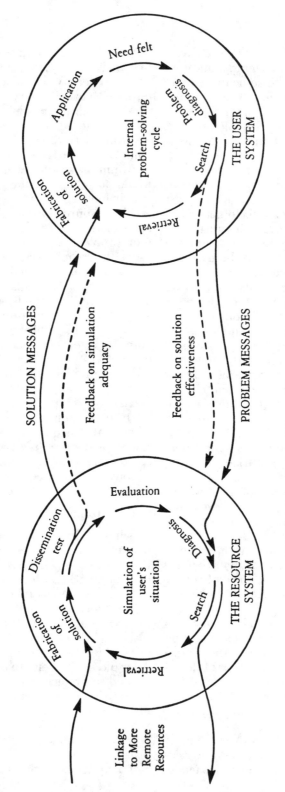

FIGURE 9-3 Linkage View of Resource-User Problem Solving Model.
Source: from Ronald G. Havelock, *The Change Agent's Guide to Innovation in Education* (Englewood Cliffs, N.J.: Educational Technology Publications, 1973), p. 166.

leaders need to realize that several views of organizations exist. Some social scientists have summarized an organization as being composed of individuals and groups who come together in order to achieve certain goals and objectives by means of differentiated functions that are intended to be rationally coordinated and directed according to some timetable.[61] This view refers in part to a bureaucratic structure.

Others maintain that the system of relations that forms the whole makes or defines an organization. If no system of relations draws the parts into a whole, then there is no organization, just free-floating parts.[62] However, the strength of the relationships and the parts can vary. Educators are coming to realize that the school is actually an organization of loosely coupled units—departments, classrooms, and persons. Also, these parts have rather flexible relationships. Although a central administration and roles are defined, most schools have little centralized control, especially over what occurs in the classroom. For this reason it is difficult for curricular change to be implemented as an edict from the central office.

Viewing implementation from an organizational stance, educators realize that organizations can create conditions that significantly influence how individuals will perceive the innovation and the ways in which they will be involved in implementing it. Chris Argyris addresses this point in a discussion of the concept of organizational learning.[63] Argyris notes that learning occurs when an organization achieves what it intended—a match between what it planned for action and the actual outcome of the implemented plans. He asserts that organizations can address learning, or what we can call effective action, by either a single- or double-loop approach. As depicted in Figure 9-4, single-loop learning takes place when an organization detects an error and corrects it without questioning or altering the underlying values of the system. It just asks whether it achieved its objectives in light of the problem defined. Single-loop learning is routine and repetitive. Argyris gives the example of a thermostat for a single-loop learner. The thermostat is programmed to detect states of "too cold" or "too hot," and to correct the situation by activating the furnace. If the thermostat were to ask itself *why* it was too cold or too hot, then it would be a double-loop learner.[64] Double-loop learning is more advanced and complex than single-loop. It involves reasoning processes among people affected by the change.

For the most part, students in school organizations learn by a single-loop approach. Generally, teachers note that students are deficient in certain skills, and they set out to correct the deficiencies through a program of change. They do not always ask *why* the students are deficient. Sometimes teachers are not successful in meeting certain objectives, but they still may not ask themselves if the objectives are indeed appropriate in light of the current times.

The Organizational Development Model depicts an information-processing change strategy. The organization engages in actions designed to improve its operational

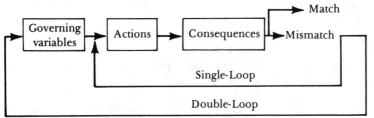

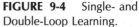

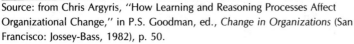

FIGURE 9-4 Single- and Double-Loop Learning.

Source: from Chris Argyris, "How Learning and Reasoning Processes Affect Organizational Change," in P.S. Goodman, ed., *Change in Organizations* (San Francisco: Jossey-Bass, 1982), p. 50.

functioning and the interactions of its members. With OD, persons within the organization work to develop the organization's members. Planned change within this model seeks to alter perceptions, attitudes, and values so that personal interactions are improved and maintained at effective levels.[65]

Blake and Mouton have expounded some principles of organizational development with applicability to education:

1. The unit of change is an organization that is autonomous and responsible for itself. The OD unit must contain within itself those persons with authority essential for setting new directions.
2. The top leadership must be actively involved in the decision making to bring about needed changes.
3. The entire human system of the organization must be involved.
4. Those responsible for managing change need to be given opportunities to learn sound concepts of leader behavior.[66]

The first and third principles draw on thinking about open systems. The principle of the open-systems concept is that the organization survives and maintains its internal order by drawing from the outside those energies necessary, and that the organization comprehends and copes with the outside forces that impinge on it. Argyris noted that open systems consist of several parts; they maintain themselves through interrelatedness; they accomplish objectives, while adapting to the environment; and through such action, they maintain the state of the organization.[67]

OD involves training groups, not individuals, in communication and problem-solving skills. It requires people to form groups and to become committed to the system and its efficient functioning. It encourages members to collaborate with one another in groups to solve their own problems. Educators who approach innovation from the OD perspective realize that the main departments and divisions of the school must

be identified, and that interlocking programs, roles, norms, and procedures must be made clear. The group is responsible for redesigning its own structure and procedures for achieving goals. The school must be viewed as a system in which actions in one part will impact actions in other parts.

Rand Change Agent Model.

This model was created by the Rand Corporation in their evaluation effort in the 1970s of four major federal programs: (1) Elementary and Secondary Education Act, Title III (Innovative Projects); (2) Elementary and Secondary Education Act, Title VII (Bilingual Projects); (3) Vocational Education Act (Exemplary Programs); and (4) the Right-to-Read Program.[68]

The Rand investigators concluded from their research that the chief barriers to change seemed to be in the organizational dynamics of a school after a decision had been made to adopt a new program or practice. The difficulty lay in the implementation of an already-developed program or procedure. For this reason, the Rand Change Agent Model emphasized organizational variables that either encourage or discourage change at all stages in the process of curriculum activity, but particularly so at the implementation stage.

The Rand Model suggests three stages in the change process: (1) initiation, (2) implementation, and (3) incorporation. In the initiation stage, change leaders work to secure the support for the anticipated change. To support a change—such as a new program—people must understand and they must agree that it is indeed legitimate in light of the organization's goals. Leaders thus require the personal backing of the individuals involved. For example, a curriculum leader or change agent needs to inform teachers about the need for change and how it might take place.

Once the curriculum leader attains the support of the members of the organization, the change activity enters the next stage. In this stage, the proposed change or program and the local school organization are modified to adapt to the program or procedure. The assumption is that the success of the implementation is a function of the characteristics of the proposed change, the abilities of the teaching and administrative staff. the nature of the local community, and the structure of the school organization.

During the incorporation stage, the changes implemented become part of the established program. Procedures are outlined and managed to ensure that the program implemented is provided with the necessary personnel and financial support so that it continues to be delivered in the intended manner. In-service and follow-up activities are essential if the program is to be incorporated. The results of the Rand study highlight the fact that successful implementation requires that a receptive group of professionals and laypersons pay attention to the organizational dynamics.

CHANGE AGENT ROLES

Any attempt at change requires change agents. Change agents may be students, teachers, administrators, consultants, state employees, university professors, parents, lay citizens, and political officials interested in education. Often such people can play different roles at different times in the change process, depending on their skills. Other persons are formally educated to assume particular roles as consultants, researchers, or systems experts. Often, the job a person holds at a particular point in time allows him or her to gain the expertise necessary to play that role in the change process.

Someone has to initiate the change process—or at least elicit a reaction to a demand. Almost anyone in the educational community can be an initiator. As we move up the administrative hierachy, there is a greater chance for an individual, because of his or her role, to serve as an initiator.

Sometimes school districts pay one or more people to be internal initiators or change agents. These persons are charged with "scanning the current scene" to detect various issues, problems, demands, or deficiencies that require attention. These persons may get others to consider change by writing papers, forming ad hoc committees to analyze particular issues, submitting proposals, or simply sending memos to staff expressing concern for some action.

In some cases, an initiator stays with the change effort during its entirety. This frequently happens when the initiator is an internal member of the organization. Other times, the initiator is a catalyst and is not actively involved in any of the stages of curriculum change. The most successful change projects always have an initiation phase with some person (or group) who is the initiator.

Teachers as Initiators.

Educators have suggested that the teacher be employed as an agent of change. The teacher should start the entire curriculum-change process by planning specific units, revising them, and then bringing the modified units to other teachers within the school system. Other educators note that in terms of being knowledgeable about the practice of teaching, teachers often represent the best clinical expertise available.[69]

Principals as Initiators.

Principals play a major role in program improvement. They can help a change be successfully implemented because they know the school organizational climate and they support those persons involved in change. Principals can also set the tone in their schools. If a principal has created an atmosphere in which good working relationships exist among teachers, and teachers are thus willing to take the risks necessary to create and deliver dynamic programs, then it is more likely that program changes will be implemented.

Berman and McLaughlin point out the

importance of the principal in their Rand Study:

The importance of the principal to both short- and long-run outcomes of innovative projects can hardly be overstated. When teachers thought that principals disliked a project, we rarely found favorable project outcomes. Some projects with neutral or indifferent principals scored well, particularly in the percentage of goals achieved; but these projects typically focused on individualization or curriculum revision, and had highly effective project directors who compensated for the lukewarm principals. Projects having the *active* support of the principal were the most likely to fare well.[70]

The principal's major contribution to implementation, according to the Rand researchers, is "not in 'how to do it' advice," which is usually better offered by project directors or consultants, "but in giving moral support to the staff and in creating an organizational climate that gives the project 'legitimacy.' "[71]

Facilitator-Coordinator.

The facilitator-coordinator, drawn from within the school organization or from outside, concentrates on the overall process of curriculum development, including implementation and evaluation. Large school districts have full-time internal facilitators who oversee curriculum activities. These persons are known as directors or coordinators of curriculum, or directors of elementary or secondary education.

Teachers and principals can also play this role. A principal can be a facilitator when he or she works to build a productive organizational unit that allows for cooperative planning and group deliberation.[72] In such situations, individuals in the school system examine their own and each other's roles to determine who has the power and qualifications to engage in particular curricular actions. A principal is also a facilitator when he or she creates a climate that fosters professional growth and leadership skills among the staff. The principal plays this role when allowing staff opportunities to accept and discharge various leadership responsibilities. If teachers are to be actively involved in curriculum development, then principals and others must "free" them from some of their regular duties so they can accomplish their new tasks.

Supervisors.

The processes of curriculum development and implementation must be supervised. Someone must monitor just what is occurring and determine whether these actions are appropriate. Frequently, the word *supervision* is associated with instruction. Certainly, instructional supervision is important, especially at the level of implementation, but, in fact, the entire process of curriculum development needs to be supervised. Moreover, during the implementation phase, not only the manner of teaching but also the content that is actually being addressed need to be supervised as well.

The supervisor provides direction and guidance, and makes sure teachers have the skills to carry out the change. Those charged with supervising curriculum development and implementation are responsible for overseeing or directing the work of others. This requires making certain decisions, engaging in particular actions, and interacting with others involved in the change effort.[73]

Effective supervisors realize that they must alter their tactics depending on the situation and the participants. Supervisors can place much responsibility in the hands of seasoned, experienced, professional teachers. However, they might have to provide beginning teachers with much more structure. They might need to schedule more opportunities for guidance and more in-service training for such staff members to deliver the new curriculum.[74]

Ronald Doll points out that supervisors have three major tasks: (1) assisting the total faculty in determining the purposes of education and monitoring the actions of professionals to see that these purposes are adhered to in the delivery of the program; (2)

furnishing democratic instructional leadership; and (3) keeping channels of communications within the school organization and between the school and the community open.[75]

Supervisors can carry out their responsibilities in numerous ways. A few popular ways are classroom observation, supervisor-teacher conferences, group work, and demonstration teaching. In demonstration teaching, the supervisor assumes a training responsibility for reeducation activities that will lead to more effective delivery of the curriculum. Frequently supervisors engage in demonstration teaching to make recommended ways of delivering the curriculum known to all involved teachers.

If supervisors are effective, it is likely that the teachers within the system will feel committed to and comfortable with the new program being implemented. Teachers will be satisfied, and thus the organization will run smoothly.

CONCLUSION

Those who understand that implementation is much more than handing out new materials or courses of study, realize that if a new curriculum is to be successfully implemented, then those involved need to be able to visualize the purposes of the program, the roles people will play within the system, and the types of individuals who are to result from the interaction with the new curriculum. Such persons also realize that even though planning is central to the change and implementation process, the process cannot be entirely or rigidly planned. Human beings require plans that are flexible; we must be able to adapt the plans to unintended consequences of implementation efforts. Also, because change is a process—not an event that happens at a point in time, but a series of engagements, behaviors, and procedures that continue over time—we are never really finished with

the implementation task. Successful implementation of a program or procedure requires perpetual fine tuning.[76]

All persons who have worked on creating a new curriculum or a new course are anxious to have it implemented and accepted with enthusiasm by all involved in the school or school district. However, new curricula often fail to become established in the school or school district because the importance and complexity of the implementation stage of curriculum development were not understood.

We have presented this chapter in hopes of making the case that curriculum implementation is crucial. We have shown that curricularists can bring various perspectives to implementation and that they can employ numerous strategies.

We have presented implementation as a change process. We have pointed out the complexity of change and that planned change is essential if innovation is to occur systematically in the school. Those in charge of change strategies must understand the relationship of change to planning and the interaction of individuals, groups, and systems.

Notes

1. John I. Goodlad and Frances Klein, *Behind the Classroom Door* (Worthington, Ohio: Charles A. Jones, 1970); Gene Hall and Susan Loucks, "A Developmental Model for Determining Whether the Treatment Is Actually Implemented," *American Educational Research Journal* (Summer 1977), pp. 263–276.
2. Glenys G. Unruh and Adolph Unruh, *Curriculum Development: Problems, Processes, and Progress* (Berkeley, Calif.: McCutchan, 1984).
3. Leslie J. Bishop, *Staff Development and Instructional Improvement: Plans and Procedures* (Boston: Allyn and Bacon, 1976).
4. Michael Fullan and Alan Pomfret, "Research on Curriculum and Instruction Implementation," *Review of Educational Research* (Winter 1977), pp. 391–392.
5. Elihu Katz, Martin L. Levin, and Herbert Hamilton, "Tradition of Research on the Diffusion of Innovation," *American Sociological Review* (April 1963), p. 240.

6. Keith A. Leithwood, "Implementing Curriculum Innovations," in K. A. Leithwood, ed., *Studies in Curriculum Decision Making* (Toronto: Ontario Institute for Studies in Education Press, 1982), pp. 65–78.

7. Edgar L. Morphet, Roe L. Johns, and Theodore L. Reller, *Educational Organization and Administration* (Englewood Cliffs, N.J.: Prentice-Hall, 1982).

8. Meredyth G. Hughes, Peter Ribbins, and Hywell Thomas, *Managing Education: The System and the Instruction* (Philadelphia: Taylor Francis, 1985).

9. Ronald C. Doll, *Curriculum Improvement: Decision Making and Process*, 6th ed. (Boston: Allyn and Bacon, 1986).

10. Wayne K. Hoy and Cecil G. Miskel, *Educational Administration: Theory, Research, and Practice*, 2nd ed. (New York: Random House, 1982); Daniel Katz et al., eds., *The Study of Organizations* (San Francisco: Jossey-Bass, 1980).

11. Michael Fullan, *The Meaning of Educational Change* (New York: Teachers College Press, Columbia University, 1982).

12. David Johnson, *Reaching Out: Interpersonal Effectiveness and Self-Actualization*, 3rd ed. (Englewood Cliffs, N.J.: Prentice-Hall, 1986).

13. Fullan, *The Meaning of Educational Change*; John I. Goodlad, *The Dynamics of Educational Change* (New York: McGraw-Hill, 1975).

14. Seymour B. Sarason, *The Culture of the School and the Problem of Change*, 2nd ed. (Boston: Allyn and Bacon, 1982).

15. Dan C. Lortie, *SchoolTeacher: A Sociological Study* (Chicago: University of Chicago Press, 1975), p. 235.

16. David Heath, *Maturity and Competence: A Transcultural View* (New York: Gardner, 1977).

17. Bruce R. Joyce, Richard H. Hersh, and Michael McKibbin, *The Structure of School Improvement* (New York: Longman, 1983).

18. Susan Loucks and Ann Lieberman, "Curriculum Implementation," in F. W. English, ed., *Fundamental Curriculum Decisions* (Alexandria, Va.: Association for Supervision and Curriculum Development, 1983), pp. 126–141.

19. David P. Crandall et al., *People, Policy and Practices: Examining the Chain of School Improvement* (Andover, Mass.: The Network, 1982).

20. Gordon McCloskey, "Principles of Communication for Principals," *National Association of Secondary Principals* (September 1960), pp. 17–23.

21. Robert Maidment, *Straight Talk: A Communication Primer* (Reston, Va.: National Association of Secondary School Principals, 1980).

22. James A. Beane, Conrad E. Toepfer, and Samuel J. Alessi, *Curriculum Planning and Development* (Boston: Allyn and Bacon, 1986); Doll, *Curriculum Improvement: Decision Making and Process.*

23. Philip Phenix, "Barriers to Academic Communication," *Teachers College Record* (November 1957), p. 88.

24. H. Dickson Corbett and Joseph J. D'Amico, "No More Heroes: Creating Systems to Support Change," *Educational Leadership* (September 1986), pp. 70–72.

25. Karen Louis, *Findings from the Study of the R & D Utilization Program* (Cambridge, Mass.: Harvard University Press, 1980).

26. Gordon L. Lippitt et al., *Implementing Organizational Change* (San Francisco, Jossey-Bass, 1985).

27. Charles E. Silberman, *Crisis in the Classroom* (New York: Random House, 1970).

28. Milbrey W. McLaughlin and David D. Marsh, "Staff Development and School Change," *Teachers College Record* (September 1978), p. 69.

29. Bill Kerewsk, "The School Community Planning Process," *Clearing House* (November 1985), pp. 113–117.

30. Mario D. Fantini, "Adaptions to Diversity: Future Trends in Curriculum," *National Association of Secondary School Principals* (May 1985), pp. 15–22; Allan C. Ornstein, "Redefining Parent and Community Involvement," *Journal of Research and Development in Education* (Summer 1983), pp. 37–45.

31. McLaughlin and Marsh, "Staff Development and School Change."

32. Leonard C. Burello and Tim Orbaugh, "Reducing the Discrepancy between the Known and the Unknown in In-service Education," *Phi Delta Kappan* (February 1982), pp. 385–388; Margaret W. Cohen, "Research on Motivation: New Content for the Teacher Preparation Curriculum," *Journal of Teacher Education* (May-June 1986), pp. 23–28.

33. John I. Goodlad, *A Place Called School* (New York: McGraw-Hill, 1984); James M. Lipham, Robb E. Rankin, and James A. Hoeh, *The Principalship: Concepts, Competencies, and Cases* (New York: Longman, 1985).

34. Laurence Iannaconne and Richard Jamogochian, "High Performing Curriculum and Instructional Leadership in a Climate of Excellence," *National Association of Secondary School Principals* (May 1985), pp. 28–35; Allan C. Ornstein, "Curriculum, Instruction, and Supervision: Their Relationship and the Role of the Principal," *National Association of Secondary School Principals* (April 1986), pp. 74–81.

35. Lortie, *SchoolTeacher.*

36. Daniel U. Levine, Rayna F. Levine, and Allan C. Ornstein, "Guidelines for Change and Innovation in the Secondary School Curriculum," *National Association of Secondary School Principals* (May 1985), pp. 9–14.

37. Ibid, p. 14.

38. John T. Lovell and Kimball Wiles, *Supervision for Better Schools*, 5th ed. (Englewood Cliffs, N.J.: Prentice-Hall, 1983).

39. Warren Bennis, *Changing Organizations* (New York: McGraw-Hill, 1966).

40. Robert Chin, "Basic Strategies and Procedures

for Effecting Change," in E. L. Morphet and C. O. Ryan, eds., *Planning and Effecting Needed Changes in Education* (Denver: Designing Education for the Future, 1967), pp. 39–57.

41. John D. McNeil, *Curriculum, A Comprehensive Introduction*, 3rd ed. (Boston: Little, Brown, 1985).

42. Roald F. Cambell et al., *The Organization and Control of American Schools*, 5th ed. (Columbus, Ohio: Merrill, 1985); John P. Miller and Wayne Seller, *Curriculum: Perspectives and Practice* (New York: Longman, 1985).

43. Edgar Z. Friendenberg, *Coming of Age in America* (New York: Random House, 1965).

44. Sydney Rosenblum and Keith Louis, *Stability and Change* (New York: Plenum, 1981).

45. Everett M. Rogers, *Diffusion of Innovations* (New York: Free Press, 1962).

46. Dorwin Cartwright, "Achieving Change in People," in W. Bennis, K. Benne, and R. Chin, eds., *The Planning of Change* (New York: Holt, Rinehart, 1976) pp. 36–67.

47. William W. Savage, *Interpersonal and Group Relations in Educational Administration* (Glenview, Ill.: Scott, Foresman, 1968).

48. Ben M. Harris, *Supervisory Behavior in Education*, 3rd ed. (Englewood Cliffs, N.J.: Prentice-Hall, 1985).

49. Neal Gross, "Basic Issues in the Management of Educational Change Efforts," in R. E. Herriott and N. Gross, eds., *The Dynamics of Planned Educational Change* (Berkeley, Calif.: McCutchan, 1979), pp. 20–46.

50. Michael Argyle, "The Social Psychology of Social Change," in T. B. Burns and S. B. Saul, eds., *Social Theory and Economic Change* (London: Tavistock, 1967), p. 95.

51. Ibid., p. 94.

52. Harold J. Leavitt, "Applied Organization Change in Industry: Structural Technology and Humanistic Approaches," in J. G. March, ed., *Handbook of Organizations* (Chicago: Rand McNally, 1965), pp. 1159–1171.

53. Gene E. Hall and Susan Loucks, "Teacher Concerns as a Basis for Facilitating and Personalizing Staff Development," *Teachers College Record* (September 1978), pp. 36–53; Hall and Loucks, "The Concept of Innovation Configurations: An Approach to Addressing Program Adaptation." Paper presented at the annual meeting of the American Educational Research Association, Los Angeles, April 1981.

54. Neal Gross et al., *Implementing Organizational Innovations* (New York: Basic Books, 1971).

55. Gross, "Basic Issues in the Management of Educational Change Efforts," in Herriott and Gross, eds., *Dynamics of Planned Educational Change*, pp. 20–46.

56. Glenys G. Unruh, "Curriculum Politics," In F. W. English, ed., *Fundamental Curriculum Decisions* (Alexandria, Va.: Association for Supervision

and Curriculum Development, 1983), pp. 99–111.

57. A. Michael Huberman and Matthew B. Miles, "Rethinking the Quest for School Improvement," in A. Lieberman, ed., *Rethinking School Improvement* (New York: Teachers College Press, Columbia University, 1986), pp. 61–81; Susan F. Loucks and Ann Lieberman, "Curriculum Implementation," in English, ed., *Fundamental Curriculum Decisions*, pp. 126–141.

58. Ronald G. Havelock, *The Change Agent's Guide to Innovation in Education* (Englewood Cliffs, N.J.: Educational Technological Publications, 1973); Havelock, *School-University Collaboration: Supporting School Improvement* (Washington, D.C.: American University Press, 1981).

59. Ibid.

60. Richard S. Schmuck and Matthew Miles, eds., *Organizational Development in Schools* (Palo Alto, Calif.: National Press Books, 1971); Schmuck et al., *The Second Handbook of Organizational Development in Schools* (Palo Alto, Calif.: Mayfield, 1977).

61. Lyman W. Porter et al., *Behavior in Organizations* (New York: McGraw-Hill, 1975).

62. Kenwyn K. Smith, "Philosophical Problems in Thinking about Organizational Change," in P. S. Goodman, ed., *Change in Organizations* (San Francisco: Jossey-Bass, 1982), pp. 316–374.

63. Chris Argyris, "How Learning and Reasoning Processes Affect Organizational Change," in Goodman, ed., *Change in Organizations*, pp. 47–86.

64. Ibid.

65. William G. Cunningham, *Systematic Planning for Educational Change* (Palo Alto, Calif.: Mayfield, 1982).

66. Robert R. Blake and Jane S. Mouton, "OD Technology for the Future," *Training and Development Journal* (November 1979), pp. 54–64.

67. Argyris, "How Learning and Reasoning Processes Affect Organizational Change," in Goodman, ed., *Change in Organizations*, pp. 47–86.

68. Paul Berman and Milbrey W. McLaughlin, *Federal Programs Supporting Educational Change, Vol. 4: Summary* (Santa Monica, Calif.: Rand Corporation, 1975). See also Daniel C. Neale et al., *Strategies for School Improvement-Cooperative Planning and Organizational Development* (Boston: Allyn and Bacon, 1981).

69. Theodore J. Czajkowski and Jerry L. Patterson, "Curriculum Change and the School," in A. W. Foshay, ed., *Considered Action for Curriculum Improvement* (Alexandria, Va.: Association for Supervision and Curriculum Development, 1980), pp. 158–175.

70. Paul Berman and Milbrey W. McLaughlin, *Federal Programs Supporting Educational Change, Vol. 8: Implementing and Sustaining Innovations* (Santa Monica, Calif.: Rand Corporation, 1980), p. 75.

71. Ibid.

72. Ann Lieberman, "Collaborative Work," *Educational Leadership* (February, 1986), pp. 4–8.

73. Robert J. Alfonso et al., *Instructional Supervision, A Behavior System*, 2nd ed. (Boston: Allyn and Bacon, 1981).

74. Lovell and Wiles, *Supervision for Better Schools*; Peter F. Oliva, *Supervision for Today's Schools*, 2nd ed. (New York: Longman, 1984).

75. Doll, *Curriculum Improvement: Decision Making and Process*.

76. Goodman et al., *Change in Organizations*.

chapter 10

CURRICULUM EVALUATION

Few educators would dispute the importance of curriculum evaluation. Even though evaluation is widely discussed, however, those charged with actually evaluating curricula do not always consider it a useful process. Many school districts, in fact, do not provide adequate resources to conduct evaluations. Moreover, many school personnel have come to regard evaluation as nonproductive behavior because evaluation results are frequently ignored. Programs judged to have value and to address particular students' needs are often discontinued, whereas programs that are questionable are often maintained because teachers and the community are comfortable with them.

It is difficult to pinpoint the reasons for the discrepancy between verbal proclamations that evaluation is crucial in all phases of curriculum and instruction and actual behavior. Part of the difficulty might be that the term *evaluation* itself is confusing because it has a variety of meanings.

Basically, anything in the schools can be evaluated in terms of its contribution to the students' overall learning and its cost. For example, school personnel can evaluate the basic worth of a program's objectives in addition to how well students attain those objectives. They can evaluate the contents, the activities, the plans, the materials, or the methods that are incorporated and ultimately delivered in the curriculum. They can evaluate the teachers' skills or behaviors, or the students' performance. Evaluation occurs at a variety of levels—classroom, school, school district, state, even nation—and involves many people serving a variety of roles.

THE NATURE AND PURPOSE OF EVALUATION

Although a simple definition of the concept of evaluation can be misleading, it can nonetheless serve to clarify the term for our discussion. Evaluation is a process or cluster of processes that people perform in order to gather data that will enable them to decide whether to accept, change, or eliminate something—the curriculum in general or an educational textbook in particular. In evaluation people are concerned with determining the relative values of whatever they are judging. They are obtaining information that they can use to make statements of worth regarding the focus of the evaluation. They are interested in conducting evaluation to determine whether the expected or the planned for has occurred or is occurring in relation to the intended. Applied to curriculum, evaluation focuses on discovering whether the curriculum as designed, developed, and implemented is producing or can produce the desired results. Evaluation serves to identify the strengths and weaknesses of the curriculum before implementation and the effectiveness of its delivery after implementation.

The purpose of gathering such data about strengths and weaknesses is to allow curricularists to either revise, compare, maintain, or discontinue their actions and programs. Evaluation enables them to make decisions, to draw conclusions, and to furnish data that will support their decisions regarding curriculum matters. Not all evaluation efforts are aimed at securing data and making judgments regarding students' success in a program. Often, evaluation efforts center on determining how to modify the staff's in-service education. Sometimes evaluation is directed toward making judgments on just how educators can communicate with and educate the community.

Evaluation Questions.

Harriet Talmage has pointed out that a good part of educators' disillusionment with evaluation results because they misunderstand what it can and cannot do for them.[1] We have perhaps been asking unrealistic or inappropriate questions of evaluation. Talmage discussed five types of value questions pertinent to evaluating curricula. An individual's approach to evaluation depends on which question or set of questions he or she poses.

The Question of Intrinsic Value. This question addresses the goodness and the appropriateness of the curriculum. It deals with the curriculum as it is planned and also with the finished curriculum as it is delivered. Essentially, if a school were dealing with a new language arts curriculum, it would ask whether the curriculum incorporates the best thinking to date on what is known about the content of language arts, the arrangement of that content, and the presentation of that content. Would specialists in linguistics, composition, grammar, and communication give the curriculum planned "high marks"?

But raising such questions is not a simple matter of getting experts to analyze the curriculum document. People bring to this question of intrinsic value their philosophical and psychological views. They perceive the curriculum in light of the purpose of education they see as paramount (Should we stress critical thinking, citizenship, or preparation for employment?) and what learning theory they prefer. (Behaviorists, cognitivists, and humanists have different views about content and methods for presenting it.)

The question of intrinsic value is difficult to process precisely, partly because there are subject areas in the school whose underlying principles are not carefully formulated. In science, there are underlying scientific principles about which most scientists and science educators agree. In contrast, bilingual educators would most likely express more diverse opinions about the underlying principles of their area of study.

The Question of Instrumental Value. This question posits, "What is the curriculum good for, and who is its intended audience?" Educators deal with the first part of this query by attempting to link up the curriculum planned with the goals and objectives stated for the program. Essentially, they judge whether what is planned in the program is going to address the goals and objectives stated. They can make this evaluation judgment by looking at the finished document; they also raise this question once the curriculum has been delivered.

The question of instrumental value also addresses whether what is planned in the curriculum will be attained, or to what extent, and by which students. In addition, this question concerns whether the philosophical or psychological orientation of the curriculum will be maintained, given the suggested contents, materials, activities, and methods. If a curriculum developer is a humanist, he or she might ask if the specifics planned for the curriculum are going to be instrumental in fostering in students a humanistic orientation toward themselves and others. A behaviorist, on the other hand, might ask if the encounters planned in the program are such that students will attain the specific behavior at the intended level of competence.

The audience to be evaluated must be identified at the outset. The second part of the instrumental value question addresses this audience factor. Not all curricula planned may be of value to all students. Evaluation efforts should identify the types of students who are likely to benefit the most from the curriculum being planned.

The Question of Comparative Value.

This question is often asked by those faced with possible new programs. Is the new program better than the one it is supposed to replace? Usually, new programs are created because people feel that the existing program is inadequate. Often when dealing with the question, people get caught up in making comparisons between different programs with different goals. Is a program that stresses skill training better than a program that stresses contemplation of the world? Certainly, the two are different. Whether one is better than the other relates to the values people hold as educators. But, still, if the program being suggested for implementation is of the same type as the existing program, the question of comparative value should be considered.

Educators need to consider this question, in fact, more than just in terms of student achievement. They need to compare the two programs' ease of delivery, cost, demand on resources, role in the existing school organization, and responsiveness to expectations of the community.

The Question of Idealization Value.

When dealing with evaluation, educators are not just concerned with determining whether what was planned actually happened. They are interested in engaging in actions that will furnish data that can help them decide how to make the program the best possible. They are concerned with taking their information on how the program is working and asking themselves if there are alternative ways to make the program even better—to heighten students' achievement or to involve students more fully in their own learning. This question requires continued action throughout the delivery of the new program. Educators must constantly ask themselves how they might "fine tune" the program's content, materials, methods, and so on, so that students can derive optimal benefits from experiencing it.

The Question of Decision Value.

If the previous four evaluation questions are addressed, the decisions made should be quality decisions. The evaluator and the curriculum decision maker should now have evidence documented in such a manner that they can decide whether to retain, modify, or discard the new program. Decisions have consequences, however. The question of decision values keeps the curriculum evaluator cognizant that the value of the decision or decisions made needs to be assessed as the curriculum is delivered in the school classrooms.

Definitions of Evaluation.

The questions presented in the previous section suggest that evaluation is a process by which evaluators can make decisions.

But, just what is evaluation? Worthing and Sanders have defined evaluation as "the determination of the worth of a thing. It includes obtaining information for use in judging the worth of a program, product, procedure, or objective, or the potential utility of alternative approaches designed to attain specified objectives."[2]

Bruce Tuckman has defined evaluation as ". . . the means for determining whether the program is meeting its goals: that is, whether the measures/outcomes for a given set of instructional inputs match the intended or prespecified outcomes."[3]

Daniel Stufflebeam has defined evaluation as ". . . the process of delineating, obtaining, and providing useful information for judging decision alternatives."[4]

All the preceding definitions view evaluation essentially as a process of identifying and gathering information that will help decision makers choose various courses of action for creating and delivering curricula. The definitions all point out that decision making is central to evaluation. It is by way of decision making that educators identify alternative curricular actions and determine various combinations of curricular elements to ensure the greatest likelihood of student learning in light of overall program goals.

Measurement versus Evaluation.

Sometimes educators confuse measurement with evaluation. Other times they use the terms interchangeably to denote a general process of appraisal. Fred Kerlinger defines measurement as "the assignment of numerals to objects or events according to rules."[5] He points out that a numeral is a symbol of the form: 1, 2, 3, ... It has no quantitative meaning unless someone chooses to give it such. People use symbols to label objects, such as boxes of strawberries or learning packets. It is important to remember that they must also assign value and meaning to numerals. For example, an evaluation of 70 percent means nothing unless someone has stated that 70 percent

means "passing" or "successful performance."

Measurement is really nothing more than the description of a situation or a behavior using numerical terms in order to avoid the value connotations that people can easily associate with words. A gym teacher can thus measure the number of times a student does pushups; a reading teacher can record the number of pages per hour a person reads; or a classroom teacher can indicate the score a child gets on a language skills test.

Measurement enables educators to record students' degrees of achieving particular competencies. Nonetheless, educators must do something with the data gathered; they must decide whether doing so many pushups is good, whether reading so many pages per hour indicates reading ability, whether a certain score denotes success or failure. They must evaluate the data and make value judgments. Such judgments will be influenced by their understanding of the purposes of the program in particular and of education in general.

APPROACHES TO EVALUATION

Evaluation is a methodological activity that really is not content specific. The same procedures are used to evaluate the effectiveness of a teaching method, a coffee maker, or the blueprints for a house. Essentially, evaluation consists of gathering and combining data in relation to a weighted set of goals or scales so as to allow people to make judgments about worth.[6] In determining the value of a curriculum plan, educators must eventually ask whether the results they expect to obtain are worth what the cost of delivering them is likely to be.

How people specifically go about processing data is influenced by their philosophical and psychological postures. If they are behaviorists or if they believe in approaching evaluation from a prescriptive or sequenced orientation, they are likely to want to spell out specific entities of curriculum and instruction. They will want to have clearly stated objectives so that they can enact procedures that will furnish them with precise indicators of whether they—or, more precisely, their students—have achieved the intended outcomes of the program. If they are humanists they are likely to be more interested in determining whether the situations planned have enabled students to improve their self-concepts. They may not pay as much attention to the students' specific achievements demonstrated by particular objective tests.

Whether educators are looking at achievement or self concept, they will realize that an evaluation will still involve a managerial aspect as well as a decision-making dimension. They have to plan how they will obtain the data necessary for making judgments; how they will communicate to students and to others the effectiveness of the curriculum; how they will manage themselves and their evaluation actions as well as the actions of others who might be involved; and how they will determine the criteria they will employ to judge some aspect of the program. Lee Cronbach separated three types of decisions for which evaluation could be used: (1) decisions about course improvement; (2) decisions about individuals, teachers, and students; and (3) decisions about administrative regulation—actually judging how good the school system is and how good individual staff members are.[7]

When evaluation is focused on course improvement, its direct purpose is to ascertain what effects the course has and how these match with the intended effects. Evaluation focused on course improvement determines aspects of the course for which revision is desirable. It also attempts to furnish data so that evaluators can comprehend what in the course or program is producing the effects and what parameters influence its effectiveness. Sometimes, evaluators discover through evaluation that the teacher's behavior with or attitude toward a certain content is influencing the degree of student attainment of that content. At other times, they discover that only certain types of students

with particular learning styles are doing well with the new content, and they attempt to determine why this is so. Evaluators also assess the administration of the total sequence of courses—the content and/or experiences—district-wide.

Scientistic and Humanistic Approaches.

More recently, Cronbach identified two basic approaches to evaluation: the scientistic ideals approach and the humanistic ideals approach.[8] He presents these approaches as opposite extremes on an evaluation continuum. Advocates of the *scientistic* end prize experiments; advocates of the humanistic approach consider experiments misinformative.

Cronbach presents the scientistic ideals person as a believer in the true experiment:

A true experiment . . . concentrates on outcome or impact and embodies three procedures: 1) Two or more conditions are in place, at least one of them being the consequence of deliberate intervention. 2) Persons or institutions are assigned to conditions in a way that creates equivalent groups. 3) All participants are assessed on the same outcome measures.[9]

Persons in this camp tend to concentrate their efforts on the learners. Data, frequently in the form of test scores, are employed to compare students' achievement in different situations, each controlled as much as is feasible. Information collected is quantitative, so it can be analyzed statistically. The decisions about the program or programs are made on the basis of the comparative information gained through the evaluation effort.

Cronbach describes the *humanistic* ideal as very different from the scientistic ideals approach:

Writers at the humanistic extreme find experiments unacceptable. For them, naturalistic case studies are the panacea. A humanist would study a program already in place, not one imposed by the evaluator. If persons are assigned to a treatment, that is because the policy under study calls for assignment; assignments are not made for the sake of research. The program is to be seen through the eyes of its developers and clients. Naturalistic investigators would ask different questions of different programs. Benefits are to be described, not reduced to a quality. Observations are to be opportunistic and responsive to the local scene, not prestructured.[10]

Those who approach evaluation from a humanistic or naturalistic posture analyze data collected in a way that differs significantly from that found in a scientistic evaluation. The data gathered in a naturalistic investigation are more qualitative than quantitative in nature. The evaluator relies more on impressions of what was observed. He or she engages in what are called "thick" descriptions of actual incidents that were observed during the evaluation effort. Data gained from interviews and discussions with participants are included in the evaluation. Patterns observed from the many observations form much of the data for analysis.

Few people follow these two extreme approaches to evaluation. Curriculum evaluators usually settle on an approach that is somewhere between the two extremes. Regardless of approach, however, evaluations contain the common thread of decision making.

Intrinsic and Pay-Off Evaluation.

Evaluators can study the curriculum plan separately or they can study the effects of the curriculum after it is delivered to the students. Michael Scriven calls the first type *intrinsic evaluation.* The criteria for evaluation are not usually operationally formulated; evaluators are merely trying to answer the question, "How good is the curriculum?"[11] The criteria employed in such evaluation refer directly to the curriculum itself. Evaluators assume that such criteria do impact educational effectiveness or results. Scriven uses studying an axe as an example of intrinsic evaluation. To examine an axe, an individual might study the design of the bit, the material used, the weight distribution, and the shape and fit of the handle. People assume that an axe of appropriate design and material will effectively cut trees, but they do not measure that fact directly.

To evaluate curricula intrinsically, evaluators study the particular content included, the way in which the content is sequenced, the accuracy of the content, the types of experiences suggested for dealing with the content, and the types of materials to be employed. They might assume that if a curriculum plan has accurate content and a firm basis for its particular organization, it will be effective in stimulating particular student learning.

Although it may seem obvious that evaluators need to engage in intrinsic evaluation—that is, they must determine if the curriculum as written has value—some persons do neglect it. Rather than asking the prior question, "How good is the curriculum?" they ask, "How well does the course or curriculum achieve its goals?" Unless educators have some judgment about the worth of the goals and objectives, and the attendant content, they cannot be sure that attaining the goals through a particular course or curriculum is a good thing.

Once the basic worth of a curriculum has been evaluated, its effects when delivered must be examined. Scriven calls this *pay-off evaluation.* Often the outcomes are operationally defined. Evaluators can consider the effects not only on the students but also on teachers, parents, and perhaps administrators. This approach to evaluation may involve making judgments regarding the differences between pre- and post-tests and between experimental group tests and control group tests on one or more criterial parameters. Pay-off evaluation draws the most attention from educators. Its defenders assert that it is really the only one that counts, because it supplies information that allows them to determine the effects of the curriculum or course on learners.

Advocates argue that with their present state of knowledge, evaluators can only do "arm-chair" intrinsic evaluation. They cannot unequivocally defend the worth of some content or experience, but they can document whether in fact learners have attained a stated objective. Supporters of the intrinsic approach would counter that the important values do not really show up in the outcomes noted in a curriculum—outcomes to which pay-off people limit themselves. This is partly due, intrinsic people argue, to the deficiencies of present test instruments and scoring procedures. Also, the results reported in pay-off evaluation studies are usually short-term results of a curriculum. Little attention is given to the long-term outcomes of a particular program. If educators wish to have an idea of the relevance and perhaps elegance of a curriculum, they will best look at the materials directly, not at students' test scores.

Formative and Summative Evaluation.

Another way to view evaluation is to distinguish between formative and summative evaluation. *Formative evaluation* encompasses those activities undertaken to improve an existing program. Evidence is sought so that decisions can be made about how to revise a program while it is being developed. That is, data are collected during the developmental phase of the program in order to modify the program before it is implemented in the total district. During the developmental and early piloting stages of a curriculum, the evaluation effort provides frequent, detailed, and specific information to guide the developers. Formative evaluation takes place at a number of specified points during the curriculum-development process. For example, some time during a curriculum's creation evaluators check whether a particular content is enabling students to learn a particular concept or certain material. If the content does not seem "valid"—that is, if it does not seem to enable students to learn a particular goal or objective—then the content is modified by the developers.

How educators conduct formative evaluation varies widely. If they are evaluating only one unit plan, their manner of evaluation may be very informal, perhaps only involving those persons teaching the unit. However, if they are engaged in creating a new program for the entire school district, then the procedure of formative evaluation may be more formal and systematic. However, the process has some flexibility.

Because curriculum development takes place over time, formative evaluation is especially well suited for guiding the creation and fine tuning of a curriculum. According to Norman Gronlund, it allows the teacher and others involved in the evaluation not only to determine what intended effects are occurring, but also to record and examine the presence of unintended effects. It uses the process of feedback and adjustments and thus keeps the curriculum development process "open."[12]

Summative evaluation aims at getting the "total" picture of the quality of the produced curriculum. It is usually undertaken after the project has been completely developed and after it has been implemented school-wide or district-wide. It focuses on the effectiveness of the total curriculum or the total course within the curriculum. Summative evaluation's major purpose is to enable the involved parties to draw conclusions about how well the curriculum or particular curriculum unit has worked. The name *summative* has been applied not because of any particular method employed but rather because this type of evaluation obtains evidence about the "summed" effects of various components or units in a particular curriculum.[13]

Although summative evaluation is performed at the "end" of the project, it should not be perceived as happening only once. It can, for example, be conducted several times at the "ends" of particular unit plans. Comprehensive summative evaluations should, in fact, be planned for certain strategic "end" points during the curriculum development process, such as at the end of the piloting stage, before final implementation district-wide stage. Engaging in summative evaluation at crucial mission points allows educators to get a total picture of the evolving curriculum product.

In contrast to formative evaluation, which often uses informal methods and frequently focuses on processes, summative evaluation is likely to use more formal means of gathering data for analysis. Tests for measuring attainment of objectives will be more carefully designed. Surveys given to assess teachers' reactions to the new curriculum will be formally prepared. Tests for students will be designed for use at the end of the course or at the end of the school year.

EVALUATION MODELS

Evaluation is not a product of this century; formal evaluation, in fact, has a very long history.[14] The ancient Chinese were giving civil service examinations to candidates as early as 2000 B.C. And early Greek teachers, such as Socrates, employed verbally mediated evaluation in their teaching.[14] Much more recently, the first evidence of formal evaluation was reported in the United states, in Joseph Rice's 1897 to 1898 comparative study of spelling performance of over 30,000 students in a large school system. Also, Robert Thorndike's contributions to the issue of evaluation in the early 1900s cannot be ignored. Called the father of educational testing, Thorndike was instrumental in getting educators to measure human change.

"The Eight-Year Study" Evaluation Model.

Perhaps the first major evaluation effort directed at curriculum was conducted under the direction of Ralph Tyler in "The Eight-Year Study" from 1933 to 1941.[15] This study was sponsored by the Progressive Education Association to address the need to free the secondary school curriculum from college dominance. (Up to that time the key curricular emphasis in high schools was the college-preparatory program.) The study was concerned with the total process of curriculum development, and evaluation was an integral part of that concern. It is one of the largest-scale longitudinal studies that has ever been conducted in education.

The study used a variety of tests, scales, inventories, check lists, questionnaires, pupil logs, and other means of obtaining data. Thirty high schools were involved in the project. Tyler, through his efforts as research director of the study, greatly influenced—and still influences—the planning of evaluation studies.[16] Tyler's recommendations were for evaluators to:

1. Establish broad goals or objectives;
2. Classify objectives;
3. Define objectives in behavioral terms;
4. Find situations in which achievement of objectives can be shown;
5. Develop or select measurement techniques;
6. Collect student performance data; and
7. Compare data with behaviorally stated objectives.[17]

These steps encourage evaluators to attend primarily to objectives. Are the objectives achieved? If so, then make these decisions. If not, then engage in these decisions and actions. Tyler maintained that evaluation is a recurring process, and that evaluation feedback is used to reformulate or redefine objectives. Information gathered can be plugged into the system to modify the objectives and the program being evaluated. This recycling keeps the evaluation system dynamic. Modifications in the objectives and in the program keep the program functioning at an optimal level; decisions made are based on data.

Metfessel-Michael Evaluation Model.

In the late 1960s Metfessel and Michael presented the academic community with a variation of the Tylerian model. Their model presents eight major steps in the evaluation process. Evaluators should:

1. Involve both directly and indirectly members comprising the total educational community—teachers, professional organization members, students, lay citizens.
2. Develop a cohesive paradigm of broad goals

and specific objectives and arrange them in hierarchical order from general to specific outcomes.

3. Translate the specific objectives produced in step 2 into a form that will be communicable and applicable to the conduct of the curriculum program.
4. Create the instrumentation necessary to furnish criterion measures from which individuals can draw inferences regarding the program's effectiveness in light of the objectives stated.
5. Conduct periodic observations throughout the implementation and maintenance of the program using tests, cases, and other appropriate instruments.
6. Analyze the data gathered employing appropriate statistical procedures.
7. Interpret the data in terms of particular judgmental standards and values that reflect the philosophical orientation of the curriculum. The conclusions derived from such interpretation will enable those involved in the evaluation to judge the direction of learners' growth, their progress in specific areas of education, and the overall effectiveness of the total program and its impact upon all affected parties.
8. On the basis of information gathered, generate recommendations that will furnish a basis for further implementing the program or for modifying the elements of the curriculum, broad goals and specific objectives, specific content, experiences, and materials. At the conclusion of this step, the process is ready to be repeated.[18]

Arranged as a system of activities, the paradigm looks like Figure 10-1.

Provus's Discrepancy Evaluation Model.

The model developed by Malcolm Provus combines evaluation with systems-management theory and consists of four components and five stages of evaluation. The four components are as follows: (1) determining program *standards*, (2) determining program *performance*, (3) *comparing* performance with standards, and (4) determining whether a *discrepancy* exists between performance and standards.[19] This is shown in Figure 10-2. Discrepancy information is reported to decision makers who in turn must make a decision (or act) at each stage. The choice of decisions is: To go to the next stage, recycle to a previous stage, start the program over, modify performance or standards, or terminate the program. It is the job of the evaluator to report to the decision maker, and to identify problems and suggest what corrective actions are possible. When discrepancies exist the decision maker is the key person in the Discrepancy Model.

There are five stages in the Provus model, and they are described in Table 10-1. In all five stages, program performance is compared to program standards—criteria which have already been established.

FIGURE 10-1 The Tyler-Metfessel-Michael Model.

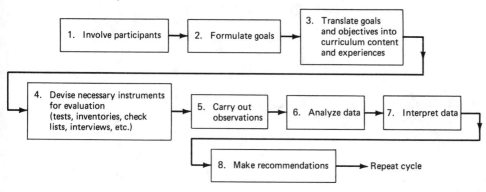

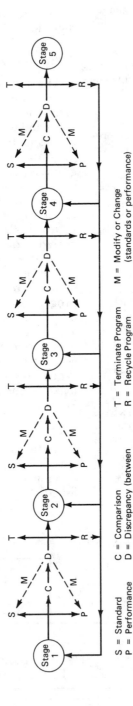

FIGURE 10-2 Components of Provus's Discrepancy Evaluation Model

Source: from Malcolm Provus, "The Discrepancy Evaluation Model," in P. Taylor and D.M. Cowley, eds., *Readings in Curriculum Evaluation* (Dubuque, Ia.: Brown, 1972), p. 118; Provus, "Evaluation of Ongoing Programs in the Public School System," in R.W. Tyler, ed., *Educational Evaluation: New Roles, New Means.* Sixty-Eighth Yearbook of the National Society for the Study of Education, Part II (Chicago: University of Chicago Press, 1969), pp. 252–253.

TABLE 10-1   Stages of Provus's Discrepancy Evaluation Model

Stages	Performance	Standard
1	Design	Design Criteria
2	Installation	Installation Fidelity
3	Processes	Process Adjustment
4	Products	Product Assessment
5	Cost	Comparisons and Cost-Benefit

Source: from Provus, "The Discrepancy Evaluation Model," p. 118; Provus, "Toward a State System of Evaluation." *Journal of Research and Development in Education* (September 1971), p. 93.

1. *Design.* This involves a comparison of the program's design with a design standard or criteria. The program is examined to determine if it is internally sound (adequacy of space, personnel, resources, materials, etc.) and externally sound (comparisons with similar programs that seem to work). The initial problems of the program are identified. Any discrepancy that exists between the program design and design standard is reported to the decision maker who must decide whether the program should be rejected, modified, or accepted.

2. *Installation.* The actual operation of the program is compared with the installation standard or fidelity criteria. The characteristics of the program are evaluated, including facilities, media, methods, student abilities and staff qualifications. Discrepancies between program installation and installation criteria are noted and reported to the decision maker for appropriate action.

3. *Processes.* Specific program processes are evaluated, including student and staff activities, functions, and communications. If the processes are inadequate, they should be reported to the decision maker who should make the appropriate adjustments.

4. *Products.* The effect of the whole program is evaluated in terms of the original goals. The products to be assessed can be in terms of student and staff products, as well as products related to the school and community. The information gained will assist decision makers about whether the program is worthwhile and should be continued as is, modified, or terminated.

5. *Cost.* The program products should be compared to products of similar programs; also, it should be evaluated in terms of cost-benefits. The methods of cost-benefit are not clearly explained. However, we must always ask whether the results are worth the cost—not only in terms of money but also morale and time taken away from other tasks. This answer has economic, social, and political implications.

Provus claimed that his evaluation plan could be used to make evaluations of ongoing programs, in any stage, from the planning stage to the implementation stage. It could be used at the school level, school district level, and regional or state level.

Stake's Congruence-Contingency Model.

In his discussion of evaluation, Robert Stake distinguishes between formal and informal evaluation procedures. While recognizing that educational evaluation continues to depend on casual observation, implicit goals, intuitive norms, and subject judgment, he notes that educators should strive to establish more formal evaluation procedures. Formal procedures are objective rather than subjective and aim at furnishing data so that descriptions can be made and judgments rendered regarding the program being evaluated.[20]

Stake indicates that evaluation specialists seem to be, and rightly so, increasing their emphasis on providing full objective descriptions and on collecting and reporting hard data. Stake asks that evaluators collect and process more extensive types of data and that they consider the dynamics among the people involved in the curriculum process. Not only should evaluators assess the roles various people play, but they should be sure to allow those people more extensive participation in judging programs. Stake further maintains that those involved in curriculum evaluation must make judgments in addition to reporting data; they should even take positions on the worth of the program being evaluated. Many evaluation specialists note that they are willing to let the local community make judgments about worth. Stake accepts that making judgments is difficult, but points out it is part of the professional role of the evaluator.

Stake maintains that data can be organized into three bodies of information: antecedents, transactions, and outcomes. An *antecedent* is any condition that exists prior to teaching and learning that may impact outcomes. Antecedents are such things as the status or characteristics of the students prior to their lessons: their aptitudes, previous achievement scores, psychological profile scores, grades, discipline, and attendance. Antecedents also include teacher characteristics such as years of experience, type of education, and teacher behavior ratings. Antecedents are "entry behaviors," sometimes described as "inputs" by other evaluators.

Stake notes that *transactions* occur between and among students and teachers, among students and students, and among students and resource people. Transactions are interactions the students have with certain curriculum materials and classroom environments dealing with time allocation, space arrangements, and communication flow. Transactions comprise what is commonly called the "process" of teaching and instruction.

In our approach to evaluation, we have been concerned with *outcomes*, also called "products," of programs—particularly achievement, sometimes attitudes and motor skills. Evaluators also need to attend to such outcomes as the impact of a new program on teachers' perceptions of their competence. They need to evaluate the influence of a program's outcomes on the actions of administrators. They also need to consider outcomes that are not directly evident at the conclusion of a program. And they should attend to long-range effects too. Stake contends that outcomes are the consequences of education—immediate and long-range, cognitive and conative, personal and community-wide.[21]

Stake's model for planning an evaluation study provides an organizational framework that points out data to be considered and contrasts what is planned and what has occurred. This model arranges the three types of data into a matrix. Figure 10-3 shows the matrix. The model shows the an-

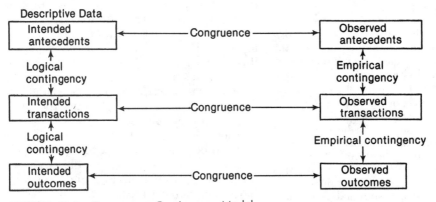

FIGURE 10-3 Congruence-Contingency Model.

Source: from Robert E. Stake, "Language, Rationality, and Assessment," in W.H. Beatty, ed., *Improving Educational Assessment and an Inventory of Measures of Affective Behavior* (Washington, D.C.: Association for Supervision and Curriculum Development, 1969), p. 20. Used with permission.

tecedents, transactions, and outcomes—the elements of evaluation—both intended and observed. The evaluator collects various judgments from different parties, students, teachers, support staff—and community members—and makes descriptions to fill in the matrix. The challenge to the evaluator is to identify contingencies, and later congruencies, among these antecedents, transactions and outcomes. *Contingencies* are the relationships among the variables in the three categories: antecedents, transactions, and outcomes. Ideally, it should be demonstrated that the outcomes are a result of antecedents and transactions. If it can be shown that transactions are related to prior antecedents, then the transactions are logically contingent on the antecedents. Similarly, the outcomes should be logically contingent from the transactions. In short, one category is expected to lead to observable and/or measurable variables in another category. The evaluator is challenged to identify the outcomes that are contingent upon particular antecedent phenomena occurring in specific transactions.

The model shows that the evaluator is also concerned with *congruence* between the intended and the observed outcomes. In dealing with congruency, he or she strives to match what is intended and what is observed. Did what was intended actually happen? To be completely congruent, all of the intended antecedents, transactions, and outcomes would have to occur.

Stufflebeam's Context, Input, Process, Product Model.

Perhaps the most important contribution to a decision-management-oriented approach to educational evaluation has been that presented by Daniel Stufflebeam.[22] His approach to evaluation is recognized as the CIPP (Context, Input, Process, Product) Model. This comprehensive model considers evaluation to be a continuing process. The general logic behind it is depicted in Figure 10-4.

The influence on decisions of management operations relating to the curriculum is evaluated; these decisions in turn impact on program *activities* or operations, which in turn are *evaluated*. This is a continuous process. The loops at the bottom of the figure show that the evaluation process includes three steps—*delineating* the information necessary for collection, *obtaining* the information, and *providing* the information to interested parties. Any evaluation study must include these three steps.

Stufflebeam and members of the Phi Delta Kappa National Study Committee on Evaluation noted that four types of decisions are required in evaluation efforts: (1) planning decisions, (2) structuring decisions, (3) implementing decisions, and (4) recycling decisions. Corresponding to these decision types are four types of evaluation: (1) context, (2) input, (3) process, and (4) product. Figure 10-5 shows these types of evaluation in relation to the four decision types.[23]

Context Evaluation. Context evaluation involves studying the environment in which the program is run. Stufflebeam maintains that "context evaluation is the most basic type. Its purpose is to provide a rationale for determination of objectives."[24] It defines the relevant environment, portrays the desired and actual conditions pertaining to that environment, focuses on unmet needs and missed opportunities, and diagnoses the reason for unmet needs. Context evaluation is really a "situation analysis"—a reading of the reality in which individuals find themselves and an assessment of that reality in light of what they want to do. The diagnosis stage provides the basis for developing objectives.

Context evaluation is not a one-time activity. It continues to furnish baseline information regarding the operations and accomplishments of the total system.

Input Evaluation. The second stage of the model, input evaluation, is designed "to provide information for determining how to utilize resources to meet program goals."[25]

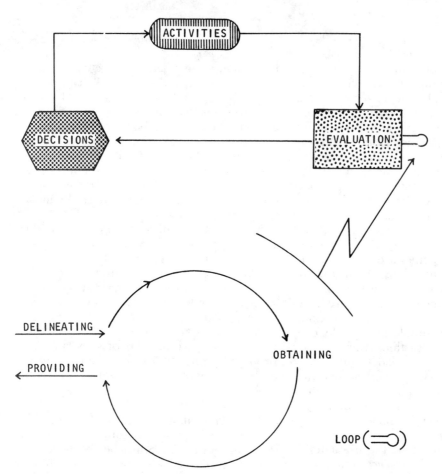

FIGURE 10-4 The Relation of Evaluation to Decision Making.
Source: from Daniel L. Stufflebeam, *Educational Evaluation and Decision Making*
(Itasca, Ill.: Peacock, 1971), p. 134.

	INTENDED	ACTUAL
ENDS	PLANNING DECISIONS to determine objectives	RECYCLING DECISIONS to judge and react to attainments
MEANS	STRUCTURING DECISIONS to design procedures	IMPLEMENTING DECISIONS to utilize, control and refine procedures

FIGURE 10-5 Types of Decisions and Evaluation. Source: from Daniel L. Stufflebeam, *Educational Evaluation and Decision Making* (Itasca, Ill.: Peacock, 1971), p. 135.

nput evaluators assess the school's capabilities to carry out the task of evaluation; hey consider the strategies suggested for chieving program goals, and they identify he means by which a selected strategy will be implemented. At this stage, they evaluate lternative designs in terms of how they will contribute to the attainment of objectives tated and in terms of their demands upon esources, time, and budget. They consider hem in light of the procedural feasibility.

In contrast to context evaluation, input evaluation is ad hoc and microanalytic ather than systematic and macroanalytic. It s placed into action in light of the conclusions reached from context evaluation. It evaluates specific aspects of the curriculum plan or specific components of the curriculum plan. Input evaluation asks many questions: Are the objectives stated appropriately? Are the objectives congruent with the tated aims and goals of the school? Is the content congruent with the aims, goals, and objectives of the program? Are the instructional strategies appropriate? Do other strategies exist that can also help meet the objectives? What is the basis for believing hat using these contents and these instructional strategies will enable educators to successfully attain their objectives?

This stage of evaluation can range from being easy and simple to being complicated and difficult. The actual complexity depends in part on the magnitude of the curriculum evaluation effort. If a school is talking only about creating a new course, then this stage would be rather simple and involve few people. But, if it is undertaking a total revision of a K-12 program, then the procedure would be quite complex.

Process Evaluation. This stage addresses curriculum implementation decisions that control and manage the plan or program. It is used to determine the congruency between the planned and actual activities. Stufflebeam has presented three main strategies for process evaluation: "The first is to detect or predict defects in the procedural design or its implementation during the diffusion stages, the second is to provide information for programmed decisions, and the third is to maintain a record of procedures as they occur.[26]

In dealing with plan or program defects, or the first strategy, it is important for educators to identify and monitor continually the potential sources of the project's failure. They must pay attention to the logistics of the entire operation, and they must maintain communication channels among all affected parties. They must also consider the adequacy of the resources, the physical facilities, the staff's preparation, and the time schedule.

The second strategy "involves projecting and servicing preprogrammed decisions to be made by project managers during the implementation of a project."[27] In this step, evaluators might make decisions regarding test development prior to the actual implementation of the program. Some decisions may require that certain in-service activities be planned and carried out before the program's actual implementation.

The third strategy addresses the main feature of the project design—for example, the particular content selected, the instructional strategies planned, or the time allotted in the plan for such activities.

Process evaluation, which includes the three strategies, occurs during the implementation stage of curriculum development. It is a piloting process conducted to "debug" the program before district-wide implementation. From such evaluation, project decision makers obtain information they need to anticipate and overcome procedural difficulties and to make preprogrammed decisions.

Product Evaluation. Product evaluators gather data to determine whether the final curriculum product now in use is accomplishing what they had hoped. To what extent are the objectives created being attained? Product evaluation provides evaluators with information that will enable them to decide whether to continue, terminate, or modify the new curriculum. It allows them to link actions at this stage of the model to other stages of the total change process. For example, a product evaluation might furnish data that shows that the science curriculum planned for talented science students has successfully allowed students to attain the program objectives. The program is now ready to be implemented in other schools in the system in which such students exist.

As noted previously, Stufflebeam relates evaluation to a decision-making process. He has outlined the objectives, the methods, and the relation of each type of evaluation to decision making in the change process.

Stufflebeam's Macro (Total) Evaluation Model.

Stufflebeam has proposed a total evaluative program, which is presented in Table 10-2. The model provides for systematic context, input, process, and product evaluation.[28]

We have already discussed the four types of evaluation shown in the model. But the model also shows four types of decisions (in the hexagons): planning, structuring, implementing, and recycling. Figure 10-6 shows that (1) planning decisions are enacted after context evaluation; (2) structuring decisions are initiated after input evaluation; (3) implementation decisions follow process evaluation; and (4) recycling decisions are made after product evaluation.

Stufflebeam and his associates note that decision making occurs in four different settings: (1) small change with high information; (2) small change with low information; (3) large change with high information; and (4) large change with low information.

The different settings in which decisions can be made generate four types of change activity:

1. *Neomobilistic change* occurs when someone attempts to make a large change on the basis of low information. In such a case, an innovation is being attempted with little evidence that the change will work.

2. *Incremental change* refers to a series of small changes also based on low information.

3. *Homeostatic change,* the most common in education, is a small change that is based on much information.

4. *Metamorphic change* is great change supported by much information. It is so rare that Stufflebeam did not include it in his CIPP model.

The CIPP model, which depicts a comprehensive view of the evaluation process, can show the entire process of program design, development, implementation, and evaluation. For this reason, it perhaps has implications for wider use than just evaluation. It is, however, rarely examined in basic curriculum texts, probably because it is somewhat complicated.

Eisner's Connoisseurship Evaluation Model.

The previous models draw heavily on the quantitative, technical posture of evaluation. Elliot Eisner has recommended a process, called educational criticism and connoisseurship, that will supposedly produce more than hard data and outcomes. It will furnish a rich or qualitative description of educational life as a consequence of new programs.[29] Eisner notes that to employ the procedure of educational criticism, evaluators should ask such questions as "What has occurred during the school year at a particular school as a result of the new program? What were the key events? How did such events arise? How did students and teachers participate in these events? What were the reactions of the participants to these events? How might the events have been made even more effective? Just what do the students learn from experiencing the new program? These questions focus on process, on school life, and on school quality. They differ in kind from questions raised in the quantitative camp.

Eisner's case for educational criticism and connoisseurship draws heavily from the arts. Eisner states that if an individual is to

TABLE 10-2 Four Types of Evaluation: Context, Input, Process, and Product

	Context Evaluation	Input Evaluation	Process Evaluation	Product Evaluation
Objective	To define the existing context, to determine the needs and opportunities present, and to diagnose the problems underlying the needs.	To identify and assess the school system's capabilities, the presence of input strategies, and the various designs for implementing strategies.	To identify or predict, in process, defects in the procedural design or in the implementation plan; to maintain account of actions taken.	To gather and communicate information regarding outcome information about objectives achieved and content covered; to relate findings to the previous three stages of evaluation.
Method	Describing the context, comparing the actual and intended inputs and outputs, gathering data to compare probable and possible system performance, and determining why certain deficiencies exist.	Describing and analyzing available human and material resources, solution strategies, and systems designs in light of the course of action being suggested.	Monitoring the actual implementation of the plan with its related activities to determine potential procedural barriers; gathering information to describe the actual procedures employed.	Defining operationally and measuring criteria associated with the objectives; comparing the results exhibited with predetermined standards; interpreting the overall results relative to the previous three evaluations.
Relation to Decision Making	Used to decide the setting to be served, the goals to be addressed, and the particular objectives to be considered.	Used to decide what sources of support are required, what solution strategies are appropriate, and what procedural designs can be employed to initiate the program change desired.	Used to make decisions regarding implementing and refining the program.	Used to gather information to determine whether to continue, terminate, or modify the program.

Source: from Daniel L. Stufflebeam, "The CIPP Model," in G. D. Borich and R. P. Jamelka, *Programs and Systems: An Evaluation Perspective* (Orlando, Fla.: Academic Press, 1982) p. 11.

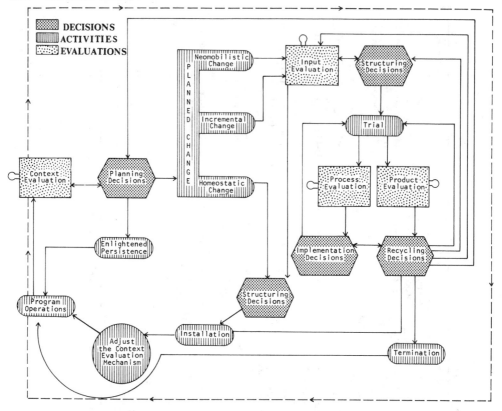

FIGURE 10-6   An Evaluation Model.

Source: from Daniel L. Stufflebeam, *Educational Evaluation and Decision Making*
(Itasca, Ill.: Peacock, 1971), p. 140.

be an illuminating critic of painting, opera, theater, film, or even wine, he or she must first be a connoisseur—that is, he or she must possess a great deal of knowledge about and experience with the type of phenomenon he or she is to criticize. A good critic has an awareness and appreciation of the subtle qualities of the situation; he or she can detect and write about the nuances of the situation in ways that help others to become more aware of the phenomenon under consideration.

Eisner points out that educational connoisseurship is "the art of appreciating the educationally significant."[30] But such appreciation is made public through criticism— the description, interpretation, and assessment of the situation. In discussing his

approach to evaluation, Eisner relies on referential adequacy and structural corroboration instead of scientific validity. *Referential adequacy* requires the critic to check that critical observation and interpretations are empirically grounded. The reader is allowed to experience the evaluated phenomenon in a new and better way. Eisner defines *structural corroboration* as continuous inquiry about whether the various parts of the criticism fit together as a consistent whole.

Eisner would have the evaluator engaged in such qualitative activities as being participant classroom observers and asking many questions about the quality of the school and the curriculum. An evaluator following Eisner's model would also engage in a detailed analysis of pupils' work. He or she would use films, videotapes, photographs, and audio tapes of both teachers and students in action; he or she would also note what is done, what is said, and, perhaps more importantly, what is not done and not said. The evaluator would strive to describe the "tone" of the curriculum in action.

Eisner makes the point that evaluation should allow for some form of communication to some public—parent, school board, local or state agency—about what has been and is occurring in the school. The evaluator presents or describes the educational scene. To some extent, such evaluation takes on a subjective and aesthetic approach; for this reason, it is considered controversial by those who believe in objective and scientific documentation. Finally, the Connoisseurship Model has many characteristics of what is sometimes called Responsive Evaluation.

Stake's Responsive Evaluation Model.

Responsive evaluation is a term popularized by Robert Stake, and is more concerned with evaluating curriculum or program activities and processes than intents or outcomes; it relies more on informal and natural communication than formal and standard communication.[31] Like with the Eisner evaluation model, the Responsive approach is more concerned with the "portrayal" of the program than standardized data, test scores, and goals—what some people might label as methodological or objective data. Responsive evaluation requires planning and development, but it relies less on formal statements and research-oriented information than do technical-scientific models of evaluation. Using the responsive approach, the evaluator tells the story of the program, presents its features, describes the clients and personnel, identifies major issues and problems, and reports the accomplishments. The evaluator assumes the posture of a critic reviewing a play or a painter depicting a landscape scene.

To conduct responsive evaluation, Stake maintains that the evaluator develop a plan which deals with the scope and activities of the program. He or she must arrange for people to make observations, prepare narratives and portrayals, and provide product displays. Because all of us have particular biases, the various audiences of the report must be identified; their feelings and expressions of what is worthwhile and important should be considered. The data reported must be analyzed in terms of the audience's biases, and they (as well as personnel of the program) must have a chance to react to the findings. To perform this task, the evaluator will probe and ask questions. Various participants and audiences may become defensive and seek to avoid or confront the evaluator. However, important questions about quality must be examined and processed.

Stake outlines the steps of responsive evaluation as applied to evaluating a curriculum. (Nine steps are listed; number four is the authors' based on interpretation of the entire model.)

1. Negotiate a framework for evaluation with the sponsors.
2. Elicit topics, issues, and/or questions of concern from the sponsors.
3. Formulate questions for guiding the evaluation.
4. Identify the scope and activities of the curriculum; identify the needs of clients and personnel.
5. Observe, interview, prepare logs and case studies, etc.
6. Pare down the information; identify the major issues or questions.
7. Present initial findings in a tentative report.
8. Analyze reactions and investigate predominant concerns more fully.
9. Look for conflicting evidence that would invalidate findings, as well as collaborative evidence that would support findings.
10. Report the results.[32]

Many of these steps are related to goal-free evaluation which is concerned with the biases of evaluation. In goal-free evaluation, the evaluator is expected to be objective, not influenced by the goals or objectives of the program or the values of the program developer or sponsors.[33]

PRACTICES OF EVALUATION

The previous models involve a variety of practices. Although there is some disagreement about the precise steps that evaluation would take, some notion of how to proceed through the evaluation process is useful. Presented next are phases of evaluation that educators can follow. These steps draw heavily from the technical-scientific approach to curriculum. But, even a humanistic approach to evaluation, such as Eisner's, or Stake's, would have to focus on the curricular phenomena being evaluated. Evaluators would also need some means, whether objective or subjective, of collecting the information.

Phases of Evaluation.

As just mentioned, to carry out an evaluation, an evaluator must have a plan of action. Much has been written on what steps are necessary to accomplish this. The following steps seem to be common to most evaluators' discussions:

1. *Focusing on the Curricular Phenomena to be Evaluated.* In this step, evaluators determine just what they are going to evaluate and also what design they will use. They determine the focus of the evaluation: Will it be the total school system or a particular school? Will it be one particular subject area or grade level within that school?

   In this connection, evaluators spell out the objectives of their evaluation activity and identify the constraints and policies under which the evaluation will be conducted. They identify the level of decision making necessary to carry out the evaluation as well as a target date or schedule for the various aspects of the evaluation. They also identify criteria for determining alternative decisions and action paths, and for assessing the results of the curriculum components.

2. *Collecting the Information.* In this step, evalua-

tors identify the sources of information essential for consideration and also the means they can use to collect that information. They also map out stages for collecting the information in terms of their time schedule.

3. *Organizing the Information.* Here evaluators organize the information so that it becomes interpretable and usable to the final intended audience. They note means of coding, organizing, storing, and retrieving the information.

4. *Analyzing the Information.* At this stage, evaluators select and employ appropriate analysis techniques. The specific techniques they choose depend on the focus of the evaluation.

5. *Reporting the Information.* Here evaluators decide the nature of the reporting, keeping in mind the audience for the report. They might engage in an informal reporting such as giving opinions and making judgments based on general perceptions. They might, however, decide that their evaluation should more rigorously collect, treat, and report the data. The final report would have detailed statistical data.[34]

6. *Recycling the Information.* The need for current information involves continuous reevaluation and reassessment—a continuous attempt to improve the curriculum. Even if the curriculum appears to be viable, continuous feedback, modifications, and adjustments are necessary because forces impacting on the schools are always changing.

In relaying information to the intended audience, the evaluators need to do more than just report—that is, tell the results. They should also relay their interpretations of the data, drawing from the analysis stage, and their recommendations for action. Sometimes the evaluators themselves are the audience. If so, they need to determine just how they will use the information and the results they gathered. They need to make judgments. If they have been working for those responsible for the overall curriculum-development and evaluation effort, then they may just submit their recommendations to the curriculum decision makers to do with as they wish. Sometimes, evaluators are also charged with ensuring that their recommendations are carried out. This is especially true when the evaluators are working directly for the central office. In such instances, evaluators may indicate means by which their recommendations can be accomplished.

Of course some person or persons must be in charge of these phases of evaluation. Schedules and budgets have to be determined. Ideally, the management aspects of evaluation should be carefully planned at the outset of the evaluation effort, whereby various stages of evaluation are outlined with timetables, divisions of labor (people assigned to tasks), and cost allocations per task and then totaled.

METHODOLOGICAL ISSUES OF EVALUATION

A diversity of views characterizes discussions about what evaluation is and to what purpose it should be put. Part of the reason for such diversity of opinion is that people often bring to the evaluation process different purposes—that is, they wish to employ evaluation to satisfy different needs. They argue, for example, over how much control is necessary in evaluation; they disagree about the definition of evaluation; and they debate the appropriateness of various sampling techniques. Evaluators may even contest what the issues confronting the field are. Mindful of this, we present the following issues as representative of the field of evaluation.

The Nature and Form of Objectives.

A common focus of evaluation has been to determine the extent to which objectives have been achieved. In this context, evaluators must first make clear what they mean by objectives. Perhaps during the last fifteen years, one issue in curriculum which has received much attention has been the value of and the appropriate form for objectives.[35] Part of the reason for such continued interest in objectives is philosophical. Behaviorists believe that an objective must specify the exact behavior that the learner will display as a consequence of experiencing the curriculum. At the other extreme are individuals who state that the curriculum must have a humanistic bent and, therefore, that objectives must "evolve" from the experiences of individuals. Each student has the responsibility of forming his or her own objectives.

Although a particular behavior can specify that an objective has been attained, the behavior can denote covert as well as overt action. Some curriculum specialists have noted that an objective really should show the educational intent rather than indicate realization of the intent.[36] These educators maintain that when creating objectives, evaluators should also consider why they want students to perform these actions. Having a student run a mile in eight minutes indicates a behavior (run), a situation (a mile), and even the criterion of performance (eight minutes). But the objective does not indicate *why* they would want a person to run a mile in the first place, much less in eight minutes.

Part of the problem of determining just what objectives are or should be and how to write them is that groups do not always consider sufficiently the many purposes of objectives. Objectives also can be listed at several levels. Curriculum objectives, for example, can be written to communicate general direction for the entire curriculum or for only the grade or subject level. Also they can be more specific—designed to guide the selection of particular contents and instructional experiences at a unit or lesson-plan level.

It is likely that discussion will continue to center on objectives. But few persons would accept that objectives should not be used at all. Most consider them to be valuable guides for curriculum planners and evaluators. How specific someone is in forming objectives is impacted by his or her curriculum orientations and philosophical views. Objectives, however formed, give evaluators a "view" of just where they think they are going—which will help them realize when they have "arrived."

Measurement of Student Exit Requirements.

Evaluators need to measure how students are performing at the conclusion of the program. But some evaluators distinguish between evaluating the *program* and evaluating the *students*. Program evaluation centers on instructional outcomes in the program and determines whether these outcomes are the result of groups of students' experiencing the program. The thrust of such evaluation is on the program. It assesses the worth of the program and holds those who deliver it accountable.

Student evaluation, in contrast, involves gathering data about students' performances to decide whether they are qualified for course completion or, for that matter, for graduation. The burden of responsibility shifts to the individual student. If evaluators take this stand, they really have no reason to modify the program or to hold teachers accountable. The student failed, not the program. Who an evaluator holds accountable, of course, can generate a good deal of conflict; it often reflects the individual's philosophical and political views of schools and society.[37]

Intended Outcomes versus Goal-Free Evaluation.

Mauritz Johnson, who states that curriculum is a series of intended learning outcomes, argues that evaluators should indicate at the outset just what they want their program to accomplish in order to determine how to evaluate it.[38] Tyler has also, on occasion, told educators that they must define the objectives of a program and to indicate the situations in which students would be given the opportunity to accomplish the objectives. Most evaluators favor using objectives for this purpose.

This seems logical, especially if evaluation is considered purposeful behavior—actions meant to determine the worth of the curriculum, or whether the curriculum allowed students to attain the objectives

stated. But for many years Scriven has been advocating a "goal-free" approach to evaluation.[39] Scriven argues that sometimes people wish to engage in evaluation just to examine the effects of an educational innovation and to judge the quality of the effects produced. He calls such evaluation goal-free evaluation; its purpose is to determine the actual effects of the program by recording and interpreting what occurred during and as a result of the program.

Taking this approach, an evaluator does not confine his or her energies to the stated objectives of the new program, but instead gathers data to assess and evaluate the outcomes—whatever they may be. The educator employs a wide variety of measures to do this. He or she uses both quantitative and qualitative measures to get a "picture" of the program in action and also a "reading" of what has happened to students from having experienced the program. The evaluator might focus his or her attention on both the teachers and the community to see what resulted from the implementation of the new curriculum.

It is also noted that evaluating programs based on program goals may be misleading.[40] Goals are often more political than educational in character. Frequently they are so vague that they are not useful: They misrepresent the curriculum. If educators employ goal-free evaluation and, along with their quantitative measures, use ethnographic techniques, they may get a more accurate picture of both the intended and the unexpected results of how the curriculum functions. The trouble is, many educators are not goal-free; they are compelled by strong views about schools and society—and have already made up their minds about the worth of certain programs and curriculum before the outcomes are known.[41]

Norm-Referenced and Criterion-Referenced Measurement.

Most evaluations of the curriculum involve achievement testing. Many norm-reference tests, sometimes called standardized tests, have been created to discriminate among individual students. Although testing such discrimination is important in certain situations, testing discrimination among curricula is necessary as well.

Two basic approaches to testing dominate curriculum evaluation. Norm-referenced measurement is the most common. In this approach, the student's performance on a particular test is compared with the performance of other students who also took the same test—the norming group.

Standardized achievement tests, probably the most well-known norm-referenced tests, identify persons of varying ability. They have, however, questionable value for measuring the quality of a curriculum. They do not, for instance, address the goals or content of a particular curriculum; rather, they produce scores that are fairly global in nature, such as for "reading comprehension" and "math computation."[42] They are also not designed for a particular audience or for target students. What they do measure is what a student knows in relation to other students at a given time. In addition, despite their limitations, standardized tests are often administered to determine the success of the curriculum in place or a new curriculum.

The alternative to the norm-referenced test is the criterion-referenced test. Criterion-referenced tests report how a student stands with respect to some fixed criterion. Such tests indicate a learner's status with respect to a learning task that can be stated in some specific educational objective, such as ability to identify particular examples of certain concepts or ability to multiply two-digit numbers.[43] With the criterion test, a student is given a score that indicates either mastery or nonmastery of each objective. There may be a total score for the test, but the global score is not really of interest.

Criterion-referenced tests indicate what the students can and cannot do with regard to specific content, skills, and attitudes. In effect, they indicate changes in learning over time, compared to normative tests that measure learning at a specific time. The student has either learned or not learned to do something, understands or does not understand something, or shows progress in understanding something as a result of experiencing the curriculum.

Criterion-referenced tests focus on the specific tasks and competencies that have been stressed in a particular curriculum. Because these tests are curriculum-specific, they have special value to those who wish to evaluate a new curriculum in their school district. Evaluators can use such tests to gather data that will enable educators to determine what has been taught and the overall effectiveness of the curriculum.

In addition to showing the overall success of the curriculum, criterion-referenced tests can also reveal whether a student has mastered particular material. Thus, these tests can be used for student evaluation as well as program evaluation.[44] Educators can use the results of such tests to determine what specific "remedies" are necessary for particular students. Also, test results can be employed to indicate that students are ready to proceed to other stages in the curriculum.

Even though the criterion-referenced test enables educators to correct some of the "shortcomings" of the norm-referenced test, it does have some problems or disadvantages of which educators should be aware. One is that they address specific objectives. A great number of such tests—up to ten or fifteen—are thus necessary to get a thorough picture of the curriculum.[45] Second, it is not easy to determine the standards for acceptable performance that criterion test items are supposed to measure. Just what is the cut-off score for mastery of an objective? However, educators usually get around this difficulty by setting the cutting score arbitrarily—for instance, they may require the student to get three out of four correct. But, is three out of four really mastery?

Table 10-3 presents a comparison of these two types of tests. The comparison in-

TABLE 10-3 Comparison of Norm-Referenced and Criterion-Referenced Measurement

Norm-Referenced Measurement	Criterion-Referenced Measurement
1. The main function of norm-referenced measurement is to ascertain the student's relative position within a normative group.	1. The main function of criterion-referenced measurement is to assess whether the student has mastered a specific criterion or performance standard.
2. Either general or conceptual outcomes (usually done) or precise objectives may be specified when constructing norm-referenced measurement.	2. Complete behavioral objectives (i.e., planning objectives) are specified when constructing criterion-referenced measurement.
3. The criterion for mastery is not usually specified when using norm-referenced measurement.	3. The criterion for mastery must be stated (i.e., planning objectives) for use in criterion-referenced measurement.
4. Test items for norm-referenced measurement are constructed to discriminate among students.	4. Test items for criterion-referenced measurement are constructed to measure a predetermined level of proficiency.
5. Variability of scores is desirable as an aid to meaningful interpretation.	5. Variability is irrelevant; it is not a necessary condition for a satisfactory criterion-referenced measurement.
6. The test results from norm-referenced measurement are amenable to transportation to the traditional grading system (A, B, C, D, F).	6. The test results from criterion-referenced measurement suggest the use of a binary system (i.e., satisfactory-unsatisfactory; pass-fail). However, criterion-referenced measurement test results can be transposed into the traditional grading system by following a set of specifically constructed rules.

Source: from Mary-Jeanette Smythe, Robert J. Kibler, and Patricia W. Hutchings, "A Comparison of Norm-Referenced and Criterion-Referenced Measurement with Implications for Communication Instruction," *Speech Teacher* (January 1973), p. 4. Reprinted by permission.

dicates the functions, advantages, and disadvantages of both tests.

Evaluation Standards.

Evaluation is concerned with making judgments—determining what is valuable and assessing how well students and others have done. Making judgments requires having a clear set of standards as to what is success. Standards imply value structures, however, a value structure may be unclear. Determining criteria for success—criteria on which to build standards—is difficult if mastery levels for those criteria are vague. Also, in a pluralistic society such as ours, multiple values exist. The question often is whose values or standards to apply.

What often happens is that the criteria of success are derived from evaluating what

most people or students are doing or know and attempting to get the target group of students to do the same or better. This is the approach when using norm-referenced tests. Educators judge how well their students are doing in relation to the norm group. But, the norm group only indicates what is; it does not report what could be. In a sense, what could be can only be answered by philosophical reflection.

Robert Zais has discussed four standards for evaluation that we can consider—absolute maximum standard, absolute minimum standard, relative standard, and multiple standard.[46] The *absolute maximum standard,* set arbitrarily, is only obtainable by a few students. For example, 90 to 100 percent performance may represent excellence in achievement. Theoretically, all normal students with appropriate effort can attain this standard, but in reality few do.

The *absolute minimum standard,* also set arbitrarily, represents a point that ensures success for virtually all students experiencing the curriculum. This standard is used in programs that emphasize minimum competency. Such a standard may be most valuable in situations in which basic skills are being taught.

The *relative standard* employs the concept of "normal curve." In using this standard, curriculum evaluation compares the performance of each student to the performance of other group members. The group's mean performance is appraised. Using this standard encourages competition among students and assumes that all students can compete equally.

The *multiple standard* measures the growth of each student during the program. This standard provides data on each individual's actual performance at the program's outset and at the point of evaluation. Also, the teacher gains information that allows him or her plot each student in relation to other students. This standard addresses individuals' idiosyncrasies. However, it is virtually impossible to measure the legions of students' traits or behaviors at program implementation for the purpose of obtaining base-line data. Also such gathering of data would take an inordinate amount of time. Sometimes educators use this standard in situations that stress highly restricted training.

ROLES PLAYED IN EVALUATION

Over two decades ago, Hilda Taba maintained that evaluation is a cooperative activity. This cooperation is as necessary to the process of evaluation as it is to the various activities of the total curriculum.[47] It is necessary in forming the overall evaluation plan, in selecting the instruments and evaluation model to be applied, and in carrying out all stages of evaluation from formulating objectives to writing the report.

In a school-wide evaluation effort, teachers, administrators, and evaluators need to cooperate to determine what is necessary to make judgments regarding the curriculum. They need to coordinate the gathering and formating of data. Evaluation decisions are not made by one teacher or one administrator in isolation, and they are not made about only one aspect of the curriculum. Usually, such decisions relate to the entire curriculum and all the people responsible for delivering it, including teachers and administrators.

Taba indicated that perhaps the best reason for cooperative evaluation of the curriculum is that such a "collective" effort allows all involved to get a total curriculum picture. For example, teachers can work together to provide evidence of the effects of the curriculum on various types of students. If they work alone, teachers only realize how the program worked with their own students. If they collaborate, they can ascertain the program's effectiveness with all types of students.

The Evaluator.

Cooperation among all parties engaged in curriculum development and delivery is necessary. Even though various people can play particular roles in an overall evaluation, it is wise to have one person in charge. This person—the evaluator—works closely with the central school office, which administers the curriculum.

The evaluator can be a member of the school system. There are several advantages to this; the person knows the system and its goals. It is usually less expensive to conduct an evaluation if the evaluator is already on the school payroll. Because the person is an insider, the results of his or her evaluation may be accepted more easily. However, there are also disadvantages to having an insider as the key evaluator. An insider may not be willing to issue an evaluation report that is critical of the system. He or she may also have too many other responsibilities to be able to undertake a major evaluation effort. Furthermore, his or her expertise might not be considered to be at the same level as that of an "outside expert."

The evaluator, or one of the agents of the evaluation team, is usually an observer. He or she designs the means of gathering data so that knowledge can be supplied to decision makers. Note that the evaluator does not supply the values with which the data gathered will be used; rather he or she helps the decision maker to clarify his or her values so that they can be addressed.[48]

In theory the evaluator serves as the eyes and the ears of the decision maker. In this role, he or she furnishes data gathered from observations about how the curriculum is functioning in the school. It is up to the curriculum coordinators, curriculum advisory committees, and the teachers to take the data gathered, to judge their value, and to then act upon them. The evaluator is essentially a support person to the curriculum-development and implementation efforts.[49]

Teachers.

Teachers are perhaps the most obvious professionals who assume evaluation roles. But, often they have only worked alone in evaluating the curriculum. Also, they frequently do not evaluate the curriculum but rather their instructional skills in delivering that curriculum. Indeed, teachers should be involved in cooperative curriculum work, and they should be part of curriculum advisory committees, which have partial responsibility for program evaluation. Effective teachers realize that they can play several roles in evaluation.[50]

Committees.

Because curriculum development is a cooperative effort, numerous committees may be involved. Most, if not all, schools should have a curriculum advisory committee and a special committee responsible for evaluation policy and procedure. This special committee serves an advisory function to the person in charge of program evaluation. Its membership can be similar to that of curriculum advisory committees—that is, participants could be teachers and administrators and representatives of the lay community. Depending on the school district and the curriculum level, students might also serve on this committee.[51]

Consultants.

It is sometimes wise for a school district to hire an outside consultant to conceptualize the evaluation approach and to coordinate the evaluation effort. Often small schools do not have any staff persons trained especially for evaluation. When they require such activity, a common procedure is for them to bring in an outside person. In fact, some educators argue that the evaluator of a new program should always be an outsider.[52] Such a person, having no "professional turf" to guard, can be much more objective and truthful in reporting findings.

The resources of the school district, the extent of the evaluation effort, and the level of the staff's expertise should guide educators deciding whether to bring in an outside consultant for evaluation. Certainly, an outside consultant will have expertise, but he or she may be viewed as an intruder from outside the system or as a representative of the central office, which would impede the evaluation process. The person in charge of the curriculum-development effort must take these factors into consideration.

CONCLUSION

This chapter dealt with curriculum evaluation. It began with a discussion of the nature and purpose of evaluation, and it addressed the key questions that evaluation sets out to process. Several definitions of evaluation were presented, as were various approaches to it. We made the case that evaluation is an essential aspect of curriculum development; it requires expertise and resources, just as the other major stages in curriculum development.

Evaluation is a complex stage. We discussed major models that have been developed, and their advocates and critics. The field of curriculum evaluation is not without argument. To illuminate some of the dynamics of the field, we discussed methodological issues relating to evaluation. These ranged from selecting and forming objectives to choosing the types of tests to employ when gathering data. The chapter closed by pointing out various roles that people can play in the evaluation effort.

Notes

1. Harriet Talmage, "Evaluating the Curriculum: What, Why and How," *National Association for Secondary School Principals* (May 1985), pp. 1–8.
2. Blaine R. Worthing and James R. Sanders, *Educational Evaluation: Theory and Practice* (Worthington, Ohio: Jones, 1973), p. 19.
3. Bruce W. Tuckman, *Evaluating Instructional Programs* (Boston: Allyn and Bacon, 1979), p. 1.
4. Daniel L. Stufflebeam, *Educational Evaluation and Decision Making* (Itasca, Ill.: Peacock, 1971), p. xxv.
5. Fred N. Kerlinger, *Behavioral Research: A Conceptual Approach* (New York: Holt, Rinehart, 1979), p. 413.
6. Michael Scriven, "The Methodology of Evaluation," in J. R. Gress and D. E. Purpel, eds., *Curriculum: An Introduction to the Field* (Berkeley, Calif.: McCutchan, 1978), pp. 337–408.
7. Lee J. Cronbach, "Course Improvement through Evaluation," *Teachers College Record* (May 1963), pp. 672–683.
8. Lee J. Cronbach, *Designing Evaluations of Educational and Social Programs* (San Francisco: Jossey-Bass, 1982).
9. Ibid., p. 24.
10. Ibid., p. 25.
11. Scriven, "The Methodology of Evaluation."
12. Norman E. Gronlund, *Measurement and Evaluation in Teaching*, 5th ed. (New York: Macmillan, 1985); Harold Mitzel, ed., *Encyclopedia of Educational Research*, 5th ed. (New York: Free Press, 1982).
13. Robert M. Gagné and Leslie J. Briggs, *Principles of Instructional Design*, 2nd ed. (New York: Holt, Rinehart, 1979).
14. Robert L. Thorndike, *Applied Psychometrics* (Boston: Houghton Mifflin, 1982); Worthing and Sanders, *Educational Evaluation: Theory and Practice*.
15. H. H. Giles, S. P. McCutchen, and A. N. Zechiel, *Exploring the Curriculum* (New York: Harper and Row, 1942).
16. R. E. Smith and Ralph W. Tyler, *Appraising and Recording Student Progress* (New York: Harper &

Row, 1942). Also see Ralph W. Tyler and Richard M. Wolf, *Crucial Issues in Testing* (Berkeley, Calif.: McCutchan, 1974).
17. Ralph W. Tyler, "General Statement on Evaluation," *Journal of Educational Research* (1942), pp. 492–501.
18. Newton S. Metfessel and William B. Michael, "A Paradigm Involving Multiple Criterion Measures for the Evaluation of the Effectiveness of School Programs," *Educational and Psychological Measurement* (Winter 1967), pp. 931–943.
19. Malcolm Provus, *Discrepancy Evaluation for Educational Program Improvement and Assessment* (Berkeley, Calif.: McCutchan, 1971).
20. Robert E. Stake, "The Countenance of Educational Evaluation," *Teachers College Record* (April 1967), pp. 523–540.
21. Ibid.
22. Stufflebeam, *Educational Evaluation and Decision Making*.
23. Ibid., p. 236.
24. Ibid., p. 218.
25. Ibid., p. 222.
26. Ibid., p. 229.
27. Ibid., p. 230.
28. Ibid., p. 236.
29. Elliot W. Eisner, *The Educational Imagination on the Design and Evaluation of School Programs*, 2nd ed. (New York: Macmillan, 1985).
30. Ibid., p. 226.
31. Robert E. Stake, *Evaluating the Arts in Education* (Columbus, Ohio: Merrill, 1975).
32. Robert E. Stake, *Program Evaluation, Particularly Responsive Evaluation* (Kalamazoo, Mich.: Evaluation Center of Western Michigan University, 1975); Robert E. Stake and James A. Pearsol, "Evaluating Responsively," in R.S. Brandt, ed., *Applied Strategies for Curriculum Evaluation* (Alexandria, Va.: Association for Supervision and Curriculum Development, 1981), pp. 14–28.
33. Glenys G. Unruh and Adolph Unruh, *Curriculum Development: Problems, Processes, and Progress* (Berkeley, Calif.: McCutchan, 1984).
34. Francis P. Hunkins, *Curriculum Development: Program Improvement* (Columbus, Ohio: Merrill, 1980).
35. Gronlund, *Measurement and Evaluation of Teachers;* John D. McNeil, *Curriculum: A Comprehensive Introduction*, 3rd ed. (Boston: Little, Brown, 1985).
36. David Pratt, *Curriculum: Design and Development* (New York: Harcourt, Brace, 1980).
37. Allan C. Ornstein, "Accountability Report from the U.S.A.," *Journal of Curriculum Studies* (December 1985), pp. 437–439; Ornstein, "Accountability: Trends and Policies," *Education and the Urban World* (February 1986), pp. 235–239.
38. Mauritz Johnson, "Definitions and Models in Curriculum Theory," *Educational Theory* (April 1967), pp. 127–139.
39. Scriven, "The Methodology of Evaluation."
40. David M. Fetterman, "Ibsen's Baths: Reactivity

and Insensitivity," *Educational Evaluation and Policy Analysis* (Fall 1982), pp. 261–279.

41. Allan C. Ornstein, *Education and Social Inquiry* (Itasca, Ill.: Peacock, 1978).

42. Mary J. Allen and Wendy M. Yen, *Introduction to Measurement Theory* (Monterey, Calif.: Brooks/ Cole, 1979); Jerome M. Stattler, *Assessment of Children's Intelligence and Special Abilities,* 2nd ed. (Boston: Allyn and Bacon, 1982).

43. Ibid.

44. W. James Popham, *Modern Educational Measurement* (Englewood Cliffs, N.J.: Prentice-Hall, 1981).

45. Norman E. Gronlund, *Stating Objectives for Classroom Instruction,* 2nd ed. (New York: Macmillan, 1978); Gronlund, *Constructing Achievement Tests,* 3rd ed. (Englewood Cliffs, N.J.: Prentice-Hall, 1982).

46. Robert S. Zais, *Curriculum: Principles and Foundations.* (New York: Harper & Row, 1976).

47. Hilda Taba, *Curriculum Development: Theory and Practice* (New York: Harcourt, Brace, 1962).

48. Stufflebeam, *Educational Evaluation and Decision Making.*

49. Peter F. Oliva, *Developing the Curriculum* (Boston: Little, Brown, 1982); John P. Miller and Wayne Seller, *Curriculum: Perspective and Practice* (New York: Longman, 1985).

50. N. L. Gage, *The Scientific Basis of the Art of Teaching* (New York: Teachers College Press, Columbia University, 1978); Philip W. Jackson, *The Practice of Teaching* (New York: Teachers College Press, Columbia University, 1986).

51. Decker Walker and Jonas F. Soltis, *Curriculum and Aims* (New York: Teachers College Press, Columbia University, 1986); Stake, "The Countenance of Educational Evaluation."

52. James A. Beame, Conrad E. Toepfer, and Samuel J. Alessi, *Curriculum Planning and Development* (Boston: Allyn and Bacon, 1986); Ernest House, *Evaluating with Validity* (Beverly Hills, Calif.: Sage, 1980).

chapter 11

CURRICULUM THEORY

Curricularists have often written about curriculum theory without providing clear examples of what it is and how it can help the practitioner. Although curricularists are concerned with curriculum theory, because curriculum as a field presents many theoretical and perplexing problems, these people are in an exploratory era in theory building. This is true partly because curricularists have not accepted either a clear-cut definition of theory nor criteria to distinguish curriculum theory from other theory in education.

But their lack of clarity about what curriculum theory is has not diminished discussion of or writing about it. Elizabeth Maccia has pointed out that talking about theory is, itself, theorizing.[1] Dorothy Huenecke indicates that even though no one would assert that the field of curriculum has any full-blown theories, an abundance of theorizing activity is aimed at exploring aspects of curriculum.[2] James Macdonald has mentioned

that curricularists might expect that such theorizing would focus upon a clearly identified realm of phenomena. But, such is not the case, partly because curricularists cannot agree about just what curriculum is.[3]

THEORETICAL PERSPECTIVES

Curriculum is a complex phenomenon. Although few curricularists agree on all theoretical aspects of the field, they realize that they must advance their understanding of it if they are to conceptualize and develop curricula of value for students.

Over time, people have divided, subdivided, and classified their experiences into categories so as to comprehend them and to manage the masses of data associated with them. These divisions are called disciplines, areas, or realms of knowledge. Within each discipline, statements explain, describe, and/or predict the phenomena of central interest. Such explanations can be called theories.

Knowledge of reality has also been grouped into more general categories. George Beauchamp has asserted that all theories are derived from three broad categories of knowledge: (1) the humanities; (2) the natural sciences; and (3) the social sciences.[4] These *divisions of knowledge*, shown in Figure 11-1, are well established as the basic realms of knowledge. For example, under the humanities are the disciplines of philosophy, music, art, and literature. Under the social sciences are the disciplines of history, sociology, psychology, and anthropology, among others. Under the natural sciences are the disciplines of chemistry, physics, botany, geology, and so on.

Beauchamp argues that from these basic knowledge divisions come areas of *applied knowledge*—architecture, medicine, engineering, education, and law, to name a few. Although some curricularists question the validity of these categories, and their continued usefulness, many writers in curriculum do accept them as, if not valid, at least useful. What distinguishes applied realms of knowledge from disciplines is that applied realms draw their content and indeed their authority from theory in the disciplines. Education, for example, draws from psychology, sociology, and history and uses information from biology when referring to human growth and development. It takes much of its emphasis from philosophy. What makes education a field of knowledge is the manner in which it combines knowledge from various disciplines and formulates rules and procedures for making the combinations and using the knowledge.

Beauchamp has identified a series of subtheories in education—administrative theories, counseling theories, instructional theories, evaluation theories, and curriculum theories. There are two major categories of curriculum theories—design theories and engineering theories. *Design theories* address the basic organization of the curriculum plan. For this, curricularists draw on philosophy as well as on social and psychology theory. Design theories of curriculum content are influenced by various theories of knowledge.

Engineering theories explain, describe, predict, or even guide curriculum-development activities. They involve specific plans, princi-

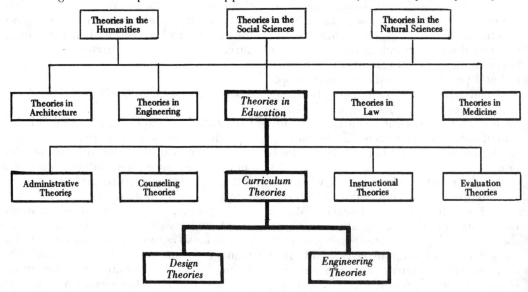

FIGURE 11-1 Curriculum Theory in Perspective.
Source: from George A. Beauchamp, *Curriculum Theory*, 4th ed. (Itasca, Ill.: Peacock, 1981), p. 5.

ples, and/or methods or procedures. Engineering theories of curriculum are also partially based on principles of measurement and statistics.

The Meaning of Theory.

Despite the myriad works on the nature and function of theory, and on the differences between theory and practice, curriculum specialists have not produced a universal definition of theory. This is not too surprising because the three basic realms of knowledge—humanities, social sciences, and natural sciences—all look at reality differently and generate definitions of theory that reflect their interests.

Although differences exist among the major types of theory, some commonalities are evident as well. Most definitions of theory deal with sets of events or phenomena and the relationships among these events. Abraham Kaplan provides a useful general statement defining theory: "A theory is a way of making sense of a disturbing situation so as to allow us most effectively to bring to bear our repertoire of habits, and even more important, to modify habits or discard them altogether, replacing new ones as the situation demands." Theory will appear as the device for interpreting, criticizing, and unifying established laws, modifying them to fit "data unanticipated in their formation, and guiding the enterprise of discovering new and more powerful generalizations."[5]

Richard Snow states that "a theory is essentially a symbolic construction that is designed to bring generalizable facts or laws into systematic connection." The theory itself consists of a set of units that can be "facts, concepts, or some variables, and a noting of relationships among the units identified."[6]

Another social scientist offers another view, that is "a theory is primarily a form of insight, a way of looking at the world." Theories represent perspectives about the world that are not necessarily true or false, but help clarify certain facts or forces. "When

we look at the world through our theoretical insights, the [results] we obtain will evidently be shaped and formed by our theories."[7]

In all of these definitions, theory is a set of related propositions that sheds light on why events occur in the manner that they do. The propositions identify concepts by pointing out the relationships between them.

Scientific Theory. Natural scientists in this century have made great advances in their realm of knowledge, largely because of their extensive utilization of what is called scientific theory. In many instances, scientific theory has been given the status of exemplar for theory formation and statement. In other words, it exemplifies the "true" nature of theory. Although some curriculum specialists argue that scientific theory is not appropriate for explaining or guiding curriculum work, curricularists nevertheless still need to understand such theory.

Within the natural sciences, the term *theory* sometimes refers to a set of propositions inductively derived from empirical findings. These generalizations refer to various facts, laws, or hypotheses that are related to each other in a systematic way and that form a type of whole—an entity. Scientific theory, then, is comprised of general facts, laws, or hypotheses related to each other.

Perhaps the most widely accepted definition of scientific theory is delineated by Herbert Feigl and includes:

[A] set of assumptions from which can be derived by purely logicomathematical procedures, a larger set of empirical laws. The theory furnishes an explanation of these empirical laws and unifies the originally relatively heterogeneous areas of subject matter characterized by those empirical laws.[8]

According to this definition, theory is a cluster of logically connected statements that generalize to and offer explanations of particular cases. In its explanations of the various cases to which it refers, theory unifies myriad data and those propositions relevant to those data.

Fred Kerlinger asserts that the basic aim of science is theory—that is, the aim of science is to identify basic statements that explain natural events. He notes that theories are general explanations that enable scientists to understand the phenomena studied.[9] Instead of attempting to explain every separate event—for example, the behavior of students in one activity—scientists formulate general statements about similar events or behavior so that they can link many events or behaviors. Instead of describing how different children each solved a particular science problem, the theorist would derive from his or her observations a general explanation of most, if not all, kinds of problem solving. The investigator would then present the general statement as a theory of problem solving.

Philosophical and Humanistic Theory.
Scholars in the humanities use theory to formulate consistent and logical explanations of humans' place in the world. Such theories produce a set of assumptions or beliefs that *explain what ought to be.* These assumptions, derived inductively from the scholars' professional experiences and knowledge of the world, contrast their thinking with that of colleagues in specific disciplines. Philosophers' theories describe their outlooks—their views of reality and their place within it. One example of such theory is Plato's theory of the ideal; reality as we know it is really an imitation of the ideal.

Much of the theory that relates to education, and specifically to curriculum, stems from the philosophical and/or humanistic orientation.[10] A tenet of existentialism is that to become fully human, or at least more human, people must be engaged actively in their world; without engagement, individuals become detached and isolated. This "theory of engagement" is based on ethical matters rather than scientific validation.

Philosophical and humanistic theory fits into the category Herbert Kliebard has identified as a concern for systematic analysis of a set of related concepts or problems.[11] Theory at this level is essentially the result of an attempt to clarify the nature of concepts and problems, and their understanding does not depend on empirical support. Empirical considerations play only a minor role. Rather, "validation" of the theory relies on the logic of various positions and the articulation of values.

Philosophical and humanistic theory is largely normative (based on values). It essentially indicates what should or should not be included or done in some action. Using such theory, curricularists should have "guidelines" about what to do or not do in creating the curriculum—that is, about what they should include in and perhaps what they should exclude from the curriculum.

But some curriculum theory is largely an attempt to identify the important factors or variables that comprise the phenomena that we are investigating in some given discipline.[12] Here the focus is on using theory to identify certain variables without having any insights about the relationships among the variables attracting interest. Such theory does not indicate precisely the relationships extant among identified variables. There are many instances when curriculum specialists advise individuals to look at particular variables of curriculum but they give no precise explanation of the relationship of the variable to, say, student achievement or the formation of attitudes. Such theory gives an orientation toward reality, but it does so without empirical support.

The Functions of Theory.

Educators may ask, "Why do we need theory at all?" As stated earlier, the aim of science is to understand phenomena studied. Certainly, most people would accept this statement in relation to theory. Even philosophers require theory to question what is knowledge, what is reality, and what is of value?

Theory comes from the Greek word *theoria* connoting "wakefulness of mind." It is a type of "pure viewing" of truth. Theory explains reality; it makes people aware of their world and its interactions. Many writers have ascribed four functions to theory: (1) description; (2) prediction; (3) explanation; and (4) guidance.[13] Although some writers disagree about which function is paramount, most view all as important and as closely related.

DESCRIPTION. Description provides a narrative classification of knowledge in a particular theoretical field. It furnishes a structure through which individual's interpretations of complex activities can be verified. It organizes and summarizes knowledge. A theory "tells" us that there are certain variables and that they interact in particular ways or have certain relationships to other variables; it does not indicate why certain variables are important nor why they are interrelated. Theory presents an account of events. It unifies phenomena and arranges the information so that the scope and internal relationships, though not explained, are at least visible.[14]

PREDICTION. The second function of theory is rather obvious. A theory can predict the occurrence of as yet unobserved events on the basis of explanatory principles embedded in it. Perhaps this is the ultimate function of theory. Of course, cautious people always regard a theory with some degree of tentativeness, for a theory, regardless of the accumulated data to support it, cannot account for all situations. If it did, it would not be a theory but a law. Nonetheless, the more diverse observations a theory can explain, the greater should be people's confidence in using it to predict the phenomena in question.

EXPLANATION. Explanation addresses "why." It not only points out the relationships between phenomena, but suggests either explicitly or implicitly the reasons for the relationships. The best explanations relate to what people know as opposed to what they may mistakenly believe. For example, an explanation of students' learning difficulties in terms of "evil spirits" would be less believable than an explanation stressing students' motivation and interests.

GUIDANCE. Theory also acts as a guide. It helps researchers choose data for analysis and make economical summaries of the data. The theory generated guides further investigation. In essence, it serves a heuristic function. Many scientists assert that this is the true or primary responsibility of scientific theory—to serve as the guide for further study. One educator addressed this heuristic function when he stated, "What is important is that laws propagate when they are united in a theory; theory serves as matchmaker, midwife, and godfather all in one."[15]

Theorists cannot divorce themselves from their values and knowledge when addressing the heuristic functions of theory. Values will influence, suggest, even prescribe what their behavior should be. Collecting the facts is a necessary first step in theory building—but what facts, whose rendition of the facts? Without theoretical orientations, people cannot decide what facts to gather or what issues to address. Their values influence what facts and relationships are relevant to them. Their values, in other words, guide their theorizing. As one educator put it: Theory is "a set of rules which guide or control actions."[16]

THEORY BUILDING

Essentially, the process of theory development is tied to inductive and deductive thinking. Sometimes, these are considered to be two different approaches to theory generation, but typically both are employed together to create theory.

Induction means building a theory by accumulating and summarizing a variety of inquiries. People using induction rely rather heavily on empirical data. They form propositions on the basis of research that began as tentative hypotheses they tested and validated.[17]

Deduction, in contrast to induction, is the

process of inferring necessary conclusions from a combination of premises whose truth has either been accepted as given or assumed to be true. People employing deduction develop theory by constructing logical sequences.[18] They proceed from the general to the specific.

Steps in Theory Building.

George Homans listed six rules of theory building:

1. Look at the obvious, the familiar, and the common. In a science that has not established its foundations, these are the things that best require study.
2. State the obvious in its full generality. Science is an economy of thought only if its hypotheses sum up in a simple form a large number of facts.
3. Talk about one thing at a time. That is, choose words (concepts) that refer not to several classes of facts at the same time but to only one. Corollary: Once you have chosen your words, always use the same words when referring to the same thing.
4. Cut down as far as you dare the number of things about which you are talking. "As few as you may; as many as you must" is the rule governing the number of classes of facts you take into account.
5. Once you have started to talk, do not stop until you have finished. That is, describe systematically the relationships between the facts designated by your words.
6. Recognize that your analysis must be abstract, because it deals with only a few elements of the concrete situation. Admit the dangers of abstraction, especially when action is required, but do not be afraid of abstraction.[19]

Defining Terms. One of the basic rules in theory building is to be clear about terms. According to Beauchamp, agreement on terms is an essential ingredient in the work of a theorist. The terms theorists employ and the concepts implied by those terms are the building blocks of the theory. Selecting terms is governed by two rules: (1) The wording must be clear, and (2) the terms, once defined, must be used consistently.[20]

Terms define what is to be observed. They refer to concepts, and they are the variables between which empirical relationships are to be sought. Concepts are either nominal or operational. *Nominal* definitions present the attributes associated with a term or concept. The term is thus explained by the boundaries of its interpretation. In contrast, *operational* definitions indicate the conditions under which a concept is used. Operational definitions assume an "if-then" property. If certain conditions are present, then the statement within which the term is used is correct.

Some terms really cannot be defined either by referring to nominal attributes or by referring to other operationally defined terms. Yet they are a critical, basic part of theory. These so-called *primitive* terms are accepted by those who use them in their theoretical work. In mathematics, for example, the terms "point" or "straight line" are primitive terms. They really cannot be nominally or operationally defined; all we can say is that a "point" is a point. In education, such terms as "felt needs" and "experience" are primitive terms.[21]

Although theorists may not always be able to refrain from using primitive terms, they should try to use them as infrequently as possible.

Another category of terms used in theory is *theoretical* terms or operational constructs; theories with any degree of sophistication contain such terms. A construct is a concept that represents relationships among things and/or events and their properties.[22] Theoretical terms cannot be defined directly by observing particular events. Rather they can be defined by their relationships to other terms that are operationally defined. Educators use a large number of such terms—motivation, cognitive dissonance, attitude, perceptual structuring, set, and social need.

Classifying. The second activity in theory building is classification. At this stage, theorists attempt to organize and integrate what they know about the areas being theorized. They begin summarizing discovered uniformities of relationships between two or more variables or concepts.[23] Their classifications or statements of classifications can have varying degrees of precision, but this does not diminish their place in theory building. Classification allows theorists to discover voids in their knowledge that must be filled through research activities if they are to give meaning to their theorizing.

When classifying information, theorists group facts and generalizations into homogeneous groups. However, even if categories seem to be taking shape, explanations of the interrelationships among the categories or of the relationships among the facts and generalizations within any single information cluster may still be lacking.

Interpreting. To interpret the information, theorists may approach their data inductively or deductively. The inductive process tends to produce philosophical or prescriptive types of theory; the deductive approach tends to generate logical types of theory. Both processes are necessary to generate meaningful theory; both enable theorists to generate general statements.

But producing general statements is not the end of the interpretation task. Theorists must also make inferences from their general theoretical statements. In other words, they must use the statements to go beyond what they know or have observed. They must make additional assumptions, create hypotheses, perfect generalizations from additional observations, and deduce other conclusions from observations and generalizations. They must, in effect, suggest new theories that will require additional testing to determine their soundness.

Models.

Sometimes, persons involved in theorizing activities engage in *model building* as a means of summarizing the phenomena investigated. Although the term model is sometimes used as a synonym for theory, it is not. Models are representations of aspects of a theory. Models aid comprehension and theory building. They are useful for economically organizing and explaining vast amounts of data. Models help theorists understand how their theories are shaping up. They also trigger questions whose answers are requisite to generating theory. Models in science act like metaphors in language. They enlighten us by suggesting arguments by analogy from known resemblances to so-far unnoticed resemblances.

Of course, models do have some disadvantages. They can: (1) invite overgeneralization; (2) entice people into committing logical fallacies; (3) show the relationships between variables incorrectly; (4) exhibit faulty assumptions about constructs; (5) stress invalid data; and (6) turn useful energy into nonproductive activity.[24]

LINGUISTIC MODELS. Models, in terms of language, serve to organize a person's thinking by helping to describe, categorize, and conceptualize his or her knowledge and experiences. According to Philip Phenix, language is used to process thought, and so do theories and models of a discipline or field of study. Linguistic models represent a fundamental vehicle of human thought by which people make the complex and puzzling become more familiar and more readily understood.[25]

In discussing linguistic models, we are speaking of verbal concepts and abstractions. Most people use verbal models in everyday speech. The various systems and processes in this book to describe curriculum making are to a large extent examples of verbal models. Teachers, also, rely on verbal models in their classrooms for transmitting learning experiences to students, especially cognitive learning. The art and science of presenting information and ideas, what some of us might call "pedagogy," are based on verbal transmission.

PHYSICAL MODELS. Verbal models may sometimes be a bit complex to understand, but physical or working models are usually quite easy to comprehend. They are usually three-dimensional and show the actual "thing" in a reduced scale. We all are familiar with model airplanes; they look like real airplanes—some even fly—but they are not real airplanes. Chemistry students have all seen models of molecules or atoms, usually made of different colored balls. Physical models enable theorists to visualize the variables or parts under consideration and to note their interrelationships.

MATHEMATICAL MODELS. Sometimes, the best model for depicting the component parts or variables under consideration is a mathematical model. Such models reduce complex interactions of phenomena to the regularity of mathematical expressions. They are common in the physical sciences. Chemical equations that describe and predict the consequences of particular chemical reactions are mathematical models. Einstein's equation $E = mc^2$ is a well-known mathematical model. In decision theory, mathematical equations denote the probability that certain actions will be decided, given a particular situation.

GRAPHIC MODELS. Throughout this book we have used a fourth kind of model—the graphic model. This is perhaps the most common type of model. It can be a picture, drawing, or diagram of some of the major components, and their interrelationships, of the concept being described. Graphic models help illustrate our verbal text or narrative. The old saying, "A picture is worth a thousand words" applies with good graphic models.

CURRICULUM THEORY

Theory as we have defined it is a set of statements so worded that it can be used as a means of communication among people and as a directive to those who wish to study the field of curriculum. Macdonald has noted that because curriculum theory and theorizing are in a rather formative stage, we have no generally accepted and clear-cut criteria to distinguish curriculum theory and theorizing from other educational actions.[26] Some, like Kliebard, have argued that we do have curricula theory,[27] whereas others, like Joseph Schwab, have stated that

not only do we lack theory, but we should not strive to have one either. Schwab maintained that the crisis in the curriculum field was due to overreliance on curriculum theory.[28]

The challenge to curricularists is to make sense out of the complexity of the field of curriculum and to determine whether they should create their own curriculum theory or theories, borrow theories from other disciplines—such as psychology, sociology, anthropology, philosophy, and so on—or do both. To create a single curriculum theory that would describe, and more importantly explain, curriculum is perhaps an unrealistic goal; curriculum covers too many aspects of education.

Curriculum theory has been the subject of conversation and the focus of reflection by many concerned with curriculum. Even in the early years when the field of curriculum was gaining identity and stature, curricularists were concerned with defining a theoretical basis.

Early Theory in Curriculum.

The publication of Franklin Bobbitt's *The Curriculum* can probably be cited as the starting point of theorizing in curriculum. It also represented one of the early books in scientific theorizing. The entire scientism movement in education established a major approach to theory. Bobbitt urged his fellow educators to borrow from the new technology to guide educational functioning. He believed strongly that the principles of management and the application of "theory" could help educators be more precise and efficient in creating and managing their programs.[29]

Scientific theory was viewed by many to have the quality of objectivity. Theory could serve to describe and explain what is. Theory of phenomena would allow educators to predict the consequences of putting certain phenomena into action. The Lincoln School was initially set up at Teachers College, Columbia University, as an experimental school where theoretical approaches to education could be investigated. Although other teachers colleges organized their own experimental schools (sometimes called laboratory schools) for examining educational practice, according to Robert Schaefer, these experimental schools were "conceived less as laboratories for inquiry and more as exemplars of particular proscriptive theory."[30]

Many educators believed that scientific theory would add to our understanding of curriculum. However, people like Charles Judd, who certainly supported the methods of science, were somewhat concerned that persons untrained in the discipline of science would conduct trivial and poorly conceived studies. William Bagley warned that while using the scientific method, educators had to be careful to adequately conceptualize the problems to be investigated and not to draw unwarranted conclusions from poorly conducted investigations.[31]

Many new discoveries in testing and statistics furnished those who wished to engage in theory building with some tools that enabled them to manage more carefully investigations and process more precisely data gathered. Persons in curriculum theory drew guidance from the context of the times. This was especially true of Bobbitt and Charters, both of whom were expert in the field of research and evaluation. Both theorists linked the idea of activity analysis with formulating curriculum decisions. The idea was to correlate the objectives of the subject with specific activities—those tasks and skills that students had to learn to prepare for productive living. However numerous these activities were, educators had to make decisions about which activities were to be stressed in school.[32]

During the last years of the nineteenth century and the early years of this century Dewey was engaged in creating a curriculum theory. Even though Dewey may not have considered his work to be a curriculum theory, but rather a science in education, it still holds interest for curriculum theorists.[33] Dewey's theory draws on the notion that the development of the individual and the development of the human race are similar in their overall stages. His theory attempts to show the relationship between schools and society and the various aspects of experience and education as they relate to the learner.[34]

Dewey urged educators to tie knowledge in the curriculum to human experiences relevant to children; moreover, he urged that children experience knowledge through various activities. The experience-centered curriculum, which we discussed in Chapter 7, drew much of its theoretical support from this "theory" advanced by Dewey. It also gave rise to the entire activity movement. Following his reflections on theory, Dewey actually attempted to reproduce in his experimental elementary school at the University of Chicago the actual conditions of social life. Children would learn about the industries of life—how humans processed their realities. Children would be involved in doing.

Educators might well ask, then, if persons such as Bobbitt or Charters approached curriculum from various theoretical stances, and Dewey attempted to test out theory in his school, why did curriculum theorizing remain undeveloped?[35] Perhaps because educators have talked a "better game" of theory than they have "played." The Lincoln School at Teachers College conducted many "experiments" to test out its theories, but it did not really produce any objective accounts of the results. The University of Chicago hired many educators interested in theoretical proposals of education, but most curricularists who dominated during the 1920s and 1930s tended to be child-centered and had little interest in either formulating theory or "fleshing out" scientific principles in curriculum.[36]

Theory at Mid-Century.

Much of the early talk about curriculum did not consider theory per se. However, in the 1940s, curriculum writings began to discuss actual theory. The first major discussion on the topic took place at the University of Chicago in 1947. The various participants at this conference produced a paper addressing curriculum theory, but no curriculum theory emerged from the meeting. The papers, which appeared as a monograph *three years* later, did conclude with a challenge: "As a further effort in hastening the communications between groups of interested people and in the development of more adequate theory, someone might spend some time trying to describe the nature of such theory, its tasks, its subject matter, its tests, and its uses."[37]

Tyler, some might argue, took up the challenge in his book's presentation of the basic principles of curriculum and instruction. But Tyler's approach, if it can even be considered theoretical, was more attuned to curriculum development than to an overall theory of curriculum.[38] Beauchamp, however, was instrumental in adding to the field of curriculum theory.[39] His 1950 book, *Curriculum Theory*, addressed the topic. Even so, although the book has gone through four editions, it still leaves us without an agreed upon curriculum theory. Some of the major theories that have evolved are as follows:

Maccias' Theory. During the last twenty-five years, the "formative" years of curriculum theory, a more diversified view of curriculum theory has evolved. Elizabeth and George Maccia, for example, presented four different kinds of curriculum theory. They noted that curriculum specialists speculate about forms, events, values, and practices. Consequently they organized theory as formal theory, event theory, valuational theory, and praxiological theory.[40]

1. *Formal Theory.* This theory deals with speculation about the structure of the disciplines that comprise the curriculum. Curricularists usually draw their understanding of such theory from philosophers and members of the particular disciplines in question. Such theory is nonvaluational; it deals with what is and what exists, rather than what ought to be.

2. *Event Theory.* This theory, very similar to what we have been discussing as scientific theory, refers to speculation about occurrences. It attempts to predict what will occur given certain circumstances.

3. *Valuational Theory.* This theory involves speculation about the appropriate means to attain the objectives most desired and to include the content judged to be the best. In contrast to event theory, valuation theory does involve values or norms. It deals with "ought-ness."

4. *Praxiological Theory.* Such theory refers to speculation about appropriate means to attain what is considered valuable. It is about practices. It can support the creation of curriculum policy, the means we employ to adopt particular objectives, and specific practices in schools.

The Maccias asserted that curricularists could use theory to guide their building of a definition of curriculum, as well as in the planning and development of curriculum.

Johnson's Model. In contrast to the Maccias, Mauritz Johnson stated that curriculum specialists should first define curriculum and curriculum making and should then direct their energies at theory building. He argued that most past efforts to build curriculum theory had centered on programs, with the result that attention was really on curriculum development.[41] As shown in Figure 11-2, Johnson distinguished between the curriculum plan and the process of curriculum development by defining the former as an output of the latter; he also revealed the differences among curriculum, instruction, and teacher behavior. His attention to objectives puts him in the behavioral-rational camp. Although curricularists may not agree with Johnson's definition of curriculum—an intended series of learning outcomes—they should realize the usefulness of distinguishing between theorizing about curriculum as a plan and theorizing about the means by which such plans are generated. Johnson did not actually present a theory, but he has provided a useful model.

Macdonald's Model. Macdonald, a major curriculum theorist, has presented a

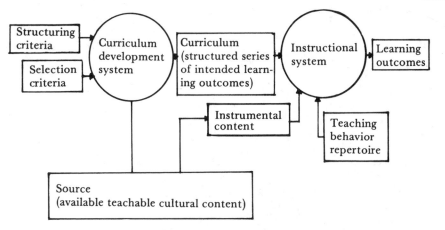

FIGURE 11-2   Curriculum as an Output-Input of One System.
Source: from Mauritz Johnson, "Definitions and Models in Curriculum Theory," *Educational Theory* (April 1967), p. 23.

model of the major systems in schooling: curriculum, instruction, teaching, and learning.[42] Although the model depicted in Figure 11-3 is just that—a model, not a theory—it does at least point out possible key components involved in the dynamics of curriculum and instruction. It presents a map indicating the key "features" of the educational landscape.

Though curriculum is quite large in the drawing, Macdonald's model shows it as one of four interacting systems. Macdonald defines *curriculum* as the social system that actually produces a plan for *instruction,* which he in turn defines as another social system within which formal teaching and learning take place. *Teaching* is different from instruction, and is defined as a personality system—the teacher—acting in a particular manner to facilitate learning. *Learning* is defined as a personality system, too; the student becomes involved in specialized task-related behaviors. All of these systems come together in the center, depicted in Figure 11-3 by a shadowed spot. At this juncture, the curriculum goals become operative in the instructional encounter because of the efforts of the teacher and the behavior of the students.

Macdonald considered space V as concomitant learning—that is, learning that accompanies the direct learning, but is not

part of the stated objectives. Space VI involves teachers' actions aimed at modifying such behavior in response to the immediate feedback about the institutional or school situation. Space VII refers to in-service experiences for teachers, while space VIII suggests supervision experiences for them. Macdonald noted that he had few ready examples for spaces IX and X, but they might deal with pupil-teacher planning experiences.

We still do not have theory. Macdonald's model does, however, clarify the interrelationships between teaching, learning, instruction, and curriculum. It points out that each can be considered a system in its own right, but that in the reality of the school, the systems interface with each other so as to produce some specialized subsystems. Still, the model leaves theorists without answers about how they would determine the nature and scope of the curriculum. The reality of the curriculum in action is certainly more complex than depicted by this model.

Wilson's Open Access Curriculum Model. Craig Wilson noted that for a public school curriculum to have more clarity than the larger society's vision of its destiny often requires a good deal of insight. He notes that theory should reflect this insight. He maintains that a curriculum theory really should

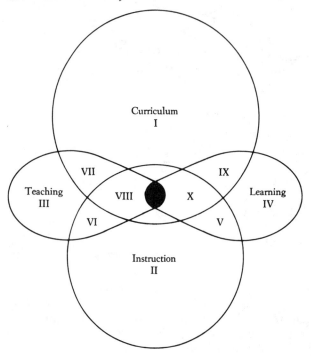

FIGURE 11-3 The Interaction of Four Systems.
Source: from James B. Macdonald, "Educational Models for Instruction," in J. B. Macdonald and R. R. Leeper, eds., *Theories of Instruction* (Washington, D.C.: Association for Supervision and Curriculum Development, 1965); p. 95.

be a combination of *knowledge theory* about the organization and structures of knowledge, *environmental theory* (how people interpret their space), and *management theory* (what procedures people use to manage or control the organization). He calls this the theory of open access curriculum.[43]

Wilson's model, shown in Figure 11-4, displays three dimensions of knowledge: facts, contested truth, and open exploration. In dealing with facts, the teacher would primarily use lecture and controlled reading. For processing contested truth, the teacher would employ seminars. Open exploration would be processed by students involved in research. The model exhibits both the curricular (fact, contested truth, open exploration) and instructional (lecture, seminars, etc.) dimensions of education. It also suggests that the students can enter the curriculum system at the open exploration stage and then proceed through contested truth and fact. The pathway through the curriculum can be varied to meet the students' needs, interests, and abilities.

Wilson argues that the critical features of a curriculum organized according to this model are: (1) multiple- rather than single-entry points; (2) an increased scope of content; (3) no precise sequence for all to follow with related tracking of students; (4) learning styles related to both the nature of the discipline and the methods of inquiry; and (5) teachers' playing differentiated teaching roles.

Current Attempts at Theorizing.

Educators might wonder, given that their actions in past years have not created a theory, why they should continue to reflect and to theorize. Perhaps they have taken to heart Dewey's statement on theory: "Theory is in the end the most practical of all things, because this widening of the range of attention . . . eventually results in the creation of wider and farther-reaching purposes and enables us to use a much wider and deeper range of conditions and means than were expressed in the observation of primitive practical purposes."[44] Educators continue to

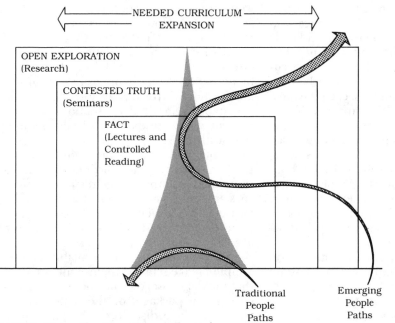

FIGURE 11-4 The Open Access Curriculum.

Source: from L. Craig Wilson, *The Open Access Curriculum* (Boston: Allyn and Bacon, 1971), p. 19.

believe that theory can produce hypotheses that can be tested in the world of concrete experience. They believe still that theory can enable them to describe reality and, more importantly, to begin to explain it. It also can serve as a policy map suggesting what they should do.

But, the challenge is immense. Gail McCutcheon states that few examples of curriculum theories really integrate data resulting from analyses, interpretations, and understandings of curriculum phenomena.[45] She has argued that curriculum persons need more examples that have a clear value for them and that draw from multiple disciplines, such as psychology and sociology. Other curricularists have also addressed this issue, focusing on how the various psychological theories can contribute to curriculum thinking and action.[46]

Jean Anyon has noted that curriculum investigation and curriculum theorizing are intimately related to social science theory. She argues that theory must be socially explanatory—that is, it must situate social

data in a theory of society, it must be systematic, and it must explain what is socially systematic. If curriculum theory is to be part of social science theory, then it must be situated in a larger theory of society.[47] (Many radical and reconceptualist theorists note that "theories" of curriculum are in conflict with what they consider the ideal of society.)[48] Although Anyon does not present a curriculum theory, she notes that in curriculum, a unified field theory would identify the interconnections between school knowledge, school process, contemporary society, and historical change. Such theory would identify the reasons for exploitation and pain in our society and our schools, and it would then furnish directives for eliminating such exploitation and pain.

Some curriculum theorists state that educators must derive curriculum theory from their analyses of curricula-in-use. Decker Walker has faulted many in the curriculum field for being too concerned with prescribing procedures for creating curricula that they have not paid sufficient attention to how curricula are created or to the nature of the programs generated.[49] He argues that curriculum theories can help curricularists view curriculum in a different light and thus generate novel interpretations of curriculum. He suggests that theories can be conceived as clustered in families, each having a different purpose and perhaps a different form. But, all theories focus on rationalizing, conceptualizing, and explaining practice. Walker notes that some theories being advanced fit into the current society without question, whereas others are being presented within a context of a new and better, as yet unformed, society. He cites Paulo Freire as one person who is relating "curriculum theory" to a better society still in need of creation. Programs are rationalized on the basis of their enabling society to attain such "utopias."

Tom Barone also argues that curricularists should be concerned with analyzing how curricula are created and used.[50] Theory, if well conceived, can directly help practitioners plan and use actual curricula. The kind of curriculum theory that Barone envisions will arise from the qualities of students' experiences of, and their interactions with, educational encounters. It will be derived, too, from the meaning students deduce from the curriculum they experience. It is important therefore, that those studying the curriculum-in-use attend to the students' perspectives of the curriculum and how it relates to their lives.

Barone places the kind of theory he is advocating within the critical tradition of social inquiry. He notes that because the theory carefully attends to "real-world" phenomena, the type of inquiry that leads to it is empirical. Simultaneously, because such theory views the curriculum reality from the perspectives of those for whom it was designed, it is phenomenological.

Such theory does not report the relationships between complex phenomena. Rather, the theorist attempts to portray relationships in their full complexity and to denote recurring patterns among them. Such theory corresponds to reality, its meaning woven into specific contexts. What we have as a theory statement is more of a story, and the reader must judge whether he or she can deduce any generalities to relate to other situations. The "theoretical statement" reports what happens in certain situations and so provides an idea about what can happen in similar situations. We are presented with probable possibilities rather than with precise predictions.

Finally, Elizabeth Vallance notes that curriculum theory is practical and based on real situations; such theorizing in curriculum occurs in every school.[51] Taking this stance, curricularists are encouraged to survey, analyze, synthesize, and test the knowledge available about curriculum problems. They should look at the data available and attempt to make sense of them. Vallance notes that the data observed may be part of a new curriculum package, or the textbooks just purchased by a district, or the political climate of the school, or even competing views of what a school is. Even though the data that theorists might view could be different data than classroom teachers might value, the process of theorizing is similar.

METAPHORS AND THEORETICAL CAMPS

Some curriculum theorists have argued that theoretical problems stem from faulty or nonproductive conceptions of curriculum. Dwayne Huebner has urged that educators discontinue their use of logical-rational language that stresses effectiveness, objectiveness, and behavioristic principles of learning and instead employ a language that centers on the economic and political policies that impact on education.[52] He wants educators also to use language that will direct their attention to how learners are provided with choices in subject matter—for example, how can a teacher best involve a student with the myriad cultures of the world so as to enhance the student's world-mindedness? Huebner has argued that educators have used a language that encourages control over the students, rather than liberation.

Metaphors.

Kliebard suggests that a way in which educators can perhaps cure their myopia is to use different metaphors from those that currently influence their thinking.[53] Because a technological orientation to curriculum essentially dominates in this century, for example, the metaphor of factory and production is common. Kliebard would propose substituting a metaphor that would enable curricularists to reconceptualize their view of the school and its curriculum. He notes that some social reconstructionists employ the metaphors of culture as a form of capital.

Paulo Freire has used the metaphor of education as banking. Education in this metaphor would be an action of deposition. The students are the depositories and the teacher is the depositor.[54] Note, however, that following a metaphor too closely can be dangerous. According to a banking metaphor, for instance, the student is considered a passive receiver of the deposit; he or she is only to receive, memorize, and repeat. Moreover, this metaphor also brings into focus that educators should ensure that "cultural capital" is deposited equally into each student's account.

Somewhat recently, Arthur Foshay discussed metaphors used in curriculum talk. He cited five common metaphors about children—the child as flower; the child as enemy; the child as cog; the child as machine; and the child as reasoner.[55] The child as *flower* (first conceptualized by Rousseau) is perhaps the most popular metaphor among elementary teachers. Accepting this metaphor means viewing the child as a growing plant. All that a child needs is good soil, nourishment, and warmth in order to grow to his or her full potential. If children are left alone, they will develop as they have been programmed by nature.

The child as *enemy* metaphor views the child as a force to be shaped. It draws much of its thinking from the military; teachers are to "attack" learning difficulties. However negative this metaphor might seem, it does allow educators to see that they do need plans in order to educate their students.

The child as *cog* metaphor assumes that the child only has meaning as he or she fits into the overall system. Some of the emphasis on doing one's part in a particular team effort comes from this perception of the child. The child as *machine* metaphor considers that once educators know the machine they can predict what it will do in particular situations. Also, it assumes that the machine will not function unless there is a person (teacher) to turn it on and also to run it. The child as *reasoner* centers on the rational abilities of the child. The child is a thinker.

Theoretical Camps.

People do not usually think consciously about the conceptual systems by which they organize their world. In most of the things they do, they just act and think more or less automatically along pathways that have become comfortable to them. But, if they think about their language, they find themselves in conceptual (and metaphorical) camps that organize their realities. William Pinar has presented conceptual organizers that group curriculum persons into three camps and John McNeil has recently elaborated on these camps.[56]

Traditionalists. Pinar defines traditionalists as those individuals who value service to practitioners above all other concerns. These individuals view the curricula as plans and stress those procedures requisite for creating such plans. They are more concerned with the practical dimension of curriculum matters than with theoretical concerns. A close relationship exists between traditionalists and school personnel. But, this closeness of interests has prevented them from creating new ways of talking about curriculum that may, in fact, enable more productive educational programs. Pinar places such persons as Ralph Tyler, Daniel and Laurel Tanner, Robert Zais, and John McNeil in this camp. We would probably add to this list Hilda Taba, John Goodlad, Galen Saylor, and Malcom Provus.

Traditionalists are concerned with the implementation of curriculum-development strategies; they are also interested in theorizing. Dorothy Huenecke has described them, in fact, as being involved in *structural theorizing*,[57] which focuses on identifying elements in the curriculum and determining their relationships. It also centers on the decisions and decision makers (sometimes called players or engineers) involved in curriculum planning. Huenecke indicates that those who focus on curriculum development and the structure of curriculum attest to the centrality of human rationality. People in this camp tend to be what we call behaviorists and intellectual-academics.

Structural theorists contend that educational practice is not an art but is rather, and to an extensive degree, a science. Accepting this, they assume that all that occurs within the dynamics of education can be identified, described, and, to some extent, controlled. Understanding the theories resulting from such activity can provide theorists with insights into the components of curriculum development. It can describe and explain their actions, and it can serve as a policy map for creating new programs.

Conceptual Empiricists. These persons, according to Pinar, are often in the social sciences and view their primary mission as engaging in research that will be theory producing. They argue that scientific knowledge of human behavior, including the curriculum, is possible. They claim that the research and the resulting theory are of practical value because they enable school practitioners to articulate the reasons for their actions. This, in turn, increases the likelihood that they will realize the traditional goals of the school.

People in this camp, as Pinar perceives it, are George Posner, Richard Schutz, and Jerome Bruner. We would also add Ronald Doll, Robert Stake, and Dan Stufflebeam. All these people are actively exploring the application of cognitive science to curriculum and instructional research as well as to cognition and learning to guide the arrangement of curriculum content and its delivery in the classroom.

Huenecke asserts that people who are in the conceptual empiricist camp engage in *substantive theorizing*.[58] The theory activity is designed to highlight appropriate content for the curriculum. Conceptual empiricists, engaged in substantive theorizing, analyze current situations and suggest alternatives to current patterns of content and experiences that comprise most curricula. They question why teachers are teaching what they are teaching and why they have arranged the school content in the ways they have. People in this camp tend to coincide with those in what we call the systems-managerial and intellectual-academic approach to curriculum.

Reconceptualists. Curricularists who are in this camp maintain the view that intellectual and scientific distance from curriculum practice are required if those in charge of education are to effectively critique and theorize about existing programs. They need to establish a distance between themselves and their worlds. They need, as Pinar states, to reach a perceptional point from where they can make their own personalities the "objects" of their focus.[59] Understanding does not lie in the external or objective world, but in the internal and subjective. The way to improve the world, a major goal of education, is not to improve the public world, but rather to improve oneself.

Presently, the reconceptualists are focusing on a critique of the field, which they believe is too immersed in the practical, technologically oriented approaches to understanding and action. They feel that true understanding will come from aesthetic, humanistic, and existential postures. Focusing on understanding oneself will lead to truly heightened consciousness.

Pinar seems to be the most visible of the reconceptualists, but James Macdonald has been credited with coining the term *reconceptualist*. Macdonald had argued that curricularists were far too concerned with logic and rationality in approaching their work, and so they often totally ignored the aesthetics of the curriculum.[60] They needed to reconceptualize—to take a new focus—to furnish new direction and to deemphasize providing practitioners with prescriptive formulas for efficiently delivering curricula.

We might classify the reconceptualists as *generic theorizers*. As Huenecke defines this category, generic theorizers focus on the outcomes of the curriculum rather than on its development or various elements. They focus on the cumulative effects of schooling on the total person. They thus attend to the total educational environment—within both the school and the larger society. They maintain that we can get a clearer picture of educational reality by looking at sources outside of education. These curricularists would coincide with our reconceptualist and humanistic approach to curriculum.

A theme common to much of the work and writings of reconceptualists is liberation. Some people, who draw heavily from existentialism and phenomenology, propose that liberation comes from within the person. Both Macdonald and Pinar recommend a method of self-analysis by which learners can study their own responses to life—and, therefore, to educational situations.[61] The method for doing this involves: (1) recalling and describing the past and then analyzing its psychic relation to the present; (2) describing one's imagined future and determining its relation to the present; and (3) placing this analytic understanding of one's education in its cultural and political context. We draw from this that learning is highly personal and unique for each of us. Individuals need a method for processing their experiences such that they derive meaning from them and control over their lives.

Others, such as Michael Apple and Paul Freire, question the dynamics of power, control, and influence.[62] They raise questions about "who is in charge" of the educational system—and for what purpose? Who controls the type of knowledge that is to be experienced in the school? Who controls the amount of knowledge that will be presented to various groups of students? Who creates the criteria that will determine success? How do we liberate schools and society from the political and economic establishment? Such curriculum people are drawing on what some call critical theory.[63]

To the critical theorist, liberation or emancipation means freeing one's self from the accepted ideology of current social conventions, beliefs, and modes of operation. It uses theory to get individuals to reflect on the current scene and to realize that it needs modification. People need to organize socially so that they will have the power to create new worlds and new societies. Students must be empowered by the curriculum to question the values of the current social and political scene. They are to analyze the current reality and then reflect on those beliefs and ideas that contribute to their psychological lives.

Critical theorists contend that individuals' places in society result not from their free choices, but rather from the actions performed by the economically elite who control our competitive society. Critical theorists argue that individuals are enslaved in our highly capitalist system. People strive to obtain meaningless certificates to the point that they are more interested in the document than in intelligence. Students, for instance, are more interested in passing tests than in gaining knowledge. The system forces us all to be passive recipients of the rewards. Critical theorists wish to use theory to enable curriculum developers to create programs that will free students of this form of existence. The main aim is to make students fully aware of themselves and of the fact that society must be altered to allow both self-freedom and collective freedom.[64]

DIRECTIONS FOR THE FUTURE

Curriculum theorizers, regardless of their particular camp, do share a common concern, namely, to make sense out of human experience and human knowledge in order to promote in people those competencies, skills, understandings, and values that will enable them to grow and prosper. As one observer indicates, to account for quality in human experience is no small task, for such experience is an extraordinarily difficult thing about which to theorize.[65]

In many respects, *experience* is a vague theoretical term—one that really cannot be precisely defined or described but which nevertheless must be considered. Experience designates an amazingly wide and complex set of human phenomena that taken together comprise life. Because experience really refers to the totality of life, it is not likely that any one theory about the nature of experience can guide us. Yet, educators are challenged to create curricula that will enable individuals to be successful in their life experience.

Curriculum Inquiry.

Curricularists are confronted with making sense of the world, not only to describe it but to manage it in the present and to entertain and initiate ways of modifying it in the future. The reconceptualists have suggested that curricularists take on a psychoanalytic posture in order to discover their inner worlds before describing and guiding their outer worlds. Decker Walker, who is classified by some as a conceptual curricularist, has outlined five questions:

1. What are the major features of a given curriculum?
2. What are the personal and social consequences that a given curriculum feature elicits?
3. What accounts for the stability and change in curriculum features?
4. What accounts for people's judgments of the merit or worth of various curriculum features?
5. What sorts of curriculum features should be part of a curriculum designed for a particular purpose?[66]

Walker apparently views curriculum as a practical field of study that is to create some product that, when experienced by students, will make a difference in their learning. However, Walker's concept of a "curriculum feature" is vague. Perhaps, however, a precise conception is not possible because there are so many definitions and conceptions of the curriculum.

To make sense out of the dynamics of the curriculum field, curricularists need to analyze the total educational environment in which experience occurs. This includes the school and the outside community. A "good" theory of curriculum cannot ignore the influence of the surrounding environment or the meaning generated by the theory will be incomplete. Even when approaching curriculum from a global or macroanalytic stance, however, curricularists will not be able to explain the total picture or use such theory to control the total educational drama. At best, they will be able to plan or modify portions of the curriculum and the environment impacting upon them.

Conceptualizing the Task.

There is much diversity of thought about what curriculum is, what it should be, and how it should be theorized. Debate exists, too, about what is the unit of analysis in curriculum theorizing and related research. Is it the school district, the school, the classroom, or the student? Is it the interacting network extant between the school and the local community? Is it the content, experiences, or values we are trying to convey?

Talk about metaphors relates to the issue of conceptualizing the curriculum. A person's view of the curriculum will influence what he or she thinks to be appropriate ways to create it, to deliver it, and to evaluate it. Different notions of the curriculum, and therefore its development procedures, will force curriculum specialists to center on new approaches to curriculum. They will have to look for new ways to understand and assess the delivery of programs. Different views about the purposes and goals of education generate various concepts of what the curriculum is within the educational context.

Peter Lemish has presented curriculum development as action occurring in uncertainty. His approach to curriculum development has involved parties' posing problems that challenge the apparent operations of the school.[67] Teachers are challenged to reflect upon the assumptions, values, and meanings of the activities within the school. They are challenged to engage in what Schwab has called "fluid inquiry"—inquiry about the bases, the history of current actions, to see if in fact they are still of value.[68] Teachers are involved in critical inquiry. They question the current scene; they try to plot the consequences of their situations. From such analyses they have a better idea of the curriculum and the roles they and their students play in it.

William Reid has taken a similar posture. He explains curricular action as action concerned with practical uncertain problems. Curriculum decision makers realize that they really can only control a small portion of education; there is much uncertainty.[69] Moreover, they are required to deal with this uncertainty to lessen it. The reason for such action is not so much to advance the field of curriculum as it is to deal with the practical aspects of everyday education.

The task of curriculum theorizers is to theorize about the many dimensions of curriculum. They can theorize about the total curriculum field: where the field is going and why—its overall dynamics. Or, they can theorize on a *micro* level—about various elements or aspects of curriculum—say curriculum design, curriculum development, or curriculum evaluation.[70] Whether they ap-

proach the field of curriculum in its totality or they break it down into its major elements, a diversity of approaches exists that depend on the "mind sets" they bring to the inquiry.

A Balanced Approach to Curriculum Theorizing.

The traditional school of curriculum theorizing has been dominant for most of this century. Especially in research, this school has relied primarily on quantitative inquiry. Empirical investigation has been the norm, and the classroom has been viewed as a laboratory in which variables are to be manipulated in a controlled atmosphere.

Although this type of research is valid in the curriculum field, and will add to the "polishing" of existing theories, much information can also be gained from qualitative inquiry in the schools. Playing "participant observers" in classrooms, theorists can note the types of materials used, the nature of classroom interactions, and the consequences for learners. Employing methods of ethnography, sociology, and history, they can ask the key questions: "What do schools do?" "What are schools for?" "How do students learn?"

Curricularists are beginning to realize that in order to generate any theories within the curriculum realm, they need to discover and describe how teachers manage content and how students manage school experiences. If they observe what is occurring they will obtain a more accurate sense of education. They will see what is being done regarding the curriculum, and they will begin to realize what should be done.

People in the traditional camp using well-established quantitative procedures are still influenced by their values and their views of the world. This is also true of qualitative researchers, according to McCutcheon. Because many qualitative researchers use a phenomenological approach, they interpret events in light of the meanings they bring to those events.[71] As Bernice Wolfson states, "Each human-being-in-the-world speaks from a unique perspective reflecting a particular history, a private construction of the world, and a personal set of beliefs and values."[72] She also notes that persons speak in a particular context that exists within a certain time frame. Both quantitative and qualitative camps are approaching reality through their own perspectives—whether they are scientific or philosophical, empirical or aesthetic.

Qualitative researchers outline stories for a variety of purposes. Theorists can use these narratives to derive a sense of the field of curriculum and to thus behave in particular ways. Qualitative efforts can contrast what is with what ought to be.

The focus of most, if not all, of this curriculum research is to discover useful generic principles. But focusing on the total field often only gives information accurate at the general level, not at the specific level—for example, a particular subject or grade level.

To get a picture of a particular subject or grade, theorists need to engage in action research, which is done in the classroom by teachers faced with particular problems. The value of action research is not judged by whether a new general principle is formulated, but rather by whether the "guideline" deduced from such research will lead to improved classroom practice.

Curriculum specialists Gordon MacKenzie and Hilda Taba involved teachers in the research process. They guided teachers to observe their classrooms and to gather data that would enable them to conclude what were promising procedures and meaningful arrangements of content.[73] Even though many teachers do not have extensive formal backgrounds in curriculum design and curriculum development, they are still confronted with making curriculum decisions daily. Increasingly, researchers are recognizing that teachers are, or at least have the potential to be, meaningful theorists and researchers in their own right. Ideally, teachers and scholars in curriculum will begin to work more and more as team members concerned with advancing the field of curriculum and delivering effective programs to students.

CONCLUSION

In this chapter we discussed the state of curriculum theory. We presented the nature of theory by outlining the various types of theory possible and the different functions that theory could serve. It is not likely that total agreement about the nature and purpose of theory will be forthcoming in the near future. Hopefully, there is some level of agreement about the steps necessary for theorizing. The first step is conceivably the greatest challenge: to come to some kind of agreement about what terms to use. Until theorists have some consensus on the meaning of major terms in curriculum, they are going to be hard pressed to produce many theories of high utility.

Although the "slipperiness" of terms has perhaps prevented a dominant curriculum theory from arising from the field, models depicting the curriculum and its various components are certainly not lacking. We presented several in this chapter to give readers a "feel" for the diversity of opinion, as well as to note the common elements that draw the attention of curricularists.

Common curricular elements do interest theorists, but they nonetheless still have diverse approaches to theorizing. Some of them are traditionalists, others are conceptual empiricists, and still others are reconceptualists. But even these classifications are not firm. Theorists can also be substantive theorizers, generic theorizers, or structural theorizers.

Where do we go from here? What is the future of curriculum theory? Some theorists will likely continue to study curriculum from a macro perspective, and others from a micro perspective. Regardless of approach, a balance will be needed; not only a balance of approach, but also a balance among the types of professionals involved in theorizing and a balance among curricularists in schools, colleges, universities, and even in state, regional, and federal agencies.

Notes.

1. Elizabeth S. Maccia, *Curriculum Theory and Policy*, Occasional Paper 65–176 (Columbus, Ohio: Ohio State University, 1968).
2. Dorothy Huenecke, "What Is Curriculum Theorizing? What Are Its Implications for Practice?" *Educational Leadership* (January 1982), pp. 290–294.
3. James B. Macdonald, "Curriculum Theory," in J. R. Gress and D. E. Purpel, eds., *Curriculum: An Introduction to the Field* (Berkeley, Calif.: McCutchan, 1978), pp. 44–56.
4. George A. Beauchamp, *Curriculum Theory*, 4th ed. (Itasca, Ill.: Peacock, 1981).
5. Abraham Kaplan, *The Conduct of Inquiry* (San Francisco: Chandler, 1964), p. 295.
6. Richard E. Snow, "Theory Construction for Research on Teaching," in R. M. Travers, ed., *Second Handbook of Research on Teaching* (Chicago: Rand McNally, 1973), p. 78.
7. David Bohm, *Wholeness and the Implicit Order* (London: ARK Paperbacks, 1983), pp. 4–5.
8. Herbert Feigl, "Principles and Problems of Theory Construction in Psychology," in W. Dennis, ed., *Current Trends of Psychological Theory* (Pittsburgh: University of Pittsburgh Press, 1951), pp. 182–195.
9. Fred N. Kerlinger, *Foundations of Behavioral Research*, 2nd ed. (New York: Holt, Rinehart, 1976), p. 10.
10. Ira J. Gordon, ed., *Criteria for Theories of Instruction* (Washington, D.C.: Association for Supervision and Curriculum Development, 1968).
11. Herbert M. Kliebard, "Curriculum Theory: Give Me a 'For Instance,'" *Curriculum Inquiry* (Summer 1977), pp. 257–268.
12. Ernest Nagel, "Philosophy of Science and Educational Theory," *Studies in Philosophy and Education* (Fall 1969), pp. 5–27.
13. Max van Manen, "Edifying Theory: Serving the Good," *Theory into Practice* (Winter 1982), pp. 44–49; O'Connor, *An Introduction to the Philosophy of Education*.
14. May Brodbeck, "Logic and Scientific Method in Research on Teaching," in N. L. Gage, ed., *Handbook of Research on Teaching* (Chicago: Rand McNally, 1963), pp. 44–93.
15. Kaplan, *The Conduct of Inquiry*, p. 20.
16. D. O'Connor, *An Introduction to the Philosophy of Education* (New York: Philosophical Library, 1957).
17. Kenneth R. Hoover, *The Elements of Social Scientific Thinking* (New York: St. Martin Press, 1984).
18. C. E. Noble, "Induction, Deduction, Abduction," in M. H. Marx and F. E. Goodson, eds., *Theories in Contemporary Psychology*, 2nd ed. (New York: Macmillan, 1976), pp. 300–308.
19. George Homans, *The Human Group* (New York: Harcourt, Brace, 1950).
20. Beauchamp, *Curriculum Theory*.
21. Gordon, *Criteria for Theories of Instruction*.
22. M. H. Marx, "Theorizing," in Marx and Goodson, *Theories in Contemporary Psychology*, pp. 261–285.
23. Beauchamp, *Curriculum Theory*.
24. Carter V. Good, *Introduction to Educational Research*, 2nd ed. (New York: Appleton-Century, 1963); O'Connor, *An Introduction to the Philosophy of Education*.
25. Herbert M. Kliebard, "Curriculum Theory as Metaphor," *Theory into Practice* (Winter 1982), pp. 11–17.
26. Macdonald, "Curriculum Theory," in Gress and Purpel, eds., *Curriculum: An Introduction to the Field*, pp. 44–56.
27. Kliebard, "Curriculum Theory: Give Me a 'For Instance.'"
28. Joseph Schwab, *The Practical: A Language for Curriculum* (Washington, D.C.: National Education Association, 1970).
29. Franklin Bobbitt, *The Curriculum* (Boston: Houghton Mifflin, 1918).
30. Robert J. Schaefer, "Retrospect and Prospect," in R. M. McClure, ed., *The Curriculum: Retrospect and Prospect*, Seventieth Yearbook of the National Society for the Study of Education, Part I (Chicago: University of Chicago Press, 1971), p. 19.
31. Ibid.
32. Bobbitt, *The Curriculum*; W. W. Charters, *Curriculum Construction* (New York: Macmillan, 1923).
33. Kliebard, "Curriculum Theory: Give Me a 'For Instance,'" pp. 257–268.
34. John Dewey, *The School and Society* (Chicago: University of Chicago Press, 1900).
35. Kliebard, "Curriculum Theory: Give Me a 'For Instance.'"
36. Daniel Tanner and Laurel N. Tanner, *Curriculum Development: Theory into Practice*, 2nd ed. (New York: Macmillan, 1980).
37. Beauchamp, *Curriculum Theory*. p. 35.
38. Ralph W. Tyler, *Basic Principles of Curriculum and Instruction* (Chicago: University of Chicago Press, 1949).
39. Beauchamp, *Curriculum Theory*.
40. Occasional papers by Elizabeth Maccia and George Maccia (Columbus, Ohio: Bureau of Educational Research and Service, Ohio State University, 1963–1965).
41. Mauritz Johnson, "Definitions and Models in Curriculum Theory," *Educational Theory* (April 1967), pp. 17–32.
42. James B. Macdonald, "Educational Models for Instruction," in J. B. Macdonald and R. R. Leeper, eds., *Theories of Instruction* (Washington, D.C.: Association for Supervision and Curriculum Development, 1965), pp. 93–98.
43. L. Craig Wilson, *The Open Access Curriculum* (Boston: Allyn and Bacon, 1971).
44. John Dewey, *Sources of a Science of Education* (New York: Liveright, 1929), p. 161.

45. Gail McCutcheon, "What in the World Is Curriculum Theory?" *Theory into Practice* (Winter 1982), pp. 18–22.

46. Bernice J. Wolfson, "Psychological Theory and Curricular Thinking," in A. Molnar, ed., *Current Thought on Curriculum* (Alexandria, Va.: Association for Supervision and Curriculum Development, 1985), pp. 53–72.

47. Jean Anyon, "Adequate Social Science, Curriculum Investigations, and Theory," *Theory into Practice* (Winter 1982), pp. 34–37.

48. Michael Apple, *Education and Power* (Boston: Routledge & Kegan Paul, 1982); Henry Giroux, *Ideology, Culture and the Process of Schooling* (Philadelphia: Temple University Press, 1981).

49. Decker F. Walker, "Curriculum Theory Is Many Things to Many People," *Theory into Practice* (Winter 1982), pp. 62–65.

50. Tom Barone, "Insinuated Theory from Curricula-in-Use," *Theory into Practice* (Winter 1982), pp. 38–43.

51. Elizabeth Vallance, "The Practical Uses of Curriculum Theory," *Theory into Practice* (Winter 1982), pp. 4–10.

52. Dwayne Huebner, "Toward a Remaking of Curricular Language," in W. Pinar, ed., *Heightened Consciousness, Cultural Revolution, and Curriculum Theory* (Berkeley, Calif.: McCutchan, 1974), pp. 36–37.

53. Kliebard, "Curriculum Theory as Metaphor."

54. Paulo Freire, *The Politics of Education, Culture, Power, and Liberation* (South Hadley, Mass.: Bergin and Garvey, 1985).

55. Arthur W. Foshay, "Curriculum Talk," in A. W. Foshay, ed., *Considered Action for Curriculum Improvement* (Alexandria, Va: Association for Supervision and Curriculum Development, 1980), pp. 82–94.

56. William Pinar, "Notes on the Curriculum Field 1978," *Educational Researcher* (September 1978), pp. 5–12; John McNeil, *Curriculum: A Comprehensive Introduction*, 3rd ed. (Boston: Little, Brown, 1985).

57. Huenecke, "What Is Curriculum Theorizing? What Are Its Implications for Practice?"

58. Ibid.

59. William Pinar, "Heightened Consciousness, Cultural Revolution and Curriculum Theory: An Introduction," in Pinar, ed., *Heightened Consciousness, Cultural Revolution, and Curriculum Theory*, pp. 1–15.

60. Macdonald, "Curriculum Theory," in Gress and Purpel, eds., *Curriculum: An Introduction to the Field*, pp. 44–56.

61. James Macdonald, "Curriculum and Human Interests," in Pinar, ed., *Curriculum Theorizing: The Reconceptualists*, pp. 283–298; William Pinar and Madeline Grumet, *Toward a Poor Curriculum* (Dubuque, Ia.: Kendell-Hunt, 1976).

62. Apple, *Education and Power*; Freire, *The Politics of Education.*

63. William H. Schubert, *Curriculum, Perspective, Paradigm, Possibility* (New York: Macmillan, 1986).

64. Ibid.

65. George Willis, "Curriculum Theory and the Context of Curriculum," in Pinar, ed., *Curriculum Theorizing, the Reconceptualists*, pp. 427–444.

66. Decker Walker, "What Are the Problems Curricularists Ought to Study?" *Curriculum Theory Network* (Vol. 4, 1974), pp. 217–218.

67. Peter Lemish, "The Technical Approach and the Praxis Orientation to Curriculum Development." Paper presented at the annual meeting of the American Educational Research Association, New York, 1982.

68. Schwab, *The Practical: A Language for Curriculum.*

69. William Reid, "Practical Reasoning and Curriculum Theory: In Search of a New Paradigm," *Curriculum Inquiry* (Spring 1976), pp. 261–285.

70. Richard D. Hawthorne, "An Empirical Approach to Curriculum Theory Building," Occasional Paper (Kent, Ohio: Kent State University, 1982).

71. McCutcheon, "What in the World Is Curriculum Theory?"

72. Wolfson, "Psychological Theory and Curriculum Thinking," in Molnar, *Current Thought on Curriculum*, p. 58.

73. Gordon Mackenzie, "Why a Strategy for Planning Curricular Innovation?" in M. Lawler, ed., *Strategies for Planned Curricular Innovation* (New York: Teachers College Press, Columbia University, 1970), pp. 5–23; Hilda Taba, *Teaching Strategies and Cognitive Functioning in Elementary School Children* (San Francisco: San Francisco State College, 1966).

chapter 12

CURRICULUM ISSUES AND TRENDS

Various trends and events that have impacted curriculum in recent years are likely to continue to impact it in the near future. Many issues related to these trends confront curriculum workers, and they are all important in their own right. In this chapter, we raise questions about four broad curriculum issues: (1) censored curriculum; (2) compensatory curriculum; (3) irrelevant curriculum; and (4) emerging curriculum. The latter can be further divided into three topics: sex education, multicultural education, and handicapped education.

CENSORED CURRICULUM

A certain amount of curriculum censorship has always existed, not as a matter of policy or law, but rather as a customary practice. During the eighteenth and nineteenth cen-

turies, content in curriculum was restricted to traditional American values that centered around the family, church, work, and nation. Textbooks portrayed, according to authorities, the Puritan morality, work ethic, individualism, achievement,[1] American patriotism, and the melting pot theme.[2]

As late as the mid twentieth century, history, civics, and English literature textbooks barely included—or even excluded—such topics as poor people, immigrants, minorities, women, and organized labor. Many even ignored our Democratic presidents. In a strict sense, the curriculum was not censored. Rather, it only included information educators considered appropriate. Readers or textbooks presented an idealistic American society with traditional, patriotic, and majority core values. Information considered too sensitive or too controversial was simply excluded. This policy elicited no fanfare or controversy—just occasional criticism. The problem was, however, that some of the content in the textbooks was racist and sexist. It mirrored what has been called a "hidden curriculum"—the interests of dominant groups.

Today, publishers exercise self-censorship to appease dissenting factions and to avoid alienating pressure groups. As a matter of practical concern, textbook editors must have a keen sense of the educational marketplace and they must be highly cognizant of a variety of pressure groups. Like other businesspeople, publishers attend to what their customers want, and they are sensitive to the wishes of textbook selection committees.[3] Current data show that all the major textbook companies conform to the preferences of the larger educational markets—the most populous states, such as California, Illinois, New York (which together accounted for more than 23 percent of the total national expenditure on curriculum materials in one recent year)[4]—or to the major adoption states—California, Texas, and Florida.[5] These few states greatly impact the books available for study in other states; most other school systems have little choice but to go along with the dictates, specifications, and price maintenance of a handful of school systems in a few states.

Recent Censorship.

As the 1970s unfolded, covert censorship changed to overt censorship, and criticism began to mount. Widely publicized textbook battles and school library book battles fanned censorship flames in many parts of the country. Kanawha County, West Virginia, was one of the first places where community groups successfully banned books. The outcome was that no text or curriculum would be supported if it: (1) raised questions about the sanctity of the family; (2) questioned belief in a Supernatural Being or fostered religious disbelief; (3) encouraged skepticism or attacked the laws of the nation, state, or local community; (4) criticized the free enterprise system; (5) fostered

anti-Americanism or disrespect toward traditional American values; or (6) implied that formal rules of grammar were inappropriate.[6]

Community groups in different states focused on issues of concern in their respective states. In Florida, the issue was sex education programs; in Indiana and New Jersey, it was obscene language; in Illinois, Ohio, and New York, the issue was racial (criticism from both blacks and whites depending on the particular books); in Rhode Island, the issue involved the danger of overpopulation and its religious implications; and in California and in many parts of the South, the issue was creationism versus evolution. Antireligious or nonreligious books raised other issues involving separation of church and state.[7]

More recently, a zealous husband and wife team in Texas organized a school book censorship group known as "Educational Research Analysts." By tirelessly campaigning across the state and elsewhere the group has successfully pressured many schools—through their parent groups—to ban certain books alleged to instill disrespect for American values, the family, and church. Similarly, in the twenty-two "adoption" states that prepare lists of instructional materials mandated or recommended for use in the public schools, the trend is growing to "limit what students shall read."[8]

The ban on books, which has spread to school libraries, curriculum councils, and classrooms across the country, has involved all types of school districts: suburban and city; rich and poor; predominantly minority and predominantly white, and so on. Various community groups, parent groups, and taxpayer groups involved with censorship concerns have exhibited different "zones of tolerance," ranging from heated school-community conflicts and serious watch-dog committees to mild newspaper editorials and questions at PTA meetings.

Today, almost any book that contains political or economic messages, obscenity, sex, nudity, profanity, slang or questionable English, ethnic or racially sensitive material, or that is considered by a pressure group as antifamily, antireligious, or anti-American is subject to possible censorship. The list of books for potential censorship has included: *Madame Bovary, Soul on Ice, Grapes of Wrath, Mary Poppins, Catcher in the Rye,* and even such classics as Shakespeare's *Hamlet* and Mark Twain's *Huckleberry Finn.*[9]

Caught in the middle of book-censoring controversies are publishers of school texts and materials, who are forced to compromise; boards of education, both state and local, who are pressed by special-interest groups to censor books; and librarians, teachers, and school administrators, who are afraid to stir citizen wrath. On one side are some parents and other community members, who contend that certain passages or pictures in textbooks or library books are warping traditional American or community values that should be "inculcated" in students; on the other side are advocates of intellectual freedom and most education associations, who say that schools and libraries should be forums for ideas that students can question and examine.

In general, the current community-school conflict over censorship has several causes. One is the schools' unwillingness to recognize the role of the community in selecting books. A second is the schools' inability to define or clarify the community's role in the selection process. A third cause is that certain community groups may be overzealous in pushing their ideas on other parents and public institutions.

One way to deal with this confrontation is to recognize the citizens' reasons for concern and their right to express views about the merit and appropriateness of the school curriculum and materials. Such concerns should be communicated to school authorities and responded to promptly and professionally. Censorship battles will continue, but appropriate selection policies with well-defined procedures worked out in advance by school and community representatives should alleviate some of the fury that has erupted in the past over curriculum materials and textbooks.

COMPENSATORY CURRICULUM

A massive movement into compensatory education, begun in the 1960s and 1970s, was designed to overcome the educational (and to some extent social and psychological) deficiencies or disadvantages of lower-class and minority children. The movement was widespread and intense; it took on more than just bandwagon status. Nonetheless, surprisingly little mention is made of this trend in other curriculum texts.

The various programs and projects can be categorized by *target population* (kindergarten through college, student or teacher), *treatment* (remedial, enrichment, and therapeutic), *service* (curricula, instructional, counseling, school-wide, and community), *setting* (urban and rural), and *policy* (local, regional, state, and national).[10] Most compensatory programs were experimental or additive, and were not designed for fundamental or system-wide reform. They operated from the theoretical premises that cognitive, social, and psychological development are mainly the consequence of environmental influences, and that improving the environment of the child can reverse whatever learning deficits exist. Most compensatory programs and projects stressed enriching experiences at home and in school, and making changes in the formal curriculum to meet the special needs and problems of the child. Beginning with the Johnson administration, special personnel and services were usually funded by the federal government, under Title I of the Elementary and Secondary Education Act (ESEA). Chapter I was introduced (to replace Title I) by the Reagan administration.

Programs and Practices.

Following is an overview of the major compensatory activities. They emphasize curriculum and related methods and instructional strategies.

1. *Infant Education.* Research indicates that parent-child and family interactions are ex-

tremely important influences on children's cognitive and school development. Many infant education and parental programs that evolved stress various auditory, visual, and motor activities. They encourage proper nourishment for the children. They also help the mother teach her child at home, by altering her language and interaction techniques with her child, to improve family stability.

2. *Early Childhood Education.* Operations Headstart and Follow-Through are the most well-known programs under this category. Headstart attempts to help disadvantaged children achieve "readiness" for first grade. Follow-Through concentrates on sustaining the readiness and supplementing whatever gains are made by the children who participate in Headstart. Because environmentalists and compensatory advocates emphasize counteracting disadvantaged children's cognitive deficiencies as early as possible, a great deal of school money and effort were devoted to early childhood programs.

3. *Basic-skill Programs.* Poor academic achievement is linked to inabilities in basic reading and language areas. More than half of the compensatory programs, regardless of grade level, deal directly with improving reading and language skills using various materials, methods, and personnel. New readers and new technologies were developed, and a variety of individualized and small group methods were introduced that emphasized basic-skill acquisition.

4. *Materials and Media.* Basic readers, workbooks, and textbooks have been revised to make them more relevant to the experiences and interests of disadvantaged children. The all-white, middle-class world of library and school books has been replaced by one replete with multicultural and multiethnic materials. The media have also been updated to include more culturally "relevant," remedial, and audio-visual aides.

5. *Instructional Packages and Approaches.* A variety of kits containing multisensory, diagnostic, and detailed materials and programs have been developed. They include lesson unit plans and programs that consist of various individualized, self-instructional, and self-paced activities. Most are extensive and carefully designed; they stress mastery learning,

direct instruction, continuous learning, and other behaviorist and teacher-directed approaches. In addition, the use of such language laboratories, programmed materials and machines, instructional television, and computer-aided devices for purposes of teaching basic skills has sharply increased.

6. *Guidance and Counseling Programs.* Various social, psychological, and vocational services have been provided for disadvantaged children as well. Social workers, psychologists, and community aides have been involved in bridging the gap between school and home. Parent involvement in counseling and mental health programs has been encouraged, too.

7. *Tutoring Programs.* Individual and small-group tutoring programs have been greatly augmented. This has involved both volunteer and paid student tutors, as well as volunteer and paid community people and aides. At the public school level the programs usually also provide a positive older student or adult model. Many schools have also developed after-school programs and summer programs to provide extensive instruction and assistance in basic subjects and cultural enrichment.

8. *Auxiliary School Personnel.* The recruitment and training of teacher aides and paraprofessionals, along with nonpaid volunteers, have increased in some schools. The emphasis is on employing low-income adults from the local community to reduce the student-adult classroom ratio, enhance school-community relations, and provide jobs to improve the economy in low-income neighborhoods.

9. *Parent-linkage Programs.* Parents have been encouraged to volunteer as teacher aides in classrooms and schools to help teachers perform instructional, clerical, and supervisor tasks. They have also been urged to acquire skills to help their children with homework and other basic-skill activities at home. Parents have been encouraged to attend on a regular basis parent-teacher meetings aimed at improving their children's learning, to join parent clubs (usually on grade levels) and parent associations (usually school-wide), and to participate in various advisory committees to enhance school-community relations. When parents are unable to visit the

school, teachers and social workers have made home visitations to improve communication and collaboration between parents and school officials.

10. *School Organization.* Many schools serving the disadvantaged have received funding for a variety of organizational plans ranging from extended school days and extended school years to flexible scheduling, team teaching, nongraded programs, and open classrooms.

11. *Community-centered Programs.* The curriculum has been expanded to include several community-centered programs that provide a place: for community recreation, leisure, and fun activities; for expressive art, music, and drama activities; for influencing and enhancing community policy related to housing, health, and legal aid; for developing social-welfare and mutual aid programs; and for extending vocational, citizenship, and continuing education. In this connection, the school has also been extended to include afternoon, evening, weekend, and summer hours.

12. *Dropout Prevention and Vocational Programs.* Along with vocational and career education a number of programs have aimed at preventing students from dropping out. Numerous work-study programs, on-the-job training programs, and financial incentives have been offered. Some of these programs have been incorporated into the regular school program; others have been offered in special centers; some in the daytime, others in the evening or summer. The most noted of these programs have involved neighborhood youth corps manpower development and training programs, and community-action programs.

13. *Higher Education Programs.* Special programs in this area include: (1) identifying students of college potential and enriching their learning experiences; (2) accepting lower academic scores for college admission; (3) using admission criteria that allow open enrollment, eliminate test-performance data, and credit life experiences; (4) providing transitions to increase the probability for success for disadvantaged youth admitted into college; examples are summer programs, tutoring, reduced course loads, and remedial courses; and (5) providing special scholarships, loans, work-study opportuni-ties, and jobs based on financial need and minority status.

14. *Adult Education.* The most rapidly growing sector in education is adult education. Much of the focus is on illiterate adults and others who need training in basic job skills and citizenship education. Programs are usually offered at public schools, libraries, community colleges, private industries, and special centers located in various parts of cities and metropolitan areas.[11]

Problems and Prospects.

Much of the effort during the first two decades (1960s to 1970s) of compensatory education was shown to be ineffective in raising the cognitive levels of disadvantaged students. Basically, four failure trends emerged:

1. In many of the best-known and heavily funded programs, such as Headstart and Follow-Through, no significant differences showed in learning between the target children and matched controlled groups.

2. In the early stages of compensatory funding, input increments had a discernible effect, but they gradually diminished until input was wasted because there was virtually no increase in output. The conclusion was that the programs had reached a "flat area"—less output in relation to input, or even worse, no return.

3. Longitudinal studies of several programs also revealed a "fade out" process—that is, the early gains made by these youngsters (if any) eventually leveled off and, after a few years of schooling, were equivalent to gains made by those without such funding.

4. Many so-called "successes" were generally based not on hard data, but on impressions and testimonies (in many cases suspect). When evaluated on the basis of measurable data, most of these programs proved to be ineffective.[12] For example, of the more than 1200 projects evaluated in the early 1970s, and originally judged to be successful, only ten were found to be effective on the basis of statistical reanalysis.[13]

The same problems were exhibited in the

late 1970s and early 1980s, when several well-publicized and so-called outstanding early-childhood programs were analyzed and proved to have limited cognitive outcomes despite early claims of success. Some programs tended to be subject to "fade out" within a few years; others had no data available with which to verify successes or to conduct critical reviews in scientific journals.[14] What educators experienced in the early stages of compensatory programs was reality. Intervention efforts of a few hours a day in one or two school years could not compensate for several years of impoverishment, despite the claims of many environmentalists and behaviorists of the 1960s.[15]

In general, compensatory education has been criticized for: (1) its hasty planning and piecemeal approach; (2) its mismanagement and misappropriation of funds; (3) its dependence on unethical grantspeople who justify their conduct on the basis that "everyone does it"; (4) the large consultant fees charged for unaccomplished or shoddy work; (5) its use of inadequately trained personnel at the state and local levels; (6) the high salaries it pays people at the administrative levels; (7) its disregard for and lack of teacher participation; (8) its vague objectives; (9) its poor evaluation procedures; and (10) the increased quantity of services it substitutes for change in the quality or content of the program.[16]

In addition, opponents have criticized the attitude of educators that the money was there for them to give away even if they expected no real benefits. Lawmakers who allocate funds for compensatory programs have become increasingly concerned about putting money into areas in which little worth has been empirically shown.

Advocates of compensatory spending claim that most of these problems can be remedied over time, and that the real problem is the concern that disadvantaged children will not succeed. Americans are obligated to find solutions that will reach these children and provide them with the necessary equality of opportunities. Moreover, advocates contend that, in most instances:

(1) money was made available in such haste that the quality of planning and development was limited; (2) many programs have been operative for too brief a period to be effectively evaluated; (3) many programs were funded at insufficient levels; and (4) some student successes have been reported in the affective domain.[17]

A number of recent studies have identified the characteristics of successful compensatory programs: (1) clearly stated goals and objectives; (2) reductions in adult/child ratios; (3) a climate of high (but also realistic) expectations for students; (4) structured and step-by-step learning approaches; (5) matching instruction to children's needs; (6) emphasis on basic-skill instruction; (7) greater time spent on tasks; (8) more frequent monitoring of student progress; (9) greater parental involvement; and (10) appropriate staff development and teacher inservicing.[18]

What seems to work, to some extent, is a compensatory program that provides teachers with positive expectations of students, and technical assistance and support. This program's institutional activities provide direct instruction and mastery-learning opportunities—that is, prescriptive and diagnostic approaches, emphasis on basic-skill acquisition, monitoring of student progress, and prompt student feedback. Carl Bereiter writes: "The kind of research that holds out the most promise for giving direction to compensatory education is not research on the nature of educational disadvantagement but research on the nature of instruction."[19]

Also, the programs that exhibit the most promise tend to be well organized and targeted toward preschool and primary grade children.[20] This approach coincides with traditional and technical data, which suggest that environmental influences and intervention are especially critical in early stages of human development, because the most rapid period of cognitive development, according to Benjamin Bloom, is in the initial years (50 percent by age 4).[21] The trouble is, however, that most compensatory education programs do not exhibit positive findings because they are not well organized, and because changes in human characteristics are not easy to effect.

As we approach the 1990s, then, the question is to what extent compensatory funding will increase or decrease. Federal monies for education decreased approximately 33 percent between 1980 and 1985, after twenty years of uninterrupted increases (from $1.7 in 1960 to $25.6 billion in 1980), a reflection of the "new federalism," which reduces federal funding in education and shifts most education responsibilities to the states. Note however, that during the same five year period, compensatory funding increased in actual dollars—from $2.9 to $3.7 billion annually.[22] This increase reflects successful pressure from minority and liberal groups and from the educational establishment in general. Whether these groups will continue to experience success in the future is difficult to predict, given the increasing trend toward cost effectiveness in education. Moreover, the present stress on excellence in education may plague compensatory policy in the future, especially if the pursuit of quality education becomes a code word for a retreat from equality.

IRRELEVANT CURRICULUM

Almost everyone likes to criticize the schools. And such critics often claim that the curriculum is irrelevant in some way or another. When people say that the curriculum is irrelevant, they often mean either that it does not meet the needs of the social situation or the students and so the subject matter needs to be modified. Such a broad view permits educators to consider the irrelevant curriculum in several ways: (1) The curriculum is *fixed* or not relevant to society, which suggests that the sweep of change in society is more rapid than that in curriculum; (2) the curriculum is *antiseptic*, which connotes that the materials or textbooks are divorced from the students' sense of reality; and (3) the curriculum is *trivial*, which implies that

its facts and figures are remote, meaningless, and/or nonessential to students.

The Fixed Curriculum.

This interpretation suggests that a relationship exists between changes in society and changes in the curriculum. It is rooted in Dewey's interpretation of the *curriculum as experience*, which links curriculum to the importance of perpetuating, transferring, and reconstructing society. "The scheme of a curriculum must take into account . . . the intention of improving the life we live in common so that the future shall be better than the past,"[23] asserted Dewey. This idea suggests that the cumulative knowledge and total culture of society must be reflected in the curriculum, what such reconstructionists as B. Othanel Smith and his colleagues called *curriculum as race experience*. They wrote: "The curriculum is always [or should be], in every society, a reflection of what the people think, believe, and do . . . [A] universal relationship [exists] between the curriculum and the culture of a society."[24]

The idea that the curriculum had become static or fixed was proclaimed by another early reconstructionist as well. In 1939, Harold Benjamin described a society whose curriculum was based on perennial beliefs—dating back to the Paleolithic era. The wise men of society argued that "the essence of true education is timeless . . . something that endures through changing conditions like a solid rock standing squarely and firmly in the middle of a raging torrent."[25] Benjamin's message was simple: Eventually the curriculum became outdated.

Today's explosion of knowledge, and the swiftness of change, underscore the need for curricula to be relevant. Some educators have contended that a curriculum can become obsolete every few years. This claim is based on the facts that knowledge increases exponentially and that the rate of obsolescence of scientific knowledge equals that of an automobile.[26] This premise is somewhat questionable, however, because it assumes that the explosion of knowledge can go on indefinitely, and it does not consider that trends change or that the rate of change varies over time. Moreover, it considers our resources to be limited.

The effects of the knowledge explosion on curriculum are tempered by the fact that new knowledge is assimilated as existing knowledge is revised and modified to accommodate it. In the same vein, new subject matter is systematically incorporated into existing subject matter, and new teaching and learning methods are fused with existing methods to produce new instructional approaches. These curriculum and instructional processes are continuous, and to some extent reflect new knowledge in the social sciences. In assessing the onrush of new knowledge, Orlosky and Smith contend that as "knowledge continually expands so does the curriculum. Old areas grow and new ones emerge. . . . These developments give rise to new perspectives, new goals,"[27] and, if we may add, new content. Indeed, if schools are to maintain their health and vitality, the curriculum cannot remain fixed in a world of change.

The Antiseptic Curriculum.

An antiseptic curriculum is safe and sterile; it does not deal with student or societal reality. The stories, characters, and illustrations in reading material tend to be one-dimensional or monolithic, not multicultural (in terms of ethnicity, religion, sex, and class).

The term antiseptic curriculum was first used to describe basic readers in the 1960s— when they were considered to be irrelevant to the social realities and culture of disadvantaged (minority and low-income) groups. These readers portrayed an almost exclusively white and middle-class world, and they treated the few minorities they did include as exotic or different—not part of the American landscape. The Indians, for example, were called "Big Horn" or "Shining Star," and peddlers or organ grinders wore red scarves, not ties, and ragged clothes, not suits. Their appearances or names were typically Italian,

Greek, or Polish. When "Dick and Jane" or "Johnnie" visited their grandmothers in the South, or in the country, either no mention was made of blacks or one black boy might be inserted in the background. Yellow or dark people were depicted in the illustrations for the stories about China, India, and Africa, but they were always different in appearance and custom. Women were usually portrayed as mothers, nurses, or teachers, and religion was rarely mentioned except, perhaps, in relation to church attendance on Sunday mornings. In short, these readers were presented with a monocultural view of our society. Put in different words, in 1960, approximately 6.5 million nonwhite children were learning to read books that either scarcely mentioned them, or omitted them entirely.

According to Fantini and Weinstein, life was depicted in these books in terms of "happy, neat, wealthy, white people whose intact and loving families live only in clean, grassy suburbs. . . . Ethnic groups comprising so much of our population are often omitted," or else they are included under "units as 'Children From Other Lands.' "[28] Fantini and Weinstein concluded that these books had no relationship to the culture or reality of the disadvantaged child.

Otto Klienberg was more outspoken in his review of the most popular readers of the period. Americans, when illustrated, were almost exclusively white and blonde, were relatively comfortable financially (but not wealthy); were nicely dressed; lived in clean, pleasant homes with nice furniture; and provided their children with toys, bicycles, and spending money.[29] Every family had a father and mother at home, and usually a grandmother or grandfather to visit. The parents always had time to take their sons to ballgames or their daughters shopping, or to take both children on train rides to visit relatives, on car rides to learn about farmers, or to the seashore on family vacations. In summary, life in America was portrayed through a white, middle-class lens; life was comfortable, frustrations were rare, and people were invariably generous, kind, honest, and hardworking. Other kinds of people did live in the world, and some of them may have had problems, but they lived far away, and had no place in the American scene. For Klienberg, the basic readers displayed both "ethnocentrism" and "socioeconomic-centrism."[30] Critics argued that the great distance between the schools' curricula and reality for minority and poor children contributed to their academic failure.

Most of these abuses were corrected by the late 1960s to the extent that Harry Passow could summarize the instructional materials as being: (1) multiracial, multiethnic, and multisocial class; (2) urban-oriented rather than suburban or rural; (3) historically and culturally accurate regarding the contributions of various minority groups; (4) nationally and internationally pluralistic; and (5) positive in the treatment of emerging and third-world nations.[31]

Today, readers, workbooks, and textbooks unquestionably exclude racial, ethnic, religious, and sexual stereotyping. Obscenity, violence, and sexual topics are still generally avoided, as are such unpleasant issues as disease and death. Story characters and pictures tend to be well represented by major racial and ethnic groups, including the handicapped and elderly. Girls now rarely play with dolls, and women are depicted as airplane pilots, police officers, construction workers, lawyers, and doctors. Blacks, Hispanics, and other traditional minorities have professional and managerial jobs. Minorities are not basketball players or musicians, unless surrounded by a host of whites, and boys rarely play baseball—and least not without girls.[32]

Finding good literature, or good texts, that meet all these requirements (and many more) is difficult. To accommodate some of the new criteria, many classic works of literature have been eliminated from the curriculum, and many bland texts and instructional materials have been included. "The idea is to please all and offend none [and thus] many textbooks [and related materials] have no clear point of view."[33] Although many new books portray the majority and minority populace more accurately, however, they remain sterile and safe; they tacitly perpetuate the antiseptic curriculum. This, in turn, can lead to student boredom. Considering that readers, workbooks, and/or textbooks have become the basis for curriculum and classroom instruction and that they represent 70 to 95 percent of the total curriculum program (depending on the subject), this is a serious problem indeed.[34]

The Trivial Curriculum.

A trivial curriculum is one that emphasizes rote learning and irrelevant facts and figures that teachers must insist that students learn. Teachers may ask students, for example, to memorize a good deal of nonessential and meaningless information, such as the names of all the American presidents in order, the capital of each state, the products of Brazil, the lines to the "Highwayman" or the "Rhyme of the Ancient Mariner," or the coefficient of an angle. This type of teaching and learning is almost useless, and it occurs at the expense of important academic time that could be utilized more efficiently by introducing significant content.

Most students have had facts and figures drummed into them repeatedly during their school careers, perhaps even in college. Most of them cannot remember what they memorized for their last exams, much less what they memorized a year or more ago. More than 75 percent of various kinds of facts learned in a subject is forgotten over a twelve-month period of time.[35] For a single lecture, as contrasted with a whole course, retention over one hour is also unimpressive—as low as 60 percent.[36] Obviously, the drop-off or loss of retention differs for students with varying ability. Bright students retain more than slow students, and college students do better than elementary school students. For content, what is perceived by the learner as trivial material—useless, arbitrary or disconnected—the ability to recall data declines very rapidly—often within minutes.

David Ausubel makes a critical distinction

between rote and meaningful learning. He argues that, to the extent that instruction concerns simple rote learning and meaningless data, the curriculum is essentially irrelevant to the learner, and little is learned.[37] In contrast to memorizing a host of facts or words (for a short period of time), meaningful learning takes place if the curriculum relates to what the learner already knows, deems personally useful, and considers relevant to his or her personal experience.

If trivial facts and figures have little value or relevance to adults, how can we expect them to have meaning for children? Information—including the names of the American presidents, state capitals, coffee beans, sonnets, and quadratic equations—can have meaning to students, *if* it can be related to existing ideas in the students' cognitive and affective backgrounds, or *if* it can be subsumed within existing mental and personal structures. If data are learned only as random facts, or only because of the dictates of the formal curriculum, students' memory-storing processes will be limited and what they remember will be remote and arbitrary.

Using satire, Harmin and Simon illustrate how teaching facts can dominate the entire curriculum, and how educators' misplaced ingenuity can stifle real learning. Their scenario takes place during "the year the schools began teaching the telephone directory" to the seventh grade.[38] Each seventh grade teacher, working in conjunction with his or her immediate supervisor, was responsible for developing appropriate methods to make this memorization task easier. The students began from A to Z: " 'What is Gregory Arnold's phone number?' asked the teacher. 'Who lives at 174 N. Maple?' "[39] (Everyone knew because it was the principal's address.) The task continued, with frequent quizzes, a midterm through M, and a final exam at Z: "Oh the cram sessions which were organized by eager mothers, the withheld allowances which were used as bludgeons, the diligent studying which went on! Never before did so many telephone numbers, addresses, and

names get committed to so many memories."[40]

Students who did not learn the phone book were labeled as slow learners and were placed in remedial classes the following term. In general, the telephone directory curriculum was deemed a success and was admired by the entire community. It was even extended down to the sixth and fifth grades the following year. To integrate subject matter, sixth graders were required to memorize the Paris, France, telephone directory as well. To make learning more relevant, fifth graders were also assigned the local community directory. New seventh graders were assigned the "exciting" task of learning the state capitol directory.

Although Harmin and Simon's criticism is directed at reforming the curriculum, their wit has implications for the way teachers still require students to commit to memory much trivial information. The real issue is how educators can help students move from memorizing random facts to developing useful concepts and problem-solving skills. Learning useless or arbitrary facts in isolation—a process that characterizes a good deal of classroom activity—is not conducive to real learning; that is, to concept thinking or problem solving. At best, a trivial curriculum can encourage students with good memories to retrieve information, in order to please the teacher or pass an examination. But computers can now do a better job of retrieving information than students. Learners must instead be taught to think and solve problems.

EMERGING CURRICULUM

An emerging curriculum is one that is evolving currently, or has evolved in the recent past, and that constitutes new curriculum content and areas of study. These areas of study are innovative; they break from traditional subject matter, and they reflect social and political changes. An emerging curriculum tends to be learner-oriented and value-oriented; it tends to implement what is relevant or important for the period that is emerging.

The first authority to identify the "emerging" curriculum by name was Gail Inlow, who identified five such curricula for the early 1970s: (1) mental health education; (2) educational creativity; (3) sex education; (4) drug-abuse education; and (5) black studies.[41] Inlow also examined innovative content in traditional subject matter fields and noted that the issue between what is emerging or traditional really boiled down to the old question: "What knowledge is of most worth?" He maintained that traditional subject matter was too formal, that it overemphasized the abstract and theoretical, and that it was not sensitive to changes in society, or what he called "present realities." He failed to point out, however, that the opposite criticism could be made about the emerging subject matter; that is, it was too informal and that, in its desire to be relevant, it overlooked major hierarchies of learning, such as abstract and theoretical content.

In his statement of what constitutes a balanced curriculum for secondary education, William Van Til listed sixteen emerging areas of study: (1) war, peace, and international relations; (2) overpopulation, pollution, and energy; (3) economic options and problems; (4) governmental processes; (5) consumer problems; (6) intercultural relations; (7) world views; (8) recreation and leisure; (9) arts and aesthetics; (10) self-understanding and personal development; (11) family, peer group, and school; (12) health; (13) community living; (14) vocations; (15) communication; and (16) alternative futures.[42] Van Til maintained that even though the secondary school was still subject-centered, the curriculum needed to be "opened," and personal and future alternatives needed to be considered.

Writing during the early 1980s, Allan Ornstein identified ten emerging subject areas: (1) career education; (2) environmental education; (3) ethnic education; (4) bicultural-bilingual education; (5) drug-abuse education; (6) metric education; (7) sex education; (8) nonsexist education; (9) law-related education; and (10) consumer education.[43] He concluded that these curricula were affected by the movement away from traditional disciplines to more interdisciplinary and multidisciplinary approaches.

Although many curriculum trends are emerging today, we only discuss three in this chapter: (1) sex education; (2) multicultural education; and (3) handicapped education. These are controversial trends and current curricula that demand attention today to them and will demand continued attention in the future as well.

Sex Education.

Sex education frequently provokes controversy. Some conservative groups have objected to the topic even being part of the curriculum. They claim that the study of sex education might encourage teenage pregnancies, lesbianism, and homosexuality. Counselors and other educators have maintained that schools must fill an information gap or at least counteract teenage misinformation about sex. Traditional instructional units in biology, hygiene, home economics, and physical education have been supplemented with comprehensive explanations and prescriptions about dating, marriage, parenthood, and health problems. Whereas the topic of sex was once considered taboo in the classroom, it now surfaces regularly in literary, historical, cultural, and philosophical discussions.

Approximately 1.1 million teenage girls become pregnant each year, and the total number is still on the upswing. Four in ten girls get pregnant before the age of 20, and two in twenty have babies. Approximately 7 million teenage boys and 5 million girls are sexually active; on the average, they start having intercourse at 16.4 years of age. In some rural and inner-city areas the average age is 14 years.[44]

Related to this sexual activity among youth is a steady increase of unplanned pregnancies, abortions, and venereal disease, and an increase in single-headed and female households (directly related to poverty), especially among black and Hispanic teenagers. The victims are not only the pregnant adolescents, but their families, their local communities, their states (which are further taxed to provide care and services for the mothers and the offspring), and also society in general.

Educators argue whether the emphasis in sex education should be taught in the home, church, or school. They argue about the so-called appropriate school role, and about whether alternative modes of sex education are more appropriate than the school's delivery system. The basic dilemma is a question of responsibility: Who should do what in the delivery of sex education? Who is accountable for whom and for what? And who has the authority to decide? Moreover, in times of budget cuts and increasing fiscal constraints, the economics of proposed or ongoing sex education services also become important factors. To be sure, sex education can be viewed as a health issue; a matter of moral values or religious beliefs; a family concern; a social, psychological, or physical matter; an educational issue; or a community issue. In our changing and pluralistic society, all of these views have merit.

Sex education can be viewed from many perspectives. Some parent groups protest the development of any sex education program in the schools or elsewhere in their communities; others just as forcefully fight to have sex education programs included in the school curriculum or implemented through some other community agency. Some parents want to handle their children's sex education themselves in the home; others feel far more comfortable delegating the responsibility to trained professionals in the field, relying on the schools, or seeking advice from such diverse sources as religious organizations, youth groups, medical institutions, or mental health agencies. Some parents think sex education should be related to physical development, personal health, or biological or medical concerns. Others believe sex education

should be closely related to moral or religious convictions, personal beliefs, and family values. Still others perceive that sex education should consider a combination of social and psychological issues. Questions, controversies, and even conflicts often accompany the development and delivery of sex education programs. The diversity inherent within any community is fully reflected in the differing demands, expectations, and fears that surround sex education.[45]

Mario Fantini suggests that a program of sex education should include four criteria: (1) it should be geared to the needs of the learner; (2) it should involve cooperative planning among all interested parties; (3) it should be flexible and involve a range of choices for families and communities; and (4) it should be committed to fostering school-community cooperation.[46] According to Sol Gordon, sex education is a moral issue and must be taught within a context of a value system.[47] The question of whose values, of course, can lead to controversy.

After reviewing twenty exemplary sex education programs across the country, Vincent Rogers, and his colleague, defined the major curriculum content and topics they thought should be included in a full-scale sex education program: (1) physiology, including human reproduction, pregnancy, and childbirth; (2) sex-related activities, including dating, necking and petting, the advantages and disadvantages of premarital sex, the range of normal sexual behavior, and alternative lifestyles; (3) sexually transmitted diseases; (4) myths about masturbation and sexual relations; (5) values, including attitudes and feelings about sex roles, as well as long-range goals; (6) pressure and exploitation, including peer pressure, assertive techniques, and avoiding unwanted sexual experiences; (7) contraception, including advantages and disadvantages, fears, family planning, and religious issues; (8) skills, including how to resolve sex-related conflicts with peers and parents; and others.[48]

This curriculum outlined by Rogers et al.

could be criticized for suggesting the provocative nature of sex and sex education. Nevertheless, it is becoming increasingly important for children and youth to understand the various aspects of sexuality. Given today's trends toward teenage marriage, unwanted pregnancy, abortion, veneral disease, even AIDS,[49] it is likely that curricula on sexuality will increasingly appear within the schools.

An important consideration is that sex education reflect the norms and values of the community—that is, that it be designed to best suit the needs and feelings of the clients, their parents, and their community. Also, because genuine differences of opinion surround sex education, sex education in schools should be voluntary; students and parents should be informed before topics or courses are introduced so that they can decide whether to participate; and parents, community members, and religious groups should be involved in developing the programs. For the schools to introduce sex education programs without input from parents, community, or religious institutions is to invite unnecessary conflict.

Multicultural Education.

America is a pluralistic society, a nation with many different ethnic groups and cultures. For most of our history, we have perceived of our country as a *melting pot* whose different peoples have joined to form a "new" race. We expected the schools to contribute to this melting pot process by socializing and acculturating immigrant children to the American ways and by instructing them in English. Today the melting pot concept is in disfavor, because it is perceived as stripping different ethnic groups of their cultures and identities. In contrast, *cultural pluralism* calls for understanding and appreciating differences among people, so that ethnic groups can maintain their customs, folk mores, and languages and still work together with other groups. Ideally, cultural pluralism promotes a sense of wholeness within society, based on

the strengths of each of its parts or groups, and maintains that ethnic group interests can coincide with the interests of the nation.

Multicultural education values and believes in the ideal concept of cultural pluralism; it seeks the cultural enrichment of all children and youth through the curriculum, and at all levels of education—kindergarten to grade 12. In particular, national professional associations, state and local education agencies, colleges and universities, and curriculum developers have introduced various guidelines for promoting constructive multicultural education. In general, they have emphasized curriculum materials and instructional techniques. They have specifically proposed: (1) introducing materials that are multiracial, multiethnic, and nonsexist; (2) teaching values that promote cultural diversity and individuality; (3) incorporating various cultural and ethnic activities in the classroom and school-community program; (4) encouraging multilingualism and multiple dialects; and (5) emphasizing multicultural teacher education programs.[50]

What began in the late 1960s with political demands by traditional minority groups—that their heritage and experiences be reflected accurately and positively in the curricula—has now extended to other ethnic groups and to all aspects of education. We discuss three basic curricula trends next: ethnic studies, multicultural instruction, and bilingual education.

Ethnic Studies. That a rapid growth of curriculum offerings in various ethnic studies came on the heels of black studies is not surprising. The sense of being neglected and overlooked, the need for identity and recognition, and the search for heroes and jobs are by no means limited to blacks. Ethnic studies programs started as simple and supplementary units or lessons on heroic deeds and ethnic feasts, on the virtues of ethnic cuisine, and on ethnic celebrations and quaint folk customs. Eventually, the content developed into a series of courses that constituted a program of ethnic studies.

Many, if not most, of the programs were poorly and hastily conceived, overlooked basic principles of learning and pedagogy, and were criticized as "soft" in content and academic standards.[51]

Early ethnic studies courses aimed at correcting distortions of existing curricula about ethnic experiences, ethnic stereotyping, and ethnic omissions—which are no longer problems in most current textbooks or materials. These courses encouraged ethnic identity, ethnic culture, and ethnic politics; they were (and, to some extent, still are) "crisis"-oriented—that is, based on placating pressure groups rather than on detailing sound curriculum and instructional practices. Moreover, disagreement continues about who is to speak for which ethnic group, which ethnic version of contemporary history of English is to be taught, where mention of lowered academic performance is "racist" or "ethnocentric" talk, or whether relevancy is more important than substance. As long as this is so, problems of content and learning will persist—a legacy of the 1960s and 1970s.[52]

Some positive results of the rise of ethnic-related courses are that these programs lead to greater understanding among different groups, and that they enhance the concepts of cultural richness, cultural diversity, and ethnic self-esteem. Two negative results are that these programs may trivialize the curriculum rather than enrich it, and that they may promote diversity and loosen the ties that bind society together.

The focus on ethnic study programs varies from state to state. Some states have little interest whatsoever in ethnic studies, whereas others introduce considerable legislation encouraging institution of various programs. In some cases, even though no state-level laws or defined policies have been established, considerable local activity exists. As of 1980, nearly forty states had published materials on the subject of ethnicity, nearly thirty states had formed policy statements on ethnic studies, and nearly twenty states had mandated ethnic studies in school

curricula.[53] In some states, however, ethnicity and cultural pluralism are still applied, somewhat misleadingly, to programs for officially recognized minority groups only—for example, blacks and/or Hispanics.

At the same time, some educators are concerned that ethnic studies may have a short history and that ethnic education will need a new partner during the 1980s; that is, global education. This concept views the United States as a world leader that deals imaginatively and constructively with different countries and cultural groups. Much of the attention on ethnic and multiethnic education to date has been justified on the basis of its promoting democratic ideals; its future, however, will require that it provide long-range plans, practical models of curriculum design, more rigorous subject matter, and demonstrations of effectiveness (both in terms of student performance and costs).[54]

Multicultural Instruction. Educators are also trying to identify effective instructional approaches for teaching students of various racial and ethnic backgrounds. Some of the more important approaches have been concerned with student learning, or what is called a "biocognitive" approach to student learning. For example, Ramirez and Castañeda concluded that Hispanic students tend to be more "field sensitive" than nonminority children.[55] Field sensitive children are described as being more influenced by personal relationships and by praise or disapproval from authority figures, including teachers, than are "field independent" students, who are more abstract thinkers. A field sensitive curriculum is "humanized through use of narration, humor, drama and fantasy," and should be "structured in such a way that children work cooperatively with peers or with a teacher in a variety of activities."[56]

Another effort to identify instructional approaches suited to students' ethnic backgrounds has been provided by researchers who have worked with native Americans.[57] These researchers conclude that schooling for native American children would be most successful if the curriculum took better account of their "primary learning" patterns (learning outside the school) and organized instruction in a manner more compatible with these patterns. These researchers contend that primary learning tends to take place in personal communication with emotionally important individuals and in tutorial (face-to-face) situations in which learning is adaptive (linked to the concerns and needs of the community). Primary learning also includes verbal instruction, exploratory play, and concrete (as opposed to abstract) learning. It involves monitoring the activities of elders who are particularly important to the children—say, uncles or aunts.

Some caution is necessary. The value of field-oriented and primary learning approaches is not well documented. What appears to be as or more important, according to some observers, are the basic, old approaches—friendliness, understanding, democratic teacher behaviors, positive teacher expectations, English proficiency, and parental support for the students.[58]

Bilingual Education. Bilingual education, which provides instruction for non-English speaking students in their native languages, has been an expanding activity in public schools in the United States since the late 1960s. Although the federal and state governments fund bilingual projects for more than sixty groups speaking various Asian, Indo-European, and Native American languages, the large majority (70 percent) of children in these projects are Hispanics.[59]

Bilingual education has been expanding for various reasons: (1) partly because of the United States Supreme Court decision in the *Lau* case, which requires that school districts initiate some type of bilingual program if they enroll more than twenty students of a given language group at a particular grade level; (2) partly because of the subsequent pressure of the federal Office of Civil Rights (OCR), which insisted that educational opportunities be provided for limited-English speaking (LES) and non-English speaking (NES) students; and (3) partly because of the continuous federal funding of bilingual programs, even today, even though other categorical programs are being merged within block grants. The push for bilingual programs assumes particular importance if we consider the growing non-English-speaking population, which is expected to increase from 30 million in 1980, to about 40 million in 2000,[60] and to approximately 60 million in 2020.[61] To be sure, bilingual education is intertwined with such sensitive issues as our attitudes toward immigrants; namely, our accepting or rejecting those legal and illegal immigrants who work for less money and thus replace American-born citizens on the job, and our deciding who can enter the United States, and who is a political refugee, economic refugee, and/or undocumented worker.

Controversies over bilingual education have become somewhat embittered emotionally as federal and state guidelines have led to the establishment of various programs. Those who would "immerse" children in an English-language environment argue with those who believe initial instruction will be more effective in the native language; and both of these groups argue with those who wish that a mixture of both English and the native language be taught in school. Ethnic and community leaders have engaged in bitter struggles over the establishment of bilingual programs in the public schools.

Educators and laypeople concerned with NES and LES students also argue whether emphasis should be placed on teaching in the native language over a long period (maintenance) or proceeding to teach in English as soon as possible (transitional). On the one side are those who favor maintenance because they think it will help build or maintain a constructive sense of identity among ethnic or racial minorities.[62] On the other side are those who believe that cultural-maintenance programs are harmful because they separate groups from one another or discourage students from mastering English well enough to function successfully in the larger society.[63] The latter or transitional approach is reflected in current federal guidelines.

Adherents and opponents of bilingual education also differ on the related issues of whether bilingual programs sometimes or frequently are designed to provide teaching jobs for native language speakers and whether individuals who fill these jobs are competent in English. Observers who favor bilingual/bicultural maintenance tend to believe that the schools need many adults who can teach LES or NES students in their own languages; many observers who favor transitional programs feel that relatively few staff are required for a legitimate program.

Another major controversy involving bilingual education concerns whether this approach is effective in improving the performance of low-achieving students. Most scholars who have examined the research agree that bilingual education has effected little, if any, improvement in the performance of participating students.[64] Other scholars partially disagree; they argue that programs implemented well can result in significant achievement gains and enriched cultural experiences.[65] In general, however, educators agree that much more than bilingual/bicultural education is needed to improve the performance of economically disadvantaged LES and NES students. Some researchers have summarized the literature by stating that, on the whole, bilingual education is too frail a device in and of itself to significantly change the learning experiences of the minority-native tongue. Many other factors not related to language explain why such children achieve poorly. Removing only the language problem does not usually change the situation, regardless of the approach.[66]

Handicapped Education.

Children are different from each other. Some are more intelligent or creative than others, some are socially and emotionally gifted, and some possess outstanding physical traits. On the other side of the bell-shaped curve, unfortunately, are some who are less intelligent, some who have social and emotional problems, and some who have physical handicaps.

Of most concern to educators are children who are handicapped and who thus need special educational personnel and services. Table 12-1 shows, by handicap, the number of handicapped students receiving public education services. The table shows that the number of handicapped students has increased from 1977 to 1983. This does not mean that more students are handicapped, but rather that more students are being identified and served, particularly through Public Law 94-142 (The Education for all Handicapped Children Act), which was passed in 1975.

PL 94-142 sets forth a national policy whose goal is to provide: (1) free appropriate public education to handicapped students as their fundamental right; (2) valid testing and assessment of handicapped students; (3) Individual Education Plans (IEP), both short range and long range, to meet the needs of each handicapped student; and (4) all students an education in the "least restrictive environment."[67] In many cases, this environment has been judged to be the regular classroom. As a result, an increasing number of curriculum specialists and classroom teachers must now deal with handicapped children.

Coinciding with several federal mandates, special education expenditures have steadily increased from $115 million in 1975, to $834 million in 1980, to $1.2 billion in 1985.[68] Since 1980, over 90 percent of these federal funds has been earmarked for the states to disseminate to local schools. More than 4 million handicapped students now constitute about 11 percent of public school enrollment. The average cost of educating handicapped students is more than twice the average for nonhandicapped students, which is approximately $3000. Today, at least 80 percent of the nation's handicapped are receiving special services, as

TABLE 12-1 Number of Students Receiving Public Educational Services by Type of Handicap, 1977 and 1983

Type of Handicap	1977	1983
Speech impaired	1,302,666	1,134,197
Mentally retarded	969,547	780,831
Learning disabled	797,213	1,745,871
Emotionally disturbed	283,072	353,431
Crippled and other health impaired	141,417	52,026
Hard of hearing and deaf	89,743	75,337
Orthopedically impaired	87,008	57,506
Visually handicapped	38,247	31,096
Deaf-blind and other multihandicapped	NA*	68,032
Total	3,708,913	4,298,327
Percent of public school population	8.33	10.98

*NA = Not applicable category in 1977.

Source: from *The Condition of Education, 1985* (Washington, D.C.: U.S. Government Printing Office, 1985), Table 4.1, p. 182; *The School-Age Handicapped* (Washington, D.C.: U.S. Government Printing Office, 1985), Table 1, p. 61.

compared with less than half before PL 94-142.[69]

Classification and Labeling of Students.

Although the federal government mandates local school districts to provide free appropriate education for all handicapped students, it provides only a few hundred dollars per child to help make this possible. The result is that many school officials are somewhat reluctant to search out handicapped students because of the extra costs involved in educating them. On the other hand, what teachers consider to be learning or behavioral problems may not even be problems in terms of valid and reliable student classifications. Existing learning disability programs, for example, sometimes become "dumping grounds" for many academic- or discipline-problem students whom classroom teachers cannot handle.

Many educators, in fact, view learning disabilities as an umbrella category for children who experience a variety of learning problems, even though some of these labeled children exhibit normal intelligence and no demonstrable physical, emotional, or social handicap. It is difficult to be certain, for example, whether a slow-learning student is mildly retarded, and could thus benefit from special education services, or is simply a slow learner who requires additional motivation or guidance to learn. Also, the authorities disagree on what constitutes a "learning disability" or "handicap" that requires special education as well as on what services should be provided for a particular disability or handicap.[70] Similar problems are evidenced in distinguishing, among other categories, between mildly and severely emotionally disturbed, partially deaf versus nonhearing, and severely myopic versus visually impaired and legally blind.

Uncertainty in classifying students accurately is connected with fundamental questions regarding appropriate treatment for a given child, as well as the effects of labeling a student as handicapped. Many educators question the special classification approach, on the grounds that isolating mildly handicapped children from other students generates feelings of inadequacy and inferiority, and that placing students in classes organized under such labels as "emotionally disturbed" or "mildly retarded" may mean teaching them at a slow pace or, even worse, impairing their abilities to function in the larger society. Critics are also concerned about the large numbers of minorities funneled into special education programs and about the effects of culturally biased tests on placement. In addition, they are concerned that handicapped classifications may lead children to "self-fulfilling" prophecies: Handicapped labels may not only be unfair, but they may also lower labeled children's self-expectations and thus present additional disadvantages to them.

Mainstreaming the Handicapped. Researchers who have reviewed studies on labeling have concluded that the overall negative effects of having special or separate classes or programs for the handicapped are not well established. However, neither has it been proved that placing handicapped children in separate classes or programs is more beneficial than placing them in regular classes.[71] Less restrictive settings are generally supported for moral and legal reasons.

Every handicapped student should, in fact, be placed in the regular school program to the fullest extent possible. Efforts to place handicapped students in regular class settings, referred to as "mainstreaming," have been encouraged and carried out throughout school districts since the passage of PL 94-142. In general, mainstreaming means integrating handicapped children into regular schools and classrooms to maximize their opportunities not only to join school activities but also to be "counted" among the nonhandicapped. Unfortunately, because nonhandicapped students frequently perceive handicapped, especially severely handicapped, students as possessing many negative characteristics, they prefer to socialize with other nonhandicapped students.[72] Although mainstreaming provides the opportunity for nonhandicapped students to learn about handicapped and disabled children, so both groups can grow and function together in

society, social realities sometimes prevent the attainment of this ideal.

Researchers who have reviewed the data on special-class placement and mainstreaming find that the data on the effectiveness of either approach are mixed. If neither approach is carried out very well, the research shows both approaches to be ineffective and neither to be superior.[73] The research also indicates that regular classroom teachers are not adequately trained or prepared to work with handicapped students in regular classes; teachers assigned to regular classes that comprise even a couple of handicapped students are thus frustrated.[74]

Curriculum for the Handicapped. Even though research has not yet identified or documented the most effective approaches to providing instruction for handicapped students in the "least restrictive environment," much has been learned concerning the types of practices that are most likely to enhance learning. For example, researchers who have reviewed the literature on "concerns and strategies" for mainstreaming students with special educational needs have summarized what appear to be the most promising instructional strategies:

1. Greater emphasis should be placed on meeting the social and emotional needs of *all* students, including the handicapped.
2. Careful, regular evaluation based on individual performance criteria should be used to ascertain students' progress.
3. Class placement should be based on careful preassessment of each child's problems and capacity.
4. Better assessment procedures should be developed; they should be used only by professionals skilled in their interpretation.
5. A team approach including the classroom teacher should be utilized to determine if a child is in need of special services, what services are to be provided, and how best to provide such services.
6. Class size should be limited to a realistic number so that individual needs can be satisfied.[75]

This list suggests that developments dealing with the education of handicapped children have been related to—and have influenced—general trends in curriculum and instruction. Assessing needs and monitoring progress, for example, are not only relevant for educating handicapped students but are also important for educating all students. Using a mastery learning and/or a diagnostic-prescriptive approach provides each child with structured instruction based on his or her individual learning needs.[76] These approaches have gained popularity for all students, not only the handicapped. In addition, Individual Education Plans (IEPs), required for handicapped students by PL 94-142, are frequently desirable for all students.

Implementing PL 94-142, and related legislation, is helping educators, policy makers, and curriculum designers learn more about the problems they are likely to encounter and the steps they can take to bring about fundamental improvement in the schools. For example, researchers who have studied the development and implementation of legislation dealing with special education have learned they need to carefully prepare local personnel; specially redefine the roles of all personnel involved in an innovation; implement desirable policies to ensure that parents and community representatives retain a real voice in curriculum development and implementation; and introduce strategies that take into account bureaucratic obstacles to change.[77]

CONCLUSION

This chapter has been concerned with contemporary philosophical, social, and political issues in curriculum. Indeed, the search to improve school curricula is a continuing process that reflects current issues and trends impacting on schools and society. The curriculum trends noted in this chapter are controversial. Surely debate over them will continue in the near future.

Censorship battles will continue, for example, even though schools having appropriate selection policies with formal procedures will offer a wise compromise. Since 1965 more than $60 billion has been spent for compensatory curricula ($40 billion alone for Title I activities), but the cost and effects of these programs are still questionable.[78] Irrelevant curricula remind us that many mindless and miseducative experiences creep into our classrooms and schools. Finally, emerging curricula address broad educational concerns—sex education, multicultural education, and handicapped education—and give people a chance to redefine who they are, what kind of schools they want, and what social and political choices they want to make about curriculum.

Notes

1. Harold Hodges, *Social Stratification: Class in America* (Cambridge, Mass.: Schenkman, 1964); George D. Spindler, "Education in a Transforming American Culture," *Harvard Educational Review* (Summer 1965), pp. 145–156; and Spindler, "The Transmission of Culture," in G. D. Spindler, ed., *Education and Cultural Process* (New York: Holt, Rinehart, 1974), pp. 274–310.
2. Robert A. Dahl, *Democracy in the United States*, 3rd ed. (Chicago: Rand McNally, 1975); Hans Kohn, *American Nationalism: An Interpretative Essay* (New York: Macmillan, 1957); and Michael Novak, *The Rise of the Unmeltable Ethnics* (New York: Macmillan, 1972).
3. Ron Brandt, "On One to Blame," *Educational Leadership* (April 1985), p. 3; P. Kenneth Komoski, "Instructional Materials Will Not Improve Until We Challenge The System," *Educational Leadership* (April 1985), pp. 31–37; and Harriet Talmage, "Creating Instructional Materials: The Textbook Publisher as Connecting Link," *Curriculum Review* (September–October, 1986), pp. 11–13.
4. Ray Gerke, "American Textbooks: Perspectives on Public Controversies and Censorship," *High School Journal* (October–November 1983), pp. 59–64; Sherry Keith, "Politics of Textbook Selection." Paper prepared for the Institute for Research on Educational Finance and Governance, Stanford University, 1981.
5. Raymond English, "The Politics of Textbook Adoption," *Phi Delta Kappan* (December 1980), pp. 275–278; John Maxwell, "The Future of Textbooks," *National Association of Secondary School Principals* (May 1985), pp. 68–74.

6. Fenwick W. English, "Contemporary Curriculum Circumstances," in F. W. English, ed., *Fundamental Curriculum Decisions* (Alexandria, Va.: Association for Supervision and Curriculum Development, 1983), pp. 1–17.

7. "Censorship in the Schools," *Today's Education* (November–December 1980), pp. 56–60; Joel J. Kupperman, "Why Some Topics Are Controversial," *Educational Leadership* (December 1984–January 1985), pp. 73–76; and Allan C. Ornstein, "Curriculum Trends for the 1980s," *Contemporary Education* (Summer 1985), pp. 242–249. Also see *Education Week*, September 10, 1986, p. 14.

8. "Censorship vs Selection—Choosing the Books Our Children Shall Read," *Educational Leadership* (December 1981), pp. 211–213; *Fifty-State Survey of Textbook Adoption Procedures and Policies* (Washington, D.C.: Education Commission of the States, 1984). By 1985-86, 130 censorship incidents were reported in 44 states, up 35 percent from the previous year and 117 percent over four years. See *Attack on Freedom to Learn: 1985–86* (Washington, D.C.; People for the American Way, 1986).

9. Frank R. Kemerer and Stephanie A. Hirsh, "School Library Censorship Comes Before the Supreme Court," *Phi Delta Kappan* (March 1982), pp. 444–448; Kupperman, "Why Some Topics Are Controversial."

10. Edmund W. Gordon and Doxey A. Wilkerson, *Compensatory Education for the Disadvantaged* (New York: College Entrance Examination Board, 1966); Allan C. Ornstein, Daniel U. Levine, and Doxey A. Wilkerson, *Reforming Metropolitan Schools* (Pacific Palisades, Calif.: Goodyear, 1975); and A. Harry Passow, "Urban Education in the 1970s," in A. H. Passow, ed., *Urban Education in the 1970s* (New York: Teachers College Press, Columbia University, 1971), pp. 1–45.

11. Allan C. Ornstein, *Education and Social Inquiry* (Itasca, Ill.: Peacock, 1978); A. Harry Passow, "Compensatory Instructional Intervention," in F. N. Kerlinger and J. B. Carroll, eds., *Review of Research in Education*, Vol. 2 (Itasca, Ill.: Peacock, 1976), pp. 145–175; and Benjamin D. Stickney and Laurence R. Marcus, "Education and the Disadvantaged 20 Years Later," *Phi Delta Kappan* (April 1985), pp. 559–564.

12. Daniel U. Levine and Robert J. Havighurst, *Society and Education*, 6th ed. (Boston: Allyn and Bacon, 1984); Milbey W. McLaughlin, *Evaluation and Reform: The Elementary and Secondary Act of 1965/Title I* (Cambridge, Mass.: Ballinger, 1975); Harry S. Miller, *Social Foundations of Education*, 3rd ed. (New York: Holt, Rinehart, 1978); and *National Assessment of Education Progress, Has Title I Improved Education for Disadvantaged Students* (Denver: Educational Commission of the States, 1981).

13. Richard L. Fairley, "Accountability's New Test," *American Education* (June 1972), pp. 33–35. See also *Compensatory Education and Other Alternatives in Urban Schools* (Washington, D.C.: U.S. Government Printing Office, 1972); Daniel P. Moynihan, *Coping: On the Practice of Government* (New York: Random House, 1975).

14. Consortium for Longitudinal Studies, *As the Twig Is Bent* (Hillsdale, N.J.: Erlbaum, 1983); *Lasting Effects after Preschool* (Washington, D.C.: U.S. Government Printing Office, 1979); and R. M. Stonehill and J. I. Anderson, *An Evaluation of ESEA Title I* (Washington, D.C.: U.S. Government Printing Office, 1982).

15. Arthur R. Jensen, "Compensatory Education and the Theory of Intelligence," *Phi Delta Kappan* (April 1985), pp. 554–558; Perry Skerry, "The Charmed Life of Head Start," *Public Interest* (Fall 1983), pp. 18–39; and Edward Zigler and Winnie Berman, "Discerning the Future of Early Childhood Intervention," *American Psychologist* (August 1983), pp. 894–906.

16. Allan C. Ornstein and Daniel U. Levine, "Compensatory Education: Can It Be Successful?" *National Association of Secondary School Principals* (May 1981), pp. 1–15.

17. Consortium for Longitudinal Studies, *As the Twig Is Bent;* Edmund W. Gordon, "Education of the Disadvantaged: A Problem of Human Diversity," in N. F. Ashline, T. R. Pezzullo, and C. I. Norris, eds., *Education, Inequality, and National Policy* (Lexington, Mass.: D. C. Heath, 1976), pp. 101–123; and Allan Odden, "Sources of Funding for Education Reform," *Phi Delta Kappan* (January 1986), pp. 335–340.

18. David L. Clark, Linda S. Lotto, and Martha M. McCarthy, "Factors Associated with Success in Urban Elementary Schools," *Phi Delta Kappan* (March 1980), pp. 467–470; Daniel U. Levine and Joyce Stark, "Instructional and Organizational Arrangements that Improve Achievement in Inner City Schools," *Educational Leadership* (December 1982), pp. 41–48; Virginia R. Plunkett, "From Title I to Chapter I: The Evolution of Compensatory Education," *Phi Delta Kappan* (April 1985), pp. 533–537; and Robert M. Stonehill, "The Sustained Achievement of Chapter 1 Students: A Summary of Findings." Paper presented at the annual meeting of the American Educational Research Association, Chicago, April 1985.

19. Carl Bereiter, "The Changing Face of Educational Disadvantagement," *Phi Delta Kappan* (April 1985), p. 541.

20. *Federal Programs Affecting Children* (Washington, D.C.: U.S. Government Printing Office, 1983); Lawrence J. Schwienhart et al., "The Promise of Early Childhood Education," *Phi Delta Kappan* (April 1985), pp. 548–553; and David P. Weikart

et al., *The Effects of the Perry Preschool Program on Youths through Age 19* (Ypsilanti, Mich.: High/Scope Press, 1984).

21. Benjamin S. Bloom, *Stability and Change in Human Characteristics* (New York: Wiley, 1964).

22. Allan C. Ornstein, "The Changing Federal Role in Education," *Kappa Delta Pi Record* (Spring 1985), pp. 85–88; Plunkett, "From Title I to Chapter I: The Evolution of Compensatory Education."

23. John Dewey, *Democracy and Education* (New York: Macmillan, 1916), p. 125.

24. B. Othanel Smith, William O. Stanley, and J. Harlan Shores, *Fundamentals of Curriculum Development*, rev. ed. (New York: Harcourt, Brace, 1957), pp. 4–5.

25. Harold Benjamin, *The Saber-Tooth Curriculum* (New York: McGraw-Hill, 1939), pp. 43–44.

26. Bentley Glass, *The Timely and the Timeless* (New York: Basic Books, 1979); Joseph J. Schwab, "The Concept of the Structure of a Discipline," *Educational Record* (July 1962), pp. 197–205.

27. Donald E. Orlosky and B. Othanel Smith, *Curriculum Development: Issues and Insights* (Chicago: Rand McNally, 1980), p. 192.

28. Mario D. Fantini and Gerald D. Weinstein, *The Disadvantaged: Challenge to Education* (New York: Harper & Row, 1968), p. 133.

29. Otto Klienberg, "Life is Fun in a Smiling, Fair-Skinned World," *Saturday Review* (February 16, 1963), pp. 75–77, 87.

30. Ibid.

31. Passow, "Urban Education for the 1970s"; A. Harry Passow, "Urban Education for the 1980s: Trends and Issues," *Phi Delta Kappan* (April 1982), pp. 519–522.

32. Dennis Doyle, "The Unsacred Texts," *American Education* (Summer 1984), pp. 3–13; Connie Muther, "What Every Textbook Evaluator Should Know," *Educational Leadership* (April 1985), pp. 4–8.

33. Muther, "What Every Textbook Evaluator Should Know," p. 7. See also Connie Muther, "Reviewing Research When Choosing Materials," *Educational Leadership* (February 1985), pp. 86–87.

34. Dolores Durkin, *Is There a Match Between What Elementary Teachers Do and What Basal Readers Manuals Recommend?* (Champaign, Ill.: Center for the Study of Reading, University of Illinois, 1983); Patrick Shannon, "The Use of Commercial Reading Materials in American Elementary Schools," *Reading Research Quarterly* (Fall 1983), pp. 68–85.

35. J. P. Guilford, *General Psychology*, 2nd ed. (Princeton, N.J.: Van Nostrand, 1952); Ralph Tyler, *Constructing Achievement Tests* (Columbus, Ohio: Ohio State University, 1934).

36. John McLeish, *The Lecture Method* (Cambridge, Eng.: Cambridge Institute of Education, 1968).

37. David P. Ausubel, *Educational Psychology: A Cognitive View* (New York: Holt, Rinehart, 1968); Ausubel, "In Defense of Advance Organizers," *Review of Educational Research* (Spring 1978), pp. 251–257.

38. Merrill Harmin and Sidney B. Simon, "The Year the Schools Began Teaching the Telephone Directory," *Harvard Educational Review* (Summer 1965), pp. 326–331.

39. Ibid., p. 327.

40. Ibid., p. 328.

41. Gail M. Inlow, *The Emergent in Curriculum*, 2nd ed. (New York: Wiley, 1973).

42. William Van Til, "What Should Be Taught and Learned through Secondary Education," in W. Van Til, ed., *Issues in Secondary Education*, Seventy-Fifth Yearbook of the National Society for the Study of Education, Part II (Chicago: University of Chicago Press, 1976), pp. 1–29.

43. Allan C. Ornstein, "Change and Innovation in Curriculum," *Journal of Research and Development in Education* (Winter 1982), pp. 27–33; Ornstein, "Innovation and Change: Yesterday and Today," *High School Journal* (May 1982), pp. 279–286.

44. Catherine S. Chilman, *Adolescent Sexuality and the Human Service Professions* (New York: Wiley, 1982); James Walters and Lynda H. Walters, "The Role of the Family in Sex Education," *Journal of Research and Development in Education* (Winter 1983), pp. 8–15.

45. Mario D. Fantini, "Sex Education: Alternative Modes of Delivery," *Journal of Research and Development in Education* (Winter 1983), pp. 1–7.

46. Ibid.

47. Sol Gordon, "The Case for a Moral Sex Education in the Schools," *Journal of School Health* (April 1981), pp. 214–218.

48. Vincent Rogers, Kay Merriam, and Michele Munson, "Sex Education—Curriculum Issues," *Journal of Research and Development in Education* (Winter 1983), pp. 45–51.

49. According to the Surgeon General, the key to stemming the spread of AIDS is through sex education, which should begin in the early elementary grades, "so that children can grow up knowing the behavior to avoid to protect themselves from exposure to the AIDS virus." See Everett Koop, *Surgeon General's Report on Acquired Immune Deficiency Syndrome* (Washington, D.C.: U.S. Government Printing Office, 1986).

50. *Multicultural Education: Commitment, Issues, and Applications* (Washington, D.C.: Association for Supervision and Curriculum Development, 1977); *No One Model American: A Statement of Multicultural Education* (Washington, D.C.: American Association of Colleges of Teacher Education, 1972); and *Standards for the Accreditation of Teacher Education* (Washington, D.C.: National

Council for the Accreditation of Teacher Education, 1982).

51. Harry S. Broudy, "Educational Unity in a Pluralistic Society," *School Review* (November 1977), pp. 70–81; Geneva Gay, "Multiethnic Education: Historical Developments and Future Prospects," *Phi Delta Kappan* (April 1983), pp. 560–563.

52. Stanley D. Ivie, "Multicultural Education: Boon or Boondoggle?" *Journal of Teacher Education* (May–June 1979), pp. 23–25; Edith W. King, "Aspects of Ethnicity and Multicultural Teaching," *Multicultural Teaching* (Spring 1984), pp. 33–35. See also Christine I. Bennett, *Comprehensive Multicultural Education: Theory and Practice* (Boston: Allyn and Bacon, 1986).

53. Allan C. Ornstein, "The Ethnic Factor in Education," *High School Journal* (December 1981), pp. 74–81.

54. James A. Banks, "Multiethnic Education at the Crossroads," *Phi Delta Kappan* (April 1983), p. 559; Gay, "Multiethnic Education"; and Kerry J. Kennedy and Gilbert McDonald, "Designing Curriculum Materials for Multicultural Education," *Curriculum Inquiry* (Fall 1986), pp. 311–316.

55. Manuel Ramirez and Carlos Castañeda, *Cultural Democracy: Biocognitive Development and Education* (New York: Academic Press, 1974).

56. Ibid., p. 142.

57. Paul E. Greenbaum, "Nonverbal Differences in Communication Style between American Indian and Anglo Elementary Classrooms," *American Educational Research Journal* (Spring 1985), pp. 101–116; Vera John Steiner and Larry Smith, "The Educational Promise of Cultural Pluralism." Paper prepared for the National Conference on Urban Education, St. Louis, 1978.

58. James A. Banks, *Multiethnic Education: Theory and Practice*, 2nd ed. (Boston: Allyn and Bacon, 1985); James Lynch, *The Multicultural Curriculum* (London: Batsford, 1983).

59. Allan C. Ornstein and Daniel U. Levine, "Multicultural Education: Trends and Issues," *Childhood Education* (March–April, 1982), pp. 241–245.

60. John Fallows, "The New Immigrants," *Atlantic* (November 1983), pp. 45–68, 85–89; *The Prospects for Bilingual Education in the Nation, 1980–81*, Fifth Annual Report of the National Advisory Council for Bilingual Education (Washington, D.C.: U.S. Government Printing Office, 1982).

61. L. F. Bouvier and C. B. Davis, *The Future Racial Composition of the United States* (Washington, D.C.: Population Reference Bureau, 1982); Allan C. Ornstein, "Urban Demographics for the 1980s," *Education and Urban Society* (August 1984), pp. 477–496.

62. Jose A. Cárdenas, "The Role of Native Language Instruction in Bilingual Education," *Phi Delta Kappan* (January 1986), pp. 359–363; Carlos J. Orando, "Bilingual/Bicultural Education: Its

63. Noel Epstein, *Language, Ethnicity, and the Schools: Policy Alternatives for Bilingual-Bicultural Education* (Washington, D.C.: George Washington University Press, 1977); Nathan Glazer, "Pluralism and Ethnicity," in M. Ridge, ed., *The New Bilingualism: An American Dilemma* (Los Angeles: University of Southern California Press, 1982), pp. 55–70.

64. Keith Baker, "The Ideological Dictates of Research in Bilingual Education." Paper presented at the annual meeting of the American Educational Research Association, New Orleans, April 1984); Epstein, *Language, Ethnicity, and the Schools;* and Russell Gertsten and John Woodward, "A Case for Structural Immersion," *Educational Leadership* (September 1985), pp. 75–79.

65. Joseph E. Barry, "Politics, Bilingual Education and the Curriculum," *Educational Leadership* (May 1983), pp. 56–60; Glen T. Dixon and Susan Fraser, "Teaching Preschoolers in a Multicultural Classroom," *Childhood Education* (March–April, 1986), pp. 272–275; and Robert Miller, "The Mexican Approach to Developing Bilingual Materials and Teaching Literacy to Bilingual Students," *Reading Teacher* (April 1982), pp. 800–804.

66. Baker, "The Ideological Dictates of Research in Bilingual Education"; Joshua A. Fishman, "Bilingual Education—A Perspective," *IRCD Bulletin* (Spring 1977), pp. 1–5; and Tracy Gray, "A Comparative Evaluation of Immersion and Foreign Language Programs." Paper presented at the annual meeting of the American Educational Research Association, New Orleans, April 1984.

67. David Galloway, *Schools, Pupils, and Special Educational Needs* (Dover, N.H.: Longwood, 1985); Stuart M. Losen and Joyce G. Losen, *The Special Education Team* (Boston: Allyn and Bacon, 1985).

68. *The Condition of Education, 1985* (Washington, D.C.: U.S. Government Printing Office, 1985), Table 4.5, p. 190; *Digest of Educational Statistics, 1983–84* (Washington, D.C.: U.S. Government Printing Office, 1984), Table 144, pp. 174–175.

69. *Digest of Educational Statistics, 1983–84*, Tables 64–65, pp. 79–80; *Projections of Education Statistics to 1990–91* (Washington, D.C.: U.S. Government Printing Office, 1982), Table 4, p. 32; and *Seventh Annual Report to Congress on the Implementation of the Education of the Handicapped Act* (Washington, D.C.: U.S. Department of Education, 1985).

70. Daniel U. Levine and Allan C. Ornstein, "Some Trends in Educating Handicapped Students," *Journal of Curriculum Studies* (July–September 1981), pp. 261–265; Maynard Reynolds, "Classification of Students with Handicaps," in E. W. Gordon, ed., *Review of Research in Education*, Vol. 11 (Washington, D.C.: American Educational Research Association, 1984), pp. 63–92; and Eileen M. Senior. "Learning Disabled or Merely Misla-

beled?" *Childhood Education* (January–February 1986), pp. 161–165.

71. Mary F. Hanline and Carol Murray, "Integrating Severely Handicapped Children into Regular Public Schools," *Phi Delta Kappan* (December 1984), pp. 273–276; Gaea Leinhardt and Allan Paulay, "Restrictive Educational Settings: Exile or Haven?" *Review of Educational Research* (Winter 1982), pp. 556–578; and Rosemary A. Thompson, "Public Law 94-142: A Critical Review," *High School Journal* (October–November, 1985), pp. 50–54.

72. Douglas Fuchs et al., "Bias in the Assessment of Handicapped Children," *American Educational Research Journal* (Summer 1985), pp. 185–198; Hanline and Murray, "Integrating Severely Handicapped Children into Regular Public Schools"; William Steinbeck and Susan Steinbeck, "Nonhandicapped Students' Perceptions of Severely Handicapped Students," *Education and Training of the Mentally Retarded* (April 1982), pp. 177–182.

73. Janet Learner, *Learning Disabilities: Theories, Diagnosis, and Teaching*, 4th ed. (Boston: Houghton Mifflin, 1985); Cecil D. Mercer and Ann R. Mercer, *Teaching Students with Learning Problems*, 2nd ed. (Columbus, Ohio: Merrill, 1985).

74. Thomas E. Linton and Kirsten D. Juul, "Mainstreaming: Time for Reassessment," *Educational Leadership* (February 1980), pp. 433–435; Nancy A. Madden and Robert E. Slavin, "Mainstreaming Students with Mild Handicaps: Academic and Social Outcomes," *Review of Educational Research* (Winter 1983), pp. 519–569.

75. Levi Lathen, *Developing a Comprehensive Special Education Service Delivery System* (Lanham, Md.: University Press, 1983); John Salvia and James E. Ysseldyke, *Assessment in Special and Remedial Education*, 3rd ed. (Boston: Houghton Mifflin, 1985).

76. Benjamin S. Bloom, *All Our Children Learning* (New York: McGraw-Hill, 1980).

77. Carol Milofsky, "Is the Growth of Special Education Evolutionary or Cyclic?" *American Journal of Education* (May 1986), pp. 313-321; Richard Weatherby and Michael Lipsky, "Street-Level Bureaucrats and Institutional Innovation: Implementing Special Education Reform," *Harvard Educational Review* (May 1977), pp. 171–197.

78. Launor F. Carter, "The Sustaining Effect Study of Compensatory and Elementary Education," *Educational Researcher* (August/September 1984), pp. 4–13.

chapter 13

FUTURE DIRECTIONS FOR CURRICULUM

Two hallmarks of this century are the rate and nature of change and the corresponding degree of uncertainty. It is because of these hallmarks that persons responsible for creating and managing the curriculum have at times faced what certainly must have seemed to be insurmountable problems. However, in dealing with the various changes, and the social demands for changes, many curricularists have come to realize that the relationship between the school and society reflects a mutual give and take.[1] During this century society has been forcefully dynamic. It is thus dangerous and misleading for educators to base education—specifically, the curriculum—on any static portrait of society, whether in the present or at some particular point in the future.[2]

The ultimate purpose of education is to present programs and thus opportunities for students to gain the knowledge, skills, competencies, attitudes, beliefs, and values that will enable them to create productive lives for themselves and others. The central question curriculum planners ask is: "What kind of educational program will achieve this central goal?" How they respond to this central question rests on their understanding of current and, more importantly, future times. They need to consider what one futurist has called a fan of alternative futures; they need to identify which of the potential futures could at any time emerge into reality given the probabilities of the different possibilities under existing trends and cycles.[3] They must not just ask what are the *likely* futures, but what are the *desirable* futures. It is pointed out that social scientists, and we might add educators, should ask: "When, where, by whom, how intensely, under what conditions, and with what consequences are different futures desired?" To deal with these questions, educators need to analyze innovations and educational trends in terms of their overriding frameworks and their histories.

Curricular activities, by their very nature, should be future-oriented. All education, to be relevant, should consider some image or images of the future. What educators think appropriate for the future will be influenced by their visions of the future. If their visions or images are inaccurate, then the education they design will miss its mark.

In general, they can deduce their images of the future from their knowledge of the past and their reading of the present. The accuracy of our views will impact upon what we project for the future. Alvin Toffler notes that people cannot totally view their images of the future as predictive in the sense that what they see is what they will get. He points out that the possible future is not singular, but plural. It is not the result of one event, or one decision, but the results of choices that people make from a myriad of options. Also, their future or futures may result from factors that they cannot control or about which they have little choice.[4] Their choices for dealing with and identifying possible and desirable futures are still limited by the tools they currently have. Even so, they do have available some methods that will allow them to discern which lines of development are more likely than others.

FUTURE AND FUTURISM

The industrial age is ending; it is being replaced with the information age. John Naisbitt asserts that society is caught between two eras—the age in which industry was the leader and an age built on information.[5] The second wave of industrial might is being swept aside by the third wave, which the information industry will lead.

Many futurists place the beginning of the third wave in the mid 1950s, when, for the first time in American history, white-collar workers in technical, managerial, and clerical positions outnumbered blue-collar workers. For the first time, more people in our society worked with information than produced material goods.[6]

Being caught between two eras, in a time of transition, disturbs many people. The rate at which the information, or postindustrial age, has appeared has clouded their images of the future. They have to generate new paradigms to organize their social and work worlds. This makes many people unclear about the roles they are to play. Indeed many are finding that their secure jobs are being phased out and that they have to almost "start again."

Discomfort is also accompanying this transition because it has occurred so rapidly. The European shift from an agricultural to an industrial society took several centuries; the same shift evolved over a century in the United States. The shift from an industrial to an information society has occurred in only two or three decades! Such rapidity of change has not allowed us either the time to reflect on the nature of the change or the "breathing room" in which to react.

Our view of time has been affected, too. During the agricultural period, our time orientation was to the *past;* during our industrial period, we looked to the *present;* in the information age, our time orientation is the *future.* This change in time orientation has interested many educators in the concept of the future. Curriculum planners, for instance, are confronted with creating programs that enable students to adapt to the future.

Although educators may not have perfected the tools for dealing with all aspects of the future, they do have the means for viewing and creating futures. These tools partly comprise the field of *futuristics,* sometimes called *futurism* or *future studies.* Whatever it is called, it embraces both the science of forecasting and the art of imagining.[7] This discipline views both technological and social events not as separate and independent occurrences, but as twin components linked in a system or process. Reality and the events comprising it are holistic. Events impact other events, which in turn impact still other events. Knowing the strength and direction of an interaction allows people to "preview" what are the likely consequences of such interactions—to "visualize" the future.

Futurism is a systematic attempt to meld creative forecasting, planning, and action. Those engaged in this new field, and curriculum leaders should be among them, are studying and developing alternative futures and generating supporting scenarios elaborating specific areas of society including its institutions. From the projected tentative futures, these professionals draw significant variables likely to influence events or behavior and then deduce the kinds of educational programs that have a high probability of meeting the projected conditions.

Using the tools of educational futurism, educators can proact rather than react. In the past, educators reacted to events impacting on the school and its programs. They still do this when dealing with public demands for a "responsive" or "relevant" curriculum.[8]

Part of the problem in processing or shaping the future is that people have experienced what Alvin Toffler calls "future shock"—individuals' disorientation that results when their past experiences are not adequate or effective for understanding or making decisions for today or tomorrow.[9] Future shock characterizes our rapidly changing times.

The Importance of Uncertainty.

Our world has become complex. It is difficult to project whether our interpretations of events are accurate or that our anticipation of future occurrences is on target. In addition, the costs of failure have become high. If educators "misread" the future, they may create curricula that do not address students' needs. They may even educate students in ways that will add to social problems—for example, by preparing students for obsolete jobs and thus unemployment.

Kenneth Boulding points out that a de-gree of uncertainty exists in much of decision making.[10] This is because the rate of change is increasing; with this increase come new problems—and thus uncertainty—with which educators have to cope. Boulding suggests that educators need to be mindful of this element of uncertainty. Decisions made under uncertain conditions are very different from decisions made under certain ones. If a situation is certain, educators only have to decide to achieve whatever it is that they want to maximize and then focus their resources and time to do it. However, Boulding cautions that in the real world, life is not so simple; the real world is uncertain. Realizing this, educators should strive to make decisions that are "liquid, flexible, and adaptable."[11] They should realize that sometimes, it is best to postpone decisions. At other times, it is good procedure to leave options open and to denote contingency plans. Being unsure about what the future may demand, they should arrange for possible options—that is, they should suggest several programs that can be delivered in a multitude of ways. They need to anticipate problems and ways of dealing with them.

Areas of Instability.

Educators have perhaps changed the most with regard to their attitudes and views. A major attitudinal shift concerns the notion of unlearning the past. Educators have been concerned with getting the right answers, Herman Kahn asserts, a stress that was in part influenced by their view that the future would be very much like the past—nothing more than a linear projection of the past. Answers that were correct in the past would be appropriate for the future;[12] knowing the answers to past questions would enable educators to function effectively in the future. Educators had little more to do than to use the curriculum to pass on accumulated culture.

But the future is not a linear extension of the past. In many instances, in fact, the future perceived is nothing like the past. Answers that were correct are frequently now wrong—and students who successfully learned the answers might have to "unlearn" them. The explosion of knowledge has indeed furnished new information that has challenged the validity—even the occurrence—of previously held conclusions. It is difficult for people to abandon existing answers and perceptions; nonetheless, unlearning is a crucial first step in dealing with unanticipated futures. The successful student of the future may be that person who can "change" his or her mind and identify those situations that require such change.

Another attitudinal shift that has already occurred, and that will likely continue, is the push for personalized pluralism. Educators are striving to make individuals fully unique and in control of themselves and their destinies.[13] The belief that the school, like society, is a melting pot, tended to homogenize all students into a new type. According to this view, the school played an integral role in reducing cultural and ethnic differences among people in order to bring about a common American culture. Educators created programs that devalued individual uniqueness; they focused on creating curricular tracks for students and on delivering such curricula in similar fashion to all.

Now, however, educators are stressing cultural pluralism. They realize that they need to adjust the school curricula so that students can develop their individual talents. They are now thinking of modifying the schools to fit the students rather than demanding that the students change to fit the schools. Increasingly, they are creating specialized environments to meet individual needs, and they are contemplating specialized support services that will address the unique needs of the students. According to Mario Fantini, educators are considering more interdisciplinary programs, varied program options and alternatives, multiple-career programs, and early skill development programs.[14] Educators, also, are now willing to recognize different forms of intelligence—not just in the cognitive domain—but also musical, artistic, spatial, kinesthetic, and interpersonal.

Instability relates to more than just attitude shifts. Attributes change as well. Educators will likely face students whose attributes have changed. The experiences students have prior to coming to school and while in school may actually alter their ways of processing information. Future students may indeed have different language forms. Daniel Bell believes students will skillfully communicate with computers and visual images in ways we can only vaguely anticipate. Reading and writing were the recorded language forms of yesterday; today, speaking is the primary language form. The spoken word has also been augmented with visual images, especially through television, videotapes and discs, satellite dishes, and telecommunication devices. Our technology has enabled us to use the spoken word to influence people literally from all over the world.[15]

Observation as a basic skill is just beginning to be introduced as well. So much information is being displayed on video screens that students' observation skills may well be crucial to their interpreting their world.

It is also likely that students will shift their learning styles. They may actually want to arrange information in ways that differ significantly from what is considered logical and sequential today. Students of the future, quite conceivably, will think more multidimensionally and creatively—utilizing visual, computer, and communication tools to enhance the way they process and utilize information. Many students in the future will think and process information in ways that may challenge, and even differ from, their teachers, who might still rely on traditional thinking patterns.[16]

Areas of Stability.

Some people are overwhelmed with so much instability. Certainly, some things of the present will continue into the future, and we can make forecasts based on that continuity. For example, we can take some comfort in the realization that in the future we will continue to have students, teachers, schools, and parents. The basic organizers for our thinking most likely will continue as well. Despite, in some circles, the cry to deschool society, society will probably keep its schools, because schools are the most efficient means of bringing students into contact with their culture, with themselves, and with others. (Of course, the organization of the schools, and even who attends them, can change.) And, with schools continuing, we will have to have curricula. We may not recognize the content, but we will have content, and we will plan experiences for students.

Schools are, however, likely to play a less important role, or at least a shared role, in learning. More learning will occur as a result of students' interacting with the mass media, especially television and tapes. But, the mass media will not be a few media sources presenting a rather common "picture." Rather the media is likely to be what Toffler calls demassified.[17] The media industry will create both written and visual materials for specialized markets. Already in the United States, mass magazines are no longer a powerful influence in national life. Such magazines as *Life* and *The Saturday Evening Post* have even been phased out as an explosion of minimagazines address particular audiences. The media also cover an expanded range of topics: addressing young children, teenagers, middle-aged persons, and senior citizens. These trends are likely to continue.

The same trends characterize television and radio. No longer are there just three major channels; there are potentially hundreds. No longer does just one radio station play rock music; numerous stations specialize in all rock of all styles—from soft to hard.

With the rise of the personal home computer, individuals now have access to vast amounts of information and a multitude of means for processing it. And people interact with the computers; they are not passive observers. This certainly has implications for the manner in which we can expect students to learn in schools.[18]

With such demassification of the media, it is likely that people's opinions will not only be enriched, but that they will also become less uniform. Individuals will "tune into" and interact within their "sections" of the information world.

Another reason educators can anticipate that schools may perhaps have less influence on learning is that we are entering an age in which people will require lifelong learning.[19] More individuals will be engaged in formal learning long after high school and even after college. Elementary and secondary schools will probably only be responsible for a brief period of an individual's total formal learning. Other agencies will provide the continued learning required for people to interact with the future world.

DIRECTIONS FOR THE 1990s

This century, as already noted, has been characterized by unprecedented change in every aspect of life. More change has occurred in this century, in fact, than has occurred in all the previous centuries of human existence.[20] Harold Shane notes the rapidity of change. He notes that, from a historical point of view, it seems reasonable to conclude that for the first time in human history, we have been propelled from yesterday into tomorrow with no familiar "today" during which we can become acclimated to change.[21]

Toffler states "at the rate at which knowledge is growing, by the time the child born today graduates from college the amount of knowledge in the world will be four times as great. By the time that same child is fifty years old, it will be 32 times as great and 97 percent of everything known in the world will have been learned since the time he was born."[22] Toffler's projection, however, assumes a linear extrapolation of current events. It does not consider changes in either rate or direction (see Chapter 5), nor does it consider unseen variables or events, what some people call system breaks. Still, it is safe to accept that the knowledge explosion, though it may not be as dramatic as Toffler indicates, will still be formidable.

Daniel Bell has noted that today's world seems to be becoming increasingly empirical, worldly, secular, humanistic, pragmatic, utilitarian, contractual, epicurean, and hedonistic. Bourgeois, bureaucratic, and meritocratic elites also seem to be forming. More and more decisions are being made by fewer and so-called highly qualified individuals. Scientific and technological knowledge is accumulating that leaves many areas of decision-making beyond the scope and participation of many people.[23]

Michael McDaniel has listed seven factors that have contributed to the rapidity and nature of change. They basically deal with social and cultural trends and the way society is undergoing change:

1. *Demographic change*: sex and age patterns, death rates, lifespans, family size, balance of youth versus old, and so on.
2. *Technological innovation*: adaptive changes in existing machines and productivity.
3. *Social innovation*: new arrangements, systems, or styles in educational, political, economic, military, and other dimensions.
4. *Cultural-value shifts*: changes in cultural axioms or values and ideas.
5. *Ecological shifts*: changes in the natural ecology, catastrophic events, pollution of rivers.
6. *Information-idea shifts*: scope, quality, and manipulability of knowledge; new conceptions of how things work.
7. *Cultural diffusion*: transfer of ideas, values, or techniques from one culture to another through war, invasion, advertising, and increased travel.[24]

John Naisbitt has popularized ten megatrends that are impacting educators planning curricula: (1) changing from an industrial society to an information society; (2) going to a situation that requires high technology corresponding with a high level of human interactions; (3) moving from a national to a world economy; (4) changing from short-term planning and action to long-term planning and action; (5) going from centralized to decentralized services and government; (6) emphasizing self-help instead of institutional help; (7) going from representative democracy to participatory democracy; (8) changing from organizations that represent hierarchies to organizations that are examples of networking; (9) engaging in a demographic shift from the north to the sun belt, and (10) going from either/or choice situations to situations with multiple options.[25] Reflecting on Naisbitt's list can enable educators to identify their challenges, the questions they must raise, and the possibilities that will result from processing such questions.

Dealing with the Future.

Curriculum decision makers need more than just different concepts of the future; they require knowledge of and skill in actually forecasting the future. "The need for all types of future-planning to 'create' tomorrow in education should be evident to all but the most perversely 'misological' of U.S. citizens."[26] For example, forecasting is the window through which one can survey potential happenings. By their glances through such windows, curricularists can get direction about what to avoid, about what to modify, and toward what to strive. The task is easier—and more accurate—when they make short-range forecasts about what the program will be next month, or at the end of this year, than if they forecast for years or decades in advance.[27]

The majority of futures techniques are really types of forecasting. Note that *predictions* are statements about occurrences that are to happen in a specific future. *Forecasts* tell us not what will happen, but rather what can happen if certain conditions or certain events occur or continue. The accuracy and inclusiveness of forecasts depend on the data fed into the deliberations, the systems of logic applied, the diversity of the techniques utilized, and the energies expended.

One researcher has provided a useful overview of the major approaches to future planning. These approaches involve either exploratory forecasting or normative forecasting. *Exploratory forecasting* means processing data to discover possible capabilities, changes, opportunities, and problems that may or are likely to appear in the future, assuming the continuance of certain events. Attention is given to identifying likely futures. Often such forecasting expands various trends that have been identified. *Normative forecasting* deals with attending to various goals or norms to be actualized in the future. Here forecasters are "inventing" the future of their choice. They actually set the norms for the future and then indicate what needs to be accomplished to attain such norms or goals.

Following is a listing of some major approaches to forecasting:

Simulation Forecasting. This technique generates the future by activating models of known physical, social, and environmental laws and determines how they will most likely impact the future. The models, designed and used to predict future probabilities, denote sets of variables or entities and their interactions.[28] They allow forecasters to study the interactions and to discover what can be or should be controlled, what can be or needs to be designed, and ultimately what needs to be forecasted.

For example, educators might create a model of the future school system denoting the key variables and then, using various mathematical formulas, design a computer program that will enable them to project results of current actions, or to identify and then evaluate alternative actions that might result from making particular choices. Using this technique, educators might be able, for example, to accurately picture what might happen if all the students in a school experienced a common curriculum. By obtaining a readout of possible consequences, educators can decide whether to enact their current plans—in this case, require all students to take a common curriculum.

Trend Forecasting. To use this procedure, an educator plots mathematically the path of discovered events and extends them into the future. Such forecasting assumes

that the rate of change noted in the past and present will continue uninterrupted into the future. For example, educators may be interested in the amount of new knowledge that is being discovered in a subject or discipline. The number of discoveries can be either plotted on a graph or compared against specific points in time—such as decades, years, or months—and arranged in increasing order. Arranging the information in this manner, educators can see if the variable—for example, the number of discoveries in biology—is increasing or decreasing with time. A straight line may be fitted to the points and then extended beyond the most recent point. If the line denotes an increase, then educators can forecast that they will likely need to expand coverage in the biology curriculum, or at least to think of ways to integrate the content to ensure that the students encounter current information.

Intuitive Forecasting. This procedure is something everyone can do. It relates to the images or "feelings" people have about the future. These perceptions of what is to come influence their decisions and actions, such that many of their views become reality. For example, someone may feel that in the future there will be a greater need for more science and mathematics courses in light of the increasing technological nature of our society. In other words, their intuition about the increasing technology becomes essentially a tool for their forecasting what will be a useful educational future.

Delphi Forecasting. Along with brainstorming, Delphi forecasting is perhaps the most well-known futures procedure. It is a process of extracting "expert" intuitive opinions about the future and then furnishing the "experts" with the preliminary results. This process is repeated several times until the "experts" achieve consensus of opinion regarding the future.[29] According to one observer, "Delphi . . . operates on the principle that several heads are better than one in making subjective conjectures about the future, and that experts . . . will make conjectures based on rational judgment and shared information rather than merely guessing, and will separate hope from likelihood in the process."[30]

Educators might use a Delphi technique to obtain a "reading" of what they believe the future will demand of the curriculum with regard to specific content to be covered. Each educator might be given a questionnaire that asks him or her to note ten major content areas that will be needed for future education. An analysis of the results of the first questionnaire is used to develop a second questionnaire. This second questionnaire is sent to the same group of educators with the results of the first questionnaire, to indicate those areas considered essential for inclusion in the curriculum. Educators are asked to respond to this second questionnaire after considering the responses of the "experts" to the first questionnaire. They are also asked to indicate why they revised their responses if they did so.

A third questionnaire is then created to summarize the previous responses and the reasons individuals changed those responses. As before, the educators are again asked to consider the questionnaire items, to revise their responses if they think it necessary, and to explain their actions. Ideally, by this third round, educators have a fairly good consensus of how they and their colleagues "read" the future.

Scenario Forecasting. This procedure is also quite well known to the public. It involves creating a scenario, which is basically a well-thought-out story or description about how a possible future state of affairs might occur. The story must draw on current happenings and likely trends. Often it notes how people can go from the present reality to some possible future period.[31] Scenario writing puts into prose form innovative, imaginative, and plausible utopias for people to contemplate.

There is really no one method for creating a scenario, but there are certain approaches to scenario forecasting. Usually, the general process requires those involved to begin with a checklist of the aspects of so-

ciety that deserve attention. The scope of the checklist depends on the writer's definition of the system that is to be the focus of the scenario. If, for example, a teacher is going to write a scenario about the schools of the future, the list will be much more detailed than if he or she is writing a scenario about only one subject area in the curriculum. A checklist for a curriculum might include such areas as: (1) Content, (2) Teaching methods, (3) Instructional media, and (4) Staff support.

The writer would then propose specific questions on the checklist items. For curriculum, they might include: What new contents might be produced? How will the new contents be organized? What old contents are likely to remain? How will these old contents be organized? What are some likely new teaching methods? How will computers interface with students? What new staff members will be needed? How will change agents, researchers, and instructional designers be used in formulating curriculum? The writer reviews the answers to these questions for accuracy and arranges them in chronological order or in a time period. This arrangement of the responses to the questions really forms the basis for the scenario. In essence, the scenario writer has created an outline for his or her "story."

Force Analysis Forecasting. To use this procedure, educators note and analyze forces (sets of events, pressures, problems, and/or social events) and their probable impact on particular future events or areas. For example, people start out by selecting a topic—say, an area of the curriculum. Next, they define a force as a "set of events, pressures, or technologies, whose impact upon the curriculum will impel those who design the curriculum to make modifications in it. Next, they ask persons knowledgeable about the curriculum to scan the present and immediately past environment for forces, as they have defined them. Recent discoveries in knowledge might be listed as one force, and the public's increasing demands that certain contents be covered might be another. National needs might also be noted, as could the changing nature of students.

Once these forces have been selected, each is described. After descriptions have been written, the forecasting team draws upon data gathered and the inferential summaries made to describe the nature of each force and the impact it has previously had on, in this case, the curriculum. Last, the forecasting team uses the data gathered to forecast the nature of each force and how it will impact the curriculum in the time frame indicated.[32]

Although the preceding discussion has listed six types of forecasting, it is not all inclusive. Nonetheless, it does indicate that educators have options. Rarely would they employ just one technique; rather, they would usually combine various types of forecasts to obtain a useful reading of a possible future.

But forecasting the future is still challenging, because the future is the consequence of the dynamics between events current and events yet to happen. The future, in a real sense, is always evolving. For this reason, a curriculum that is to be responsive to the times must also be evolving. Shane asserts that humans have, in the physiological sense, achieved the capacity to share in their own evolution. He extends this thinking to curriculum: "In an intellectual, interactive sense man can likewise engage in the act of deliberately shaping educational change."[33]

Traditional Subject-Centered Design.

Because it is the most pervasive design not only in the United States but also in the rest of the world, it is unlikey to disappear in the future. Subject-centered designs regard intellect as central to humanness, even though they have partly resulted from historical accident, institutional inertia, and social demand.

At the elementary grade level, the subject-centered design comprises such subjects as language and communication skills, social studies, mathematics, science, and the arts. At the secondary level, the traditional academic subjects are English, mathematics, science, social studies, and foreign language. Although these subject divisions are not likely to change, the specific content and experiences can and will.

Other Designs.

Most schools in the United States use some version of the traditional subject-centered design. But some schools organize content according to students' interests; such schools are likely to remain few in number. Indeed, their numbers might even diminish as mastering the basics and preparing for a technological society become dominant educational concerns.

"Other" curriculum designs are humanistic, because their main theme is to "humanize" learning. They generally feature student-centered curricula and instructional patterns to encourage students to be more in control of their learning. The curricula are geared to the maturational levels of the students; teachers work as facilitators and catalysts rather than as transmitters of knowledge.

Many curriculum designs classified as "other" can be grouped under what Eisner calls a personal "relevance orientation."[34] This orientation to curriculum emphasizes the primacy of personal meaning. Teachers develop educational programs in concert with the students rather than from administrative mandates or outside sources—as they often do with subject-centered designs.

Many of these "other" designs draw on existentialist, moral, and spiritual ideas, what some call "Third Force" psychology. Abraham Maslow, a pioneer in humanistic psychology, considered this type of psychology to be a transitional preparation for a "higher" Fourth Force or *transpersonal* psychology. Transpersonal psychology focuses on the cosmos, rather than on human needs and interests, and on intuition and transcendence.[35] Through intuition, an individual thinks creatively and views the world holistically.

Perhaps one reason not many new curricular designs stress these new humanistic and transpersonal orientations is the difficulty of precisely organizing the content to address the inner realms of an individual. Reflecting back in this century, we can see shades of experience or child-centered curriculum designs. The new curricula are different, however, because they really strive to do more than just make the curriculum interesting to students. These new designs seek to include higher-level psychological, philosophical, and religious experiences.

New Curricular Areas.

The curriculum in the future will no doubt contain some entirely new areas of information. Currently, for example, we have the beginnings of several new content areas.

Informatics. Informatics deals with computers and their use. It has been described as a science of techniques for dealing with information. The computer, a central aspect of this new discipline, will afford students access to vast amounts of currently unattainable information. Students will be able, for example, to process documents written in other languages, because the computers will translate them. Computers will also enable students to "network" with other students in other schools, even in other countries. Joint investigations by students in different states or countries can become commonplace.

Informatics can be a method or cluster of methods of thought that are applicable to a wide range of subjects and activities.[36] As students think of ways to program their computers, they will begin to conceptualize different ways of organizing information. "Presenting" the computer to students will really give them power and control over the curriculum. If they control the machine, they can control the information; if they control the information, they may in effect gain increased influence in the classroom. This shift in classroom power from teacher to student could be a real system break in how school is "played": Learning could come to dominate teaching.[37]

Most schools and classrooms have been and still are arranged in a hierarchy. With the computer in place, teachers and students could well restructure this institution. They could change the school and classroom from a hierarchial, pyramidal, managerial system to one characterized by horizontal decision making shared among students and teachers. Writes one educator, "In the year 2000, the learning environment will combine automatic and human teaching in a variety of settings to accommodate many learning styles, allow for new definitions of literacy, and foster life-long learning skills. The advent of this technology will make research, [and] study and communication skills the new basics of education."[38]

The computer is much more than a tool. Indeed, it can be a "partner" the students can use not only for "joint" inquiry but even for suggesting and creating new curricular areas into which they can delve. The computer has the potential of personalizing the curriculum of the future.

Not all learning with the computer will occur in schools. Much of it will occur in the home, or perhaps in public learning centers. Closed circuit and cable telecourses should be commonplace by 2000, and video and/or auditory discs and tapes should replace many textbooks and written materials. Students may even have available a dial-access facility that permits access, via laser or a telephone, to a central learning center equipped with high-speed computers that can communicate with computers in any home or learning center anywhere in the world.[39]

The Future as Curriculum Content. It would seem unusual if future curricula did not include courses on the future itself. Such courses already exist in a few secondary schools. Some objectives of future studies courses are to give students a more sophisticated approach to thinking about the future and to help students learn forecasting techniques. Such courses will most likely increase in number; they may also extend into elementary schools.

Draper Kauffman has presented six areas of competence that could comprise a possible future-oriented curriculum: (1) having access to information; (2) thinking clearly; (3) communicating effectively; (4) understanding humanity's environment; (5) understanding the individual and society; and (6) enhancing personal competence.[40]

As part of the future studies curriculum, students should learn about planning procedures, the nature of decision making, various types of heuristics for dealing with information, and procedures for handling stress caused by the rapidity of change. They should learn not only how to think critically about the future, but also perhaps how to "break" boundaries between logic and nonlogic.

New Areas of Content. Whereas some courses on the future are predictable, other courses on the future are not so predictable. Nevertheless, we venture some predictions. Many courses may reflect hybrid fields of study—courses in biostatistics and molecular biology, for example. In addition, courses in humanistic psychology and corporate psychology should increase, as will courses in satellite astronomy or the politics of satellites.

Courses in dieting and exercise should increase as we become more health conscious. Research linking good nutrition and exercise for children with positive social behavior and academic achievement should encourage the schools to incorporate increased nutrition and exercise into the curriculum—and possibly lead to the elimination of junk food (especially excessive sugar and fats) from school vending machines and lunch counters.[41]

Some new courses may deal with the changing nature of society. Courses in aging, for instance, may become commonplace because students will be faced with an increasingly large "maturing" populace. Eventually the curriculum should treat many of the problems of aging as a form of discrimination, as another "ism." This emphasis should parallel changes in the curriculum concerning racism, "ethnicism," and sexism.[42] Special courses may offer students the opportunity to study about lifelong education and the ways in which it can be accessed.

As society continues to become culturally and ethnically pluralistic, more courses will deal with international and global education. Courses in valuing will appear so that students can gain insight into the attitudes, feelings, and emotions of themselves and others.[43]

Not all new courses will be related to emerging fields in the public sector. Some new courses may deal with the brain and ways of thinking. Secondary schools may assign textbooks on courses entitled "Your Brain," "Metacognition," "Left-Brain/Right-Brain Thinking," and "Transductive Thinking." Specific courses in self-management of one's intellect, emotions, and stress are probable as well. Courses in "inner awareness," T-groups, and encounter groups may reappear.

New courses which focus on problems might deal with the causes of famine, disease, flood, and so on, and their social and economic consequences. A new course entitled "frontiers" may include the geography of the ocean, perhaps the universe. Courses in the sociology of crime or the nature of conflict may be in more and more public school curricula. So may formal courses on the nature, complexity, and challenges of change—and how to address them. The possibilities are endless.

CHALLENGE OF DEALING WITH THE FUTURE

We mentioned at the outset of this chapter that all education springs from some image of the future. We have also stressed repeatedly that the way people deal with their images optimally is through planned change. Assuming the posture of futurists, educators should be able to anticipate and even manage future directions for the schools so that their programs are responsive to students' needs not only in the practical sense of application to job situations, but in the totally humanistic sense of allowing them to understand, manage, and appreciate their realities.

This is no small order because, historically, schools have been assigned a highly conservative role by society—that of guardian of continuity. The school is to guarantee, as much as possible, that each new generation is enough like the previous one to maintain existing institutions, social arrangements, and methods for dealing with people.[44]

Schools require organization so that they not only keep current with the rapid present change, but also can manage the nature and rate of change. Schools should no longer be managed by a few who make decisions about what is good for the masses. Toffler points out that no educational institution today can address the challenges placed upon it until all its members, including students, subject their views of the future and related challenges to critical analysis. Toffler cautions: ". . . to design educational systems for tomorrow . . . we need not images of a future frozen in amber, as it were, but something far more complicated: sets of images of successive and alternative futures, each one tentative and different from the next."[45]

Our images of the future are influenced by our ideological stances. But most of us, although we may have different particular future images, do believe that we should continue to create educational programs that emphasize individualism, rationalism, and a realistic sense of family, religion, and nationhood. In the final analysis, the educational future we design and develop should not focus on one prescribed, preferred, or predicted type of future. Rather we need "to realize a future of alternative choices for all people."[46]

The challenge is for curriculum designers and developers to create programs so that all students will be able to function optimally in a just future society. The task is difficult and complex. perhaps at times unmanageable. But, those with curriculum

responsibilities should realize that they must rise to the challenge—society depends upon it.

CONCLUSION

In this chapter, we have attempted to define what futurism is and to relate it to the field of curriculum. Futurism was presented as a systematic attempt to meld creative forecasting, planning, and action. In using futurism, educators can proact rather than react to events. Certainly, educators have past habits to break, because it has been their posture to react to events impacting on the schools and their programs. Often educators are unaware of how to influence the future, how to modify public or client demands to more manageable dimensions, or how to be more in tune with accepted purposes of education.

We live between eras, and we have uncertainty in our lives. Nonetheless, we need to approach this uncertainty as a plus rather than a minus. Uncertainty forces people to engage in decision making that is liquid, flexible, and adaptable. This should encourage the creation of more diverse curricular offerings.

In this chapter, we discussed various directions of the 1990s and beyond that appear likely for our world. We mentioned such factors as demographic change, technological innovation, social innovation, and cultural value shifts, which are all influencing the direction of our schools and our overall society.

We discussed procedures that we can muster that will enable us not only to react to directions but also to play a role in their creation. We presented various forecasting procedures for consideration. We presented, too, a general overview of some of the developments within the curriculum field. We briefly mentioned what might be expected in new curricular areas.

We ended this chapter with a brief section identifying challenges educators face in dealing with the future. The challenge is to generate images of the future and then to fit schools and their programs into those images so that the curriculum that is actualized serves the needs and desires of all those within the school and society. To attain this is no small task. The health and vitality of society depend to a significant degree on how well curricularists meet this challenge.

Notes

1. Robert G. Scanlon, "Policy and Planning for the Future," in L. Rubin, ed., *The Future of Education: Perspectives on Tomorrow's Schooling* (Boston: Allyn and Bacon, 1975), pp. 83–96.
2. Draper L. Kauffman, *Teaching the Future* (Palm Springs, Calif.: ETC Publications, 1976).
3. Wendell Bell, "Social Science: The Future as a Missing Variable," in A. Toffler, ed., *Learning for Tomorrow: The Role of the Future in Education* (New York: Vintage Books, 1974), pp. 75–102.
4. Alvin Toffler, "The Psychology of the Future," in Toffler, ed., *Learning for Tomorrow*, pp. 3–18.
5. John Naisbitt, *Megatrends* (New York: Warner Books, 1982).
6. Ibid.
7. Harold L. Strudler, "Educational Futurism: Perspective or Discipline?" in Toffler, ed., *Learning for Tomorrow*, pp. 173–180.
8. Walter G. Hack, "On Confronting the Future," in W. G. Hack, ed., *Educational Futurism, 1985* (Berkeley, Calif.: McCutchan, 1971), pp. 2–19.
9. Alvin Toffler, *Future Shock* (New York: Bantam Books, 1970).
10. Kenneth E. Boulding, "Predictive Reliability and the Future: The Need for Uncertainty," in Rubin, ed., *The Future of Education*, pp. 57–82.
11. Ibid., p. 59.
12. Herman Kahn, "The Great Transition," in F. Feather and R. Mayur, *Optimistic Outlooks* (Toronto: Global Futures Network, 1982), pp. 57–70.
13. Harold Shane and Bernadine Tobler, *Education for a New Millennium* (Bloomington, Ind.: Phi Delta Kappa Educational Foundation, 1981).
14. Mario D. Fantini, *Regaining Excellence in Education* (Columbus, Ohio: Merrill, 1986).
15. Daniel Bell, *The Third Technological Revolution* (New York: Basic Books, 1984).
16. See Alfred Bork, "Computers in Education and Some Possible Futures," *Phi Delta Kappan* (December 1984), pp. 239–243; Neil Postman, "Engaging Students in the Great Conversation," *Phi Delta Kappan* (January 1983), pp. 310–316.
17. Alvin Toffler, *The Third Wave* (New York: Bantam, 1981); Toffler, *Previews and Premises* (Boston: Sound End Press, 1983).
18. Frederick G. Knick and Kent L. Gustafson, *Instructional Technology: A Systematic Approach to Education* (New York: Holt, Rinehart, 1986).
19. Harold G. Shane, "A Curriculum for the New Century," *Phi Delta Kappan* (January 1981), pp. 351–356.
20. Harold G. Shane, "Future-Planning as a Means of Shaping Educational Change," in R. M. McClure, ed., *The Curriculum: Retrospect and Prospect*, Seventieth Yearbook of the National Society for the Study of Education, Part I (Chicago: University of Chicago Press, 1971), pp. 185–218.
21. Ibid.
22. Toffler, *Future Shock*, pp. 157–158.
23. Daniel Bell, "The Year 2000—The Trajectory of an Idea," *Daedalus* (Summer 1967), pp. 642–644.
24. Michael A. McDaniel, "Tomorrow's Curriculum Today," in Toffler, ed., *Learning for Tomorrow*, pp. 103–131.
25. Naisbitt, *Megatrends*.
26. Shane, "Future-Planning as a Means of Shaping Educational Change," p. 189.
27. Earl C. Joseph, "An Introduction to Studying the Future," in S. P. Henley and J. R. Yates, eds., *Futurism in Education: Methodologies* (Berkeley, Calif.: McCutchan, 1974), pp. 1–26; Marilyn Ferguson, *The Aquarian Conspiracy* (Los Angeles: Tarcher, 1980).
28. Roy Amara, *Some Methods of Future Research* (Menlo Park, Calif.: Institute for the Future, 1975); Elizabeth Vallance, "Ways of Knowing and Curricular Conceptions," in E. Eisner, ed., *Learning and Teaching the Ways of Knowing*, Eighty-Fourth Yearbook of the National Society for the Study of Education, Part II (Chicago: University of Chicago Press, 1985), pp. 199–217.
29. O. Helmer, *Analysis of the Future: The Delphi Method* (Santa Monica, Calif.: Rand Corporation, March 1967).
30. John W. Sutherland, "Architecturing the Future: A Delphi-Based Paradigm for Normative System Building," in H. Linstone and M. Turoff, eds., *The Delphi Method* (Reading, Mass.: Addison-Wesley, 1975), p. 467.
31. Amara, *Some Methods of Future Research;* Department of Defense, *Military Standard: Human Engineering Design Criteria for Military Systems* (Washington, D.C.: U.S. Government Printing Office, 1981).
32. Joseph, "An Introduction to Studying the Future," in Henley and Yates, *Futurism in Education*, pp. 1–26.
33. Shane, "Future-Planning as a Means of Shaping Educational Change," p. 216.
34. Elliot W. Eisner, *The Educational Imagination*, 2nd ed. (New York: Macmillan, 1985).
35. Jerry L. Patterson, Steward C. Purkey, and Jackson V. Parker, *Productive School Systems for a Nonrational World* (Alexandria, Va.: Association for Supervision and Curriculum Development, 1986); Roger Walsh and Frances Vaughn, *Beyond Ego* (Los Angeles: Tarcher, 1980).

36. Harlan Cleveland, "Educating Citizens and Leaders for an Information-Based Society," *Educational Leadership* (March 1986), pp. 62–63; M. Francis Klein, "Beyond the Measured Curriculum," *Theory into Practice* (Winter 1986), pp. 1–17.

37. Ibid.

38. Marvin Cetron, *Schools of the Future: How American Business and Education Can Cooperate to Save Our Schools* (New York: McGraw-Hill, 1985), p. 114.

39. Decker F. Walker, "Computers and the Curriculum," in J. A. Culbertson and L. L. Cunningham, eds., *Microcomputers and Education.* Eighty-fifth Yearbook of the National Society for the Study of Education, Part I (Chicago: University of Chicago Press, 1986), pp. 22–39.

40. Kauffman, *Teaching the Future.*

41. Judith Herr and Winifred Morse, "Food for Thought: Nutrition Education for Young Children," *Young Children* (November 1982), pp. 3–11: Allan C. Ornstein, "Controversy and Trends in Curriculum for the 1980s," *Contemporary Education* (Summer 1985), pp. 242–251.

42. Allan C. Ornstein, "What Are We Teaching in the 1980s?" *Young Children* (November 1982), pp. 12–17.

43. Ibid.

44. Kauffman, *Teaching the Future;* Alex Molnar, "Tomorrow the Shadow on the Wall Will Be that of Another," *Journal of Curriculum Theorizing* (Fall 1986), pp. 35–42.

45. Alvin Toffler, "The Psychology of the Future," in Toffler, ed., *Learning for Tomorrow,* p. 5.

46. David W. Livingstone, *Class Ideologies and Educational Futures* (Sussex, England: Falmer Press, 1983), p. 216.

NAME INDEX

SUBJECT INDEX

D